The Barefoot Sisters

WALKING HOME

The Barefoot Sisters

WALKING HOME

Lucy and Susan Letcher

a.k.a. Isis and jackrabbit

STACKPOLE BOOKS

For the hikers, maintainers, trail angels . . .
and especially for the dreamers.
—Isis and jackrabbit

Copyright © 2010 by Elizabeth Letcher and Susan Letcher

Published by
STACKPOLE BOOKS
5067 Ritter Road
Mechanicsburg, PA 17055
www.stackpolebooks.com

Printed in the United States of America

10 9 8 7 6 5 4

First edition

Cover design by Caroline Stover

Library of Congress Cataloging-in-Publication Data

Letcher, Lucy.
  The barefoot sisters walking home / Lucy and Susan Letcher, a.k.a. Isis and jackrabbit. — 1st ed.
    p. cm.
  ISBN-13: 978-0-8117-3529-2
  ISBN-10: 0-8117-3529-X
  1. Hiking—Appalachian Trail. 2. Appalachian Trail—Description and travel.
  I. Letcher, Susan. II. Title.
  GV199.42.A68L48 2009
  917.4—dc22

                                                    2008032957

CONTENTS

PREFACE

Isis

On a wet, buggy midsummer's day in 2000, my sister and I set out to hike the Appalachian Trail southbound, from Maine to Georgia. Our preparations consisted of three or four enthusiastic telephone conversations over the past few months, a trip through the dried foods aisle of our local health food store, and a quick visit to a local sports outlet store to supplement the camping gear we'd accumulated over the past few years and stored in our mother's garden shed. We carried fifty-pound packs, pared down to what we considered the absolute essentials: tent, sleeping bags, mattress pads, stove and cooking pot, water filter, first aid kit, rain gear, clothes for every temperature from ten to ninety degrees Fahrenheit, and bug nets for our heads. A slim volume of poetry for me, and a penny whistle for my sister. Our food bags bulged with twelve days' worth of food, including hot cereals, dried lentils, and more peanuts than I ever want to see again in my life. As we set out on the first morning of our journey, we stuffed our shoes into the remaining few inches of pack space; we'd decided to try hiking barefoot.

The Barefoot Sisters: Southbound gives the details of our southbound adventures. From the steep granite ridges of Maine and New Hampshire to the southern balds, from summer thunderstorms and fall hurricanes to the ice storms and blizzards of a surprisingly harsh winter in southern Virginia and Tennessee, our southbound journey brought us more than we bargained for. We put on shoes in Shenandoah during our first ice storm, after 1,300 barefoot miles, and shortly afterward we were wearing boots and snowshoes. Injury, illness, and hiking through deep snow for a few months slowed us down: the 2,168 miles, which hikers normally cover in five or six months, took us eight and a half. Our southbound hike was also a demanding emotional journey. The hardships that we faced revealed strengths and weaknesses we had never suspected, and, at times, sorely tested our friendship. Despite the difficulties, we stayed on the Trail. The kindness of friends and strangers and the beauty of the landscape were enough to sustain us. We reached Georgia in the beginning of March, just as the northbound hikers of 2001 were setting out.

After such a brutal winter, we felt we owed it to ourselves to see spring on the Trail. Besides, we had to get home somehow. Our original plan had been to buy a used car in Georgia and road-trip back. Instead, we decided to spend the rest of our savings hiking home to Maine. Northbound, we'd be walking with the seasons, from spring into summer. All the seasonal hostels and restaurants would be open, and dozens of trail angels would be waiting to work their magic for the nobo crowd. Besides, we were trail-hardened veterans, our bodies and minds conditioned and ready for the task at hand. It would be easy—or so we thought.

Besides the familiar demons of hunger, hypothermia, and quarrels we'd never resolved, hiking north brought its own set of challenges. The shelters were crowded, bears and rattlesnakes were emerging from their winter dens, and winter was far from over in the Smoky Mountains. On top of all this, our barefoot hike southbound had earned us a sort of notoriety that we weren't prepared to deal with; at first, many of our fellow hikers treated us as celebrities rather than friends. We'd envisioned the trip as a sort of victory tour, but we found that we were, in many ways, simply starting over.

CHAPTER 1

Homeward Bound

Isis

For the second time in a week, we stood at the southern terminus of the Appalachian Trail. The low, wooded summit of Springer Mountain seemed unchanged—the same bare oak limbs, dripping with cold rain, and the same glowering sky. Some obliging northbounder took a photo of us by the plaque that marks the summit: jackrabbit's smiling in spite of the weather, putting on a brave face for the start of our expedition. I look glum: *Let's get this over with. I don't see the point. We had our picture taken in this same spot last week, wearing the same outfits. If we don't start hiking soon, my toes will go numb.*

After we finished our southbound hike, our friend Lash had invited my sister and me to spend a few days with his family in Asheville, North Carolina, while we prepared for our return to the Trail. His father and brother welcomed us graciously, and his mother treated us like long-lost daughters, cooking elaborate meals for us, fussing over our ragged clothing, and driving across town to buy us some baklava, because I'd mentioned that I liked it. Lash took us to his favorite bars and cafés. It was strange to be back in a town for so long—every morning when I woke up, it took me a few minutes to realize that there were walls around me, and no trees.

The days passed in a flurry of activity. We finished our taxes; shopped for new gear to replace the things that had worn out or broken on our southbound hike; treated our Gore-Tex with a spray to restore its waterproof finish; washed our sleeping bags. I finally bought a new backpack, a light, sturdy Arc'teryx model that fitted to the curve of my hips and spine as if it had been made for me. Lash took us to a huge co-op food store, where we bought enough whole wheat couscous, dried veggie chips, and organic energy bars to send mail drops to the towns with limited vegetarian options. We made a collage of photos from the last few weeks of our southbound hike to send to friends and trail angels, telling them that we'd finally reached Springer and thanking them for their support. As the envelopes stacked up, I marveled at how many new friends the past year had brought us, and how many strangers had surprised us with their kindness. In all, we sent out 153 copies.

A few days before we planned to leave, jackrabbit got an e-mail from Miss Janet. She had heard through the trail angel grapevine that the Family from the North was due to finish the Trail on March 11. We had meant to leave Asheville early that morning, but with all the last-minute phone calls, packing, and goodbyes, we didn't get on the road until midafternoon. Our gear filled up the back of Lash's father's station wagon, emitting a powerful hiker odor in the enclosed space.

Lash rolled down a window. "Dude, one thing I'm not gonna miss is that *smell*."

We pushed the speed limit on the winding mountain roads through North Carolina and Georgia, but dusk was already falling by the time we turned off the main highway. The network of logging roads in Lash's atlas bore as little resemblance to reality as the elevation profile of a Virginia ridge. As darkness gathered, we got lost in the maze of gravel roads around Amicalola Falls State Park. We drove up to an abandoned cabin, an Army Rangers base, and a 4-H camp, none of which appeared on the map. The tired-looking caretaker at the 4-H camp gave Lash the directions that finally got us to the logging road that crossed the A.T. near Springer.

Jackrabbit and I raced up the path from the parking lot in the dark, hoping that the children hadn't gone to sleep yet. It would be so good to see them again and hear the stories from their last month on the Trail.

The shelter was empty except for a few nobos in shiny new wind pants and jackets, trying to figure out how to light their stoves.

"Family?" they asked, blinking at us. "There was a *family* hiking the Trail?"

We skimmed through the register. Nothing. I kept expecting to hear a patter of small footsteps, children's laughter echoing through the night. At last, a young nobo who'd been getting water when we arrived confirmed that the Family had finished the Trail earlier that day.

"Saw them on the summit about four in the afternoon, just after I got here. Didn't stay long. Went off with some woman in a van. Nope, no idea where they were headed."

Anywhere else on the Trail, jackrabbit and I would have known where to find them. What town they were going to, and probably what hostel. But there were no hostels near Springer. I thought of the pile of letters we had sent out, over the past week, to all our friends and helpers along the Trail. The Family had been closer to us than any of them. We didn't always agree—didn't always get along, even—but we owed each other our thru-hikes, and perhaps our lives. Now they had vanished, and we had no way to contact them. Alone among our Trail friends, the Family had no address, no phone number, not even a last name.

Our northbound hike began, like our southbound hike, in a downpour. A few miles from Springer, I noticed that my Gore-Tex jacket was darkening, growing heavier, sticking to my skin. The waterproofing spray that we had painstakingly applied, following a complicated series of instructions, didn't seem to have done a thing. I picked up my speed a little and managed to stay warm—the air wasn't as cold as it had been the day we hiked Standing Indian southbound. I worried about how we'd dry out, though, and whether the temperature would stay mild. And beyond that, what on earth we would do for rain gear for the rest of our trip.

We ate a late lunch at Hawk Mountain Shelter, chatting with some nobos who had already spread out their sleeping bags in the shelter loft. A cheerful young woman called Skelator, with pale blond hair and a pretty, dimpled face, perked up her ears when she heard that we were from Maine. It turned out that she had grown up in a town just across the bay from the island where we lived. We reminisced about our hometowns: the gray-shingled houses with lilacs in their dooryards, the general stores that served ice cream in summer, the smell of the docks. I would have liked to talk longer—I would have liked to stay the night and dry out our gear—but jackrabbit was eager to go on.

"It's our first day. This will set the tone for the rest of our northbound hike. If we hike eight-mile days when we could be doing fifteens, we'll take as long to hike northbound as we did to hike south. We can't afford that. We don't have time."

If this is setting the tone for the rest of our hike, I thought as I pulled on my dripping jacket and stepped back out into the rain, *I'm not sure I'm going to like it. At all.*

We hiked another seven miles before stetting up camp on the bank of Blackwell Creek. Gooch Gap Shelter was only a few miles farther on, but we knew that it would be packed with nobos trying to get out of the rain. Better to camp in a nice patch of forest by ourselves than to set up our tent in the mud beside a shelter. Besides, neither of us was in a mood to be the center of twenty strangers' attention.

I had just taken my food bag out of my pack and started digging the stove out, when I heard jackrabbit shout.

"Look out! Behind you!"

I spun around, hiking stick in hand, expecting to face a charging bear or a rabid dog. Instead, I was just in time to see my smooth, cylindrical, and thoroughly stuffed food bag topple off the edge of the bank and into the flooded stream. Without really thinking about what I was doing, I dropped my hiking stick and leaped after the runaway food bag. I slid down the muddy bank into the churning, waist-deep water. Luckily, the bright purple silicone-nylon bag, one of our Asheville purchases, resisted water well enough to float. It caught on a fallen tree trunk just a little ways downstream. I was able to grab it, toss it to jackrabbit, and then use the fallen tree to pull myself out of the water.

Water swirled around inside the legs of my rain pants as I climbed back up to our tent site. The pants seemed to hold the stream water in much better than they had been holding the rain out. I pulled them off to shake out the water, grimacing at the feel of the cold, sopping cloth sliding up my legs. Even with my wool shirt on under the wet jacket, I still felt chilled. I wanted nothing better than to crawl into the tent, pull my newly washed, fluffy sleeping bag up to my ears, and forget about the rain until morning. Maybe, by then, it would stop.

Food, I reminded myself. *Must eat before sleeping.* Ever since the fiasco in the Bigelow Mountains in Maine, where we'd gotten so tired and hypothermic that we'd gone to bed without eating anything, we'd made it a rule to cook supper no matter what happened. *Maybe some hot food will help*, I thought, feeding twigs into the smoking Zip stove with my numb fingers.

We ate our couscous as fast as we could, then propped our packs against a tree, pack covers up. *Finally*, I thought, *I can get out of this rain*. I started toward the tent and almost tripped over our food bags; I had forgotten to hang them for the night. The string to suspend them was somewhere in the bottom of my backpack. It seemed too great an effort. My hands were trembling uncontrollably—they looked gray in the light of my headlamp. I couldn't feel any of my fingers. I had to get warm.

"I th-think I-I'll just put th-the food bags in the t-tent vestibule t-tonight." I said to jackrabbit. "If anything t-tries to g-get them there, I'll h-hear it and I'll ch-chase it off."

She nodded agreement, and we both dove into the tent.

I woke to a rustle of plastic and the insistent grating sound of rodent teeth. A mouse. In our food. I unzipped the tent screen and punched the nearest food bag, and something scampered away through the dead leaves. I closed the screen and lay back down. A minute later, the mouse was back. Sighing, I crawled out of my sleeping bag. I couldn't bear the idea of putting on my wet clothes, so I stepped out of the tent naked, grabbed the food bags, and strode over to my backpack to get the string. The rain had stopped; mist rose from the forest floor and swirled through the beam of my headlamp. The cool, wet air felt soft against my skin. I found a suitable branch, threw the string over it, hauled the food bags up, tied off the string. Then I turned off my headlamp and stood still for a moment, letting my body blend into the night, before I returned to the tent.

The next time I opened my eyes, sunlight dappled the roof of our tent and the fly flapped in a brisk wind. The stream, clear now and half as deep as it had been the night before, gurgled peacefully in the background. After we'd hung our wet shirts and jackets on branches to dry, jackrabbit found a perfect place to sit down for breakfast. The retreating waters had exposed a small sand beach, with a washed-up log for a bench.

I retrieved the food bags and inspected them for damage. The mouse had chewed a big hole in the side of mine, straight into a package of homemade cookies our mother had sent—the best food that either of us was carrying. At least there didn't seem to be any mouse poop among the remaining crumbs. Jackrabbit and I ate them for our first course.

We were on to the granola course when a shadow fell across the beach. We both looked up; a dark, roiling cloud was bearing down on us, driven rapidly along by the wind.

"You don't think it's going to . . ." jackrabbit's voice trailed away.

"It wouldn't!" I said, but even as we spoke, the first huge drops splattered onto the surface of the stream. We dashed around, tugging our half-dry clothes out of the trees.

"Don't put anything past Murphy," said jackrabbit, as we ducked into the tent, pulling our gear in behind us.

"Murphy? Aren't we a little far south for him? I thought he was the evil weather poltergeist of the White Mountains," I said.

"Maybe he's on vacation," jackrabbit answered. "Maybe he flew all the way down here just to visit us."

Our recent reunion with Waterfall had reminded me of the appropriate word for the occasion. "Notch Murphy!" I said.

"Notch him to notch!" jackrabbit agreed.

jackrabbit

We hiked another day in rain and fog, pursued by the glowering spirit of Murphy, and camped at Slaughter Gap. The next morning, thankfully, dawned bright and sunny, with a brisk wind ripping through the thin cover of trees. The Georgia mountains, now that we could finally see them, looked just the same as when we had left for Asheville—a thousand shades of brown and gray. Leafless trees clung to the rounded shoulders of the ridges, and occasional patches of snow lingered in the deep shade.

Camped on the shady side of the ridge, out of the wind, we woke late. As we sat on a fallen tree, eating granola out of our camping cups, we heard a man coming up the trail, singing an old bluegrass song at the top of his lungs:

> The longest train I ever saw
> Was on that Georgia line.
> The engine passed at six o'clock,
> The cab went by at nine . . .

He had a fine tenor voice. We paused with our spoons in midair to listen.

"Wow," Isis said. "After all the glum, silent types, it's great to hear a nobo having a good time."

"Yeah. Anybody who sings to himself in the woods can't be half bad."

The sound of the voice came closer, and we saw a young man with bright, shoulder-length, red-gold hair and a beard of the same shade. He was tall and stocky, carrying a tiny green pack and wearing grungy tennis shoes.

> In the pines, in the pines,
> where the sun never shines,
> and we shiver when the cold wind blows . . .

He stopped when he saw us, and looked up without a hint of embarrassment. "Morning, ladies. Great day, isn't it? I'm Nate, by the way."

"I'm jackrabbit. Thanks for the music."

"Jackrabbit? Say, are you guys the Barefoot Sisters?"

"Yup. I'm Isis," she said through a mouthful of granola.

"Man!" He shook his head. "I've been hearing crazy rumors about you guys. It's good to meet you. So is it true? Are you yo-yoing?"

"Yeah, it's true. We finished our sobo hike last week, and now we're back for more."

"Far out! And you really hike barefoot?"

"When it's warm enough," I said.

"That's awesome. Man, I hope I get to hike with you guys before you pass me. I mean, you must be in great shape from your southbound hike and all."

"I don't know," I said. "After the first couple weeks, when you get in shape, I think pace is more a matter of pack weight. I mean, we can hike fifteens and occasional twenties now, but with all the heavy gear we've got, it's tough to sustain more than that." I glanced at his streamlined green pack. "Once you get going, I wouldn't be surprised if you end up pulling twenties on a regular basis. You'll probably pass *us* in a little while."

He shrugged and smiled. "I don't know. I've done a lot of hiking out West. My dad and I are section-hiking the PCT. Out there, we can do twenty-five, thirty miles a day, but this trail is something else. All these crazy little ups and downs."

A Pacific Crest Trail hiker, I thought. *That would explain the lightweight pack and footwear.* "Thirties!" I said. "You'll pass us in no time!"

"Aw, you never know . . . Say, are you guys missing a filter bag? I found this by the spring back there." He held up a familiar-looking piece of gray nylon.

Isis frowned. "Goodness. I don't think it's ours." She rummaged around in the top of her pack, and took out our water filter—without its stuff sack. Her face reddened. "I can't believe we just left it there. Really, we're not like that."

"Thanks," I said, shamefaced, taking it from him. "Man. After all this time on the Trail, you'd think we would have learned to look after our gear."

Nate smiled. "No biggie. People forget their stuff all the time. See you down the trail, ladies."

As the sound of his singing faded into the gray woods, I reflected on our first few days as northbounders. I had imagined that we would return to the Trail strong and confident, ready for anything it could throw at us. Instead, we'd had another brush with hypothermia, nearly lost a food bag in Blackwell Creek, and left a piece of gear by the side of the trail. So far, it was a less than auspicious start; if I had learned anything, it was how much more I needed to learn.

We came to Neel's Gap in the late morning. A crowd of exhausted-looking northbounders surrounded the Walasi-Yi Outdoor Center, lounging on the steps and filling every corner of the patio. A few sat in groups with their boots off, comparing their blisters. Thirty miles into the Trail, these nobos didn't yet have the look of long-distance hikers. Their packs and boots were brand-new, with just a few scuffs and mud stains, and their bodies, for the most part, still carried excess pounds. Isis and I, with our ripped clothing and well-developed hiker funk, stood out from the crowd. People moved aside when they smelled us coming, and eyed us with a certain trepidation: *Is that what we'll turn into on the Trail?* A few people noticed our bare feet as we passed, but hardly anyone spoke directly to us. Instead, a whisper traveled through the crowd: "Barefoot! It's them, the Barefoot Sisters!" It was more than a little unnerving.

At the far side of the patio, we saw a familiar head of brilliant red-gold curls. I was glad—here, at least, was one nobo who wouldn't be afraid to talk to us. Nate was chatting with a pair of tall, thin men, who sat on the stone retaining wall with their feet up on their packs. When he caught sight of us, he grinned and waved us over.

"Hey, Barefoot Sisters! This is Joel—" he indicated the man with graying hair and a short salt-and-pepper beard "—and Reid." The other man, with dark hair and a mustache, gave a tired smile. He looked like a young version of Garrison Keillor. "I've been telling them all about you guys."

I sighed. "This is how rumors get started. Yes, we hike barefoot. No, we wear boots when there is snow on the ground. Usually. Yes, we're yo-yoing the A.T. And yes, we are crazy."

Reid and Joel laughed. I noticed how similar their smiles were, both turning up crookedly at the left corner. "Are you guys brothers?" I asked.

"Cousins, actually," Joel said. "It's funny, I've had this dream of hiking the Trail since I was about ten. I called Reid up last year to tell him I was planning to do it. There was about ten seconds of silence at the other end of the phone. And meanwhile I'm thinking, what's happened to him? Is he okay? Did I give him a heart attack, or what? Then he says, 'I'm starting March 10, 2001.'"

Reid chuckled. "I'd been planning it for two years already."

At the outfitter's store at Walasi-Yi, Isis and I bought a few extra snacks to supplement the food we had brought from Asheville. We also invested in new rain gear: Frogg Toggs, a recent innovation made from a waterproof, breathable material similar to Tyvek house wrap. They were the cheapest option available (short of garbage bags), and the salesman gave them high marks. He had field-tested them earlier in the spring.

"They repel snow, rain, and everything in between," he said. "The week I was out, it was mostly the in-between stuff. You know, sleet, freezing rain, snow that melts when it hits."

"Nasty," I said.

"My least favorite kind of precip," the salesman agreed. "When I hiked northbound in '96, we had about three weeks of it in Georgia and North Carolina, right off the bat. A bunch of people quit. But it takes all kinds," he said, shaking his head. "We had a lady come in here a couple days ago who must've been carrying seventy-five pounds. She said, 'I just have to get rid of some of this weight!' We spread out all her gear—t-shirts, sweatshirts, big heavy stove, a couple of Tom Clancy novels. A couple of them! Plus all kinds of other things. Makeup, even. We went through it all, item by item. And every single one, she said, 'Oh, but I can't possibly part with that!' So you know what she did? She got rid of her rain gear! She said, 'I never hike in the rain anyway.'"

"Man. That's about the last thing I'd get rid of," I said. "What if she gets caught in a storm somewhere between shelters? You know, up in the White Mountains, the weather comes in like—"

He gave a wry smile. "I don't think we have to worry about that. I give her about three more weeks before she quits."

"It's hard to predict," I said. I told him about Highlander, who had taken twenty days to get through the Hundred Mile Wilderness. "For all I know, he's still on the Trail back there. And then there's the Family from the North. You must have met them . . ." All of a sudden, I couldn't go on. I had a lump in my throat.

On the way out of Neel's Gap, Nate hiked with us, telling stories of his adventures along the Pacific Crest Trail.

"I'm really curious about this barefoot thing," he finally said. "What's it like?"

"You can't really describe it," Isis said. "It's like another sense that you didn't know you had."

Nate considered for a moment. Then he stopped by the trail and took off his ratty tennis shoes.

"This isn't the best kind of ground to try it on," Isis cautioned. The red dirt was littered with gravel and small twigs. Even for us, accustomed as we were to barefoot hiking, this kind of surface took an inordinate amount of concentration. It was hard to avoid landing on the points of sharp rocks.

"I've got to try it," he said. He followed us for almost a mile up the steep slope out of the gap, with his shoes in one hand. At the crest of the next ridge, though, he stopped to put them back on. "Wow. That was far out. You're right, it's like you experience the trail in a whole different way."

"Are you a convert, then?" Isis asked.

He shook his head ruefully. "I think I'd need a whole lot more practice. I've got to say, I'm pretty impressed with you guys." He laced up his shoes. "I just don't think it's my way, you know?"

"Yeah," I said. "Hike your own hike. But I'm pretty impressed with *you* for trying it. See you down the trail."

We picked up our pace and he fell behind in a few minutes. The March sunlight looked pale and washed-out, cascading through the bare branches of oaks on the hillsides. At every overlook, we could see the long ridges stretching to the horizon, cloaked in gray trees. Once, only once, I permitted myself to think about Katahdin, our endpoint, out in the hazy distance. I pictured the sharp silver blade of the mountain springing from the horizon. Then I thought about the months and miles in between, the seasons of unknown hardship and joy ahead, and I forced my mind back to the present. I looked down at the red clay trail and kept moving.

We came across Reid and Joel, setting up their tents beside the trail while the sun was still high. Reid sat in the dead grass, pounding a recalcitrant tent stake into the ground. His shoulders slumped with fatigue. He was wearing ace wraps on both his knees.

"Hey, it's the Barefoot Sisters!" Joel said.

"Yep," I said. "And you must be the Shod Cousins." They both laughed. "You guys camping here?"

"Yeah," Reid said. "My knees are really bothering me. I don't know how much farther I'd get tonight."

"Figured we might as well stick together," Joel said, but I could see a hint of frustration in his eyes. He looked considerably less tired than Reid.

I thought back to the first weeks of our southbound hike, when I had chafed at the slow pace Isis set. Now, if anything, she was the stronger hiker; winter had taken its toll on me. "It's tough hiking with somebody if your pace is different," I said. "But if it means a lot to you, you'll find a way to stay together."

"We'll see," Joel said. "We never planned on hiking the whole Trail with each other."

"Yeah, we'll see how it works out," Reid said. "Do you ladies want to share this campsite? There's plenty of space."

"No thanks," Isis answered. "We're going to get a few more miles behind us. See you down the trail."

Isis and I stealthed at Hogpen Gap, alone, under gathering rain clouds. The dark trees, the drifted shoals of oak leaves, the slow-flowing spring and the marsh, looked just the same as when we had stayed there with the last of the sobos, just a few weeks ago. I could imagine their familiar voices in the clearing, and the jumble of well-worn tents. I wondered where they all were now—Lash must be home in Asheville, Heald en route to the New Hampshire coast for the summer, Tim back in Virginia. Spike and Caveman would be apartment-hunting in New York City. Without them, the tent site felt empty and almost desolate. I half-hoped that Nate or one of the nobos from Neel's Gap would catch up, but no one did. A light rain began tapping on the tent as we lay down to sleep.

The rain continued all through the next day, along with a thick fog that deadened sound and locked us into a tiny island of visible landscape. Trees in the middle distance, festooned with straggling vines, materialized out of the white haze as we walked forward. When I glanced back over my shoulder, I saw fog swallowing the woods behind us. It was warm enough to go barefoot, just barely. We had to move fast to keep the numbness from creeping into our toes.

We stopped for an early lunch at Low Gap Shelter. We were only four miles into our hiking day, but we were already hungry and we wanted to eat lunch out of the rain. The next shelter would be another seven miles. Once again, I had such a clear memory of this spot that I could almost hear my sobo friends' voices: Lash, exhausted from hauling five liters of wine, had wanted to spend the night right there. Only Tim's derisive laughter—"Don't be such a wuss, Lash!"—had convinced him to hike on. As he stumbled up the trail, he had muttered, "Dude, Heald better appreciate this!"

Now, in the fog, three disconsolate nobos sat in the back of the shelter. A petite gray-haired woman occupied the far corner, surrounded by heaps of gear. She was reading a thick novel, and it looked as though she had not moved for quite a while. On the near side of the platform, a slim young woman with glossy brown hair folded a shirt neatly and placed it in her pack. The man beside her, with close-cropped dark hair and a square jaw, scowled irritably. "Come on, Linda. We've been here all morning; let's get a move on." His own gear, I noticed, was still scattered around the shelter.

"I'm working on it, honey," she said in a sweet, patient, voice.

Then he noticed us. "Oh, good morning."

"Hi," Isis said as she unbuckled her wet pack. "I'm Isis."

"Jackrabbit," I said, scrambling onto the shelter platform, out of the rain.

"You must be those Barefoot Sisters we hear so much about," the man said. He looked at Isis's feet, wet and pink from the cold. She had lost her big toenails in the fall, wearing too-tight sneakers, and they were still growing back. "Hmph," he said. "Tell me, does it help to have half your toenails missing?"

She stood there open-mouthed, searching for a reply. The elderly woman in the corner, barely visible behind her pile of gear, spoke up in a bright, cheery voice. "Hello! I'm Hoo-rah, and I hope you have a hoo-rah day!" Something in her tone (not to mention her timing) reminded me of a kindergarten teacher.

"Pleased to meet you," Isis said, choosing to ignore the young man, who went back to berating his girlfriend.

"Useless weight!" he snorted. "I don't see why you carry those things around."

I looked over at her. She was folding up another shirt, carefully wrapping it around two delicate porcelain teacups. "I like them," she said helplessly. "It's just so necessary to have something, you know, *elegant* out here. Something that doesn't look like it was designed for a military base."

The man gave me a conspiratorial glance. I wasn't sure how he'd decided I was an ally. "She's such a softie."

"Two cups," I said levelly. "I suppose you drink your coffee out of one in the morning, too."

"What a beautiful day to be in the woods!" Hoo-rah said with enforced cheerfulness. "Of course," (her brightness faltered a little) "I don't hike in the rain."

"Never?" I asked. Considering the amount of precipitation we'd had in the past week, I wondered how long it had taken her to get this far.

Hoo-rah shook her head with a tight little smile. "Never. I don't even carry rain gear," she said with pride. I noticed suddenly that her cheeks were rouged, and her prim mouth had a ring of pink lipstick. *This must have been the woman the salesman at Neel's Gap was talking about*, I thought. *It does, indeed, take all kinds.*

The rain cleared up toward afternoon, and we had an easy hitch into Hiawassee at Unicoi Gap. An oversize pickup, emblazoned with the logo of a construction company, pulled into the lot almost as soon as we stuck out our thumbs.

"Hop on in," the driver said. "Y'all enjoying the Trail?"

"Yeah, you bet!" Isis told him as we stowed our sticks and packs among the joint compound buckets in the back.

"When'd you start?"

"Well, we actually started last summer, back in Maine." Isis gave a brief account of our adventures as we hurtled down the winding road.

"Well, I'll be," the driver mused. "I've been pickin' up hikers for years, and I've never heard a story like that."

"You do any hiking?" I asked.

"I do a little bit, here and there." He adjusted the visor of his baseball cap. "I like goin' off-trail. You get away from the crowds, and you see all kinds of things. I been tryin' to find all the waterfalls around here. I found one that's just a half mile off the main road, but it don't show up on any maps." He chuckled. "Took me all day just to get there, though. You'd be amazed how tough it is to get through a laurel slick. There's places around here, some coves and hollows, nobody's ever crossed, so far as I know."

As we descended into the valley, patches of green grass began to appear along the roadside. A few trees showed the faint pink mist of thickening buds. "I was out last summer," the driver continued, "in a place called Dismal Cove. Might even be on your maps. Folks around here just call it The Dismal. It's only five, six miles acrost it. I figured I'd take six days' worth of food to be on the safe side. I told a buddy of mine where I was gonna be, and I headed out.

"Well, I'd never seen anythin' like it. I got back in there, and the whole place was one big laurel slick. So thick you couldn't see the sky. And steep! Twice I almost fell off a cliff afore I saw it. All kinds of waterfalls back there. It was the most peaceful place I ever seen. But three days went by, and as near as I could tell, I'd only gone a mile into it.

"Gettin' out was harder. I had to get through all those branches goin' uphill this time. I didn't bargain on how hard it'd be. It was the better part of a week afore I got out of there, and my food was all gone. I'd sort of lost track of time back in there. Turned out I'd missed a couple days of work.

"Well, when I got back home, I called up my buddy, who was supposed to come lookin' for me if I was out late. He just about started bawlin' when he heard my voice. He said, 'Jeff, I thought you was a goner.' I said, 'What happened? Weren't you gonna come after me?' And he said, 'I tried.' He found where my truck was parked, and he got about a hunnert yards back in there afore he hit the first cliff. Then he figured if he didn't get out right then, there wasn't gonna be just one corpse in The Dismal, but two." He laughed.

"Wow," Isis said. "And you thought *our* story was something. The A.T.'s pretty tame, compared to The Dismal."

I remembered many places where the Trail was a tunnel hacked through dense rhododendron thickets. The story of The Dismal gave me a new appreciation for the trail maintainers' efforts.

In town, we resupplied at the market where Lash had bought his box of wine, and then hitched out to a hostel called the Blueberry Patch. (It hadn't been open when we came through as sobos.) The hostel was crowded with northbounders. Hikers sprawled on benches around the room, reading *National Geographic*, doctoring their blisters, or conversing in low voices.

"Fifty miles," one man said.

"Fifty point seven," his companion corrected.

"Whatever. If this is what fifty miles feels like, I don't know how in hell I'll make it two thousand." He groaned and leaned back against the bare pine boards of the wall.

"But look," a young woman pointed out. "You can see it on the map!" A fold-out map of the A.T. and its corridor hung on the wall, a strip of paper about eight inches wide and four feet long. The distance we had traversed northbound covered maybe half an inch.

I had a sudden flash of memory from the beginning of our southbound trip: sitting in the dining room at Shaw's Boarding House in Monson, Maine, studying a copy of the same map. All the twists and turns of the Hundred Mile Wilderness, all the days of mud and rain, mosquitoes and blackflies, translated into slightly more than an inch on paper. I had felt a sense of unreality settle in: *Am I really doing this? If the first inch of the map was like that, am I ready for the next four feet?* At the same time, I had felt a certain weary pride in my accomplishment. My aching muscles and itchy bug bites *meant* something. If I was capable, if I was diligent, the rest of those inches would fall as the first one had. Looking around the bunkroom at the Blueberry Patch, I could tell that the new nobos were feeling the same way. There was pain and exhaustion, and a little fear, but also determination and hope.

I heard a car pull up outside as dusk fell. Joel and Reid came through the door a moment later. Reid was visibly favoring his right knee, but both of them were in high spirits.

"Hey, check this out," Joel said with a rascally grin. "We've got wheels!"

"A vehicle?" I said. "How?"

Reid smiled. "We were coming down to the gap, and we met these section hikers going south. They were all worried about leaving their car in the lot up there. They were kind of having a fight about it, actually, when we met them."

"And just as a joke," Joel said, "I told them, 'Well, we could drive it down to town for you.' We told them about this hostel and everything. We figured we could park it here, and then they could hitch here to pick it up. And you know what?" He held up a key ring and jingled it.

There were looks of astonishment all around the room. Isis and I just smiled. We had been on the Trail long enough to know about the level of trust that develops between hikers. This was certainly an extreme example, but not without precedent.

"No way!" a young man called.

"Way," Reid said with a shrug.

"Road trip!" came a voice from the back of the room. "Mexico's nice this time of year."

"Hey, I've got an idea," I said. Three van-loads later, almost all the hikers at the Blueberry Patch were down at the Casa de Fiesta.

Isis

The day we left Hiawassee, we ate lunch at Bly Gap, leaning against the leeward side of the Georgia Oak and basking in the sun. Several other northbounders had stopped there. I thought I recognized a familiar face across the clearing, a slender woman in her early thirties with long blond hair in a French braid and tiny gold earrings. Her graceful bearing made even her hiking jacket look elegant.

"Isn't that Simply Seeking, from the Ruck?" asked jackrabbit.

It was indeed. She came to join us while we finished eating. "I'm training for my PCT hike," she told us. "I thought the best way to get in shape would be to hike a few hundred miles on the A.T. first."

"How fast are you going?" asked jackrabbit.

"Oh, fifteen, sixteen. Maybe a twenty. I'll have to hike twenty-fives between water sources on the PCT, but that trail's graded for pack horses. The ups and downs are a lot more gradual."

"Would you mind if we hike with you for a few days?" jackrabbit asked. "We're moving faster than almost everyone out here. It gets kind of lonely camping with strangers every night."

Simply Seeking's eyes lit up. "I'd love to have company! Maybe you can help me get rid of the Old Buzzard."

"The Old Buzzard?"

"He's this guy who's been after me ever since I got on at Springer. He's about my dad's age, but that's not what gets me. He's too slick. Unctuous. He never misses an opportunity to turn a normal conversation into innuendo. His real trail name's something like 'Golden Hawk.' But I think of him as 'the Old Buzzard.'" She glanced down the trail to the south. "I really ought to get going. He'll be along any minute now."

Jackrabbit and I packed quickly and followed her up the trail.

"So, the PCT. When do you plan to start?" I asked her as we started up the hillside north of the first state line.

"Not until late April," she answered, "but I'm heading out to the West Coast early to visit some relatives. I only have a few more days on the A.T."

"Well, thanks for spending this time with us," jackrabbit said. "I'm lucky enough to have my sister around all the time, but it's still a treat to hike with another woman."

"You *are* lucky to have each other," said Simply Seeking. "I did my thru-hike solo. There were whole months when all the people I was hiking with were men. Don't get me wrong, guys can be a lot of fun, but it gets a little intense being the only woman. Sometimes I felt like the focal point for a veritable maelstrom of hormones."

I tried to imagine how insufferable Tim and Lash would have been if I was the only woman they'd seen in a month. It was a scary thought.

A few minutes later, jackrabbit stopped and unbuckled her pack. "I need to pee," she said. "Go ahead, I'll catch up."

Simply Seeking turned around. "Oh, I'll wait for you. But why are you taking your pack off? Don't tell me you've been on the Trail this long, and you haven't learned to pee standing up!"

"Pee standing up?" I asked. "You mean, with one of those little funnel-and-hose contraptions?"

"No, you don't need those," she said. "It's easy. You just pull the crotch of your shorts aside, tip your pelvis forward, like this, and pee. But don't be shy about it, or it'll drip on your leg. I had to rinse off in streams once or twice when I was first learning. It was well worth it, in the end. It takes half the time, you don't have to pull your shorts down, and best of all—well, it really disconcerts the guys. When they come around a corner and see you standing there peeing, they get this shocked expression on their faces. It's like, 'Oh God, women are going to take over the world. They've learned to pee stand-ing up!'"

The three of us were sharing after-dinner tea at Big Spring Shelter the following evening when a white-haired man with handsome, craggy features sat down on the edge of the sleeping platform.

"Hello, ladies. My, you all look lovely tonight."

Simply Seeking's eyes narrowed a bit, and the cup of tea stopped halfway to her lips, but her expression remained perfectly composed as he turned toward her.

"Stacey. I've lit the candle lantern in my tent for you. It casts such a romantic glow. I hope you'll come over for a little . . . conversation, when you've finished your tea."

"No, thank you," she answered, setting down her cup. "Good night."

He slid off the sleeping platform and sauntered across the clearing toward his tent. Halfway there, he looked back, fixing Simply Seeking with his gaze. "If you change your mind, I'll be right here. Lying awake. Thinking about you."

Simply Seeking ignored him, but jackrabbit was bristling. "My God. Was that the guy who's been bothering you? You didn't tell us quite how awful he is. You've got to get away from him!"

"Can't you out-hike him?" I asked.

Simply Seeking glanced up from her teacup. "I've tried. Believe me. But he's a tough Old Buzzard."

The Buzzard was packed and ready to leave by the time we got up the next morning, but he dawdled around the campsite, poking at the ashes in the firepit, while we ate breakfast.

"Uh-oh," Simply Seeking whispered to me and jackrabbit. "I think he's going to try to hike with us. Listen, would one of you do me a huge favor and distract him if he starts talking to me? There've been a few days when he's walked along for miles, half a step behind me, just talking and talking. Stuff about his three ex-wives and his collection of champagne corks. I don't think I could take it again."

"I'm on it," said jackrabbit, punching her right fist into her left palm.

We set out single file, with jackrabbit bringing up the rear. Sure enough, a couple miles out, the Old Buzzard caught up with us and tried to pass her.

"Oh, hi," she said over her shoulder, pretending that she had just noticed him. "I didn't catch your trail name. Raptor? Buzzard? Oh, that's right. Golden Hawk. Did you give yourself that name?"

Simply Seeking and I doubled our pace, and pretty soon we were out of earshot.

"I hope he isn't boring her to death," said Simply Seeking.

"Don't worry," I said. "She won't give him a chance."

Jackrabbit caught up with us eight miles later, on the far side of Winding Stair Gap.

"Where's the Old Buzzard?" I asked her.

"Oh, he got off in Franklin. Said his knee was bothering him."

"What did you do to him?"

"Nothing! That is, I talked his ear off about my internship at the veterinarian's office last summer—"

"What internship? You've never—"

"I had a friend who did, though. I know enough about it to be quite convincing. I described a neutering operation to him, in great detail. Then I told him how much you like sword fighting. And somewhere in there, I think I mentioned that I know how to pee standing up."

We spent our last night with Simply Seeking in Wayah Bald Firetower, a square stone building perched on the top of a hill. It wasn't meant to be used as a shelter, but the splendid acoustics more than made up for the water dripping down the walls and the slanted concrete floor. We sang, drank tea, and sang some more before lying down to sleep.

Some time in the night, I woke to a soft tingling sensation on my face. Snow. Clouds of it were blowing in the doorway, and about an inch had already collected on our sleeping bags. I shone my headlamp on the walls around the doorway, looking for any hooks or protruding rocks I could use to fasten our tarp over the entrance. Smooth, sweaty rock glared back at me. Too tired to do anything else, I brushed as much of the snow as I could off our sleeping bags and wrapped the tarp around us before I fell back to sleep.

Snow blanketed everything in the morning, four inches of it, heavy and wet. I tried to unwind myself from the cocoon.

"Fuck!" cried jackrabbit, sitting straight up. My movements had sent a stream of ice water sliding off the tarp, right into her ear.

Simply Seeking sat up slowly, rubbing the sleep from her eyes. She glanced around, taking in the snow on the ground and the snow still falling.

"I think I'll leave," she said. "Hike fast to Nantahala. I have a friend who was going to pick me up there tomorrow, but I'll call and ask her to come early."

She packed in a hurry and left, wishing us a good hike. Jackrabbit and I ate a quick breakfast, put on all our layers of clothing, and followed her rapidly vanishing footsteps out the door.

The snow clung to our clothing, melting. At first I didn't notice how much I was sweating under my Frogg Toggs, but within an hour, all my clothing was soaked. I didn't dare stop, even to pee, for fear of becoming hypothermic. Uphill and downhill we trudged, as fast as we could go, through ten miles of the nasty sticky snow. Finally, we reached Tellico Gap and headed down the fire road in search of a hostel Spike and Caveman had told us about.

We ended up taking a zero day there, as the snow continued to fall. The hostel owner, a quiet, brown-haired man in his early forties, kept us well-fed with the copious supply of veggie lasagna in his freezer, and well-entertained with his collection of classic films. A little past noon, two more hikers showed up. The first, a tall man with curly hair and a round dimpled face, introduced himself as Digger.

"I'm Dan," said the second, a big, burly man with copper-colored skin and brown eyes that sparkled as if someone had just told him a good joke. "No trail name yet."

We introduced ourselves, and I asked if they were headed to Nantahala to resupply the next day.

"Yeah," said Digger. "I've got a mail drop at N.O.C."

"I don't think I'll stop there," Dan said. "I've got about twelve days of food left in my bag."

"Twelve days of food?" I asked, incredulous. "How do you fit all that inside your pack?"

"It doesn't take up that much space," he said. "This is it." He tossed me a plastic bag containing six candy bars, a pound or so of granola in a Ziploc, and some packs of broken ramen noodles. The whole package was about a third the size of my food bag.

"You're kidding," I said. "This isn't even *two* days' worth of food."

"It's twelve for me," he answered. "I just haven't been very hungry since I got on the Trail. A little granola in the morning, half a candy bar in the afternoon. Sometimes I have some ramen for supper, but sometimes I don't even want that."

"You might want to carry a little extra, just in case," I said. "The Appetite is bound to hit you sooner or later."

"Maybe. Maybe when I've gotten rid of this," he laughed, patting his gut.

The next day dawned clear and sunny. Jackrabbit and I hit the trail early. Six inches of snow still covered the ground, but the temperature rose rapidly, until it felt like it was in the high sixties. I stripped down to my shorts and sports bra, leaving my high gaiters on to keep snow from falling into my boots. When jackrabbit finished changing, she took one look at me and promptly doubled over laughing.

"What?" I asked her.

"Look at yourself. You look—" she paused, overcome with laughter. "You look like an action figure. Warrior Princess Isis."

I looked down. She was right. I was standing with my legs braced apart, to keep my balance on the slippery trail. The combination of hiking boots and gaiters looked like heavy, knee-high leather boots. The waist belt of my pack, clasped just below my belly button, could have been some kind of sword or ammunition belt. Over my black sports bra hung the badger-claw necklace that my stepfather had lent me when we started the Trail. And then there were my fierce, pronged hiking sticks. I had to join in jackrabbit's laughter.

"Okay, so I'm a warrior princess," I said. "What's my mission today?"

"How 'bout, consume a whole pint of Ben & Jerry's at N.O.C.?" jackrabbit suggested.

"Great idea. Let's go!"

The warm weather continued over the next few days. Green leaves started peeking through the brown ones on the forest floor. On the shoulder of a road, I found a cluster of tiny purple mint plants with a wonderful gingery flavor. We gathered a handful of them and saved a few for our tea that night— our first harvest of the spring.

One clear morning, as the trail skirted the edge of a valley, I saw a bluebird flying among the yellow poplar branches below us. I had been daydreaming, reciting poetry in my head, so my mind interpreted the sight with the logic of art, not zoology. I saw the bright azure shape, gliding through the trees below me, and I looked up, searching for the bird-shaped hole in the sky that it had been cut from. I had just time to wonder what I would see behind the sky—a white wall like the ceiling of a planetarium? night, with stars? a misplaced dawn from the Mesozoic Era?—before my mind snapped back to a more mundane frame of reference, and I realized that bird and sky were not the same substance.

That afternoon, we saw our first wildflower, a tiny purple violet clinging to the moss beside a stream. The next day we saw a yellow violet, and then a whole cluster of white violets. As we descended to Fontana Dam, the trilliums appeared: at first a whorl of pale green leaves, speckled with deep purplish red, poking out of the fallen oak leaves; lower down, the closed flowers like candle flames rising between the three splayed leaves; and lower still, open flowers, blood red and palest yellow, painting the whole forest floor.

jackrabbit

The shelter at Brown Fork Gap brought back many memories. I remembered the last time we'd been there, just three weeks earlier—the arrival of Tim and Lash, with his chipmunk beard. The shelter's porcupine trap, unusual this far south, reminded me, too, of shelters in Maine—the evenings of stories and songs with Waterfall, Tenbrooks, Blue Skies, and the rest of the sobos. Our southbound hike had brought us so many close friends. Northbound, aside from our few days with Simply Seeking, we had been hiking much faster than the crowd. I wondered when people would start catching up, and if they would all pass us again as they had on our southbound trek. I wondered if we would ever find a group of like-minded, like-paced hikers.

This time, when we came to the shelter at Brown Fork Gap, we found only one person there: a nobo in his mid-thirties, with long frizzy blond hair tied into a knot at the base of his neck, and a prodigious beard. He smiled up at us from behind tiny round glasses. "Hi there. I'm Basil."

We introduced ourselves.

"Is that your real name, or a trail name?" I asked.

"Oh, it's my trail name. I've worked as a chef, off and on." He sat wrapped up in his sleeping bag, with a cooking pot bubbling on a Whisperlite stove beside him.

"A chef, eh? What's for dinner?" I asked.

He looked a little abashed, as though he didn't quite want to admit what he was cooking. "Risotto with sun-dried tomatoes and parmesan. And basil, of course. I mean, I figured I could get by with ramen and Lipton dinners and all that, but it's not too much extra weight to carry some herbs. Olive oil."

"And garlic," Isis said. "I don't know what we'd do without garlic." I could tell she approved of his strategy—it was hers, too.

"Yeah. Dude, there's no reason that just 'cause we live in the woods, we have to eat like barbarians." He smiled and stretched luxuriously, and then returned to stirring his dinner. Basil and Isis traded recipes and cooking tips while I went to the spring for water. By the time I came back, they were laughing like old friends.

"I don't know when I first got interested in cooking," Isis said. "I guess growing up in my mom's kitchen, I just picked it up naturally."

"Oh, I know right when it was for me," Basil said. "It was when I got out of the service, after Desert Storm."

I was surprised—he had been a soldier when I was still in middle school. Obviously he was older than I had thought.

"I'll never forget that first civilian meal I had," he continued. "I said to myself, 'I'll be damned if I ever eat another M.R.E.' So that first night, I cooked up a huge pot of pasta with cheese, tomatoes, all kinds of herbs, garlic. All the fresh vegetables I could find. It would have been pretty good, except I just about cooked the life out of that pasta. It was, like, mush. I said to myself, 'Man, you're on your own now. You gotta learn to cook.' So I signed up for a cooking class in night school, right then." He stirred the pot of risotto again. "That was the same day I started growing my hair out," he said with a certain pride. "I've never cut it since then."

"It is kind of hard to picture you with a crew cut," I said.

"It's hard for *me* to picture it anymore. Like, where I am now is a million miles away from that kid I was ten years ago. Just a kid with big dreams. Something about saving the world. Dude, if I learned one thing out there, it's that you can't save the world with a gun. You know, if I saw that kid on the street today, maybe I'd talk to him, say, 'Man, what were you *thinking*?' And maybe I'd just let him walk on by."

Basil was still curled up in his sleeping bag when we left in the early morning. He mumbled something as we shouldered our packs.

"See you down the trail," Isis said.

Spring was finally coming to the Nantahala Mountains. The dark brown mud of the trail felt rich with promise underfoot, like the loam of our mother's garden. Among the dead leaves on the forest floor, we saw leaves and petals unfolding, yellow and purple violets, delicate bloodroot, banks of maroon and yellow trilliums with their fragile variegated leaves. In the lowest hollows, the buds of the trees swelled pink and green. At last, it seemed that we had left winter behind us. I was so thrilled by the signs of spring that I scarcely noticed the steep ups and downs of the trail. The day flew past, and before the shadows of afternoon lengthened across the mountains, we found ourselves at the edge of the giant parking lot at Fontana Dam.

We hitched a ride up the road to Fontana Village Resort with a couple returning from a fishing trip. "This place used to be quite something," the woman said. "Back when I was growing up, this was where everybody came for the summer. People are off to different things now, I guess."

Her husband had a darker view. "I don't know. This place didn't really start going downhill until that new company took it over, ten, twelve years ago. My guess is, they lose money here on purpose. Use it as a tax break."

"Well, y'all enjoy," the woman said as they dropped us off. Looking around the grounds of Fontana Village, I was inclined to agree with the man's assessment. The unmown athletic fields, disheveled hedges, run-down buildings, and the cracked asphalt of the parking lot all spoke of a place that had seen better days. We rented a room in the hotel, took showers, and went in search of food.

There were several restaurants open during the summer, apparently, but only one that served anything this early in the season. We got a table with Digger and Dan, who had arrived shortly before us. The place had an atmosphere of faded elegance, from the slightly frayed blue carpet and green tablecloths to the bouquets of yellowing plastic flowers. The menu was limited, and the vegetarian options even more so. Out the window, the greenish waters of Fontana Lake tossed in a gathering breeze and the tops of small trees danced. There was green grass outside, studded with flowers, but the Shuckstack Ridge across the way looked dead-brown with winter. I wondered whether the Smokies, hidden behind them, were still clad in snow.

"I love this trail," Dan said. "All my family, back in Miami, they thought I was crazy."

"Yeah, man, so did I, first time I saw you—"

"Shaddup, Digger!" Dan cuffed him on the arm. "But seriously, it's just so great to be out here. After spending all the time and money getting my gear together, and convincing Mom I could really do this . . . It's like, you know, one of those MasterCard ads. 'Backpack: $200. Leki poles: $180. Sleeping bag: $150. Hiking the A.T.: Priceless.'"

"Priceless!" I exclaimed. "That's you! That's your trail name!"

"Priceless." He grinned, his eyes bright. "I like the sound of that." He mused a while. "I think I'm gonna start writing those ads in the registers. 'Tuna can: $1. Piece of string: ten cents. Stick: free. A night without mice in your food bag: Priceless.'"

The waitress came over to take our orders: two burgers with fries for the meat-eaters, and two cheese quesadillas and the deep-fried vegetable assortment for Isis and me. I was beginning to long for vegetables that were not deep fried. When our plates were clean (an alarmingly short interval), she returned and we asked about dessert. Her charming Tennessee Valley drawl and her dimples seemed to have a magnetic effect on Priceless. He kept her talking as long as he could.

"We've got the key lime pie, at five dollars . . ."

"Five dollars for a slice of pie? How big are these slices, sweetheart?" Priceless managed a look of righteous indignation.

"Oh, 'bout like this." She held out her hands in a very narrow V.

"So, there's what, like, ten slices in a whole pie?"

"That's right."

We had a brief discussion. "How much for the whole pie?" Digger asked.

"Well, I don't rightly know. I can't recall anyone orderin' a whole one before. I'm gon' ask the chef; y'all sit tight." In a moment she was back again, looking apologetic. "He said he cain't sell it for less than forty dollars."

"That's one expensive pie!" Priceless raised his eyebrows. "Is it made fresh right here?"

"Well, no, it's made in a bakery in Alabama and shipped here special. It's real tasty."

"So how many people order this five-dollar pie? I mean, at that price, you can't sell too many slices."

"Well, somebody ordered a piece last week . . ."

We all fell silent, contemplating the shelf life of key lime pie, and the waitress's dimples faltered for a moment. "It keeps real good," she offered, but none of us had much appetite for pie any more.

Our hunger not quite sated, Isis and I walked over to the general store to look for dessert. The store was next to the post office in a log-cabin style building, down the road from the motel. Inside, fluorescent lights overhead cast a dingy glow over the shelves and freezer cases. The man behind the counter grunted as we came in and didn't look up from his newspaper.

With our hiker senses honed, it didn't take long to find the ice cream case. It took even less time to realize that there wasn't much there. The back of the freezer housed what looked like the beginnings of the next ice age. Jumbled pints of ice cream and boxes of popsicles were encased in a solid waterfall of ice, six inches thick in places. A few ice cream cakes stood loose in the front of the freezer, but when Isis pulled one out the expiration date read *January 1996*.

We did buy a package of cheese for our resupply, and some Gatorade. We could use the bottles to carry extra water in case the springs in the Smokies were frozen. Outside the store, Isis opened her bottle of Lemon Frost to take a swig, but she paused when she saw the writing under the cap.

"Hey, check this out!"

"Did you win something?"

"No. I think the contest was over a couple years ago anyway. But this is better than winning something. Here, read it."

She passed the cap over, and I read: STAY IN THE GAME. PLAY AGAIN.

"Georgia to Maine," she said, laughing. "That's us, sister, staying in the GA–ME."

We picked up our mail drop at the post office, a box of food we had sent from Asheville. Considering the state of the general store, I was glad we didn't need to do an entire resupply there. We sat at a picnic table by the edge of the parking lot and began pouring the boxes of cereal and polenta into Ziplocs, filling up our food bags. The amounts looked a little scant for the eight days to Hot Springs, but with the warmer weather, we had been eating less anyway.

"Hey, Barefoot Sisters!" It was Basil, walking across the parking lot with two unfamiliar hikers. "You gotta meet some friends of mine."

"Hi, I'm Luna." She was a slender, lively woman with long henna-red hair and freckles. Her worn-out purple pack, red pants, green shirt, and the bright orange handkerchief she wore across her forehead made the most colorful outfit I'd seen in a long time.

"And I'm Six-string Hillbilly." He tipped his green slouch hat. He was tall and lanky, with shaggy brown hair and a trimmed beard, and a slightly goofy smile. "Most people just call me Six-string."

"And I call him Sixy!" Luna said, throwing an arm around his waist.

He grinned. "Pleased to meet y'all."

"Good to meet you guys," I said, and it really was. Unlike many of the nobos we had met so far, who seemed uncertain and uncomfortable on the Trail, these two looked right at home. That, combined with Luna's ragged pack . . . "Have you guys hiked before?" I asked.

"Yeah, we hiked in '99," Luna beamed. "This was where we met, actually, right here in Fontana."

"We got married on the Grayson Highlands, three weeks later," Six-string said.

"Well, it was a hiker wedding," Luna added. "He gave me a bouquet of rhododendron and a ring made out of grass. I had a couple ponies for brides-maids. Counts for us, though." She gave him another squeeze. "But I want to hear about all of your adventures. You're yo-yoing, right? That's so excellent! And barefoot?"

While we traded stories with Basil, Luna, and Six-string, I noticed another hiker sitting on the porch of the laundromat, a short ways from us. He had dark hair and a neat black beard. His green Go-lite pack leaned against a column of the porch. I waved to him, but he didn't seem to notice.

Luna and Six-string talked about hiking in New Zealand, and traveling all over the U.S. and Luna's native Canada in their camper van. Finally Six-string got up and stretched. "Well, I hate to cut this party short, y'all, but my lovely wife and I have got some errands to run."

"I hope we'll meet up again on the Trail," Luna said. "This was fun."

Basil headed for the post office. Isis and I finished packing up our resupply and headed for the laundromat. The dark-haired hiker smiled when he saw us coming. "I know who you guys are," he said. "You're the Barefoot Sisters! But I know you have lots to do. I don't want to bother you. Unlike *some* peo-ple, I don't just go up and talk to famous people without an introduction." There was a certain smugness in his tone, but a gleam in his eyes let me know he wasn't entirely serious.

It always amused me to be called famous, knowing that if I went five miles off the trail, my face—and my feet—would be unrecognizable to just about anyone. "Hey, those were our friends," I said in a slightly bantering tone. "You think famous people don't have any friends?"

"Point taken, Barefoot Sister."

"Jackrabbit," I said.

He nodded slightly. "Jackrabbit. I'm Forest Phil."

Isis introduced herself.

"So what's a pair of pretty women like you doing on the Appalachian Trail?"

Something in his tone invited a sarcastic reply; he seemed like the kind of person who would appreciate the caustic humor I usually held in reserve. "Hiking," I said. "Isn't it obvious?"

Forest Phil regarded me for a moment. I hoped I hadn't misread him. Then he gave an appreciative laugh, shaking his head. "You don't suffer fools gladly, do you, jackrabbit? I like that in a person." He gave me an evil grin. "You know, a name like that is practically begging somebody to call you jack—" he spat out the syllable vindictively and paused, as if about to append the name of a different animal "—rabbit. Did you ever think of that?"

"Hmm. Can't say I did . . . Land Phil."

We stayed in town for a long time the next day, debating whether to hike out or not. Isis was set on trying to do a barefoot flip-flop within our yo-yo—hiking back to the middle of Shenandoah National Park, at least, barefoot. We had managed to hike every section of the Trail south of Fontana barefoot in at least one direction. Given the recent snowstorms, though, we knew it would be difficult, if not impossible, to hike through the Smokies without putting our boots back on. In the early afternoon, we lingered by the pay phone outside the post office.

"Maybe we should wait for a week or so before we try to hike the Smokies," Isis said. "Give it more time to melt."

"Bill and Jill said if we needed to get bailed out in the Smokies, we could give them a call."

"It's not like we need bailing out right now. We probably should tell them we're on the way through, though. This is the last phone till Hot Springs."

But there was no answer at their house. The phone rang and rang; not even a machine picked up.

"While we're here, maybe we should call home. It's been a while since we talked to our mom," Isis said.

It was wonderful to hear her clear voice, and she had good news—in a few weeks she was planning to fly down and join us while we hiked through the Roan Highlands. We had been trying to arrange her visit for a long time. At last, her schedule of meetings and obligations was free enough that she could join us.

In the end, we decided to leave town in the afternoon. It was a gorgeous, clear day, and the wind felt warm even as we crossed the Dam. The sun slanted toward afternoon by the time we headed into the woods. Priceless and Digger were somewhere up ahead. Forest Phil hiked with us briefly, but with his light pack he quickly passed us. Six-string, Luna, and Basil had opted for another night in town.

My pack felt unusually heavy with eight days of food. The four-mile uphill of Shuckstack Ridge left my legs weak and tired. Isis and I decided to take a break at the top of the ridge and check out the fire tower that was marked on the map. We dropped our packs in the brush by the side trail and went to investigate.

The tower was a decidedly rickety structure; the glass windows of its cabin had long since shattered, the paint had peeled off, and the cables that anchored it had dripped streaks of rust on the rock at its base. Some of the wooden steps were missing; the rest were silvered by the weather and looked ready to break in half. Still, Isis and I climbed the turning stairway, clinging to the handrail, placing our bare feet close to the iron supports that held the remnants of the steps.

Once we had climbed above the treetops, a bracing wind hit us. We looked off to the northeast, where we were going: row on row of mountains, rolling off into the blue-gray distance. In the clear air, the nearest summits looked close enough to touch. And all of them were pale with snow.

"Isis," I said over the roar of the wind, "I don't know about the idea of doing this barefoot."

She squared her shoulders. "We'll just have to see."

Climbing down was harder than going up; it was impossible to avoid noticing the holes in the slats, through which the ground seemed terribly far away. After a few moments of stomach-wrenching vertigo, I found the will to move downward. As the trees closed in around us again, my fear diminished. I scampered lightly down the last turn of the stairs. But the cold wind seemed to have followed us down from the tower, and the temperature kept dropping as shadows collected in the woods.

CHAPTER 2

Staying in the Game

Isis

We stayed at Birch Spring Shelter on our first night in the Smokies. A little over a month before, when we'd passed that way southbound, we'd had the shelter to ourselves after leaving the Family from the North and before we caught up with Tim and Lash. Now we shared the low wooden building with a crowd of nobos—the newly named Priceless, Digger, and Forest Phil, along with a few others I hadn't met. The row of colorful sleeping bags spread out along the wall, the smells of sweat, stove fuel, and ramen seasoning packs, and the atmosphere of nervous excitement as people traded rumors and advice about the mountains ahead reminded me of our last week in Maine southbound, preparing to enter the Whites. Then, jackrabbit and I had been part of a tight-knit group who had dreamed of staying together for the whole Trail. Now that I knew how hard it would be to match our pace to someone else's, I had no illusions about summiting Katahdin with friends we met this early in our hike. We were beginning to see the same faces for more than one night in a row, though; we might hike through the Smokies with some of these guys, or we might meet again a few states down the Trail. *Time to be sociable*, I thought.

I fought down a wave of shyness. It was much harder to break the ice with nobos, most of whom treated us like celebrities, than it had been to meet other sobos, who had experienced a lot of the same things we had. As a compromise, I turned to Forest Phil. Jackrabbit and I had already spent some time around him in Fontana, and he seemed to take pride in ignoring our celebrity status.

"Hey, Forest Phil. What's on your menu tonight?"

"I haven't decided yet," he answered, his voice slow and solemn as if he were mulling over a complicated mathematical formula. "Angel hair pasta, Alfredo sauce, garlic, parmesan, some red onion, and perhaps the spinach . . ."

Red onion? Spinach? I wondered if he had dehydrated all of his own food. Even the co-op in Asheville hadn't had anything that good.

"Yes, the spinach," he continued. "The weather's colder than I expected it to be, and if I don't eat the spinach now, it might freeze."

He reached into his Go-lite pack and took out what looked like half a pound of fresh spinach, followed by a large red onion and a head of garlic.

"Some of this might be nice, too," he mused, producing a huge, glossy red pepper.

My mouth watered. I forced my attention back to the polenta and beans I had been cooking. A moment before, it had seemed like quite a delicacy, because I had a clove of garlic and some dried tomatoes to add to it.

Jackrabbit came up, bringing a few Nalgenes of water to boil for our hot water bottles.

"Man, you eat well," she said to Forest Phil. "I'd never have guessed that you could fit all that fresh stuff into that tiny pack."

Forest Phil's chest swelled. "*Some* people have a stereotype about ultralight hikers. *They* think that we don't carry enough food for ourselves—" his voice rose with righteous indignation "—that we *mooch* off other hikers. *I* make a point of always carrying more food than I need, just to prove them wrong. And I'd *never* mooch. Even if I made a mistake, and hiked out short-supplied, I'd go hungry for a week, rather than mooch. *I* have my honor!"

His black eyes flashed, and he thrust his chin forward in an expression that reminded me uncannily of Blade. Jackrabbit and I looked at each other. Considering how cold the air was growing, and how much the temperature affected our appetites, we were probably short-supplied for the eight days to Hot Springs. And our packs were twice as heavy as Forest Phil's. *Well, I prefer his attitude to Charlemagne's*, I thought, laying one thin slice of cheese on each side of our pot of polenta.

jackrabbit

I had a hard time in the Smokies. The morning we hiked out of Birch Spring, the cold clamped down. It was winter again; ice crystals formed in our water bottles even as we walked. We hadn't yet reached the snow line, though, so we tried to go barefoot. My body protested the bitter weather and our low food supply—after hiking fast for two hours, I still couldn't feel my feet.

I threw down my pack by the side of the trail. "Isis, I can't do this any more!"

She stopped and looked back. "So put your boots on."

"Are you going to?"

"No, my feet are fine," she said shortly, and kept walking.

I sat down on a bank of frozen red earth at the edge of the trail and tried to rub some life into my toes. They were still faintly pink—no danger of frostbite—but so cold I could barely feel my hands on them. I untied my boots from the outside of my pack and found a pair of socks. I watched Isis walk up the path, diminishing with distance, still barefoot, and I felt myself diminished, too. *I'm weak*, I thought. *I don't belong here.* Inside my boots, my feet warmed up and began to throb painfully with each step. *It's just what you deserve*, said an ugly little voice in the back of my head. The hunger gnawing at my belly had awakened other demons.

I caught up to Isis at the top of the ridge. There were meadows of tawny grass on both sides of the trail, half-grown in with bushes and small trees. Distant snow-covered mountains showed between the branches. The leaves of the rhododendrons, even in the sun, curled up tight, and snow clung to the ground.

"I'm going to have to put my boots on, too," she said softly. "I thought I could do it, but I just can't."

"So don't bitch to me about it," I snapped. "You don't have to prove that you're tougher than me. We know that already, don't we?"

She whirled to face me, her eyes flashing. "Damn it, this isn't some macho thing! *I'm* not out here to prove anything. You can have your little delusions if you want—" She stopped as the sound of voices came up the trail.

"Shit," I said. The last thing I wanted was to have our petty arguments overheard. We sat in glum silence as the other hikers drew closer.

It was Luna and Six-string. "No, I'm sure that meadow was where we stealth-camped, that first night," Luna was saying. "Remember? We left our dishes out after dinner and came up the ridge to watch the sunset. Then we hid out when that ranger went by, and he confiscated all our cooking gear." Six-string mumbled something. "No, you're on crack!" she responded. "I swear it was that meadow—" she looked up and noticed us. "Hey, Barefoot Sisters! Guess where we are!"

Her enthusiasm helped lift my spirits a little. "We must be near Thunderhead Mountain by now," I said.

"This is Rockytop!" she told me. "You know, like in the Tennessee fight song."

A dim memory stirred in my head. "Oh, yeah. I had a friend in college from Tennessee who used to go around singing that."

Luna looked at Six-string, and they began to sing, in glorious harmony.

> I wish I was up on Rockytop,
> up in the Tennessee hills.
> Ain't no smoggy smoke on Rockytop,
> ain't no telephone bills.
>
> Rockytop, you'll always be
> Home sweet home to me-ee-ee
> Good old Rockytop, Rockytop Tennessee,
> Rockytop Tennessee.

"How's the rest of it go?" Six-string said, half to himself. "There's that one verse about moonshine, and one about a girl . . . oh, and then my favorite verse. The one about the guy in the city. Wish I'd written that one myself!" They started singing again.

> Corn don't grow at all on Rockytop,
> Dirt's too rocky by far.
> That's why folks who live on Rockytop
> Get their corn from a jar!
>
> Once I had me a girl on Rockytop
> Half bear, the other half cat
> But she was as sweet as soda pop—
> I still dream about that!
>
> I've had years of cooped-up city life,
> Trapped like a duck in a pen.
> All I know is it's a pity life
> cain't be simple again.

By the last chorus, I was able to join them, filling in the harmonies.

Rockytop, you'll always be
Home sweet home to me-ee-ee
Good old Rockytop, Rockytop Tennessee,
Rockytop Tennessee!

Six-string finished off with a masterful bluegrass air guitar riff.

"Thanks, guys," I said. "You came at a really good time. I've been having kind of a crappy day."

"Yeah," Isis said, starting to smile.

Luna and Six-string told stories from their first thru-hike and offered us more granola bars to supplement our meager lunch. It was amazing what a difference a little food made. Suddenly I could see the beauty of the day around me: the saturated blue of the sky overhead, cloudless from horizon to horizon; the shapes of the mountains visible between the trees, outlined in snow, a line of flowing sculptures like standing waves in a river. I was so grateful I wanted to weep.

Over the next few days, the temperatures stayed bitterly cold. High clouds began gathering, casting a halo around the sun; we knew that bad weather was on the way. I was beginning to feel desperate—if we were caught in a shelter, icebound, now, we'd be eating our bootlaces by the time we reached Hot Springs.

The only consolation was the presence of Luna and Six-string. They were full of wild adventure stories and bluegrass songs, and their constant good humor helped to keep our spirits up. Also, Isis and I had an unspoken pact not to argue in front of other hikers. The four of us walked together in a line, talking and laughing, and the miles seemed to fly past.

Isis

We caught up with Forest Phil at Mount Collins Shelter, just before Newfound Gap. He was setting up his stove in a corner when we hiked in. I sat down near him and started sorting through our meager supplies, trying to decide how much I could allocate for this meal. Out of the corner of my eye, I saw Forest Phil pull an entire head of broccoli out of his pack.

"This is a lot of broccoli for one person," he said to himself. "Maybe I should share some of it."

Broccoli! Not just food, but a fresh vegetable. I couldn't think of anything that would taste better. I held my breath.

"Isis, would you like some of this?" Forest Phil asked.

Black Forest's old expression, "Do I have an ass?" came to mind, but I remembered Forest Phil's opinion of moochers. I forced myself to come up with a more measured reply.

"I'd love some," I said, "but are you sure you can spare it? I don't know about you, but this cold doubles my appetite."

"You have a point," he answered. "Maybe I should keep it." He fell silent for a moment, reflecting. "I could give you just a few florets . . . No, I don't think I will, after all. I'm hungry enough to eat the whole thing." By this point in the monologue, he had chopped the top of the head into a pile on a plastic bag. "Well, that is a lot of broccoli," he said. "I hope it will fit in my pot, along with the onion, rice, and cheese. He turned to me. "You know, you can use the stems also," he said. "But I don't think I will. I think I'll save them for tomorrow."

Jackrabbit arrived with the water. We ate our small pot of rice and beans, washed down with a large pot of tea. Five minutes later, my stomach felt empty again. I thought about asking Six-string and Luna if they had any extra dinners, but I couldn't bring myself to do it in front of Forest Phil.

He came out and stood beside us as jackrabbit and I brushed our teeth. "I could hardly finish my supper," he announced. "I guess I should have given you some of that broccoli after all."

"Broccoli?" jackrabbit asked after he left. "He had broccoli? God, I'd sell my sleeping bag for a piece of broccoli right now." She turned and limped back to the shelter, her head bent and her shoulders slumped with fatigue.

I don't give a shit what he thinks of me, I said to myself as I lay down to sleep, knees curled tight against my cramped and empty belly. *Tomorrow, I'll ask Luna for another granola bar. If not for myself, for my sister.*

I waited until Forest Phil had packed up and left before explaining to Luna and Six-string just how desperate we were, and asking if they still had extra food. After holding out for that long, I didn't think I could face Forest Phil's scorn.

"Sure, Isis," Luna said. "Take all you want." She dumped out her food bag, spreading an assortment of dried fruit, candy bars, and packaged dinners across the shelter floor. "We might be getting off at Newfound Gap anyway."

"Hey, no fair," said Six-string. "If you're gonna lighten her food bag, you gotta help lighten mine too!" He took out half a jar of peanut butter, several baggies of granola, and a bar of cheese, and added them to the pile in front of us.

Jackrabbit and I looked over the food, trying to pick something inexpensive. Finally, we each took a granola bar; there seemed to be a lot of those.

"Here, take these, too; they're real good," said Luna, pushing a bag of dried apricots toward us.

"And if you take some of these oriental ramens, and mix them with some peanut butter and sesame seeds, it makes halfway decent fake Thai food," said Six-string, stacking the ingredients in front of me as he spoke. "Oh, and a few shakes of soy sauce. I've got some of those packets of it around here somewheres."

jackrabbit

We came to the parking lot at Newfound Gap at midmorning. A few tourists huddled near their cars, pointing video cameras at the surrounding mountains. A brisk wind whistled through the parking lot and thick snow clung to the ground; the weather didn't seem to have changed at all since February.

"Listen, y'all," Six-string said. "We're probably going to get off at the Gap. Looks like some nasty weather's headed this way. We've got some friends in Cullowhee, down in the valley past Cherokee. We could probably stay there. Y'all are welcome, too."

"Are you sure?" Isis said. "I mean, we wouldn't want to impose . . ."

"Oh, it's totally fine," Luna said. "They're raft guides. Kind of like hikers. They'll take us in. And I have to get back there anyway; I left my van with them. I was planning to hitch down from Hot Springs and pick it up, but this'll be easier."

All four of us stood by the edge of the road with our thumbs out.

"I discovered the trick to hitching on my first thru-hike," Luna said. "Nobody wants to pick up a glum hitchhiker. So you beam sunshine at them. Anybody who drives by, you smile like you've just heard the best news in the world."

We tried to beam sunshine, but it didn't seem to be working. The few cars that passed us sped up. "This isn't goin' so well," Six-string finally said. "Nobody's got space for four hikers. Maybe it'd be better if just two of us hitch at a time."

"Where can we meet you?"

They thought for a moment. "Cherokee," Luna said. "We'll go pick up the van, and you can meet us, let's see . . . There's a little restaurant, Grandma's Kitchen or something like that, over on the east side of town. Yeah. Meet us there, in, like, a couple hours?"

"Sounds good," I said. We stepped back into the fringe of trees.

In a few minutes, a rust-streaked white Plymouth pulled onto the shoulder. A wild-eyed man with stringy brown hair leaned out the window. "Where ya headed?" They got in, and the car took off with a screech of tires, slaloming down the center of the narrow road.

Isis and I caught a ride down the mountain a few minutes later, with a kind retired couple on vacation from Indiana. The road down from Newfound Gap twisted and turned, banking around sharp corners as it descended. It offered breathtaking views of the valley and the mountains beyond. My appreciation of the beauty was diminished by my worries for Luna and Sixstring—I half-expected to see the wreckage of a white car in the underbrush. When we came to the outskirts of Cherokee, the first souvenir stands and cheap hotels, I breathed a sigh of relief. At least they'd gotten down the mountain safely.

The main street of Cherokee was a strip of trading posts selling brightly colored feathers, arrowheads, tomahawks. Several painted teepees stood in the parking lots, next to roadside stands selling boiled peanuts. Neon signs advertised motels, tattoo parlors, and a twenty-four-hour wedding chapel. In the bright glare of late morning, the town looked gritty and run-down. But there was something in the place that seemed much more real, more human, than the garish extravagance I remembered from Gatlinburg, across the mountains. (On the way to Jill and Bill's house in winter, we had driven through that town. Its bizarre concatenation of faux-Alpine resorts, mini golf, theme parks, and upscale shopping malls had been a disturbing contrast to the spare beauty of the mountains in winter.) On one side of Cherokee's main street, the clear golden water of the Oconaluftee River leaped and sparkled like a vein of life in the middle of the hardscrabble town.

"Now, where was it you-uns wanted to go?" the driver asked us.

Isis remembered the name of the restaurant. The woman found it on their tourist map of the town and dropped us off with a cheery wave. "You-uns stay safe now, you hear?"

The restaurant was mostly empty; the breakfast rush was over and lunch had not yet started. We stowed our packs and hiking sticks in a corner and settled into a red Naugahyde booth.

The waitress came over immediately. She was a short woman with a wide, intelligent face and warm brown eyes. "Y'all want coffee?"

"Yeah. Thanks." We turned over our mugs.

"I have to ask, what are y'all doing with those huge packs?"

"We're hiking the Trail," Isis said.

"One of the trails in the park?"

"No, the Appalachian Trail. It does run through the park, though."

"Wow," she breathed. "The whole Trail? That one that runs from way up north down to Georgia?"

"Yup," I said. "We went down from Maine to Georgia, and now we're headed back up."

"Well, I'll be! I've never met anybody who's hiked that whole Trail before. And y'all are planning on hiking back? That takes the cake! I'm Michelle, by the way. It's a real pleasure to meet y'all."

"I'm Susan," I said. My real name felt strange on my lips.

"Lucy," Isis said, and that was even stranger.

"I'm surprised you don't see more hikers in here," I said. "The Trail runs right along the top of the ridge there, in the Smokies. You can almost see it from the sidewalk out there."

"Do you do any hiking?" Isis asked her.

Michelle gave a quick laugh. "Oh, not me. My people, the Cherokees, we were great walkers. Walked all around these hills. But these days, it's all I can do to hold a job down, take care of the kids. Y'all are lucky to be out there."

We ate fried eggs, thick pancakes, and hash browns that tasted suspiciously of lard. I was so hungry I didn't care. When we had finished, Michelle came by our table again. "What's it like out there on the Trail?" she asked. "It must get cold sometimes . . ."

"What's it like?" Isis said. "It's so hard to describe. Every little aspect of life on the Trail is so different from town life. You always have to worry about carrying enough food, enough water; staying warm enough. But the people out there are so wonderful. There's this . . . interconnectedness that you don't find in many other places."

Michelle glanced surreptitiously around the restaurant. The rest of the tables were empty. She pulled a chair up to the end of our booth and sat down. "My boss doesn't like it when I take too much time chatting with the customers," she said. "But there's nobody else here right now; I guess it won't matter. And I want to know about that Trail. Now, what time of year was it when y'all started?"

We talked until the lunch customers began trickling in. Michelle asked question after question, her deep brown eyes shining. Finally she sighed and stood up. "I've got to get back to work. But do me a favor, y'all?" She wrote something down on a napkin. "Here's my number. Call me when you finish the Trail, okay? Tell me what it's like up there in the North."

Isis took the paper. "We will. Good to meet you, Michelle."

We stepped out of the restaurant just as an enormous blue camper van with Manitoba plates pulled into the lot. Luna leaned out the window. "Hey, Barefoot Sisters! Hop on in!"

We climbed into the back of the van, stepping over boxes of hiker food, clothing, and various camping equipment, and settled on velvet-upholstered cushions behind the driver's seat. Inside, the van seemed even larger than it had first appeared. Paisley curtains covered the windows, steeping the interior in a warm red light, and a smoldering stick of incense on the dashboard filled the air with the sweet reek of patchouli.

"Welcome aboard, y'all," Six-string said.

Luna leaned back over her seat. "Man, I'm glad it was us that got that first hitch, and not you. It was big-time sketchy. The guy had hotwired the ignition. I think he was strung out on something, too. He was all over the road. And he kept going on about his wife, and how evil she was, how all women are out to do you wrong."

"Do ya wrong!" Six-string said in a harsh nasal tone, scowling and hunching over the steering wheel. He glanced around with shifty eyes.

"Yeah, just like that," Luna said, laughing. "Hope you guys got a better ride."

Down in the valley, green grass sprouted from the roadsides. Flowers in the undergrowth made blurs of color as we drove past, and a few trees were misted with pale green leaves. The sun was warm and the sky looked cloudless as we arrived in Cullowhee.

"This is the place," Six-string said, carefully maneuvering the van down a rutted driveway. A small trailer home with peeling vinyl siding sat on cinderblocks in a patch of brilliant red earth.

We piled out of the van, stretching our cramped legs. A young man with a white-blond ponytail stood in the doorway, smoking. He crossed his arms. "We don't want no stinkin' guitar-playin' hippie hiker trash 'round here," he said, but he couldn't help cracking a smile.

"James!" Six-string said. "Hey, my man, long time no see."

"Yeah, all of an hour or so." James grinned. "Glad you found your friends, man. Glad that van of yours didn't break down again."

"James, these are the Barefoot Sisters," Luna said, introducing us with a flourish.

"Good to meet y'all," he said.

A woman rode up the driveway on a bicycle and stopped beside us. "Hey, I'm Julia," she said. She was compact and muscular, with dark curly hair and a profusion of freckles. Isis and I introduced ourselves.

"I figured you guys would be back for the van one of these days," Julia said to Luna.

"Actually," Luna told her, "we were kind of hoping we might be able to stay here for a little while. There's a storm coming in the mountains."

James and Julia glanced at each other. He shrugged. "Sure," she said. "It's all good."

"Man, it'll be just like last summer," James said. "All of us in the guides' cabins at N.O.C., hanging out after work. Those were some good times."

"Yeah, too bad the river's still too cold," Julia said. "I know where we can find some killer rapids. You guys kayak?" she asked Isis and me.

"I've been out sea kayaking," I said. "The only whitewater I ever did was on a raft. Oh, and a bit of, like, class two in a canoe."

"That's cool," Julia said.

"All of us were guides on the Nantahala last summer, rafting and kayaking," Luna said. "That's where we met these guys."

"That sounds excellent," I said. "Spending all day on the river . . ."

"It's kinda like hiking, in a way," Six-string said. "Sometimes it's really awesome, and sometimes it just sucks. There's days when you wake up, and it's cold and nasty outside, raining or whatever. All you want to do is pull your sleeping bag back over your head, and you still have to go out there and tell a bunch of morons, 'Paddle! Backpaddle! High side!' But then there's days when you get out on the river in the early morning with the fog still coming up. It's so pretty it makes up for all the rest of the shit you put up with."

"The community's kind of like hikers, too," Luna said. "I mean, not the tourists and everything. The guides. People help each other out. We share all our stuff, like, food, clothing, alcohol, pot, whatever."

James grinned. "There's also this whole cleanliness thing. Lack thereof. From what these guys said, I guess it's like that on the Trail, too. But there's this old joke—how do you starve a raft guide?" Julia glanced at Luna and rolled her eyes—she had probably heard this one far too many times. "You hide his money under the soap!"

"Bad James, no biscuit," Julia said.

He ducked the punch that she slung his way. "I wish we could get out on the water now. But the river's, like, forty-five degrees. Snowmelt. Dude, we wouldn't last long."

"What do you do in the off season?" I asked.

"Right now, we're both in school," James said. "We're taking this Woofer course—Wilderness First Responder. Julia's taking some history and stuff, too."

She shrugged and smiled. "Mostly we just wait around till the weather gets warm." She leaned her bike against the side of the trailer and headed for the door. "Come on in. Make yourselves at home."

James and Julia were gracious hosts, sharing their space like hikers in a shelter, even though it was their own home. After a few days in Cullowhee, though, we began to feel that we'd worn out our welcome. Luna and Six-string were getting restless, too. With six people inside the cramped trailer, there was hardly room to move. In the late afternoon, James, Julia, Luna, Six-string, and I shared the couch, watching *Return of the Jedi* for the fourth time. Six-string played along to the Ewok music on James's mandolin. Isis was in the kitchen, baking bread. The driving rain, which had begun the day after we arrived, continued as hard as ever outside.

"Dude," Luna said suddenly. "We've got to get back to the Trail."

"Didn't you see the weather this morning?" Julia asked her. The TV weather map had shown a massive storm system still hovering around the peaks of the Smokies.

"Yeah," she said, "but I just feel like, I don't know, like I've got to get *moving* again."

"You did yoga all morning," James said, flipping his pale blond hair back from his face.

"You know you're welcome to stay as long as you need to," Julia said. "Like, it's fun having you guys here and all."

"We really appreciate it," Isis said from the kitchen. The warm aroma of baking bread was beginning to permeate the room, rising above the stale smell of smoke.

"Yeah. Thanks," Luna said. "It's great to see you guys again. But it's time to move on, you know?"

I extricated myself from the pile of people on the couch and started pack-ing. It didn't take long; most of my gear was still stowed away. By the time the bread came out of the oven, we were ready to go. Isis left a loaf of oatmeal bread with James and Julia, and we split the other one with Luna and Six-string for our resupplies. We thanked our hosts and climbed into the van.

Back in Cherokee, we found out that the road up to Newfound Gap was closed. Apparently the rain in the valley had fallen as ice on the higher peaks.

"Maybe we can find a hotel in town," Luna said. "If we all split a room, it'll be cheap enough. There's this place that I've always wanted to stay at, just 'cause of the name. It's called the Pink Fairy Motel." But there was no room at the Pink Fairy Motel, the Twilite Motor Court, the Bide-a-Wee Lodge, or even the Ramada Inn. Finally we drove to the Riverside Cabin Court, a run-down complex of hotels and tiny cottages at the edge of town.

"Alls I got is one double room," the manager said.

Luna and Six-string looked at each other. "You guys take it," Luna said. "We can always sleep in the van."

"What's the big event?" Six-string asked the manager. "This must be, like, the last hotel room in town. I don't get it. It's a Thursday night."

"It's the casino," he said. "It's like this jest about every night."

Isis and I paid for the room and ducked back into the rainy parking lot to fetch our gear from the van.

"Well, I guess we'll see you down the trail," Luna said. "We're gonna take the van up to Hot Springs and hitch back, I think. I don't know." She shrugged cheerfully, rain running off the shoulders of her jacket. "We never know what we're gonna do, day by day. It's all a big mystery, eh?"

"That's for sure," I said. "Hey, thanks for inviting us along."

"Oh, sure. That was fun."

"You guys take care."

"You, too."

The morning dawned overcast in the valley, but the rain had ended. The TV weather map still showed an angry stain of clouds across the Smokies—sleet, ice, and winds of sixty miles an hour were predicted for the afternoon. And the road to Newfound Gap was still closed. We tried to get a room for that night, but the manager shook his head. "Sorry 'bout that; I'm booked full."

We stayed in the motel as late as we could, then packed up and walked into town along the highway, stopping at a general store to add a few extra granola bars and crackers to our food bags. It felt strange to walk along a main road in my hiking garb, with my heavy pack and sticks; I felt like a pilgrim from a different century cast into this world of blacktop and strip malls.

"Where are we going?" I asked Isis, shouting over the roar of passing traffic.

She shrugged. "I don't know. It's Friday now; we have even less of a chance of getting a room anywhere. I figure we can just walk up the road."

"Walk up to Newfound Gap? But that's, like, twenty miles! Not to mention the elevation gain."

"It's an auto road. It'll be an easy grade. We can go as far as we get tonight and just camp off to the side. They'll open the road in the morning. Somebody'll stop for us."

I didn't really like the plan, but I couldn't think of anything better. "All right," I said.

The sun began to break through the clouds as we crossed the Oconaluftee River and headed down the main street of Cherokee. There seemed to be more traffic today as the town geared up for the weekend. A crowd of tourists was gathering near one of the painted teepees in front of a souvenir store, where two men in feathered headdresses and elaborate buckskin outfits had set up a stage under an awning. One of the men picked up a megaphone. "Hey, you girls with the big sticks!" he called across the street. "Where are you going? Come on over and watch us dance!"

I looked at Isis. She shrugged. "Might as well check it out." We crossed the street, slung off our packs, and sat down in metal folding chairs by the platform among the crowd of tourists.

The man with the megaphone picked up a drum and stood at the edge of the stage. "Welcome to Cherokee!" he said, to a smattering of applause. "I hope y'all are having a good time. Today my friend Wagoo and I are going to show y'all some traditional dances of the Native people here. Now, I'm going to pass a bucket around, and I want y'all to be generous, be kind to your Native brothers, because Uncle Sam sure hasn't been!" He gave a great laugh, and there were a few uncertain outbursts of laughter from the audience. Someone passed the bucket back, and bills rustled into it. "Remember, all this land around us, all this continent—all this used to be Native peoples' land. Now, we're not angry, we're not bitter. We just say: remember. We were stewards of this land for a thousand generations. We say, take good care of it, because it doesn't really belong to you. It doesn't belong to anyone." There was a pause, punctuated by the sound of the river and the traffic on the road behind us. "Now, who wants to see some dancing?" The tourists around us began to applaud again.

The man who had spoken started beating the drum and singing. An older man, with rows of feathers fastened to his arms like wings, did a dance imitating the flight of an eagle. It was nothing I had expected. He whirled about the stage, light on his feet, turning in time to the steady drumbeat and the mesmerizing voice. He seemed to transcend his surroundings—the flimsy plywood stage, the crowd of tourists in the parking lot, the grimy streets and strip malls, the storefronts full of tacky souvenirs—like a bird of prey rising on a thermal. The music and the dancing were *real*, and everything else became suddenly insubstantial around them. *It was worth coming to Cherokee just for this*, I thought. *Even if we have to walk all the way up that road to Newfound Gap, it'll be worth it.*

After the performance, Isis and I went up to talk to the man with the drum. The dancer had vanished shortly after the show ended, ducking back into the souvenir store.

"That was awesome," I said.

"Aw, thanks." He was older than I had thought, probably in his mid-thirties, and a little overweight. He looked tired as he sat back on the edge of the stage. "It's a pretty good living, singing for the tourists."

"Everybody probably asks you this," I said," but were those traditional Cherokee songs and dances?"

He looked off into the distance. "Not really. Most of what we had in this tribe was lost with the forced relocation. Trail of Tears, white people call it." He picked up the drum and slid it into a buckskin carrying case. "You know, the Cherokees here in town are the ones that wouldn't march. The rebels. All the people that hid out in the woods. That's why we got a town full of troublemakers." He laughed.

"Where'd you learn those songs and dances, if they're not Cherokee traditions?" I asked.

"Powwows. It's mostly Plains Indians stuff. They kept their traditions much better than we did. Wagoo and I, when we were younger, we used to do the whole powwow circuit. Every year we'd be on the road six, eight months; dancing, drumming, singing. These days, we stay closer to home."

"I'm glad we got to see your show," Isis said. "Thanks for inviting us over." We gave our names—our real names.

"I'm Jonathon," he replied. "Thanks for coming. It's not every day I see a pair of women with packs and big sticks going down the road. I said to myself, 'I wonder what those two are up to. There's got to be a story there.'"

"We're hiking the Trail," Isis said. "The Appalachian Trail." She gave a brief synopsis of our journey so far. Jonathon listened, exclaiming softly every once in a while. "And now we're heading back to Maine."

"*Hiking* back?" He shook his head. "Either you've got a lot of guts, or you're crazy."

"Yeah," I laughed. "Sometimes I can't even tell which it is."

"Where are you headed now?" Jonathon asked. "You're not going back to the Trail, are you? I saw the weather this morning. Looks like it's going to be nasty up on top the mountains. The road's closed, too."

"We were going to stay in town another day," Isis said, "but with so many people here for the casino, we couldn't find a room. We were just planning to camp by the road somewhere, maybe."

"Naw!" Jonathon said. "There's always room in town. You just have to know where to look." He thought for a moment. "My old middle school principal, he's got rooms to rent over his shop. This might be a bit early in the season, but I'll give him a call."

We spent that night in a lovely furnished suite above the Half Moon Trading Post, overlooking the river. The clean and spacious suite, equipped with a full kitchen, was $20 cheaper than our tiny room at the Riverside. As I drifted off to sleep that night, I thought about the strange turns my path had taken. When we started the Trail, more than nine months earlier, I had expected months of solitude, rugged mountains, deep woods. I had never imagined the people we would meet. But now I knew that when I saw a map of these southern mountains, I would picture Luna and Six-string, Michelle, James and Julia, Jonathon. The memory of their kindness would last much longer than the memory of struggling up Rockytop in the cold with my stomach growling.

Isis

The past five days of storms had made the trail into a maze of blowdowns. Every fifty feet, it seemed, we had to climb over, duck under, or scramble through the crown of an enormous old hemlock. The branches, twisted at odd angles and slick with ice, felt like a cruel parody of a jungle gym. My hiking sticks caught in the twigs, and the small amount of upper-body strength I had gained by carrying the heavy maple poles lasted me only as far as the third blowdown. After that, my arms burned with lactic acid each time I tried to pull the combined weight of myself and my pack through an ice-covered tree canopy.

When I was able to think beyond my pain, I wondered what was happening to the forest. These were old trees falling. Was something weakening them, acid rain or insects, so that winds they had withstood for centuries could blow them down like a row of dominoes? I remembered an essay I had read before hiking, in an anthology of A.T. stories, about the changing of the Eastern woodlands. The author described the chestnuts that once dominated the forests of the South: the sound of rain on their broad leaves, the taste of their nuts, the perfect domes of their canopies, like the trees in old engravings. And the dogwoods, vanished from much of their former range, whose clusters of flowers looked like white altar cloths in cathedrals of hemlock and pine. Would the hemlocks themselves be the next to go?

Suddenly, the hemlocks seemed like the most wonderful trees in the forest. Where else would we find shelter from a quick rainstorm, or dry, resinous twigs to start our Zip stove when everything else had been wet for days? Deep in the South, where everything else but the rhododendrons lost their leaves in winter, the occasional stand of hemlocks had cheered us with its enduring green. If my children hiked the Trail, would there still be hemlocks to shelter them and brighten the winter woods?

We ate lunch on a narrow ridge just past Icewater Spring Shelter. We'd expected to get farther before taking a break, but the five miles from Newfound Gap had left us both trembling with exhaustion. We had oversupplied at the Cullowhee supermarket to make up for the three days we'd gone hungry before getting off with Luna and Six-string. We'd bought lots of treats, including an onion, a zucchini, and two apples. Forest Phil may have driven me to tears with the broccoli saga, but I was grateful to him for giving me a new perspective on Trail food. One or two pounds of fruit and vegetables didn't make a lot of difference in my pack weight, especially now that I was carrying ten pounds less than I had carried in midwinter. Like the candle lantern in winter or the tradition of evening tea, I knew it would make all the difference in our comfort.

I split one of the apples with my pocket knife and sliced cheese onto bagels. They were squishy and crustless, the only kind of bagels available this far south, but the cheese, a kind of havarti full of little flecks of vegetables, looked delicious. I gave jackrabbit her sandwich and bit into mine. Somehow, it wasn't quite what I'd expected. The cheese had a smoky, salty taste, and another flavor I couldn't quite place. I was halfway through my sandwich when I noticed that I was chewing on something rubbery. Gristle. I looked more closely at the cheese. Along with the flecks of pepper and onion, it was full of chunks of what looked like the cheapest, greasiest sort of pepperoni—something I hadn't eaten since I was sixteen. From the grimace on jackrabbit's face, I could tell that she had made the same discovery. We were both so hungry, though, that we finished the sandwiches anyway.

We ran into Digger and Priceless that evening at Peck's Corner Shelter. They had gone down the other side of the mountain, to Gatlinburg, to avoid the storm, and they regaled us with stories of wild evenings at the bars, and days spent in the local theme park, Dollywood (named for its owner, Dolly Parton). Priceless's Trail appetite had finally caught up with him there; he'd consumed so many corndogs that the impressed vendor had given him the tenth one free.

"Hey, guys, would you like some cheese?" I asked them. "I have to warn you, it's kind of gross. It's got pepperoni in it."

"Cheese?" asked Priceless, his eyes widening. "You carried cheese all the way out here, and now you don't want it?"

"Cheese and pepperoni. That's almost a pizza," said Digger. "I can't think of anything I'd like better."

I cut the block of havarti in half, handing a chunk to each of them. Beatific smiles spread over both their faces as they bit into it.

"Mmm, this is great," Digger said through a mouthful. "I can't believe you're willing to part with it."

"I've also got a zucchini," I said, "if you want a little of that." I didn't really want to share the zucchini, but, remembering how I'd coveted Forest Phil's broccoli, I felt bad about eating such a delicacy in front of other hikers without offering them at least a few slices.

"A *zucchini*?" Priceless's eyes got even wider. "I can see why you'd carry cheese, I mean, it's got a lot of calories, and it tastes good. But a vegetable?" He shook his head. "You keep it."

"Yeah," said Digger. "You can keep the zucchini. If you packed it all the way out here, you must want it. For some reason."

The clouds had lowered the next morning, almost to the tops of the mountains. Strange hollows and undulations pocked their still, voluminous bellies, like the petals of Georgia O'Keefe's white morning glory blossoms. On distant ridges, the gray treetops seemed to form a thin, transparent membrane over the snowy ground. Close up, the Smokies blazed with color. Moss glowed green on the hemlock trunks, and beech saplings still clung to their pale golden autumn leaves. Streaks of yellow lichen brightened the red cliffs that fell away steeply on either side of the trail. Mica-filled pebbles glittered in the meltwater streams, dark silver and red-gold.

The rain began about ten in the morning, and continued, heavy and steady, for the rest of the day. We ate our lunch without stopping: bagels that turned soggy in our cold, spongy hands. The six or seven inches of snow that lingered in the trail turned to muddy slush; for most of the afternoon we waded ankle deep in it. With so much humidity in the air, jackrabbit had to stop every few minutes to defog her glasses.

In spite of soggy boots, wet bagels, and jackrabbit's glasses, we kept each other in good spirits all day. We told stories as we walked, as we'd often done to entertain the children of the Family. *Isis and the Fugitive Food Bag. How Lady Jackrabbit Vanquished the Evil Buzzard.* (In order to draw out the suspense, I imbued him with sorcerous powers akin to Murphy's, and made him the cause of the snowstorm that caught us on Wayah Bald.) We reminisced about the friends we'd been hiking with the last time we'd passed through this part of the Smokies, pointed out bright patterns of lichen on the rocks beside the trail, and speculated about the signs of spring we would see in Davenport Gap. At least once every hour, one of us reminded the other that we had an onion to put in our polenta, and an apple left over from lunch.

We stayed the night at Mount Cammerer firetower, alone, and sang all our old songs by candlelight. In the morning, the sun shone through the tower windows, though a sea of clouds filled the valleys and lapped around our small island of laurel and stone. We ate breakfast on the balcony, watching the clouds twist loose from the hills below us, like layer upon layer of veils. By the time we had packed up to leave, we could see all the way down to Davenport Gap, where a green and purple haze of swelling buds covered the treetops.

jackrabbit

As we descended the long shoulder of Mount Cammerer, heading down into Davenport Gap, spring unfolded around us like a stop-motion video. We saw first a few green leaves peeking through the leaf mold on the forest floor. Then the flowers began: spring beauties, with their pale pink-veined blooms, leathery leaved trailing arbutus, yellow trout lilies, violets, trilliums in light yellow and maroon, hepatica, anemones, and the splayed white petals of bloodroot. Every step down the mountain brought a new kind of flower, a new intoxicating fragrance on the wind. The temperature warmed rapidly, too; the sun dried out the lingering dampness in the air, and we began to shed our outer layers of clothing. By the time we were halfway down, we had stripped to bare feet, shorts and sports bras, and we were still sweating.

"This is impossible," Isis said. "How are we ever going to hike in summer if it gets this hot in spring? It must be eighty degrees out!"

"We could camp during the day and night-hike. I heard of some nobos who did that when it got hot."

"Then we'd miss the flowers."

"We'd still smell them . . . You know, it's funny; after this winter I never thought I'd complain about being too hot again. Even last week, I would have given anything for warm weather."

The hot air pressed in around us, stifling and thick. I paused every few steps to wipe the sweat off my forehead with a handkerchief. Worse than the heat, my left knee ached horribly. It was an old injury that had bothered me several times on the Trail, but never like this. I had slipped on a patch of ice yesterday, throwing it a little out of whack. At first it had just felt tender and watery, but with the constant downhill it began to throb with each step. We came to the burned area, where John had asked about dragons, and heat shimmered from the charcoal-black ground. My knee felt as though a nail had been driven into it. By the time we reached the Pigeon River and the I-40 underpass, I was gritting my teeth together to keep from shouting expletives.

"Isis, I've got to take a rest," I said, as she headed into the woods across the road.

She looked back. "Yeah. Heat getting to you, too?" Then she paused, seeing my face. "Are you okay?"

"I think so. Hope so. It's my fucking knee again."

For once she didn't say anything about my swearing. "Let me see." Her forehead wrinkled with concern.

I sat down on the bank of red earth by the trail, dripping sweat, and held my leg out for inspection. The knee was slightly puffy and red on the outer side. Isis put a warm hand on it, feeling gingerly for damage. "That doesn't hurt? Is it okay here? . . . There's nothing wrong, as far as I can tell. It's just swollen. I'm no expert, though. Can you get to Hot Springs?"

"How far is it?"

"Like, thirty-five miles."

"I don't know. I think so, if we go slow. Maybe it'll be better on the uphills."

The uphill was less excruciating, and the beauty of the climb almost made up for the pain. Redbuds had begun blooming, great sprays of purple blossoms in the understory. Nodding drifts of flowers covered the hillsides in the hollows around little streams. The buds of rhododendrons were still curled tight, but the leaves had unfurled, spread wide and upturned as though drinking the light. I had to stop every once in a while to rest and breathe through the pain, but I could keep hiking. We made another slow six miles that night, before the sun dipped below the Smokies behind us.

In the morning, while I filtered water, I soaked my knee in a pool of the cold creek that tumbled past our campsite. The swelling had gone down a little overnight, though the joint was still puffy and sore. Isis took some of the heavier items from my food bag—granola, rice, Lipton dinners—and put them in her own pack. I still had to lean heavily on my hiking sticks on the downhills. The pain was tolerable, though, never as immediate and fierce as it had been the day before.

We came to Max Patch in time for lunch. I remembered the ice fog that had blown across the open summit, clinging to the trees and posts like white feathers, when we were southbound. It had been almost impossible to see from one trail marker to the next. Now, on a clear, warm, spring day, the posts marking the path seemed almost laughably close together. Aside from an S-curve of old, granular snow that clung to the shady side of the slope, every aspect of the bald had changed entirely. A thin thatch of grass had sprung up, almost hiding the blackened ground on the burned side of the mountaintop. We stopped at the height of the land to look out over the valleys on either side. Fields of full green lay quiet under the sun. The patches of woodland that cloaked the rolling hills were just beginning to soften into their spring colors: a subtle mist of pink, green, purplish gray. A warm wind, smelling of fresh-cut hay, sighed in the low grass. It seemed like a short while, an eyeblink of time, since we had stood here and seen nothing but swirling ice fog.

I took my pack off and sat down to rest. Physically, I felt horrible; the effort of suppressing the pain in my knee was wearing me down. Tension had collected in my shoulders and neck; my temples throbbed. But mentally, I felt better than I had in a long time. I was able to see past my pain to the beauty of things, and this gave me hope.

"Hey, are you guys the Barefoot Sisters? Far out!"

"We heard about you all the way back in Georgia!"

Two hikers, young men with lightweight packs, had come up the trail behind us. They were both tall and rangy, with the slim, muscular physiques of serious athletes.

"Yeah, that's what they call us," I said, lifting up a grimy foot for their inspection.

"Sweet!"

"You guys northbound?" Isis asked.

The younger guy grinned. "Actually, we're just on a training hike. Springer to Damascus."

"Then we're headed out west," the other added. He was wearing a cowboy hat, which seemed to be one of his heaviest pieces of gear.

"Pacific Crest Trail?" Isis asked, and they nodded, their smiles broadening. "I'd love to hike the PCT some day," she said. "Twenty-five hundred miles. Wow."

"You guys must have come about that far by now," said the guy in the hat.

I did a quick mental calculation. "Yeah, just about. But it's taken us nine months."

The younger guy smiled. "Hiking through winter and everything. Man, you guys are tough. I'm glad we caught up with you."

I gave a rueful laugh. I wasn't feeling tough right then; I felt worn-out, exhausted. "Catching up with us isn't too hard. Every single southbounder last year managed to do it."

"That's not true!" Isis protested. "There were a few people behind us."

"People who got off the Trail," I said.

"But maybe that's the point," the hiker in the hat said. "Like, you guys stayed on-trail through all of that. And you're still out here. Dude, it's unreal. It's, like, an honor to meet you guys."

"Uh, thanks," I said. I was still uncomfortable with this kind of hero-worship. It was flattering, but each time it happened I felt a little awkward. I knew I couldn't live up to the expectations that people had built up: jackrabbit, the tough barefoot hiker, who walked through snow and ice. Jackrabbit, the beautiful blond Amazon. Instead, I was just me: jackrabbit, slumped against my pack, wondering if I could muster the energy to get to my feet and keep hiking. Jackrabbit, scruffy and muddy, with my hair—which could hardly be called blond anyway—in an oily braid, my body reeking from two days of sweating in the heat.

All afternoon, I played word games in my head to distract myself from the pain. We walked in and out of gaps with tantalizing names: Kale Gap, Lemon Gap, Walnut Gap. *I could really go for some kale with lemon and walnuts*, I thought. *Or even spinach. Some kind of green vegetable.* And then a fantastic vision came into my head, unbidden: a heaping bowl full of lettuce and sprouts, with cucumbers, tomatoes, strips of pepper, and feta cheese. Tahini dressing with poppy seeds. Elmer's salad. It was a vision that had kept me from leaving Hot Springs for four days in winter, and now it drew me inexorably toward the town. *Less than twenty miles, now*, I thought. *It was twenty exactly from Max Patch.*

We wouldn't get to town that night, and as the afternoon wore on, I began to wonder if we would even make it the next day. My knee swelled up and sent a hot jolt of pain up my leg with each step. It was almost as bad as it had been coming down into Davenport Gap. Downhills were the worst. I began to dread the final approach into Hot Springs, three miles of steady descent off the ridgeline.

When the sun dipped below the trees, we set up camp in a meadow halfway up Bluff Mountain, still ten miles from town. I wanted nothing more than to curl up in my sleeping bag and forget everything. My strength was almost exhausted. I was afraid that I might have done some serious damage to my knee. I was angry, too—at myself, for letting this happen. Angry at the universe. *Just when I'm beginning to enjoy this hike again*, I thought. *Just when things get beautiful, when spring comes. It's like when we were southbound—I finally got into shape, and then, bang! Down for the count.*

I was pounding in the last tent stake, using my boot for a hammer, when another hiker came into the meadow. He was short and muscular, with light blond hair that stuck out in all directions and a bushy beard. He tossed his pack down in the grass.

"Hi, I'm Toast," he said. He spoke in a Southern accent with a slight twang.

We gave our names.

"Oh, the Barefoot Sisters! I think I met y'all before. Back when you were still southbound, in Georgia. At least, I passed y'all on the Trail. It was back around Chattahoochee Gap, in that area."

"You must have started the Trail pretty early, then," Isis said. "Have you been hiking since February?"

"Well, I actually started in November. Hiked the first twenty miles or so. Then I called it quits till spring, started back up at the end of February." He gave a sly smile that reminded me of Tim. "I like to take things slow."

I tried to recall our meeting. His pale blond hair and bearded narrow face were fairly distinctive, but I couldn't summon up the memory. "I wish I could remember meeting you," I said. "There were so many people on the Trail, though . . ."

"Well, we didn't really stop and talk," Toast said. "It was pretty crappy weather; raining and cold. One of y'all was barefoot, that's all I noticed." He laughed. "It was one of those things. Y'all went by, and about five minutes later, I thought, 'Well, damn! One of those ladies was barefoot!'"

"Wait a minute," Isis said. "Chattahoochee Gap? And one of us barefoot, and the other in shoes? It must have been right after Lash brought the wine!"

"Wine?" Toast said.

Isis told the story.

"Man. That's a good one. I wish I had me some wine right now. A nice red wine. Maybe I'll pick some up in town." He opened his pack and took out a tarp. "That's how I got my trail name, actually. South of Fontana, I was hiking with a couple, Luna and Six-string—"

"Oh yeah, we hung out with them in the Smokies," I said.

"Good people."

"Definitely."

"Well, coming out of Wesser, I packed out a Nalgene full of merlot. First night out of town, at the shelter, Six-string said something funny, and I said, 'I'll drink to that.' I passed the wine around. They decided to call me Toast." He raised an invisible glass to us. "Here's to wine in Hot Springs!" He started setting up his tarp, using his hiking poles for support.

I lifted up my water bottle. "I'll drink to *that*. I hope we make it there tomorrow."

"It's only ten miles."

"I know. I've been having knee problems."

"I'm real sorry to hear that, jackrabbit. Anything I can do to help y'all? My pack's real light; I can take some weight from you." His sturdy red pack didn't look very light—it was stuffed full, and it had landed with a solid thump when he'd thrown it down.

"That's really kind of you to offer, Toast," I said. "But my pack weighs hardly anything right now. Isis took most of my heavy stuff."

Isis spoke up. "You know what you could do for us . . . Where are you planning on staying in town?"

"Well, I'm not real sure. I guess I'll find out what's open when I get there."

"Could you swing by Elmer's and ask him to save a space for us?"

"Sure."

We arrived in Hot Springs in the late afternoon, having hiked less than two miles an hour all day. Spring had come to the valley, with new green grass in the lawns and tulips and crocuses beginning to open. The tall maples around Elmer's house were unfurling their tiny yellow-green leaves and flowers. I limped up the driveway, feeling weariness settle over me.

Elmer was on his knees by a flowerbed in the side yard, wearing gardening gloves. "There you are! I was starting to wonder. Good thing you sent that fellow ahead; we've got a full house tonight. I made beds for you on the upstairs porch."

"Thanks, Elmer," Isis said. "It's good to be back."

He smiled. "I'm glad you're here." He turned to the flowerbed again, deftly pulling weeds from among the crocuses. "Leave your sticks outside— but you know that. Take your boots—" he looked up at us, shook his head with a wry grin. "Wash your feet. The hose is out back."

Elmer wasn't kidding about a full house. The stack of mail drops on the side porch almost reached the ceiling now. There were groups of hikers sitting in the sun in the backyard, and more on the porches. I could hear a steady hum of voices from inside the house. When we were southbound, seventeen had been a crowd. Now there was easily twice that many at Elmer's alone, and probably many more in the other hostels around town.

Inside the kitchen, a complex blend of wonderful smells drifted through the air. There were two people at the stove, stirring huge pots of food, and one chopping vegetables on the sideboard. Perhaps the number of helpers explained Elmer's relative calm.

"Hey, Barefoot Sisters!" It was Bob, the young man with white-blond dreadlocks who had been there in the winter. "So you really are yo-yoing? That's radical! Hey, this is Ben—" a tall, lanky young man with dark hair and a beard, who nodded with a grin "—and Jack."

Jack tipped his hat. He had blue eyes and long dark blond hair pulled back into a ponytail, and he was shirtless in the heat of the kitchen. "Good to meet y'all."

"Good to meet you guys," I said. "And it's great to be here. This feels like the Promised Land."

Ben laughed. "Milk in the fridge, honey in the cupboard. But you have to wait for supper to get any."

"What I need right now is some ice, if you can spare some," I said.

"Sure. What happened?" Bob asked, as he reached into the freezer.

I showed him my knee, which had swollen to nearly the size of a grapefruit. He whistled. "Dude, that does *not* look comfortable." He gave me a blue ice pack.

I sat on a stool in the corner of the kitchen with the ice on my knee, while Isis took our packs to the upstairs porch. The guys entertained me with a steady stream of bad jokes while they chopped vegetables and stirred spices into the vat on the stove. I recalled a joke I'd heard in Georgia. "What're a redneck's last words?"

"Oh, not this one," Jack groaned.

I put on my best backwoods accent. "'Hey, watch this!'"

Ben gave a slow grin. "And you know what his brother's last words are?" (Jack groaned again.) "'Hell, I can do that!'"

When the ice pack began to thaw, I washed its cover and returned it to the freezer. "Shower's free!" someone called from the next room, and I hurried to take advantage of it. It was glorious to wash off the grime and sweat of the past few days. Though I was still limping, I felt renewed. I made a beeline for the music room.

There was a crowd of hikers there; every chair was occupied. But no one was playing. They were all listening to the bluegrass music that drifted through the open doors from the front porch. At first I thought it was a tape—the guitar picking was so skillful, and the three voices harmonized so well, that I was sure it couldn't be live. When I got to the porch, though, I found two familiar hikers perched on the railing, bent low over their guitars: Six-string and Nate, the red-haired nobo we had met on Blood Mountain. Luna sat on the porch swing, rocking gently and singing along.

> I wish I was on some foggy mountaintop
> I'd sail away to the west
> Oh, I would fly like a little bird on high
> To the one I love the best.

When the song ended, Luna looked up. "Jackrabbit!"

"Luna! Six-string! Nate! You guys sound awesome!"

"Aw, thanks." Nate flipped a strand of red-gold hair out of his eyes. "I've got a trail name now. They call me Tha Wookie. 'Cause I'm so hairy, I guess."

"So you guys know each other?" Luna asked me.

"Yeah, we met in Georgia. Tha Wookie hiked barefoot with us. He kept up with us for like a mile."

"Yeah," he said with a slightly shamefaced grin. "It hurt like hell."

"Hey, it's great to see you again," Luna said. "We heard you were coming into town. What's this rumor about a bum knee?"

"No rumor, for once. It's the truth. I might have to take a couple zeros."

Six-string plucked a few chords on his guitar. "Man, that sucks. Just when it's getting nice out."

"Tell me about it!" I said. "But I don't want to interrupt the music. You've got half the house listening to you."

"Come sing with us," Luna said.

"I don't have a great voice," I told her. "And I don't really know any songs . . ."

"You sounded fine on 'Rockytop,'" Six-string said, and before I knew it, I was singing along to the old bluegrass standard.

Dinner that night was as delicious as I remembered: curried tomato soup, fresh bread, spicy tofu with vegetables and rice, and of course the famous salad. The only difference was the number of people—instead of one long table, there were four. The chairs were packed as close together as possible. Luckily Elmer suspended the rule of not eating until everyone had answered the dinner question. Tonight's question ("If you could have a tattoo, what would it be and where?") brought out some bizarre and hilarious responses; laughter rose like a tide in the room.

Afterwards, feeling sated, I made my way back to the music room with Isis. "Sing your song!" someone shouted as we entered. A chorus of other voices joined in. "Barefoot Sisters! Sing the dig-a-hole song!"

"Oh, man. I guess our reputation precedes us," I said, surveying the crowd. The voices died down. "Okay," I sighed. "The dig-a-hole song. You guys have to join in on the chorus, though."

We sang through all fourteen verses, ending with our journey through North Carolina and the verse I had finally written on the day we finished our southbound hike:

> And the Smokies during February sure are great;
> every skinny ridge has got a view (of fog!)
> But when the last of the sobos meet the first of the nobos
> you've got to wait in line for the loo!
>
> Dig a hole . . .
>
> Well, I stood on Springer Mountain on the third of March
> Nobody can say that I'm a quitter—
> But I just had to run to the woods when I was done,
> 'cause the summit's not provided with a shitter!

I was getting less nervous about singing it in front of people, and I thought again about the Trail Days talent show.

"Bravo, Bravo!" There was loud laughter and applause. Elmer stood among the back row of hikers, with an amused smile on his face. "Encore," he said.

We sang one of the songs that Isis had written in the winter, a serious ballad about companionship in hard times. "Somebody else's turn!" I said when we finished. Someone took up a guitar, and we faded back into the crowd, grateful that the attention had turned elsewhere.

A young man, probably in his late teens, came up to us. He was tall and gaunt, with a black crew cut. "I think I'm going to call you the Shitter Sisters from now on," he said.

I didn't mind the name—I guess we deserved it—but there was something about him, his oddly emotionless face and uninflected voice, that set my teeth on edge. "Nice," I said. "And who are you?"

"Roadrunner."

"Are you northbound?"

"Yes. My parents dumped me off at Springer three weeks ago with a pack and a credit card. They said, 'See you in Maine.'"

"Three weeks? That's just about when we started. I'm surprised we haven't run into you before." I was surprised, too, that he'd been able to start out at such a fast pace. Most northbounders took a few weeks to hit their stride. Isis and I, in shape from our sobo hike, had managed fifteen and sixteen-mile days from the beginning.

He shrugged. "I hike at night a lot. That's why people don't see me."

The longer he talked, the less comfortable I was. I tried to ignore the feeling and be kind to him—after all, he was another hiker. The prickles on the back of my neck persisted, though. There was something deeply strange about him. I needed an excuse to get away.

"I'm gonna go play some music," I said, and took a seat across the room, picking up a set of bongos.

Another hiker came in from the porch. "I am Greensinger!" he announced to no one in particular. He was young, probably eighteen or nineteen, with a slight build. His curly shoulder-length brown hair and old-fashioned leather hat gave him the look of a Renaissance troubadour.

I introduced myself, since I was near him. "Where'd you get your trail name?" I asked.

"Well, it's actually the English translation of my Sindarin name—" he said earnestly, and spoke a long, mellifluous word full of F's and L's. "I didn't think many people would speak Elvish on the Trail."

"Cool," I said, a little amused. Some of the other hikers, behind Greensinger, were rolling their eyes. He sat down next to me and picked up one of the guitars, which he played with great enthusiasm. Someone else took the banjo, Bob played a set of conga drums, and a young woman with dreadlocks played the didgeridoo.

The jam session continued late into the night, and people gradually dropped out. Eventually, it was down to me, tapping on bongos, and two guitarists: Greensinger and a guy named Chris. He was tall and lanky, and had short dark hair and square yellow-tinted glasses that made his eyes look jaundiced. He hadn't said much the whole evening; he just sat back against the wall and strummed his backpacker guitar nonchalantly. The chords he threw out jived with the music about half the time, but he seemed to prefer dissonance.

"Let's play a twelve-bar," Greensinger suggested.

"D?"

"Sounds good to me."

"You can sing," Chris said, indicating me with a lazy glance.

"Sing what?"

"I don't know; make shit up. Flow with it, whatever's cool, you know?"

"Sure, whatever." I tried to look nonplussed. Greensinger laid down the chords, and I tapped out a rhythm on the bongos, heavy on the backbeat. Chris was soloing. He extended the harmonies so far that the underlying chords broke apart, spinning out a line so idiosyncratic that it hardly seemed related to the basic progression Greensinger strummed.

I let the words flow, trying to draw a melody out of Greensinger's chords:

> "I been walkin' since morning,
> hot sun beating down—
> I been walking since morning,
> ain't another soul around.
> Left town in the morning,
> leavin' all my friends behind,
> eight o'clock in the morning
> with a six-day resupply—"

Greensinger stopped playing.

"Why'd you stop?" Chris asked. "It was cool, she was flowing with the words, it was all fitting."

"Well, it wasn't really fitting. You've got to play inside the chords." Greensinger tinged his voice with righteous indignation. "I mean, you have to follow the basic structure for a meaningful collaboration."

Chris bristled in response. "Structure undermines creativity."

I had to agree with Greensinger. "Structure is essential for communication," I said. "It's fine to extend your chords into the stratosphere if you're playing by yourself. Throw in all the nines, elevens, thirteens, flat sixes you want. But if you want to play in a group, there has to be an *understanding*—"

"Structure stifles the individual's contribution," Chris reiterated. "The construction of a teleological paradigm prevents the expression of uniqueness." It was obvious he wasn't interested in arguing music theory; he was just in it for the argument. Greensinger rose to the bait.

"You're just talking semantics," he said. "On one level, there is 'structure' as constraint, 'structure' in the societal sense, but on the level that I am arguing, there is 'structure' as *basis*. At one extreme, as you so correctly stated, it prevents the development of the individual's contribution, but properly applied, structure is fundamentally essential to effective communication . . ."

They continued in this vein for several minutes, their speech peppered with arcane terminology and roundabout syllogisms. *In college*, I thought, *I would have jumped right in*. But it was late, and I was exhausted. College had ended months ago, almost a year ago. All I wanted to do was play music, and it was obvious there wouldn't be much more of that tonight.

Finally Chris retorted, "You're just conflating the synthesis of independent particulars!"

"That's it," I said. "When 'independent particulars' get broached, I usually head for bed." (I was tempted to say something about intellectual pissing matches, but I held back.)

Chris and Greensinger both stared at me for a moment as though they had just remembered I was in the room. Then they turned back to their argument. I heard their insistent voices rising and falling behind me as I climbed the stairs to the upper porch, leaning on the banister to favor my sore knee.

I got an appointment at the clinic in town the next day. After a long wait among other hikers nursing knee and ankle injuries, a sullen teenager who coughed constantly, and two mothers with colicky babies, I went into the doctor's office. The nurse, a pale woman in her late thirties, brought out a clipboard and asked a few questions in a blasé tone.

"Are you on any medication?"

"No."

"Any chance you're pregnant?"

"No."

"Do you smoke?"

I shook my head.

"Chaw? Dip?"

Oh, man, I'm in the South now, I thought.

The doctor prodded my knee and turned it at uncomfortable angles. "Don't worry; it's not permanently damaged. Yes, you'll be able to keep hiking," he said with a wry look, before I could even ask. He'd obviously seen a lot of hikers in his time. "You've injured it before, haven't you? There's a little bit of tendonitis. Get some rest in the next couple days; ice, ibuprofen. Keep it elevated. I expect you know the drill. Oh, and try to keep your pack weight down."

"Thanks," I said, automatically translating his advice into hiker terms: zeros. Slacking. It sounded like the perfect thing right now—but lodging and food in town were expensive, and slacking shuttles cost money, too.

Back at the hostel, Isis and I talked to Elmer. "Is there any chance we can do some work-for-stay?" I asked him.

He stroked his chin, frowning. "What kind of work are you looking for?"

"I've gardened in the summers since I was fourteen," I said. "I can do some carpentry, too."

"I can cook," Isis said.

Elmer's frown deepened. "I don't usually let anybody but my helpers into the kitchen. A lot depends on my cooking—I've got a business to run here."

"I cooked professionally for a summer," Isis told him. "I don't want to intrude on your kitchen. I mean, I could just make bread or something. I make a really good braided challah with sesame seeds."

Elmer sighed. "I guess so. We have thirty-six people here for dinner tonight, so be sure you make enough."

"I will. Thanks." Her eyes were shining. I knew she loved to make bread almost as much as I loved to play music, and it was a skill she didn't often get to exercise on the Trail.

Elmer set me to work in one of the flower beds out back, digging up the sturdy tubers of Jerusalem artichokes for transplanting. It was a perfect spring day. The light breeze carried the scent of flowers and fresh-cut grass across the lawn, and the sun streamed down through the tiny new leaves of the maples. The first insects had emerged from their winter dormancy. Flies buzzed lazily in circles on the patio; improbably huge bumblebees, fully the size of my thumb, somersaulted in the tulips and made drunken lines in the air. Something in their boxy, rectangular bodies and loud drone reminded me of my father's old Volkswagen bus, and I had to laugh out loud. I felt more content, more at home, than I had almost anywhere on the Trail.

I was so engrossed in my work that I hardly heard the footsteps come up behind me. "Hello, jack . . . rabbit."

I turned and squinted up into the sun. "Land Phil! Long time no see."

"Elmer said to tell you that's enough artichokes. You're with *me* now." He gave a cartoon villain's laugh.

"Oh boy. What're we doing?"

We sat on the patio, resetting panes of antique glass into frames for storm windows. Forest Phil showed me how to scrape the old paint and detritus from the surface with a razor blade, set the panes into the wood with glazier's points, and seal the edges.

"I thought you'd be pretty far ahead by now, with your light pack and all," I said, working at a particularly tough streak of paint.

"Naw." He shrugged. "I had a bit of trouble with my ankle on the way into town. I've been here five days already."

"Five days? So you must've stayed in the Smokies through that storm. We got off at Newfound Gap; that's why it took us so long to get here."

"Yeah, I was out there in that storm." He shook his head at the memory. "Not one of the smartest things I've done in my life. I was at Icewater Spring the morning it hit. It looked nasty when I left the shelter—the sky was kind of purple, and it was blowing hard—but I wanted to hike." He looked a little ashamed. "I didn't have enough food to just hang out." He took another pane of glass and began scraping. "Well, by the time I got up on the ridge by Charlie's Bunion, it was sleeting so hard I couldn't see five feet ahead of me. Trees were falling left and right. Then the thunder started."

"Thunder?"

"Yeah. Thunder and lightning, all around me. And I got to thinking, there I was, with my two metal hiking poles—"

I began to laugh at the horrible pun that came to mind.

"What?" he said, with mock outrage. "I was out there risking my life, about to get fried, and you think it's funny?"

I gave him an evil grin. "Forest Philament."

I came back into the house in midafternoon to find the kitchen almost empty. Isis stood at the stove, stirring something, and Ben was at the sideboard chopping potatoes.

"Hey, Ben," I said. "What's for dinner? And where'd Bob and Jack get to?"

He looked up with a slightly guilty smile. "Well, Jack went out for a hike. Bob's girlfriend is here for the weekend, so I doubt we'll see much of him. I didn't really want to do the whole meal on my own. Your sister here kind of took charge."

"Pumpkin soup with toasted walnuts and coriander, challah, mixed vegetables in African peanut sauce with couscous, green salad, lemon tart," she said, half to herself. "Are the potatoes ready, Ben?"

"Yeah, here you go." He shook his head. "Man, Elmer's gonna flip when he finds out about this. A hiker cooking dinner."

I wished them luck and headed into the music room. In a few minutes, I could hear Elmer's voice from the kitchen, a low rumble of disapproval. It wasn't until dinner that night—when he tasted the subtly flavored soup and the hearty bread—that his frown began to soften. By the time he took the last bite of his lemon tart, he was smiling broadly.

"Isis, you can cook for me any time you want!"

After a few days in Hot Springs with an ice pack on my knee, glorious long days of sun and light winds, I felt ready to try slacking a section. My knee looked almost normal again, and we needed to put some miles behind us. We had planned to meet Miss Janet in Erwin four days from now, to help her prepare the annual Easter feast she arranged for thru-hikers. Also, our mother would be meeting us to hike the Roans in less than a week.

Jack drove us out to the trailhead in his rusty blue pickup. We planned to cover about twelve miles, going south, making it back to town in time for supper.

"I love this time of year," Jack said. "All the flowers come out, everything wakes up." There was a fading garland of wildflowers hanging from the rearview mirror, souvenirs of his hike a few days before, and he identified all of them for us. "Hey! Check it out!" He pointed at a stand of trees beside the road. The gray branches were still leafless, but plate-sized starbursts of white petals hung in the air like motionless fireworks. "Cucumber magnolias, blooming already."

He turned off the main road onto a narrow, meandering track of crumbling asphalt that ran beside a creek. "Man, this spring has been so crazy. It's like, a week ago it was still winter, and then all of a sudden, whoo-ee! Spring! Eighty degrees! I pity anybody with allergies, though. Everything's blooming at once. The pollen counts are off the scale. Whoa!" He swerved the truck to avoid a box turtle in the road, and then pulled over. "Be right back!" He jumped out and carried the turtle to the bank of the stream. "I'd hate to see that little fellow end up roadkill."

The section we slacked was harder than I had remembered. I wasn't carrying much—a few sandwiches for lunch, a water bottle. (Isis carried some extra water, the first aid kit, warm clothes and a headlamp in case of emergency, and our filter.) By the end of the day, even with such a tiny load, my knee hurt again. The downhills were slow and unpleasant.

Six-string, Luna, Toast, and Tha Wookie passed us on their way out of town, singing in four-part harmony. I was happy to see them hiking together, but somehow, when they passed, I felt desolate. It brought back the feeling of despair I'd had so often as a southbounder, watching our friends walk on ahead and knowing I was not strong enough, not fast enough, to keep up.

We stopped by a spring a few miles outside of town to filter more water. In the heat, we'd been guzzling it down at a rather alarming rate. I sat on the forest floor by the pool, trying not to crush any flowers, and unscrewed the cap of Isis's water bottle. It was the one she'd bought in Fontana Village, and the lettering under the cap now leaped out at me: STAY IN THE GAME. PLAY AGAIN. *That's exactly what we're doing*, I thought. *Staying in the GA-ME. But can I keep going now? Is it even worth it?*

Then I looked up. On the far side of the pool, a dwarf iris lifted its grasslike leaves and fragile purple petals to the light. Its reflection shimmered in the clear water. I remembered Spur's photographs at the Ruck, and I remembered what I had thought: *Maybe I'll hike until I see a dwarf iris. Maybe then I'll be able to go home.* I stared at it for a long time. *Is this a sign from the cosmos that I've done enough?* I wondered. *Can I leave the Trail now? If I stay, will I just be beating myself up for no reason?* I shook myself. It was just a flower; full of beauty, meaning nothing. I set the intake valve of the filter and began pumping.

We came into town that night a few minutes before the dinner bell at Elmer's. I had been slowing down all day, and now it was all I could do to keep pace with Isis on the sidewalk.

A truck came to a halt beside us. "Hey, Barefoot Sisters!" It was Joel, the nobo we had met at Neel's Gap. His cousin Reid waved from the passenger's seat.

"Hey, it's the Shod Cousins!" I said. "How are you guys?"

"And how did you get a vehicle again?" Isis asked.

Joel shrugged and grinned. "You're not going to believe this."

"What, another pair of section hikers just handed you their car keys?" I asked.

"Um, actually, yeah. They needed somebody to pick them up at the Pigeon River in a couple days. And I figured, while I'm in the area, it'd be fun to have some wheels." He gave a disingenuous smile. "I don't know why they picked me. I guess I just look like a nice guy." Reid pantomimed a fit of helpless laughter.

I shook my head. "Some people have all the luck."

"Reid and I are headed over to Asheville to check out the music scene. There's supposed to be great bluegrass at this little bar in town. You want to come?"

I did, but I wanted to rest more. Take a shower, ice my knee, and rest. "I wish I could. I'm kind of a mess right now, though."

"Sorry to hear about your knee. The guys at Elmer's told me."

"Oh, thanks. Have fun in Asheville."

Reid rolled his window down. "I'll request a song for you. 'Darlin' Corey'—do you know it?"

"No," I said.

He started to sing, barely suppressing his laughter.

> Wake up, wake up, Darlin' Corey,
> What makes you sleep so sound?
> The revenue men are a-comin',
> Gonna tear your stillhouse down.

When he hit the chorus, I could see why he'd chosen the song:

> Dig a hole, dig a hole in the meadow
> Dig a hole in the cold, cold ground
> Dig a hole, dig a hole in the meadow
> Gonna lay Darlin' Corey down!

I almost fell over laughing. We waved to the Shod Cousins as the truck pulled away.

That evening after supper, I found Elmer in the kitchen, helping Ben put away the dishes.

"Elmer? Can I talk to you about something?" I said. I felt like he was someone I could trust, and someone with the wisdom to help me make the decisions I needed to face.

He hung a pan up on the rack and looked at me. "Sure." We went out to the front porch and sat on the swing.

I tried to explain the mixed feelings I'd been having recently about the Trail. "We've been out here nine months now. Nine months of waking up in a different place every morning, not knowing where I'm going to lay my head that night. And I've been afraid, I've been cold, hungry, exhausted . . . and now this knee. It's like the last straw. Sometimes I think, well, it seems like a signal telling me, this is enough. It's time to quit." I told him about the dwarf iris, and how I had felt in the moment I saw it.

He waited a while before answering. "There's a time and a place for all things," he said finally. "People come out on the Trail for a lot of different reasons. But one thing I know is, you can't find the answers out there. You find the answers inside you; they're waiting there all along."

I sighed. It was an answer, but not the kind of clear answer I had hoped for. "I've just had this feeling recently where I want to settle down somewhere, put down roots. I'm so tired of being transient. And this place, this town . . . it feels more like home than any other place I've seen on the Trail. I feel like I could fit in here." I hadn't meant to ask him for a job, but somehow the words came out. "If I did get off the Trail, could I work here?"

He was quiet. I hoped I hadn't overstepped my bounds. "I mean, I'm sorry," I said. "That was awfully forward of me. You must have people ask you that all the time."

"Fairly often," he said with a touch of amusement, but his voice was kind. "You're a hard worker. Good with people. Can you cook?"

"Not like Isis. But yes, I can cook."

"I might have an opening in June, when Jack goes hiking," he said. "Stay close to what you feel. Give the Trail another chance. If you still feel like settling down in June, you are welcome here."

A cricket began chirping in the dark by the porch; the twang of the banjo came from inside. The swing creaked gently. I imagined leaving the Trail and coming here, and the thought brought me great peace. June. Another two months.

"Thank you," I said.

Isis

Jack dropped us off at the trailhead and waved goodbye. As usual, it had taken us a long time to pack our gear before leaving town. We sat down for lunch in a rhododendron thicket less than a mile from the road.

"How's your knee?" I asked jackrabbit, as I sliced avocado, cheese (not havarti this time), and onion onto our bagels.

"Still on the Forest Phil diet plan, are we?" She eyed the avocado appreciatively. "My knee's okay. But this heat is killing me."

"Yeah, me too," I said. "Little Laurel Shelter's only five from the road. I'm tempted to crash there and hike on in the cool of the morning."

"We have to make more miles than that," jackrabbit answered. "We told Miss Janet we'd meet her in Erwin in three days to help with her Easter party." She ate a few bites of her sandwich, then looked up at me, her eyes gleaming. "Hey, what if we just take a nap at the shelter," she asked. "And then night-hike?"

Night-hike? Now that we finally have enough daylight that we don't have to? I thought of the endless miles of winter trail we had covered before dawn and after dusk, the world circumscribed by our headlamp beams. And I remembered our first night-hike, through a treacherous rock field in southern New Jersey. There had been some good moments: the sound of a deer pawing the dry leaves, the lights of towns clustered in the valleys below us. We'd felt strong and proud of ourselves when we reached the shelter, but we'd also been covered with scrapes and bruises. I wasn't sure we should risk it with jackrabbit's sore knee.

A faint breeze rustled the rhododendron leaves, and cooled my sweat-drenched skin for a moment. Then the heat settled over us again, like a thick itchy blanket. *If the alternative is walking another ten or twelve miles in weather like this,* I thought, *we might as well give night-hiking another try.*

We didn't get to take a nap at the shelter. A few nobos were already camped in the clearing when we arrived, and we both got caught in conversations. We did rest, though, lounging on our foam pads, reading through the register, sharing tea and cookies with the other nobos, and eating an early, leisurely supper. As the sun settled into the hazy horizon, we packed up our gear and hiked out.

The cool air on my skin felt as refreshing as a shower. All my senses sharpened with the fierce concentration that it took to set my feet down safely on the darkening trail. I heard a mouse rustle through the undergrowth a hundred yards away; I smelled the smoke of a campfire long before we came to Camp Creek Bald. The twilight had deepened to indigo as we stepped into the open air of the bald. A few stars appeared in the cloudless sweep of dark blue. Perhaps twenty yards from the trail, five or six nobos clustered around a small fire, eating their suppers. I could just make out the dark trapezoids of their tents, scattered among the trees. A headlamp beam arced through the campsite, briefly illuminating the tent flies: purple, purple, green, blue. A woman with short dark hair, carrying two bottles of water, walked over to the group around the fire. Jackrabbit and I passed close beside them, our feet silent in the dewy meadow grass. No one looked up.

The night darkened until my feet hardly showed against the surface of the trail. With each step, I saw only a glimmer like a fish swimming by, far beneath the water. The ground felt soft and cool, clay soil varied here and there by a patch of fine sand. A warm wind from the valley washed over us, bearing a scent like honey. Slick rhododendron leaves brushed my shoulder, and I looked up just in time to see the silhouette of an owl glide across the stars. Close by, something low-slung and heavy trundled through the leaves on the forest floor: a raccoon or opossum. A herd of deer, downhill from us, stamped in alarm as they caught our scent, then walked away slowly.

We passed one more tent a few hours after dark. The fragile walls glowed orange with the beam of a flashlight or candle lantern. For a moment, the warm light drew me in. I wanted to call a greeting to the tent's occupant, to step out of the shadows and set up our tent beside his. Before I could open my mouth, though, I realized how much my voice would startle him—coming out of the night, suddenly, it would sound like the cry of a wild animal much too close.

An hour later, we stopped for a snack break and put our headlamps on. I felt like a shape changer who had just shed her animal skin: suddenly awkward, my senses of smell and hearing dulled by the returning primacy of vision. I chewed my granola bar self-consciously, feeling the eyes of the night world staring at me from just outside the radius of the lamp. When we stood up to leave, I wanted to turn it off, but I felt suddenly vulnerable. How had we set our feet down with such clean certainty, between all the rocks I could now see, scattered over the trail? I wasn't sure I could recapture the strange trance that had allowed me to find the path by touch.

Jackrabbit agreed; we were both tired, and it was better not to risk injuring our feet. We walked on, two humans in a hurry, closed in our capsule of light. Around three in the morning, we set up our tent on a bare patch of ground next to Flint Mountain Shelter. We crawled inside just as the moon rose, curled up back to back, and slept.

The next day brought many kinds of flowers: small yellow lilies with splotchy red and purple leaves, and clusters of tiny pink and white anemones, the source of the honey smell the night before. I recognized them from Anonymous Badger's descriptions—trout lily and spring beauties.

About three miles into the morning, the trail zigzagged up a long valley, crossing and recrossing the lively stream that tumbled down it. A riot of new greens covered the earth under the still-bare trees: the feathery bluish foliage of Dutchman's breeches, the pale, translucent umbrellas of mayapple, the glossy arched stalks of lily of the valley. Trout lilies and trillium, and, higher up, drifts of spring beauties so thick that the ground seemed to be covered with a light, sweet-smelling snow.

The profusion of flowers so changed the landscape that I felt as if I had walked into a different world, not just another season. No spring I'd ever seen had prepared me for this one; it looked as if someone's bulb garden had gotten loose, filling up the forest with a thousand shades of leaf and petal. It was hard to picture this valley as it would have looked in February, when we had passed through it southbound. I remembered the curve of the stream, though, and the yellowish-red soil. When we stopped for a snack, I checked the map. I was right; we were in Devil's Fork Gap, the valley we'd been hiking through when Yogi had described the spring wildflowers to us.

For the rest of the day, we hiked along dry ridges. Here and there, a few lilies of the valley or a clump of spring beauties brightened the forest floor, but in most places, only a few green leaves rose out of the dead ones. The clouds thickened, sinking closer to the ridge tops. Jackrabbit's limp grew more and more pronounced as the day wore on, and when we stopped for lunch at Hogback Ridge Shelter, I noticed the purplish circles around her eyes, and the muscles standing out along her neck and jaw. Her hands trembled as she took the bagel I offered her. We ate in silence; I was afraid to ask how much pain she was in, afraid to find out if she would have to quit the Trail. And somehow I couldn't muster the energy to make conversation about a more cheerful topic to distract us both.

As we packed up to leave, a tall, skinny hiker wearing headphones strode up to the shelter. He looked at us, tapped the radio in his breast pocket, and said, "It's gonna snow," as a greeting. "Big storm," he added solemnly.

"Maybe we could hitch to town from Sam's Gap," I said to jackrabbit. "It's only a few miles from here."

"The road through there's a freeway," jackrabbit sighed. "No one would stop."

"Maybe Miss Janet could pick us up. The *Companion* says there's a restaurant half a mile down the road from the trail crossing. We could try calling her from there."

"I hope we get through," jackrabbit said, her voice almost a whisper. She picked up her hiking sticks and used them to lever herself to her feet. "I don't think I can get much farther on this knee."

At the gap, we followed the freeway shoulder downhill to the east, where the *Companion* claimed that there was a truck stop restaurant. We walked for half an hour, passing nothing but a run-down farm. After forty-five minutes— long enough that we must have walked more than a mile, even at our slowest pace—we came to a gravel parking lot with two or three abandoned buildings around its perimeter. One of them had a sign in the window that read, "Dottie's Pancakes and Coffee," but to judge by the sagging roof and the long grass growing up through the porch, Dottie had made her last pancake at least five years earlier. Jackrabbit sat down on the rotting steps, her left leg stretched out in front of her.

"I don't think I can walk much farther," she said. "Not on asphalt, anyway."

"Okay," I said. "You can wait here. I'll go a little farther down the road and see if I can find a phone to borrow. It looks like there's a house near that next bend."

As I got closer to the house, I noticed the broken window pane, the torn, faded curtains, and the screen door flapping open and closed in the wind. *I'll knock, anyway*, I decided. *It looks a bit run-down, but maybe someone still lives here.*

I had just started up the driveway, when I heard a car pulling in behind me. *Oh good, they're home,* I thought, followed by, *I hope they don't think I'm a thief. They must not get a lot of visits from strangers.*

The van pulled up beside me and the passenger door opened. There sat jackrabbit, grinning. Miss Janet, in the driver's seat, turned around and beamed at me.

"I was hopin' to find y'all," she said. "I figured y'all'd be headin' through Sam's Gap about now, and I was wonderin' if you'd like to slack the last twenty miles to Erwin."

"We'd love to," I said. "Thanks so much. But . . . how did you know where to find us? I mean, we must be a mile and a half east of the gap, and you were coming from the west."

She gave a little shrug, accompanied by an impish smile. "Oh, I just knew."

CHAPTER 3

Nobo Stories

jackrabbit

D own in Erwin, dogwood trees bloomed in every front yard, their clouds of pink and white flowers like flocks of butterflies in the branches. Tulips and daffodils added their colors to the riot of spring. All the trees in the valley were leafing out. The soft green color of new foliage had begun to spread into the mountains around town, diffusing upward.

We took a couple of zero days in Erwin. Miss Janet's house was full of hikers; a crowd of nobos, mostly men in their twenties, lounged in the backyard or watched movies in the living room. Some of them, like me, were injured, but most were just enjoying a few days off. We took turns buying food, cooking, and washing the endless stream of dishes. Miss Janet herself was hardly ever home. She spent most of her time on the road, shuttling hikers to restaurants and stores. Isis and I supervised the production of food for the Easter party: vats of cole slaw and potato salad, baked sweet potatoes, corn fritters, bread and rolls.

One afternoon, we walked into town to pick up our mail—a beat-up cardboard box emblazoned with the usual "please hold for thru-hikers"—and opened it on the bench outside the old brick post office. It was mostly food our mother had sent: a few gourmet freeze-dried dinners, some dehydrated rice and beans, pilaf, quinoa in various flavors, pasta, and crackers. There was a small pile of letters: two magazine solicitations, a credit card application, a postcard from a college friend. At the bottom of the stack was a small envelope with familiar writing, so thick and slanted it was barely legible. The return address was a hotel on Maui.

"Black Forest!" I said.

"I wonder what he's up to these days," Isis mused.

I slit open the envelope, and a faint scent of cologne drifted up through the spring air of Erwin. Turning the paper forty-five degrees to decipher his handwriting, I read: *Aloha Hikerchicks! Imagine an A.T. thru-hiker and self-declared badass (German one) is sitting on an island, got nothing better to do than thinking of two chicks out of the woods with no shoes on and an extremely "natural" odour, which turns a well balanced guy like me into an emotional wreck—damn you! . . .* He continued in this vein, letting us know how he had almost been thrown out of the Atlanta airport for being a bum, after hiking a thirty-mile day and hitching sixty miles, and most of all how insufferably boring Hawaii was without our presence. He signed off, *still begging for sex (and still with little success)—Black Forest.*

"He hasn't changed," Isis said, shaking her head. "He leaves us behind to finish the Trail—"

"—doing his eight-hundred-mile death march—"

"—and get to Hawaii—"

"—with his *grandparents*!"

"—and then he complains about how much he misses us!" Isis shook her head again and rolled her eyes. "Silly German!"

I did miss him, though. I thought back to the feeling of his bony frame lying beside me, the slow smile that lit up his enormous blue eyes. He could be insufferable, immature, annoying, but at least we had shared that time, side by side without speaking, feeling the steady rhythm of each others' breath. Perhaps it was not him I missed so much as the idea of closeness. Seeking fellowship in the wilderness.

We took stock of the food we had, closed up the box and hefted it into Isis's empty pack, and walked to the supermarket to complete our resupply. Miss Janet's gray van (the "Shaggin' Wagon") came into the lot with a load of hikers, who all waved to us. I spotted Reid and Joel, Toast, Tha Wookie (easily visible with his head of bright red curls), Priceless, and a young couple from Maine who we had met that morning. Johnny, a middle-aged man from Florida with one of the lightest packs I had ever seen, was sitting on the wheel hub. Every time I'd seen the van in the last three days, he had been in that same place. There was one hiker I was less than happy to see: Roadrunner, the guy who had tried to dub us the "Shitter Sisters" in Hot Springs.

Kaitlin, the youngest of Miss Janet's daughters, tumbled out first and came running to meet us. "Mom wants me to get the eggs for the Easter party! Can I come with y'all?"

"Sure thing." Isis grabbed a cart and we headed into the crowded aisles. Kaitlin followed, offering suggestions and advice.

"Chocolate Pop-tarts are the best! Priceless told me the frosted ones crumble in your pack, though . . . oh, if you don't like Pop-tarts, then you can always get your chocolate from Cocoa Pebbles! The only thing is, they make your milk turn kinda purple . . ."

We turned a corner in the produce section, and there was a barrel of the biggest pickles I had ever seen. Cucumbers probably eight inches long and as thick as my wrist floated in clear brine. A diamond-shaped red label proclaimed, "Black Forest Pickles."

Isis spotted it about the same time I did.

I could almost hear Sharkbait's voice on the phone, in that Front Royal hotel room so many months ago. *He says he'd like to give you his pickle, too.* "I didn't know what I was missing," I gasped, and we both burst out laughing uncontrollably, leaning against each other to keep from falling over. Kaitlin came running, her white-blond hair flapping behind her.

"What is it? What'd y'all find?"

"Oh, just some funny looking pickles. Aren't they huge?" I couldn't explain the whole story to a twelve-year-old. Even a twelve-year-old like Kaitlin.

We loaded back into the van with all our groceries, a tangle of shopping bags, long legs, and scruffy clothing. Johnny was still perched on the wheel hub. It looked as though he hadn't moved.

"You got your resupply, Johnny?"

"Yesterday, actually. I'm just along for the ride."

"You even been out of the van since this morning?" somebody asked.

Johnny gave a small smile and shrugged. "Naw. I like ridin' in the van."

"Trail name! Trail name!" I shouted, and other hikers took up the cry. Suggestions rained in from all sides.

"Van Man!"

"Van-derbilt!"

"Van Morrison!"

"I-van the Terrible!"

"Van-Go," I said.

"Hey, that works," Johnny grinned. "I get in the van, and I go. And I'm an artist, too."

"Just as long as you don't cut your ear off."

"No worries."

I spent the rest of the afternoon in the kitchen. The food was all ready (except for the ham, which would bake on the day of the party), but there were six dozen eggs to dye. Kaitlin, Van-Go, Isis, and I decorated most of them, drawing designs in crayon and dipping them in vats of vinegar and food coloring. We drew leaves and flowers, bunnies, spirals, mountains. I made a few eggs with trails of bare footprints wandering their smooth surfaces. Van-Go attempted a *Starry Night* egg, but it came out looking more like an impressionistic rendering of lawn clippings.

"Crayon on eggshell ain't my best medium," he said.

Miss Janet's friend Blondie decorated a couple of eggs, too. She was a tall, raw-boned woman in early middle age, with a mass of blond hair piled above her narrow face.

"I got the name when I hiked with my husband—ex-husband now; good riddance," she said. "He was Dagwood 'cause of the huge sandwiches he made in town, so everybody called me Blondie. The name just stuck with me. I tried to get another trail name, I really did. But I'm such a blond." She giggled. "I guess it fits."

"When did you hike?" Isis asked her, as she stirred another few drops of color into the vat of blue dye.

"Oh, five years ago. I miss it. That's why I love hanging out with hikers." She giggled. "Plus I get to check out all these sexy young guys."

"Yeah, that's a definite advantage to Trail life," I said.

A car pulled up outside. It didn't sound like the Shaggin' Wagon; the engine was too quiet, and I didn't hear a crowd of hikers climbing out.

I looked up as the door opened and nearly dropped the egg I was holding. "Tuba Man?" I said when I caught my breath.

He grinned. I hadn't exaggerated the lines of his face in memory; no, he was ten times as gorgeous in person as anything I could have imagined. "I told you, you never know when you'll see me and my tuba," he said, gathering me up in a hug.

I was too stunned to even hug him back; I stood there with my mouth open like an idiot. At Hawk Mountain, when he had disappeared into the morning fog, I had resolved that the next time I saw him, I would tell him what he meant to me. But here he was, and I was suddenly tongue-tied, stupid, too shy to even look at him.

"Well, hello there," Blondie purred. "Miss Janet's told me all about you."

That evening, Isis and I spread out our sleeping bags on the living room floor. Tuba Man and Blondie were still in the kitchen. I could hear the rise and fall of their voices, occasional laughter. I sat on the couch with an ice pack on my knee, sulking. *She's practically old enough to be his mother*, I thought, *and she's flirting with him like a co-ed. Shameless.* Mostly, I wished I had as much nerve as she did. *All those winter nights, when I looked up at the first damn star and wished for this. And here's my chance, and I don't take it.* I lay down next to the wall and put a pillow under my sore knee, and fell asleep.

The day of the party dawned clear and beautiful again. I woke up to the sounds of hikers on the lawn outside, and the mingled scents of pancakes frying and fresh-mown grass. Looking across the living room, as my eyes adjusted to the brightness of the day, I saw Isis's empty sleeping bag and the inert forms of a few other hikers. Near the doorway, Tuba Man was still asleep in his puffy blue down bag—with his arm around Blondie. She was snoring softly in her fleece liner beside him. Her wide mouth hung open. *She looks her age*, I thought sourly as I stepped past them.

In the kitchen, Isis stood at the stove, flipping pancakes. She gave me a sympathetic look that I pretended not to notice. *Sometimes the best way to deal with misery is to ignore it*, I told myself. "Thanks for making breakfast!" I said. "These look great!"

She handed me a plate. "No problem." There was a question in her eyes, but she didn't ask it. I was grateful.

Miss Janet drove countless vanloads of hikers to the Nolichucky Hostel, a complex of buildings and fields down by the river. There was an outfitter's store, several cabins, a bunkhouse, and racks of canoes, kayaks, and rafts set back under the greening woods. Isis and I went with the first load, and spent nearly an hour hiding Easter eggs and hauling wood to the firepit for a bonfire that night. By the time we had finished, a huge crowd of hikers had assembled in the dining hall. Miss Janet and Blondie served lunch: coleslaw and potato salad, green salad, macaroni, turkey and ham, beans and fried okra, fresh fruit, and a huge array of desserts. Afterward, when the stupor of too much food had worn off, someone brought out Frisbees and hacky-sacks. A volleyball game began. Tuba Man and Tha Wookie were formidable opponents on the court, thwacking their serves over the net like cannonballs. Joel and Reid played on the same team, shouting like kids, diving into the sand for some impressive saves.

In midafternoon the Easter egg hunt began. Digger and Priceless raced each other, running around the perimeter of the field checking every log and stone. Forest Phil stalked over the ground, bent low, hunting methodically. Luna and Six-string, who had come into town this morning, searched as a team, and Toast tagged along behind them, picking up the eggs they missed and laughing at their inattention. A crowd of other hikers crisscrossed the field. Tuba Man and Tha Wookie eventually abandoned their volleyball rivalry to join the search when they saw the prizes that the Nolichucky Outfitters were offering: water bottles and energy bars, but also a handsome fleece jacket, a new water filter, and a rafting trip for two. Clouds came over the sun and a scattering of rain touched the surface of the river, but no one seemed to mind.

I enjoyed the party more than I had expected to. It helped that Blondie flirted indiscriminately, batting her long eyelashes at any male hiker who walked past. Tuba Man didn't seem to be paying any special attention to her, either. In the middle of the afternoon, when the rain showers had cleared up, he took his tuba from the trunk of his car and serenaded us all. Warm, liquid sound filled the clearing. Charisma's bell had been straightened, pulled back into its proper curve, but marks on the metal still showed where it had been bent. I remembered watching him play by the campfire at the Gathering. Snow, the first snow of this long winter, had collected in his beard and drifted in the crumpled tuba bell. *Why can't I accept what I realized then?* I thought. *He flirts with everyone. It's just his way of addressing the world; I shouldn't take it personally.*

And then he turned to look straight at me, his eyes full of warmth. "This next song is for a special friend of mine. Jackrabbit, of the Barefoot Sisters!" I was sure I was blushing so red the entire crowd could see. He lifted the tuba and began to play *Summertime*. The slow, sweet notes floated in the air. It seemed like the most beautiful sound I had ever heard.

"Thanks," he said to the crowd of hikers when he finished. "You've been a great audience."

I stood there stammering and incoherent for too long, before I managed a tiny, "Thank you."

"And now I hate to leave this party," he was saying, "but I've got a rehearsal tonight at seven, and it's a four-hour drive." The hikers applauded loudly and called for encores. He flashed his glorious smile and bowed again. "I really wish I could stay. Good luck; happy hiking!" He waved and turned to walk away.

I was stunned. I had thought he would stay for the night, or for the bon-fire at least. I had thought I would have more time to figure out what to say, how to say it. Instead, I followed him to his car, my heart racing, my mind blank.

"Hey, this was really fun," he said.

"Yeah. Thanks for coming." I squared my shoulders and the words came out—not the cool, eloquent words I had hoped to prepare. Not at all. "You're the sexiest man I've ever met," I blurted.

His jaw dropped. For the first time since I'd met him, he was speechless. "Um, ah, thanks. Uh, nobody's ever said that to me before." He opened the trunk of his car and put the tuba into its case.

I wanted to say something else, but my capacity for speech had failed me.

He looked back at me. "I have to go. I wish there was something, I mean . . ." he rooted around in his glove compartment. "Here." He handed me a photograph. "So you can remember me."

"I don't need a picture to remember you."

"I, uh, thanks. I don't know what to say. You're really kind." He smiled. I felt as though my knees would give way. "I'll see you later, okay?"

I waved numbly. "Bye." And I wondered if I would ever see him again. I wondered whether I would be able to face him if I did. I looked down at the picture; he was standing at the edge of the ocean, with his tuba balanced above his head on one hand.

His little blue car pulled away, up the gravel road and onto the asphalt.

At the fire that night, melancholy settled over me. I watched the faces of people around me talking, laughing, drinking, having a good time. Greensinger waltzed by unsteadily, exclaiming about the colors of starlight. Six-string and Tha Wookie had found a guitar somewhere, but their music was almost drowned out by the din of the crowd. Once or twice, as I looked across the firelight, I saw Roadrunner staring at Isis with a disturbing intensity. All these things registered only dimly, though. I was missing Tuba Man, wish-ing he was beside me instead of all the drunken nobos who staggered past. I drank a few cups of wine and a shot of whiskey, but it didn't seem to help.

Toast sat down heavily on the log beside me and put an arm over my shoulders. "It sure is nice to sit next to a beau'ful woman on a night like this . . ." He had a Nalgene with a few inches of red wine sloshing in the bottom. I could smell its pungent sweetness on his breath.

"That's awful kind of you, Toast," I said wearily. Any other night, perhaps, I would have flirted and played along. But I felt empty and conflicted from all that had happened—and not happened—with Tuba Man. I slipped out from under Toast's arm, steadying him at the last minute so he wouldn't fall off the log. "Good night."

I staggered across the grass, leaving the circle of firelight and the boisterous laughter of the crowd. Most of the other hikers had set up tents and tarps around the edge of the field, but Isis and I had left our tent at Miss Janet's, so we'd decided to sleep in the bunkhouse. As I came into the dark building, I turned off my headlamp so I wouldn't wake my sister. I felt my way across the room; my eyes began to adjust to the dim moonlight as I reached the bunk where I'd left my sleeping bag. On the top bunk, Isis mumbled something and turned over in her sleep.

Footsteps clattered on the porch. There was a shadow in the doorway, and a familiar, strangely unmodulated voice. "The Barefoot Sisters." It was Roadrunner. I froze. Something in his tone made the hair on the back of my neck stand up.

"Hello, Roadrunner." I kept my voice calm with an effort.

"I knew you and your sister would be here," he said in that odd voice. "Alone."

My tipsiness faded and full alertness rushed into my veins with the pumping adrenaline. So he knew we were both here. He'd been watching us. He filled up the doorway, a few inches taller than me, all muscle and sinew. He had every advantage—height, weight, surprise. And he knew it. But I was trained.

I forced my muscles to relax, ready to whip into lethal action. I kept my voice level and quiet. "Roadrunner, do you know what a flying side kick is? How about a spinning back hook kick?"

"What's that?" His voice was flat, analytical.

"That is what I will do if you take one step through that doorway. You'll end up on your ass in a lot of pain, with your jaw and several ribs broken. If you come into this room, you are *my* victim. Don't make me hurt you."

"I'm scared shitless," he said without emotion. He stayed where he was.

I took a step forward, my hands raised in a fighting stance. "Leave now," I told him, with all the weight of authority I could bring to my voice.

Slowly, he backed away. I heard his footsteps going down the porch stairs, and a muffled curse as he tripped on something. Then he stumbled into the grass and began to run.

I put my sleeping bag in the bunk nearest the door. For a long time, I lay awake, my heartbeat thudding against the wooden bunk frame. I listened hard:

the sounds of the river, scraps of laughter and shouts from the crowd at the bonfire, the crackle of flames. No more footsteps came to the porch, and eventually I fell into an uneasy sleep.

We had meant to slackpack the next day, but we woke up to snow. Perhaps an inch clung to the ground, even here in the river valley, covering the new leaves and the flowers. It was still falling. The crowd of hikers came into the kitchen in the morning, huddling in their warmest clothes and cursing, while Isis cooked up a huge batch of pancakes and started up the coffee maker.

I shared a table with Luna, Six-string, and Toast. Six-string looked decidedly the worse for wear. He leaned his head on the table, groaning occasionally.

"April sixteenth," I said, spitting out the words. "Even up in Maine it hardly ever snows this late."

Toast shrugged. "Some winters are just like this," he said philosophically. "I've seen snow as late as May in these mountains."

"This damn weather! It feels like we just can't escape winter, no matter how long we wait, how fast we hike."

"It is kind of nasty out there," Luna agreed. "But hey! It's a good excuse to stay in town another day."

Six-string mumbled something and put his head back down.

Luna patted his hair. "Yeah, I think we'd be taking a zero today, regardless. Last night—" she shook her head. "Oh boy. We were gonna change his trail name to Sick-string."

Six-string grunted something else, and Luna translated. "Yeah. At least he found a dumpster. No puking in the bushes for this guy. Always a gentleman." She patted him again. "Drink your coffee, hon. It's good for you."

"Toast was pretty far gone, too," I said. "He was after all the ladies at the campfire, eh, Mr. Toastee?"

Toast blushed a little, his face bashful behind his blond beard. "What'd I do this time?"

I put my arm around him and leaned in close. "'It sure is nice to sit next to a beau'ful woman on a night like this . . .'"

He blushed a little redder. "Did I really?"

Isis cooked the last of the pancakes and came to join us.

"Thanks for cooking," Luna said.

"Oh, no problem. Say, do you guys have any idea where Miss Janet is this morning?"

"Yeah," a hiker at the next table told us. "She's driving up to Damascus."

"Damascus!" I said. "In the snow?"

"Yeah. Apparently there's this guy, a total yellow blazer." (This was a Trail expression for someone who skipped big chunks of the A.T. by hitchhiking.) "He wanted to leave town in a real hurry for some reason."

"Who was it?" Isis asked.

"Guy named Roadrunner."

Isis

Ever since we had turned around to hike north, our mom had been planning to come down and hike a section with us. She met us on our last day in Erwin. Petite (at least compared to her daughters), fine-boned, and nearing sixty, our mother might not have seemed like the best candidate to jump on the Trail for a six-day stint with thru-hikers. She's tough, though—in her mid-twenties she went on long sailing trips and climbed over glaciers to reach unnamed mountains in Alaska. Now, nearing retirement, she keeps up a quarter-acre vegetable garden, and whenever she can take the vacation time, she works as a grip on our stepdad's film expeditions.

We planned to hike ten-mile days while she was with us, perhaps working up to twelves by the end of the week. We knew that slowing down to a beginning hiker's pace might be frustrating, but this would be a good time to do it. The slower we walked, the faster jackrabbit's knee would heal.

On our first day out of Erwin, we left Nolichucky Gorge just after lunch. I hoped that would give us time to make the four miles to Curly Maple Gap Shelter. It was almost all uphill, but I figured that our mom could handle it as long as we went slowly. She'd slacked ten miles in the snow, over lots of little ups and downs, the day after Miss Janet picked her up at the airport.

We made better time than I expected. In spite of a half hour spent gathering nettle shoots for soup, several stops to admire the redbuds, and a snack break halfway up the hill, it was only three-thirty when we reached Curly Maple Gap.

"Is this it?" our mom asked, as we lined our packs up against the shelter wall.

"This is the shelter," jackrabbit answered, "but I don't think we'll stay here tonight. It's too early to stop."

Hey, wait a minute, I thought. *That's not what we planned. And if this were my first day on the Trail, it's not what I'd want to hear.* I thought of the day I'd earned my trail name, on my first backpacking trip. I had budgeted my energy very carefully to reach the place where we planned to camp, and the prospect of hiking even one mile farther had filled me with dread. Ignoring jackrabbit, I asked our mom how she was doing.

"Great!" she answered. "I'm really enjoying this, and I'd like to hike a bit farther this afternoon. Susan's right; it's too early in the day to stop."

Jackrabbit shot me a triumphant glance, over our mom's shoulder. I smiled and shrugged, trying to hide my irritation. Not that I minded hiking on—it was a lovely clear day, with temperatures in the low sixties, and we had more than three hours of daylight ahead of us. I just minded the way that jackrabbit had announced the change in plans, precluding any discussion. I minded the fact that she was gloating. And I really minded my own reaction—a seething resentment that took a long time to calm, hard as I tried to reason my way out of it. I caught myself wishing that jackrabbit's knee would act up again, so that she'd regret her insistence on making miles. *Quit it*, I told myself. *You should have grown out of "nyah-nyah, I told you so" about twenty years ago. It's as though having our mom here has turned us both into children.* But I couldn't help feeling a slight twinge of satisfaction when, three miles later, jackrabbit's limp returned.

We camped at Indian Grave Gap, eight and a half miles from Nolichucky Gorge. Our mom set down her pack and glanced around the stealth site.

"Look, girls! There's a firepit," she exclaimed, delighted. "I'll go gather some wood!" She took a step toward the pines and laughed, her bright voice filling the clearing. "I feel so light without my pack on. I feel as if I could float." She lifted her arms slowly, like a hawk stretching its wings on a thermal. "Do you always feel this way when you take your packs off?"

To my surprise, I realized that I did. The sense of levitation had become so familiar, though, that I hardly even noticed it any more. I nodded, feeling the bad mood lift off my shoulders as easily as a pack. Our mom walked into the forest, singing "She'll Be Coming 'Round the Mountain" to herself. Jackrabbit started unpacking our tent, while I hung a bear line for our food bags. When I got back to the clearing, I noticed that jackrabbit was limping, even with her pack off, as she set up the tent. My chest tightened. *Oh no. My stupid, spiteful wish has come true. What if she has to get off the Trail?*

"I can finish that, if you want," I offered. "You can sit by the fire and rest your knee."

"I'm fine," she shot back. "Worry about your own chore."

Our mom set up her tent and built a fire, while I picked out one of the gourmet backpacking dinners she had brought for our resupply. Jackrabbit finished with the tent and joined us, sinking onto a rock in front of the firepit with a sigh.

"I'm sorry I've been such a bitch today," she said to me. "I just thought that with all the time we've taken off, and all the slacking, my knee would be better by now."

"Maybe I can try some Qi Gong on it," our mother suggested.

"Chee what?" I asked.

"Qi Gong. It's a Chinese healing art. I just started taking classes five or six months ago, so I don't know that much. But there's a simple way to gather *qi*, the vital energy—" she paused, noticing our skeptical expressions, and laughed. "Okay, I know it sounds kind of woo-woo. But it feels like it works—to me, anyway."

"I've tried everything that the Hot Springs Clinic suggested already," jackrabbit answered. "Rest, ice, and ibuprofen. None of it seems like it helped much. I may as well try this."

Our mom sat up straight, took a deep breath, and began moving her hands apart and then back together, like clapping in slow motion. After repeating the gesture five or six times, she turned her palms downward and held them in the air over jackrabbit's knee. A slow smile spread across my sister's face, and then she broke into laughter.

"That feels funny!" she giggled.

"You can feel something?" I asked her.

"Yes. It . . . *tingles*."

"Do you want to try it?" my mom asked me. "Cup your hands a little, like this. Bring them out to the sides, then bring them close together, gathering *qi* between them."

I repeated the gesture a few times.

"That's good," my mother coached. "Imagine the *qi* forming a ball between your palms."

Perhaps it was the power of suggestion, but I did feel a warm, tingling sensation in my hands. I held my palms over jackrabbit's knee. The tingling continued. I focused all my concentration into my hands. *Please, Goddess*, I prayed, *let this help.*

We tried to let our mom set the pace the next day, but she insisted that we walk ahead. "I'll keep up," she said, and—to my amazement—she seemed to have no trouble doing so, even on the uphills.

It was a perfect day for hiking. Pale sunlight filtered through the trees, giving the woods the soft, dusty radiance of a hand-tinted photograph. Anemones covered the forest floor and tangled in the grasses of the bald at Beauty Spot. On Unaka Mountain, the new grass shone under the trees, and the scent of spring beauties mingled with the sharp perfume of spruce. Even on Little Bald Knob, which I remembered as an unmitigated PUD, clumps of trillium nodded in the breeze, deep red, yellow, and greenish white. On the north slope, just before the road, we found our first wild larkspur: fans of leaves surrounding a foot-high tower of deep blue blossoms.

We camped by a stream, a few miles farther on. I checked the map—we'd hiked a fourteen.

"Fourteen. That's not bad," jackrabbit said. She took the map and studied it for a minute. "If we can average fifteen for the next three days, we'll be at Kincora."

I felt a flicker of anger. *She's only thinking of herself. As soon as she can make fifteens, we all have to.* I'd noticed that she hadn't been limping all day.

"Fourteen's a pretty long day for someone who just started," I told her, keeping my voice level. "Remember how long it took us to work up to our first thirteen, in the Wilderness?"

"Your packs were a lot heavier than mine is," our mom put in. "I'm only carrying thirty-five pounds."

"What about your feet?" I asked her. "Any blisters?"

"I think there might be one on my little toe. But it's not really bothering me. Oh, girls, look at that sunset!"

I caught jackrabbit's eye, shrugged my shoulders, and smiled. *Okay, maybe we will make fifteens.*

We got an early start the next morning, and I found myself sharing jackrabbit's confidence that we could hike long miles. Perhaps we could even make it to Overmountain. The old tobacco barn, with its view of sloping fields and distant mountains, was one of my favorite shelters on the Trail. How far was it? Sixteen? Seventeen? As long as jackrabbit's knee stayed healthy, it would be an easy day for us. As for our mother, I was beginning to believe that anything was possible.

By the time we stopped for our first snack break, the day had turned hot and muggy. I checked the map, and discovered that Overmountain would be nineteen miles from the place we'd camped. Better give up that plan. Stan Murray Shelter, at fifteen, was a much better prospect. I wasn't nearly as enthusiastic about staying there; I remembered it as a small, dank building painted Forest Service brown, perched on a narrow ridge without much space for tenting. Not exactly one of the highlights of the Roans that I'd been hoping to share with our mother.

We hit the long ascent of Roan High Knob in the early afternoon, the hottest part of the day. Our mom never complained, but I noticed that she hiked more and more slowly as the trail climbed. She didn't comment on the views or the wildflowers as often as she had in the morning. When we finally reached the peak, the sun had sunk close to the horizon. Its light already had the amber cast of evening. We ate our granola bars, drank from a cold spring that tasted of spruce trees, and headed down toward Carvers Gap.

The air felt cool under the evergreens, and the song of running water filled the woods. To my delight, I discovered that my feet had regained almost all of their summer toughness; the old gravel road that the trail followed hardly hurt them at all. Jackrabbit didn't seem to be faring as well. Every once in a while, I heard a muffled curse from behind me. *Oh, come on, not in front of our mother*, I thought. But I didn't want to let her spoil my good mood.

Horizontal rays of sunlight slanted through the trees by the time we came to the stream at the bottom of the gap.

"It's getting late," I said to jackrabbit, as we took turns filtering water into our bottles. "I guess we won't make our fifteen today. We'd better carry some water to cook with, and stealth somewhere up on the balds."

"Stan Murray Shelter's only three more miles," she answered testily. "We'll night-hike if we have to."

"Stan Murray's a tiny shelter. It'll be packed with hikers by the time we arrive, and I don't remember many tent sites around it."

"We've only hiked twelve miles! That's less than we hiked in winter on this stretch, with the whole Family in tow!"

"We were planning to hike tens, remember?" I glanced over at our mom, who was leaning against a tree, her eyes closed, sipping out of her water bottle. She had taken off her shoes to cool her feet, and I noticed that the blister she'd mentioned the day before seemed to cover her entire toe, swelling it to twice its size.

"You mean *you* were planning," jackrabbit answered. "I just went along with it because there's no use arguing with you, once you decide what we're going to do. You decide how fast we're going to go, where we're going to stay, and who we're going to hike with. You want a zero, we take a zero. Well, I'll tell you what I want. I want to get to Katahdin in September. And there's no fucking way we're going to get there hiking twelves."

Our mom opened her eyes. "I don't mind night-hiking," she offered. "I have a headlamp. I don't want to interfere with your hike."

"That's just the problem," jackrabbit growled. "It isn't *our* hike, and it never has been. It's *hers*."

I was embarrassed to quarrel in front of our mom, but I couldn't hold back any longer. "I'd like to see how far you would have gotten without me," I snapped. "Who else would have carried the heavy food for you, and done all the chores in winter when your hands were too cold?"

"We wouldn't have gotten caught by winter in the first place, if you'd hiked a bit faster through Mass and Vermont! If you'd kept up with Waterfall—"

"We got behind Waterfall because you got injured, remember? She was two weeks ahead of me, hiking twenties, by the time you left—"

"You still could have hiked more than ten miles a day!"

"I slowed down so that *you*—" Suddenly, I remembered that our mother was sitting right next to us, a captive audience to all our petty grievances. I turned to her. "I'm sorry we're having this fight. Now. When you're here. I wanted to show you all the good things about the Trail, how much fun we have . . ."

"Yeah," jackrabbit said. "We don't fight like this all the time. Maybe two other times, on the whole trip. I don't know why it came up now."

Our mom sighed. "I'm not surprised. Having family around can do that to you. Break down your defenses, like Kryptonite does to Superman. That's the way *my* sister puts it."

So hiking with my sister all the time is like Superman hiking with a big block of Kryptonite hung around his neck, I thought. But all I said was, "Sun's almost down. I guess we'd better get going, unless we want to camp *here* tonight."

"Where to?" asked jackrabbit, an edge of suspicion creeping back into her voice.

"I don't know," I sighed. "Here, hand me that bottle. I'll bring some cooking water, and we can see how far we get."

"I'll carry the water," jackrabbit answered.

We reached Jane Bald just at sunset. At this elevation, the grass hadn't even begun to turn green. Matted and bleached by the snows, it looked like the coat of a mangy lion. The late light threw each tussock into relief and mottled the bald with their shadows. Row upon row of mountains, tinged orange, mauve, and gray, circled the horizon. I felt like the argument had wrung all the strength from my body. I couldn't imagine putting one foot in front of the other for two more miles, in darkness. I took off my pack. Our mom sighed as she set her pack down next to mine, then sat in the grass, leaning against it.

"I feel like I could just curl up right now and go to sleep," she said, wrapping her arms around her knees.

"I'll put the tent up," jackrabbit conceded.

The wind rose as the sky darkened; all night it rippled through the tent flies and guy lines. The sound of the flapping cloth reminded me of nights on a sailboat, far from shore, in my early childhood. It woke me at least once every hour. I had to reassure myself that it was not a sail luffing before I could fall back to sleep.

In the pale, cold hour before dawn, I woke to the sound of a tent fly unzipping; my mother was getting up already. Had she slept as little as I had? By the time I'd put on my long underwear and slipped out of our tent, she was walking away up the bald, following the trail northward. She paused at the brow of the hill, and I caught up with her.

"Morning walk?" I asked.

"Qi Gong," she answered. "There's a meditative exercise I do every morning to welcome the sun. Want to join me?"

I stood beside her, copying her movements, as the stars faded and the sky flamed pink and gold over the low blue mountains. The slow, dancelike exercise worked the stiffness from my limbs, and by the time the sun lit the dome of Round Bald behind us, I felt ready to hike a twenty.

"Looks like this'll be another short day," jackrabbit said to me, as we fluffed up the grass where our tents had stood, hiding the traces of our encampment.

"Why's that?" I asked. "Is your knee bothering you?"

"My knee's fine. Take a look at the map, though."

She handed it to me, and I saw what she meant. Twelve to Apple House Shelter, and then . . . eight or ten miles of Campbell territory, starting with the road where she and John had nearly gotten hit by a truck.

"Apple House?" I asked her.

"Apple House it is." She paused, and looked at me. "I'd like to hike the fifteen to Moreland Gap tomorrow, but it's full of nasty PUDs. We could stealth at a stream if we had to, once we got off of Campbell land."

"Last time we hiked that section, we had sixty-pound packs and five inches of wet snow to wade through," I said. "It's probably not as bad as we remember."

We hiked a leisurely day through the last of the Roans, stopping for naps and an early lunch at Overmountain. A bright sun shone in a sky the color of a robin's egg, and new grass brightened the lower balds. In the last few miles of the day, a slow, gradual downhill, we gathered ramps—a kind of wild leek with a powerful garlicky flavor—and nettles to add to our pasta primavera.

"Holy shit, it's the Barefoot Sisters!" a young man with frizzy blond hair exclaimed, as we walked up to Apple House Shelter.

A middle-aged man with a reddish-blond mustache and a cowboy hat scanned our muddy feet, stained clothing, and flyaway hair. "So, you're the ones who call yourselves the Barefoot Sisters."

I could hear the murmur of voices rising in the shelter behind him.

"Barefoot Sisters?!"

"They're here?"

"Does that mean they're real?"

I peered into the dark shelter opening. No one I recognized. Farther down the Trail, I knew, all of these people might become good friends. At the moment, though, I really didn't feel like playing the celebrity for them. I glanced over at jackrabbit. She was smiling and greeting the man with the frizzy hair, but, to judge from the set of her jaw, she didn't feel any more sociable than I did.

I waved to the shelter in general. "Hi, I'm Isis. That's my sister, jackrabbit. Yes, we're real. Anyone with doubts on that subject, please address them to our mom, Patty."

I tried to listen to the chorus of names and questions that came back to me, but my mind seemed to be working too slowly to catch the words. *Did that guy say he was Jeff, or Josh? Wait a minute, the woman in the twill hat just asked me something. Something about cabbages? No, calluses. I think.* Finally I gave up and waved again, smiling as sweetly as I could. "We've got to go set up our tents, but it was great to meet all of you. See you in the morning, or somewhere down the trail!"

Jackrabbit caught up with me and our mom as we headed around the corner of the shelter. "Thanks for getting us out of there," she said. "Nothing against the kid I was talking to, but I just can't deal with strangers right now. Where are you planning on camping?"

"Looks like all the official tent sites are right by the shelter," I answered. "But they're kind of gravelly, and most of them are taken. I was thinking we could camp in that abandoned orchard across the stream. I feel like I need some kind of moat tonight."

The orchard stretched farther back than I'd realized: fifty or sixty trees, all in bud or in blossom. Beneath the trees, thousands of violets bloomed in the thick, pale grass. We gathered a few handfuls of the peppery flowers to spice our pasta, then sat around our stove as supper cooked, enjoying the trilling song of an unfamiliar bird.

Jackrabbit and I woke late the next morning. Our mother greeted us cheerfully as we crawled out of our tent; she appeared to have been up for hours. She'd already retrieved our food bags from the tree where I'd hung them, and filtered water for breakfast.

Just as we sat down to eat, a scruffy young man carrying his shoes in his hand waded across the stream and headed for our camp.

He stopped a few yards away, and gave me an uncertain smile. "Hi. One of the guys in the shelter told me you were here. I hope I'm not interrupting your breakfast." He had a charming British accent.

I still wasn't in a mood to deal with the public, but if this guy had crossed the stream to see us, I felt that I owed him a courteous reception.

"Not at all," I said. "Please join us. I'm Isis, by the way."

"I know. I'm Ox."

Suddenly I recognized him, through the short, dark beard and the layers of mud and ashes. Ox, the British sobo who we'd last seen in Duncannon in October. Both jackrabbit and I jumped to our feet and flung our arms around him.

"Ox, how've you been?"

"A fellow sobo! I can't believe it!"

We sat together for almost an hour, catching up on each other's hikes. Ox had taken a few months off in the middle of the winter and gone home to England. Ever since he'd gotten back on the Trail, he'd heard rumors of our yo-yo, but he hadn't really believed them.

"Will you be at Trail Days?" jackrabbit asked him.

"I hope so. I'm planning to finish the Trail in the first week of May and hitch back up to Damascus."

"We'll see you there, then," she said. "Have a great hike!"

After Ox had walked back across the stream, jackrabbit turned to our mom. "I hope we didn't bore you, talking Trail for an hour straight."

"Don't worry," our mom said. "I enjoyed hearing about your hike. And I'm glad you had a chance to catch up with an old friend."

"You know what's funny?" I mused. "We spent all of one evening together, before today. Drank a few beers with him in a Pennsylvania bar. We hardly know him, but it feels like we really are old friends."

"He's a sobo, man," said jackrabbit.

The weather changed quickly as we headed up the ridge across from Apple House. Clouds blew in, and a few miles from the road, a steady drizzle began to fall.

"Looks like Murphy's in league with the Campbells," jackrabbit said to me.

"Probably just buddying up to them so he can steal their moonshine," I answered.

"Who's Murphy?" our mom asked. "Another sobo?"

Jackrabbit and I burst into laughter, which we spent a good part of the next mile trying to explain. I had gotten deep into Reverse Applications of Murphy's Law, telling our mom why we wore our pack covers even when it wasn't raining, when I heard a soft crunch, and her startled voice saying, "oh!"

I turned around. She had slipped on a muddy embankment and fallen with one ankle twisted beneath her. Before I could reach out a hand to help her, though, she had planted a hiking stick in the ground and pushed herself to her feet.

"I'm fine," she said, taking a step forward to prove it.

"Are you sure?" I asked. "It looked like your ankle got pretty badly twisted. Maybe I should take a look at it. We can hitch out on that road through the trees there, if we need—"

"No, we can't," jackrabbit said, her voice grim. "That's Campbell Hollow Road."

"I'm fine," our mother repeated, more firmly. "Let's go on."

"Okay," I said. "As long as you go ahead. Set a pace that you're comfortable with."

She walked on ahead of me, her back straight and her steps even. No sign of a limp. The only indication that anything might be wrong was her pace. We seemed to be walking more and more slowly, until I found myself counting *one-and two-and-one-and two* . . . the way I'd counted steps on long hikes when I was a child, to keep myself going.

At long last, we came to a gravel road winding steeply down from the ridge.

"It's two-thirty already," jackrabbit said. "How 'bout some lunch?"

I checked the map. Buck Mountain Road. We'd come only four miles from the place where our mom had twisted her ankle, and those four miles had taken us three and a half hours.

"How's your ankle doing?" I asked her.

"It doesn't hurt," she answered, cheerful as ever.

"We're going one mile per hour," I said.

"Oh." Her smile faltered a little.

"May I take a look at it?"

"I guess so . . ."

I carefully rolled down the sock, revealing a red and purple lump the size of an egg, sticking out right in front of her ankle bone.

"*This* doesn't hurt?" I asked.

She looked down. "Well, a little," she admitted.

Jackrabbit knelt down to inspect the lump. "My God! That looks awful," she said. "What are we going to do?"

"Walk down this road until we find a phone," I said. "And then see if Bob Peoples can drive over from Kincora and bail us out. At least, that's the best plan I can think of."

We had just started down the hill when I heard the crunch of wheels on gravel. A hitch! Without thinking, I turned around and stuck my thumb out. The vehicle, an enormous slate-gray pickup, ground to a halt in the middle of the road. A middle-aged man with a dark mustache jumped out over the driver's seat. He was dressed in camouflage from head to toe, and he clutched a hunting rifle across his chest.

I froze. *Oh shit. Campbell territory. How could I have forgotten?*

"Hi there. I'm Joe. Can I help you ladies?" the man called out. His raspy Tennessee drawl sounded friendly and mildly curious, not the least bit threatening. Still . . .

"Don't mind the get-up," Joe continued. "I was just doin' a bit of turkey huntin', before headin' down to town to see my son's Little League game. Now, lemme stow this gun in the rack, and I'll have plenty of room for y'all."

Twenty minutes later, jackrabbit, my mom, and I were sitting in a red Formica booth at the Roan Mountain Diner, sipping milkshakes while we waited for Bob to arrive.

"My flight home is scheduled for tomorrow morning," our mom said.

"Tomorrow morning? We'd never have gotten you there on time."

She shrugged. "I know. I was planning to miss the flight. Hike with you as long as you wanted me to, and then change my ticket home. But now that this has happened, I might as well fly out on schedule."

Kincora looked the same as ever, except for the tower of mail drops on the porch and the throngs of unfamiliar hikers lounging on the steps and filling the living room. I felt even less inclined to deal with strangers than I had the day before. This was the last we'd see of our mother for five months, and I didn't want to waste the time letting people poke our feet.

"I've reserved you three bunks in the corner," Bob said as he ushered us inside. He turned to the people in the living room, most of whom were staring at us with unabashed wonder. "This is Isis, and jackrabbit, and their mom, Patty. Good friends of mine. Please, make them at home." The hikers smiled, greeted us, and then returned to the conversations they'd been having when we arrived.

As Bob led us up the stairs, I caught sight of his copy of the collage of photos I'd sent out to friends when we finished the Trail southbound. It was pinned to the wall in a corner of the stairs, among hundreds of other finishing photos.

"I'll expect another when you reach Katahdin, mind you," Bob said with a smile.

I remembered how distant Springer had seemed, the last time I'd stood in that room. Katahdin was three times as far. It seemed much more reachable, though, than Springer had. Gentle seasons stretched before us: spring, summer, and early fall. I knew every step of the path. And whenever I thought of the Mountain, I felt a tug behind my breastbone, a strong, fine line connecting me to the place where my hike began. I had no doubt that we would reach Katahdin.

"We'll send you a picture," I told Bob. "As soon as we get home."

jackrabbit

The day after our mother left, we slacked the stretch from the Buck Mountain Road to the hostel. I remembered it as a snowy wasteland of nearly insurmountable PUDs, punctuated by garbage dumps. In the spring, though, when all we carried were daypacks full of sandwiches and water, it didn't seem nearly so awful. Weak sunlight broke through the clouds, illuminating the gray-green forest. The pale enormous blossoms of cucumber magnolias hung like stars in the high branches. Drifts of flowers on the forest floor obscured the piles of old rubbish: red and yellow columbine, trout lilies, hepatica, anemones, dwarf irises, painted trillium with its sunbursts of pink and white. Flooding streams leaped and sparkled under rhododendron thickets in the valley bottoms. I was less paranoid than I had been in winter, too; the kindness of the man who had given us a ride down the mountain had reassured me.

Back at Kincora, a crowd of northbounders filled the hostel. They were mostly men in their twenties, fast, loud, confident hikers with light packs. The only one we knew was Forest Phil. It was strange to be at Kincora without the Family. The children's artwork still hung on the walls and filled the first few pages of the register. I wondered again where they were, and what they were doing. Thinking about them, and our mother's sudden departure, I felt a bittersweet sadness welling up in me. *I take things for granted too easily*, I thought, *never knowing what I'll miss until it's gone.*

Bob came over that night to address the hikers. "Now, most of you guys know, I'm a trail maintainer for this section. I like to bring hikers out to work on the Trail, 'cause it's a good way for you to see what goes on behind the scenes. Another side of the whole Trail experience. There's a work trip this Saturday, if anyone's interested. We're goin' up to Jane Bald. It'll be a good time." There was a chorus of assenting voices. "Now, the other thing is, who wants to slack tomorrow?" A louder shout came back. "I've only got so much space in my vehicle, so try to organize yourselves so we can get out early in the morning."

"I can run shuttles, too," came a voice from the back of the room. It was an older man, heavy-set, with thick glasses and long graying hair in a ponytail.

"Great!" Bob said. "So if you want to slack, come see me, or . . ."

"Hacksaw," the other man said. "I'm Hacksaw. Got my truck out front. I was goin' to hike over into Damascus from here, but my knees are botherin' me. So I'll be drivin' instead, I guess."

A crowd of hikers gathered around Bob, so Isis and I went to talk to Hacksaw.

"Y'all want to slack tomorrow?" he asked us.

"Yeah, we were hoping to do that twenty from the middle of the ridge between here and Damascus," Isis said.

"I can take y'all out there first thing in the morning," Hacksaw said. He sighed. "Wish I could be out there hiking myself. I've only got these few weeks of vacation."

"What happened to your knees?" I asked.

"Oh, it's an old injury. Bunch of old injuries. I used to race motorcycles, back when I was young and too dumb to know better. Got in a bad wreck." He laughed. "I got pins in just about every bone they can put pins into. I was all set to hike for a few days, but I went out yesterday, full pack, and I only got about five miles before the pain got bad. Must've busted a tendon or something. I had to hitch back here."

On the way out to the road in the morning, Isis and I sat in the front of Hacksaw's monstrous brown pickup. A load of other hikers had piled into the back, under the cap.

"Mind if I ask y'all something?" Hacksaw said.

"Not at all," I told him. I expected a question about barefoot hiking, or surviving the winter.

"What are y'all's real names?"

I hesitated, surprised.

"I mean, I don't want to be too forward or anything," he said. "It's just that, somehow, when all you know is somebody's trail name, it's like you only know a little piece of them. Y'all remind me of my daughter."

"I'm Susan," I told him.

"Lucy," Isis said.

"Lucy! A friend and I used to have a shop called Lucy's. My buddy did tattoos; I did screen printing, airbrushing, custom details on cars and bikes, that kind of thing."

"Where'd you get the name from?" Isis asked him.

He shrugged. "Just picked it out of a book, actually. Liked the sound of it."

The slack over the ridge back to Kincora went much faster than I had expected. In winter, it had taken us two full days to cover the distance. I remembered watching Joy struggle up hillsides, up to her waist in snow. Now, with a warm breeze off Watauga Lake and the trees beginning to leaf out, it looked like a different place. We skimmed along the trail, barefoot in the soft mud. I hardly recognized any landmarks along the ridge until we came to Vandeventer shelter. I shivered, remembering the story of the woman's voice and the bird that landed in the firepit. But in the light of day, with green grass beginning to spring up in the ground around the shelter, the place looked benign and innocent. The only ghosts were the memories I carried with me.

The place that had changed most with the seasons was the shore of Watauga Lake. We came down the last slope as the shadows lengthened toward evening. I had hated this section of trail in the winter; as we hiked the meandering ups and downs in a sleet storm, it had seemed the least attractive landscape I could imagine. Spring had transfigured it. A heady golden light filled the trees, reflected in the still, glassy surface of the lake. The understory was a riot of flowers: blue spikes of larkspur; trilliums in white, pink, yellow, and maroon; pale red bleeding hearts; a delicate lily I didn't recognize, with twisted yellow-green petals. I hardly noticed the slight elevation changes in the trail.

Saturday came, the day of the work trip to Jane Bald. Surprisingly, most of the strong young hikers had cleared out the day before. (A few of them, cackling like maniacs as they packed up, had planned to night-hike the forty-one miles to Damascus. I wished them luck and shook my head. *Nobos.*) On the morning of the work trip, it was Bob, Hacksaw, Forest Phil, a guy who had injured his ankle and spent almost two weeks at Kincora, and a couple of section hikers in their fifties and sixties. The only representatives of the twenty-something thru-hiker crowd were Isis and myself, and a lanky young man named Sleepy the Arab.

I ended up next to Sleepy in the back of Bob's truck. "How'd you get your trail name?" I asked him. With his hazel eyes, light brown hair, and freckles, he hardly looked Arabic.

He sighed. "Everybody asks me that."

"Everybody asks *me* why I'm barefoot. Most of them ask me if I'm insane, too. I've gotten to the point where I just say yes. I'm curious, though, Sleepy. Where did you get that name?"

"Well, the Sleepy part is pretty obvious. I'm not usually functional before 10 A.M.," he said with a yawn. It was a little past eight. "The trouble was, on my first hike, in '98, there were about six Sleepys on the Trail." He made a face. "I hate redundancy. Luckily I found the rest of my name pretty fast. The bugs were really bad that spring. I started wearing a t-shirt wrapped around my head. Somebody said I looked like a character out of Lawrence of Arabia. So, Sleepy the Arab I am." He made a bow, or at least as much of a bow as it's possible to make while sitting in the back of a pickup truck with six other hikers. "You know, I'm getting really tired of telling that story. I think I'll impose a moratorium. Yes." He smiled. "No more explanations of my trail name until I reach the Vermont border."

"Well, I'm honored," I told him. "I guess I got the last one for a while."

"Ninety-eight was a good year," he said in the tone of a wine connoisseur. "One of the outfitters that year made up a t-shirt with all the answers to the questions everyone asks, you know, 'what do you eat? where do you sleep?,' et cetera. It cut down considerably on the amount of time spent explaining things to dayhikers."

"Oh, I remember seeing those," one of the section hikers said. "It said stuff like, 'In the woods. Ramen, Liptons, Pop-tarts, and granola bars. Every week or so.' You could just point at the right answer."

"Yeah," Sleepy said. "This year, I'm always tempted to come up with different answers. You know, 'what do you eat?'" He put on a deep backwoods accent. "Roots. Berries. Squirrels." Then, with a deranged grin, "slow dayhikers."

Spring had come to Jane Bald in the week since we had camped there with our mother. New blades of green poked up among the old grasses, and some kind of small white flower showed here and there. This high in the mountains, the buds of the trees were still tiny and clenched, but we could see the soft green wash of new leaves filling the valleys and beginning to climb the slopes. A warm wind rustled the grass.

All day, we filled buckets with gravel from piles along the trail, and spread it in the muddy ruts, along with plastic webbing designed to anchor it in place. At first I had mixed feelings about spreading gravel on the trail—as a barefoot hiker, I would much rather walk on the soft mud we covered than the sharp stones we left on top of it. Bob's explanation made sense, though.

"I took this gravel up here with a forklift when the ground was still frozen," he told us. "You can see how the treadway gets eroded without it. People don't want to walk in the mud, so they start a new path next to the Trail. The ground's so soft up here on the balds. Pretty soon the new trail's a rut like the old one, and it just spreads out. This place seems to see more use every year." He rolled a stone into an old rut beside the path. "I just hope we can get this gravel down before the rhododendrons bloom. It'll be a couple more weeks. That's when the tourists show up in full force."

A few thru-hikers came by while we shoveled gravel onto the trail. Some of them pitched in, carrying buckets or picking up a shovel or rake. One nobo who stopped was an attractive young woman, probably in her late teens. Forest Phil was very solicitous, helping her carry the bucket and tip the gravel out.

"Can you stay around a while?" he asked her. "It's so good to meet you."

"Sorry; this was fun, but I've got to get back to the Trail." She flashed him a sweet smile and hefted her pack.

Forest Phil watched her walk off. He sighed.

Sleepy the Arab came up beside us to fill his bucket. "You go for the young ones, don't you . . . Forest Philanderer?"

"That's not funny," Forest Phil said. He loaded another shovelful of gravel into his bucket and walked off in a huff. I looked over at Sleepy. Both of us were laughing.

In the evening, my shoulders aching from the strenuous work, I looked back at the stretch of trail we'd been working on. Perhaps a quarter mile of the A.T. was covered in dark gravel. Farther back, more piles of it loomed by the path, dotting the slope like giant anthills.

"How much gravel did we move today?" I asked Bob.

"Well, let's see. Each of those piles was around two tons. We got ten of 'em outta the way."

"So twenty tons?"

"Yup, just about. And with the ten of us here, that's about two tons apiece."

"No wonder I'm tired!"

The next day we bid farewell to Bob and Kincora. Hacksaw took our packs to Damascus so we could slack the remaining twenty-two miles into town. From the days of hiking short distances with our mother, resting, and slacking, my knee felt almost entirely healed. I was still nervous about hiking into Damascus, though, for some strange, irrational reason. We had almost left the Trail there in winter. I could remember how the town's name had taken on mythical proportions in my mind during the storm on the Grayson Highlands: *All we need to do is get to Damascus. When we reach Damascus everything will be fine.* And it had turned out to be true; the town had given us the strength we needed to continue. But getting there had nearly cost us everything. Even in spring, it didn't seem possible that we could simply walk into Damascus like any other Trail town.

Once again, it was strange to pass the places where we had stayed as sobos: Double Springs Shelter. Abingdon Gap. I remembered how we had packed into the cramped cinderblock-sided shelters, the Family, Lash, Heald, Anonymous Badger, Isis, and me, using every inch of floor space. I remembered breaking trail in the knee-deep snow, gathering firewood every night, sleeping with my water bottles so they wouldn't freeze. In the warm spring sunlight, it hardly seemed like something that had happened to me. It seemed like a legend, a story out of the distant past.

It was almost dark when we came down the ridge outside Damascus and started following the blazes along the wide, smooth trail by the river. I still had a vague sense of disquiet: *It shouldn't be this easy.* But everything was calm. Frogs sang in the pools, a faint wind stirred the new leaves. The white blossoms of dogwoods stood out among the trees like swatches of moonlight. An owl called. The lights of town came into view in the distance. Then we were turning the street corner by Cowboy's Exxon, going up Laurel Avenue past Mount Rogers Outfitters. We had come, once again, to Damascus.

My stomach growled. "Let's get some food," I said.

"We really ought to get cleaned up first."

"We took showers yesterday! This is only one day's worth of sweat. Besides, I'm hungry."

Isis sighed. "I guess the restaurants here are used to hikers anyway."

There was a loud, boisterous crowd at Quincy's Pizza. I didn't think there would be space for us, but Hacksaw waved to us from a table in the back, near the bar. "Come on over," he called above the hubbub. Forest Phil and another hiker were just leaving his table; we took their chairs.

The harried-looking waitress came to take our order: an extra-large veggie pizza, breadsticks, two sides of onion rings, and two sweet teas.

"Good hike today?" Hacksaw asked.

"Yeah," Isis said. "This is a great time of year to be in the woods."

"I wish I could be out there," he said quietly. "There was a time when I thought I could section-hike the whole Trail."

"You probably still could," Isis said, but he shook his head.

"I guess I just started too old. My knees are busted up, and I've put on too much weight . . . and now I can't get rid of the weight, because exercise hurts my knees. Catch-twenty-two. I'm just glad I can still be a part of it, you know? I figure I'll drive shuttles till I'm pushin' up daisies." He took a sip of his coke. "I want to hear some stories from y'all's hike."

We told him about Hiker Box Stew, and night-hiking into Harpers Ferry from both directions. Then the food arrived, and it was his turn to talk.

"Y'all're so lucky to be doing this so young. Me, it took me years to get my head on straight. Right out of high school, I got drafted. And after that, well, it kind of . . . that war kind of tore me apart. In the head, I mean. Mentally. I used to be a big drinker, gambler. Got in fights." He took another drink. "I don't know why I'm telling y'all this."

"It's okay," I said through a mouthful of pizza.

"Y'all seem like such good people. Like you got a lot of things figured out. At your age . . ." he shook his head. "Y'all're lucky. And I was lucky, too, but it took a hell of a lot longer. After the accident I told y'all about, where I busted my knees, I hit the bottle pretty hard. But somewhere in those years I had a daughter. She's the best thing that ever happened to me. She lived with her mom most of the time, but every time she saw me, she'd try to get me to sober up. Took a while, though. When she got married, I was so hung over I missed the wedding. I didn't hear from her a long time after that. Then she called me up, out of the blue, four years ago last week. Told me she had a son, and she wanted me to see him. That did it. I wanted to be someone my grandson could be proud of. I haven't touched a drop since. I started hikin' the Trail instead. It helps me clear my head like nothing else."

The crowd of hikers in Quincy's began to disperse. Most of the noise now came from the bar at the back of the restaurant, where someone had fired up the jukebox.

An old man slid off his barstool and wobbled over to our table. He leered at Isis and me. "How come you got two of 'em?" he said to Hacksaw. It took a moment for me to make out his words. "Hey! How come you got two of them bitches? I ast you a question!" the man hissed in Hacksaw's face. His lips twisted into a snarl. "You wan' take it ou'side? Do ya? Do ya?"

Hacksaw sat there, patient, imperturbable, saying nothing. He folded his arms in front of him. He was twice the size of the old drunk, and the man seemed to realize this after a few moments of silence. He backed off a step. Finally Hacksaw spoke. "I want you to leave these ladies alone." His voice had an edge to it. "You don't ever treat a woman like that. It's time for you to get outta here. Go on."

The old man regarded him for a moment longer, then spat on the floor and shuffled back to his barstool.

Outside, as we walked down the street to the hostel, I thanked Hacksaw for dealing with the drunk. He shrugged it off. "Nobody deserves to get treated like that. Y'all are like family to me. I couldn't just sit back and let him say that."

"I was really impressed with the way you handled things, though," I said.

He gave a weary laugh. "You know, ten, fifteen years ago, I would've taken him out in the alley and kicked his ass. But I'm getting too old for that kind of thing. There's better ways to deal with stuff."

Isis

Hikers crowded around the doorway of Mount Rogers Outfitters, packing new gear, sorting through mail drops, and sharing half-gallon boxes
of ice cream from the Damascus Minute-ette in the bright midday sun. We set
down our packs and hiking sticks, donned sandals and tank tops, and walked
inside.

"Well, if it isn't the Barefoot Sisters!" Damascus Dave's weathered face
broke into a rare smile, as he stepped around the counter to greet us. Steve
and Jeff excused themselves from the customers they were helping, and they,
too, hurried to the front of the store to welcome us.

"Man, it's great to see you guys again!" jackrabbit said, after we'd all
exchanged hugs and handshakes. "Our rescuers! I don't think we can ever
thank you enough for picking us up that day at Elk Garden."

"It's just what we do," said Damascus Dave. "Try to help the hiking community a little, 'cause we're part of it. Anyway, you'd already gotten through
the hard part by the time we picked you up."

"I just hope that family you were with thanked you," said Jeff. "You probably saved their lives."

"We all saved each other," I said. "I might have given up if it hadn't been
for them."

"I don't know," Jeff continued. "Don't know what those parents were
thinking, hiking with children in a blizzard like that. They'd have died up
there, if you hadn't been with them."

"None of us knew what the weather would be like," I said. "It was totally
calm in the morning, down in the shelter of the trees. If we'd had any idea,
we never would have hiked into that storm."

"We made the best decisions we could, based on what we knew," said
jackrabbit, "and that day we all made a big mistake. One that probably would
have ended our hike, if you guys hadn't rescued us the next day."

"You're the heroes," Steve said quietly. "You saved those kids."

The throng of hikers around the counter had fallen silent, staring at us
with their mouths half-open and their eyes shining. My cheeks burned. I
could already hear the rumor taking shape: *The Barefoot Sisters, blond goddesses
six and a half feet tall, carried a bunch of children off a mountain in the snow.* I
wished that I could tell them all how it really was—the mistakes we'd made
and the help we'd received, unexpected and sometimes unhoped-for, at every
turn of the trail. The complex web of interdependence that had brought us
Arctic Sobos through the winter, and allowed most of us to reach Springer in

the end. I knew, though, that it would take too long to explain. For most of these people, nobos nearing the five-hundred-mile mark, the best explanation I could give them would be to let them finish the Trail. There are no heroes; there's only the stranger who shares water with you even though she herself is running short, the friend who offers to carry your tent when you have a stress fracture, and the out-of-work stone mason who drives you thirty miles to the airport when you have to go home for a funeral. No heroes; or, if you choose to see it another way, there are heroes everywhere.

To celebrate our first quarter of the Trail northbound, we treated ourselves to a night at the Lazy Fox Inn. We had hoped to share the luxury with our mother, but even in her absence, returning to the warm, clean B&B where we'd recovered from the blizzard felt like a homecoming. Ginny greeted us with mugs of steaming dark coffee, and Ben sat on the porch with us, telling stories of the days when trains had run along the tracks beside the river, and Damascus had been a working mill town.

The next morning, after we'd eaten all we could of Ginny's sumptuous breakfast spread, Hacksaw picked us up and drove us to Elk Garden. His knees were still too painful to hike on, so he'd offered to slack us for another day. We decided to take advantage of the fair weather and slack the twenty-four from Elk Garden all at once.

Hacksaw took a different route than we'd taken with Damascus Dave in winter: a road that wound past farms and villages and a white clapboard church whose plastic signboard read *FORBIDDEN FRUITS MAKE BAD JAMS.*

Spring had come to Elk Garden; trout lilies dotted the ground beneath the trees, and the scent of spring beauties hovered in the still, warm air. A few hundred yards up the trail, we met a long line of neatly dressed women, strolling through the trees. They turned out to be a local ladies' aid society, out for their spring wildflower walk.

"This is just such a lovely, peaceful place," said the woman I'd stopped to talk to. "I look forward to coming here so much!"

I shivered, remembering the same hills covered in three feet of snow, and the bitter wind rattling the branches over our heads. "It is lovely," I said to her.

We walked fast on the soft trail, skipping and vaulting on our hiking sticks when we came to meadows. Even in the high places, where we had burrowed our way through chest-high snowdrifts, wildflowers studded the new green grass. Late in the afternoon, we left the A.T. for the blue-blazed Virginia Creeper Trail, an old railroad bed that had been converted to a trail. Like the road we'd taken in the morning, the Creeper Trail passed through farmland as well as forest: small towns where children ran from yard to yard playing hide and seek, and pastures where graceful, long-legged horses grazed in the evening light. We reached Damascus just as darkness fell.

We planned to stay in The Place that night, a hiker hostel run by the local Methodist church. Hacksaw had promised to drop off our gear there and reserve us a couple of bunks. As we approached the hostel, I noticed four men standing under the porch light, engaged in what appeared to be an altercation—or at least a very animated discussion. By far the smallest of the four was a policeman, who stood with his back stiff and his shoulders shrugged up around his ears. The other three—tall, powerfully built men with flowing beards, whose ripped jeans and black cotton t-shirts made them look more like bikers than backpackers—faced him, scowling. Jackrabbit and I stopped in the middle of the parking lot, watching the exchange.

"I tell you, he's a thief," said one of the men, who wore a bandana around his forehead, over waves of unruly salt-and-pepper hair. He crossed his heavily tattooed arms and stared down at the policeman.

"How do you know?" asked the officer.

"Of course I know he's a thief; he's been hangin' out with *us* all day," the man with the bandana repeated, flinging out his arms in a gesture of frustration.

"We saw 'im stealin' tips offa the tables, over at Dottie's place," offered the heavyset, gray-haired man on his left. The officer took out a small notepad and began writing as the man continued. "We made him put back the money, but if we seen 'im stealin' once, we reckon he'll steal again, soon as nobody's lookin'."

"Yeah, and we can't have that in a hiker town," said the blond man on the right, who appeared to be the youngest of the group by at least twenty years. "Hikers trust each other, leave their stuff all over. Let one thief loose in Damascus, and five or ten people'll be without their resupply money come morning."

Just then, the man wearing the bandana glanced up and noticed us. He waved, and called out a greeting. "You ladies stayin' at The Place tonight? Come on over. Excuse us blockin' the door here. We're just keepin' a bit of law and order in this town." He turned to the police officer. "So, you got our description, and we told you where to find the guy. Why don't you just pick 'im up and give 'im a lift outta town before there's any trouble."

The policeman stuck his notepad in a pocket and scurried away down the street. Jackrabbit and I approached the three men cautiously.

"I'm Pirate," said the one with the bandana. "Bet y'all're wonderin' how a gentleman like me landed himself a trail name like that." He opened his eyes wide and shrugged his massive shoulders.

The blond man snorted with laughter. "I'm Lone Wolf," he said. "And you're—holy shit, you must be the Barefoot Sisters!"

"You watch your mouth around them, Lone Wolf," the gray-haired man said, cuffing the younger one on the shoulder. "They're ladies. And on toppa that, they rescued some children last winter. Damascus Dave was tellin' me about it." He turned to us, smiling. "It's an honor to meet you. I'm Wee Willie, Prince of Whales, and here's my business card."

I looked down at the rectangle of paper he'd handed me. In the center was a heraldic crest, divided into four quadrants. One contained a peace sign, another a cross, the third a smiling, spouting whale. The fourth was left blank. *Wee Willie, the Prince of Whales, on a walk about the World*, the card said. The only other printing on it was a Web address, www.hobocentral.com.

"Hobo Central?" I asked.

"Sure, don't you know about the Hobos?" Pirate said.

"You mean the guys who used to ride around the country in box cars?" I asked, skeptical.

All three men burst into guffaws.

"Naw," said Pirate. "The hikin' Hobos of the Appalachian Trail."

"'Course, we hike other trails, too, whenever we have a mind to," put in Wee Willie, Prince of Whales.

"Hobos . . ." mused jackrabbit. "I think I remember Maineak telling me something about the Hobos. Wait a minute. Lone Wolf." She fixed him with an inquisitive stare. "I met you five years ago, at a party at Maineak's, around the time Isis and I went down to Peru with him. You're the guy who supported him on his speed hike, aren't you?"

Lone Wolf nodded, looking a little bemused.

"Of course, you wouldn't recognize me," jackrabbit added quickly. "I was only seventeen."

"So, you got roped into one of Maineak's adventures when you were only seventeen?" Lone Wolf asked her. "Man, you must've been born with one foot on the Trail."

The thief must not have had time to raid The Place—all our gear was piled on two painted plywood bunks in the dormitory at the top of the stairs, just where Hacksaw had told us that he'd leave it. We put our hiking sticks on top of the pile and ran the half-block to the Minute-ette to pick up sandwich material, apples, donuts, and ice cream for supper. After we ate, I forced myself to stand upright long enough to take a shower, and then went straight to bed.

I woke in the middle of the night with my hip and shoulder crunched uncomfortably against the planks of the bunk. *I must've gotten soft from tenting so much*, I thought. *It's a good thing I wasn't so wimpy in the middle of winter, when we had to sleep in shelters all the time.* I rolled to my other side and fell back asleep. A few hours later, I woke up again. It felt as if there was no air in my mattress. *Valve must've come loose.* I pulled the mat out from under me, blew a few breaths into it, and screwed the valve back down. By morning, my Thermarest was completely flat again. I couldn't see any holes in its surface, but it wasn't holding air.

"Bad news," I told jackrabbit. "My sleeping pad's sprung a leak."

"Maybe the guys at M.R.O. can fix it," she suggested. "We can stop by there after breakfast."

Half an hour later, Hacksaw joined us at the Sidetrack Café, a charming little restaurant with red gingham curtains and a mural on one wall of mountains with a train winding through them. I told him what had happened, and asked if he'd mind waiting while we stopped by the outfitter's store.

"I'll come with you," he said. "I got nothin' better to do, as long as my knees keep givin' me trouble. And besides, I enjoy your company. You girls remind me so much of my daughter."

"Thanks," I said, touched. "From what you've told us about your daughter, that's quite a compliment."

After a few more plates of pancakes, eggs, and grits, the three of us trooped over to M.R.O. with the mattress pad.

"Sure, I can fix that," Steve told me. "Just come back in a couple hours and I'll have it good as new."

"A couple hours?" jackrabbit asked, dismayed. "We were planning to hike out today."

"Well, I have to hold it under water and look for bubbles, to figure out where the leak is. I'll mark the leak with a permanent marker, wait for it to dry, and put a drop of tent seam sealant on it. Then the sealant has to dry— yeah, two hours at the least."

I looked at Hacksaw. "Can you wait that long?"

"I could," he said, "but I've got a better idea. How 'bout I slack y'all over the Grayson Highlands, and y'all can come back and pick it up tonight?"

The clear sky and soft spring breeze couldn't quell the uneasiness I felt as we crossed the small stretch of bald beside the road. A few miles up the trail, dark spots began dancing across my vision. The ground wobbled and seemed to rush toward me, but when I caught my breath, I discovered that I was still standing upright. I sat down on a log and tried to quiet the rhythm of my breathing, concentrating on the bright, solid colors of the woods around me. Blue sky. Green leaves under the small, twisted trees. Yellow fields to my right. Suddenly, I recognized the pasture as the one in which Lash and I had almost lost the Trail on our way down the mountain.

"What's wrong?" jackrabbit asked. "Are you sick?"

"I don't know. I'm a bit dizzy. I think I'm just scared of this place."

"Yeah, join the club," she said, her voice grim.

The dizziness passed, but the prickles on the back of my neck intensified as we crossed the bald to Thomas Knob Shelter. I didn't want to stop there, but I forced myself to go in. Warm sunlight spilled through the window of the empty loft, and dust motes swirled in the air. *What had I been expecting? Ghosts? Snow?* Only the even pattern of cracks around the eaves, where cold drafts had swept through the tiny room, matched my memories.

The biggest shock came when we left the shelter. Instead of going through the gap in the fence, the way we had come to Thomas Knob in winter, the trail took a sharp right turn into a patch of woods.

"I don't remember this forest," jackrabbit said.

"No," I answered. "We were lost."

Almost a mile later, we came out of the trees where the trail crossed a small dirt road and an empty gravel parking lot. In winter, the parking lot had been buried deep under snow, but I recognized the Forest Service sign that marked its western edge.

The balds stretching away beyond it bore little resemblance to the white, windswept desert that still haunted my dreams. Dwarf rhododendron bushes spread their coppery leaves to the sun, and tiny, stunted wild pear trees blossomed among the crags of black rock. Wild ponies dotted the hillsides, grazing. Their bright coats stood out against the tawny bald, each one a different color: white with gold splotches, black or bay or speckled. New colts frisked around their mothers or slept in the shade of rhododendron thickets. A few of the ponies trotted over to us, and jackrabbit fed them salt from the Ziploc of condiments in my food bag.

We saw the white tree a quarter mile before we came to it. A wild pear as tall and straight as if it had grown in the middle of the forest, it was so covered in flowers that it looked like a solitary, motionless cloud perched on the bald. When we walked closer, I recognized it from December. A huge lightning scar marred the smooth gray bark, and one enormous branch, a third the width of the whole tree, had split from the trunk. It lay twisted along the ground, connected to the rest of the tree by only a few splinters of wood and an eight-inch-wide strip of bark. In winter I had thought the tree was dead— all trees looked dead then, and this one's injuries had seemed too severe for a living thing to bear. As I struggled past it with the snow lashing my face, I had felt a moment of wonder that the tree had grown straight in such a fierce climate. A moment of pity that this old, strong tree had endured hundreds of blizzards, only to be struck down by a lightning bolt. Deep gratitude for the white blaze painted beside its severed limb—the second blaze I had seen in the last three miles. Then I had walked on, glad of my chance to escape that brutal wasteland.

In the sunlight, the whole tree shone with flowers, the brightest sign of life in a landscape full of the soft tints of spring unfolding. As we came abreast of it, I saw that even the severed branch, barely connected to the roots, was covered in blossoms.

jackrabbit

Evening painted the maples gold as we passed Old Orchard Shelter on the way down from the Grayson Highlands. I meant to just stop and sign the register, but I heard a familiar voice.

"Isis! Jackrabbit!"

"Hey, Luna! What's up?" I said. "I thought you guys would be miles ahead by now. We've been so slow the last couple weeks."

She grinned. "We went to Merle Fest."

"What's that?"

"You guys don't know about Merle Fest? It's the best music festival in the Southeast! All kinds of good bluegrass. Doc Watson was there, and Dolly Parton, and Gillian Welch . . . Six-string had a friend on the festival committee, so we all got jobs on the stage crew: me and Six-string, Toast, Basil, and a couple other guys. It was so awesome. We got to hang around backstage and meet all the performers, and there was all kinds of free food. I wish you guys could've been there!"

"Yeah, me too," I said. "We got to hike with our mom for a while, though. That was fun. We hadn't seen her since last June."

"You guys didn't even go home for Christmas? That's hard-core!"

"Or just crazy, depending on your point of view. So where's the rest of the Stage Crew?"

"Oh, they're all camped around here." Luna gestured to the meadow in front of the shelter, where six or seven tents stood in the tall grass. Basil and Toast waved from beside the firepit.

"Hey, are you guys going back to town tonight?" Luna asked.

"Yeah. Hacksaw's slacking us. Isis's Thermarest sprung a leak. The guys at M.R.O. said it'd be ready by tonight, and it was too pretty a day to just sit around in town."

Luna adjusted the orange handkerchief across her forehead. "Could you do us a big favor?"

"Sure. What is it?" Isis asked her.

"Me and Six-string are running a little low on food. Do you think—"

"All we've got left is a candy bar," Isis said with regret, digging into her mostly empty pack.

"No, that's okay; we're fine for tonight. We were just hoping to stay out here for a few days, instead of hitching into town. You know how that is . . . We've got a bunch of food in the camper van. If I give you guys the keys, do you think you could bring us, like, three or four days of stuff?"

"Definitely," Isis said. "Where are you parked?"

Luna described where she had left the van and handed the keys to Isis. I'd seen this level of trust among hikers all along the Trail—after all, two different pairs of section hikers had lent their keys to the Shod Cousins. It still amazed me, though.

"We'll see you at the road at ten tomorrow, then?" Luna said. "Great."

Over the next few days, we hiked with the Stage Crew. It reminded me of the happier times with the Family from the North; sometimes we all hiked in a line together, with someone singing or telling a story as we walked. Luna and Six-string had an inexhaustible supply of bluegrass music. Toast and Basil had learned a few of the songs, and Isis and I eventually picked up the choruses. On the steep uphills, where nobody had the breath to sing, Toast, Six-string, and Basil traded ribald jokes.

On the night we stayed at Trimpi Shelter, Toast taught me how to play Spades. Luna and Six-string teamed up against the two of us. A thunderstorm was gathering in the hills outside, rumbling and muttering behind the trees. I began to pick up the rudiments of the game—enough to tell that I'd been dealt a lousy hand. "I don't have a single good card, Toast," I told him. "You'll have to take this round."

Toast shook his head. "Haven't I taught you anything, jackrabbit? That's not how you play Spades. This game's mostly just a chance to exercise your vocabulary. First lesson. Repeat after me: 'Who *dealt* this shit?'"

The storm came closer. Basil looked up from his cooking pot and scooted his sleeping bag farther back into the shelter. "Sounds like a freakin' monster truck rally in the sky."

Isis cooked up a huge pot of what she called "pasta ramp-a-vera": Lipton fettuccine Alfredo with wild ramps and nettle leaves we had gathered along the trail that day. The new greens tasted wonderful, even though I knew my sweat would reek of ramps for several days. As we ate, I saw a huge millipede patrolling the sleeping platform. Its plated carapace was blue-black and shiny, fully the size of my little finger. I wondered what other beasts would be sharing our sleeping quarters, and I thought for a fleeting moment about setting up the tent. It was almost dark, though, and thunder still growled around the hills. Late that night, when the storm broke above us and rain poured down like a fire hose from the sky, I didn't care what kind of animals might wander into the shelter. I was just happy to have a roof over my head.

Isis and I woke up before dawn, planning to cover the ten miles to Partnership Shelter by lunchtime. The lure of pizza was as strong as ever. The Stage Crew had elected to sleep in; the night before, Isis had offered to take their orders and have the pizza ready by the time they arrived.

"Don't be late, or we'll eat yours, too!" I called as we left the shelter.

The sun broke through the early mist as we came down the end of the ridge. Trees in their new green glowed with the miraculous, restored light that comes after a storm. We passed the derelict school bus in the meadow, where Heald had contemplated moving in. The grass came almost as high on the hubcaps as the snow had in winter. Next to the bus, someone had placed a cow's skull on one of the old fence posts. It looked like the shrine of some bizarre cult.

We had underestimated our pace. It was not even ten o'clock when we reached the shelter. We found two hikers there, one about my age and one just a kid, eleven or twelve.

"I'm Joe!" the boy said. "My brother and I are hiking all by ourselves!"

"I'm Fiddler," the older one said. He was tall and slight, with soft brown hair. "Good to meet you."

I noticed the violin case strapped to the outside of his pack. It looked like it weighed five or six pounds at least: heavier than a tent. "You must play pretty well to want to lug that thing up the trail," I said.

He shrugged. "I'd miss it too much if I didn't have it."

"Will you play something for us?" Isis asked him.

He gave a sad smile. "I'd love to, but my A string broke yesterday. I asked mom to send one in our next mail drop. It'll be a few weeks, though."

"There has to be something you can play on three strings," I said. I thought back to college, all the violin recitals I had accompanied. "I've got it. The Brahms D minor sonata, second movement. You can get through the first page, anyway, without your A string."

His face lit up. "I hadn't thought of that one!" Soon the violin was out of its case, and the clearing filled with rich amber sound. I sat down at the picnic table and pretended it was a piano. The notes soared above the trees, transporting me to a place beyond the Trail. Somehow, impossibly, he played the whole movement on three strings. When he put the bow down, there was a moment of stunned silence before we applauded.

"That was amazing," I said.

"Thanks. I was a double major in music and philosophy in college. Seems like I don't get to use either one very often, out here on the Trail."

"I was music and bio," I said. "But unfortunately I never learned to play a portable instrument."

"You sounded good, bro," Joe said, swinging from a rung of the ladder that led to the loft. "Now let's go get some pizza!"

We walked across the parking lot to the pay phone, only to find that the pizza place didn't open for another two hours. The greasy menu posted above the phone whetted my appetite. *Eggplant sub*, I thought, *veggie pizza. Then maybe some tiramisu. I wonder if they deliver ice cream.*

While we waited, we played a dice game that the brothers carried. Joe patiently explained the rules. "See, you roll all of these, and if the ones of the same color have the same number on them, then you lose your turn. If not, then you add up these, and multiply by this one . . ." It seemed to me like a sneaky way to make a twelve-year-old practice his math, but it kept us entertained.

Luna, Six-string, Toast, and Basil came to the shelter around 11:30, a little red-eyed and bleary. They started to sing a song, but collapsed in laughter halfway through.

"Hey, where's the pizza, man?" Basil said. "I've got the munchies big-time."

"Place doesn't open till noon," Isis told him.

"Argh! I'm starving!" Toast tossed his pack down.

"Be cool, man, it's all cool," Luna said vaguely. Six-string gave a stoned giggle.

We called the pizza place at noon. Busy. We sat next to the pay phone, trying to place the call every five minutes. It wasn't until 12:50 that a live voice answered the phone (and a good thing—it was our absolute last quarter). It took about five minutes for Isis to give our order. I wondered if they would need more than one car to deliver it. Everyone was ravenous by this time, and our orders had grown larger with the passing minutes. *I really could eat a twelve-inch sub* and *a large pizza right now. Why not some onion rings, too?*

"It'll be about half an hour," Isis told us.

"Half an hour! This is too much!" Basil ran back to the shelter. The rest of us followed. I was a little curious to see what he would do. I expected him to eat some food from his pack, but instead he began searching through the hiker box. *Of course*, I thought, remembering the 501 Shelter in Pennsylvania. Slim pickings: a bag of mouse-chewed rice, some jerky, and several of the worn-out Ziplocs of unlabeled white powder that seem to breed in hiker boxes.

"That jerky looks okay," Toast said.

Basil sighed. "I know, man, but I'm a vegetarian." He lifted out one of the sacks of powder. "This doesn't look too bad."

"Yeah, but what *is* it?" Toast said.

Basil opened the bag for a cautious sniff. "Hmm. Vanilla. I think it's some kind of vanilla drink mix, you know, one of those power drinks." He poured some into his cup and mixed it up with a little water. It fizzed suspiciously.

"Man, it looks just like cake mix," Luna said. "I bet that's what it is."

"Vanilla shake," Basil said. He took a sip. An expression of dismay crossed his face momentarily. "Hmm. Anybody else want some?"

The food didn't arrive until almost two o'clock. By then, we were all so hungry that we shoveled it in, rapidly and indiscriminately. It was the first thing I had eaten since my scanty bowl of granola at dawn. Even on the Trail in winter, I had never eaten so much, so fast. I devoured an entire large pizza, most of a sub, and half a box of onion rings before I slowed down. My stomach was distended as though I'd swallowed a watermelon. It pressed painfully against the waistband of my shorts. The clearing in front of the shelter was littered with the evidence of our gluttony—grease-spattered boxes and napkins, a few scraps of food. I gathered the trash into a pile. Suddenly I knew that if I looked at it any longer I would be sick.

"I've got to take a nap," I said, staggering back to the shelter. My belly felt like an enormous lead-filled beach ball. I lay down on the cool pine boards. There was no comfortable position; my stomach felt as if it was about to burst no matter how I turned. Finally I curled up on my side.

The sun was low over the trees when I woke up. The first thing I realized, coming to wakefulness, was that I was still full. Still too full, in fact. Luna and Six-string, beside me, groaned as they sat up and stretched.

"I feel like a beached whale," Luna said.

Basil sat up slowly, holding his head in his hands. "Oooh. I guess I shouldn't have had that vanilla power drink."

"Admit it, man," Luna told him. "It was cake mix."

Isis and I decided to hike a few more miles before setting up camp for the night. I had to loosen the waist strap of my pack by several inches. It was still uncomfortable across my swollen midriff. I wobbled down the trail, feeling hungover, and I vowed that I would never eat that much again. This was even worse than being hungry.

We filtered water from a spring by a Forest Service road. There were lovely campsites there, flat green meadows with big firepits—but I remembered Heald's warning about camping near roads in the South. Looking closer, I saw broken glass among the ashes and crumpled beer cans glinting in the underbrush.

At the top of the next ridge, only a few miles from Partnership, the dark caught up with us. We found a clearing just big enough for the tent. Needless to say, neither of us felt like eating dinner.

The food-induced stupor continued the next morning. I woke up with a headache and a cottony mouth. All my muscles felt like rubber bands that had been stretched out and snapped too many times. I was slow packing up, and even slower to get moving. My bad mood magnified the little ups and downs of the ridge top. The heat didn't help. Even on the highest ridges, where a light wind blew through the maples and hickory, the air shimmered with warmth.

The Stage Crew caught up with us in midmorning. "Hey, ladies," Six-string said. "Y'all want to stop for milkshakes in Atkins?"

"Milkshakes?" I asked him.

"Yeah, there's a great little café at the hotel there. Luna and I stopped there on our first hike. It was late June, one of those days where you feel like you're made out of sweat . . . That little place was like heaven."

"I thought it would be a while before I stopped for town food again," I said.

"Pizza's one thing," Luna said.

Toast groaned. "Don't say the P-word!"

"Sorry," she said. "But you have to admit, milkshakes are, like, the anti-pizza. They're light, and sweet, and cool . . . Chocolate, strawberry . . ." By the time we reached the fields outside of Atkins, where hawthorns and apple trees bloomed in extravagant pink sprays from the fencerows, Luna and Six-string had convinced us all.

We settled into a red vinyl booth in the café, sweaty and probably reeking. The waitress, to her credit, pretended not to notice. "What can I get for y'all today?"

The milkshakes arrived quickly, and were just as good as Luna and Six-string had said. But a strange thing happened—about halfway through my cup, I found that my appetite was gone.

Luna toyed with her cup. "You know, this is crazy. I actually can't finish this."

"Dude, me either." Basil gave up his half-hearted attempt on his chocolate shake. "I feel like I'm not living up to my hikerness, or something."

Six-string pushed his cup away. "You know, we oughta just get a room here. I don't really feel like hiking."

"Hey, that sounds pretty good." Basil sounded more lively than he had in a while. "Toast, are you with us?"

"Come on, you guys!" Luna sighed. "We've hiked, like, ten miles today!"

"It's clouding up," Toast said, glancing out the window. It was true; a few clouds had come over the sun while we ate.

Six-string sat back with his hands on his belly. "Looks like rain." This was something of an exaggeration; the sky was still mostly clear. "You know, this looks like the kind of day to just lay back and have a good time. Think I'll draw a nice bath, lay in the water all afternoon, smokin' a fatty. Then I'll watch a movie, and maybe, I don't know, smoke me another one . . ."

"Sounds like my kind of day," Basil told him. "I'm goin' over to the office to get us a room. Anyone want to finish this?" He offered his cup around, but for once, there were no takers. We sat back in the booth, feeling lethargy settle in, watching old Star Trek reruns on the TV mounted above the door. Isis and I planned to hike on—a bath and a movie sounded pretty good, but smoking up was not our thing. Also, we were eager to get some more miles behind us. We tried to convince Luna to hike out with us for a ladies' night at Knot Maul shelter. She decided to stay with the rest of the Stage Crew instead.

The waitress came by. "Anything else for y'all?"

"No, I think we're all set." Toast told her.

"All righty. Oh, I got a message here to give to a hiker by the name of Jim Anderson. Y'all know him?"

We looked around the table. Everybody drew a blank. I realized I didn't know the real names of any of my friends here—even Luna, who had lent us her car keys.

"You know his trail name?" Luna asked the waitress.

"Nope; didn't say."

"Maybe Basil knows him." I got to my feet, feeling a minor echo of the lead-balloon sensation in my belly. I met Basil in the parking lot. "You know a guy named Jim Anderson?"

"Know him? He's me!"

Isis

After trying for twenty minutes to persuade the Stage Crew to come with us, we hiked out of Atkins alone.

"I wonder if they'll catch up with us this time? Man, I'm gonna miss them if they don't," jackrabbit said, as we crossed a pasture beyond the maze of truck stops and highway intersections. "It's too bad their pace doesn't match ours."

"Yeah, they're fun people," I answered.

What qualifies as "our pace?" I wanted to ask. *The eight- and ten-mile days that we hiked all winter? The fourteens and fifteens that we could easily cover barefoot? The twenties that most of our sobo friends had hiked from Vermont to Virginia?* We'd had this argument many times, most recently in front of our mother. It never seemed to get resolved. I'd give in, and we'd hike fast until someone got injured. Jackrabbit would grudgingly agree that we needed to zero or slow down until the injury healed, but after a few days she'd be impatient to make up for the lost miles. Caught in this cycle, we rarely had the leisure to stop anywhere just because it was beautiful, or because our friends were there. And we never hiked enough consistent long days to reassure jackrabbit—to convince her that we would reach Katahdin on time, that she *would* complete a thru-hike. *We'll hike fast in summer,* I told myself. *When our packs are lighter.* But a nagging voice in the back of my mind asked, *Will I ever be comfortable hiking twenties? Will I even be able to do it, when the time comes?*

A flash of bright orange against the forest's pale green caught my eye, startling me out of my thoughts. Two or three yards downhill from the trail, clusters of two-inch-wide, lily-shaped flowers hung between the forest floor and the canopy like bowls of fire suspended in midair.

"Look! Flame azaleas!" I said to jackrabbit. Waterfall had told us about them, long ago—wild azaleas of the Southern mountains that bloom in all the colors of fire.

"I know," she answered, sounding a bit surprised. "We've been hiking past them for a mile."

"Why didn't you say something?"

"I thought you would have noticed them already. You're the one who usually stops for flowers."

I'd been so busy thinking about our pace that I hadn't even seen them.

We made good time that afternoon, hiking all the way to Knot Maul Shelter, fourteen miles beyond Atkins and almost twenty-four from the place we'd stealthed the night before. I remembered that section of the trail as a grueling stretch of PUDs, so at first, I was surprised at how quickly it flew by. Somewhere on the third hill, I figured out why—this section had been constructed with northbounders in mind. We climbed gently graded uphills, followed by swift descents into the valleys. For sobos, this translated as a steep, tiring hike to each summit, and tiers of pointless switchbacks on the other side. *Maybe I will be able to hike fast, and still enjoy the views*, I thought. *Northbound, the seasons are with us. And it looks like the Trail is with us, too.*

jackrabbit

At the side trail to Jenkins shelter, I paused. We had only come three miles, and the day before had been a short one: Knot Maul Shelter to Davis Path Campsite, sixteen miles in the heat. I was torn between wanting to make time—the Stage Crew was still behind us, but they might pass us any minute now if they had stealthed on the ridge—and wanting to see this place again. It was the shelter where we had spent Christmas. At least we could go and look at it, write a few memories in the register . . .

The squat brown Forest Service building was just as ugly as I remembered. Someone had taken down our wreath and garlands—a good thing, I decided, since they would be dry and ratty by now anyway. I dropped my pack and jotted a note in the register (just a few days old—I wondered if Pilgrim and Gollum had gotten theirs back yet). Isis leaned against the wall, her pack still on.

Just as we turned to go, I heard a voice coming up the spring trail. "Isis! Jackrabbit!"

"Highlander!" We rushed to embrace him. He looked strong and fit, and he wore the same grungy white shirt, pants, and hat that he'd worn when we last saw him, at the RPH shelter in New York. His beard was longer and his hair was shorter, but the merry light that danced in his brown eyes was the same.

"Where've you been? Where are you headed? What did you do over winter?"

When the flurry of questions ended, Highlander addressed them all in his usual unruffled way. "I got off in November, in Front Royal. The weather was just too much for me. So I spent the winter in Florida, near Cape Canaveral—"

"Did you see the space shuttle?"

"Yes, blasted thing just about knocked my house over when it took off! I got back on the Trail in late March, in a snowstorm—" here he gave an eloquent shrug "—headed south. Here I am. And what about the two of you? I've heard rumors here and there . . ."

"I think Florida was a better deal than Virginia and Tennessee this winter," I said grimly. Isis and I recounted a few of our winter adventures, culminating in the trip across the Grayson Highlands. "So after all that, we decided it would be silly to just drive home. So here *we* are."

"And where are you headed today?"

"Oh, we'll probably head for Helvey's Mill, or stealth somewhere."

A shadow crossed his face, fleetingly. "Then I may not see you again."

"You'll be at Trail Days, won't you?" I asked.

"Or you could come with us, hike backwards for a while."

He gave a look of distaste. "I wasn't so fond of those ridges, the past few days."

"Oh, I remember those," Isis said. "Ick. We used to call them fibrillating ridges."

"Fibrillating. I like that. But I couldn't really imagine crossing and recrossing them . . . You could come south, with me, for a day?"

"We're kind of with a group right now," I explained.

"What if we stay here?" Isis said suddenly. "I'm pretty sure we could convince the Stage Crew to stop, too—"

"Doesn't take much!" I said with a grin.

"—and that way we can finish our Trail Days outfits today!" Isis and I had heard rumors about the hiker parade at Trail Days—apparently hikers try to out-do each other with bizarre costumes. We had already made handkerchief miniskirts to wear in town when all our other clothes were dirty, and for the parade we had started sewing skimpy bikini tops from matching bandanas. We left a note for the Stage Crew at the foot of the blue-blaze trail, and spent the day with Highlander, telling stories, laughing, singing our new songs, and sewing. Nobody came to the shelter all day. It was overcast and cool, good hiking weather, but I was glad, for once, not to be hiking. I was glad to be right where I was.

Toward evening, we heard footsteps coming up the path. I looked up, expecting the Stage Crew, but it was a solitary hiker. He was tall and wiry, with reddish blond hair and constellations of freckles on his clean-shaven cheeks, and he carried a green Go-lite pack. He looked about thirty, though it was always hard to tell with hikers.

"Hi! I'm Breaking Wind!" he said with a silly grin.

"Breaking Wind? Must be the Lipton and Pop-tarts diet," I said. "Jack-rabbit. Pleased to meet you."

We introduced ourselves. Highlander was the first one to ask, "Whence the name?"

Breaking Wind shrugged and looked slightly abashed. "Actually, my mother gave it to me. I was at dinner with my family a few weeks before I left for the Trail. We started talking about trail names, so I said, 'I'd better choose one before I go, so I don't get saddled with something really horrible.' And then my mom said—well, you have to understand, when I was little I had this problem with gas. Really bad. I mean, I was like a little Hindenburg, ready to go off at any moment—so my mom said, 'How about Breaking Wind?' And I said, 'Thanks, mom.'"

"And you kept it?" I asked.

He flashed me a look of mock reproach. "Of course I kept it. It was a gift from my mother, after all." He shrugged off his light pack and sat down on the edge of the shelter platform, and we began the standard round of questions.

"So, when did you start?

"April 15."

"That's less than a month ago!" I did the math, roughly, in my head. We were maybe a hundred miles north of Damascus, so about 550 miles into the

Trail. He would have to be averaging well over twenty miles a day. "Man, we were in *Erwin* on April 15. You must have been in pretty good shape when you started."

He shrugged again. "Not as good of shape as I like to be in. I was in better shape for swimming than walking, anyway."

"What do you do for a living?" Isis asked.

He gave a wry grin. "Well, I used to be a professional windsurfer. I did stunts, wave jumping, and that sort of thing."

"Awesome!"

"It was a pretty good career. Then last winter, I decided I didn't want to compete anymore. I'd built my life around competition, and one day it just didn't matter to me. So I quit."

"And what do you do now?" Highlander asked him.

"I swim with dolphins."

"Really?"

"Really. Up till April, I was house-sitting for a guy I know on Maui, and every day I'd go out and swim with the dolphins. There were bottlenoses and Hawaiian spinners. Have you ever seen a spinner?"

I remembered a *National Geographic* story I had read at a hostel somewhere. "Are those the ones that leap up and whirl around like tops?"

"Yeah! They're the most beautiful animals on earth," he said with quiet conviction. "It's wild, you know, people think we're so well-suited to living on the earth, but we need all this technology, all this *stuff*—" he hefted his green pack, and I reflected that he probably carried half as much stuff as I did "—just to get by. When you see an animal like a dolphin, that just lives in the water, just eats enough to survive on, and doesn't hoard things . . . I couldn't help thinking when they leapt out of the water like that, that they know something about happiness that humans can't begin to understand.

"I used to swim out there every day. The house was right on the coast, and I'd go down the cliffs and dive in and just swim out as far as I could. At first the dolphins wouldn't get close to me. It was like they were teasing me, I think—they'd come around behind me, and jump out of the water, and then they'd stay just out of reach, always swimming away from shore. One time I got so angry that I couldn't reach them. I just kept swimming after them as hard as I could, and they stayed maybe twenty feet away, just going slowly out to sea. After about an hour I could feel my strength going, and I looked back, and the shore was just barely visible. I knew I wouldn't make it back there. I turned around and I started swimming but I was sinking . . . and then I felt the dolphins all around me. One of them came up underneath me and helped me float."

"What does their skin feel like?" I asked.

"Cool. Smooth. It has a kind of give to it, like silk stretched over springy rubber. They came around me, five or six of them, and they all turned and took me back to shore. After that, they would come right up to me. I would try to dive under and swim with them, but they're so fast . . . I think they thought of me as some bizarrely crippled thing. People move in water about as well as walruses move on land. They tolerated me, though. They would rush up to the surface and jump out right next to me. Sometimes they'd jump over me, and I'd look up and see this huge, heavy body just spinning in midair above me . . . I was never afraid, though. They had so much skill."

We traded stories as evening drew on. Isis talked about seeing wild elephants in Burkina Faso, when she went to visit a friend who was serving in the Peace Corps, and Highlander regaled us with tales of the late sixties in San Francisco. I listened to all the narratives unwind, amazed at the wealth of experiences and perspectives brought together in this rickety wooden structure in the middle of the forest. I thought of all the stories that go unheard in the wider world, in the silence of subway cars and bus stops.

It grew dark. Outside, the woods gathered blue-green shadows, and the liquid calls of a hermit thrush began to echo down through the branches. An owl hooted softly, twice.

I had forgotten how beautiful the next few miles were. After we climbed over a small ridge, the trail dropped down on a steeply slanted sidehill path under the green light through the leaves, and crossed and recrossed Little Wolf Creek. The thickets of rhododendrons were blooming here and there, and the olive-green water of the creek flowed knee deep.

At the end of the valley the trail crossed a little bridge and a woods road, and there we found Joe, Fiddler, Breaking Wind, and a man we didn't know. The guys perched on the edge of the creek, a congregation of skinny limbs, knobby knees, sunburned shoulders, and pale backs. They were rinsing out their filthy socks and shirts in the leaping clear water.

"Hey, ladies!" Fiddler grinned. "There's a great swimming hole just upstream. Come join the party! Have you met Ian?"

The unfamiliar hiker nodded. He was short and compact, with thinning ash blond hair and a reddish complexion. "You must be the Barefoot Sisters," he said in a British accent. "Good to meet you."

We swung our packs to the ground and leaned our sticks against them. The water was barely past my knees, but it felt cool and refreshing. I managed to get all wet by scrunching up like a human cannon ball. As I waded to the bank, dripping and happy, I saw a huge crayfish lurking by a rock. "Crawdads! Too bad it's too early for lunch!"

"We were thinking about hitting Bastian for lunch," Fiddler said. "It's another seven miles, but it's all flat once you hit the ridgeline."

"Yeah, sounds good." I didn't remember the ridge being all that flat, but I knew that without its knee-deep snow cover it would certainly go faster than it had in winter. Beside the sparkling creek in the warm May sunshine, I reflected on how easy this northbound hike had been. Certainly, we'd had days of snow, days of cold driving rain. My knee injury had been difficult to bear. But the majority of the hike had been beautiful and trouble free. I knew that without the bad times, I wouldn't be able to appreciate this nearly as much.

Breaking Wind hiked out with us, a few minutes after Joe and Fiddler left. We headed up the hill, on a fragrant carpet of pine needles, between pink clouds of rhododendron blossoms. Isis and I went barefoot, feeling the sun-warmed rocks and the pine needles with their straight smoothness and prickly points.

"I want to hear more of your stories," Breaking Wind said.

"We've already told you our best Trail stories," I said. "Here's our craziest story of all, though. Isis—the snake in the whirlpool?"

"Yeah!"

"Okay. Summer that I was seventeen—"

"—and I was twenty—"

"—we spent three weeks in Peru with our friend Scott Grierson. Maineak."

"He has the third-fastest speed record on the A.T.," Isis said. "Something like fifty-two, fifty-three days. Insane."

"So, it was us, Maineak, two of his hiking buddies from the A.T., and three guides. We spent a couple days in Cuzco, acclimatizing, and four days in the Andes, hiking into Machu Picchu. For the rest of the trip we followed the Urubamba River down into the headwaters of the Amazon. We spent a couple days in whitewater rafts, and then we built rafts out of balsa logs and floated down through the jungle."

"And when Maineak said balsa rafts," Isis broke in, "I was picturing, you know, big logs, floating above the water. But they were these little rafts, maybe ten feet long and three feet across, made of logs that size—" she indicated a skinny oak tree near the trail, hardly as big around as her calf muscles "—and they rode pretty low in the water."

"Running rapids in a balsa raft is an interesting experience," I said. "The raft stays perfectly level, and goes smoothly down, and the waves wash over you. So we had all our gear lashed down in dry bags, and we sat three or four to a raft, just floating on down. We steered with poles of cane—"

"—we traded some fishhooks for a paddle with a family living on the riverbank, way out in the jungle, so we did have one paddle."

"There were a lot of rapids, at the upstream end of things. Every time the river went around a bend, there'd be cliffs on one side, big red clay bluffs, and shallows on the other. You couldn't go down too shallow, because you could hang up on the gravel and flip the raft, and lose all your gear—"

"—if not your life!" Isis interjected. "You could get caught under the raft and dragged down."

"—and you couldn't go down too close to the cliffs, either, because sometimes there'd be rocks sticking out from the base of the cliff, and whirlpools. In a few places, dead trees would make snags on the cliff side . . . There was an art to reading the river," I said, remembering. "You had to judge where the center of the rapid was, and go just to the outside, just to the shallow edge, because it was safer to err on that side than to get caught in a whirlpool."

"And Maineak told us that sometimes the cliffs collapse, too, and you can get trapped under the clay if you're too close."

"But some of our guides," I continued, "didn't know much about river-running at all. They were all from the mountains, and one of them, Leo, I think he was actually afraid of the river."

"Leo was kind of, you know, imperious, too," Isis added. "He liked to be in control of things, even when he didn't really know what was going on."

"Yeah. So Leo was on the back of the raft with two other guides on it, pretending he knew how to steer. Maineak and the two of us were on a raft just behind them. We started heading down into a big rapid. The guides were running way too far to the inside. We had the paddle, so Maineak steered us over into the eddy on the other side, and we drifted back upstream so we could help in case something happened. It was just awful to watch. The raft hit the cliffs and two of the guides fell off. Leo managed to climb back on, but the other guy, Bambi, was swept downstream."

"He wasn't wearing a lifejacket or anything," Isis added.

"He went under for a long time. Then he was up, but he disappeared again. I couldn't stop watching. You know how your stomach just kind of clenches up? But he came out again, and he was alive, clinging to the rocks at the foot of the rapid. He was kind of lying there, half in and half out of the water. And then the raft went by—"

"—the other guys were okay; they were still hanging on—"

"And the raft went right over Bambi's legs. I thought for sure he'd get swept down again. There was a big whirlpool just behind the rock, and there was no way he'd get out of that alive. But somehow he hung on, and the raft floated off. So there we were, Isis and Maineak and I, with one paddle for the three of us, and there was only one thing we could do. We shoved off from the bank, and Isis paddled as hard as she could on the downstream side. Maineak somehow kept the bow pointed into the current, and we ferried across, right for that whirlpool. We landed just on the downstream edge of it, where the current wasn't as strong. I held onto the raft and the bank."

"Maineak and I jumped out to rescue Bambi—"

"—and just as they were leaving, I saw a medium-sized brown snake of some kind uncoil itself from the bank and slip into the water right next to the raft. I was lying there, hanging onto the raft and the rocks with all my strength, trying to keep out of the main current on one side and the whirlpool on the other, and kind of wondering what'd happened to that snake, and whether or not it was poisonous."

"We climbed over a couple cliffs and got to Bambi," Isis said, "and he was okay. It was pretty amazing, after what he'd been through. He was weak from all that time underwater, and his legs were pretty scraped up where the raft had run over him, but he could walk . . . we got him back to the raft, and I tried to paddle out, but we got caught in the whirlpool."

"So there we were, in the middle of the jungle, no towns or people around for miles, getting sucked into a whirlpool. Bambi was lying across the raft. We were all getting tossed around quite a bit. My life was kind of flashing before my eyes, you know?"

"We swung around three times, and I didn't have the strength left to paddle out. So I tried to hand the paddle to jackrabbit, but I dropped it. It went under the raft."

"We were all reaching around under there, trying to grab the paddle—"

"—and finally I caught hold of it, and handed it to jackrabbit. She had the strength to get us out of there and back into the main current."

"Then we were drifting down the middle of the river, between those green walls of jungle, and everything had that adrenaline clarity. Like you could see every twig on every branch, and hear every sound the water made. Like you could feel every photon of light hitting your shoulders. And I turned back to Bambi, to ask if he was really okay, and he started to say yes, and then he turned really pale. We were all asking him what was wrong, and he told us he'd just felt a snake of some kind slipping past his legs."

Isis delivered the clincher. "So all the time that we were reaching around for the paddle, that snake had been under the raft."

Breaking Wind whistled. "That's a good one." He paused for a sip of water. "What've I got to match that one for the adrenaline factor? Let's see . . ."

We had almost reached the top of the ridge now, cruising along a smooth trail laden with pine needles. Occasionally we could glimpse the valley and the mountains beyond through gaps in the trees. Higher up, the woods still showed pink and yellowish green with spring. In the hollows, the darker green of summer was beginning to gather.

"How about this?" Breaking Wind said. "You guys remember Hurricane Iniki?"

"Wasn't that the one that hit Hawaii in the early nineties?" I said. "It took people by surprise. Nobody thought it would be that strong."

"Right. It was the biggest storm to hit the islands in the past century. It was supposed to go past us, but it slammed right into Oahu and Kauai. Lots of people lost their homes. Millions of dollars of damage."

"So where were you during the storm?" Isis asked him.

Breaking Wind cackled gleefully. "Windsurfing."

"What?!"

"Well, Maui didn't get the worst of it. We were just outside the storm's track. But we did have the most gnarly waves I've ever seen. Thirty-five, forty feet high at Puunene. The sky was all dark, sort of purplish colored, and there was torrential rain off and on. Lots of wind, sixty, seventy, eighty miles an hour. But those waves . . . it was just too much. I had a bunch of crazy friends, and we took our boards down to the beach. Paddling out into the water was the hardest part. The beach was pretty torn up. Luckily there's a deep place there, where it doesn't break as hard, and we got in there.

"I had my tiniest little storm sail on, reefed down as far as it would go. It was intense. These waves were like walls, like buildings four stories high. They didn't even look like water any more, more like steel. Slate colored. Oily looking. You could see things inside the waves sometimes, pieces of seaweed or big fish, or bits of rock getting tossed around . . . We were zipping in and out of the break zone, riding the curls. Sometimes you'd look down and see this drop-off, right below you. You had to scoot down the inside of the wave, on one little edge of the board . . . What you had to do was get out just ahead of the break. Squirt out like a watermelon seed. If one of us had gotten caught against that reef, nobody ever would have found the pieces. The waves hit that coral with a sound you could feel all through your bones, and there was so much spray in the air it looked like fog. All these guys were pros, though. We thought we knew what we were doing.

"I was riding one wave, the biggest one yet. I came skimming down the inside, down that drop-off toward the trough, going so fast my eyes were watering. And all of a sudden I looked ahead, to where I was going, and there was no water down there. There was the reef, a big ledge of old coral, sticking six feet out of the water. Little waterfalls coming off it. That wave was so huge, it had sucked the reef dry." He paused, and I imagined myself caught between a wall of water and a wall of rock, trapped. The suspense was too much to take.

"So what did you do?" I asked, and Isis voiced the same thought almost in unison.

Breaking Wind laughed. "You know it's a good story when you can't stop to take a breath. Well, I looked at that chunk of reef up ahead of me, as I was screaming down the face of the wave, and it took me a second to even realize what it was. Then I thought, 'Shit, I'm gonna die!' And then I gathered all my strength, and bent my knees, and I jumped. I bunny-hopped that board right over the reef and rode it out the other side, with the whole wave slamming down behind me like a mountain collapsing."

He grew quiet for a while, and when he spoke again his voice was more reflective, older. "Then I got out of the water. I'd had my moment. I'd felt those icy hands on my shoulder. It's things like that, when you get so close to death, when you gamble like that . . . well, it makes life seem so much more real and important for a while. And some people become junkies for that sort of thing. One of those guys that was with me that day, he was killed in a sky-diving accident the next year. Some people are just driven by that feeling of pushing things to the edge. For me, that wasn't what I was in it for. I just loved the . . . *purity* of it. Like sometimes when you catch the wind and the current just right, and your timing is perfect, it's like flying. Like you could go forever."

Breaking Wind took off ahead of us after a while, loping easily along the ridge top. The trail hit a gravel road, newly crushed dark gray stones that were uncomfortably hot and sharp underfoot. We put on our sandals and walked along the shady edge of the road. Suddenly the world opened out before us into a panorama of stone and asphalt. I had forgotten the extent of the highway cut that led to Bastian and Bland, but now as I stood before it, I could remember how the wind-driven sleet had funneled through it in winter, with gritty blasts of slush and gravel turned up by passing cars. Today, the road and the dynamited slope of reddish rock lay quiet, shimmering with heat.

I turned to Isis. "Hey, it's still early. We could hitch into Bastian for lunch, like Joe and Fiddler said."

"Yeah. I haven't heard much traffic, though." It was true—all the way down the ridge road, I hadn't heard any cars pass.

"We could wait a couple minutes and see what goes by," I said. "I mean, we have enough Trail food to get us to Pearisburg . . . but Isis, they might have pizza." After the fiasco at Partnership Shelter, I had thought I would never eat pizza again. It had only taken a few days, though, for it to regain its former allure. A good veggie pizza was about the only readily available town food that could satisfy our cravings for fat, salt, bread, and vegetables at the same time.

"Okay," Isis said, "we can wait a few minutes."

The heat settled over us, and nothing moved. Cicadas made their electric buzzing sounds, suddenly loud in the cleared land. After a few minutes, a vehicle appeared at the bottom end of the long curving road: a rattletrap Ford station wagon, driven by a woman in her mid-sixties. We stuck out our thumbs, but she swerved and sped up as she passed us, with a look of distaste. A few minutes later, a yellow school bus chugged its way up the hill.

"Slim pickings," I said.

"Maybe we should just start walking."

We shouldered our packs again and took a few steps down the road, when a rusty pickup hove into view.

"That's more like our style!"

We stuck out our thumbs and the truck pulled over. "Y'all hop in!" the driver called, and in seconds we were perched in the back of the pickup, sitting on our packs. I could see the road going by underneath us through the holes in the truck bed. On the way into town, we passed Joe and Fiddler walking by the side of the road. We waved. Fiddler shook his fist at us, but he was smiling.

We thanked the driver and jumped out by the gas pumps in the parking lot of the Bastian General Store. The deli was at the back of the store, dimmed with Venetian blinds, with a creaky overhead fan circulating air around the orange vinyl booths. Breaking Wind and Ian looked up from a table littered with napkins and paper plates, and mumbled greetings through mouthfuls of pizza.

Isis ordered a veggie pizza and onion rings, while I refilled our water bottles from the tap in the bathroom. Waiting for the food, we sat at the ketchup-smeared table, poring over our maps and planning for the next week.

"I think we can get pretty far past Pearisburg before Trail Days," Isis said.

"Oh, easy. It's what, like, forty miles from here?"

"Yeah."

"Trail Days doesn't start till the eighteenth. And today's the ninth. So, make it two and a half days to Pearisburg, max . . . that gives us almost a solid week of hiking up past there. Where would that put us?"

"We don't have those maps yet. Our mom's sending them to Pearisburg." I swore softly.

"Want to borrow my *Data Book*?" Ian asked. "Bloody useful, the thing is."

"Thanks, man." He passed the book over to our table. It was a thin, half-size volume, less than a hundred pages. Inside, there was little more than a list of shelters, road crossings, and water sources, with a table of distances. It seemed almost impossible that the whole Trail could be encapsulated in such a small form.

I followed the columns of numbers. "We could get up to Catawba, going really slow. Troutville with fifteens."

"That's doable in this terrain," Isis said.

"But the thing is, do we know anybody up above Pearisburg? Walrus and Roots are there. I'm pretty sure they're going to Trail Days."

"And Playfoot. He lives pretty close by too."

"Right. But who do we know up above there? Should we just plan on hitching down?"

Isis shrugged. "Things have a way of working themselves out."

"I like to have a plan," I protested, and the edge of the old argument surfaced; plans versus spontaneity, the goal versus the journey, but just then the pizza arrived and put an end to our discussion.

Joe and Fiddler came in as we finished our lunch. "Girls get easy hitches!" Fiddler huffed in mock exasperation. "We must have stood there for twenty minutes, and then nobody would pick us up on the road while we were walking."

"It's just luck, man," I said.

"Completely," Isis told them. "We'll hitch out with you guys, and then you'll see how hard it is for us, too, most of the time."

On the way out of town, the first pickup stopped for us.

Up in the mountains, flame azaleas filled the undergrowth: pink, yellow, peach, orange, bronze, red, in colors so rich they almost crackled in the humid air. The trees were leafing out, faster and faster, and now a dappled shade covered even the tops of the ridges. The breeze tasted of greenness and growing things, sweetened with the sudden cinnamon fragrance of azaleas.

After a day of navigating the bumpy ridgeline, we came down into the valley as the golden light lengthened across the fields. From the swinging bridge at Kimberling Creek, the still gray water showed the new leaves of maples and the pink azaleas on the bank with such perfect symmetry that it was easy to become lost in the reflection. Overhead, and inverted in the stream, tiny flecks of cloud gathered almost imperceptibly into a patchwork in the upper air.

"Hey, Isis. Ian's *Data Book* said there was food on this road. Point-six west. You wanna go?"

Once again, the lure of pizza and ice cream proved too strong for us. We strapped our sandals on and walked down the gravel shoulder of the road, to a gas station where the man behind the counter followed our every move with his narrowed blue eyes. There was pizza, soggy-crusted and scantily-cheesed, but inexpensive and filling. Before we left, I stopped in the restroom to refill our water bottles. A sign beside the cracked mirror read: *Hikers: Do Not Steal Our Toilet Paper!*

That night, we camped at Dismal Falls, at the end of a short side trail. In the clear spring light the creek looked anything but dismal; azaleas bloomed in a rainbow of colors under the fragrant red pines. The white rocks by the stream and the pale gray trunks of oaks, maples, and sassafras glowed with evening. We had stopped along the path to dig sassafras for tea, pulling the sweet-smelling red-barked roots from the leaf mold.

A group of rowdy teenagers had already laid claim to the near bank of the creek, so we crossed in the shallows above the falls and found a campsite. Joe and Fiddler sat nearby, making Chef Boyardee pizza. Fiddler mixed the dough in a plastic bag while Joe opened a tiny can of tomato sauce with his pock-etknife. The Dutch oven was heating over their Zip stove; the scent of wood smoke drifted across the little clearing.

"That's the most complex camp cooking I've seen on the whole Trail!" I said. "And it looks a whole lot better than the pizza at the gas station back there."

"We get one of these in every mail drop!" Joe said, with a grin that stretched from ear to ear. He was perched on the ground, feeding twigs into the stove. With his skinny twelve-year-old arms and legs, he seemed to be made of twigs himself. He brushed back his fine brown hair with a sooty hand. "We carry the cheese out from town, but the sauce mix and all, Mom sends to us."

Fiddler finished assembling the pizza and set it to bake. "So you guys went to that place on 606?" he asked.

"Yeah. It was kind of . . . I don't know, I felt like the guy was glaring at me the whole time," Isis said.

"Breaking Wind told me he had the same experience when he hiked in '98. My brother and I thought about going in there, but after his story we decided against it."

I told him about the sign by the mirror. "I was kind of pissed that somebody would assume that just because we're hiking, we're going to steal something."

Fiddler gave a wry smile. "A lot of people assume things like that about hikers. Maybe they had bad experiences in the past, maybe they just don't like the way we dress, the way we smell—"

"—and we sure do reek!" Joe said, laughing and wrinkling his nose.

"It doesn't necessarily do people any good, to see us that way, but maybe it does *us* some good," Fiddler said.

"How so?"

"Look at us. How many white, middle-class Americans know what dis-crimination feels like? Maybe if we realize what it's like to be followed by stares and whispers, we'll be less likely to do it to somebody else."

When the tent was pitched and our food bags hung, Isis and I made our way to the falls. We walked gingerly along the pale ledge and down the side of the falls, avoiding broken glass that had gathered there from past revelry. The falls cascaded, six or eight feet down and half again as wide, over a jumble of broken stones. The sound was more musical and intimate than the roar of a larger cascade, and the spray felt cool on our sweat-stained faces. At the foot of the falls was a wide pool, deep enough for swimming.

I waded in on a rock ledge and found the water shockingly cold. Thoughts of swimming disappeared—twilight was settling, and a slight chill was in the air. Isis dove in, though, and splashed around in the green water. I rinsed my face and arms and reached down to scrub the grime off my legs. When I looked up, someone was waving from the far bank. He wore a cotton tie-dyed shirt and jean shorts—hardly hiker apparel—and his hair was shaved close, but I recognized him instantly.

"Playfoot?"

Isis emerged from underwater. "Playfoot?"

"Hey, ladies. Want to go to Florida?"

"Florida! How?"

At camp that night, Playfoot explained his plan. "Well, my housemate Larry's sister has a beach house in Florida. They rent it out all summer. Normally Larry gets a bunch of friends together and heads down there this week, but he couldn't find anybody on short notice this year. Then he got a last-minute call about a meeting he has to attend, so offered the place to me, and he said I could bring friends. It gives us just enough time before Trail Days. And I thought, since you're in the area . . ."

"Playfoot, you're awesome," I said. "How can we thank you?"

"Well, there's another person to thank for the plans. He was really the one who suggested bringing you guys along. He was going to be here tonight, but he has to play in a brass quintet."

"No way . . . Tuba Man?"

He nodded. I felt like a character in a soap opera. Conflicting emotions danced around inside me: a girlish elation—*He remembers me! Maybe he likes me!*—and an equally girlish sense of deflated hopes—*But he's not here tonight; maybe I'll never see him again.* At the back of my mind, a cynical voice dismissed all these whirling hopes and speculations: *I'm too old for schoolgirl crushes. Silly infatuations like this never lead anywhere.*

"But he will be joining us in Florida," Playfoot said.

I must have let out a shriek of delight, because Isis said, "jackrabbit, dear, get a hold of yourself," and I blushed scarlet in the gathering dark.

As I fell asleep to the sound of the waterfall, all kinds of thoughts ran through my head. The last thing I remember thinking was, *Isis was right. As for Trail Days, things will work themselves out.*

CHAPTER 4

Spring Break

jackrabbit

Playfoot ferried our packs to the Woods' Hole Hostel so we could slack the next ten miles of ridgeline before we left for Florida. It was a splendid day—rhododendrons budding out, azaleas glowing in the understory, and all the trees unfurling their foliage. Even on the highest ridges, the last oak trees had put forth their tiny, curled, pinkish leaves. I remembered how stark these ridges had seemed in winter, with rows of empty trees and the black-and-white view of the valley. I had mixed feelings about going to Florida. It had been so magical to see spring arrive in the Southern mountains, gradually spreading upward from the coves and hollows; to walk in and out of the season with the changes in elevation. I wanted to see summer come in the same way. Also, I was nervous about seeing Tuba Man again. The last time I'd talked to him, at Miss Janet's Easter party, I knew I'd made a fool of myself. Beneath these hesitant regrets and fears, I felt a giddy, unreasonable joy. *I'm going to Florida! Spring break! And Tuba Man will be there!* In a way, it seemed like a reward for all the trials of winter on the Trail.

Playfoot met us on the gravel road at Sugar Run Gap, in his Jeep with the TRL MGC license plate. I remembered the first time I had seen the vehicle, after our night of drunken revelry in Duncannon in fall. Dimly, I recalled something about the turn signal coming off in Black Forest's hand, and an illegal left turn on the freeway.

"Hey, ladies. Ready to go?"

"Oh yeah," I said, loading our packs into the back. "Talk about trail magic! This is awesome. More than awesome."

He shrugged. "Trail magic is what it's all about."

The Jeep bounced down the red, rutted gravel road, passing woods, overgrown fields, the gray planks of half-tumbled barns. Then a paved road, a tiny, winding mountain road, then a wider one, and finally the freeway, a vast waste of gray concrete that zipped past us at an alarming speed. Over the sound of the motor and the roar of wind flapping the Jeep's cloth paneling, Playfoot asked about our northbound hike. The stories lasted all the way to the border of Virginia.

"What's new with you?" I finally asked him.

"Well, I'm getting a house built," he said.

"No way! Aren't you a little young to settle down?"

He grinned. "I might look like it. No, I just felt like I was tired of moving from apartment to apartment. Never knowing where I'd be the next year. I love the Blacksburg area; I knew I wanted to settle down there. Then when I heard about this intentional community—don't give me that look! It's not a commune or anything. No, it's a bunch of people, just regular people, who wanted to live in a more, I don't know, community-focused kind of way. You know how most subdivisions are—everybody with his little half-acre of lawn and his driveway. It's so isolating. The place I'm moving into, people own their own houses, their little plots of land, but there's also a patch of woods that's community property. A neighborhood park, kind of. And a garden. And there's going to be a meeting house where we all get together every few weeks to talk things over." A semi passed, the rush of sound making conversation momentarily impossible. "It's kind of like the Trail, I guess," Playfoot said. "The way people share things, I mean. I miss that."

When I saw the exit sign for Greensboro, North Carolina, my heart gave a little skip inside my chest. *Tuba Man!* I knew he was studying at the university there. Would he remember what I had said? Would he think of me as an idiot?

"This is the place," Playfoot announced, as we pulled up in front of a nondescript two-story house on a cul-de-sac. "Frisbee House. Tuba and a bunch of his friends are renting it together. He said he'd be here to meet us, unless his rehearsal goes late."

And there he was, stepping out onto the curb, the golden boy. "Hey! You made it! Awesome!" He hugged us all. "You're just in time for barbecue night. I told 'em to put some more chicken on the grill for you guys."

"Uh, thanks," I said, suddenly tongue-tied and probably blushing.

"We're actually vegetarians, pretty much," Isis told him, unloading her pack from the back seat.

"Oh, no prob. I'll see if I can scrounge up some veggie burgers."

The whole night, I watched Tuba Man from a slight distance. He flirted with everyone—me, Isis, the handful of women who showed up at the barbecue, and the girls next door, who gave us some ice to keep the beer cold. His powerful charisma was directed everywhere and nowhere. I wondered if I had made any impression on him at all.

Playfoot drove for most of the next day. I sat in the back with Tuba Man. He fell asleep leaning against me. The warmth of his shoulder filled me with a joy so intense it bordered on melancholy. Eventually I drifted to sleep too, trying to imagine the days ahead. Florida. White sand beaches, the sound of the ocean. And Tuba Man. I could hardly believe this was happening to me.

I woke up when the sound of the engine changed. Playfoot was pulling off the highway, down an exit ramp where a huge billboard proclaimed *Bob's Discount House of Fireworks! All styles, all sizes—we will not be undersold!*

"It wouldn't be a vacation without some wanton pyromania," Playfoot said cheerfully.

"I didn't think fireworks were legal in Florida," Isis said.

"They're not. That's why we're stopping in good ol' South Carolina to buy them."

We stocked up on bottle rockets, sparklers, Catherine wheels, and Roman candles, plus a few larger ones: a "Good Fortune Unicorn Fountain" and something by the unlikely name of "Phoenix Tail Howl." We also bought peaches, the only nonincendiary item in the store. A heaping basket of them stood next to the register, looking too ripe and delicious to ignore.

"Where are the peaches grown?" I asked the man at the counter. A few of them were wrinkly and irregular, and they all lacked supermarket produce stickers. I thought they might be local.

"Georgia," the man said, ringing up our purchases. Georgia. Of course. The Peach State, wasn't it? But it was hard to reconcile my memories of Georgia—leafless trees, dead grasses, snow on the humpbacked mountains—with this basket of ripe fruit.

We stopped for dinner somewhere in north-central Florida, amid a flat expanse of strip malls and palm trees. In the mall parking lot, the air felt weighted, dense, sticky with accumulated heat and moisture. Thunderheads were stacking up on the wide sweep of horizon.

"Tokyo Grill," Playfoot said. "That looks promising. You guys ever been to a Japanese steakhouse?"

"Yeah, a long time ago," I said. "When I was, like, ten."

Tuba Man grinned. "Is this one of those places where they chop stuff up and cook it right at your table? Where they juggle vegetables and stuff? Yeah, right on!"

Inside, the place was packed with high school students. The boys sweated inside rented tuxedos; the girls looked bored and unassailable in strapless satin gowns, sequins, bows, corsages, pancake makeup, flammable quantities of hairspray: prom night.

Playfoot maneuvered his way to the cash register. "It'll be a few minutes," he reported back to us. "I gave them my name."

We stood in the parking lot. Isis and I were ravenous; our hiker appetites were still in force, even though we'd been sitting in a car for the past day and a half. We ate the last of the peaches. Playfoot was rummaging the glove compartment in search of a candy bar when we heard a voice from the restaurant: "Streaker, party of four."

"Playfoot, you didn't!" Isis said.

He gave a mischievous grin. "Sounds like our number's up."

We walked in to find about forty pairs of eyes focused on the door. There was a distinct sigh of disappointment as we passed by, fully clothed, and sat down at a table in the back.

The chef cooked our food on a large grill set into the center of the table. He was a master of surprise, balancing an egg on his knife blade and then flipping it to crack it open in midair; constructing a smoking volcano from half an onion and some sauce; juggling bottles of condiments; setting things on fire and extinguishing them with an easy flick of the wrist. Our steaming platters of rice, vegetables, and tofu (meat for the guys) tasted great, but the flavor was almost secondary to the fun of watching him cook.

"It's getting kind of late," Playfoot said as we piled back into the car, "and we still have, like, three hours to go. Maybe we could look for a motel somewhere."

"Hey, we could stay with my sister in Tallahassee," Tuba Man said.

Playfoot looked skeptical. "I didn't know you *had* a sister in Tallahassee."

"Yeah. I'm sure she wouldn't mind. I haven't seen Paige in, like, forever."

"You know how to get there?" Playfoot asked him.

"Oh, totally. At least, I think I remember. Maybe if I drive. . ." Playfoot handed over the keys, and Tuba Man screeched out onto the highway, accelerating at an alarming rate. "Hey, sweet car, bro."

Heat lightning crackled around the horizon, illuminating the bellies of the clouds with brief purple flashes. After perhaps half an hour, Tuba Man turned off the main road into a maze of small residential streets. The outlines of unfamiliar tropical trees loomed darkly under intermittent streetlights. "It's somewhere back here," he said, half to himself. "Aha!"

The headlights had caught the figure of a delicate blond woman standing outside a garage, holding a small dog. Tuba Man leaned on the horn and pulled into the driveway right in front of her. She froze, petrified.

"Paigey-boo!" Tuba Man yelled out the window.

"Scott?" she said in a tiny voice. "God, you almost gave me a heart attack! Why do you never call ahead when you come to visit me?"

"I didn't mean to scare you," Tuba Man said in his best innocent voice. "Aren't you happy to see me?"

"Oh, Scott." She shook her head. "You never change, do you?" But she hugged him as soon as he got out of the car. Then she noticed the rest of us. "Little brothers," she shook her head sadly. "I hope none of you have little brothers. This one—" she reached up and tousled his hair "—has already taken years off my life expectancy." The little dog in her arms started yapping. "Hush, Baby! She always gets excited when there are strangers around. Well, if I know Scott, you guys are on the road somewhere. Up to some kind of mischief." She smiled, a quick, bemused expression almost like her brother's. "And you need a place to stay." A few fat raindrops hit the pavement, and thunder rumbled in the distance. "I can't turn you out on a night like this."

We thanked Paige and set out in the early morning, with the sun just illuminating the rain-washed pastels of the neighborhood. By midmorning, we had reached the Gulf coast. The gray-green water, hardly marred by a ripple, stretched out to meet the pale sky. It was my first glimpse of the sea in a long time. We stopped at a roadside market for more peaches, and Isis bought an enormous bottle of wine and some citrus to make sangria.

Tuba Man read the directions Playfoot had brought. "Okay, now we make a left. It should be about a quarter mile up here, on the right . . . holy shit! Is *that* it? The huge one?" There was only one house on the stretch of beach that matched the directions: an elegant two-story home with blue siding, just at the back of the dunes. The house number was right, too. We drove into the built-in garage, hardly daring to believe our luck.

Inside, the house was full of light. Sun streamed through huge bay windows and skylights in every room, reflecting on the polished wood and settling in soft rectangles on the nautical colors of the furniture and carpets. We opened the screen doors and let in the sea breeze. I felt a lingering sense of disbelief: *is this really my life?*

Isis and I changed into the handkerchief bras we'd sewn for Trail Days. They were perfect as bikini tops, though our shorts left something to be desired. After a brief stop to slather on sunscreen, we ran down the weathered wooden boardwalk to the beach. It was exactly as I had pictured it: fine white sand like sugar snow, thin grasses in the dunes, the clean blue arc of the sky and the greenish sea stretching to meet it at the horizon. The long curve of beach was almost deserted; most of the houses stood empty, and we only saw a few other people in the miles of glistening sand. Tuba Man tried, unsuccessfully, to make a volleyball net with some driftwood and a piece of washed-up netting. Instead, we played Frisbee among the waves. In the afternoon, Isis mixed up the sangria in a huge bowl she found in the cupboard, and we drank it steadily from frosted glasses.

All day, I tried to figure out what to say to Tuba Man. The longer I waited, the more awkward I felt. That evening, Playfoot winked at me and said, "Hey, Isis. Do you want to come into town for groceries?"

"Sure," my sister said, with a too-wide grin that suggested they'd planned it.

"It's kind of a long drive," Playfoot said. "We might be gone a while."

After they left, the sound of the surf seemed twice as loud, echoing in the rooms of the house. I looked over at Tuba Man, who lay on the couch with his feet up, watching a football game on TV.

"Do you want to go watch the sunset?" I asked him, hearing my voice go high-pitched and ridiculously breathy.

"What? Oh, yeah. Sure." He switched off the TV. I poured us two more glasses of the sangria—the enormous bowl was now less than half full—and we went to the upstairs balcony. The sun hovered just above the horizon, a slightly flattened oval of intense red. Lines of color flared out into the high clouds, and refracted in brilliant, glittering points from the tops of the waves.

"It's weird to watch the sunset over the ocean from the East Coast," I said. "I mean, it's like we're in California or something. I know it's the Gulf coast, but still . . ." I realized I was blathering, and shut up.

"Yeah, I guess it is kind of strange," he said. "It's like that scene in *The Patriot* where they're sitting on the beach, watching the sun go down over the ocean, except I think that was supposed to be in North Carolina. No sunsets over the ocean there, as far as I know." He put his feet up on the railing and leaned back in his chair.

I noticed a tattoo of three Greek letters on his ankle. "What's your tattoo stand for?"

"Oh, that's my frat. Phi Gamma Delta. Fiji, for short. We used to throw these great beach parties."

"Where'd you go to school?"

"Vermont. UVM."

"Wait a sec. Beaches in Vermont?"

He grinned. "We'd bring in, like, a truckload of sand. Put it in the frat house basement, or the living room, or something. Then we'd have barrels full of rum punch, daiquiris. All kinds of girls in bikinis. Fiji parties were legendary."

"Carleton didn't have any frats," I said. "What'd you do, other than throw parties?"

He looked a little surprised. "Parties were the main thing. We did some community service type stuff, too. Painting the Girl Scout headquarters and that kind of thing. Mostly, I just met a bunch of cool people. Slept with lots of random women."

The last sliver of the sun sank under the edge of the water. High up among the clouds, the first star appeared. Bizarrely, I found myself staring at it and wishing for Tuba Man. Not the half-drunk frat boy beside me, beautiful as he was, but the Tuba Man I had wished for all winter: strong, sensitive, clever; the one who could draw such splendid music from such an unlikely piece of brass.

We talked about movies for a while, a safe subject. Eventually headlights cut through the gathering dusk. The Trail Magic Jeep pulled into the garage.

"Fire up the grill!" Playfoot shouted up to us. "We're making shrimp kabobs!"

"I like fire," Tuba Man said. He swung his lithe body over the railing of the balcony and dropped neatly onto the deck below, perhaps ten feet down.

"Jump, jackrabbit," he called up to me, grinning, but I shook my head. After so many glasses of sangria, I didn't trust myself. Instead, I went back into the house. In the bright kitchen, Isis was pulling a bag of charcoal briquettes from one of the cupboards. She gave me a questioning glance as I passed. I shrugged.

Soon the aroma of roasting seafood and vegetables began to drift back through the house. We ate out on the deck, and emptied the rest of the sangria bowl. I felt mellow and hazy, a few degrees separated from the rest of the world.

"It's such a perfect night," Tuba Man said, leaning back against the railing. The sound of the surf washed over us, serene and constant; the half-moon hung in the indigo sky. The strong breeze off the water carried a scent of salt and iodine. "Hey, we ought to set off some fireworks!"

"The wind's pretty strong," Playfoot said doubtfully.

"No, this is perfect! Where are those bottle rockets?" He ducked into the house and emerged a few minutes later with a plastic bag full of fireworks. "Give me that lighter, Playfoot." He took out one of the bottle rockets and tried to light the fuse, but the wind kept putting out the lighter flame. "This isn't working too good. I bet the barbecue's still hot enough, though!" Before anyone could stop him, he took a few steps across the deck and stuck the firework into the glowing coals. I ducked, bracing myself for an explosion, but by some miracle, only the fuse caught. He tossed the bottle rocket into the air and watched the bright trail of sparks bloom over the bay and disappear. "That worked great. Come on, let's light some more!"

By then, though, Isis had hidden the bag of fireworks. Playfoot reached over and closed the lid of the grill. "I think that's enough for tonight," he said.

The next day was another long stretch of white sand and sea wind, the hours marked off by the steady progression of the sun across the blazing dome of sky. My shoulders and back were beginning to burn, no matter how much sunscreen I used, and my pale stomach was turning pink. Once again, I tried to figure out what to say, and how to say it, but I couldn't find the right words. The moment never came.

That night after supper, we drove out to an even more deserted stretch of beach to light off the rest of the fireworks. The "Phoenix Tail Howl" lived up to its name, spouting showers of blue-green and white sparks and giving an unearthly shriek as it zipped across the sky. I held a few Roman candles, feeling the slight recoil and rush as the red and green balls of fire shot out.

"I don't know why we didn't set off more fireworks last night," Tuba Man said, lighting another bottle rocket and tossing it into the air. "The coals were plenty hot enough."

I was astounded. "But don't you see? If it was hot enough to light the fuse, it was probably hot enough to make the whole *thing* go off!"

"Oh," he said in a contemplative tone. "I didn't think of that."

On another bright, hot day, we rented a couple of two-person kayaks and went to a wildlife refuge down the coast. It was a narrow peninsula of the ubiquitous white sand, open to the sea on one side, with a brackish marsh on the other. Tuba Man had an eye for wildlife. He spotted a great blue heron, motionless among the reeds, and the knobby brown snout of a small alligator before it vanished into the murk.

Isis and Playfoot shared a kayak. They paddled out far from shore, giving a wide berth to me and Tuba Man. This was the moment, I decided. I hoped it would go better than last time.

We paddled along in the shallows. Tuba Man pointed out skates and rays on the sandy bottom, and after a while we made a game of guessing where their diamond-shaped leathery bodies would erupt from the sand, scooting away like cloud shadows on a windy day. We also found horseshoe crabs, following their strange prehistoric shapes across the ripples of light on the sea floor.

Finally I had to speak. "I'm glad I got to spend this time with you," I said. "It's good to get to know you a little." I turned halfway around in the kayak so I could see him.

His blue eyes were fixed on the horizon. "Yeah. It's been fun."

"Somehow I expected you to be different," I said.

"Different? Like how?"

"I don't know. More . . . sensitive, I guess. Since you're a musician, I mean, I kind of expected—"

"I am sensitive," he protested. "I'm completely sensitive. Ask my mom. It's not like I go around moping about things. I'm not artsy-fartsy or anything like that. But sure, stuff affects me more than most people. After I got off the Trail, I was really depressed. It took me a couple months to get over it. I guess most of the time, I handle things by just laughing it off. Staying positive. 'Cause that's the only thing you can really influence. Your attitude about things."

For a while, the only sound was the distant surf and the dip and splash of our paddles. "I remember what you said to me in Erwin," he said finally. "I've been thinking about it."

"And?"

"And I don't think I want to get involved with you. It's not that you're bad-looking or anything, 'cause you're not. It's just, well, I'd rather be friends. I can imagine us hanging out together in, like, twenty years, talking about the Trail or whatever. And I think, in general, long distance relationships are a bad idea."

"Yeah," I said. "I guess so." And I hadn't expected anything else, not after the way he had acted the past few days. I wasn't even sure that I would want a relationship with this man. He was so different from what I had imagined him to be. Still, I felt a loss. It was hard to let go of a dream I had carried with me for such a long time.

"I had a girlfriend when I started the Trail," he said. "And we were really happy together. At least, I thought so. She broke up with me the weekend of the Gathering."

"The Gathering! You seemed so happy then."

"That's what I mean about the way I deal with stuff. I figured, why be sad about it? And of course I was sad, inside, but I didn't show it. I played my tuba for everybody, and I acted happy."

And flirted with me to distract yourself. Nice, I thought, but I didn't say it.

"After a while I *was* happy. I didn't have to act any more. Hey, there's another horseshoe crab! I'll paddle. See if you can grab him."

His childlike enthusiasm was so catching that I had to smile. My hands closed around the edges of the slick brown shell, and I held the creature out of the water. The long spike of a tail flapped back and forth; the many legs waved feebly.

"Awesome!" Tuba Man said. "I think that's the biggest one yet. Can I hold him?"

I passed the horseshoe crab back to him. His warm hand closed over mine for a second, and I pretended not to notice. *Maybe his way of dealing with things is best,* I thought. *If I can act like I don't care for long enough, maybe, eventually, it will be true.*

The next day we were on the road again, heading back to Damascus for Trail Days. I slept in the back of the Jeep for most of the way, waking occasionally for a view of gray concrete streaming past, or the hubcaps of a semi. Each time I woke, I wondered whether the past week had been another crazy dream. Only the tight, itchy pain of my sunburned back convinced me otherwise.

Isis

We drove into Damascus late Thursday afternoon. Three weeks earlier, we'd been surprised by the number of nobos filling The Place and crowding around the counter at M.R.O. The town's population seemed to have doubled since then; small groups of people gathered on every street corner, some wearing clean cotton shorts or summer dresses, others still carrying packs and hiking poles.

Tuba Man took one of the last two parking spaces next to the flower shop, and before we'd finished unloading our packs, a tiny white car pulled up beside him. A familiar, lanky figure unfolded from the driver's seat—Stitches! We introduced her to Tuba Man, and the four of us headed over to M.R.O.'s new hostel, where Steve and Jeff had promised to reserve us a room.

Even though jackrabbit and I were wearing sandals, "going incognito," we drew stares as we walked along Laurel Avenue. Strangers smiled and waved as we passed. Whispers rose up in our wake: *Do you think that's . . . ? Oh wow; I heard, but I didn't believe . . .* Our clothes had more tears and stains than most other nobos', our faces were dark tan from the winter's harsh sun (not to mention the past few days in Florida), and I carried hiking sticks the size of small trees. We'd been living in the woods for eleven months, and we looked it. Still, I wouldn't have thought that we stood out that much among the motley throng of hikers, hikers-to-be, and trail angels converging on Damascus for the weekend.

I turned to say something to Stitches, and discovered the source of the excitement. Tuba Man was most definitely not incognito. He was striding along behind us, his pack slung over his shoulder and his tuba cradled in one arm. He waved at the crowds with his free hand and flashed them a grin straight out of a toothpaste commercial. He seemed to revel in the steady stream of whispers and shy waves that his presence elicited. I smiled to myself as I ducked into the hostel. For once, the attention was focused on someone who was happy to accept it.

We spent a peaceful evening at the hostel, chatting with Stitches and listening to a private concert from Tuba Man. (After we went out for pizza at Quincy's, even he seemed to have had enough notoriety for the day.) Around nine, Nimblewill Nomad, the Eastern Continental Trail hiker who we'd met in Hanover, stopped in. He'd successfully completed his hike from Cape Gaspé to the Florida Keys, and he read us passages from his journal. With his long, rippling white beard, emaciated body, and shining eyes, he looked like a holy man just returned from a pilgrimage. He flung out his arms in expansive gestures, and his thin face glowed as he described wading through mangrove swamps in a hurricane on his way to the sea.

"We just finished the southern half of the E.C.T., too," jackrabbit told him, her eyes sparkling. "But we yellow-blazed from here to Florida. Man, I'd love to hike it someday."

"I dunno," said Tuba Man. "That much saltwater might be bad for Charisma. But the E.C.T., with a tuba—I bet that'd make a few headlines!"

Nimblewill Nomad caught his eye and winked. "I'm sure it would. I was the first person to hike the whole E.C.T., back in '98. And last year, I was the first to hike it southbound. The A.T.'s been hiked backwards and forwards, by a blind man and an eighty-year-old and a speed-hiker who averaged forty miles a day. The E.C.T., though, it's wide open ground." He turned to me and jackrabbit. "You two are pretty famous already, but if you were to hike the E.C.T. barefoot . . ."

"We haven't even hiked the whole A.T. barefoot," said jackrabbit, "and we already get more attention from strangers than I know what to do with."

I nodded my head in agreement. Both Tuba Man and Nimblewill Nomad stared at us, incredulous.

"But—they're not strangers," Nimblewill Nomad said finally. "They're people who love you."

All day Friday, hikers poured into town. We met Waterfall in the morning, and the three of us walked around town looking for other friends. Miss Janet's enormous cabin tent, under a banner reading "Trail Daze 2001 Luv Shack," proved to be a nexus for the current northbound crowd: we ran into Reid and Joel, Priceless, Toast, and Van-Go there. Around noon, we headed back to town in search of lunch. The two-block journey took us almost two hours. The streets and sidewalks were packed with people, and they all seemed to know us. Some were old friends—we stopped for half an hour on a street corner, talking with Ox the British sobo, and we shouted a greeting to P.A. Mule, an impassable half-block away from us. Others were acquaintances, people who we'd passed on the Trail or met once in a hostel. I struggled to remember their names, and when I couldn't, hoped that jackrabbit would speak first. Many people knew us only through rumor. I couldn't help wondering, as we introduced ourselves and answered their questions, whether we lived up to whatever expectations they had of the famous Barefoot Sisters. The press of people and the repeated questions reminded me of the White Mountains; I found myself longing for a stealth site hidden in swirling fog where we could make cocoa and read *Harry Potter* by flashlight.

The lunchtime crowd had cleared out a bit by the time we reached the Side Track Café. The small, cheery room seemed like a haven after the noisy streets. Miss Janet waved us over to the table she was sharing with Priceless and Tha Wookie. Highlander, who had spotted us from across the room, hurried over to join us. He had just hiked in; his worn pack sat in the corner with his Tilley hat perched on top of it. Waterfall leaned over and hugged him as he sat down.

"Oh, Highlander, you smell like a hiker," she sighed. "Y'all won't believe it, but I even miss that smell."

For the rest of the afternoon and most of the next morning, jackrabbit, Waterfall, and I hid in the flower shop, where the proprietor let us play the rickety upright piano in the corner. We made up elaborate choreography for "Dig a Hole" in preparation for the talent show. I bought some bandanas from M.R.O. and sewed Waterfall a skirt and halter top to match ours. When we had to cross town, we tried to find a back way, cutting through the alley between the hostel and the funeral parlor, or taking the Creeper Trail from Hobo Camp to the concession stands on the Green.

On one such excursion, jackrabbit and I crossed paths with Baltimore Jack, legendary for having hiked the Trail northbound five years in a row. I recognized him immediately—a middle-aged man with a few days' worth of salt-and-pepper stubble on his grizzled face, a cigarette dangling from the corner of his mouth, and a ratty black t-shirt with a single white blaze painted on it. I had heard that he was thru-hiking a sixth time this year. It didn't look like the trip was going very well, though; he had an air cast on one ankle and he walked with a pronounced limp.

"Hey, Jack," called jackrabbit. "How are you?"

We'd been introduced to him briefly, eight months earlier, at the bonfire at the Gathering. He had been drunk at the time, and he'd snapped something rude and then ignored us. I was afraid we'd get the same reaction this time, but instead he stopped and gave us a quizzical smile.

"Good morning," he said, squinting into the sunlight. "Do I know you ladies?"

"I'm Isis," I said.

"Jackrabbit."

"Oh," he answered, sounding a trifle disappointed. "You're the ones people call the Barefoot Sisters."

"Yes."

"How's your ankle?" jackrabbit asked him, trying to steer the conversation away from our feet.

His mouth turned down at the corners, in a grimace worthy of a Shakespearian actor.

"It's broken," he said, drawing out every syllable. Without waiting for a response, he turned and hobbled away in the direction of Hobo Camp.

Late that night, we ventured down to Hobo Camp ourselves. Pirate greeted us with heaping plates of venison, which Wee Willie was roasting over a campfire. The fresh meat smelled so good that we couldn't refuse. Even though we're usually vegetarians, we do eat organic meat or wild game every once in a while.

"It's outta a friend's freezer," Pirate said, sounding apologetic. "Shot it last fall. Most years we serve fresh roadkill, but we drove all over the county yesterday and couldn't find none."

"This tastes great to me," jackrabbit reassured him.

I looked around to see if I could spot Lone Wolf, but the shadows just beyond the firelight seemed to be full of broad-shouldered, bearded men. They were all gnawing on venison, swigging a clear liquid from unlabeled plastic milk jugs, and telling jokes and stories in voices the size of bass drums. Below their words, the river's steady murmur filled the darkness.

Suddenly, the high, clear tones of a violin vibrated through the night air, and all the men fell silent, their faces tilted toward the sound. I might have expected good bluegrass music out of that night, in that place, but after a few tuning notes, the invisible musician broke into Mendelssohn. (We knew it wasn't Fiddler; in town that afternoon, he'd lamented that he was still missing his A string.) The music swept through the hushed clearing, sharp as the stars glittering over us, resonant as the river's song. No one clapped when it ended, but a sigh rose from the audience, as if we had all set down our packs at once after a long day's hike. A pause, and then the bow leapt into the familiar strains of "Rockytop." A rich tenor voice joined in, and soon, half of the hikers in the clearing were singing along. An hour later, the chorus of "Shady Grove" followed us as we walked back over the bridge to town.

By Saturday afternoon, we'd gathered enough energy to face the crowds in the Trail Days Parade. It was easier than I'd expected to get through town; for once, everyone in the street was headed in the same direction. We met Sheltowee and P.A. Mule on the way over, and in the parking lot where the parade started, we found Highlander busy tying bandanas to the top of his hiking stick to make a banner. Basil wandered by handing out beers, with one leg of his pants rolled up to the ankle and the other rolled up above the knee. Miss Janet snapped pictures while her daughter Kaitlin dodged through the crowd, spraying everyone with a water gun. Fiddler walked by with a pack full of water balloons, which Joe was tossing indiscriminately into the crowd with loud laughter. The splash of cool water felt delicious in the heat of the day. Sharkbait hurried over to greet us, looking much more at home in the steamy parking lot than he had been in the frosty Virginia woods, where we'd last seen him. His bright blue nail polish and the matching turquoise necklace he wore over his bare chest fit right in with the gaudy costumes that hikers had made themselves for the parade. Tiny Tim had one of the best: he had cut open a Tyvek priority mail envelope and duct-taped it around his waist. He'd written *FRAGILE, HANDLE WITH CARE* on the front, with a somewhat suggestive drawing of a wine glass, and *PLEASE HOLD FOR A.T. THRU-HIKER* on the butt. A matching Tyvek bow tie, a pair of sandals and a two-foot-long green-and-orange Supersoaker completed the outfit.

Perhaps it was meeting so many old friends at once, or perhaps I'd finally gotten into the spirit of the event. When strangers lining the sidewalks pointed at our bare feet and shouted our names, I felt lifted by their voices, turned into someone flawless and glossy as a star on a magazine cover. It was the same feeling I'd had in high school plays, when the warmth of the lights and the sea of upturned faces in front of me completed my transformation from an unpopular, desperately shy child into a queen or a cabaret singer. Only this time, I was playing a role I had created: Isis the Barefoot Hiker. I waved and laughed, tossing my long hair over my shoulder so that it caught the sunlight. I knew what they were asking for, when they called my name—courage and craziness that broke through the boundaries of everyday life, beauty too rich for use. For once, I felt that I could give it to them, that I could embody the legend of myself.

That mood carried me through the talent show the next day, when jackrabbit, Waterfall, and I got up on stage in front of several hundred people, wearing our bandana skirts and halter tops, and sang "Dig a Hole." None of us had spectacular voices, and out of the corner of my eye, I could see our attempted choreography falling apart. Still, we belted out the verses, feeling the audience's laughter tumble over us like confetti with every joke in the lyrics. On the choruses, a hundred voices joined ours, and at the last verse, when we linked arms and swayed back and forth on the stage, the whole front row got up and swayed with us. Afterward, the applause buoyed us down the stairs and followed us in sporadic bursts as we skipped across the Green. Just as we reached the place where Miss Janet had saved seats for us, a surge of clapping greeted the next performer. I sank down on the grass, grateful to have felt the full force of the crowd's enthusiasm, but even more grateful to be able to pass it on to someone else.

Some of the acts that followed—semiprofessional bluegrass bands and clear-voiced singer/songwriters whose lyrics evoked the beauty of the mountains—made ours look like an eighth-grade play. The mysterious violinist from Hobo Camp, a young northbound woman who, rumor had it, was preparing for a recital in Carnegie Hall, took an easy first place with a wild fiddle rendition of a local folk song. There was a time, not long past, when I would have been humiliated to discover that I had pitted my weak voice against the talents of real musicians. Now I didn't care if I'd made a fool of myself in front of hundreds of people. I'd given them five minutes' entertainment, and they'd responded as generously as if I'd been a famous comedian. In the end, we even won something: seventh place, which included a hammock, two hats, and a stuff sack.

As the audience drifted apart, back to tents and concession stands, a slightly built man whose neatly combed gray hair and spotless clothing contrasted with the general hiker aesthetic, fell into step beside me.

"Thank you for your song," he said, his eyes sparkling behind small oval glasses. "That was quite clever."

"Thanks," I answered.

There was something familiar about his clean-shaven face, round and smooth as a boy's, but I was sure I hadn't met him on the Trail. In fact, he didn't look like he'd ever *been* on the Trail. Far too tidy. Maybe he was a prospective hiker, who'd come to Trail Days to pick up a few practical hints about fulfilling a long-held dream. I wondered whether anyone had warned him about the hygiene situation.

"Are you hiking now?" he asked me.

"Yes, my sister and I are on the northbound leg of a yo-yo."

He nodded; apparently, he'd spent enough time in the Trail community to understand the nomenclature.

"And you?" I asked. I was pretty sure I knew the answer, but I didn't want to insult him if, by some odd chance, he was a hiker.

"I hiked southbound last year," he said.

A 2000 sobo? Even if I'd never met him, I should have seen his photo at Harpers Ferry or in one of Rusty's albums.

"My son and I hiked together," the man continued. "He's up in a tree somewhere, but I expect he'd be interested to meet you when he comes down."

"Pilgrim?" I asked, hardly daring to believe it. "And Gollum's here too?"

Jackrabbit turned around. "Pilgrim? Sobo 2000? This is awesome! I never thought we'd get to meet you! Where's Gollum?"

Pilgrim looked somewhat taken aback by our enthusiasm, but he led us over to an oak at the end of the Green. A young man with a thick beard and long, wavy brown hair sat on a branch eight or ten feet above the ground, drinking a cup of lemonade. When Pilgrim waved to him, he swung down and landed in front of us without spilling his drink. He wiped a hand on his shorts and held it out to me.

"Wow! Gollum! You and your dad were such an inspiration to us," I said, taking his hand. "We read your register entries all the way down the Trail!"

"Yeah, those riddles you wrote in the Hundred Mile Wilderness—" jackrabbit began.

"And that time in Shenandoah, when you packed in apples and honey for Rosh Hashanah, and wrote a prayer for peace in the Middle East—"

"And Christmas! We found one of your registers in Jenkins Shelter, where we stayed on Christmas Eve. We were hiking alone at the time, and it was like spending the evening with old friends."

"We've wanted to meet you ever since Maine," I said, "but as soon as you started pulling thirties, we realized we'd never catch up."

"Yes, well, it's good to meet you," said Pilgrim. "We promised a friend we'd be at the Side Track in half an hour, so we'd better head over there."

"I'd love to talk with you some more," I blurted out. "Is there any chance we could meet for breakfast?"

"I'm afraid we already have plans for breakfast. Good luck with the rest of your hike!"

As Pilgrim and Gollum walked off, I realized that I had reacted to them the same way so many strangers had reacted to us. They didn't owe us their time in return for our admiration. I may have spent months following their register entries, but they didn't know me from Eve. We were fans, not friends, of theirs.

The next morning, I found a note slipped under our door, in Pilgrim's fine handwriting. *Gollum and I will be at the Side Track for breakfast at nine. We would love to meet you there, if the time is convenient.* At the bottom of the page, there was a post script: *My wife just mailed me the Jenkins Shelter register. It must have arrived right after we left home. We very much enjoyed your Santa Claus poem.*

I nudged the half-asleep jackrabbit. "Look at this! Pilgrim and Gollum want to meet us after all! Your Christmas poem reached them just in time!"

As we put on our town clothes and packed up our sleeping bags, I vowed to be more patient with the strangers who knew us through rumors and registers. To answer their questions, but also, to give them a chance to become friends.

After breakfast, we headed to Carvers Gap to join a work trip that Bob Peoples had organized, repairing the eroded trail through the Roans. Lash, who had gotten to Trail Days just in time for the talent contest, gave us a ride down. As he navigated the mountain passes in a morning thunderstorm, he told us about his life since the Trail. He'd moved in with his family and worked odd jobs, still doing his best to avoid putting his business degree to use.

"I don't know if I'll ever be fit for life off-trail," he told us. "Like, for instance, the bathroom's just down the hall, but at night I still pee in a bottle."

"Lash!" jackrabbit sounded scandalized. "You lazy bum."

Lash blushed even redder than usual, and quickly changed the subject. "Did you all ever see the Family again, after the Smokies?"

"No, did you?" jackrabbit asked him.

"Yeah, I visited them last winter. They were staying in a cabin somebody had lent them in exchange for Paul doing some carpentry. Down in Georgia, near Springer."

"Do you think they're still there?" I asked. *So close*—I was already trying to figure out a way we could get there, if I could persuade jackrabbit to take a few days off to see them one more time.

"No," Lash answered. "They were just staying through the winter, working so they could save up and move on. They kept talking about going back to the island where Paul and Mary met—somewhere in the Carribean, I think."

"I wonder how they'll get there, with no I.D.s," jackrabbit mused.

"I don't know," I answered, "but I bet they will. When they make up their minds to something, I doubt even an ocean could stand in their way."

We met Bob, Highlander, and Forest Phil on Jane Bald, along with half a dozen other volunteers. All afternoon we heaved buckets of gravel up the hill, spread them over the trail, and moved rocks into place to form water bars and shore up the embankments.

Jackrabbit ended up next to Forest Phil on the bucket chain, and the bad joke war that ensued kept us all entertained through the heat of the day.

"Nice buckets, jack . . . rabbit."

"Thanks, Forest Philanderer. Buckit!" she exclaimed as she dropped one.

By sundown, we had moved another ten piles of gravel—again, almost two tons per person. We gathered around the Jane Bald sign, making muscle poses, while Bob took group photos. Then we drove back to Kincora for supper: lasagna, salad, and garlic bread courtesy of Baltimore Jack. His stress fracture had prevented him from joining the work trip, so he'd spent the day cooking for us. The lasagna had a few minutes to bake when we arrived, so I offered to whip up some gingerbread for desert.

Jack stood at the counter, pulling what looked like quarters of onions out of the salad bowl, slicing them finely, and then putting them back in.

"Let me ask you something," he said, holding up a large chunk. "Is this the size of onion you would want to find in your salad?" Without waiting for an answer, he shook his head and put the onion down on his cutting board.

"People want to help you, and you can't really refuse," he continued. "But most kids these days don't know the first thing about a kitchen." He looked up at me sharply. "What are *you* doing here?"

"Making gingerbread. I hope I won't be in your way."

"You know how to cook? Well, then, you can't be all bad."

"Funny, that's just what I was thinking about you," I said. It was true; the delicious, complex aroma of his lasagna cooking had almost made me forget that this was a man who'd been gratuitously rude to me the first time I met him.

He cracked a smile. "You're sharp, too. I'd almost like you, if it weren't for the barefoot thing."

"What's wrong with going barefoot?" I asked.

"Publicity stunt," he spat. "Using the Trail to make yourself famous. You oughta hike the Trail for the Trail's sake, not for any record book. It's sacrilege to use it that way."

I laughed. "If we were doing this for a record, we would have given up in November, when we hit our first ice storm. We hike barefoot because we like to. We grew up doing it. I didn't expect the publicity. To tell the truth, I'm not very comfortable with it most of the time."

"Well, then. I guess I'll think better of you. If your gingerbread's edible."

Kincora was even more crowded than it had been when we hiked through a month earlier. Along with the members of the work crew, there were eight or ten nobos, a few section hikers, and some old friends of Bob's staying there for the Trail Days weekend. Luckily, Baltimore Jack had made enough food to go around. I heaped my plate with veggie lasagna and salad, then sat down on the porch swing next to a slender, slightly built black man who had just hiked in. His pack, which rested against the rail beside him, looked almost as big as mine had been in winter. Once we'd both had time to take the edge off our hiker appetites, I introduced myself.

"I'm Patch," he said. "It's a pleasure to meet you."

"Patch?" I asked. "How'd you get your trail name?"

"I gave it to myself. When I started at Springer, I was carrying ninety-one pounds." *Ninety-one pounds?* Fifteen pounds more than I'd carried for the longest resupply of the winter. Patch looked like *he* weighed only a hundred and ten or a hundred and twenty.

"My family made me promise to carry all the food I needed for the first month," he continued, "because they were worried about me hiking through Georgia alone. They didn't want me to have to hitch into towns there. In my first few weeks on the Trail, a lot of people wanted to name me for my pack weight. Box Turtle, or Heavy Duty." He laughed. "I didn't keep those names, because I didn't think pack weight was the defining factor in my journey. I carry what I need to, what I can. I don't think about it very much.

"One evening, I hiked up to Max Patch right at sunset. I felt like I was standing at the heart of the Earth, with the full moon rising in the east and the hills all around the horizon brown and golden. I set up my tent there, and I stayed all the next day, just to see the sunset again. I named myself Patch after Max Patch, because that's what I want to remember about the Trail. It's the most beautiful place I've ever lived. I don't think I'd get tired of it if I spent my life out here."

"I know what you mean," I told him. "My sister and I are yo-yoing, because we couldn't get enough of it in one hike." I gestured to jackrabbit, who had just sat down on the other side of me with a second plateful of food.

"So, you've hiked the whole Trail already? You must have some wonderful stories," Patch said.

We spent the rest of the evening recounting the highlights of our southbound hike, in answer to Patch's questions. His eyes lit up when I described Max Patch in winter, with ribbons of ice rime clinging to the blackberry canes. I would have guessed that his age was somewhere between eighteen and twenty, but he looked even younger when he smiled. He had a sense of wonder that few people keep beyond the age of ten—it reminded me of John from the Family.

After we told him about the blizzard on Grayson, he shook his head slowly. "You're some of the strongest women I've ever met," he said softly. "If I ever have daughters, I hope they'll be just like you."

It seemed like a strange thing for someone so young to say, but it was also one of the most generous compliments I'd ever received.

"Thank you," I said.

jackrabbit

Bookworm, a '99 hiker who we had met on the work trip after Trail Days, drove us back to the Woods' Hole Hostel. The forest was a darker shade of green now, lush and summery, but flame azaleas and rhododendrons still gleamed among the low branches, pink, red, yellow, and purple. Little streams, swollen with gold-brown water, were carving new ruts in the gravel roads. The sky darkened as we drove. When we piled out of the car on the lawn in front of the hostel, stretching our cramped legs, we could see thunderheads towering over the ridge between us and Pearisburg. The air had a prickly, damp weight.

"That sky doesn't look too friendly," Bookworm said. "You might want to hunker down here for the day."

"We were planning to meet Walrus and Roots in Pearisburg tonight, though," I said. "I don't know if there's any way to get a message through."

The hostel was a converted barn with a front porch of silver-weathered wood, across the lawn from a red-roofed log cabin. Several hikers sat on the porch, watching the approaching storm, and there was evidence of many more: food bags, packs, rain gear, and clothing hung from every possible surface, drying out.

A slender woman in a green apron came out onto the porch of the house. She had a halo of curly white hair. "Hello there," she called to us. "Welcome to Woods' Hole. I'm Tillie Woods. Are y'all the Barefoot Sisters?"

"Yes," Isis told her.

"I've got a message for y'all. A man by the name of Walrus called up. He says y'all shouldn't hike today; there's s'posed to be bad storms." She looked up at the sky, which was turning a strange purple color over the clearing. "I'm inclined to agree with that." She smiled. "Make yourselves at home."

"Thanks," Isis said.

We moved our packs inside, claimed bunk space in the loft, and went back out to the porch. I could see a gray wedge of rain extending down from the underside of the nearest anvil-shaped cloud. It advanced over the mountain, rapidly obscuring the view behind it. Lightning lanced out. Then came a sudden close rumble of thunder, and the clatter of rain on the leaves. In a moment, the air was so thick with falling water that we couldn't see the other side of the clearing.

A few minutes after the rain began, two more hikers, both young women, came to the hostel. The older one wore a purple shirt and bright red and yellow sarong, now plastered down with rain, and the younger one had more typical hiker apparel: khaki shorts and a gray tank top. Both of them had dark brown hair, curling in the dampness, and gray eyes, and remarkably similar happy-go-lucky smiles.

"Are you guys sisters?" I asked.

"Yeah," the older one said, beaming. "I'm Wood Nymph."

"And I'm Sarah." She was younger than I had thought, probably still in high school. "I'm not really hiking the Trail. I just came out for a week to spend time with Amanda. Wood Nymph." It sounded like she was still getting used to her sister's trail name.

"Awesome. It's good to see other sisters out here," I told her.

"This rain is crazy," Isis said. The sky had turned a shade darker, and the hammering on the roof intensified.

Wood Nymph rolled her eyes. "Tell me about it! Of course, it's been like this for two solid weeks."

"We were off-trail," I said, a bit guilty. "We had . . . kind of a vacation. Then we went to Trail Days."

She gave a rueful smile. "You picked the best time to miss."

When the storm had passed, I put on my rain jacket against the lingering drizzle and went to get water from the pump in the yard. For once, I didn't need to use the filter—it came straight from Tillie's well, pure and sweet and cold. I collected Zip stove wood from the edges of the clearing, peeling the wet bark off the twigs so they would burn.

Isis and I cooked dinner on the porch with Wood Nymph and Sarah. The clouds passed over, leaving a smudgy red sunset. Sarah looked up from the stack of photocopied papers she had been studying. "It's just not fair. I told all my teachers I wouldn't have time to do this while I'm hiking. I *said* I'd make it up when I got back. And they *still* gave me all this stuff. I have, like, six problem sets from Mr. Miyares, and a three-page paper for Ms. Leamon—"

"Wait a minute," I said. "John Miyares? The bane of all pre-cal students? Becky Leamon, the most awesome teacher to ever walk the halls of—"

"MDIHS," we finished together. Mount Desert Island High School, the public school of perhaps five hundred kids, where Isis and I had both graduated.

"No way," Wood Nymph said. "I went there too. I heard a rumor you guys were from Maine, but nobody said exactly where. So you guys are really from the Island?"

"Yeah," I said. "We grew up in Southwest Harbor. Our parents are divorced now, but they both still live on the Island."

"No way! That's so crazy. What are the chances of four MDI kids meeting up in the middle of Virginia?"

"Miyares would probably want me to calculate it," Sarah said, a bit sourly, as she flipped to the next page.

"What year did you guys graduate?" Wood Nymph asked.

"Ninety-five," I said.

"Ninety-four," Isis told her. "We're old."

"You might have met our little sister Claire, though. She graduated last year."

"Claire, with the really long hair? No way! I sat next to her in physics!"

We stayed on the porch until dusk settled, reminiscing about Island life. The Trail had brought us many bizarre coincidences, but this was one of the strangest yet.

Tillie served a magnificent breakfast the next morning: eggs, sausage for the meat-eaters, fruit salad, biscuits, and little crystal bowls of homemade raspberry jam. While we ate, she told us how the hostel had started. "My husband, Charlie, found this little cabin in the forties. He was a wildlife biologist. He studied elk."

"Up in the North?" someone asked her.

"Oh, no! Right here in these mountains. You'd hardly believe it now, but there used to be a good number of elk here. Disease got them, and overhunting. But Charlie always loved this place. He said, 'Tillie, when I retire, let's move to that little cabin up by Sugar Run Gap.' And that's exactly what we did.

"He fixed up the house and the barn. Both of them are prob'ly more than a hundred years old—all these beams are chestnut." She patted one of the sturdy house timbers. "We had the first hikers here in 1970, I think it was. A couple of young men passing through. They asked if they could stay in the barn, and we said, 'Well, sure.' After that, it seemed like more and more people found the place. We didn't much use the barn for hay anymore, so we decided to just turn it into a hostel. More biscuits, anyone?" She handed the basket around.

"When Charlie passed away a few years ago, I decided I'd keep the place running. I guess it's helped me, in a way, to have some kind of continuity. You know, every year the gear's different, and the names are different, but hikers are pretty much the same."

Bookworm took our packs down to Pearisburg in the morning so we could slack the ten miles into town. It was a clear day, with soft sunlight coming through the wet leaves. Tiny streams had swollen to brooks; springs near the trail gushed with golden water. Flame azaleas still glimmered red and gold and orange in the underbrush on the highest ridges, though their petals were beginning to fade. Rhododendrons scattered the fat pink cones of their blossoms across the trail. Tillie had told us that it wasn't a particularly good year for the "rhodies." I had no standard of comparison, though, and it seemed like a pretty good year to me. At least every other rhododendron bush sent up extravagant clusters of blooms, almost hiding the slick green leaves. On Angel's Rest, above the valley of the New River and the town of Pearisburg, the woods glowed pink with their fragile blossoms.

We stopped for a drink of water, looking down through the trees. By the river, the colors of summer softened the harsh grid of gray streets in town. Ranks of miniature houses, schools, and shopping malls stood among the green fields and trees, perfected by distance and the mellow, forgiving light. Even the factory, with its plumes of steam and smoke, its cylindrical tanks and coils of pipe, looked almost beautiful through the leaves and flowers on the ridge. I remembered hiking out of Pearisburg in winter, topless, and I laughed to myself. I wondered where we would be for Summer Solstice, the proper Naked Hiking Day. *As long as it's not a state park on a weekend*, I decided, *we'll probably be fine.*

Walrus and Roots met us at the road, smiling like proud parents. "It's so great to see you guys again!" Roots caught us both in a hug.

"Great to see *you!*" I said.

"After that winter, you guys have got guts to turn around and hike back," Walrus said. "I'll never forget that little voice on the phone: 'Hello. Walrus?'" He laughed. "I'm glad you guys thought to call us."

"I'm glad, too," I said. "I don't know what we would have done without you."

They took us to the supermarket to resupply, and then cooked an excellent spaghetti dinner. Isis made a large batch of cookies—some for our hosts, and some to carry with us. Over the afternoon and evening, we told Walrus and Roots about our adventures since December. It was hard to believe all that had happened in that time, from our reunion with the Family to our Florida trip.

"Life's good on the Trail," Walrus said. "When the kids finish college, and we get some money together, we might just head back out there."

We called Playfoot that night, since he lived nearby. "How about we meet for breakfast at Gillie's?" he said.

I checked with Walrus and Roots. "Sounds great," I told him. I had fond memories of the breakfast I'd eaten there in winter. "Nine o'clock?"

"Excellent."

After supper, Walrus showed us his collection of A.T. memorabilia: photos and newspaper articles, a walking stick that a friend had carved for him, and a set of *Data Books* for 1995–2001.

I picked up one of the data books. "These things must be pretty useful," I said. "We've always gotten by with just maps, but I can see how this would come in handy for long-range planning."

"Oh, you can have it," Walrus told me.

"No, you're too generous! You need it for your collection."

"Take it," he insisted. "It would make me happier to know that it was being used out on the Trail."

"Thanks," I said, touched by his generosity. I took the last book in the set and stowed it carefully in my pack, in the Ziploc that held my journal and a few other sheets of paper. "I'm sure it will come in handy." I was already planning how I could use it, calculating our mileages and setting goals for the rest of the Trail. Maybe we would finish by September after all.

Breakfast at Gillie's was as good as I remembered. We got a table by the window. Playfoot came in a few minutes late, in high spirits. "I drove by to see my house site on the way here," he said as he slid into his seat. "I just couldn't resist. It's going to be such an awesome place. You've got to see it!" He ordered two eggs over easy, hash browns, and toast. "Hey, are you guys interested in slacking today?"

"Slacking?" Isis asked. "Have you got time?"

"Well, I'm doing contract work right now. Computer stuff. I just finished up a big project last night, so I'm due for a day off. I could take you guys out to Route 635, maybe. It's, like, twenty miles."

I looked over at Walrus. "Karen's got to work the night shift today," he said reluctantly. "And I've got to be at work early tomorrow. I'd love to have you stay again, but I don't know."

"There's a hostel in Pearisburg," Playfoot offered. "It's a four dollar dona-tion. I stayed there southbound. The guy who runs it can be a little, well, gruff, but he's okay."

The waitress came over. "More coffee, anybody?" She looked at me and Isis. "I have to ask. Are y'all the Barefoot Sisters?"

My jaw dropped. Blacksburg wasn't a Trail town at all; we were probably thirty miles from the A.T. corridor. "Yes, we are," I told her when I could talk again. "But how in the world did you know about us?"

She smiled. "I heard of y'all when I hiked a section down in Georgia this spring. Apparently I was just a few days behind y'all. When I saw all y'all coming in here this morning, I thought, well, those two look like hikers. And they look like sisters. Then I noticed—" she pointed to our sandaled feet "—y'all don't have a sock tan." She poured coffee for everyone. "I just wanted to say, good luck to y'all. Have a great hike."

"Thanks," I said, still blinking in astonishment.

We hugged Walrus and Roots goodbye and climbed into the Trail Magic Jeep. Playfoot was planning to drop us off at Route 635 and take our gear to the Pearisburg Hostel so we could slack. Before we started, he showed us the site of his new house. He turned onto a narrow, winding road at the outskirts of Blacksburg, through fields and small patches of woods. Subdivisions were springing up all around, cul-de-sacs and carefully managed lawns encroaching on the small amount of remaining undeveloped land. He stopped where the road became a muddy gravel track leading into a larger patch of woods. I could hear the sound of heavy equipment in the forest.

"Hey, they're digging my basement!" Playfoot said. "Come on, let's check it out!"

Back under the trees, the air felt cool and damp. The dappled green light between the branches made a soothing contrast to the heat of the late May morning and the glare of the open fields. It seemed like a much better place for a house than a flat acre of open sod.

Playfoot showed us the cellar hole, a pit of red earth where a backhoe labored. "They only had to take down twelve trees for the house," he said over the engine sound. "I sent them to a sawmill. I'll use them for trim."

We walked around the woods and fields, and Playfoot pointed out where all the houses and the community center would eventually stand. "And the rest of the woods will be a park." From the field, we could see that the stand of woods stretched back for a long ways. "More than ten acres. Most places would just subdivide it and put up a house on each lot. We figured, why not put the houses closer together and save the woods?"

Playfoot dropped us off at the trailhead in late morning. We had twenty miles to cover, so we put on our sandals to move fast. It was another clear day, with a lively wind over the ridges. Enormous cumulus clouds soared past overhead, their shadows racing across the valleys. Up on the ridge, the fields and power line cuts were full of early summer flowers: buttercups and daisies, Indian paintbrush, and a host of others I couldn't name. In one field, a herd of spotted cattle grazed.

Slacking south, we passed droves of northbounders—apparently "the wave," the huge crowd that had started in early April, had caught up with us in the two weeks we'd been off-trail. Isis handed out cookies to nearly twenty hikers before her supply ran out. One thing was odd about this crowd of northbounders: many of the men wore skirts. Sarongs, precisely; brightly-colored wraps like the one Wood Nymph had worn. I had seen a booth selling them at Trail Days. I wondered why the men, and not the women, had picked up this particular fashion.

Another pair of young men in skirts came up the trail. After a brief round of introductions, I decided to ask them. "I think I've seen more men than women in skirts today. What's up with that?"

The taller one gave a toothy grin. "No chafing. I wore shorts for the first 450 miles. This is *so* much better."

The other one snickered, just audibly. "Free Willy."

Isis

As we hiked down the last long hillside to Pearisburg, the stench of the Celanese factory rose to meet us. A sound like a distant, endless shriek of metal scraping over metal accompanied the nauseating, sour-sweet odor. Perhaps it was some chemical in the air, or perhaps it was simply the power of suggestion, but my head began throbbing, and I had a hard time keeping my balance on the rocks. I remembered a long detour through PUDs at the bottom of this valley; we had four or five miles to go, all within smelling and hearing distance of the plant. Perhaps we could blue-blaze around it with a road walk. I stopped to check the map, and jackrabbit, who'd been hiking behind me, sank down on a rock. She looked even worse than I felt. Her face was white and clammy, and her breath came in short gasps.

"It's that smell," she said, noticing my worried expression. "I feel like I can't breathe."

"It's bothering me, too," I said. "Look at this, though. There's a road at the bottom of the hill, and if we walk into town on that, instead of following the Trail, we can cut two and a half miles from our hike."

She gave me a weak smile. "Blue-blazing has never looked better."

We'd barely walked a quarter of a mile down the road when a truck pulled up beside us. A huge blue pickup truck with Confederate flags waving from every corner, and more, in the form of bumper stickers, taped to the windows. Heald's warnings about Southern rednecks flashed through my mind. I thought of Patch, who had carried ninety pounds from Springer to Fontana in order to avoid going into towns. I was glad it was me, and not him, walking down this small mountain road in the dusk.

The man who stepped out of the driver's seat didn't fit my stereotype of a redneck, though. He wore a clean pair of jeans with a button-down shirt, and his silver hair was neatly combed in a wave across his forehead.

"May I offer you ladies a ride to town?" he asked, his voice full of friendly concern.

I hesitated for a minute. This would constitute yellow-blazing, a sort of infidelity to the Trail which we'd never really approved of. Besides, there were those Confederate flags—a symbol I equated with racism and possibly, also, a lack of tolerance for independent women. The man didn't sound intolerant, though. One look at jackrabbit's pale, sweaty face convinced me that this was a good time to trust a stranger.

He helped us swing our packs into the back of the pickup, then asked where in town we wanted to go.

"The supermarket would be good," I said. "We're headed to the hostel eventually, but I have to pick up something for supper." *Please*, I thought, *let him offer to wait for us while we buy our groceries. It's getting dark, and it might be hard to get another hitch.*

"I was planning to go to Pizza Hut for supper," he answered. "If y'all would care to join me, I could drive you to the hostel after that."

I looked over at jackrabbit. The color was already returning to her cheeks; it looked like just sitting down had done worlds for her.

"That sounds great," she said. "Thank you."

The three of us had just stepped into the restaurant when two hikers hurried over to greet us—a slender, muscular blond woman with a sparkling smile and tall black man whose hair was graying a little at the temples. They introduced themselves as Slow and Steady, a couple hiking the Trail to celebrate their tenth wedding anniversary.

"You must be Isis and jackrabbit," Slow said. "We heard all about you from the Stage Crew; we hiked with them for a week."

"Are you staying at the hostel tonight?" asked Steady.

"Yes," I told him. "This gentleman has offered to give us a ride up there." My heart in my throat, I introduced him to our benefactor.

"I'd be glad to give y'all a lift, too, if you could join us for supper," said the man who I'd pegged for a redneck, shaking Steady's hand. "My treat."

jackrabbit

I woke to the sound of rain drumming steadily on the roof. I was sorely tempted to turn over, go back to sleep, and write off the whole idea of hiking. Then I remembered the signs posted around the hostel. On the door: *Attention Hikers: One Night Only!* Above the kitchen sink: *One night—you're welcome here. Two nights—you're pushing your luck. Try for three—I'll throw you out.* We had heard rumors about Bill, the hostel manager. Some hikers said he was brusque to the point of rudeness; others said he was really a nice guy as long as you didn't get on his bad side. Either way, I decided, it would be better to hike out in the rain than to risk his wrath.

"Good morning, hikers!" came a great bellow of a voice from the front door. I rolled out of my bunk, yawning, put my glasses on, and went to see who it was. A huge, broad-shouldered man with graying hair stood in the doorway. Isis and the few other hikers already in the common room gave somewhat subdued greetings. "I'm Bill, the hostel manager. Let me know if you need anything. I run shuttles for a buck a mile out of town, two bucks a pop to the mall in town." He seemed cheerful enough.

Isis and I exchanged a glance. We needed to get back to the road crossing where Playfoot had dropped us off the day before. Bill's shuttle price was reasonable, and it would certainly beat trying to hitch in the rain.

"Can you take us to 635?" Isis asked him.

"Who's us?" he rumbled.

"Me and my sister."

"I suppose I could do that. Get your stuff ready in half an hour." His tone of voice didn't invite discussion.

"Sure. Thanks," Isis said. We scrambled to eat breakfast and pack in time. The rain was still pounding on the roof, sheeting down from the eaves, when we came out on the front lawn of the hostel. Bill's pickup stood in the driveway.

He rolled the window down. "You're late. Get in."

"Uh, sorry," Isis said, a bit tentatively, as we loaded our packs in back and settled into the front seat.

Bill waved it away. "Only a couple minutes late. Down, Buster!"

I noticed the tiny dog, some kind of short-haired terrier, a moment before it launched itself at me, stuck its wet nose in my ear, and started licking my face. Then it bounced away, rocketing around the inside of the cab like a charged particle, yipping vociferously. The dog seemed like the antithesis of Bill: where he was slow-moving, deliberate, stolid, the animal was frenetic.

"Buster's coming along for the ride," Bill said. "I hate to leave him home alone."

It was a quick ride to the trailhead, the rain-soaked pastures and forests sliding past. I asked Bill how long he'd been helping out at the hostel.

"Oh, I've been volunteering there since the beginning, helping keep the place clean, shuttling people around and all that. It started out in the church basement, in the seventies. Then they built the new place, about ten years ago. Seems like recently, we've had a real problem with freeloaders. Moochers. Down, Buster!" The dog gave another fit of high-pitched barking and jumped around the cab, eventually coming to rest behind Bill's seat. "Hikers would come in and stay for a week, without helping clean up or anything. We never used to ask for donations, but now we have to, on account of those few bad apples."

He turned onto the narrow, winding lane that led up the ridge to the trailhead. "A couple times, we almost had to close the place down. This spring, we had a rowdy bunch of idiots who got drunk, made a lot of noise. The neighbors had to call the police on them."

"That's too bad," I said. "I think some hikers just get this sense that while they're on the Trail, the normal rules of society don't apply to them any more."

"Yeah. Inconsiderate is what it is. Especially since we have a no-alcohol policy. That's why we put in the one night only rule, too. Seems like it's the people who stick around in town that cause the trouble."

He stopped in a little gravel parking lot. I could see a white blaze on a tree across the road. It was still pouring. "Here you are."

We put on our rain gear, picked up our hiking sticks, and fastened our pack straps. Bill regarded us for a moment with something like pity. "You know, if I was you, I would have stayed at the hostel today. I can suspend the rules for weather like this."

The rain continued all day, a constant gray curtain cascading out of the sky. It tapped and plinked on the new leaves and pounded on the muddy ground, making a stream six inches deep over the trail. It was a cold rain, too, especially cold for this time of year. After the first half hour, my feet and hands felt numb and spongy. The gray skies and the endless rain wore me down, frazzling my nerves. *I hate rain even more than I hated snow*, I thought. *At least snow was beautiful.*

"Oh, isn't this lovely!" Isis pointed to a stand of mountain laurels. Water dripped from their glossy green leaves and clusters of pink-lined flowers in the dull gray light. And it *was* lovely, I had to admit, but instead of feeling grateful to my sister for pointing it out, I only felt a vague resentment: *She enjoys the world more than I do. Too damn bad for me.*

The rain cleared toward evening. The sky lightened by degrees, and I felt better and better as wisps of blue appeared among the clouds. As the sun went down, shafts of rich amber light came between the trees, catching the mist that rose from the ground. I began to notice the brilliant colors of azaleas and rhododendrons, the detail in the pale blossoms of laurel. It was amazing, I reflected, how closely my mood was tied to changes in the weather; darkness and rain left me moping, while sunshine—usually—could lift me out of a funk. The time we had spent on the Trail, more than eleven months now, had only deepened this sensitivity.

We smelled wood smoke, and a few minutes later War Spur Shelter came into view. There were seven or eight hikers in the clearing, sitting around a low fire. I recognized some of the people we had met on our slack the day before, and Wood Nymph waved from the picnic table. Someone had strung a clothesline between two trees. Brightly colored sarongs, orange, yellow, blue, and green, steamed where the last rays of sun hit them.

"Hey, ladies," Wood Nymph said. "Have you met these guys? Hobo and Chad and Timberghost?"

"Didn't we meet you yesterday?" I said. "You were the guys in skirts."

"Yeah, we met you," the youngest of the hikers said. He had shoulder-length brown hair and a short beard, and a blue bandana tied across his forehead. "You gave us cookies! I'm Hobo. It's good to see you again."

"I'm Chad." He was probably in his mid-thirties, with short blond hair and a rascally grin. "No trail name yet."

"Timberghost," the other hiker said. He was still wearing his blue sarong. He had short dark hair and a serious, lean, tanned face.

"How'd you get that name?" I asked him.

"Oh, these fellers gave it to me. It's 'cause I like to hike pretty fast. I get in the woods, timber, you know, and I'm gone like a ghost." His blue eyes lit up with a smile.

I set up our tent at the edge of the clearing, hung my sopping rain gear on one end of the clothesline, and went to the spring. I could have gotten water almost anywhere—it was still running four inches deep in parts of the trail—but I used the official water source by force of habit.

Isis, Hobo, and Chad were cooking dinner when I returned; Timberghost munched on dry ramen and took a few sips from his water bottle to wash it down.

"Dude, a stove isn't too much extra weight," Chad told him.

Timberghost shrugged. "I've come more'n six hundred miles without it."

I had heard of hikers following the no-cook plan, but I had never met one before. "Don't you ever miss hot food?" I asked.

"I git plenty of hot food in town," he said.

"But on a night like this, when you've been cold and wet all day, doesn't it, I mean, don't you . . ."

"I guess I do miss it on occasion," he said. "But I don't miss it enough to make me add onto my pack weight."

"That's kind of the opposite of our approach," Isis said. "We've always been heavy—pun intended—on comfort."

I searched the clearing for firewood, managing to find a few dead branches that had caught in other trees as they fell, leaving them drier than the soaked wood on the forest floor. I broke them into reasonable lengths, dumped them in a pile on the ground, and sat down by the firepit, hoping to dry out a little before the chill of evening fell. I began taking the bark off some smaller twigs and breaking them up so Isis could use them for the Zip stove.

"Hi, I'm jackrabbit," I said to the man next to me. He was short and stocky, with a blond crew cut, and he wore a ripped cotton t-shirt, jeans, and heavy construction boots—an unusual costume for a hiker. His outfit reminded me of Mohawk Joe, Heald's fall hiking companion. Maybe this was another guy who had "fallen off a barstool and onto the Trail."

I waited. The guy didn't say anything. He stared into the ashes with a slightly disturbing intensity.

"What's your trail name?" I asked him.

"Fuck!" he said suddenly, in the manner of someone who has forgotten something vital. He jumped up and went to the shelter, where he dug into his olive green army surplus pack. That pack was another strange detail—the last time I had seen one like that was at Neel's Gap, where one of the starting nobos had discarded it with a curse and bought a brand-new Gregory. "Those damn army things are the least comfortable packs in creation," the salesman had told me. I wondered how anyone could have gotten this far with one of them.

The blond guy returned with a thick metal saucepan and some food. He scooped water out of a puddle in the trail and set the pan on the coals. When it began to steam and bubble, he dumped in at least a pound of macaroni.

"Are you northbound?" I asked him.

He grunted a negative.

"A *southbounder*? When'd you start?"

"April. New York. Fuck!" His pasta was boiling over. He grabbed a stick from the pile of firewood and stirred the noodles. Little bits of bark came off in his food. He wrapped his hand in a handkerchief, grabbed the pot, and poured off most of the water into the firepit. Steam rose up, the coals died back. He opened a can—*a full-sized can!*—of tomato sauce and poured it over the half-cooked noodles.

"Supper's ready, jackrabbit," Isis called.

Our hiker appetites weren't quite as strong as usual, given all the time we had taken off around Trail Days. About halfway through the pot of rice and beans, my stomach felt uncomfortably full. Isis, too, moved her spoon at half speed, and finally both spoons came to rest on the edge of the pot.

"I've lost my superpowers," I said. "I can't eat any more."

"Me either," Isis conceded. "Does anybody want some rice and beans?"

Hobo, Chad, and Timberghost perked up.

"Did somebody say food?" Chad said. Then his face turned contemplative. "Really, we oughta give the Ghost first dibs. He hasn't got a stove, after all."

"Yeah," Hobo said, a little reluctantly.

"Are you guys sure?" Timberghost asked us. "I mean, it's real kind of you."

"Oh, totally," Isis said. "I'm so stuffed."

There was a sizzle of coals from the firepit. I looked over. The odd guy with the crew cut had just dumped the remains of his pasta—perhaps half the pot—into the fire, without asking if anyone wanted some first. *He's really not a hiker*, I thought, and I wondered, with a brief prickle of alarm, exactly what he was doing on the Trail. I was glad for the company of other hikers.

In the morning, Isis and I packed up and left early. Almost everyone else was still asleep. The strange guy snored softly in one corner of the shelter. He had left the remains of his dinner in the firepit, with the tomato sauce can sitting on top. *I hope he'll clean it up before he leaves*, I thought.

It was a fine, clear day, with a light mist rising from the damp ground. Laurels and rhododendrons painted the understory, full of the lazy hum of bees, and the last azaleas sent up their sparks of color and cinnamon scent. The trees on the highest ridges still had a remnant of spring yellowness in their leaves, but we could see the dark green of summer spreading upward out of the valleys.

We stopped for lunch at Laurel Creek Shelter, where we had been ice-bound for two days in winter. Crossing the stream on the shelter side trail, I hardly recognized the place; the rhododendrons in the clearing sent up count-less clusters of watermelon pink blooms, and the forest behind them was a wall of green in many shades. I remembered how ice had clung to those branches in winter, how monotone and dead-looking the woods had been.

At the shelter, we found the firepit full of soggy day-old pasta with a tin can on top.

"This is disgusting!" Isis said. "We should pack it out."

"We can't really pack out that pasta. It must weigh, like, a pound. And it'll rot before we get anywhere."

"You're right. We should at least carry out the can, though." We ended up dumping the noodles in the privy and rinsing the can in the stream. Isis put it in her pack. "I almost feel like going back and catching that guy. Giving him a piece of my mind. We could do it; he only went six miles yesterday. Unless this was his lunch."

"I don't know. I think the less time we spend around somebody like that, the better."

Late spring had changed the mountains so much that I barely remembered where we were. Instead of the constant black-and-white views through trees to the valley floor, and the shapes of the mountains outlined in snow, we could see only a tunnel of riotous green. In the late afternoon, though, we came to a place I recognized. Open sheer slopes of gray stone, hemmed in with greenbriar and spicebush. The trail followed tiny ledges in the rock. Southbound, we had come through here just as the ice fog began to thicken, sticking to every surface. Our timing had been pretty close; any later, and the path would have been entirely impassible.

"This is Sinking Creek Mountain, isn't it?" I asked Isis.

She stopped and consulted her map. "Yeah, that would be about right."

"I heard a rumor that there're goats up here. Feral goats. They escaped from a farm a couple years ago."

Isis laughed. "That sounds like one of those Trail rumors. It probably got started because of these cliffs—it'd be easier to hike this if you were a goat. Or a Barefoot Sister." She hopped from the trail to a lower ledge and back, her strong feet easily gripping the rock.

"No, the guy swore it was true. He said they use hikers like walking salt licks. They chase you down and lick your legs." Just then, we heard a strange clopping sound. I looked back. "Isis . . ."

Three scruffy, shaggy, flea-bitten goats came trotting up the cliffs at a fast pace. They looked up at us with their slitted eyes and made little goaty sounds of anticipation.

"I'm not sure I like this," Isis said. "I don't really want to be a salt lick." We picked up our pace, but the goats followed, gaining on us.

Then we heard another sound behind us: hikers' footsteps. I chanced a look back. Chad and Hobo were trotting along at their usual four miles an hour, drenched in sweat. The goats changed direction.

"Hey, Hobo! Check out the goats!"

"Far out, man! Hey, can you get my camera? Outside pocket on the left."

"Barefoot Sisters!" Chad called. "We've been seeing your tracks all day in the mud. Wondered when we'd catch you."

"Hey, good to see you again," I said.

"Chad, dude, they're, like, licking my legs. This is trippy."

"Yeah. Feels kinda good, actually. In a weird way." Chad's legs were coated in thick goat slobber.

Isis and I decided this would be a good time to make our exit. "See you later," we called to the guys, and headed down the trail at top speed. As we rounded a bend and entered the woods, I could just hear Hobo's voice, carried back on the wind: "No! Hey! Don't lick me *there!*"

Evening gilded the ridges when we came to Niday Shelter. We heard the sound of a guitar and familiar voices singing a bluegrass tune: the Stage Crew! We raced down the trail. Sure enough, there they were: Toast and Basil, Luna and Six-string. We tossed our packs down and hugged them all. The hiker with the guitar was a tall young man with brown hair and a narrow face. He wore an orange shirt of a shade so virulent it seemed to glow.

"Hi there. I'm Fragipan," he said, extending a hand.

"Good to meet you." I said. We gave our names. "How'd you get that trail name, anyway? Isn't it some kind of tropical flower?"

"No, that's frangipani," he said, laughing. "Fragipan is actually a geology term. It's a subsurface soil horizon that's really dense and hard except when, like, everything's totally saturated with water. Like the last two weeks."

"Are you a geologist, then?"

"Yeah. I'm studying for my Master's right now."

"That still doesn't explain how you got your trail name."

"Oh, yeah. Well, when I started the Trail I went by 'Scorpion.' But the thing is, when people hear that, they think of some big tough dude with tattoos. I'm not a Scorpion. So one day I was walking along, thinking about soils—I do that a lot. I guess that's why I'm in grad school. Anyway, I was walking along, and I just thought, 'Fragipan. Now there's a cool word. I'll bet nobody's taken that for a trail name.'" He started strumming his guitar and singing:

> Here I am, the only man
> who goes by the name of Fragipan.
> Who would think a name so royal
> could be found beneath the soil?

"Excellent," I said.

"Where'd y'all stay last night?" Six-string asked us.

I sat down at the picnic table in front of the shelter. "War Spur."

"War Spur! That's gotta be where Satan was yesterday!"

I said the first thing that came to mind. "I slept with Satan and I didn't even know it?"

Toast laughed heartily. "You know, jackrabbit, you probably don't wanna get quoted on that."

"Who was Satan, anyway?" I asked.

"Blond guy," Luna said. "Kinda short. Army pack."

"Oh yeah," I said. "Dumped his dinner in the firepit?"

"That's the one."

"He wasn't exactly my favorite person, but what'd he do to deserve the name of Satan?"

Six-string laughed. "Well, the guy didn't say much. Seemed kinda shifty, to me. And then I asked him where he was hiking from, and all he said was, 'Hell!'"

"Sounds about like my experience," I told him. "I asked the guy his trail name, and he just said, 'Fuck!'"

Fragipan started playing a funky blues. "Well, now I'm gonna sing a song," he crooned, "all about Satan and how he done me wrong."

Six-string jumped in. "Poured half his dinner in the firepit; don't wanna know where that feller took a shit! Jackrabbit, you take over."

I jumped up on the picnic table and did a vampy dance. "Oh, I met Satan just the other night, and Satan, he didn't say two words to me, that's right. He said one word, and he said it twice, and that word was 'Fuck!'"

"I heard he came down from New York," Isis sang breathily.

"Yeah, I heard that about New York, too," Luna broke in.

Fragipan finished off the song. "O-oh Satan, why'd you do me wrong? Why don't you git off the Trail, go back where you belong? Go on, Satan, go on back to hell." He ended with a squeaky falsetto note, and we all collapsed with laughter.

Isis

At the road crossing a mile past Niday Shelter, we found our old friends Walrus and Roots serving up a trail magic breakfast. They'd brought gallons of orange juice, tea and coffee, donuts, pastries, and, best of all, a whole box of fresh fruit. Much better than the dry milk and granola I'd eaten half an hour before. I filled a plate and sat down in a lawn chair between Fragipan and Wood Nymph.

"What luxury!" I said to Walrus, as he refilled my orange juice cup. "This is so kind of you guys."

"Oh, this is just the beginning." He winked at me. "We're going to set up a lunch picnic on Route 620, eight and a half miles from here. Would you like us to slack you over there?"

It was a hot day, full of small, steep hills, and I was grateful to be free of my pack. The prospect of another real meal made our feet fly. We hiked past noon without stopping for a snack, even though our stomachs began growling. As we walked down the last quarter mile of ridge, the smell of frying meat greeted us, along with a babble of voices. By the sound of it, this party was even better attended than the morning one had been.

"Isis! Jackrabbit! Welcome to the party!" Luna came skipping up the trail, followed by Six-string. Behind them, I could see Basil and Toast, along with most of the hikers we'd shared the shelter with the night before.

"Stage Crew!" jackrabbit laughed. "We meet again."

"Come on over and help yourselves to potato salad," called Walrus. "I'll put a couple tofu dogs and some veggie burgers on the grill."

"There's some cookies and brownies over here," Roots said, "if you want dessert first."

"Where are you headed tonight?" I asked Luna as I set down my pack in the shade of a pine.

"Right about here looks fine to me," Six-string suggested around a mouthful of brownie. He leaned back against a tree, his eyes half-closed.

"Catawba's only another thirteen," Luna said. "It'd be a push, but I bet we could make it to the Home Place in time for dinner."

Six-string's eyes snapped open. "The Home Place? I'd forgotten it was so close. Y'all ever been to the Home Place?" he asked me and jackrabbit.

I shook my head. "What's that?"

"Best country cookin' along the whole Trail," Six-string said. "We gotta go there tonight."

"Can we camp there?" jackrabbit asked. Since we'd decided to yo-yo, we had a lot less leeway in our budget for random bed-and-breakfast stays.

"They've got a couple gazebos," Six-string said. "Last I checked, they let hikers sleep in 'em."

Walrus walked over, bringing two plates full of veggie burgers, tofu dogs, and potato salad. "Did I hear you say you're headed to the Home Place tonight?" he asked.

"Sound's like that's the plan," jackrabbit told him.

"Great place. Karen and I try to get over there at least a few times every summer. We were talking about going tonight, too." He started to walk back to the grill, then turned around. "We could slack you there," he offered.

jackrabbit

The Home Place Restaurant was a sprawling two-story mansion surrounded by sloping green lawns and gazebos. The crowd of people waiting for tables was an interesting mix, evenly divided between sweaty north-bounders in ragged clothing and local families in weekend finery. The hikers waited in the gazebos, sprawled on benches and chairs, while young children raced each other over the grass and their parents stood in loose circles, chatting. A loudspeaker announced names occasionally as tables became available. Walrus and Roots had called ahead to get us reservations, so when we arrived, our party—Isis and me, the Stage Crew, Fragipan, and a few other hikers who had enjoyed the day of trail magic—was seated almost immediately.

"Welcome to the Home Place," the hostess said in a gracious Southern accent, seating us around a large oval table. The décor reminded me of my grandmother's house in Virginia: solid wood furniture, starched linens, cabinets of china and silver on the walls. There were seven or eight tables in this room, and I could hear the low hum of conversation from the next room, too. I wondered how many diners the old house could hold.

"Are y'all hiking the Trail?" the hostess asked.

There was a chorus of assent from the table. Aside from Walrus and Roots, we all had such scruffy clothes and unwashed bodies that it was fairly evident—but I still thought it was polite of her to ask.

"Y'all probably know we let hikers sleep in the gazebos out back." She smiled sweetly. "A lot of people say they can hardly walk ten steps when they leave here, so we like to give y'all a place to stay. Have any of y'all been here before?" she asked.

Most of us answered in the negative.

"Well, here at the Home Place, we do things a little differently. All our food is served homestyle; that's why y'all don't have menus. We'll just bring out all the fixin's for a good old-fashioned Southern dinner, and if y'all want more of anything, all you've got to do is ask."

"The two of us are vegetarians," Isis said, indicating me.

"I am, too," Basil told her.

She gave us an accommodating smile. "I'll tell them to give y'all's table a little less meat and more vegetables, then. I hope y'all enjoy."

The food arrived promptly. Luna, Six-string, Toast, and a few others went straight for the platters of pork chops and fried chicken. Basil, Isis, and I depleted the basket of enormous biscuits, and the bowls of mashed potatoes and string beans. The beans, in particular, were delicious. The waitress brought out a second bowl, smiling, as soon as the first one vanished. Among the green pods, a large piece of unidentified, gristly meat floated up as Basil spooned another helping onto his plate. He sat back from the table, looking queasy.

"Think I'll wait for dessert."

Isis and I exchanged a glance. We were hardly pure vegetarians, after all; we'd grown up eating meat. We still ate fish, from time to time, and a token amount of turkey at Thanksgiving. We had even eaten venison at Trail Days.

I shrugged. "We can eat around it."

Basil scooted the bowl over to us. "Suit yourselves. I think I've had all I want."

Now that I noticed the meat, it seemed to be everywhere. Little bits of pink flesh dotted the heap of string beans on my plate. Even the mashed potatoes congealed suspiciously as they cooled, and the biscuits had an unusual density to them, like the griddle cakes my dad used to fry in bacon grease. My appetite declined as well. At the other end of the table, the plates of fried chicken and pork chops had been reduced to scraps and oily heaps of bone. Looking at the grisly evidence, I remembered once again why I was usually a vegetarian.

Dessert arrived, generous helpings of blackberry cobbler with ice cream. Aside from the cream and the butter in the crumble topping, there didn't seem to be any animal products in this course. I ate four bowls; Basil had seven.

After supper, we wobbled out to one of the pavilions across the restaurant's lawn. Rain clouds threatened; we strung tarps across the up-wind side and set out our foam pads on the wooden floorboards. Nobody was quite as stuffed as we had been at Partnership Shelter, but nobody really felt like moving very fast, either. Walrus and Roots joined us for a while.

Fragipan strummed his guitar, improvising a soundtrack for the day:

> Trail magic for breakfast, trail magic for lunch,
> Home Place for dinner—Walrus and Roots, we love you a bunch!
> Talkin' bout trail magic, oooh!

> Looks like it's gonna rain soon, but here we're dry and warm;
> Gonna sit here playin' my gui-tar in a thunderstorm,
> Talkin' bout trail magic, oooh!

Walrus and Roots smiled. "Thanks for the serenade," Roots said. "We'd better get going, though. I've got to work an early shift tomorrow." All the hikers in the pavilion cheered and waved as they walked away.

Six-string brought out his pack of cards just as two other hikers came up to our gazebo. "Hobo and Chad! Y'all wanna play some Spades with us?"

Chad shook his head. "No thanks, man. We got us a table comin' up soon. Just figured we'd hang out here till they call our names."

"That's cool." Six-string dealt out the cards for himself, me, Toast, and Luna.

"Hey, thanks for distracting the goats up on Sinking Creek Mountain," I said. "You guys came just in time for us to make our getaway."

Hobo laughed. "Yeah; at first it was like, 'Cool! Goats!' Then they started, you know, gettin' friendly."

The restaurant's loudspeaker crackled to life. "Zeigler, party of two."

"That's us, dude," Chad said.

Six-string broke into a grin, his eyes gleaming as though he had just thought of a particularly awful joke. "Ziggler? Which one of you is named Ziggler?"

"That would be me," Chad said.

Six-string clapped him on the back. "Chad, my man, you just got yourself a trail name. Ziggler. *Zirk* Ziggler."

"Zirk." He shook his head and laughed. "Yeah, I could be a Zirk. Come on, Hobo. Time for some serious eating."

They left, and I turned my attention to the pile of cards in front of me. It was the lousiest hand I'd seen yet. "Damn it, who dealt this shit?"

Toast gave me a slow, appreciative smile. "Now that's how you play Spades."

We were halfway through the game, with Toast and me losing miserably, when we heard a commotion from the front patio of the restaurant. A man came over to the gazebo and drew one of our tarp curtains aside. "Y'all hikers oughta see this," he said, with the attitude of someone with fascinating gossip to share. By then, we had all rested long enough to partially overcome the food-induced inertia. Most of us got up, staggering a little as we rose to our feet, and followed him back across the grass. It was getting close to dusk; the rain clouds had parted to reveal a glimpse of the low, blood-red sun.

The circle of people on the patio parted a little to make room for us. At first I didn't see anything; I wondered why people were staring so intently at the bricks. And then I spotted it: a tiny snake, barely six inches long. Its mottled brown body, the color of raw earth and dead leaves, twisted into a threatening S-shape. It swayed its flattened triangular head back and forth, hissing.

I overheard a few whispers from the crowd.

"Copperhead," someone said.

"—little ones are the most dangerous—you cain't spot 'em."

"—and if there's one, there's prob'ly a nest of 'em somewheres close by."

"Watch him! There he goes!"

The little snake slithered into the flowerbed by the side of the building and vanished, blending with the ground. I was nervous, suddenly aware of my vulnerable feet in their sandals, wondering where the nest of copperheads might be. Hopefully not too close to the gazebo where we would be sleeping that night . . . But I was also, in a strange way, elated. It was the first poisonous snake I had ever seen, outside of a zoo. *Even here*, I thought, *among these manicured lawns and flowerbeds, there is still something wild. Something that, small as it was, commanded respect.* I looked up at the darkening hills, the long rows of serrated ridges on either side of the valley. The forest suddenly seemed thicker, stranger, in the twilight, the leafy branches still holding some inviolable mystery.

I remembered the time I had spent at Elmer's, and my thoughts of leaving the Trail. *It'll be June in a few days*, I thought. *I could leave now, if he's got a job opening; hitch down to Hot Springs* . . . but I rejected the thought almost as soon as it crossed my mind. More than anything, I wanted to stay on the Trail now. *Whatever's out there in the mountains, whatever that mystery is, I want a chance to understand it.*

Isis

We hiked up McAfee Knob in the foggy dawn after a night of rain. At first, it looked as if the rain would return; clouds hung in the trees like dirty cobwebs. As we climbed, though, the sky lightened from pewter to white. Then the sun broke through, making the misty forest glow like a palace carved in emerald. Five months of winter, and now all this green! When the sun transformed the woods so unexpectedly, I felt as if I'd just woken from one season into the other.

At the summit of the Knob, pools of water on the cliffs mirrored the bright sky, and dew sparkled in the white and pink tufts of laurel blossoms. Clouds lifted from the rippling crests of ridges, caught the breeze, drifting slowly away across the valley. The lines of low mountains shone a clean blue, like shadows on freshly washed linen.

We rested there as long as we could afford to, taking pictures of each other posed on the lip of the cliff, eating granola bars with our legs swinging over the edge, as if we were children in chairs much too high for us.

By the time we hiked on, the sun had burned away the last of the morning's haze and the pleasant day had turned hot. The trail followed the crest of the long ridge between McAfee Knob and Tinker Cliffs with a maddening exactitude: up and over each little bump or rocky outcropping. The ground underfoot was comfortable, though—soft mud quickly turning to dust, and drifts of last year's fallen leaves, their surfaces smooth as tile. I let myself slip into a trance, practicing the poems I'd memorized.

My right foot hit the sharp end of a cut sapling beside the trail. I felt a quick jolt of pain beneath my little toe, in the small space of soft skin between the calluses. It would make a bruise, probably. *Careless of me.* I walked on a few steps before noticing the slickness of the fallen leaves. I looked down. Blood pooled on the dry earth, spattering the leaves with bright autumn color. *How did this happen?*

"Wait a sec, I've got a cut," I called to jackrabbit, who had walked on ahead of me. "I'm going to put on a band-aid." I took off my pack and poured some water over my foot to wash it out. The blood mixing with water cascaded to the ground in a brilliant scarlet plume.

"That looks bad," jackrabbit said, hurrying back to me. "You might need more than a band-aid."

"Yeah," I said, "it might need some gauze to soak the blood up." I found a gauze pad in my med kit and slathered it with antiseptic ointment, since the wound was still bleeding too liberally to put the ointment directly into it. I taped the pad down, crosswise between the toes and several times around my foot. Over top of it all, I tied a spare handkerchief to put a little more pressure on the cut. Then I gingerly pulled a sock over the bandage and stuffed my foot into my loosened sandal.

"Okay," I said to jackrabbit. "That's the best I can do for now. Let's go on."

I tried not to think of what else I might need to take care of the injury: a long time off the Trail. I had cut my foot that badly once before, when I was twelve, and that time it had taken two weeks to heal.

The ridge before Troutville lasted one and a half PUDs too long. My foot throbbed steadily. The bandage worked loose on each uphill; I had to stop many times to retie the slippery bandana. I'd used up most of my water rinsing the cut, and I hadn't wanted to stop for more at the last shelter; if we stopped, I was afraid that I'd have a hard time getting up again. At this point, I would have walked four miles back to that stream if I'd had the strength. My tongue felt thick and cottony with dehydration.

In the valley to my right, I could see a long, narrow reservoir fringed with pines—so much like the lakes at home in Maine. Water. Perhaps it would be a good thing if I had to leave the Trail. I'd carried my pack long enough, through plenty of blackflies and snowstorms and smog. I wouldn't mind taking an indeterminate number of zeros right about now. I remembered the lazy summers of my childhood—swimming all day, picnicking on the seashore, sleeping in a featherbed and waking to the smell of waffles cooking.

By the time we hit the last, long downhill, all the fight had gone out of me. I would have given my pack away for a drink of water. Even more than I wanted water, I wanted to go home. *Give me a bus station, give me a road.* But the sun that had seemed so harsh on the dry ridges was slanting westward now, its light turning soft and rich. It reminded me of the morning's enchanted glow, but golden now instead of green. At the bottom of the hill, we walked into a valley full of blooming honeysuckle, its scent hanging heavy in the warm, calm air. Bees spun in drunken circles over the flowers and warblers sang in the trees. Jackrabbit found mulberries, almost ripe. The taste of the fruit slaked my thirst enough that I could forget it for a while. At last, with nothing but level ground between me and the road, I didn't want to get there. I wanted to stay on the Trail.

CHAPTER 5

In Which We Learn to Fly

Isis

We spent one night at the Troutville Best Western, sharing two rooms with the Stage Crew and Fragipan. Washing my cut foot in the sink, I tried to estimate the extent of the damage. The sharp stick had sliced in just beneath my little toe, where the skin was relatively thin, and it had continued cutting into the ball of my foot, leaving a ragged laceration about an inch long and nearly half an inch deep. As I washed it, the cut began to bleed again. Yes, this would take a while to heal. But my cursory inspection showed that it wasn't quite as bad as I'd thought. Deep as the cut was, only half of it extended beneath the dermis. The rest showed a cross-section of callus, pliant yellowish skin almost twice as thick as the leather of my boots.

In the morning, Luna called a few of her Troutville connections. In less than half an hour, she'd found a trail angel who was willing to drive us the forty miles to Lexington, where our Aunt Nancy could pick us up. We bid a fond farewell to the Stage Crew, who looked like they were settling in for a zero. (Six-string was drawing a bath; Basil, dressed in his freshly washed hiking shorts, was testing the water in the leaf-filled outdoor pool; and Toast was preparing to walk over to the supermarket to buy a bottle of wine.) I smiled to myself—if they continued at this pace, we might catch up with them when we got back to the Trail.

We had half a day to spend in Lexington before Nancy could pick us up. We ate a couple pizzas for brunch, stopped by the chocolate shop, then wandered over to the used book store. My right foot felt hot in its wad of bandages, and I walked a little awkwardly, trying to keep the weight on my heel.

I wondered if I could have stayed on the Trail, hiking slowly, until it healed. After all, jackrabbit had walked sixty miles into Hanover, barefoot, with a much worse injury. And Baltimore Jack was hiking with a stress fracture. *It would be hard to keep an open wound clean,* I told myself. *I only have one spare bandana and two pairs of socks.* Maybe I was a wimp where pain was concerned, compared to my sister and a lot of the other hikers out there. But I felt that I had a contract with my body. It didn't complain very often. When it did complain, I did my best to take care of the problem. In return, it had served me well, adapting gracefully to each change in season and terrain. This time, I was asking a lot of my body: *heal before jackrabbit gets sick of waiting and hikes on by herself.* Giving it a week's rest, without dirt or sweat getting into the bandages, seemed like a better bet than limping down the trail at ten or twelve miles a day.

We stayed at Aunt Nancy's farm for four days. After I had made sure that the cut was clean—no flecks of leaf or gravel caught beneath the skin—I soaked it with comfrey from Nancy's herb garden. Comfrey was one of the most useful discoveries I'd made in many years as an amateur herbalist. Experimenting on myself, I'd found that a poultice of the leaves could cure a deep bruise in a matter of days, and I'd read that early settlers even used it to heal broken bones. Most of my herb books counseled against using it on open wounds: it worked so quickly that dirt and splinters could get sealed under the skin, causing internal infections. I had a long ways left to hike, though, and a limited amount of time. I decided to take the risk.

Fragrant steam rose from the long, spear-shaped leaves as I poured hot water over them. Not a sweet smell, but wholesome, like the scent of the forest floor after rain. I leaned back on the couch, closing my eyes, while jackrabbit read aloud from the copy of *Huckleberry Finn* that we'd picked up at the used book store.

The comfrey worked its usual magic. On the second day, I was on my feet all afternoon, washing our laundry and hanging it on the line, then helping Nancy cook supper. On the third day we worked together in the orchard, picking the wormy fruits off the apple and peach trees. Summer had reached the mountains; already, the green apples were the size of babies' fists. The peaches, Nancy told us, would be ripe in less than a month.

"Sure you don't want to stick around?" she asked. "I could use some help with the harvest. All the peaches you can eat, all day long."

Fresh fruit every day. It was certainly tempting. One thing about staying on the Trail for eleven months at a stretch—the kinds of food that you could carry easily got less and less appealing. It wasn't just peanuts anymore. Jackrabbit was sick of almost every brand of granola bar readily available, and I felt the same way about squishy Southern bagels.

I shook my head, smiling. My foot was healing faster than I'd believed possible, even with the help of comfrey. At the end of this line of round blue mountains, Katahdin waited. What were a few more bad lunches, between here and there?

"Maybe another year," I told Nancy. "Thank you."

"We'll stop by in six or seven days," jackrabbit said. "When we get near here on the Trail. Will anything be ready for harvest then?"

"Strawberries should be ripe in a day or so," Nancy answered.

"Great!" Jackrabbit laughed. "We'll hurry back!"

The next day, we caught a ride back to Troutville with a neighbor of Nancy's who had some business there. I brought a few comfrey leaves with me, though I was pretty sure I wouldn't need them. Already, a thin ridge of scar tissue filled the cut, between the flaps of callus. I would wear sandals for a day or two, to keep twigs from poking into the wound, but for all other purposes, it was completely healed.

We left Troutville in the early afternoon, striding easily up the long, gentle ridges. We passed the Fullhardt Knob Shelter, where I'd expected to spend the night, at three in the afternoon, without so much as a sidewise glance. That night, we stealthed on the bank of Curry Creek, eleven miles from Troutville.

Late in the evening, as I fed twigs into the Zip stove, jackrabbit pored over the *Data Book* that Walrus had given her. She flipped back and forth through the pages, writing neat little columns of calculations in the margins. A few minutes before the couscous was ready, she set the book aside, smiling.

"What's the plan?" I asked her.

"Well, if we hiked an eleven today, starting at one o'clock, we should be able to hike twenties on a regular basis."

By force of habit, I opened my mouth to protest. Then I thought better of it. It was summer. Our packs weighed so little that I felt as if I were slacking, even at the beginning of this six-day resupply. If we would ever be able to hike twenties easily, this was the time.

"If we average fifteens from here to Vermont—" jackrabbit continued.

"*Average* fifteens," I interrupted. "That means four twenties before we can take a day off."

She nodded, looking me straight in the eye. "We can slow down to tens and elevens through the Whites and Maine."

"That sounds good," I told her. *May as well try it*, I said to myself.

To my surprise, I found that jackrabbit was right. In this season, on this section of trail, we could fly. We hiked a twenty-two the following day and averaged nearly twenty for the next four days. Neither of us got injured, or even very tired. We set up camp before dark every night and had plenty of time to read *Huckleberry Finn* by firelight. At last, we were hiking jackrabbit's hike, light and fast, the ridges lining up behind us like waves in a ship's wake. In camp she smiled to herself, tallying the miles in the margins of her *Data Book*. And I was glad, also, feeling my muscles stretch into this new rhythm of fast walking, discovering how easy it was, after all.

jackrabbit

On the ridges around Cove Mountain Shelter, a few days north of Troutville, the woods began to look strange. At first we saw scattered bits of leaves lying in the pathway, as though someone had made confetti of them. Then the bits of leaves piled up in thick drifts. The June sun came down strongly between the branches, and I looked up to see trees as bare as they had been in winter. I could almost picture the way ice had clung to the branches. Behind the trees, the far ridges looked hazy and insubstantial behind a curtain of smog. Something about the scene raised the small hairs on the back of my neck—the combination of leafless trees and summer heat felt so unnatural.

"Isis, what do you think it is?"

She stopped, an expression of absolute disgust on her face, and pointed at a nearby oak. "Gypsy moths." Several enormous fuzzy caterpillars were inching their way down the runneled bark. When I looked closer, I could see many more of them on the surrounding trees.

"Ick!" Most insects don't really bother me, unless they're trying to suck my blood, but gypsy moths are an exception. I remembered reading about them in an ecology class in college. Native to Europe and Asia, gypsy moths were introduced to the U.S. in the late 1800s by an entrepreneur who wanted to develop a domestic silk industry. Their silk proved unsuitable for spinning, but the moths themselves escaped and thrived. They defoliate millions of acres of trees in the U.S. and Canada every year. Although I had only seen pictures of gypsy moth caterpillars before, I recognized them instantly: long brown bodies with spots of red and blue and orange, and patches of mangy-looking bristles. Knowing their history made them doubly repulsive. I watched the trail carefully as I walked on. The thought of putting my bare foot down on one of these outsized caterpillars was enough to turn my stomach.

Luckily, there was only a small patch of defoliated woods here. The trail led us back under the shade of the intact forest. The green light and the cool, leaf-scented air soothed me as we descended from the ridgeline, and I quickly forgot the ugliness of the scene we had left.

Down in the valley, we crossed a two-lane highway and came to the little creek where we had gotten water to carry to Cove Mountain Shelter in the winter. A few hikers were swimming in the shallow pools, and more sat on the gravel beach, soaking their feet. I heard the voices of other nobos in the woods.

"I could almost camp here," I said to Isis. Although the sun was still above the trees, we had already hiked a respectable seventeen miles.

"Possibly," she said, "but it's pretty close to the road. And besides, where would we fit the tent?"

I looked back into the trees: eight tents, two tarps, and a hammock filled up the level ground, leaving hardly any flat space open. It made me almost nostalgic for our days of solo hiking as southbounders.

A young hiker, who had overheard our conversation, swam over to the bank. "Y'all could sleep under the bridge," he suggested, with a glint of laughter in his eyes.

"Dude, that is *such* a bad idea!" said another swimmer. "Did you hear about the guy that slept there a couple years ago? He got bit by a copperhead!"

"That must've sucked," the first guy said. "No sleepin' under the bridge, I guess. But y'all've got to take a swim here, anyway. The water's great."

We took off our packs and splashed into the pool in our shorts and sports bras. The water was colder than I had expected, and the current stronger, but it felt good to scrub the grime from my face and test my arm strength against the stream's flow. I swam upstream to where the creek curved under the bridge. It didn't look like a good sleeping spot at all; the bank beside the bridge abutments was wet and dank, covered with broken glass, and a vaguely foul odor floated out of the shallows. I turned and let the current carry me down.

"Who would *want* to sleep under that bridge, anyway?" I asked the guy who had told the copperhead story. "It looks pretty gross under there."

He shook his head. "I don't know. Some dude. He was prob'ly drunk as a skunk."

Refreshed by the swim, Isis and I shouldered our packs. We made another four miles that evening, coming into Bryant Ridge Shelter just before night fell. It was one of the largest shelters on the A.T., a spacious two-story wooden building made to accommodate twenty-five hikers, and when we arrived, it was nearly full.

I found a space of almost flat ground near the shelter and set up our tent, then went down to the spring with the filter, cooking pot, and an armload of water bottles. Three hikers already perched on the ground around the pool of water. I sat down nearby to wait.

"Hi, I'm jackrabbit," I said.

"I'm Strider," one of the other nobos returned.

"No, *I'm* Strider. I chose it first."

"Yeah, well, I had no idea you were up ahead when *I* chose it."

The first guy sighed. "You could've read the registers once in a while. There just can't be two Striders!"

I had to laugh. "There were about five Striders last year. Three north-bounders, two sobos."

The Striders left, still bickering, and the other hiker and I sat down by the water source. "I'm Iculus," he said. He had curly shoulder-length brown hair and dark eyes, and he looked young, probably eighteen or nineteen.

"That's a cool name," I said. "Not one you hear every day. What's it mean?"

"Well, you know the band Phish? Their lead singer has this whole mythology he made up. Iculus is . . . well, Iculus is the god of the mountains." It was hard to tell in the gathering dusk, but it almost looked like he was blushing. "I guess I was kind of arrogant calling myself that, but, you know, I thought if I took that name, maybe it would help me cope better with bad stuff out here."

I laughed. "You ought to meet my sister. She's named after an Egyptian goddess."

"Wait a minute. Are you the Barefoot Sisters? Radical!"

Back at the shelter, Isis had set up the Zip stove on the end of the picnic table. I quickly gathered a few twigs and brought them to her with the water. "Hey, Isis. This is Iculus."

"Good to meet you." She asked about his name, too, and soon they were involved in an animated discussion of world religions and mythologies. I introduced myself to the hikers at my end of the table, a man and a woman.

"Aloha," the woman said. "I'm Aloha Anne." She was tall and thin, with short graying hair and a narrow face. By the light of Isis's headlamp, I could see that her eyes were pale blue.

"I am Parypinoy," the man said with a slightly British accent. He had bronze-colored skin and black hair, and tiny glasses balanced on his nose. His smile was gentle and profoundly peaceful.

"What's your name again?" I asked him.

"Pah-ree-pee-noy," he said slowly. "I chose the name because I am a priest from the Philippines. *Pary* is the word for priest in our language, and *pinoy* is a word . . . a word we Filipinos use to describe ourselves. Like *American* for you."

"I'm from Hawaii," Aloha said. "You probably guessed as much from my name. That's one reason I chose it—the minute I say 'Aloha,' people know where I'm from. The other reason, well, it seemed so appropriate. It means hello, and goodbye, and I love you, and a couple other things, too. That's kind of what the Trail is like—hello and goodbye and everything in between, and you never know quite what's what until afterwards. Everything's in transition."

"That's pretty deep," I said.

Parypinoy laughed, a rich chuckle. "If you want to be deep, you could say the same of life, more or less. Everything is in transition in this world. The question is a transition from what? To what?" We were all quiet for a few moments; the only sound was the hiss of Aloha's stove and the murmur of conversation drifting out from the shelter.

"Would anyone like some dried mango?" Parypinoy asked.

We left in the morning while the mist was still rising from the hollows. As we climbed higher in the mountains, we began to see glorious tangles of blooming rhododendrons. In the valleys, their petals had already wilted in the late spring heat, but up on the ridges, their clusters of pink and purple blossoms were still fresh and bright. Some of the bushes grew twenty feet tall, with gnarled gray trunks as thick as my thigh. It was cooler, too, on the high ridges, and a brisk wind overnight had cleared the smog from the air. The trail led up and down the bumpy ridgeline, touching every high point and plunging into every gap. I didn't mind these elevation changes nearly as much as I had in winter. Now, with a light pack and the beauty of the early summer woods around us, the miles seemed to slip past with hardly any effort.

Toward evening, we stopped for a snack among a grove of tall white pines by a gravel road. "Where are we, anyway?" I asked Isis.

She took out the map. "Well, this must be Petit's Gap. We're about to go over our favorite little mountain: High Cock Knob." We had a good laugh at the name, as we had in winter.

"Where do you want to camp tonight?" I asked.

"It's about six miles to Matt's Creek Shelter." She glanced at the sun, which was already low. "We might have time. I think it's all downhill, a pretty easy grade, on the other side of the Knob. All we've got to do is get up it."

While I fished around in my brain for a nasty pun—*get up it, get it up*—I heard footsteps coming down the trail. It was Aloha, but I hardly recognized her. She was limping, leaning heavily on her hiking poles, and her long face was drawn and pale with pain.

"Aloha, what happened?" I asked her.

"Oh, it's just my knee," she said through gritted teeth. "I fell a couple miles back. It's been hurting ever since. All I need is a little rest."

"Do you have enough water to camp here?" Isis asked her.

She shook her head, and Isis and I made a quick inventory of our water bottles; she had half a liter, I had a little more.

"We can share our water and camp with you," Isis said. "Or we could go down this road a ways and look for a spring or something. You probably shouldn't hike if it's that painful."

"At least let us lighten your pack for you a little bit," I said. "Mine's not that heavy; I can take some of your gear."

Aloha's face was set. "No thanks," she said. "I'm sure that if I just get some rest, I'll be able to hike on. I'll get to VA 501 in the morning, down in the next valley, and I'll be able to hitch out there."

We tried to convince her to stay in Petit's Gap, but she was adamant. "I'll be absolutely fine," she said, though the dark circles under her eyes and the way she leaned on her poles suggested the opposite. She wouldn't even accept water from us.

As we walked on, leaving Aloha in the gap to "catch her breath," as she said, I felt awful. To see her suffering and not be able to do anything . . . it called to mind all the times in winter, and even before, when I had been in pain and Isis had tried to help me. I had always rebuffed her, in an attempt to maintain my independence. Now I could see how much that had hurt her. It had hurt us both.

From the peak of High Cock Knob, in the low sunlight, we could see dead patches in the forest ahead. All along the slopes down to the James River, swaths of grayish purple woods stood out, ugly and bare against the summer green, like patches of rot on the hills. It took me a moment to figure out what I was seeing. "Gypsy moths," I said. I had hoped that the small outbreak we had seen would be the only one, but looking ahead, I could see hardly any forest along the Trail route that had escaped their depredations.

"Maybe we'd better camp in the next gap," Isis said grimly. "There's a spring down there. I don't think I can face all that tonight."

"Me either."

We set up camp at Marble Spring, a mile north of the Knob. There were a few tents in the clearing already. I recognized Iculus and one of the Striders. "Hey, guys," I called.

A wiry middle-aged man sat with his back against an oak tree, smoking a cigarette. "Hi. I'm Smokey," he said. "Were you guys hiking with Aloha?" He looked worried.

"We saw her back at Petit's Gap," I told him.

"Was she okay?"

I hesitated. "She didn't look so good," I admitted. "Her knee was bothering her. We offered to camp there and share water, or help her carry her stuff, but she didn't want to do that."

Smokey gave a wry smile. "That's Aloha for you. Always one to pull her own weight."

I set up the tent and gathered firewood. Twenty minutes passed, half an hour, and there was no sign of Aloha. I went over to talk to Smokey, who sat in front of his tent, listening to his Walkman, smoking another cigarette.

"Hey, Smokey."

He took off his headphones and peered up at me. "What's up?"

"Well, you know Aloha better than I do. I'm really starting to worry about her. Do you think, I mean, would she be offended if I went back to look for her?"

He twisted his lips, considering. "She might," he finally said. "She hates it when people try to take care of her."

I gave a wry smile. "I guess I can sympathize with that."

"If she's not here before dark, though, I might just go myself," he said.

I went down to the spring as dusk fell and filtered four liters for the next day. I knew we would need extra water without the shade of leaves above us, and I was dreading the miles of bare trees.

Back at the campsite, the red glow of Smokey's omnipresent cigarette was nowhere to be seen. "Hey Iculus, where'd Smokey go?" I asked.

Iculus looked up from adjusting his stove. "The dude went back over the mountain after all. Wanted to check on Aloha."

It was late when he returned, alone, the blue beam of his headlamp bouncing down the trail ahead of him. Isis and I were brushing our teeth. I kicked a shallow hole in the leaves, spat out my toothpaste, and kicked dirt over it. "Hey, Smokey. What's the story?"

He shook his head. "She's one tough woman. She got almost all the way up the knob, and then she realized she wasn't going to make the six miles down to 501. She turned around and camped in the gap by that gravel road. She's gonna try to hitch out there, if anybody goes by. Parypinoy's with her. He found a spring somewhere down the road and brought her a bunch of water."

"Man, I hope she's okay."

Smokey looked grim. "She was in bad shape when I saw her. Couldn't put any weight on that leg. The priest'll take care of her, though. He's a good man."

I was glad we had waited for a full night's sleep before heading out into the moth-devastated landscape. Less than a mile into our hike, the green summer woods gave way to denuded trees. The sun came hot and bright through the empty branches. There was a strange background noise of tiny things falling from the canopy, a steady disquieting hiss like freezing rain. *Frass.* The word came back to me from ecology class long ago. Frass. Caterpillar shit. Little olive green pellets of it dropped out of the trees and stuck to everything. I began to see the caterpillars, too, their distended fuzzy bodies clinging to every tree branch and twig. No plant escaped them; even the laurels and rhododendrons, with their poisonous leaves, wore twitching, writhing coats of caterpillars. I put my sandals on to keep from stepping on them. The trail was slick in places with dead ones, raising a thick stench. I felt bile burn the back of my throat.

After almost four miles of the desolate landscape, we came back under the leaves. I tried to force the memory of the caterpillars from my mind, but every time I closed my eyes, disgusting scenes came back. There was something in that mindless destruction, that horrible manifestation of appetite unleashed, that was more terrifying than anything I had experienced on the Trail. And the scariest thought was to remember how this had all come about—an entrepreneur trying to get the silk industry started in America. A guy without much foresight trying to make a buck.

Isis

After the moth-ravaged landscape, the land around Punchbowl Shelter looked like a manicured park: open woods (the leaves whole and shining), a small, sloping meadow, and a pond made from a dammed mountain stream. When we walked in, an hour or so before sunset, frogs already clamored in the reeds: a chorus of peeps and ribbits punctuated by one bullfrog croaking so deep in the bass register that we surmised it must be the size of a Volkswagen Beetle.

I gathered some wood for the stove and sat down at the table in front of the shelter between a few nobo men who had arrived earlier. With the frogs singing and the low sunlight warming my shoulders, I felt like a picnicker just out for the afternoon. Too bad our supper didn't match the mood—another pot of rice and beans, unmitigated this time by cheese or onions. (I'd used up the last of our Forest Phil ingredients the night before.)

I had just set the water to boil when a man and a woman walked up the spring trail, carrying wicker baskets on their arms. Both of them were tall and slender, with tanned skin and graying hair. They looked fit enough to be hikers, but their neatly ironed cotton clothing, as well as the incongruous picnic baskets, proved otherwise. I watched them, wondering if they'd gotten lost on their way to a potluck. In spite of the parklike setting, this shelter seemed to be too far from roads for people to stroll in so casually, with baskets on their arms.

"Hi there!" The woman waved as she walked up to us. "I'm Mary Ann Williams, and this is my husband Ed."

The man nodded a greeting and began to unpack his basket, setting the food on the table. Cookies, brownies, and something elaborate that looked like miniature pies. All of us hikers looked on, our mouths watering.

"We live just a few miles over the ridge," Mary Ann went on, gesturing back toward the spring trail. "We like to walk over here every once in a while durin' thru-hiker season, and bring y'all a little somethin' to eat. Please help yourselves," she said, pulling three jars of homemade jam and a fresh loaf of bread from her basket.

We didn't need to be asked twice. As I spread black raspberry jam on a warm slice of bread, I thought back to our southbound hike through this same section. Ice storms and dry springs. Whole weeks when we saw no one but each other on the Trail. *Is this what it's like to hike northbound? If we're not careful, we're going to get spoiled*, I thought, reaching for another slice of bread.

The next morning, four smooth downhill miles into the day, we found a small camper van parked at a road crossing. A heavyset man in an apron stood in front of it, flipping pancakes and frying eggs on an enormous grill.

"What's for breakfast?" jackrabbit joked.

"Toast, flapjacks, bacon, coffee," the man answered, his voice perfectly serious. I noticed the crates of eggs stacked up behind him. "I come up here every year on my vacation and cook breakfast for the hikers. How do you like your eggs?"

The air turned muggy in the afternoon, and sweat glazed our skin on the uphills. Fueled by the trail angel's breakfast, we didn't stop for a snack until we reached an open bald, only a few miles before the gap where our aunt lived. Grass and ferns glowed emerald in the afternoon light, and all around us mountains stretched away, the colors of summer cloaking their flanks. As we sat down, I noticed a tapestry of scalloped, dark green leaves and small red berries in the grass.

"Wild strawberries!" I said to jackrabbit. "Let's pick some to take to Nancy. It's still early; we have plenty of time."

"Nancy said her own strawberries would be ripe by now," jackrabbit pointed out. "Besides, I don't like the look of those clouds."

I looked where she was pointing. Huge thunderheads billowed up to the south of us, their white crests boiling higher as I watched.

An hour and a half later, we came around the last bend of Nancy's steep, dusty driveway, a few miles west of the trail.

"Hey, girls," Nancy called to us. "I wasn't expecting you back this soon."

"We hiked faster than I thought we would," I told her.

"Well, you're just in time to help me get my clothes off the line before the storm hits," she answered, gesturing toward the mountains behind us.

Glowering thunderclouds ringed the valley, east, south, and west. Jackrabbit and I set our packs under the eaves, then hurried to help with the laundry. As we worked, the tip of one anvil cloud crossed the sun, throwing the fields around us into shadow. Lightning flashed, and a few seconds later, a long peal of thunder echoed around the hills. Then the sun came back out, coating the hillside with hazy, surreal light. We finished folding the clothes, and Nancy sent us to the strawberry patch with a small basket.

"Pick me a few handfuls for dessert," she said, "and then eat as many as you want to. I have a hard time keeping up with them this time of year."

We knelt in the warm red soil, picking strawberries, for almost half an hour. Behind the flower garden and the sloping green pastures, beyond the bright woods and distant ridges, lightning darted back and forth across the steel gray bellies of the clouds. Thunder rumbled all around us, almost continuously, but the sun still shone.

A light, cool breeze swept over us, making the grass hiss softly. The sun dimmed. Jackrabbit grabbed the basket and we retreated to the porch. Lightning touched down on a nearby ridge; a curl of smoke rose out of the trees. A gray wall of rain advanced over the hills to the south of us, obscuring everything in its wake. It hit the edge of the pasture and the cows bolted for the woods, jolting along with their heads high and their nostrils flared. The pasture vanished behind a gray curtain. A minute later, the rain hit the porch railing, and I couldn't see the bird feeder five feet beyond it. We stepped into the living room, inhaling the aroma of baking potatoes and steaming asparagus.

"It's a good night to be off the Trail," I said to jackrabbit.

"No kidding. I just hope none of our friends are camped near here," she answered.

We took the next morning off, washing our clothes and waiting for them to dry. I baked two pans of rhubarb cake, one for Nancy and one to take with us, to share with the hikers who weren't lucky enough to have family in the neighborhood. After lunch, Nancy drove us up to the trailhead at the gap.

We came to Seeley-Woodworth Shelter just before dark. Signs of the previous night's storm filled the woods; streams bubbled over their banks, and here and there a green branch lay across the trail. A newly fallen tree divided the clearing behind the shelter. Earlier, as we hiked, we had found the remains of a tree that had been completely shattered by a lightning bolt—a circle of bright, raw splinters, none thicker than my forearm, radiating out from a jagged stump a foot and a half in diameter. Some of the splinters had flown a hundred yards into the woods; others protruded from the trunks of nearby trees.

I shivered. "Good thing we got off the Trail early yesterday."

None of the hikers at the shelter that night had seen the storm; apparently it had been a pretty localized phenomenon. Jackrabbit and I walked around the campsite, handing out rhubarb cake and getting to know this new crowd of nobos. There was a couple in the shelter who had Swahili trail names; the man had been in the Peace Corps in South Africa. His wife was a marathon runner. She told us that she got up every morning at four, and jogged five miles out and back before beginning the day's hike.

"Running uses different muscles," she explained. "I have to keep them in shape."

Nearby, a young man sat in front of his tent with his feet propped up on a log, showing callused yellow soles.

"Hey, are you a barefoot hiker?" jackrabbit asked him.

"I wish I was." He gave us a rueful smile. "I grew up on a farm in the Georgia mountains, not far off the Trail. I went barefoot all my childhood. Even in college, I'd walk around campus barefoot. Got myself a bit of a reputation for it. But I didn't think it'd work out here; thought the ground would be too rough. Man, I was kickin' myself when I heard about y'all."

"You could start hiking barefoot now," jackrabbit said.

"Naw, my feet are too soft from all those miles in boots. Besides, I like to hike long days—twenties, twenty-fives. I don't suppose y'all go that fast barefoot?"

I had to admit that we didn't. Ever since my foot had healed, we'd worn sandals about half the time.

"I think I'll go set up the tent," jackrabbit said to me. "It's getting late."

"Okay. I'm going to offer some cake to that guy camped back in the woods, and then I'll make supper."

As I walked toward the solitary tent with a stooped figure cooking in front of it, I wondered if this was a good idea. Perhaps he'd set up his tent back there because he wanted a bit of privacy. Perhaps he'd had a bad day and didn't want to be bothered. *Or maybe if he's had a bad day, a piece of cake would be just the thing to cheer him up,* I told myself. *Anyway, it's too late to turn back now.*

The man crouched over his stove, his shoulders hunched as if he were cold or frightened. A lank gray ponytail hung down his back, between jutting shoulder blades. He didn't seem to notice my approach. I walked as loudly as I could, shuffling my feet in the leaves so I wouldn't startle him. I got within two feet of him, and still, he ignored me.

"Hi," I said. "Would you like a piece of rhubarb cake?"

He turned his head and squinted up at me for a long time without answering. His pale eyes didn't seem to focus; I felt as if he was staring through me or past me, instead of meeting my eyes.

"Your hair," he said finally.

Oh no. Not my hair. I could feel the blood rising to my cheeks. Before I hiked, I usually wore my hair up in public. Long and loose, it drew too much attention when I let it down. I'd become a lot more relaxed about it on the Trail, though. Trying to keep my hair hidden all the time would have been almost as difficult as trying not to let anyone see me dirty or tired. I had undone my braid to brush it when we arrived in camp this evening, and now my hair fanned out around me in the last light.

"Your hair is beautiful," the man said. "And you brought me cake!" He reached out a bony arm and selected the biggest remaining piece.

"I brought it for everyone," I said, backing away a step.

"Yes, but you came all the way over here to offer some to me!" He tipped his head to one side, and stared at me for another minute. "So beautiful . . ."

"Yes, well, I have to get back to the shelter to cook supper. Have a good evening."

His arm shot out, and I flinched, thinking he was going to grab my wrist. Instead, his hand paused in midair, open, waiting for me to shake it.

"I'm Mike," he said abruptly.

Reluctantly, I took his cool, sweaty hand in mine.

"Nice to meet you. Good night."

He tightened his grip and drew my hand toward him.

"It *is* a good night, now that you've come to visit me. What's your name?"

"Isis." No point in lying; he could have learned the name of the shorter, blonder Barefoot Sister from almost anyone on the Trail. I tried to tug my hand back, but instead of letting go, he leaned toward me.

"Icy. You don't seem very icy to me. I'll call you Rhubarb, because you made me rhubarb cake!"

I gave a harder tug on my hand, and this time, he let go. I staggered back a few steps, then turned and headed toward the shelter, moving as fast as I could without breaking into a run. Before cooking, I twisted my hair into a bun and stuck a twig through it to hold it in place.

"Jackrabbit, wake up," I whispered.

"Mrrr. Wha time is it?" She held her watch up in front of her face and blinked a few times. "It's five-thirty! Why are we getting up now?"

"I want to get an early start today. You know that guy camped by himself, behind the shelter? He's creepy. I don't want to see him again."

Jackrabbit sat up and gave me a fierce grin. "That can be arranged."

I smiled back at her. "Hopefully we can arrange it nonviolently. Outhike the guy."

"Sounds like a wonderful plan." She consulted her *Data Book*. "How 'bout a twenty to Rusty's today? Oh, and look! It won't even be a real twenty. We can blue-blaze the Mau-Har Trail and save ourselves at least three miles."

I sighed dramatically. "We were such virtuous white-blazers southbound. And now we're going to turn ourselves into Mau-Harpies?"

She winked at me. "It'd be one way to keep the creepy men away."

We hiked out just as the sun rose. The young man who'd been in the Peace Corps waved to us from the shelter, where he was already cooking breakfast, but nobody else seemed to be stirring. Early sun shone through the leaves, making them look as thin and luminous as they had been a month before, when they first opened. The trail felt pleasantly cool underfoot. Here and there, a thick, springy layer of fallen rhododendron blossoms covered the damp ground. Somewhere to the east, a strange bird called—a glorious, thrushlike spire of song, with a second note buzzing under the melody. Another bird answered, far ahead of us.

A few miles out, we stopped at an overlook to eat our dried fruit and granola. Sunbeams slanted over the ridges, leaving the valleys in deep, quiet shadow. The marathon runner waved as she jogged past us on her way back to the shelter. Still early. This would be a good day.

We came to the Mau-Har Trail early in the afternoon. The opening stretch curved along the mountainside, wide and flat as a road bed. We congratulated each other on finding such an easy way around the Three Ridges, which I remembered as a relatively steep and rocky section of the A.T.

"The Mau-Har Trail's only three miles long, right?" I asked jackrabbit, as we cruised around another shoulder of the ridge.

"Three and a half, I think."

"Close enough. At the rate we're hiking, we must be almost halfway there. We'll have all afternoon to visit with Rusty!"

Just then, we reached the first switchback; the trail turned southward and dipped down toward the valley. We glanced at each other, frowning. On the map, the Mau-Har Trail looked like it rose a gradual five hundred feet, winding along the mountain's flank. Of course, the map didn't show much detail, and there weren't any elevation profiles for side trails. Jackrabbit shrugged, and we kept going.

After the second bend, the trail gave up any pretense of switchbacks. It plunged down a steep ravine, overgrown with greenbriar and poison ivy. In places, it was so badly eroded that I had a hard time keeping my balance, even barefoot. I thought about turning back, but scrambling up the loose scree looked like it would be even harder than going down it. After an hour and a half—long enough that we must have hiked at least three miles—we found ourselves in the bottom of a deep stream valley. I undressed and rinsed off the dust in a mossy pool under a waterfall, but I didn't think I had time for a real swim. Clearly, the Mau-Har Trail was more than three and a half miles long, but how much more, I had no way of knowing. Considering that its northern end was about five hundred feet higher than the southern end, I figured that we had at least fifteen hundred feet of elevation gain ahead of us.

The second half of the trail wasn't quite as steep as the first, but it followed the stream's bank through a boulder field that put most of Pennsylvania to shame. We found more poison ivy and greenbriar, more eroded scree slopes, and, to top it all off, a long-dead, bloated possum lying across the trail near the northern end. After the possum, though, the trail leveled out, becoming just as smooth and easy as it had been for the first few miles.

Around five in the afternoon, we rejoined the A.T. at Maupin Field Shelter.

"I need a snack," said jackrabbit, throwing down her pack.

"I need a hot bath and a week of zeros," I answered. "But a snack would be good to start with."

While we ate, we took turns reading the register. Suddenly, jackrabbit dissolved in giggles. "You've got to see this," she said when she caught her breath. "Good old Sleepy."

Sleepy the Arab, only a day ahead of us, had drawn an elevation profile of the Mau-Har Trail in the register: a V that took up most of the page, with a short level stretch on each end of it. A scale at the bottom divided it into ten miles, and Sleepy had written brief captions with arrows indicating various points along it. *Miles 1–2: Nice easy stretch to fool northbounders. Mile 2 1/2: Met a funny-looking guy with horns and a goatee.* (Here he had drawn a cartoon devil, with a word balloon saying "See you at my place in an hour, Sleepy.") *Mile 3: did not realize that it was possible to ski on gravel. Mile 3 1/2: If I'd known, I would have brought skis. Mile 4: Aaaaaaaaaaaaa! Mile 5: Thump. Mile 6–8: Mahoosuc Notch. Mile 8: Carnivorous greenbriar. It's got my leg! Mile 9: Rodent of Unusual Size. I slew it. Mile 10: Nice easy stretch to fool southbounders.*

jackrabbit

We came to Rusty's in the early evening. Mist was rising out of the gardens and the wide swath of green pasture, where a few goats grazed; the windows of the wooden cabins glowed with lamplight. All around the hollow, the darkening hills stretched back to the horizon with no sign of human habitation. I felt as though I had stepped back a hundred years into the past.

A few hikers sat on the front porch. By now, most of the nobos were indistinguishable: skinny, muscular, grubby young men with longish hair and scruffy beards. A few of them recognized us, though.

"Barefoot Sisters!" One of the guys said, rising from his seat at the table. His voice was familiar, and I thought I recognized his blue sarong.

"Timberghost?" I hazarded a guess.

"Right on!"

"I thought you'd be a couple hundred miles ahead of us, with all the time we've taken off."

One of the other nobos laughed. "Who, the Ghost, man? He's been here, like, two weeks."

Timberghost gave a little shrug. "Ain't as long as Kineo. How long you been here now?" he asked a guy who was curled up in a chair in the corner.

The man looked up from the *National Geographic* he'd been reading. "Two more days, and it'll be a month. This place kinda has a vortex, you know? Rusty, he's the man."

"Where is he?" Isis asked him.

Kineo waved his hand vaguely. "Inside somewhere, I think."

"Thanks." We left our packs on the porch and went into the house. It took a moment for my eyes to adjust to the lamplight. There must have been twelve or fifteen hikers crammed into Rusty's small living room, talking, playing cards, trying to read in the dim light, or mending pieces of gear.

"Isis and jackrabbit!" came a familiar voice from across the room.

"Six-string Hillbilly!" I jumped over several hikers who were lounging on the floor, and gave him a hug. "Long time no see. Where's the rest of the Stage Crew?"

"We're down by two, y'all. My lovely wife got off to work at N.O.C. a couple weeks ago. Toast was here, but he hiked out yesterday."

"Sorry to hear that," I said.

"We're planning to all meet up and maybe hike Maine together at the end of the season. Basil's here, though. Out at the hot tub right now."

"Excellent," Isis said. "Six-string, have you seen Rusty?"

"Yeah, he's down by the fire ring, I think."

"Thanks. See you in a bit."

There were more hikers sitting on the back porch, cooking dinner, and still more trying to play Frisbee on the fields in the failing light. Down through the mist across the field, I could see the beginnings of a bonfire, with another crowd around it, and a few hikers waiting outside the wooden shed that housed the hot tub. I tried to estimate how many hikers were in the Hollow. Fifty? Sixty? It was strange to think back to the time we had spent there in winter, with just the two of us and Rusty. I wondered where he was among all these people.

We finally found him standing by the pasture fence, staring off into the shadowy woods. When he turned around, I could see new lines of grief etched into his face. "Isis and jackrabbit," he said softly. "I'm glad y'all are here."

"It's good to be back," I said. "Rusty, what's wrong?"

He sighed. "Y'all remember my little dog Punkin?"

"Yeah," I said, recalling the little golden-brown mutt that had curled up by Rusty's feet in the winter.

"He got bit by a copperhead three days ago. Died in my arms."

"Oh, Rusty, I'm so sorry."

"Punkin was the best dog I ever had. He used to wake me up in the mornings, with his cold little nose in my face: 'Wake up, Rusty! Time to start the fire!' Just like clockwork, every mornin' about five. And he was so fun to have around. I would toss him goldfish crackers, just toss 'em up in the air, and he'd catch every single one before they came down." He paused, and there was a catch in his voice when he continued. "It's so hard, y'all. I keep expectin' he'll come runnin' out of the woods, with his tail up in the air. I keep thinkin' I'll hear that little bark again. Then I realize I never will. I know I shouldn't be so broke up about it, but I am. And the toughest thing is, I don't want to be a downer for the hikers, you know? They're in the Hollow, they oughta have a good time. But it's just hard, to see all these people havin' fun, when I'm ready to fall apart."

It was almost dark now. A few fireflies sparkled above the grass. "Listen, can y'all do me a favor?" Rusty said. "Can y'all stick around a few days? I know y'all will help out. And it's a comfort having y'all here. I feel like, well, y'all know me. I don't have to put on any false pretenses of bein' Mr. Happy for y'all."

Isis looked over at me. We had an ongoing argument about pace, and specifically about how much time we could afford to take off the Trail if we wanted to finish in September. I always argued against taking zeros unless we absolutely had to—counting our break in Cherokee and Cullowhee, the zeros in Hot Springs waiting for my knee to heal, our trip to Florida, Trail Days, and Isis's convalescence in Lexington, we had already spent more than a month off the Trail since we started northbound. It seemed unwise to take any more zeros without a very good reason, because we never knew when we would be forced to take time off for illness or injury. But seeing Rusty's grief-stricken face, I had to broaden my definition of a good reason. I nodded to Isis.

"We can stick around for a couple days," she told him. "What can we do to help you out?"

Over the next few days, Isis and I shared the farm chores with a few other hikers, mending fences and hoeing the rows of potatoes, corn, and okra. Isis helped Rusty make pancakes for the crowds of hikers in the mornings, and baked bread in the woodstove one afternoon. In the evenings we chatted with the other hikers in the Hollow, trading stories and jokes. Hawkeye, an older hiker with a salt-and-pepper ponytail, recited a few long poems by Shel Silverstein, and I chimed in with *The Cremation of Sam McGee*. When the mosquitoes and no-see-ums got bad, we moved inside to play cards.

One morning, while I was finishing up the breakfast dishes in a tub of water by the front porch, I heard a car coming down the driveway. I looked up to see Pirate, one of the Hobos we had met at Trail Days, in a beat-up pickup truck. A man I didn't recognize got out of the passenger's seat. He had white hair and walked with a slight hobble, but he still looked spry as he crossed the parking lot.

"Hey, y'all," Pirate called to the hikers on the porch. "This here's Paw-paw. He's the oldest thru-hiker. Y'all show him some respect!"

People moved aside, giving him a chair at the table. Pirate stood nearby, against the wall, with his arms crossed in front of him. Blue anchor tattoos stood out on the muscles of his forearms.

"How old are you, Paw-paw?" someone asked.

"Well, let's see," he said in a deep Tennessee drawl. "I was eighty-six when I finished my hike." Someone whistled, and Paw-paw laughed. "Hadn'a been for this bastard," he gestured over his shoulder at Pirate, "I never woulda finished the damn thing."

"That ain't true," Pirate said. "I brought him some food. Hiked with him a little. But this geezer would've finished the Trail if it killed him."

"Jest about did."

"He's eighty-nine now," Pirate said, "and he still hikes. We did a couple hundred miles last month. I'm trying to get him to do the PCT with me next year."

"Reckon I'll do it, too, if I ain't bought the farm by then."

"Paw-paw's one tough bastard," Pirate said.

Paw-paw grinned, revealing several missing teeth. "I'm a real McCoy."

"Isn't that *the* real McCoy?" One of the other hikers asked, a little timidly. "I mean, don't most people say—"

"It don't matter to me what most people say," Paw-paw said, "because I *am* a McCoy, on my momma's side. Some of y'all probably heard about the feud."

"Is it still going on?" I asked him.

"What, the feud? Well, there ain't been no killin's in quite some time. But—" he spat on the ground "—I still won't have nothin' to do with them goddamn Hatfields."

Rusty seemed a little happier with each passing day; the color came back into his face, and I saw him cracking jokes with the other hikers. One afternoon, he drove a vanload of us into town to resupply and pick up mail drops. Isis and I bought a replacement cartridge for our water filter and enough food to cover the Shenandoah section. Now that the concession stands and restaurants in the park were open, we wouldn't have to carry nearly as much food as we had in winter. We planned to hike out the next day.

We packed everything up by midmorning and picked up our hiking sticks. In the parking lot at the base of the driveway, we found a bunch of hikers piling into Rusty's van for another trip.

"Barefoot Sisters!" Six-string called from the back seat. "Y'all have got to come with us!"

"Are you slacking somewhere?" I asked him.

"Naw. It's the Buena Vista Fiddle Festival! All kinds of good bluegrass music, not just fiddlin'."

Basil leaned across the seat. "You guys missed Merle Fest. You have to come."

"Isis. Jackrabbit. Y'all are in the South now," Six-string said. "Y'all need to experience some Southern culture." I almost laughed, thinking of the last time someone had used that argument on me—Yogi, in Hot Springs, passing out next to the bonfire.

"If we don't convince you," Basil said, "maybe *that* will."

I looked over my shoulder to where he was pointing. Above the roof of Rusty's cabin, a phalanx of purple-bellied thunderclouds loomed ominously, building as I watched. The clouds blotted out the sun, and a few fat raindrops splatted on the gravel around us.

I sighed. "Murphy wins this round." We stashed our packs on the porch and jumped into the van.

Down in the valley, the sky looked cloudless. We parked at the edge of the festival grounds and walked to the grandstand. Many people had set up campers in the parking area, and all around, we could hear the sounds of instruments tuning. Here and there, a phrase of music floated out.

We arrived just in time to see the finals of the "Bands Fourteen and Under" division. A quartet of skinny twelve- and thirteen-year-olds stood on stage: guitar, fiddle, mandolin, and string bass. The instruments looked comically oversized next to the kids.

The tallest boy stepped to the microphone. "We're the Sweetwater Hollow Band, from Buena Vista, Virginia." The hometown crowd gave a huge cheer, and he grinned. "Our first tune is 'Man of Constant Sorrows.'"

They began to play and sing. I was amazed—aside from the timbre of their voices, they sounded like adults who had been playing together for thirty years. The guitar and mandolin picking was clean and tight. The young girl on the fiddle spun a sweet line that blended with the voices, and the bass player held everything together, plucking his strings nonchalantly.

Six-string leaned back and closed his eyes, a smile of pure bliss on his face. "That's how it's done, y'all."

The music continued through the afternoon. I sat back in the grandstand, mesmerized, forgetting even to eat until Isis bought an enormous tub of popcorn and some chips. She offered the food around to the other hikers. Six-string, Timberghost, and a few others took handfuls of popcorn. Basil was deep in conversation with the couple seated next to him, who didn't look like hikers at all. Basil looked up. "What's that? Food? Well, thanks, Isis. Hey, you've gotta meet these people. This is Dale and Billie Ann. Guys, these are the Barefoot Sisters, Isis and jackrabbit."

"Pleased to meet y'all," Billie Ann said. She was a petite woman in her forties, with curly gray hair, wearing a comfortable cotton dress with a floral print. She seemed completely unperturbed by our strange names. "Basil here has been tellin' us all about the Trail. It sounds fascinatin'. Listen, me and Dale were about to go back to the trailer and grab a bite to eat. Y'all want to come? We've got plenty of food to go around."

"That's really generous of you," Isis said. "Do you know how much hikers *eat*, though?"

"It's no problem," Dale said. He was a robust, stocky man in his late forties, with a Nascar cap pulled down over his forehead. "My brother J.C. was s'posed to be here, but he took sick at the last minute. Way that feller eats, we always bring along a bundle of extra food. C'mon."

Dale and Billie Ann led us back through the rows of cars and trailers. The sunset above the field was a wash of high clouds stained pink and gold. Thunderheads had stacked up on the ridges, but the sky over the valley was still clear. As evening came to the campsite, we could hear more and more bands tuning, and soft voices raised in song.

"This here's our place," Billie Ann told us. "Y'all set down and make yourselves comfortable." She indicated a row of folding lawn chairs. Dale found a few more leaning against the trailer and set them up. "Lemme get y'all some food."

"What have you got?" Basil asked. "I mean, I hate to be picky, but I'm a vegetarian."

"We are, too," Isis admitted.

"Well, that's fine," Billie Ann said cheerfully. "I'll get y'all some extra potato salad and slaw and biscuits, and maybe some sweet potatoes and corn. We've got some watermelon too. And cherries. And y'all can have some extra brownies for dessert . . . how's that sound?"

Somehow, Billie Ann's supply of food was enough to satisfy even our hiker appetites. While we ate, we told stories from our hike. Dale and Billie Ann asked question after question.

"What brings y'all to the Fiddle Festival?" Dale finally asked.

Isis told him a little about Rusty. "He was bringing a vanload of hikers down here, and we decided to come along."

"We wanted to hear some good mountain music," I said.

"Well, you ain't heard the best of it till you heard our boys," Dale told us proudly.

"What do they play?" I asked.

"Jimmy plays the guitar—"

"—our younger son; he's fourteen," Billie Ann added.

"Dale Junior, he plays the fiddle. Just turned eighteen last month, so he's competin' with the big boys now."

"They've got a band with their cousin Raymond. He plays the string bass. They call themselves the Wabash Mountain Boys, on account of that's where our whole family's from."

Dale took another piece of fried chicken from the platter. "The boys have played in festivals pretty regular ever since Dale Junior was ten or so. They have a good time. This time of year, we spend near on every weekend drivin' and campin' out so's the boys can play."

"Where are they now?" I asked.

"Oh, they're prob'ly over at Raymond's trailer, gettin' ready." Billie Ann checked her watch. "They're set to play in twenty minutes; maybe we oughta head over there."

"Thanks so much for dinner," I said.

Billie Ann smiled. "Oh, it's no problem at all. Thank y'all for the stories. Good luck on that Trail. It's an amazin' thing, what y'all are doin'."

"Pretty amazing what you guys do, too," I told her. "Keeping the traditions alive. I never would have believed there were so many kids playing bluegrass. And playing it so well. Good luck to your boys tonight."

The Wabash Mountain Boys, like so many others, played with a skill and spirit that seemed far beyond their years. We never did learn how the competition ended up, though, because Rusty began gathering the hikers together for the trip back to the Hollow as dusk fell.

"I don't like to be out on the road too late," he said. "I'm gonna head out in about ten minutes. Is everybody here?"

"Where's Timberghost?" someone asked.

"What about that kid, Trouble?"

Rusty sighed. "Isis and jackrabbit, y'all know those folks?"

"Yeah," I said. Timberghost would be easy to spot in his blue sarong (which was causing much less of a stir at the Fiddle Festival than I had expected). I remembered Trouble from our conversation the day before. A skinny girl in her teens, with shaved blond hair and an impish smile, she had a knack for saying outrageous things.

"Can you go find 'em for me?" Rusty asked.

"Sure."

"I saw the two of 'em headin' for that fire at the edge of the campground," someone said.

"Thanks."

At the bonfire, a Mason jar of something obviously not water was making the rounds, and the sickly sweet smell of weed hung in the air—probably a good place to find them.

"I'm looking for a guy in a skirt and a girl named Trouble," I told a long-haired man with tattooed arms. He frowned a minute, and I began to think I'd asked the wrong person, but then he broke into a lopsided grin and pointed toward the far side of the fire.

"They went that-a-way."

Isis

After another day at the Hollow, Rusty dropped us off at Rockfish Gap in the early evening. Seven miles to the nearest shelter; we could make it if we put on shoes and hurried. We both felt pretty sluggish, though, after our three days off at Rusty's.

"The Shenandoah registration booth's five miles from here," jackrabbit said, looking at her *Data Book*. "As long as we set up our tent before that, I think we're legal."

"I don't know," I told her. "On the map, it looks like the park starts only a mile from the road." Stealth camping in Shenandoah was forbidden by park policy. Other hikers had warned us that the rangers were pretty strict about enforcing it, because they'd had a lot of trouble with poachers hunting bears at night.

"What else do you want to do? Hitch into Waynesboro?" jackrabbit asked.

"No way." I made a face. When we'd gone into town two days ago, Timberghost had met Creepy Mike at the Waynesboro Post Office. "Weird, skinny guy," he'd told us. "Said he was takin' some time off to wait for a mail drop. He asked if I'd seen you, and his eyes got all intense. I didn't tell him you was at Rusty's."

A few miles beyond the gap, an old road bed covered with soft, high grass crossed the trail and wound off into the woods.

"This looks good," jackrabbit said.

We walked down the road until we were out of sight of the trail. Jackrabbit found a level place to set up the tent while I went looking for a good limb to hang our food bags from. (We'd found that it was easier to throw the line over a branch while we still had daylight, and then carry our food bags over to it after we cooked.) Maybe a hundred yards from the tent, I spotted a good branch, leaning out across the road on the other side of a rhododendron. Just as I reached the rhododendron, I heard something moving through the bushes on the other side of it. No sound of footsteps, only the rustle of something massive displacing the underbrush. I'd done enough dayhiking in wild places to know what made that sound. A creature with feet so large and soft that they folded over twigs without breaking them. I knew, but I looked anyway.

Luckily, the bear had more caution than I did; by the time I rounded the rhododendron, she was running away from me, barreling down the road bed without a backward glance. I hurried back up the hill to tell jackrabbit.

"A bear, and I missed it?" she said. "Well, I guess we'd better pack up camp. It might be shy now, but it knows we're here. If it comes back after dark, it'll have a pretty easy time finding our food bags."

Only a mile or so farther, we found another old, grassy road bed branching off from the trail. I walked up the road for five minutes before looking for a place to hang our food bags. I'd read that it was safer to hang food a long ways from camp, so that bears wouldn't be drawn to it by the smell of cooking. *And if a bear does get into our food tonight,* I thought, *I don't want to lie awake listening to it eat.*

The walk seemed much longer on the way back. Dusk had settled under the trees; every shadow seemed to have eyes and large, silent paws. The gleam of jackrabbit's headlamp, glimpsed through the tree trunks, was as welcome as the bright windows of a hostel would have been.

"Where were you?" she asked, sounding as nervous as I felt. "I was about to go looking for you."

"I wanted to hang our bear line a long ways from camp."

"Right. Good thought."

Jackrabbit had already gathered twigs for the Zip stove. I set it up and started cooking while she read aloud from *Huckleberry Finn*. The water boiled, and I reached for the packet of rice. A flicker of light caught my eye, down the road in the direction of the A.T.—a headlamp, bobbing along as its owner strode toward us. I reached up to turn off my own light, then thought better of it. Whoever it was must have noticed us long ago. If it was a ranger, acting surreptitious wasn't likely to put us on his good side. The light came closer and closer, until the person wearing it stopped only a few feet from our tent. Leather boots, hairy, muscular legs, and khaki shorts. I couldn't see anything else about him without shining my headlamp in his face.

"Who's there?" he asked.

"Hikers," I answered.

"Phew." He unstrapped a pack from his back and lowered it to the grass. "I thought you were rangers when I saw your lights. I was coming up here 'cause it looked like a good place to stealth. I didn't notice you till I was halfway up the hill, and by then I figured it was too late to turn around. I'm Kain, by the way."

"Jackrabbit," my sister said, getting up to shake his hand. "Good to meet you. And I'm glad you're not a ranger, either."

jackrabbit

The weather continued hot and hazy as we hiked through Shenandoah National Park. Thick brownish-yellow smog blotted out the views from the overlooks. The parkway in summer was a steady stream of cars, and every parking lot and overlook held throngs of families with binoculars and guide-books. Back in the woods away from the road, I kept my eyes wide for bears—Isis had seen two on the Trail so far, and I hadn't even spotted one. It hardly seemed fair.

I didn't see any bears in the park, but deer were everywhere. They seemed to have no fear of humans. Early one morning, as we tramped through knee-high wet grass, I nearly tripped on one. It snorted and got to its feet right in front of me; another moment, and I probably would have fallen over it. The sight of that brown wall of fur rising from the grass sent a wave of adrenaline through my bloodstream. When I realized what it was, though, I began laughing uncontrollably. The deer gave me a disgusted look and ambled away, swishing its tail.

"Did you see the sign about these deer at the last road crossing?" Isis said. "The whole population apparently comes from a founding herd of thirteen."

I whistled. "Talk about inbreeding. That explains a few things!"

We camped one night at Hightop Hut, back from the trail among a grove of oaks. It was the shelter where we had stayed after our first full day of hiking in shoes in winter. I hardly recognized the place now, with ferns springing up in the understory and a thatch of dark green oak leaves shading the clearing.

The group of hikers at the shelter was almost entirely female when we arrived—a rare occurrence on the Trail. The only man, and the only person I knew there, was Parypinoy.

"How's Aloha?" I asked him.

"She is off the Trail," he said sadly. "After I camped with her that night, we found a ride down the mountain and went to a hospital."

"You went with her?" I asked.

"She did not want to be left alone," he said quietly. "She was in so much pain."

"What happened? Did they find out?"

"Her leg was broken."

"She was hiking on a broken leg?" I suppressed my expletives out of respect for the priest. "Man, she *is* tough! But she's okay now, isn't she?"

"Yes. She is sad to leave the Trail, though."

"Yeah, that's too bad."

Isis and I introduced ourselves to the other hikers. The rest of the women were just hiking sections of the Trail. Brooke, a dark-haired woman in her late twenties, was in the middle of a ten-month honeymoon. "My husband's up at the tent site," she said. "We're doing the Virginia section of the A.T., and then we're thinking about going to Thailand. I've always wanted to see Peru, too." She shrugged with a sweet smile. "We'll just see how long the money lasts before we have to settle down and rejoin the real world."

"Rejoining the real world is closer than I wish it was right now," said Robin, a tall blond with a smattering of freckles. "Kathy and I are taking the bar exam in July, and then it's off to work we go."

"Don't remind me!" Kathy said. She was a slender brunette, her hair pulled back with a headband. "We graduated from Northwestern Law this spring. We're just hiking a short section of the Trail, sixty miles or so." Dimples showed when she smiled. "I don't know how you long distance hikers do it."

"I think we've got it easier than law students do," I said. "All *we* have to do is put one foot in front of the other. No briefs and depositions and all that for us."

"So you will be lawyers?" Parypinoy asked. "I am a lawyer, too."

"Wait a minute," Brooke said. "I thought you were a priest."

He smiled. "One *can* be both." Then his face grew serious. "In my country under Marcos, the government was quite corrupt. It was difficult for political prisoners to find lawyers to defend them. And this was not because the lawyers were dishonest or lazy; it was because they were afraid. The government would come after their families if they spoke out. There were many instances of torture, rape, kidnapping. After a while no lawyer would take that kind of case.

"I decided to become a lawyer when I saw this. My parents had died some years earlier; I have no brothers or sisters. They could only come after me. And what is my life compared to the life of innocents? So I went to night school to study law."

I took the filter down to the spring to get water for the next day. As I followed the blue-blazed trail, I thought about Parypinoy. He was soft-spoken, cheerful, unfailingly polite, but beneath this calm exterior there was a strength I hadn't begun to imagine. Once again, I was amazed by the wealth of experiences my Trail friends had. I'd met alpinists, musicians, teachers, doctors, modern-day hobos, a professional windsurfer. And now a Filipino priest who had gone to law school to defend human rights.

The flat, nearly level trail in Shenandoah made for quick hiking. We covered twelve miles the next morning before we stopped for lunch at Lewis Mountain Campground. The place swarmed with tourists and cars. At the general store, we bought chips and a jar of salsa, and a frozen pizza to heat in the microwave. As we finished our greasy repast and wiped our faces with napkins, another hiker came up to our picnic table. She was medium height, stocky, with strawberry blond hair and a ruddy face. I noticed that she was limping.

"Do you know where the phone is?" she asked in a broken voice.

"I think it's over by the ranger station," I said. "Are you okay?"

She sighed. "Not really."

"Sit down and take a load off," Isis told her. "Do you want some chips?"

"Thanks." She reached into the bag. "I'm Hammock Hanger, by the way." We gave our names.

"What happened?" I asked her.

"Oh, it's an old injury, and I thought I'd taken care of it. I thought I could hike again." Her voice trembled a little. "But it's come back, and it's worse. I told my husband I'd try to hike through Shenandoah. I thought if I could get through this part of the Trail, going slowly, maybe I'd be all right . . ."

"It's really tough to hike when you're injured," I said, remembering the pain of my knee coming down into Davenport Gap. "The old stuff always comes back to haunt you. Is it your ankle? Knee?"

She shook her head. "I have a needle in my foot."

"A needle?"

"A sewing needle. I must've stepped on it when I was a little girl, and it just got lodged there. I didn't even know it was in there until I started having problems with it, down around Damascus. I went in for an X-ray, 'cause they thought it might be a stress fracture. That was when they found it."

"Can they take it out?" Isis asked.

Hammock Hanger sighed again. "No. There's a bone spur that grew up around it, or something. They said surgery probably wouldn't help, and might make it worse. The only thing for it is rest." Her brow wrinkled. "And that's the last thing I want to do. I don't understand it. I feel like I'm perfectly suited for the Trail. I never had blisters, I never even had any aches and pains getting started. And I've loved every day of it. I just think, 'Why me? Why now?' I mean, I know that's a selfish attitude, but still. That's how I feel."

I hugged her. "The Trail will always be here, you know? You've made it almost nine hundred miles. I bet with some rest, you'll make another twelve hundred and some."

"Thanks, jackrabbit. I needed that." She still looked sad, but a little light was coming back to her pale blue eyes. "I'm going to go call my husband and tell him to pick me up here. But I'll be back. I know I will."

She limped across the parking lot to the phone. It was sobering to think of the two hikers who'd had to leave the Trail in such quick succession: Aloha with her broken leg, and now Hammock Hanger. It made me realize how lucky I was to still be on the Trail, and in one piece, after so many miles. At the same time, I felt oddly guilty; these two women had been so happy on the A.T., so well-suited to Trail life. Here I was, prone to depression and injury, often miserable, yet I could continue when Hammock Hanger and Aloha couldn't.

As the day went on, huge thunderheads built up over the mountains. We glimpsed the leaden bellies of the clouds through gaps in the forest, and at every overlook we cautiously monitored their progress.

"Looks like the storm won't hit till after dark, maybe," Isis said, critically eyeing the looming cloud masses.

"Maybe," I said darkly. "Never trust Murphy."

"It might give us time to eat dinner at Big Meadows. There's supposed to be a great restaurant there. Then we can pack up and look for a stealth site."

"Are you sure it's a good idea to stealth near there? It's one of the biggest campgrounds in the park. Chances are good they'll have rangers out looking for illegal campers, and it won't be Ranger Kain this time."

"Come on. If we set up after dark and leave before dawn, nobody'll find us. And I don't want to shell out for a hotel room."

"I doubt there's space in the laundry room this time of year," I said dryly.

The clouds were beginning to roil and darken in an alarming way when we reached Big Meadows. "I don't know if the weather will hold while we eat dinner," I said, tossing my pack down on the flagstone porch outside the restaurant.

"I don't know either. But I'm not about to pass up a slice of their famous blackberry pie just for a thunderstorm. Those section hikers, Kathy and Robin, they'd only been out four days when they got here, and they said it was still the best pie they'd ever had. Imagine sweet blackberries and a flaky crust, and a big scoop of vanilla ice cream melting on top . . ."

"Okay," I sighed. "You've sold me on it." We stashed our packs beneath the overhang of the porch roof. I spotted a familiar hiker at the far end of the terrace. "Sleepy the Arab!" I called. "How are you, brother?"

"Tolerable, I would say." He grinned. "Though some find me easier to tolerate than others. Let me introduce my companions." He gestured to the two men standing beside him. "This is Polar Bear—" a rail-thin man with shaggy brown hair and a clean-shaven face "—and Johnny Steel." He was tall, big-boned, and muscular, with short brown hair in tight curls and intense blue eyes. "Guys, these are the Barefoot Sisters," Sleepy said.

Polar Bear's jaw dropped. After several seconds he regained the power of speech. "You're the Barefoot Sisters? *You're* the Barefoot Sisters?"

"Well, yes," Isis said. "What were you expecting, eight-foot-tall Amazons with broadswords?"

Sleepy gave an appreciative snicker.

"Well, um," Polar Bear stammered, "when I heard about a pair of sisters hiking barefoot, I was actually expecting you to be sixty-year-old rednecks. With no teeth."

"Watch yourself, Polar Bear," Johnny Steel said in a deadpan tone. "We still don't know whether she was kidding about the broadswords."

Sleepy, Polar Bear, and Johnny Steel invited us back to their tiny hotel room to wash up before dinner. By the time we came down to the dining room, freshly showered, wearing our handkerchief skirts and cleanest tank tops, we looked almost presentable. I was glad we'd had the opportunity to get clean; the restaurant was fancier than I had imagined, with candlelit tables and a hushed, formal atmosphere.

Just as the food arrived (asparagus quiche for Isis and me; huge plates of barely cooked steak for the men), the thunderstorm broke outside. Bolts of lightning sizzled into the hillside all around the restaurant, and thunder rattled the windowpanes almost simultaneously. The lights dimmed and flickered; the tapping of rain on the terrace intensified to a roar.

"Excellent storm!" Sleepy said, his eyes shining. He had to repeat his comment several times before everyone heard it.

"Best one I ever saw," Johnny Steel said between rumbles of thunder, "was when I was living down in Missouri on a houseboat. Lightning was hitting the water all around me, all the masts of the other boats. Hailstones the size of golf balls." He shook his head. "That was wicked."

All night, I had been trying to figure out where he was from. There was something in his speech patterns that was so familiar I almost couldn't name it. But the way he said "wicked" gave him away.

"You're from Maine, aren't you?" It almost wasn't a question. "Coastal Maine."

"Jeez. How'd you know that?"

"Lucky guess. Isis and I grew up there too. Southwest Harbor."

"Vassalboro," he said with a slightly bemused smile. "How come you guys don't have the accent?"

"Our dad's from Virginia and our mom's from southern California," I said. "Both of them cultivated this kind of anti-accent, you know, newscaster English."

"Huh. I haven't been back to Maine for about four years," Johnny Steel said. "I'm surprised you can still tell. I went down to Missouri for the fire academy. They have one of the best ones in the U.S." A rumble of thunder shook the room.

"You're a firefighter?" I asked him.

"Yeah. At least, I was, before the Trail. I don't know anymore. I love fighting fire. I'm really good at it," he said without a trace of boasting. "I have a way with fire, I guess, like the way some people have for horses or machinery or whatever. But it's a dangerous job and the pay isn't good. And I don't feel immortal any more, like I used to when I was young."

"You can't be that old," I said. "What are you, twenty-five?"

"Twenty-six." He grinned. "Old enough to know better."

The drumming of the rain abated a little. I leaned down the table to talk to Polar Bear. "Where are you from?" I asked him.

"Michigan. I'm a systems analyst."

"What does a systems analyst do, anyway?" I asked him.

"Analyzes systems," Johnny Steel cut in, poker-faced. (Thunder rang out like a rim shot, perfectly timed.)

Polar Bear cuffed him on the shoulder. "I don't know why I hang out with these guys. All they ever do is pick on me."

"Everybody needs a straight man," I said.

"He's an easy mark," Johnny Steel said. "He's a Republican."

Isis pretended to be scandalized. "A Republican? On the Trail? I never!" And it *was* rare to find them out here—almost everyone was either a Democrat or something further left on the political spectrum. In a highly unofficial poll of hikers we had conducted in the summer and fall of 2000, Nader had garnered well over ninety percent of the vote.

We waited around in the dining room until I was tempted to order a second dessert. (The blackberry pie was wonderful, indeed, but the slices were rather on the thin side.) The storm continued as strong as ever outside. Rain battered against the windows and poured from the drain spouts. It was getting late, too, for hikers; I glanced at my watch and saw that it was quarter past nine.

At last, we paid the bill and stood up. "Well, it's been fun, guys," Isis said, "but we've got to find ourselves a stealth site."

"You're going to stealth camp in *this*?" Polar Bear said. "You *are* tough."

"We could invite them back to our place," Sleepy said. "The room's not very big. There might be enough floor space for you guys, though."

"Not very big" is a pretty generous overstatement, I thought. When we had visited their room before dinner, I had wondered how the three of them would even manage to fit in the two narrow beds and the even narrower strip of space between them.

"Seriously?" I said.

Polar Bear nodded, a bit reluctantly, and Johnny Steel gave an enthusiastic grin.

"That would be awesome. Thanks." Isis and I collected our gear from the porch and followed the men to their room. We managed to pack into the tiny space. Polar Bear, ever the gentleman, insisted that Isis and I should get the beds. Johnny Steel and Sleepy took the remaining floor space, Johnny Steel in the gap between the beds and Sleepy lying in the open doorway of the bathroom. "Let's hope the toilet doesn't overflow," he said cheerfully, before pulling his mummy bag up over his face.

Listening to the rain pouring off the eaves, I was very glad to have a roof over my head. "Thanks, guys. I really appreciate this," I said.

Polar Bear mumbled something from the next room, sounding a little peeved—he was sleeping in the bathtub.

Morning dawned bright and clear. I tiptoed around Sleepy's inert form to brush my teeth and put in my contact lenses.

"Hey, do you know what day it is?" Isis whispered, her voice full of excitement. "It's June twenty-first!"

Johnny Steel sat up, grinning. "Naked Hiking Day!"

"Yes. And our one-year anniversary on the Trail!"

"You guys have been out here for a year?"

"Yup."

He shook his head. "Insane." His eyes glittered with amusement. "Are you gonna hike naked to celebrate?"

I opened the curtain and looked out. People were already milling around in the campsites: section hikers, families, Boy Scout troops. "Too risky," I said. "It's a freakin' national park. I think it's even a weekend. The rangers would be on our asses in a second."

"I've got an idea, though," Isis said.

We drew more than a few stares as we walked out of the hotel that morning, dressed in our handkerchief mini skirts and bikini tops from Trail Days.

The summer solstice was a hazy, sweltering day, even on the high ridges. Mountains that I remembered from the view in late fall were barely visible now, their outlines ghostly in the humid sky. We saw luna moths for the first time, pale green creatures as broad as my hand, with wings that seemed to be made from tissue paper. They clung to tree trunks here and there like stray spring leaves among the darker greens of summer.

It was hard to believe that a year had passed since we started hiking. It seemed like yesterday I had stood on the peak of Katahdin in a sleet storm, wondering what lay ahead. The more I thought, though, the longer the time seemed. I remembered the nights in the shelters with our southbound friends, our time alone on the ridges of Pennsylvania, the trials of winter. The Family. Our northbound hike, following spring up the spine of the Appalachian Range, and all our side trips: Cullowhee, Cherokee, Florida, Trail Days. In the end, it was hard to believe it had been only a year.

In the evening, we carried water out from one of the campgrounds and stopped to cook dinner in a day-use shelter. I read the fine print on the sign:

Byrd's Nest #3 Picnic Shelter
*Overnight camping and use between the hours
of 7 P.M.–7 A.M. strictly prohibited except in
cases of emergency or extreme weather.*

"Well, we don't have extreme weather yet, but it seems like it's on its way," Isis said rather gleefully as she unpacked the stove. She gestured toward the sky, where a bank of looming thunderheads gathered. It looked like a storm to rival even yesterday's.

"What are you cooking?" I asked. She was pouring something into a plastic bag. It didn't look like our usual supper.

"Fry bread," she answered with a grin. "I wanted to make something special to celebrate our Trail anniversary. I couldn't figure out a way to make a cake on the Zip stove. I thought this might be a good substitute."

"Excellent." I watched her mix flour and water and yeast inside the bag.

"Are you going to set up the tent?" she asked.

"I thought we could just sleep in here. If we get that much rain again."

"Look at the floor, though. It's filthy," she said.

So are we, I thought, but looking more closely, I had to agree. Mouse droppings mingled with mud and shards of broken glass. I decided it would be better to get wet than to put my Thermarest on that. I set up the tent on the highest ground I could find near the shelter.

Johnny Steel, Polar Bear, and Sleepy the Arab arrived as the sky darkened. Isis stretched the bread dough into rounds and fried it in liberal amounts of olive oil. We shared it with the guys, and they all made vegetarian dinners so we could have a potluck. As we ate, our hands and faces greasy from the delicious, oily bread, the first drops of rain began tapping on the roof.

Just after dark, the storm broke with a vengeance. Lightning crashed all around us, so bright and constant that we could see the colors of everything in the clearing: the green of storm-battered leaves thrashing in the wind, the blue of our soaking wet tent, the yellow and red of flowers at the edge of the clearing. The antiphonal chorus of rumbling thunder and the drumming of rain on the tin roof nearly drowned out the sounds of our voices, even though we all sat close together at the picnic table in the back of the shelter.

"Hey, I've got a joke for you," Polar Bear shouted between bursts of thunder.

Johnny Steel groaned.

"No, this is a *clean* joke," Polar Bear protested. "The cleanest one I know. This guy goes into a bar, and there's a lady there who's really—" he paused for a particularly loud rumble "—coming onto him, as they say. Finally she comes up and whispers in his ear, 'For two hundred dollars, I'll do anything you can say in three words or less.' So the guy looks at her, and he lays down a pair of C-notes on the bar, and he says—" thunder cracked and caromed off the clouds "—'paint my house.'"

Sleepy the Arab permitted himself a dry chuckle. "Did you hear the one about the Alabama farmer's daughter?"

We stayed at the picnic table, shouting dirty jokes over the din of the rain until after midnight. A pool of water six inches deep had formed in front of the shelter. The rain showed no sign of stopping, but all of us were becoming so exhausted we could barely keep our eyes open. Isis and I struggled out to our tent, which had a couple inches of water sloshing around in the foot of it. I lay down on my foam pad and felt the rain soak up through my sleeping bag, but I was so happy it didn't matter. *One year on the Trail*, I thought. *This is where we belong.*

Despite the storm, the weather was hot and muggy again the next day. We passed through the burned area south of Thornton Gap, which had looked so dead in fall, and found that most of the trees had survived the blaze. Here and there a trunk had been scorched all the way through, and the tree stood bare, but most of them had sent out at least a few optimistic leafy shoots. Only the blackened ground, lacking the usual thatch of dead leaves, showed clearly where the fire had been.

In the afternoon, Isis and I stopped at Elkwallow Wayside for a late lunch of veggie burgers, fries, and blackberry milkshakes. Polar Bear, Johnny Steel, and Sleepy occupied one of the picnic tables out front, surrounded by a cloud of gnats that quickly expanded to include us. We draped our wet tents and sleeping bags over the fences and trees nearby to dry out in the sun.

Johnny Steel cast a critical eye toward the line of clouds just visible above the trees. All we could see were their round, white tops. It was impossible to tell whether they were thunderheads or not.

"I don't know about those clouds," Johnny Steel said.

Polar Bear squinted up at the sky. "Those are happy clouds. Fluffy white virgin clouds."

Johnny Steel looked skeptical. "Do you know what comes from those fluffy white virgin clouds of yours?" he said, poker-faced. "The gates of hell!"

I took out the *Data Book* that Walrus had given me. "It's only five point seven to the shelter at Gravel Springs," I said. "We could probably make it there before the storm hits."

Sleepy looked at the *Data Book*, made a few quick calculations, and groaned. "The Early Risers."

"What?" I asked.

"The Early Risers. They're probably going to be at Gravel Springs tonight. Oh, they're horrible! A group of section hikers, three men and a woman. They get up at the butt-crack of dawn, hike eight or ten miles to get to the next shelter before anybody else does, spread out all their gear. They go to bed before sunset. And they *snore*."

He said the last word in such a tone of utter condemnation that I had to laugh. "Lots of people snore. What's so bad about these guys?"

"Picture the four most annoying cartoon-character snores you've ever heard. In chorus. From six-thirty P.M. onwards."

"It sounds like you had a run-in with them," Isis said.

Sleepy looked a little sheepish. "We really didn't get along," he said. "I've been going slower than slow for a few days to try to avoid meeting them again."

"What happened?" I asked.

"Well, I guess it all started when the woman asked about my trail name and I told her there was a moratorium on the explanation until the Vermont border. That really seemed to tick her off. And then, well, I hung my pack up inside the shelter, like usual. She said, 'Would you mind moving your pack?' and so I asked, 'Is it in your way?' She said—" he made a finicky face "'—Well, no, but it's blocking the airflow. And *frankly*, your pack smells.'"

We had a good laugh—one of the first facts of Trail life that hikers learn is that funk is universal. No matter how many times you wash your gear and clothes and yourself, everything you take with you on the A.T. begins to stink in short order.

"And you know me," Sleepy said. "I just had to be a wiseass about it. I turned to Kain, who was next to me, and I said, 'Did you hear that? My pack smells!'" he held up his hands in a pleading gesture. "'Why didn't you tell me?'"

"Well, Kain and I both ended up taking a short day the next day. We met up for lunch at one of the waysides. He told me he'd heard the Early Risers talking about me when they left that morning. I was still asleep, of course. He said that one of them had called me a, quote, 'fucking turd.'"

"Damn, that's harsh," I said.

"I came into the shelter that night," Sleepy continued, "and there they were. The Early Risers. And how exactly should one react toward people who have allegedly called one a 'fucking turd'? That was the crux of my problem."

"What *did* you do?" Polar Bear said. "I mean, just in case it ever happens to me."

Sleepy gave an evil grin. "Nothing. I was polite as could be. I decided that by sitting there, being peaceful, and calling no one a turd, fucking or otherwise, I had already won." His chest swelled and he made a heroic pose. "I struck a blow for thru-hikers everywhere with the Leki poles of justice and the dehydrated pellets of retribution!"

"So you really think they'll be at the shelter tonight?" Polar Bear asked, when the laughter had died down.

"It's a good bet."

"Hmm. Those clouds haven't moved since I checked them last. They look safe enough. I think I'll take my chances with the Early Risers. After all, what other options do we have?"

"We could sleep in the privy," I said, pointing out the breezeway between the men's and ladies' rooms.

Sleepy made a face. "I'd rather be *called* a turd than lie down with them. Let's hike."

The rain began just before we reached the shelter, so we arrived dripping wet, ducking under the eaves as the thunder pealed in the hills around us. It looked like there would be enough space in the shelter for all of us—if the current occupants would consolidate their gear. Foam pads, sleeping bags, clothing, stoves, and several paperback books were strewn across the lower floor of the shelter. There was a small upper platform, though, and it looked like some of the space up there might still be free. Three men and a woman sat at the edge of the shelter.

"I don't know how much space we have," the woman said, eyeing Sleepy with distaste. Then she spotted our bare feet and relented. "Oh, are you the Barefoot Sisters? Come on in. I'm sure we can make room. You guys are famous, you know."

I was tempted to turn to Sleepy and say, "Did you hear that? We're famous! Why didn't you tell me?" But I remembered the Leki poles of justice and the dehydrated pellets of retribution. And after all, these people *were* letting us in out of the rain.

Polar Bear, Johnny Steel, and Sleepy clambered up onto the second level while the Early Risers grudgingly moved their gear.

"There's room up here, Isis," Sleepy said.

"I don't know, Sleepy . . ."

"Come on, I don't bite."

She caught his eye and gave a tight smile. "Yeah, but *frankly*, Sleepy, you smell."

Isis

With all the camp stores in Shenandoah, we had enough food left to skip Front Royal. Greasy town meals—even Mexican—didn't hold the allure they had in winter. What we craved was fresh fruit and vegetables, and in this season, the Trail provided both. We found raspberries along the roads, sulfur shelf mushrooms growing out of old logs, and once, at the edge of an abandoned farm field, an enormous cherry tree, its branches laden with ripe fruit. We filled a Nalgene with them and brought it to the shelter, but only one of the other hikers was interested. I was forgetting, the nobos around us had only been on the Trail for three or four months; long enough to crave pizza and ice cream, but not enough to miss anything subtler and less caloric.

The next day, jackrabbit and I found a cooler labeled "Trail Magic" sitting on a picnic table at a road crossing. Over the table, a black mulberry tree arched its branches, thick with fruit. We checked the cooler first: a bunch of empties and one unopened beer.

"It's a little early in the morning to drink beer," jackrabbit said. "I'm not in college anymore."

"Johnny Steel and Polar Bear are pretty close behind us," I answered. "I think they'd appreciate it more than I would."

Jackrabbit smiled, looking at the tree above us. "Luckily, there's something for everyone."

We took off our packs, climbed up on the picnic table, and feasted on mulberries for half an hour.

Late that afternoon, Johnny Steel and Polar Bear caught up with us at another road crossing. "Excellent trail magic this morning," Johnny Steel boasted. "Cooler full of beer right by the trail."

"You mean a cooler with *one* beer and a lot of empty bottles," said Polar Bear. He turned to us. "I got there five minutes too late."

"Maybe you can still get a beer," jackrabbit said. "I heard there's a general store a quarter mile up this road."

I checked my *Companion* pages. *General Store, 0.1 mi east.*

"Point one! If it's that close, we may as well check it out," said jackrabbit. "Maybe they'll have bread."

It wasn't something I would have hitched into town for, but this far along in our resupply, fresh bread would certainly be welcome. The four of us set off along the highway shoulder, laughing and swinging our hiking sticks. At the top of the hill, the store came into view: an old converted barn, with plate glass windows across the front. *GENERAL STORE—GUNS—TAXIDERMY,* read a sign above the door. Boxes of apples and tomatoes filled the left-hand window, and an impressive display of guns, knives, and camouflage clothing filled the window on the right. Along the windowsills on both sides, stuffed bobcats slunk down branches, arched their backs, and snarled.

That night we camped with a big crowd of nobos at Rod Hollow Shelter, setting ourselves up for a ten-mile day through the Roller Coaster to Bear's Den Hostel.

"So, who's up for the Maryland Challenge?" asked Johnny Steel, as we sat around the campfire after supper.

"The Maryland Challenge!" scoffed a hiker named Joe, a police officer in his early thirties who we'd met in Shenandoah. "I've got too many states ahead of me to blow my knees on a forty-one-mile day."

"Not me, man," jackrabbit told Johnny Steel. "We hiked a twenty-three into Harpers Ferry southbound. *Half* of Maryland in a day was hard enough."

"What's the point?" I asked. "You hike a forty, you have to take at least a day off to recover. You might as well hike two twenties and keep going."

"But where's the glory in that?" asked Kain. "I'm with you, man," he said to Johnny Steel. They clasped hands across the fire.

"What about you?" Johnny Steel asked Polar Bear.

"I don't know. I was thinkin' I'd see how the Roller Coaster treats me first. Oh, okay. I'll hike it if you do."

Pretty soon six more men—almost everyone at the shelter—had joined the group, boasting about long days they'd hiked in the past and eagerly planning their assault on Maryland.

"Macho nonsense," muttered jackrabbit as we walked away from the fire.

"Yeah, well, they're just talking. I don't think too many of 'em will do it, when the time comes," I answered.

"I hope they don't," jackrabbit said. "If Polar Bear, Johnny Steel, and Kain all pick up and hike a forty, there won't be anyone around who we know."

I shrugged. "We'll meet new people. And I don't think they'll go through with it, anyway."

We fell behind our friends in the Roller Coaster and hiked all day alone. The interminable series of four- to eight-hundred-foot PUDs was just as tiring as I remembered, but somehow, knowing what to expect made it easier. The wild cherries helped, too. The first tree I spotted stood twenty or thirty yards off the trail, its branches bent under the weight of translucent, red–gold fruit. It looked like it belonged in a walled garden somewhere in southern France, not here in the dry beech forest miles from any cultivated land.

"Look, jackrabbit, cherries!" I cried, preparing to drop my pack and run to the tree.

"Wow. Check it out! Wait a sec—Isis, look down," she said, the enthusiasm draining out of her voice.

I looked. Between us and the tree, a tangle of poison ivy covered the ground.

"Maybe there's a stream in the next valley," I said. "If I wash off the poison ivy within half an hour, I might not get a reaction."

"What if there isn't a stream?" jackrabbit asked.

She was right. Even fresh cherries weren't worth the risk of having open, itching sores on my legs for the next three weeks. I sighed, shrugged my shoulders, and kept walking. On the very next hill, we found a cherry tree whose branches hung over the trail.

By noon, the day had turned hot—not the muggy heat that presaged a thunderstorm, but a dry, dusty heat that made our throats ache. We stopped at a stream to filter more water.

"How 'bout lunch when we get to the next ridge top?" I asked jackrabbit.

"Mmmm, ca-a-a-lories!" She scrunched her arms up in front of her chest like skinny tyrannosaur forelimbs, curling the fingers into claws. "Nice fresh calories!"

We climbed swiftly, encouraged by the prospect of food and a short break. We'd walked only fifteen or twenty minutes when the trail leveled out, following a ridge of flat, black rock. The forest canopy thinned here; the smooth rocks felt hot under my feet. I stepped into a clearing at the top of the ridge, and a flurry of pale gold moths rose up around me, spiraling through the sunbeams. It should have been beautiful, but something about the place felt wrong. The swarming insects, the bare branches, and the hard, blinding sun. I looked more closely, and I saw them. Bristling brown cocoons filled the interstices of the oak bark, and everywhere—in the trees, on the ground—curled the shriveled husks of larvae that had died of starvation when all the leaves were gone. Gypsy moths. We put on our sandals and hurried over the rocks, not stopping, or even speaking, until we were deep in the next valley, under a cool, rustling canopy of beech.

Later in the afternoon, we were walking along a sandy streambank, when I heard jackrabbit cry out in pain.

"Run!" she shouted, before I could turn around.

I sprinted away, hearing her footsteps pounding along behind me. After a hundred yards or so, I chanced a glance over my shoulder. Jackrabbit caught my eye and stumbled to a halt, red-faced and gasping for breath.

"What was it?" I asked her.

"Wasps. I must've hit their nest with my hiking stick; all of a sudden they were buzzing all around my head."

"Are you stung?"

"A couple times. On my face."

She was right; her upper lip was swelling even as I watched, ballooning until it looked like she was holding a grape underneath it. Her left eyebrow was swelling, too, and a couple of spots on her cheek. I threw my pack down and pulled out the first aid kit. No cortisone. Then I remembered. I'd hiker-boxed it in winter, and we'd never bought a new tube.

"Gold Bond cream?" I suggested.

"I don't think tho, Ithith," jackrabbit said, her voice slurred by her swollen lip. "We could try toothpathte, maybe."

Our baking soda toothpaste had really helped the time I'd gotten stung in New Jersey, but that must have been a different kind of wasp. The white cream only made the marble-sized red lumps on jackrabbit's face look infected.

"I'm sure they've got a good first aid kit at Bear's Den," I reassured her.

We hiked the last few miles as fast as we could, ignoring the viewpoints where shelves of rock protruded over still, sun-baked valleys. Jackrabbit's face continued to swell, though more slowly, the lumps on her cheek fusing into a monstrous, angry welt. At last, we walked up the gravel driveway and stood in front of the hostel. The graceful stone mansion hadn't changed since winter, but the land around it looked completely different. A profusion of red and orange day lilies leaned over the walkways, and the lush, thick lawn glowed green. I found Patti on her knees by a flower bed, busy weeding.

"Isis! jackrabbit! So great to have you back!" She jumped to her feet and hugged me.

"It's great to be here," I said. "Patti, do you have any cortisone?"

"Cortisone?" She caught sight of jackrabbit's face. "Oh. Oh, I'm so sorry. I gave our tube to a guy with bad poison ivy, just yesterday. I have it on the shopping list, but I won't be in town till tomorrow."

As a last resort, I checked the hiker box. It was almost empty: two or three granola bars, a plastic bag of rice—and one tube of cortisone ointment.

We'd intended to hike a twenty to Harpers Ferry the next day, but jackrabbit's head ached all afternoon. Her face was still swollen from the wasp stings, and her forehead felt hot when I held my hand against it. At a road crossing near the Virginia/West Virginia border, we walked a quarter mile to a grocery store to buy cold drinks. By the time we got back to the trail, the sun was setting. After our southbound experience night-hiking into Harpers Ferry, neither of us was very eager to approach the complicated maze of bridges in the dark. We ended up stealthing on the ridge just above the river.

Jackrabbit felt much better in the morning. We woke early, packed, and hurried down the last mile and a half of switchbacks before town. When we got to the river, we discovered that we needn't have worried about the bridges. The new one had been completed, and the narrow catwalk where we'd skirted around blocks of concrete had become a wide pedestrian lane with a shoulder-high railing. The old bridge, which we'd finally found on our way back into town, had vanished completely; it must have been torn down since last November. Only a scar of recently seeded turf on both sides of the river, where Canada geese nibbled the new grass blades, marked where the bridge had stood.

The town of Harpers Ferry was just waking up when we arrived; we passed a jogger, a mailman, and a few store owners unlocking their doors.

"We're early," I said to jackrabbit. "We'll have plenty of time to get our town stuff done, and hike out five or ten miles in the afternoon."

She paused a moment before answering. "You know . . . I've been think-ing about the Maryland Challenge. If we could hike a twenty-three barefoot on this terrain, we should be able to hike a forty with our sandals on."

"Riiight. Very funny."

"No, really. When else are we going to be in shape to hike forty miles in a day?"

"Just because the speedometer in your car goes up to two hundred miles per hour doesn't mean you drive it that fast."

"Come on, Isis. Speed-hiking is a perfectly legal form of entertainment."

"Entertainment?"

"Yeah. You know how much fun it is, when you stay up late and do something dumb with a bunch of great people?"

"I think my college years were a bit tamer than yours," I said.

"Maybe so. But what about that time when I was eight, and we tried to spend the night in our tree fort? Remember? We made a lamp out of pitch and birch bark in a clam shell, and we practiced our owl calls until a real owl answered, so close I almost fell out of the tree. That was fun, wasn't it?"

"Until the mosquitoes descended in force at three A.M.."

"Don't be so damn practical, Isis. It's unbecoming in a twenty-six-year-old."

"Okay, okay. It's not anything I'd do on my own, but if it means a lot to you, I'll tag along."

We spent the rest of the day preparing: eating lots of pizza and ice cream, sorting out our mail drop, and then eating some more. Laura, from the Harpers Ferry Outfitter, told us that we could sleep on her balcony so we wouldn't have to waste time packing our tent up in the morning. A little after noon, we made our way to the ATC headquarters. The young woman behind the counter took Polaroid photos of us to place in the 2001 album of hikers.

"Good luck on your hike," she called as we left the building.

Polar Bear, Johnny Steel, and a few of the other guys from Rod Hollow Shelter sat on the steps outside.

"Hey, guys," jackrabbit said. "You still up for the Maryland Challenge?"

"I don't know," Polar Bear answered. "My left knee was really bugging me yesterday."

"Maryland Challenge," said Johnny Steel, weighing the words as though he had just heard them for the first time. "Yeah, maybe. Think I'll take another zero first, though. Gotta rest up, make sure my head is clear before I make that kind of decision."

The other guys nodded in agreement. Jackrabbit spent a few minutes trying to convince them to join us, but all the men still equivocated. At last, jackrabbit gave up and turned to me.

"So much for machismo. We're on our own."

I thought that the men had made a wiser decision, but I smiled at her and shrugged. "Suits me fine. I'm not sure I'll want anyone besides you to see me in the fifteenth hour of the hike."

Laura's assistant Dandelion, a '99 thru-hiker, drove us to the nearest sizable town that evening. We bought two days' worth of good, fresh food: bread and cheese, cookies, peaches, a coffee cake, an avocado, and two tomatoes. We also bought sugar and Lite Salt (sodium and potassium chloride) to make our own energy drink mix—cheaper than Gatorade, and just as good for electrolyte replacement.

I slept lightly. Every few hours a train went by on the rails down by the river, rattling the wooden balcony with the vibration of its passage. Laura had lent us an alarm clock, but I didn't need it. At four-thirty in the morning, I was sitting up in my sleeping bag, pulling my hair into a braid. We ate a hurried breakfast of cake and peaches, and set out just as the sky began to lighten. A few other hikers had slept on Laura's porch, including Joe, the policeman who'd scoffed at the idea of the Maryland Challenge. They were all still asleep, snoring softly, when we left. I was glad of it; I didn't particularly want to explain our change of plans to Joe.

For the first few miles, I walked in a trance, not certain whether I was awake, hiking, or still waiting for Laura's alarm clock to go off. The predawn light cast a milky, blue-green glow over the landscape, as though we were walking on the sea floor a hundred feet down.

We paused for another breakfast five miles out. Jackrabbit checked her watch; we'd only taken an hour and a half to hike this far. We grinned at each other between bites of cake. In this clear, cool hour, with the sun just over the horizon, anything seemed possible.

We made good time for the rest of the morning, too, stopping for lunch fifteen miles from Harpers Ferry. *Fifteen miles before noon! A distance that we'd often considered a good day's hike, out of the way by lunch time.* I tried not to consider the twenty-five miles that lay ahead of us—more than we'd ever walked in a single day, unless we counted the meandering road walk that had completed our southbound hike into Harpers Ferry.

The afternoon was a bit harder: hot, and rocky as Pennsylvania in a few stretches. Still, we had broken our daily mileage record by three o'clock in the afternoon. We celebrated with another round of avocado and cheese sandwiches. After that, each step seemed like a minor victory, and we weren't even very tired. The sun was just setting when we stopped for some cookies at Ensign Cowall Shelter, almost thirty-one miles from Harpers Ferry.

As we packed up the remains of our snack, Joe came down the path to the shelter.

"You're hiking long miles," I said to him. "Didn't I see you in Harpers Ferry last night?"

"Yeah, well." He sounded a little chagrined. "I decided to try the Challenge after all. I'm giving up now—thirty's a long enough day for me. What about you?" he asked.

"Nine point three miles to go," said jackrabbit.

"You're going to do it? Well. Best of luck to you."

We waved goodbye to him and set off in high spirits, singing as we walked through the darkening woods.

Only the last six miles, in the full dark, were painful. As soon as night fell, time snapped loose from its moorings. Hours drifted past, forward, backward, spinning circles around us in the air. *This steep, endless uphill—wasn't I here just a little while ago? And this descent among boulders that tip when I put my hands on them—haven't I always been here, and the rest was only a long, amusing dream?*

By the time we reached the level mile of dirt road before Pen Mar Park, I was staggering along, my teeth clenched. We'd planned to cross the line, get a little way into the woods, and stealth. As we passed the park, though, a voice called out to us from a picnic pavilion.

"Who goes there? Hikers?"

"Yeah, hikers." Thinking the speaker was a policeman, I was about to add, *don't worry, we're not planning to camp in the park*, when jackrabbit spoke up.

"How far is it to the border? We're doing the Maryland Challenge."

"You're doing the Maryland Challenge?" asked another voice. "You've *done* it! The border's only two tenths of a mile away. Why don't you drop your packs here, run down and touch the line, and then crash with us? You won't even have to set up a tent."

"But isn't it illegal to camp in Pen-Mar Park?" I managed.

"Yeah, normally. But the five of us stopped here to listen to a band that was playing in the gazebo. We met this really cool policeman dude, and he said we could sleep here, as long as we cleared out before seven in the morning."

I wasn't sure that I wanted to be up and hiking before seven the next day, but I didn't really want to waste time looking for a stealth site that evening, either. Between two evils, I picked the one that offered faster gratification. *Let the morning worry about itself.*

"Let's put our packs down, and get this over with," I said to jackrabbit.

"I'm keeping mine," she answered. "I haven't carried it for forty-one miles just to slack the last point two."

"Suit yourself," I said, unbuckling my waist strap. I had to bite my tongue to keep from saying what I felt. *This whole day has been an exercise in stupidity. If you want to carry your pack when you could be slacking, go ahead. Take it to the stupid extreme.*

"Don't forget your camera," jackrabbit said, as I lowered my pack to the ground. "We'll want pictures at the border!"

I took a photo of my triumphant sister, standing behind the Mason-Dixon Line signpost with her arms upraised, but I shook my head when she offered to take one of me. I didn't think I had the energy left to plaster a smile on my face for the camera.

As we walked back to the park, my mind arced ahead of me to the place where I could lie down. Daydreaming of sleep. I would sink into sleep like lead into water, and I wouldn't care if the policeman tried to wake me at seven. I wouldn't even notice. When we finally lay down, though, sleep eluded me. Scenes from the day flickered across my mind, and I couldn't shake the feeling that there was another big day ahead of us, plans to go over. My skin itched with sweat, sharp prickles scattered all over my face and arms. Wait—that wasn't sweat. I turned on my headlamp. Tiny insects danced through the beam like dust motes. *No-see-ums.* I brushed as many of them as I could off my skin, and ducked my head under the flap of my sleeping bag liner. *Too hot. Running out of air.* I braved the no-see-ums for another few minutes. And so it went, until I drifted into restless sleep, somewhere in the early hours of the morning.

I woke at dawn to the sound of other hikers stirring. I rubbed my eyes, stretched, and looked around. Three of the people who'd gotten to the park before us were up and dressed; the other two still lay in their sleeping bags, with the fabric pulled up so that only the tops of their heads showed.

A young man with dark, tousled curls sat on a picnic bench next to me, eating breakfast. When he saw that I was awake, he turned toward me.

"Good morning, Isis." It was Iculus. "Did you guys really do the Maryland Challenge? That rocks!"

To my surprise, I felt a flush of pride. We'd just hiked a forty-one-mile day, starting at five in the morning and ending at 11:38 P.M. We'd caught up to people who were two days ahead of us, faster hikers like Iculus, and people we might never have met if we hadn't stepped through the Maryland time warp. I looked forward to getting to know them. It was six in the morning; I hadn't slept much, but I felt fine.

CHAPTER 6

Hiker-Gatherers

jackrabbit

"I still can't believe you guys hiked Maryland," Dream Catcher said. "That's unreal." One of the nobos who had stealthed with us; he was tall and lanky, with a narrow, clean-shaven face.

"It feels kind of unreal to me, too," I admitted. I stretched cautiously, leaning against a picnic table in the pavilion at Pen-Mar Park. Even in the predawn light, the temperature must have been in the high eighties. The humid air pressed in around us. Now that I was up and moving, though, the soreness wasn't as bad as I had feared.

"Where are you guys headed tonight?" Iculus asked as he rolled up his foam pad.

"I don't know," Isis yawned. "Not very far, most likely." She looked worse than I felt, with dark circles under her eyes.

"We'll probably head for Caledonia State Park," Dream Catcher told us. "It's about eighteen."

"They've got a swimming pool," Iculus said. He pantomimed diving in and doing the crawl.

Isis sighed. "I wish there was one right here in Pen-Mar."

"There's a great pizza place at Caledonia, too," I said, remembering the restaurant where Lash and Black Forest had completed their Half-gallon Challenge. "If we can get there."

We ate our breakfast of dry milk and Cracklin' Oat Bran (the most caloric breakfast cereal we had found for our last resupply), and packed up quickly. Before the first sliver of the sun rose above the trees, most of the other hikers had vanished into the woods, following the white blazes. Isis and I took one last look around the pavilion to make sure no signs of our presence remained, and started down the trail.

Considering the forty-one miles we had traveled the day before, I felt surprisingly good. We had been careful to drink enough water; our imitation Gatorade seemed to have worked. My legs were a little sore and slow to respond, but I could remember winter days a fraction of yesterday's distance that had taken a much larger toll on my energy. I smiled, feeling strong and capable. After the first mile or so, I slipped into a pleasant trance, buoyed along by the even rhythm of my footsteps.

"Hey, Barefoot Sisters!" It was Iculus, waving from the embankment beside the trail. He was waist-deep in a patch of black raspberries. "You've got to try these."

We tossed our packs down and headed into the brambles. Soon our faces and hands were stained purple. We found wineberries, too, the deep red husk-covered raspberries that I remembered from childhood summers with my grandparents in Virginia.

"Thanks for pointing these out," I said to Iculus.

He shrugged. "There's plenty to go around. You know, it's weird; all the other guys who were at the park last night just kept walking. I was like, 'Hey, guys! Come eat some raspberries!' but they were all, 'No thanks. Gotta make some miles.' I figure, what's the use of hiking if you never stop and enjoy stuff? Out in the real world, when do you ever get a chance to drop whatever you're doing and eat berries for half an hour?"

As we stepped out of the raspberry canes, I felt a bug of some kind land on my leg. I reached down to brush it off without looking.

"Shit!" I yelped. It was a bee. An angry red welt rose on my thigh.

"Jackrabbit, are you okay?"

"Yeah. Just a bee sting. Damn it, why do they always go for me?" The itchy lumps on my face from the run-in with hornets in Virginia were finally subsiding, just in time for this new sting.

"Hey, I read somewhere that bee stings are supposed to be good for arthritis," Isis said.

I glared at her. "Very funny. I'm not arthritic quite yet."

She sighed. "I'm just trying to make a joke."

"I know. I'm sorry." I spread baking soda toothpaste on the sting, and the itch subsided a little.

Maybe the bee sting did help my sore joints, because the miles seemed to pass by with little effort. Even on the infamous Pennsylvania rock piles, which were beginning to crop up among the dead leaves on the trail, my legs carried me without complaining. It was another hazy, sticky day: the neighboring ridges were barely visible at the overlooks, their edges blending with the washed-out sky. At road crossings, the blacktop shimmered with heat and little mirages floated over the surface. Under the cover of leaves, though, the heat was bearable. Every once in a while, the trail crossed a stream, and we walked through a pocket of cooler air, full of the sound of tumbling water.

Along one creek, I saw pale blossoms hanging among the low branches: the rhododendrons were still blooming. These were a different species than the ones we'd seen in Virginia. Instead of enormous bright pink flowers, they had modest petals of light pink, shading to green, with a spotting of gold freckles. In that moment, even with the heat, I felt like we had walked back into spring. Our forty-one-mile day had acted as an odd sort of wrinkle in the fabric of time, allowing us to cross back into the previous season, just as walking down from the Pennsylvania ridges in October had sometimes carried us from winter into fall.

We reached Caledonia State Park while the sun was still above the trees. Iculus, Dream Catcher, Smokey, and a few other hikers were sitting by the trailhead sign when we arrived, looking forlorn.

"What's wrong, guys?" Isis asked them.

"The pool's closed for renovations," Dream Catcher said glumly.

"We found a place to stay, though," Iculus added. "There's a hostel right down the road. Rocks and Water Outfitters. The guy said he'll bring a shuttle."

Isis and I had planned to stop at the pizza place for dinner and then stealth in the woods. "How much is it?" I asked.

"Three dollars."

"For the shuttle?"

"No, for the night."

"No way!" Hostels commonly cost twelve to fifteen dollars a night, plus extra for shuttles. A few places in the South, like Kincora, The Place in Damascus, and the Pearisburg Hostel, asked for smaller sums or donations. Three dollars was the cheapest I'd ever heard, though.

"The guy said he was just getting started, so there's not much there," Iculus warned.

"Has he got a shower?" Isis asked. Someone gave a cautious affirmative, and Isis flashed a thumbs-up sign. "That alone is worth the price of admission."

A white van with "Rocks and Water" stenciled on the door pulled into the trailhead parking lot. The driver was a young man with a blond crew cut and freckles. "Hi, I'm Jeff," he said. He hopped out and helped us load our gear into the back. "Boy, you guys sure picked a great day to be out hiking!" He wiped the sweat from his forehead.

"That's the thing about thru-hiking," someone said as we piled into the van. "You don't get to pick 'em."

Jeff laughed. "Right you are. This was a nasty one, though. Temperature hit ninety-eight in the valley here."

"What was the temp yesterday?" I asked.

"High of ninety-four."

Dream Catcher whistled. "Holy shit. These guys did the Maryland Challenge on a ninety-four-degree day."

People in the van turned to look at us. "Barefoot?" someone asked, incredulous.

"No, we wore sandals," Isis explained. "There's no way we could have gone that far barefoot. The amount of concentration it takes—" but no one seemed to be listening. My heart sank a little as I considered what was happening: the impossible body of legends surrounding us had grown another chapter.

The van stopped in front of a large outfitter's store, with racks of kayaks and canoes out front. "Welcome to Rocks and Water," Jeff said. "The hostel's right up the hill there." He pointed to a tarpaper shed behind a bank of raspberry canes. "My wife and I just opened this place in spring, and we've only had the hostel running for about a month now. It's pretty bare-bones, I'm afraid. If there's anything you can think of to improve the place, please let me know . . . Oh, the shower's out around back of the store. All we've got is cold water right now; we're working on it. What else? . . . I make a pizza run every night around seven. There's menus up at the hostel. Let me know what you want. Please, make yourselves at home."

The hostel was not elegant, certainly. Bare light bulbs hung from the ceiling; one of the windows was missing a pane of glass. It was comfortable, though, furnished with bunk beds, a few tables and chairs, an old plaid sofa, a microwave, a TV and VCR, and a shelf full of movies. Later that evening, someone turned on *Spaceballs* while we ate our pizza. I amused everyone by reciting half the puerile dialog; it had been our sister Claire's favorite movie in third grade, and I had seen it with her so many times that I'd practically memorized the script. As I lay back on the soft mattress that night, full of pizza, clean, and content, I decided that this night at Rocks and Water Hostel was the best $3 I had ever spent.

In the morning, the Maryland Challenge finally caught up with me. I rolled over and sat up, feeling completely wrung out. My head spun as I stood up; I had to hold onto the edge of the upper bunk for a moment to keep the room from fading to black around me. My legs trembled.

"Jackrabbit, you don't look so hot," Dream Catcher said.

"I don't feel so hot, either," I mumbled, staggering over to the couch. "I think I might stick around here for a while, try to get some energy together."

"Good plan," Isis said from one of the armchairs. She had been up for a while, I guessed, but she didn't look any more lively than I felt.

I ate a few slices of leftover pizza for breakfast. Yesterday's heat had diminished our appetites; Isis and I had only been able to eat about half the food we had ordered.

Jeff came up to the hostel as we packed. "Good morning. What time do you guys want to go back to the trailhead?"

There was a brief conference. "Like, eight thirty?" Dream Catcher told him.

"Sounds good." Then Jeff caught sight of Isis and me. "Are you guys okay? You look really pale."

"Oh, we'll be fine," Isis assured him. "Just a bit tired."

"I could run you a later shuttle if you wanted. Stick around here as long as you need to."

"That would be awesome. Thanks."

We slept for most of the morning. Jeff took us back to the trail in the late afternoon, after the worst of the heat had passed. We only hiked about four miles before finding a stealth site by the trail under a spreading oak tree. I tried to figure out where we were on the map and compare it to the corresponding numbers in the *Data Book*. I smiled to myself: even with this extra-short day, we'd averaged more than twenty miles a day since leaving Harpers Ferry.

It was slightly cooler in the morning, with a wind that stirred the leaves on the high ridges. I felt a little less shaky as I packed up our camp. We planned to take a relatively short day, hiking the sixteen miles or so to the Ironmasters Youth Hostel in Pine Grove Furnace State Park.

The Pennsylvania ridges had an entirely different aspect in summer than they'd had in late fall. Thick foliage now obscured the view, so it was impossible to see how skinny the ridge tops were. Tangles of black raspberries grew by the trail, tempting us to stop often. Less pleasant were the tendrils of poison ivy that twined around the trees and sprawled over the ground.

In the afternoon, as we followed the gradual downhill to the valley where the park lay, I spotted glints of red, yellow, and purple in the high branches above us: cherries! Most of the trees were forty or sixty feet high, though. On the rare occasion that a branch drooped close to the trail, we picked as much fruit as we could reach: red sour cherries with a flavor of strawberries and rhubarb, sweet yellow ones tasting faintly of peaches, pure black ones that stained our hands and faces purple and had a licorice aftertaste.

In midafternoon, we found the most beautiful cherry tree yet. It stood beside the gravel road that the trail followed, with all its limbs weighted down with glossy purple fruit. I reached for the closest branch. I could clutch a few cherries between my fingertips, but the rest sprang maddeningly out of reach. Isis watched with dismay.

"Maybe we can climb it," she suggested, laying her pack down in the gravel. The smooth-barked trunk, as thick as my waist, didn't appear to offer any handholds, but I knew my sister would be able to get up it if anyone could. She stopped at the edge of the road, though. "There's poison ivy all over the ground underneath it."

Sure enough, the shiny triple leaves were everywhere along the roadside, forming a kind of vegetative moat.

"Damn it, it's just like that cherry tree in the Roller Coaster!" I said. The fruit looked so good that I was tempted to wade in anyway.

Isis had a better idea, though. "Do you remember those apple pickers our dad made?"

"Oh, yeah." Every September, when we were kids, our dad had taken us out to gather wild apples. For our neighbors' cider-pressing party, we shook the trees and gathered the drops, not caring how bruised they got. For storage apples, though, we used the apple pickers: a bag on the end of a long bamboo rod, with a loop of wire at the end of the stick to cut the apples' stems so they would drop into the bag, unbruised.

"I bet we could make something like that." Isis furrowed her brow, concentrating. Then a smile came over her face. She took her nylon water bottle holster off the waist belt of her pack and tied it to the end of one of her hiking sticks. The edge of the bag didn't offer quite enough resistance to knock down the cherries, though, and they remained on the branch, swaying, tantalizingly out of reach.

"There's got to be a way to . . . aha!" She took out the length of string we used for hanging our food bags and threaded it through the top of the nylon bag. "Jackrabbit, when I get it positioned around a good clump of

cherries, you pull it tight." She lifted her contraption into position. "Okay
. . . now!"

I yanked on the string. Isis brought down a stained water bottle holster, a
good quantity of cherry juice and squashed fruit, and three whole cherries.

"That worked. Kind of."

We repeated the performance over and over, eating the dark fruit until
our hands were sticky with juice and our tongues were bright purple.

Isis was preparing the cherry picker for another load when I heard a slight
sound and glanced over my shoulder. I was surprised to see a hiker standing in
the road. He was slight and gray-haired, with a fine-boned face and light blue
eyes. The bemused expression on his face suggested that he'd been watching
us for a while, and still hadn't quite figured out what we were doing.

"Hello," he said. "I am Mountain Dancer."

We gave our names.

"Oh, the Barefoot Sisters! I have wanted to meet you for a long time . . ."

His slight accent was enough to tip Isis off. "*Parlez-vous français?*" she
asked, barely able to contain her excitement. I knew it had been a long time
since she had gotten to practice her French. They conversed for a few minutes. I could follow just enough of the conversation to learn that he was from
Quebec, and had been on the Trail since April. I heard something about a
sick relative. Nothing else filtered through my very poor command of French.

"I am sorry. I forget my manners," Mountain Dancer said to me after a
moment. "I am just so happy to find a speaker of French on the Trail. I am
curious, jackrabbit—what is it you are doing?"

"We're picking cherries," I told him.

"Ah."

"It's kind of slow this way," I said, as I tightened the string on another
messy bagful.

"Maybe I could help you," Mountain Dancer said. "One of you could sit
on my shoulders."

I could hardly picture it. He was wiry and thin, and about half my size. I
tried not to laugh, but a giggle escaped anyway. Mountain Dancer chuckled,
too, and in a moment we were all shaking with laughter. When we had
caught our breath, I squatted down and Isis helped Mountain Dancer climb
onto my shoulders. I straightened up slowly, feeling my spine compress. I was
accustomed to carrying another 40 pounds, but a wobbly, top-heavy 160
pounds was pushing it. The weight was tolerable as long as I didn't try to
move too much, though, and in a few minutes Mountain Dancer had filled

Isis's water bottle with fruit. I set him down carefully, and we sat on our packs on the gravel road, passing the liter of cherries around.

"This is so much fun," Mountain Dancer said. A look of regret crossed his face. "I will miss this trail."

"We're only halfway done with it," I said.

He sighed. "I forget what I said in French and what in English. I have to leave the Trail tomorrow."

"Tomorrow! After you've come so far?"

"My mother, she is not well. Someone has to look after her. She had another stroke."

"I'm sorry to hear that," I told him.

"The Trail will always be here. That is what I tell myself. I only hope that when I have the time to return, I will still have the strength to hike."

All day, clouds had been gathering, stacking up in great towers above the treetops. By the time we reached Pine Grove Furnace State Park, the sun was hidden. The air was still hot, and an oppressive silence reigned. Isis, Mountain Dancer, and I dropped our packs on the porch of the hostel, which was still closed for the day, and made a beeline for the pond. It was actually a dammed-up stream, dug out into a little swimming area perhaps ten feet deep and forty feet wide, with a beach of obviously imported white sand. I had noticed it in winter, when the still, brown water was probably a few degrees above freezing. I hadn't been tempted to swim then, but now, after days of hiking in the heat (and finding the swimming pool closed at Caledonia), I was determined to dive in. I ran down the fake beach, dodging between bathing-suited people on beach towels, barely registering the fact that nobody else was in the pool. The water came up around my legs, deliciously cool, washing off the sweat and grime. It was the most wonderful feeling I could have imagined.

"Hey! You! Get out of the water!" It was the lifeguard, yelling from her stand on the beach. "Now!" She pointed up to the sky. The swollen purple edge of a storm cloud was rushing forward, lightning lancing out into the trees. For a moment I was tempted to risk pissing off the lifeguard—and jeopardizing my life—just to prolong the transcendent feeling of that water on my skin. But common sense took over, and I waded out.

A restless wind sprang up, sucking the humid, heated air toward the mass of storm clouds. As we ran back to the hostel, the wind strengthened until the treetops whipped around and small branches came crashing to the ground.

Thunder boomed and crackled all around us. The rain caught us before we reached the shelter of the hostel porch, but for once I didn't care. It was a warm rain, sheeting down from the fierce sky, and it felt almost as good as the pond water had.

Mountain Dancer skipped and leaped on the front lawn of the hostel, his arms spread wide. "The Trail is saying goodbye to me! And I am saying, 'See you later!'"

Shawn, the hostel manager, let the hikers in at 4:30, with his usual shy smile and polite greetings. "Welcome to Ironmasters. There are bunks in the next room, showers over there . . . Isis and jackrabbit! I haven't seen you guys in ages! I heard a lot of rumors you were headed this way, though."

We stowed our packs in the bunkroom and returned to tell Shawn about our hiking adventures since we had last seen him, at the Ruck in January. He brought out pictures from that weekend. I recognized Earl Shaffer, Spur and Ready, Miss Janet . . . and there was the Family from the North. Paul and Mary, Joel, John, Hope, Joy, and little Faith. I felt a lump in my throat, thinking of all the goodbyes we had said along the Trail.

I played the piano for hours, while the storm receded gradually across the ridges. Isis made gingerbread and potato salad from the well-stocked hiker box. In the misty twilight, fireflies appeared, like a thousand low-hung constellations winking in and out over the grass.

Isis

High summer had come to the woods. On weekends, the forest swarmed with dayhikers: families out for picnics, people walking their dogs, and long lines of camp kids complaining about the heat. The day we left the Ironmasters Youth Hostel, we met two hassled-looking young men trying to herd a group of thirty or forty eight-year-olds down the trail.

"Come on, everyone, we have to move over and let these people past," one of the leaders said.

As he tried to line them up along the embankment, one little girl caught sight of our feet.

"Look, they took their shoes off!" she cried. "Why can't we?"

"Because the rules say—" the young man started to explain, but none of the children were listening to him. Instead, they were pushing forward, surrounding me and jackrabbit. The leader caught my eye and shrugged his shoulders, lifting his palms in the air.

"Do you mind if they ask you a few questions?" he asked.

I smiled at him. "No problem."

The questions were already pouring in from all sides.

"Where're you from?"

"Does everyone in Maine go barefoot?"

"How many days you been in the woods?" (This from a girl who wrinkled her nose when the crowd behind her pushed her too close to me.)

"Do you fight off bears with those big sticks?"

"Do you carry a gun, so you can shoot stuff and eat it?"

"Are you grown-ups? Or are you just real tall?"

Later that day, as we climbed through a patch of boulders on a ridge outside of Boiling Springs, a faint whiff of cigarette smoke warned me that someone was approaching. A few minutes later, I ducked around an overhanging rock and found myself facing a short, grizzled old man, jauntily dressed in a button-down shirt and vest. In one hand, he held a half-finished cigarette; in the other, he carried a dangerous-looking metal walking stick with some kind of hook at the bottom end.

"Seen any copperheads?" he asked. "I'm huntin' 'em." He twirled his metal walking stick and grinned.

I shook my head, glad that the last copperhead I'd seen was back in Virginia, a safe distance away from this man who claimed to be hunting them.

"Well, this ain't the best spot for 'em, right along the trail," he continued. "They don't like the noise of all those boots thumpin' by. But there's a good big nest of 'em near here, just a few yards into the woods. I could show you."

"Sure," I said.

He stamped out his cigarette on a rock and stuck the butt in his vest pocket.

"Katie! Carla! Tom!" he called out, and in a minute, two girls and a boy, perhaps seven to ten years of age, peered down at us from the top of a boulder. "I'm gonna show these ladies the copperheads. You comin'?" The three heads vanished behind the boulder again.

"They'll come," he said to me, leading us into the woods beside the trail. "They love seein' the snakes." He stopped in a small clearing full of stone ledges. "Used to bring my kids out snake huntin'; now it's my grandkids. Good way to get 'em interested in somethin' other than the TV."

The three children bounded into the clearing, coming to a halt behind their grandfather. "Now," he said to them, "let's see what we can find." They scattered over the rocks, peering intently into every crevice or patch of dried leaves. The old man lit another cigarette and watched them, beaming. Every once in a while, he'd take the cigarette out of his mouth and offer a bit of advice.

"Walk quietly, now, Thomas, or you'll scare 'em all away. Carla, I wouldn't poke that stick under that rock if I was you. You don't wanna go aggravatin' 'em. Oh look, there's one!"

I looked where he was pointing. I couldn't see anything but a foot-wide band of fallen leaves at the bottom of a crack in the rocks. The children tip-toed over, pointed, and whispered excitedly to each other.

"Make it move, Grandpa," begged the oldest girl.

"We're out here to look at snakes, not to bother 'em," the grandfather admonished, but he reached out his walking stick and gently tapped it against the side of the crevice. A patch of dried leaves a few inches from the stick's tip sprang forward, stretching into a two-foot-long snake that zigzagged across the ground. It was much lighter than the one we'd seen in Catawba, a golden cream color mottled with copper so bright it was almost pink. While it was moving, I couldn't believe that something so beautiful could have made itself invisible. When it froze after only a few slithers, though, its colors seemed to melt into the leaves around it. I could only find it by looking for the motion of its slim pink tongue, and following the curve of its body down from there.

"Okay, okay, that's enough," the old man said. "Let's let this one get back to sunnin' himself, and see if we can find any more."

Late that afternoon, we hiked into Boiling Springs. We sat down in the shade of a maple in the town park, in front of the ATC regional headquarters. Ishmael, the trail angel who'd taken us in when we came through in fall, was hiking out west. He'd told us to call his house anyway; his friend Becky, who was house-sitting for him, would be glad to have us visit. I was a little hesitant to call a complete stranger, but Becky sounded delighted to hear from me.

"Ishmael told me all about you guys," she said when I called. "I'll be right over to pick you up; just let me get my daughter in the car seat."

A few minutes later, a slender woman in her early thirties, with shoulder-length blond hair and freckles, jumped out of an old blue station wagon.

"Hi, I'm Becky," she called, waving to us. She turned and extracted a struggling child from the backseat of the car. The little girl dashed past us to balance on the wall beside the trout pond.

"Ooh, Mommy, a big one!" she crowed. "If I jumped right in, I bet I could get him."

"Fine with me," Becky called back. "I'll cook him up, and you can eat fish for dinner, while the rest of us have pizza." She turned to me and jackrabbit. "Pizza sound okay? There's a great Italian place just a block away from here."

"I want pizza, Mommy! I want pizza too!" The girl shouted, jumping up and down on the wall.

Becky gave us a rueful smile. "That's my daughter, Sierra. She'll calm down in a day or two. She's been with her dad for a while, and the two of them, well, they run at the same energy level."

As we walked to the restaurant, Becky asked us how we had gotten started backpacking.

"Ishmael wants me to go with him, next time he goes to Arizona," she told us, "but I don't know if I'd have the endurance. Now that one—" she smiled fondly at her daughter, who was trying to twist her paper place mat into a hair tie. "She'd have no trouble. She'd probably hike the A.T. next year if I let her go."

Jackrabbit and I took a zero the next day. We both agreed that we needed a day off to catch up with our correspondence, wash and air our gear, and send ourselves a mail drop in Port Clinton. I suspected that Ishmael's piano, one of the best on the Trail, may have influenced jackrabbit's decision that our packs needed time to air out. She played almost all afternoon, while I cooked bread and spaghetti. Becky pored over the "help wanted" section of the newspaper, circling a few ads and making calls. All three of us took turns playing with Sierra, who had calmed down enough to get through about half of a storybook before she sprang to her feet, grabbed my hand, and dashed out into the yard to show me her favorite lookout tree.

The following day was the Fourth of July. Becky offered to slack us back to Boiling Springs from somewhere to the north, so we could watch the Harrison fireworks together that night at nine. I checked the maps while jackrabbit looked at the *Data Book*.

"It's pretty flat across the Cumberland Valley, isn't it?" jackrabbit asked. "I don't remember much elevation gain there."

"Yeah, flat as a pancake," I told her. "It's pretty easy going all the way from here to Duncannon. Cumberland Valley, then a couple bumps, then a nice flat Pennsylvania ridge."

"Twenty-six miles," she mused. "We could slack that easily, as long as we wear sandals on the rocks."

"I don't know about you, but I'm planning to wear sandals all the way through Pennsylvania," I told her. "Once was enough." I turned to Becky. "Could you drive us as far as Duncannon?" I asked.

"Sure," she said. "It's only half an hour from here."

It took us longer than we'd expected to reorganize our packs for slacking, and the drive turned out to be almost an hour long. The sun was almost overhead by the time Becky dropped us off in a parking lot on the outskirts of Duncannon. Jackrabbit frowned, looking at her watch.

"It's eleven-thirty, Isis. We won't have time to stop for lunch."

"You think I'm going to hike twenty-six miles without lunch? Of course we'll have time. If we hike three and a half miles an hour, we can take half an hour for lunch and we'll still get there well before nine." I tried to sound more confident than I felt about the likelihood of hiking three and a half miles per hour. Our usual pace was two and a half; slacking, maybe three. Here on the level ridge, though, the miles fell away easily. Most of the trail was smooth-packed dirt, and with sandals on, we could skim over the occasional boulder field. The sense of balance we'd learned from hiking barefoot served us well; I found that I could tell which way a rock would tip as soon as I touched it, even through the shoe's sole. When we stopped for lunch at one-thirty, we had already hiked nearly seven miles.

We would have made it to Boiling Springs before dark, if it weren't for the cherries. First, at the base of the meadow, we found a tree of black cherries with its low branches weighted down with fruit. We gave ourselves five minutes, but we ended up taking ten. In a patch of woods just beyond the meadow, we found a tree full of tart, translucent red fruit, the flavor of the cherry pies my Virginia grandmother used to bake. And yellow cherries of the kind we'd found in the Roller Coaster, tree after tree of them. And here were black mulberries, hanging right over the trail.

Huge spires of cumulonimbus clouds gathered over the valley, darkening the sky. Thunder growled around us as we dashed across the turnpike bridge, with seven miles to go, and the first fat drops of rain slapped against the leaves overhead as we reentered the forest. We raced around the edges of fields, laughing, as the rain slid in sheets off our bare arms and lightning split the sky. The trail became a river of mud. Mulberry trees leaned out of the forest; we grabbed handfuls of the rain-soaked fruit and ate it as we ran. As the twilight deepened, a few fireflies flashed, deep in the undergrowth.

We reached Boiling Springs just as the rain slowed. It was almost nine; the low clouds, the trees, and the grass all had a bluish cast in the darkening air. Warm lights shone from a few windows on the street, but the park was deserted. As we watched, the last few raindrops spattered on the trout pond's milky surface, and the fireflies came out: thousands of them, rising from the wet grass, hovering in the trees like Christmas lights and stars. Thin mist drifted over the grass, turning the tiny lights into hazy spheres of gold.

"Let's go look for the spring," said jackrabbit. We'd heard about the spring that gave this town its name, but we hadn't bothered to look for it when we passed through southbound.

"Do we have time?" I asked.

She glanced at her watch. "We have five minutes before Becky picks us up. Come on!"

We dropped our packs on the porch of the ATC building, crossed the street, and hurried along the smooth-paved walkway beside the stream that fed the trout pond. Maybe ten yards from the road, we turned a corner and saw it—thousands of gallons of water, churning up in the middle of a wide octagonal basin. Water piled up on itself, a sliding silver mountain in the midst of the pool. I knelt on the concrete beside it and dipped my hands beneath the roiling surface. Quick currents tugged at my fingertips. I brought my hands up, full, and drank. I poured the water over my forehead, feeling the cool streams run across my scalp, through my already-soaking hair, and slide down into the hollows of my collarbones. Out of the corner of my eye, I saw jackrabbit kneeling beside me, pouring water over her own face. Her skin, in the glow of a nearby streetlight, looked silvery as the pool's surface. Her face wore a soft smile, like the face of a child deep in a good dream. After a minute, she stood up, shook her hair out of her eyes, and stretched.

"I feel wonderful," she said. "I feel like I could hike another twenty, starting now." She loped off along the walkway, and I sprinted after her.

Just as we got back to the ATC building, Becky pulled up.

"The fireworks were canceled because of the storm," she told us as we climbed into the car. "I'm sorry you're missing them."

"That's okay," I said. "We had plenty of natural fireworks."

"Even better than last year," jackrabbit said to me.

jackrabbit

Becky dropped us off in the parking lot of the Duncannon supermarket. "Good luck," she said.

"Thanks for everything. Good luck to you, too."

It was late morning; we were eager to hit the trail. We took a cart and quickly grabbed the food we needed from the shelves: granola bars, cereal, dry milk, crackers, dried fruit, a variety of Lipton dinners and instant rice dishes. Outside, we transferred the food from its boxes into Ziploc bags for easy transport. Another sweltering day; the parking lot shimmered with heat already.

"Shoot! I knew I forgot something," Isis said. "T.P."

"Good memory."

She ran back into the store while I finished packing.

"Excuse me," said a voice at my elbow. I turned to see an elderly man in a blue suit and red suspenders. "Are you hiking the Appalachian Trail?"

"Yes," I told him. "My sister and I—"

"Fascinating. Could you do something for me, young lady?"

"Uh, sure. What'd you have in mind?"

He gestured toward a bus that had parked by the curb. "The town of Duncannon sponsors a trip to this market every Tuesday for old farts like me who don't get out much." He winked. "We don't often have any entertainment. I wondered if you might step aboard for a moment and tell us about your adventure."

"Sure," I said, closing up my food bag and stowing it in my pack. I followed the old man up the steps of the bus, and looked out into a sea of curious, time-worn faces. "Hi. My name's Susan, but most people call me jackrabbit these days. My sister and I are hiking the Trail together. The Appalachian Trail."

A sort of whispered sigh went through the group. "Aren't you afraid to be out there, two young women alone?" a man in the front seat asked.

"Not really. To tell the truth, the thing that's frightened me most is the weather." This occasioned some laughs. "I mean, I don't want to make light of the dangers out there. There definitely are some scary people." I thought of Roadrunner. I remembered, too, the nine murders that had taken place along the Trail—hadn't one of them happened near Duncannon? "We've been careful not to camp near roads, not to tell random strangers where we're going . . . For the most part, though, there's a pretty amazing community on the Trail. Hikers look out for each other."

"How long have you been out there?" asked a woman with a silver bouffant hairdo.

"Well . . . we've actually been on the Trail for more than a year now. A year and two weeks." There was stunned silence. "We started in Maine, at the end of June 2000, heading south." I gave a brief summary of our hike.

The questions rained in: *What do you eat? How much does that pack weigh? Why do you carry those sticks? What did you do in winter? Do your parents know where you are?* The faces in front of me were, by turns, awed and baffled as I answered. Out of the corner of my eye, I saw Isis emerge from the automatic doors of the supermarket and look around for me. "My sister's back," I said. "I'd better go. It's been nice talking with you."

To my surprise, the whole bus erupted in applause. I grinned and waved as I stepped down. It always lifted my spirits to talk about hiking, especially to such an appreciative audience.

The bus pulled away, with people still waving from the windows. Isis and I shouldered our packs and followed the highway into town.

"Hey, I remember this corner!" Isis said. "There's the Done Cannon itself!" A WWII gun emplacement, with rust showing through its battleship gray, stood guard over the street corner and a small bed of petunias. I remembered seeing it in fall, as we walked to the grocery store to buy Netta her first-ever pumpkin pie. It seemed like half a lifetime ago. I thought about what Netta had said, as we trudged up the gravelly roadside.

"My wish is for peace. Everyone, I think, wishes for peace. Why is it, then, we celebrate war?"

We crossed the wide, shallow Susquehanna on a concrete walkway beside the freeway bridge, with a whipping crosswind and the sound of traffic ringing in our ears. Then the trail led back into the woods, up the steep slope of Peters Mountain, under the deep green leaves of oaks and maples. Here and there, cucumber magnolias grew on the lower hills, with their giant floppy leaves. I remembered how in fall they had been the last trees that held their leaves, and coming down the ridge to the valley of the Susquehanna had been like descending into a magical golden wood. Now it was a million shades of green, and no less magical.

Sweat dripped into my eyes and deerflies buzzed around us in the hot, still air. Occasionally one would land on my shoulders and bite, leaving a stinging red welt the size of a dime. Already, piles of clouds were beginning to form over the valleys, stacks and towers of cumulus. They looked innocent enough—I thought of Polar Bear's "fluffy white virgin clouds"—but I knew we would have a terrific storm before the day was over. I only hoped we would have time to get to a shelter first.

We stopped for a snack at Clarks Ferry Shelter, five miles from town.

"We could make it to Peters Mountain, anyway," I said, studying the *Data Book*. "It's another seven or so. That's what, two and a half hours? I doubt the storms'll start by then."

Isis examined the map. "It's all flat, too. I don't remember too many rocks in this section." Then she frowned. "Peters Mountain? Isn't that the one with the five million steps down to the water source?"

"I don't remember."

"You wouldn't," she said with a lopsided grin. "*I* was the one who got water that day. It's at least half a mile straight down."

"Oh." I looked at the map. "If the storms hold off long enough, we can make it down to that creek in the next gap. Thirteen miles."

She glanced critically at the sky. "Maybe."

As we left the shelter, I heard footsteps coming up the trail behind us. I turned to see a young man with short blond hair and a light pack. He was definitely a hiker, but not one that I recognized.

"Hi. I'm jackrabbit," I said.

He looked a little embarrassed, and when he gave his trail name, I found out why. "I'm Strider."

Isis and I had to laugh; this was Strider number five, at least, among this year's nobos, and the name had been popular last year as well.

"I know," he said. "I'm beginning to think I should have picked a name that nobody else would take, like Gollum or something."

"Well, actually . . ." Isis said.

Strider sighed. "Let's just change the subject." Then he brightened. "Have you ever wondered what it would be like if gravity let go for an instant? I have all these strange thoughts when I'm hiking. On the way out of Duncannon I started thinking about that. Can you picture it? What if there were no force holding things together? Would everything just drift in random directions?" He skipped along the surface of a rock field. "Can you imagine what that would feel like, to float away from the earth?"

The miles of flat ridge top seemed to fly past us as we walked in a line, sharing strange speculations and random thoughts that had come to us in the course of hiking. We came to Peters Mountain Shelter even sooner than I had predicted. Towering storm clouds showed through the trees, moving closer, but none of us wanted to stop.

"It's only another six miles to Clarks Creek," Strider said. "Six and a half. We can make it before the storms get here . . . What would you do if you could make yourself invisible?"

We continued down the ridge, laughing and talking. The sky began to darken around us, and the trees shook in a rising wind. A few large raindrops spattered down through the leaves. By now, we were just about equidistant from the shelter and the end of the ridge.

"Have you ever wondered what would happen if the storm hit the ridge while we were still on it?" I asked Strider.

KA-BLAM! A blinding flash of light filled the woods with an almost simultaneous crack of thunder. A hickory tree a hundred yards away sported a brand-new smoldering scar down its trunk.

"I hadn't thought about it," he said with remarkable calm. "Under the circumstances, I would say losing some elevation is our first priority."

We looked for a way down from the top of the ridge, but the skinny sides of the mountain had given way to cliffs here, woven with thick brambles of raspberries, greenbriar, and poison ivy. The rain began in earnest, a pelting downpour that was surprisingly cold for this season.

"We've got to keep moving," Isis said, always aware of the dangers of hypothermia.

"Okay, Plan B, then," Strider said. "We run for it." He took off, dashing down the trail, and we followed as fast as we could. The sky darkened as though someone had pulled down a shade. Several more lightning bolts hit the forest nearby. I remembered seeing a tree in Virginia that had been little more than a shattered stump, the rest of the trunk blown away in a shower of shrapnel by a direct lightning strike. I wondered briefly if I would die like a vampire, impaled on a stake. Instead of fear, this thought brought me a mad kind of joy. I laughed out loud at the sheer strangeness of life, the utter stupidity of running along a ridge in a thunderstorm. I thought of Breaking Wind's story about windsurfing in hurricane waves. What we were doing now was probably less dangerous. It was a matter of luck, rather than any skill. I felt a delicious thrill from it, though, a rush of clarity and intensity like nothing else. It was as though the idea of death's proximity had made me, for once, fully alive.

After a while, the trail dropped off to one side of the ridge. The sound of the storm faded behind us. I thought it was only a minor dip in the ridge—but no, I realized with something akin to regret, we were descending into the gap.

The rain tapered off and mist rose in the cool air. We found Strider camped at the bottom of the gap, on the opposite bank of Clarks Creek. He waved from a sandy spit of land, among huge hemlocks and rhododendrons.

"Lots of good campsites over here," he called.

"Where's the best place to cross?" Isis asked him, surveying the thigh-deep water in the bend of the creek.

He shrugged. "Anywhere."

The water was colder than I had expected, and swifter. The current tugged at my hiking sticks and my legs. On the far bank, though, was a level, sandy open space with room for many tents. Strider had already set up his tarp beneath the overhang of a hemlock and stacked a pile of firewood by the circle of blackened rocks in the middle of the clearing. *So far*, I thought, *he comes the closest to living up to his name of any of the Striders I've met.*

We lit a smoky fire and sat beside it, trying to dry out our clothes, saying little. After the storm, silence seemed the most appropriate thing. I collected twigs for the Zip stove, and Isis prepared a pot of macaroni.

"Do you want some tea?" she asked Strider, after supper.

"Sure. Thanks."

She added extra water to the pot. It was almost boiling when we heard a voice calling from the trail, on the other side of the creek.

"Hello. Do you have any idea where the Barefoot Sisters are camping?" I looked over. It was an unfamiliar man, tall, thin, bearded, with a video camera and a tripod slung over his shoulder.

"Who wants to know?" I asked him.

"I'm Lynne Whelden. I'm doing a workshop for the Appalachian Trail Conference this August. I talked to Isis in Harpers Ferry, about maybe doing an interview with the two of them."

I looked at Isis. She nodded, with a slightly guilty look—in the excitement of preparing for the Maryland Challenge, she'd forgotten to mention it.

"Do you know where they might be camping tonight?" Lynne asked again.

In response, Isis lifted up a bare, pink foot, clean for once from all the rain. "Come on over," she said.

He hesitated for a moment at the edge of the cold, swift-flowing creek. The rocks on the bottom were slick, I knew, and the mud gave way disconcertingly underfoot. Lynne stepped into the water, though, tennis shoes and all, and started wading.

I sighed. "If a guy goes to this much trouble, I guess we can give him an interview."

As it turned out, his perceptive questions and offbeat sense of humor made the interview enjoyable. He shared stories about his work, testing and designing lightweight gear for various outfitters, and we told him about our methods and motivations for barefoot hiking. When he waded back across the stream, after almost an hour, I was sad to see him go. *If all the paparazzi were like that*, I decided, *I might be tempted to seek fame in the outside world.*

Over the next few days, we traveled fast over the ridges that had seemed so interminable in fall. Our sandals made the sharp rocks easier to navigate, and our summer pack weight was much lighter. I was startled to realize that I still recognized the clearings where we had set up camp as southbounders. I knew the places by the precise configurations of rocks and trees, the shapes of low-hanging branches. When I had started hiking, more than a year ago, I hadn't noticed these details: trees were trees; one patch of forest was pretty much like another. After a summer in the woods, my brain had learned to pick out the subtle variations that made each clearing unique. I was amazed that I still knew these places, even with the change of season. When we passed one of our sobo stealth sites—and we often went by two or even three in a single day now—we would always pause briefly: this patch of ground had been home to us, for a night.

The ridges were full of fruit in this season; banks of black raspberry canes tangled beside the trail, and cherry branches occasionally hung down far enough for us to pick them. Lower down, in the gaps, mulberries grew thickly, fat purple fruits almost the size of my thumb. We grazed on the fruit as we passed, delighted to find calories we didn't have to carry.

Near noon one day, we came to PA Route 501, home of the infamous 501 Shelter.

"We're going to get pizza this time, damn it," Isis said. "Even if it *is* the middle of the day. Even if we have to hitch to town to do it."

The shelter stood empty in the noonday heat. There was no answer at the caretaker's door. We went back to the parking lot and stood on the edge of the blacktop, sticking out our thumbs to the few cars that went by. No one slowed.

"Hey, you guys want a ride to town?"

It took me a moment to locate the voice: a young man with short dark hair and blue eyes, leaning through the window of one of the parked cars at the edge of the lot. I hadn't noticed him before. We cautiously approached the car. I wondered what the guy was doing, just sitting there in the parking lot with his windows rolled down, staring into the woods. He had a friendly smile, though.

"Hi. I'm Jay," he said. "Toss your packs in the trunk; I think it's open." He must have seen the slight expression of suspicion that flickered across my face, because he laughed. "Don't worry; I'm not dangerous. You guys are probably wondering exactly what I'm doing here. The truth is, I'm kind of wondering, too. I'm supposed to be taking the bar exam right now."

"Right now?"

"The end of the month, actually." He shoved some soda bottles and fast food wrappers aside on the backseat to make room for us. "Pardon the mess. Yeah, I'm supposed to be taking a prep course in Florida this month. Taking the exam in a few weeks. I decided to take a road trip instead . . . What're your names, by the way?"

We gave our trail names, and he laughed again. "Hikers. You guys come up with the craziest names. I gave a guy a ride into town the other day, guy named Polar Bear. And I met a woman up in New Hampshire called She-Ra, Princess of Power."

"Have you been following the Trail?" I asked him as we got into the car.

"Not exactly. I've crossed it a couple times. I like hanging out with hikers; you guys seem to have your priorities straight. Me, I've just been driving around, kind of aimlessly, trying to figure out what to do with the rest of my life."

"You really don't want to be a lawyer?" Isis asked as Jay pulled out onto the road.

"No, I really don't. I was in my last month of law school, and I thought to myself, how many happy lawyers do I know? And the answer was zippo. All the lawyers I know have ulcers and migraines and trophy wives and sky-high mortgages."

"What would you rather do?" I asked him. "If you could do anything in the world, what would it be?"

"I'd be a writer. Move to Ireland and get a little sheep farm or something, and write short stories. Maybe even novels."

"That sounds pretty good," Isis said. "Go for it."

Jay sighed. "It sounds good in theory, I guess. It'd sound even better if I could scrape together the money for the plane ticket. But how in hell am I going to pay off my loans?"

The pizza was every bit as good as I had imagined. We ordered, at long last, the very things we had dreamed of on that cold October night at the 501 Shelter: a Greek salad, onion rings, and a white pizza with broccoli and onions. We also bought two eggplant subs to carry out for dinner that night.

Jay sat back in his chair, shaking his head, when the food arrived. "I thought about just getting on the Trail and hiking," he said. "But if I did that, I wouldn't even be able to afford to feed myself!"

"It takes a while for the Appetite to kick in," Isis told him.

"How long have you guys been out there?"

We told him stories from our hike, taking turns so we could both get our share of the pizza while it was still warm.

"Man," Jay said. "You guys are the ones that should write a book."

After lunch, he took us back to the trailhead. "Hey, good luck with your hike. And thanks for the stories."

"Good luck to you. Thanks for the ride," Isis said.

I waved as we headed back into the woods. "Hey, Jay, let us know when your first novel comes out."

Isis

On the ridge before Port Clinton, we decided to blue-blaze along a dirt road that paralleled the Trail, to make better time than we could have on the rocks. We hoped to get into town, sort out our mail drop, and hike a few more miles before stopping for the night. It was a hot afternoon, especially out from under the cover of trees. The sun glanced off the pale reddish dust of the road's surface; I focused my eyes on the shadows of rocks and trees around us, trying to give them some rest from the glare. There, the hard shadow of a fallen branch lay among the grasses by the road. No, it was a burned branch, its surface charred a deeper black than shadow. *Strange*, I thought, *I haven't seen any other signs of fire damage around here.*

My ankle was only a foot and a half away from the snake when I realized what it was: a timber rattler, at least two feet long and as big around as my arm. A tracery of faint, yellowish diamonds marked the black scales on its back. The snake seemed to be just as startled by the encounter as I was. It lifted its head a little, flicking its tongue out twice. Other than that, it remained motionless until I'd had time to warn jackrabbit and back away to the other side of the road. Only then did it slide into a coil, lift its tail in the air, and rattle. We stood and watched it for a moment, then walked on, examining the sides of the road more closely now.

The dry buzz of the rattle followed us until we were out of earshot. I'd seen rattlesnakes in zoos before, but this was the first time I'd encountered one in the wild, and the first time I'd heard that sound. I'd been afraid, before, that I would mistake it for a cicada or a dry leaf loose in the wind. Now, I knew, I could never confuse that sound with anything else.

This time around, we'd been careful to send ourselves plenty of food in Port Clinton. More than we needed, at the pace we were hiking. The dirt road walks, which had been the most difficult aspect of Pennsylvania

southbound, flew by now that we were wearing sandals. Without their slippery layer of recently fallen leaves, the boulder fields seemed like child's play:
weekenders and even our fellow nobos stared at us in dismay as we darted
along the tops of the teetering rocks—"flying," as jackrabbit called it. *We
must've sent ourselves twice as much food as we need to get to Palmerton*, I thought, as
I lugged our mail drop box out onto the post office porch.

Jackrabbit glanced up from the postcard she was writing. "I hope there's a
hiker box somewhere in this town," she groaned, looking at the enormous
box in my arms.

"I don't remember one," I told her, "but I could go check at the Port
Clinton Hotel. I think that's where hikers usually stay."

"Good idea," she said. "Do you think you could fill our water bottles at
the spigot while you're over there? We'll need enough to cook with."

I walked off toward the hotel, my arms full of clanking water bottles. Just
as I turned the corner onto the main road, I caught sight of a wiry, slightly
built man with wraparound shades and a long silver beard stepping out of a
restaurant. In spite of his jeans and spotless white button-down shirt, I recognized him instantly.

"Nimblewill Nomad!"

He turned and beamed at me as I ran toward him.

"Isis! What a lovely surprise to see you here." He opened his arms in
a hug that encompassed me and all the water bottles. "Is jackrabbit
around?"

I told him she was sorting through our mail drop.

"Well, why don't you both meet me at the hotel when you finish, and we
can trade some stories?"

Half an hour later, we were sitting at the bar with Nimblewill Nomad,
working our way through pints of Yuengling while he filled us in on what
he'd been doing since Trail Days.

"Staying at my cabin, mostly, working on poetry. I just finished putting
my ballads into a book; it should come out next fall. And—" He leaned in,
lowering his voice conspiratorially. "I'm planning to hike the American Discovery Trail next summer, the new trail that runs from coast to coast. Lots of
road walks; it was designed for biking, not hiking. Unless someone else gets
the same idea, I'll be the first person to walk the whole thing."

"Cool. Good luck," jackrabbit said. "I'm still wondering how you
happened to end up in Port Clinton, Pennsylvania, on the same day that we
hiked in."

"Road trip," he answered. "I'm headed over to the ATC meeting in Shippensburg. I just stopped here because it's a Trail town. I've got a lot of friends in Trail towns."

Just then the door swung open, and a heavyset man with a baseball cap pulled over his dark gray hair strode up to the bar. I knew that I'd met him at the Gathering and the Ruck, but I couldn't quite recall his name.

"Nimblewill Nomad, old buddy! And the Barefoot Sisters!"

"Bag o' Tricks!" Nomad jumped off his barstool and gave the man a hug.

"Party at Eckville Shelter tonight," Bag o' Tricks continued. "Lazee sent me over here to pick up the beer. Hope to see you all there!"

I remembered Lazee, another trail angel we'd met at the Gathering. He lived a few hundred yards off the Trail on Hawk Mountain Road, fifteen A.T. miles from Port Clinton. Eckville Shelter was a garage in his backyard, which he'd fitted with bunks and bookshelves. The place was more like a hostel than a shelter, but he maintained it for hikers free of charge.

"I don't know if—" jackrabbit began, but Nimblewill Nomad was already working out the details.

"What time? Eight? I'll give these ladies a lift over, and then I can drive them back here in the morning on my way to Shippensburg." He turned to us. "Would that work out for you?"

"Perfect," jackrabbit said. "Thanks for the invitation, Bag o' Tricks!" She took a sip of her beer and sighed, smiling. "Ever notice how well things work out on the Trail?" she said to no one in particular.

Nimblewill Nomad gave her the proud, benevolent smile of a teacher whose student has finally grasped the point of the exercise. "The longer you're out here," he said, "the better things work out. I used to be a doctor. I was not a happy person, and I wasn't very kind to the people around me. These days, I hike."

Lazee had a bonfire going by the time we arrived, and a crowd of hikers gathered around it, drinking beers and roasting hot dogs and marshmallows over the flames. (In the true spirit of the undiscerning hiker appetite, one man had put a hot dog and several marshmallows on the same stick.) Nearby, Bag o' Tricks cooked hamburgers on a grill and Lazee handed out cans of Yuengling. A cheer went up as we entered the circle of firelight.

"Nimblewill Nomad!"

He lifted his arms, palms up, and bowed his head: a gesture that expressed both humility and acceptance of their praise.

"The Barefoot Sisters!"

We smiled and waved at the eager, unfamiliar faces around the fire. In spite of the pint of beer I'd finished just an hour before, I felt shy, uncertain of how to engage any of these strangers in conversation.

"Tell us a story, Nimblewill Nomad!" one man called, and pretty soon a clamor of voices seconded the request. Nomad looked up, his eyes bright in the firelight.

"Well, this happened way up in Canada, near the mountain they call Jaques-Cartier . . ."

I smiled and relaxed, letting the mesmerizing rhythm of his voice carry me to a snow-covered mountain far away. When he finished speaking, everyone called out for another story. He smiled, shaking his head.

"I could go on talking all night, telling you all the wonderful things I've seen. But the last time I saw these young ladies, one of them recited me a Robert Service poem that would be perfect for a campfire on a night like this." He turned to jackrabbit. "Do you think you could give us *The Cremation of Sam McGee*?"

The stories and recitations continued late into the night. Hours later, the group of hikers stood in a circle around the glowing coals, swaying back and forth with our arms on each other's shoulders, as jackrabbit and I taught the crowd to sing "Dig a Hole."

We left our gear at Eckville the next morning and slacked the fifteen miles from Port Clinton, stopping for lunch at an overlook called the Pinnacle. The white cliffs jutted out like the prow of a ship, a thousand feet above the valley. Far below us, farm fields checkered the low hills, punctuated by tin-roofed barns, grain silos, and small, murky ponds.

I was reminded of the feeling I'd had, hiking the trail along the narrow Pennsylvania ridges in late fall—the sense that we were the last of a nomadic people, living in the only strip of forest left in an agricultural land. In this season, although the disparity between the wooded ridges and the farm valleys looked as sharp as ever, we could hardly think of ourselves as solitary wanderers. We shared the Pinnacle with twenty or thirty dayhikers, families and couples out for picnics, and a scattering of other nobos. Looking around at the children playing on the rocks and the young couples lounging in the shade, I realized that for the dayhikers, these cliffs and ridges were part of their home. To them, this strip of forested land connected valley to viewpoint, not Georgia to Maine, and the waves of hikers who paused for an hour and then walked on were just passing, seasonal tourists.

We cooked our dinner at Eckville that evening, chatting with a new crowd of nobos, then packed up our gear and hiked a few miles farther before nightfall.

jackrabbit

Another day of hiking over the dry ridges brought us to Palmerton, where we spent the night at the borough hall. The smudge of polluted hillside spreading upward from the smelting plant didn't look quite as bad in summer. Hints of green showed from the edges of the blasted land; evidently a few plants had found a foothold in the wasteland. The thing that worried me this time was the bank of thunderheads stacking up above the ridge. We filled all our water bottles, ate breakfast at the '50s diner, finished our resupply at the IGA, and headed out of town. I stopped by the library to check my e-mail while Isis sat on the steps outside, writing postcards.

When I returned, she cast a critical eye toward the looming clouds. "I don't want to get caught up there in a storm. Once is enough."

"Yeah," I said. "This time we wouldn't even have the shelter of the trees. We'd better hike fast." We shouldered our packs and followed the wide sidewalk out of town.

"What is it, jackrabbit? You have that little smile on your face."

I sighed. "I can't keep anything from you, can I? I got an e-mail from Tuba Man."

"Tuba Man? I thought you gave up on him after the bottle rocket incident."

"Not one of his better moments," I admitted. "But it's not like I gave up on him. We just decided it wouldn't really work out, you know? He's still fun to hang out with, though."

"What'd he say in the e-mail?"

"He's driving up the coast in a few weeks for some kind of gig in Boston. He wanted to know where we'd be so he could do some trail magic."

"Jackrabbit! Are you blushing?"

"I guess I am, damn it!"

We came to the base of the rock jumble at Lehigh Gap. I had a vague recollection of stumbling down it in fall, listening to the last of my water slosh in the bottom of my bottle. I remembered how the rocks and golden-leaved sassafras trees had glowed in the horizontal light, the image seeming to pulse in and out with my heartbeat. Even now, with the trees wearing their summer green and the benign light of midday streaming down, the place gave me a sense of foreboding. I patted the full water bottle in my hip holster and listened for the comforting slosh of the two others, stowed in the side pockets of my pack. Reassured, I started to climb.

The ascent from Lehigh Gap was faster and easier than I had imagined. We pulled ourselves hand over hand up the blocks of stone, and then stepped nimbly across the slanting, shifting boulder field near the top of the ridge. A soft wind came up from the river, cooling the expanse of blackened rocks. The clouds hung motionless in the sky. In a short time, we stood at the end of the long ridge, looking out over the desolation left by the smelter.

"It's not quite as dismal as I remember," Isis said, and I agreed. Most of the ground still lay empty, blighted, but here and there a nodding pink flower with a cushion of leaves sprouted up from the crusted soil. (*Candytuft?* I thought.) More amazingly, some of the trees that I had thought dead in the fall now bore a few leaves here and there. Twists of living bark stood out like brown ropes on their weathered stumps, feeding the stunted branches.

With sandals on, we made good time on the gravelly trail. Soon we began to see grasses among the crooked trees, and enormous, fat blueberries. I was tempted to stop and eat them, but I thought of the heavy metals in the soil and decided against it. After a while, the forest started to look more normal, with the oaks and sassafras rising straight and tall. I felt myself straighten, too, heaving a sigh of relief: we had come through the wasteland.

We spent the night at Leroy Smith Shelter, where we had eaten our pomegranate in the fall. Then, we had laughed and joked about having to stay on the Trail for months. Our predictions had been closer to the mark than we would have guessed.

The storm still hadn't broken; I felt its muggy weight in the night air around us. We found a small group of hikers at the shelter when we arrived. Two men lay on the platform, wrapped in their sleeping bags. A stocky man with gray hair and a trimmed beard sat in front of the shelter, tending a low fire. He looked up as we arrived.

"Barefoot Sisters!"

It took me a moment, but I remembered where I had seen those serious gray-blue eyes before. The Ruck, in January. "Spur?"

"Good memory," he said with a grin. "I've been trying to catch up with you guys for weeks. Then I heard a rumor you did Maryland—"

I nodded.

"Barefoot?"

"No, we actually had sandals on," Isis said.

"But still. I thought I'd never catch up."

I shrugged. "Aw, we took a couple of short days . . . I want to hear about your hike, though. When did you start? Is Ready with you?"

At the mention of his wife's name, Spur's eyes lit up. Then he gave a sad smile. "She's done most of the Trail with me, but she's taking a few days off right now. Her sciatica's really bothering her. We're going to meet up again at Delaware Water Gap and see how it goes. I miss her . . . But tell me what you guys are up to. Oh, I saw your performance at Trail Days, by the way. Well done." He winked. "I've heard all these crazy rumors. Something about Florida?"

Isis filled him in while I gathered twigs for the Zip stove. It was growing dark; I had to turn on my headlamp to make sure I didn't put my hand in a clump of poison ivy by mistake. I was a little nervous, too, thinking of the rattlesnake Isis had nearly stepped on near Port Clinton.

"Where's the water?" I asked one of the guys in the shelter. He was reading the register by the light of his headlamp. His long blond hair cascaded down in the blue beam.

He looked up at me. "Water? Ain't none. Went to all the fuckin' springs down that trail. S'posed to be three of 'em down there. Ain't a one runnin'. My brother—" he gestured to the man beside him, with an identical cascade of fine blond hair, who looked at me but did not smile. "My brother was all set to hike to that road back there, hitch out and spend another night in town. I said, 'Fuck that, man. Somebody'll have water.'" He gave a scattershot burst of laughter. I was worried, thinking of the twenty miles between here and Delaware Water Gap and the half-liter of water left in my pack, but he continued. "And you know what? Guess what?" He didn't wait for an answer. "Like an hour ago, this dude shows up with a bunch of water. It was unreal."

I noticed for the first time the five plastic gallon jugs sitting along one edge of the sleeping platform. I gave a sigh of relief. "You had me worried for a minute there."

He laughed again, and this time it had an unpleasant edge to it. "Pretty girl like you out in the woods, what you got to worry about?"

Isis and Spur were still conversing by the firepit. Spur must have overheard something, because he came to the shelter. "Jackrabbit, you guys find a tent site yet? There are some good ones up by where I'm camped."

"Thanks, Spur," I said. "I'll go set up." I was glad for an excuse to get away from these guys, and very glad that we wouldn't be sharing the shelter with them. Originally, I had planned to sleep there, knowing that the overnight rains would add to my morning pack weight, but the prospect of a wet tent didn't seem so bad now. I took the tent and ground cloth out of my pack and walked up the blue-blazed path.

It was fully dark by the time I returned to the shelter. Isis had a pot of noodles steaming over the Zip stove. The blond man yammered on, nonstop: "I never seen a stove like that. It's fuckin' weird. Where'd you pick that thing up? You ever use a normal stove?"

Spur was finished with his dinner, but he still sat by the fire. "Zip stoves aren't that rare," he said to the man in the shelter. "How long have you guys been on the Trail?"

"April," the guy said. His brother still hadn't spoken. "We started at Katahdin in April."

I nearly spat out a mouthful of noodles. Nobody started at Katahdin in April, not without a certified Maine Guide and a lot of ice-climbing experience. Most of the trails on the Mountain stay closed until the end of May or mid-June after heavy-snow winters like the one we had just hiked through.

"How'd you get the park to let you climb that early?" I asked him.

"It wasn't too tough. It's another fuckin' mountain, you know?"

I was seriously beginning to doubt his story. "Maine's a great state," I said. "My favorite part was the Allagash Range." I used the name of a river system in northern Maine for my fictitious mountains.

"Yeah. Real pretty."

In the firelight, I could see Isis trying to suppress her laughter.

"What'd you think of the new bridge over the Kennebec?" I asked, knowing that there was no bridge within twenty miles of the ferry crossing hikers used.

The guy was looking a little suspicious. "Real nice," he said. His brother beside him was scowling.

I was startled to see a headlamp coming down the path. I wondered who it could be, this time of night, crossing the empty ridge with the threat of storms close overhead. By the dim orange glow of the fire, I saw a gaunt young man with unruly short hair and a tiny pack. He threw himself down on a log in front of the shelter.

"Is there water here?" he croaked in a desperate voice.

I indicated the gallon jugs lined up in the shelter. He grabbed one that was nearly full, put it to his lips, and drank it down without stopping.

"You should've stocked up in town," I said. "That climb out of Lehigh Gap can be nasty."

He regarded me through his mop of brown curls. "Lehigh wasn't so bad. It was cooling off by the time I got there. It was the ridge around Bake Oven Knob that really got me. I'm Swampfoot, by the way."

Spur, Isis, and I gave our names; the brothers in the shelter said nothing.

"Wait a sec," I said to Swampfoot. "Bake Oven Knob? That's south of Palmerton. You didn't stay in town last night?"

"Didn't even go in," he said with a bit of pride. As the water coursed through his system, his eyes looked a little less glassy, but they still had an unhealthy manic glow. "I stayed at the Allentown Shelter last night. That's, let's see . . ." he took a dog-eared *Data Book* out of his pack. "Thirty-three point five."

I whistled. "Big day. Those ridges are pretty dry. Where'd you get water?"

"Well, I started out with almost a full liter this morning." He dug a ramen packet out of his food bag and munched it down, dry, and then reached for another jug of water.

I heard the first rumble of thunder through the trees. "I guess we'd better get in our tent before this hits," I said. "You guys take care."

In truth, I was glad to get away from the crowd at the shelter. Swampfoot seemed a little unbalanced, no doubt the result of hiking such a long day without water. As for the other two, I didn't trust them at all. The one who talked was bad enough, but his brother was even stranger. He lay there watching everything, his eyes measuring the scene, never saying a word. If it hadn't been for Spur, I probably would have packed up and hiked on a few miles, storm or no storm.

The last twenty miles of the Pennsylvania ridges were the roughest: small pointy rocks, big sharp-edged boulders, all of them tipping in random directions beneath our weight. Even with the keen sense of balance that months of barefoot hiking had given us, this section of the Trail was difficult. After the first few miles, my head ached from the concentration it took to keep from falling.

At noon, we came to Wolf Rocks, a huge, teetering pile of granite slabs sticking up above the ridgeline. During the nine days we had spent at Kincora in winter, I had come across an article about the geology of this area. Knowing the history of the landscape, I found I could make sense of the patterns of rocks and ridges around us: Wolf Rocks had been the terminal moraine of the last continental ice sheet, the mound of debris pushed up in front of the glacier as it advanced over the land. During several thousand years, the constant freeze-and-thaw cycles at the glacier's snout had fractured the rocks like frost heaves in a rural highway, leaving the infamous rock fields we had just crossed. Ahead of us was a landscape of smooth-shouldered mountains, U-shaped valleys, and little ponds: a glacier-carved landscape. Though the evergreen forests still lay far to the north, it was beginning to look like home.

We stopped for lunch on the rocks, checking carefully for snakes before settling on a big slab of stone and dangling our feet over the edge. A light wind stirred the leaves of the birches. As I munched a handful of crackers, I heard footsteps coming up the trail.

"Isis and jackrabbit?"

I looked up. It took me a moment to identify the young man who stood there. In jeans and a cotton t-shirt, he wasn't dressed like a hiker, but there was something hikerlike in his stance. He was rail-thin, pale, with short blond hair and tiny glasses.

"Nightmare?" I ventured. I hadn't seen him since Caratunk, Maine, more than a year ago.

"That's right." He smiled. "I heard rumors you guys were out here, hiking back to Maine." He shook his head. "That makes you just about as crazy as that Starman character we met."

"We aren't quite that pungent, are we?" I asked him, laughing.

He took a sniff. "Not quite."

Even though I'd hardly spent any time with Nightmare, he was another southbounder. The instantaneous sense of fellowship reminded me of what I had felt when Ox waded across the stream at Apple House Shelter in the Roans, where we had camped with our mom.

"Hey, it's great to see you, man," I said. "What are you doing out here, anyway? Out for a hike?"

"I was looking for you guys, actually. I was doing some trail magic last week, and I heard you were headed this way. Here, I brought you something." He held out two delicious-looking pastries. "Amish walnut squares. They're my favorites."

"Wow. Thanks!"

He sat down on a nearby rock. "It's just good to be back on the Trail, however briefly."

"How are things out in the so-called real world?"

"Oh, jackrabbit, the plain truth is, the real world sucks. Never go back if you can help it." He took a sip from the water bottle he was carrying. "I've had such a rough year, ever since I finished the Trail in December. My stepdad had a stroke in January. He's pretty much incapacitated. My mom's caring for him, so my salary is all they've got to pay their grocery bills and the mortgage. I'm kind of tied down right now. I keep thinking back to the Trail, when all I had to worry about was, you know, 'How far should I hike today? Where should I put my tarp? What flavor of Lipton tonight?'"

"I guess we're pretty lucky," Isis said quietly.

"Yeah," Nightmare sighed. "I've done a little hiking this summer." His eyes gleamed in anticipation of a good story. "I went up to the Whites one weekend and stealth-camped near Lonesome Lake."

"How was it?" Isis asked.

"Oh, the weather was great. But you know how weird things always happen to me when I'm out hiking?"

"Weird shit happens to everybody out here," I said. "It's part of the game."

"Well, this was more weird than usual. I went into the men's room at the hut, and there was a kid there, about ten years old, with this evil grin on his face . . . He had a Ziploc full of water, and there were leeches in it."

Isis shuddered. "Ugh! I hate leeches."

"There must have been about ten of them. The biggest, fattest leeches I ever saw."

"What did he do with them?"

"I don't know. I took off. I didn't really *want* to know, actually." He grinned. "A day in the life."

We finished our lunch, saving the Amish walnut squares for last. Glazed with honey and full of butter, they tasted every bit as good as they looked.

Nightmare walked with us down to the next road. We told stories from our hike and reminisced about the 2000 southbounders. It felt like we had known each other for years. Finally the sound of traffic came up from the gap. We reached the gravel parking lot where Nightmare's pickup stood.

"It was great to see you guys again." He sounded almost wistful.

"Great to see you, too. Thanks for dessert."

"Take care." He swung up into the cab. Then he turned back to us, grinning. He leaned out the window and did his best Starman impersonation. "'I've got forty dollars and a decision to make!'"

He gunned the motor. In a moment, the truck had vanished around a curve.

Isis

On the ridge just above Delaware Water Gap, we found the best blueberry patch yet. We took off our packs, sat down in the middle of it, and began the serious business of filling our stomachs. When we'd gone berry picking as children, I'd saved most of the fruit I gathered for pies and canning. Following my mother's example, I ate only a handful or two for every quart I contributed to the family's stores. I'd also prided myself on being a clean picker—no sticks or stems in my bucket, and absolutely no wormy berries. Now, I tried not to think of how many worms I was swallowing. We ate like bears, shoveling handfuls of sun-warmed berries into our mouths. Energy, sweet and instantly absorbed.

I ate for forty-five minutes, and still I didn't feel full. I looked at the bushes we hadn't touched yet, their green almost hidden under clusters of sugary fruit. *If only there were some way to preserve the berries and carry them with us on the Trail.* I realized that I wasn't just wishing that we'd have blueberries later on; if these past couple days were anything to go by, we'd find plenty in the next few weeks. What I missed was the process of harvest: my quick hands sorting the berries from the leaves, and the solid, satisfying weight of a full container. We could pick a few to save for the evening, anyway.

"Hey, jackrabbit, let's pick some berries for the pastor who runs the hostel," I suggested.

"Great idea," she answered. "You know, it's weird—when I was little, I used to wish that I could just eat all the berries I picked, right then and there. Now some part of my brain misses picking to save."

It took us only fifteen minutes to fill my Nalgene. I smiled to myself as I stowed it in the side pocket of my pack. Jackrabbit and I had gotten to satisfy our harvesting instincts, and at the same time, we'd found a rare opportunity to give some trail magic back to one of the people who provided it.

A buzz of voices, punctuated by rustles and clinks and the sizzle of something grilling, greeted us as we walked up the hostel driveway. A row of folding tables forty or fifty feet long stood in the middle of the driveway, covered with red-and-white-checked paper tablecloths. Next to the wall stood two more folding tables, laden with steaming soup pots and casserole dishes. Another table, pushed back a ways under the eaves, bore towering stacks of cookies and brownies. Four enormous watermelons lay in the shade beneath it. Grungy, bearded hikers milled around the tables, interspersed with townspeople—mostly older women in elegant, summery clothes. Among the hiker contingent, I recognized Iculus, Dream Catcher, Smokey, Toast, and a few others loading up plates.

The pastor walked over to greet us, her clear eyes sparkling.

"Welcome! Are you the same girls who came through here last October? What's that, you've been on the Trail ever since? Well, you must've had quite a winter. Welcome back to Delaware Water Gap. You've picked a good evening to come. My parishioners and I are having a potluck for the hikers. Please set down your packs and help yourselves to the food."

"We brought you some blueberries," I said, pulling out the full Nalgene and handing it to her. Compared to the feast set out before us, it seemed like a terribly humble gift.

Her smile widened as she took the bottle in both hands.

"Fresh blueberries! What a treat! When I was a girl I picked them every summer, but now I hardly ever find the time."

jackrabbit

Leaving Delaware Water Gap, we hiked with Toast. Isis took a picture of us in the middle of the highway bridge. I struck a heroic pose and held a bandana high as a flag while Toast pretended to paddle: Jackrabbit Crossing the Delaware.

"Man, I missed y'all," Toast said, shaking his head. "Y'all and the Stage Crew. I never had so much fun as when I was hikin' with that crowd."

"What happened to the Stage Crew, anyway?" I asked him. "I mean, I've seen Tha Wookie's register entries; he's, like, a month ahead of us. But where are the rest of them?"

Toast shrugged. "I got an e-mail from Basil the other day. He's in Massachusetts somewhere, but he said he was gettin' off to work for a while. Make some money. Luna's still down at the N.O.C. I think Six-string went back to spend the summer with her. Too bad. I miss those guys."

"Yeah, me too," I said.

We followed a blue-blaze trail up to Sunfish Pond. It was green-blazed, actually, marked with square swatches of paint the color of a luna moth's wings. It led up a stream, instead of the dry ridge that the A.T. followed, and the air was cool in the shade of giant hemlocks.

Sunfish Pond was not nearly as splendid as it had been in fall, when brilliant leaves had glowed through the fog. Today, it was opaque and rippled under a partly overcast sky, the water slate-gray, surrounded by the lush green foliage of midsummer. Groups of picnicking tourists sat along the shore. The kids dangled their feet in the water. Isis, Toast, and I sat on a log, watching cloud reflections traverse the rumpled surface. A huge blacksnake poured itself out of a dead stump nearby and slithered soundlessly across the open ground.

We walked on together, sharing memories and stories, pausing often to pick blueberries from the bushes beside the trail. The tops of the long ridges were open and grassy, with occasional oak trees and clumps of blackberry brambles. Down in the valleys, we could see red barns and silos, rolling fields, and little lakes that caught the afternoon light. The mountains here were rounded and blunt, smoothed by ancient glaciers. Their shapes were so different from the long, skinny ridges of Pennsylvania and Maryland and Virginia, or the steep water-carved mountains of the southern Appalachians.

We stopped for water at Rattlesnake Spring, a little seep among the mossy roots of an oak tree. In the nearby swamp, we saw a set of wide, clawed footprints and a patch of ripped-up skunk cabbage. Among the pungent reek of the leaves, I imagined that I could smell another kind of musk: the salty, thick stench of a large mammal. I wondered if we would see a bear. Northbounders in 2000 had told me that New Jersey was the second-best place to spot one, after Shenandoah National Park.

Toast hiked ahead and found a perfect campsite: a flat meadow, just downhill from the trail, but hidden by a clump of oaks. Loaded blackberry brambles grew on three sides of the clearing, dropping their overripe fruit into our outstretched hands.

"Y'all want to have a potluck?" Toast asked as we set up our stove.

"Sure," Isis said. "I'll make this curried vegetable couscous stuff. I got some great dried veggies out of the hiker box at the Water Gap. What're you cooking, Toast?"

He stirred his steaming pot. "Creamy pesto grits."

Isis looked doubtful.

"No, it's real good, y'all. You take a packet of pesto mix, some dry milk, and a couple packs of instant grits."

Anywhere off the Trail, the viscous, green mixture would have been almost inedible. There on the ridge top, with an orange sunset flaring above us and a light wind murmuring in the oak leaves, it tasted like the finest *haute cuisine*. With couscous *à la* hiker box for the second course and all-you-can-eat blackberries for dessert, it was one of the best Trail meals we had eaten in a long time.

In the morning, Isis and I watched the sun come up red over the ridge-line while we ate our granola, topped with handfuls of blackberries from the patch beside our camp. Mourning doves flapped and called in the oak trees above us. It was a glorious start to the day. Everything seemed perfect, at least until I began to pack up the tent.

"Ew! There are slugs everywhere!" I said, flicking several of them off the tent walls. The tall grass around our campsite was full of the slimy creatures, and they seemed to have gravitated toward our tent. I managed to get rid of them by shaking the ground cloth, but they left swatches of brown slime behind them. I had just finished scraping the worst of the slime off with a handful of dry grass when Toast emerged, looking a little bleary-eyed.

"Maybe camping in a meadow wasn't such a great idea after all," I said. "Look at all these slugs!"

Toast gave me an inscrutable stare. "Y'all had it easy. I was in a tarp with no ground cloth." He reached up and brushed a slug out of his short blond hair.

We crossed Rattlesnake Mountain in midmorning. Given the name of the place, and the name of the spring the night before, I watched the underbrush carefully. As a little kid, I had been irrationally frightened of rattlesnakes. When we visited my father's relatives in Virginia, I had always carried a stout hiking stick and thunked it against every rock by the trail before I stepped near it, in case a snake might be hiding there. I even made our sister Claire check under the living room couch and the bed in our guest room, to make sure they were free of rattlesnakes. I had never seen one in the wild, though, until Isis nearly stepped on one on the ridge above Port Clinton. Far from the aggressive, vicious animal that I had feared, the snake had been more startled than she was, it seemed. It had taken the animal a good few seconds, while she jumped across the road, to coil up into striking position and start rattling. Watching the snake from a safe distance, I had been amazed at how beautiful it was. Now, as we came down the ridge, I found myself hoping to see another one.

My wish was granted near the bottom of the valley. I heard a slight rustle in the leaves beside the path, and looked over to see an enormous dark rattlesnake crawling along, only a few feet away. He was much larger than the first one we had seen, thick-bodied and nearly four feet long. I stopped walk-ing and motioned to Isis. The snake flowed smoothly through the low brush, testing the air with his forked pink tongue, oblivious to our presence. His scales were raised triangles of burnished ebony, with crosshatched stripes of dark gold and lemon yellow. He held his rattle tipped up at an angle as he crawled. I could hear the tiny clacking sounds it made as it bumped over the ground. I held my breath as he passed, and I was overcome by the same sense of wonder I had felt when we saw the little copperhead outside the Home Place Restaurant.

Down in the gap, Isis and I stopped at a bakery by the Trail for cheese sandwiches, donuts, and iced tea. We sat on the curb in the parking lot, leaning against our packs while we ate.

"We ought to call Spike and Caveman," I said, seeing the pay phone at the edge of the lot. In an e-mail several weeks ago, they had invited us to visit them in New York City. I was so confident in our ability to hike long days now that I didn't worry about taking a few zeros. We'd left several messages for Spike and Caveman from the past few Trail towns, but so far they hadn't been home when we called.

I dialed the number. The machine picked up, and I heard Caveman's deep voice. "You have reached Jim and Dana. We're not home right now. If you are calling from the Appalachian Trail, please—" here he broke down laughing and took a deep breath before continuing, "please call your mother."

The phone rang six times before our mom answered, slightly out of breath. "Hello? Oh, hi, sweetie! So good to hear your voice. I was out in the garden. I'm glad I heard the phone. I've got a message for you here from somebody named Caveman . . . He says, call Jan Wright. He's a trail angel." She gave a number. "Where are you guys? Are you getting enough to eat? Feet holding up okay? . . . I love you, sweetie. Give your sister a big hug."

I called Jan Wright's number. A crisp female voice answered, "Sussex County Homicide Division."

"Uh, hello. Is Jan Wright there?"

"One moment, please."

There was a brief span of Muzak, and then a man's voice said, "Yeah, Jan here."

"Hi," I said. "I'm calling from the Appalachian Trail. My name is, um, jackrabbit. I'm a friend of Spike and Caveman . . ."

"Oh, yeah! Hi!" There was instant warmth in his voice. "Jim called me last night, said I should be expecting you guys. I'll take you home, my wife'll make a big spaghetti dinner, and I'll put you on a bus to the City. Sounds good? Great. Where can I meet you?"

I hadn't considered this important detail. I grabbed the *Data Book* from the top of my pack and made some quick calculations. "How about tomorrow night, at the Heaven Hill Farm in Vernon?" I had fond memories of the place, a roadside stand selling fresh fruit, ice cream, and pastries.

"Great. See you there."

It wasn't until I had hung up the phone that I realized I had miscalculated slightly. Vernon was thirty-three miles away, and it was already past noon.

Isis took out the map and studied it. "We've got to stay at Mashipacong tonight," she said. "Sheltowee said he was going to meet us there, maybe do some trail magic." He was the trail angel we had met at the Gathering, who planned to retire and hike the lower forty-eight states. We had called him from Delaware Water Gap, hoping to see him again and hear more about his plans.

"How many miles does that give us tomorrow, then?" I asked.

She frowned and traced the map with a finger. "Twenty-six."

I checked the *Data Book*, being more careful with my math this time. Twenty-six exactly.

"We could call Jan back," I suggested. We were still standing by the phone.

Isis grinned. "Or we could hike a twenty-six. We did Maryland."

I nodded. "We did Maryland. Onward!"

As we climbed out of the valley and onto the ridge of Sunrise Mountain, we found the best blueberries yet. Fat clumps of them hung in the bushes, so much fruit that the whole hillside looked bluish. I wanted to plunk myself down in the middle of the trail and just eat them, but we had to keep moving—thunderheads were thickening along the horizon, tall stacks of dark-bellied clouds.

"Blackberries, blueberries, all these great views," I said. "Now I know why they call it the Garden State. I guess all we need now to make our New Jersey experience complete is a bear sighting."

"Be careful what you wish for," Isis warned. Her voice tightened. "Jackrabbit—"

I looked up to see a huge mass of glossy black fur rise up beside the trail, not fifteen feet away. The bear, a good-sized male, stood on his hind legs, sniffing the air and regarding us with his tiny, puzzled brown eyes. He was so close that I could smell his warm, fetid animal reek. I could see the pink of his gums, his blueberry-stained tongue, his yellowed teeth. At the end of his extended forelegs, bright, curving claws gleamed between the fur of his toes. For a long moment we stood there.

"Don't mind us," I said—the first thing that came into my head. "We're just here eating some blueberries, too."

The bear dropped down to all fours and crashed away through the low shrubs on the ridge top. I stood there a moment longer, feeling the rush of adrenaline fade and my heartbeat subside back to its steady rhythm. In its wake, the fear left elation. *There is still mystery and danger in the world.*

CHAPTER 7

Old Friends and New

jackrabbit

We reached Mashipacong Shelter as thunder began to mutter and grumble behind the trees. Still thrilled from the bear sighting, I hardly felt the first raindrops pattering on my skin. By the time the deluge began, we were safe under the eaves of the old stone shelter.

Toast arrived a few minutes later, dripping wet. He was not his usual cheerful self. "Long day, y'all," he said in answer to our questions, and he barely said anything else as he hung up his pack and soaked rain gear.

"Pizza's here!" came a jolly male voice. I looked up to see Sheltowee coming up the trail from the road, holding a poncho over two pizza boxes. His red-blond hair, longer than I remembered, was curly in the damp. Behind him came a man I didn't recognize, with short curly salt-and-pepper hair and an impish smile lighting his blue eyes.

"Hi, I'm the Artful Dodger," he said with a slight Southern accent. "Most people just call me Dodger."

We made introductions all around.

"Dodger's my hiking partner," Sheltowee said.

"So you're really going through with it?" Isis asked him.

Sheltowee's grin broadened. "I quit my job two weeks ago. Everything I own is in storage, except what's in the van down at the trailhead. A month from now, Dodger and I are setting out to hike the lower forty-eight."

"You're what?" Toast gaped.

Sheltowee explained his plan to hike through all the contiguous states.

"Is there a trail that covers all that territory?"

"Not entirely," Dodger said. "We're going to hike the Big Three, of course—the A.T., the PCT, the Continental Divide. The rest of it, we'll piece together from shorter trails and road walks."

"Are you going to hike year-round?" I asked.

Sheltowee laughed. "We're not as crazy as you guys. No, we're going to take a break for about three months every year, rent a little place wherever we end up, and maybe work for a while."

"We're going to write, too," Dodger broke in. "I know we'll have some adventures worth tellin'. We'd like to make a book out of it."

"Where are you starting?" I asked.

"A trail in eastern Kentucky," Sheltowee said. "A favorite of mine—it's called the Sheltowee Trace."

"I always wondered where you got that trail name."

"There's more to it than that," he said. "Sheltowee was Daniel Boone's Shawnee name. He was adopted by the tribe, you know. The name means 'Big Turtle,' which I guess is kind of appropriate for a long-distance hiker. Carrying our homes wherever we go. But also, I feel a kind of affinity for Daniel Boone. When I was growing up, my brothers and cousins were all named for uncles, grandparents, et cetera. I was the only Dan in the family, though. I'd always ask my parents who I was named after, and they'd say 'Daniel Boone. You're going to be a great explorer, too, someday.' Now, who wants some pizza?"

"We've got wine, too." Dodger produced some paper cups and a fat gallon jug of Chianti from under his rain jacket.

"Awesome!" Toast was beginning to perk up. "Thanks y'all!"

While we ate, Sheltowee and Dodger told stories from their own A.T. hikes. Dodger, it turned out, was one of the Hobos, and spent most of his time on or near the Trail.

"How many Hobos are there, anyway?" Isis asked through a mouthful of pizza.

"Oh, quite a number," Dodger said. "You never know where one of us is gonna turn up. We like to keep an eye on things out on the Trail, you know? There was a bunch of Hobos that did trail maintenance for a while. Cutting blowdowns and that kind of thing. You ever see a mark like this on a downed tree?" He drew a pattern in the dirt in front of the shelter, a horizontal V crossed with two vertical lines.

"Oh yeah," I said. Now that I thought about it, this pattern of slashes was a familiar sight, chainsawed into the bark of blowdowns beside the trail. I had even seen it carved into a few bog bridges. I had never stopped to wonder what it meant.

"That's the mark of the Wolf Pack," Dodger said with a mysterious grin. "They used to do guerilla trail maintenance. If somebody's section was really sloppy, those Hobos would go out there with their chain saws and clean it up. They'd leave their marks on the trees they cleared. 'Course, it rubbed some people the wrong way—some maintainers didn't like these guys comin' into their sections. Felt like they were bein' one-upped or somethin'. The Wolf Pack doesn't do it anymore. Not so far as I know, at least." He winked, and I remembered seeing that mark carved into the trunk of a massive dead tree just yesterday. The sawdust had still been fresh.

"I've left my mark on the Trail, too," Sheltowee said.

"Are you a Hobo, Sheltowee?" I asked him.

"Are you kidding? Up till two weeks ago, I was Mr. Corporate America. The Hobos would never let a guy like me join the ranks."

"We'll see how he holds up over the next six years," Dodger said, amusement glinting in his eyes.

"What'd you mean about leaving your mark on the Trail?" Isis asked Sheltowee. "I hope you didn't carve your name in a shelter or anything like that."

He shook his head. "You guys remember the two-thousand-mile mark in Maine?"

"Yeah," Isis said. "That was where the first nobos wanted to take a picture of us. It kind of weirded me out. But I remember seeing that spray-painted on the road: *2,000 miles.*"

Sheltowee's grin widened. "Right before I came to that little road in '99, I'd been looking at my *Data Book*. I'd figured that it marked almost exactly two thousand miles from Springer. When I got to the road, there was a survey crew there. I was so pumped I just had to tell them. And one of the guys got really excited, too. 'You walked all that ways to get here? Well, that's the most amazing thing I've heard in months!' He ran back to the truck and grabbed a can of spray paint, and wrote it out on the blacktop, right there." Sheltowee looked a little sheepish. "The thing was, I redid my calculations at the shelter that night, and I found out I'd been off by about four miles."

The rain began to let up outside, and mist rose from the grass. I heard raised voices. A moment later, a pair of fast young nobos appeared. They were both skinny and muscular, with tiny packs, wearing soaking wet Adidas tank tops and running shorts. Their generic good looks, complete with three days' worth of stubble, made them look like escapees from a boy band.

"Flash, man, we oughta stop here tonight," one of them said in a clipped Long Island accent, swallowing his R's.

"Next shelter's only three miles, Stocks," the other returned with the same inflection.

"Yeah, but it's a half mile off the Trail."

"Come on, man. Are you tough or ain't you?" Then he stopped, catching sight of us. He came to the shelter and hung up his pack. "Hello, there, ladies. I'm The Flash." He gave a charming smile. "This here's my hiking partner, Stocks." Stocks stood back, unsmiling, with his arms crossed over his chest in a tough-guy pose.

"You want some pizza?" Isis asked, indicating the last two slices.

Stocks looked hopeful, but The Flash shook his head. "We got plenty o' food." He drew his friend aside for a whispered conversation. I overheard his earnest voice: "Let the girlies have their food, man!"

Toast looked up from his paper cup of wine. "We got wine, if y'all want some," he said, his voice a bit muzzy. The gallon bottle, I noticed, was more than half empty already. I was only on my second cup, Isis was halfway through her first, and Dodger and Sheltowee had barely had any. No wonder Toast was slurring his words.

"No thanks," Flash said. "I never drink while I'm trainin'."

"What are you training for?" I asked.

Stocks gave a tight grin. "Flash here's an Olympic hopeful. Half-marathon."

"That's awesome," Isis said. (Flash's chest swelled up with pride.) "Are you hiking a section?"

"No, we're thru-hikin'," Flash said. "And damned if I ain't in worse shape now than when I started out."

"He's always sayin' that. He's always sayin' he ain't in shape, and then he goes out and beats everybody in the trials."

"You a runner, too, Stocks?" I asked him.

He shrugged. "Not like him. I mean, I run some, but not competitive. I ain't like him."

"We're just hikin' together 'cause we have such a good time," Flash said. "We been friends since we was in sixth grade. I used to hate his guts. Remember that, Stocks? It was 'cause all the girlies liked you better. Then you refused to go out with Amanda García so she'd go out with me. We been friends ever since."

Sheltowee and Dodger took off, bearing the pizza boxes and the now-empty wine jug. It was almost dark now, and the mosquitoes came out in force. From the meadow in front of the shelter, we could see a few stars. The wind carried a scent of damp earth and torn leaves. Flash, Stocks, Isis, and I set up our tents in the meadow to guard against the clouds of insects that now whined around us, but Toast stayed in the shelter, a glazed look on his face.

"I'm gon' sleep here, y'all."

"What about the bugs?" I asked him. By the light of my headlamp, I could see mosquitoes settling on his bare legs and arms.

His eyes could hardly focus. "They don' bother me none."

"Suit yourself."

We woke up before dawn. A thin gray stripe of light painted the eastern horizon, but stars still glimmered above us. Flash and Stocks were fast asleep in their streamlined one-man tents, snoring lightly. I was surprised to see Toast awake, in the shelter, packing up.

"Morning," I whispered.

"Mornin'," he said. His eyes were red and bleary. "Hardly slept at all last night. I just laid there with the damn mosquitoes eatin' me alive, till I sobered up about an hour ago. By then, I was too tired to put up my tarp anyway. I figured I'd just pack up and get goin'."

We hiked together in a line, Isis, Toast, and I, without speaking, as dawn painted color into the grassy ridges. Every leaf shone with dew and rain, the droplets throwing back thousands of tiny sparks.

"Guess I shouldn't have drunk so much last night," Toast said softly, shifting his hiking poles into one hand and reaching up to rub his temples. "There's just times when it helps, you know? I had a rough day yesterday. I wanted to forget about it."

We'd covered more than twenty-three miles the day before, but I hadn't thought the hiking was terribly strenuous. Toast's troubled expression suggested that it was something else. "What happened?" I asked him.

He sighed. "I wasn't gonna tell y'all. But there's some stories, you know, if you don't tell 'em, they just kind of eat away at you . . . It was at the road back there, a couple miles before the shelter. Somebody had run over a raccoon. He was just a little guy, not even half-grown. And he was lyin' there in the ditch with both his back legs crushed. You could tell he wasn't gonna make it. Vultures were comin' down already. He was makin' a little whimperin' sound. And what do you do? What *can* you do when you see somethin' like that?" He paused and took a deep breath. His voice cracked. "I took a rock and I killed him. It was either that or let the vultures tear him up slowly. I keep tellin' myself that was the only thing I could've done for the little guy. But it still feels wrong."

"It's okay, Toast," I told him. "You did all you could."

"What would you have done? Would you have killed him?"

"No," I admitted. "I don't think I have the courage."

"See, that's why I got drunk," he said. "I just couldn't handle all the questions inside my head. The more I think about it, the whole damn thing feels wrong."

Isis

The next day, we said goodbye to Toast and left the Trail for a few days to visit Spike and Caveman in New York. We reached the road crossing where we'd planned to meet their friend Jan an hour or so before sunset. The farm stand had closed for the day, but there were a few benches in the shade in front of it. I sat down, dug my tank top out of the bottom of my pack, and slipped it on over my sports bra. Might as well be decorous in front of a policeman, even if he was a friend of Spike and Caveman.

Twenty minutes later, a large beige van pulled into the parking lot. A dark-haired man in his mid-thirties, with clean-cut good looks and a wide smile, hopped out of the driver's seat.

"Isis and jackrabbit? Great to meet you. Sorry I'm running so late; I just got off duty. Throw your stuff in the back, and hop on in.

"Spike and Caveman told me all about you," he continued, as I climbed into the passenger's seat. "They said you were some of the most fun people they ever hiked with, so I said, 'I've gotta meet them.'"

I may be entertaining to hike with, I thought, *but I lack Caveman's instinct for the dramatic potential inherent in everyday objects, and no sound my voice is capable of making can compare to Spike's laugh.*

"We're not exactly Spike and Caveman," I began, timidly.

"Well, you'd better be fun!" Jan said.

I'm afraid that we weren't a whole lot of fun that evening. Exhausted from our long day of hiking, we fell asleep almost as soon as we'd showered and eaten. We did tell Jan and his wife Corrine a few of our best Spike and Caveman stories over supper. The saga of All-You-Can-Eat Crab Legs Night delighted Jan, and Corrine's eyes sparkled when jackrabbit described their engagement on top of Springer.

In the morning, after a quick breakfast of toast and tea, Jan drove us over to the East Milford bus stop.

"Call when you're on your way back, and I'll come pick you up." He pressed a cell phone into my hand. "I use this phone to call my wife and tell her when I'm going to be late home from work. She's the only other person who knows the number, so you won't have to deal with any calls from strangers."

"You don't need to give me your phone," I said, trying to hand it back to him. "We can always call you from a pay phone."

"No, this is much easier. Here." He took a sheet of paper out of his pocket and unfolded it. Neat, loopy script and a column of phone numbers covered half the page. "This is our home phone, and this is my number at work. Here's my pager. Here's Corrine's cell phone number, and her work number. If anything goes wrong, call us right away. Have a great time in the City!"

Caveman had promised to meet us on the steps of the Metropolitan Museum of Art when he got out of work, so we had most of the day to wander around New York on our own. After the Trail, the press of people and buildings overwhelmed me. The cityscape looked surreal, improbable—trees growing on black glass terraces ten stories above the ground; the fluted horns of a Gothic cathedral dwarfed by the tower beside it; string upon string of enormous, flawless pearls floating behind plate glass. I tried to focus on where I was going, but my eyes kept returning to the thin strip of whitish blue sky far ahead of us, sandwiched between walls of reflecting glass. The other pedestrians flowed around us like a swift, steady river pouring past rocks.

We bought lunch in the first sandwich shop we came to, and retreated to the green shade of Central Park.

"I suppose we ought to go to a museum or something, while we're here," jackrabbit said, "but all I really feel like doing is looking for a good stealth site."

"There's one right there," I laughed, pointing to a patch of level grass under a willow by the stream. "Water source and everything."

Jackrabbit wrinkled her nose. "I think that's a purely decorative 'water source.'"

"Probably a purely decorative stealth site, too. Much too close to a road crossing to be of any use."

We didn't venture out of the park until we got hungry again, around two in the afternoon. By that time, we were feeling a bit bolder. We bought some bagels to calm our growling stomachs, then headed over to the art museum with a few hours to spare. A show of eighteenth century portraiture: pale skin with thin cracks like the surface of old teacups, and large, luminous eyes staring down at us in rooms where our footsteps echoed.

Just before five, we went out on the steps to wait for Caveman. A small crowd had gathered there, watching a troupe of street performers who spun and flipped in dizzying arcs across the concrete sidewalk, to the rhythm of hands slapping on a five-gallon bucket that they took turns using as a drum. At first, I was worried that we would miss Caveman in the throng, but soon I got so caught up in watching the acrobats that I forgot we were waiting.

Caveman spotted us first, and waved from the other side of the audience. When the performers finished, we worked our way over to him.

"Isis and jackrabbit!" He hugged us both at once. "Thank you so much for coming. It's a breath of fresh air, just seeing Trail people again."

"Thanks for inviting us," jackrabbit replied. "It's great to see you, too. And New York."

"New York." Caveman smiled fondly as he threw a few dollars into the street performers' bucket. "Sometimes the City's the only thing that keeps me sane."

I looked at him. His eyes had dark circles under them, and he'd gained ten or twenty pounds since I'd last seen him.

"Are you okay?" I asked.

"Healthy, yes. But not very happy since we got off the Trail. My job isn't much fun, and Spike's work is stressing her out, too. Never get off the Trail and come back to the real world. Just stay out there, having adventures, and I'll be happier knowing that someone got away."

Caveman led us through a maze of subways and several long streets at the end of the line. The buildings in their neighborhood looked a bit run-down from the outside—a few stories of brick covered in peeling paint, surrounded by overflowing garbage bins. Inside, though, their clean, spacious flat looked almost too elegant for hikers. Wooden bookshelves lined the living room walls, and a wrought-iron candelabra hung from the ceiling.

"That sure beats our candle lantern," jackrabbit said, admiring it. "I guess there are some advantages to living off-trail."

"Wrought iron's my weakness," Caveman said, gesturing to it. "Some people pay off their loans; others buy wrought iron."

"The books are my weakness," Spike added. "Well, both of ours. I did miss them on the Trail."

As we were talking, the phone rang. Spike hurried to the next room to answer it. To my surprise, she hurried back a few minutes later, and held it out to me and jackrabbit.

"It's Juliet," she said. "Granny Gear. Remember her from winter? I told her you were here, and she wants to say hi."

I did remember her—a tiny woman with an enormous pack, who ate a stick of butter a day and still couldn't keep enough weight on. She had never complained, in the week or so we'd hiked together, but the cheerful voice that greeted me on the phone was quite a contrast to the subdued one I remembered. It turned out that she lived near the trail in New Jersey, and she made plans to slack with us for a day when we got to Harriman State Park.

Spike and Caveman both took the following day off work and showed us around the city. We ate lunch in a Vietnamese restaurant, then made our rounds of the fabric shops near Broadway. I searched for some dark blue velveteen to make myself a cloak. I didn't find it, but I did get something more practical: six yards of silk to make new sleeping bag liners.

Just as they had on the Trail, Spike and Caveman seemed to pull everything around them into a spontaneous, ongoing comedy routine. In one fabric store, Spike wrapped herself in a sheath of red viscose with a pattern like snakeskin. Caveman draped a bright blue net of sequins over her head, and she posed demurely, holding a bolt of white linen like a baby in her arms.

"She really is Catholic," Caveman said. "That's the scary part."

Spike shot him a look of mock severity. "Look who's talking—you were Lutheran once!"

"Darling, can you ever forgive me?" Caveman dropped to one knee, and clutched the hem of her viscose robe.

In the evening, we splurged on picnic food from Dean & DeLucca and went to a free concert in Prospect Park. Spike spread out a picnic blanket. We feasted on fresh bread and goat cheese, cherries, and tiny yellow plums called mirabelles. Children danced in circles on the grass, while a dazzling soprano voice pierced the twilit air. Between the arias, Caveman entertained us by making alien faces out of the mint meringues we'd gotten for dessert: the peak of the meringue formed the nose, flecks of chocolate became eyes, and cherry stems served for antennae.

"You guys are so great," jackrabbit said. "There's nobody else like you, even on the Trail."

"It's having you guys here that brings it out," Spike answered. "We haven't had this much fun in months."

Late that night, the four of us walked from the Metro station to Spike and Caveman's apartment, laughing as we reminisced about our few weeks together on the Trail. An old man sitting in a doorway, clutching a bottle wrapped in a paper bag, shouted across the street to Caveman.

"Three pretty ladies. Well, you're a lucky man, brother."

Spike burst into wild, joyful laughter. Caveman met the man's eyes, smiled, and shrugged his shoulders.

"I really am lucky," he said.

The next day, Spike and Caveman had to go back to work, so we said goodbye to them in the morning and caught the Metro downtown by ourselves. We stopped in a bakery and bought some real bagels for our resupply, then went to a chocolate shop to buy a thank-you gift for Jan and Corrine. On our way back across the City, we stumbled on another free concert, this one featuring songs from *Batboy: the Musical*. A young man with bat ears sang about his misunderstood youth in a cave in rural Tennessee, and a group of mad scientists pursued him across the stage. We sat in on the concert for half an hour or so, and then, by mutual consent, went looking for someplace quiet where we could get out of the crowds for a while. The City had been a lot of fun, but after two and a half days of it, my mind felt saturated with sound and color. I was looking forward to spending the evening in the relative quiet of Jan and Corrine's house.

Jackrabbit noticed that the stately marble building behind the park was a public library—a perfect place to sit down for a while. *Please do not eat or drink in the library. Please turn off your cell phone before entering*, proclaimed a sign beside the door. I pulled Jan's cell phone out of my pocket, and looked for an "off" switch. There didn't seem to be one. I tried poking a few buttons, but only got a dial tone, a list of phone numbers scrolling down the screen, and an obnoxious beeping noise. *Oh well*, I thought, *only Jan and Corrine know this number, and Jan's expecting* me *to call* him *when we get on the bus.*

We walked up a few flights of stairs, opened a door at random, and found ourselves in the Genealogy Room: high-backed chairs at long wooden tables, where a few gray-haired men and women stooped over sheets of yellowed paper and five-inch-thick reference tomes. Jackrabbit looked at me and shrugged: *as good a place as any to sit down and write a letter home*. I set the day-pack Jan had lent me down on the table, and took out a pen and paper.

No sooner had I started writing than a cell phone began to ring. I looked up to see where the sound was coming from, and found all of the genealogical researchers glaring at me. It was Jan's phone. I raced out the door and down the stairs, the cell phone still ringing in my pocket. Halfway to the door, I realized that the phone would stop ringing if I answered the call. I pulled it out and pressed the "talk" button.

"Hi, Isis!" came Jan's cheerful voice. "I'm just calling to check in."

"Jan—I can't talk right now, I'm in a library!" I answered, out of breath.

I dashed up to the security guard, stammering, "I have a cell phone and I don't know how to turn it off!"

He waved me past, barely raising an eyebrow. *They must see all kinds of people in New York*, I thought as I sat down on the wall beside the library stairs, blushing furiously. I put the phone back to my ear.

"Isis, are you there? What was that all about?" Jan asked.

I tried to explain, but only felt more and more foolish.

"Don't worry about it," Jan told me. "I was just wondering what time you and jackrabbit are planning to get back. Corrine and I want to have a party tonight and introduce you to all the neighbors."

The party turned out to be at a neighbor's house, where there was a piano. At first, I was delighted; I would get to hear jackrabbit play. No Chopin or Bach, unfortunately—classical music didn't quite fit the mood. She started with some jazz improvisation, pleasant with the first round of cocktails. I chatted with a few of the neighbors, a novelist who collected cacti and a high school physics teacher.

After the first two hours, though, someone hauled out a two-hundred-page seventies songbook. For the rest of the evening, a heavy blond woman with a nasal whine proceeded to sing her way through the first half of it, her voice falling further and further out of tune as she drank successive Bloody Marys. Jackrabbit gamely played along, never missing a note in spite of two or three glasses of scotch and water. *I hope she's having fun*, I thought grouchily, as my eyes sagged closed. My head wobbled back and forth on my neck, and the conversation around me blurred into a single, irritating buzz.

I shook myself awake. Only a few minutes past midnight, by the mantle clock. At risk of being judged thoroughly un-fun, I was going to have to leave this party. I got up, unsteady on my feet, and went to look for the hostess. I found her in the kitchen, talking with Corrine.

"Thank you for the party," I told her. "I'm sorry to leave so early, but I need to get some sleep."

Corrine looked up, instantly concerned.

"Are you okay?"

"I'm fine. I think I'm just tired from traveling."

"Oh, of course! I'll walk home with you. Let me just tell Jan and your sister."

"You don't need to . . ." I began, but she had already disappeared into the living room. She returned a minute later, with a haggard-looking jackrabbit in tow.

"You poor things," Corrine said as we stumbled back up the road to her house. "You must be exhausted, after your three days in the City. I hope it wasn't too hard for you to have a party right after you got back."

"It was good to meet your neighbors," I answered.

"It was a treat to play the piano," jackrabbit said. "But thanks for rescuing me when you did. I was about to fall asleep with my head on the keys."

In spite of the party, we all woke up early. After a quick breakfast and a hug goodbye from Corrine, Jan drove us back to the trailhead—a road crossing in rural New Jersey, with a white blaze just visible through young, vine-tangled trees. Not the image I'd had in mind when I planned to hike the Appalachian Trail, but after the City, it felt like wilderness enough. More to the point, it felt like home.

jackrabbit

At the intersection of two roads in Harriman State Park, New York, more or less in the middle of nowhere, there's a pay phone. Southbound, we hadn't even known of its existence until we stepped out of the woods and saw it. At the time, we hadn't needed to make any calls, and we'd been hurrying to put some miles behind us before we got off for the Gathering. Northbound, we were counting on the phone. In our last mail drop, I had gotten a letter from my college friend Aislinn, who was living in New Jersey. She wanted to meet us on the Trail somewhere. I'd left her a message in the last town; I hoped I would get through tonight.

Dusk was gathering by the time we reached the crossroads with the phone. I stepped through the grass on the roadside, avoiding the sprigs of poison ivy that crept out of the underbrush, and dialed the number.

Aislinn answered on the first ring. "Susan? It really is you? You sound different."

"Different how?"

"I don't know. Like a big, tough outdoorswoman." She laughed. "You know, I never thought you would go through with it. Hiking the whole Appalachian Trail. Then turning around and coming back."

"I went through with the double major thing, didn't I?"

"Yeah, and you nearly fell apart in the process."

"I've fallen apart on the Trail more times than I'd like to count. And I didn't even hike the whole thing, southbound."

"Why do you do it? What keeps you going?"

I was silent for a moment. "The people. And the things you see, when you're out there in the woods all day, quiet . . . did I tell you we saw a bear a few days ago?"

We talked until the first stars appeared between wisps of cloud overhead. I told Trail stories, Aislinn described her job as a lab technician at a V.A. hospital, and we reminisced about our college days.

A car came to a halt across the street. The driver called something to Isis, and she walked over to talk to him. I kept an uneasy eye on the scene while I talked to Aislinn. Isis stayed a good distance back from the car, though, and nobody got out. After a while I relaxed and returned my full attention to the conversation.

"Can you come meet us on the Trail?" I finally asked.

"When and where?"

"We'll be at a shelter by the road in three days." I gave her the street address of the RPH Shelter. "I can't wait to see you, Aislinn. I've missed you so much."

"Missed you, too. Take care."

I hung up the phone. I was startled to see Isis, across the street, leaning into the open window of the car, talking to the men inside. I almost shouted out a warning, but she motioned me over.

"Jackrabbit, you've got to meet these guys. This is Tony—" the driver waved "—and Jake and Andy."

"Hi, guys," I said. "I'm jackrabbit. What brings you out here this time of evening?"

"We're trying to get back to the freeway," Tony said. He looked young, barely out of his teens, with dark curly hair and aquiline features. "My buddies and I were out here for a couple days, camping. I have to be back to work in three hours, and—" he gave a self-deprecating smile "—like usual, I managed to get us lost."

"What kind of job starts at midnight?" I asked him.

"I'm a firefighter in New York City."

"Cool."

"It's a pretty good job. The pay's not great, but I feel like I'm helping out, you know? Like I'm doing something good for society. And I get a fair amount of time off, too. Time to hike and camp and daydream. I'd love to do the Trail someday. Your sister was telling me about all of your adventures. It sounds so awesome."

We spent perhaps another half hour talking to Tony and his friends, and we exchanged e-mail addresses. "Let me know when you hike the Trail," I told him. "Maybe Isis and I can come hike with you for a few days, or at least send you some cookies or something. Take care. Oh, and good luck finding the freeway. I think it's that way."

"Thanks." The guys waved and pulled away, and in a moment the taillights of the car disappeared around a bend in the road.

It was fully dark by now. Isis and I hiked perhaps another mile into the woods. We were planning to meet Juliet at the Arden Valley Road, five miles away, in midmorning. Night-hiking with headlamps was not as simple as it had been in winter, though; the lights attracted clouds of insects, from miniscule gnats to large, buzzing hawk moths. They bumped against our faces and flapped in our eyes. We decided it would be easier to wake up early than to deal with another few miles of insect bombardment, so I found a flat space beside the trail and set up the tent.

The broad, open savannahs of Harriman State Park sparkled with dew in the early light. Twice, we startled herds of deer, which bounded away through the wet grass, white tails held high. Hunting hadn't been allowed in the park since it was established, in the 1920s, and the landscape was shaped by their presence; I didn't see a single tree that looked younger than thirty years. There were hardly any bushes, even, except for the low-growing blueberries. Everything that might have served as winter browse for deer had been eaten away long ago. I wondered how many of them died of starvation each winter, in a park too small to sustain a population of natural predators. I thought of Toast's dilemma—was it more humane to let an animal die an agonizing, slow death, or to end its life quickly? What about cases where, by overpopulation, the animals threaten to topple the very ecosystem that sustains them? Looking around the empty ground beneath the trees, it seemed to me that reintroducing hunting in Harriman State Park would be a very good idea.

We reached the road a few minutes ahead of schedule, after making good time on the smooth ridges and soft, dusty trail. Juliet was waiting for us, sitting by the road with a small daypack. Her red hair was in two braids. She had gained some much-needed weight since she finished the Trail, filling out her wiry, petite frame with muscle.

"Isis and jackrabbit!"

"Granny Gear!"

She grinned. "It's good to hear my trail name again. It's been too long."

"Yeah, it's been ages since we saw you. When did you finish your hike?"

"March eighth. It must've been while you guys were off-trail. I was so sorry to miss you."

"And Big Ring?"

"Sam and I aren't speaking any more. We haven't actually seen each other since I got on the bus in Atlanta."

"I'm sorry . . ."

"No, it's a good thing, jackrabbit. We weren't really together for most of the Trail. We just hiked together out of, I don't know, force of habit or something. He was so strong-willed. I guess I let myself be pulled in too much, roped into his way of doing things."

"It's so hard to make compromises on the Trail," I said. I thought of all the times in winter when I had wanted to go ahead of the Family and carry a lighter load. In the end, it had been easier to just acquiesce to Isis's plans; it took more energy to try to argue than it did to hike her hike. I wondered if Isis felt the same resentment about all the days that we had hiked fast, skipping beautiful campsites and overlooks in order to make more miles.

"I think you have to learn how to compromise, though," Granny Gear said. "If you don't, and you try to walk together anyway, it kind of destroys your hike. After I finished the A.T., I actually thought I didn't like backpacking. Then some friends convinced me to go for a week in Shenandoah this spring. It was so great. We took it slow, and stopped to enjoy things. There was no 'We have to make twenty miles today' or 'You have to carry forty pounds of food so we can stay out for twelve days.' We were just walking in the woods, having a good time."

Less than half an hour into our hike, we came across a giant banner hung beside the trail. *FAT FEST 2001*, it read. *Hikers: come stuff your faces with all the greasy, tasty things you've been craving. Turn right at the next road and walk a half mile.*

"Fat Fest!" Isis exclaimed. "I heard about it from nobos last year. It's supposed to be the biggest trail magic feast on the whole A.T.! Granny Gear, want to get some free food?"

She smiled. "I don't have my hiker appetite any more. But I'll do my best. I'm working as a rock-climbing and kayaking guide right now. I get pretty hungry from that, too."

Tantalizing smells of food drifted down the road long before we reached the Tiorati Circle Picnic Area. There were other groups picnicking there—families, Boy Scout troops—but we spotted Fat Fest right away. A horde of thru-hikers occupied one of the gravel picnic sites, all carrying plates heaped high with food. Four enormous grills stood side by side, smoking, with a small army of people flipping burgers and steaks. Three picnic tables, pushed together, bore vats of salad and fruit salad, pastries, muffins, and bread.

"Thru-hikers?" A young man at the grill called to us. He was tall and lithe, with long dark hair and bronze skin. "Come and get it! What's your pleasure? We've got steak, hamburgers, veggie burgers, fried eggs, scrambled eggs, sausages . . ."

"This is awesome," I said, picking up a paper plate. "Who arranges all this?"

"Me and my cousins." He gestured to the other men behind the grills, who grinned and waved. "I'm Nite Eyes, northbound in '99. We had so much awesome trail magic when we hiked, we decided to pass it on. This is the second year we've done it. I guess word travels; we've got about twice as many hikers this year."

"Do you guys take donations?" Isis asked him.

Nite Eyes waved the money away. "Keep it. You're hiking; you probably need it more than we do. Our family runs a catering business in the City. We get a good discount on all this stuff."

"Thanks so much!"

We loaded our plates with veggie burgers and went back to the table for salad and condiments. I recognized some of the thru-hikers: Timberghost, still in his blue sarong, had finally left Rusty's. He would probably pass us for good in a few days, at the rate he traveled. Hawkeye, the older man who had recited poetry at Rusty's, arrived as we finished our second plates of food. When we were halfway through our fourth plates, a truck pulled up and several hikers got out.

"Sleepy the Arab!" I called.

He waved. He was even thinner than I remembered. The bones of his freckled face showed clearly through the skin. "Jackrabbit! Fancy meeting you here!"

"Where are you on the Trail?" I asked him.

"Vernon."

"You've got to catch up, Sleepy. That's only thirty-five miles back. We miss you."

He sighed. "I miss you guys. I don't know about catching up, though. I have to get off for a friend's wedding in three days, and then . . . I just don't know. I might not finish my hike this year, either."

"I thought you finished in '98," I said.

Sleepy shook his head. "Wildcat Mountain was my Waterloo. I got about halfway up it, and I was out of food, out of steam, bone-tired, and injured to boot."

"Wildcat? In the Whites?" I remembered the knee-jarring descent, the swirling pall of mist. "That was where I hurt my foot southbound. My Waterloo, too, in a way . . . You'll make it this year, Sleepy. Second time's the charm."

"I thought that was third time," he said dryly. He grabbed a plate and began to load it up with food. "Hey, is that steak? Better than dehydrated pellets any day!"

After five plateloads (three for Granny Gear), we were satisfied. I was tempted to eat more, but I remembered our experience at Partnership Shelter. We still had another ten miles to hike to the Bear Mountain Inn, where Granny Gear had left her car. We thanked Nite Eyes and his cousins, and took off down the trail.

"So you're working as a rock-climbing guide now?" Isis asked.

"Yeah," Granny Gear said. "I lead trips for the outfitter's store where I— whoa!" She jumped back, and a moment later I heard an unmistakable angry buzzing from the brush beside the trail.

"Man, what a beautiful snake!" she said with remarkable calm. She moved aside so Isis and I could see. The rattlesnake wasn't quite as large as the one we had seen in New Jersey. It was gorgeous, though, with jagged rings of light brown, black, and goldenrod yellow, shading to pale gold on its belly. The tip of its tail, near the rattle, was darker brown and black.

"Is it a different species?" Isis asked "The ones we saw before were dark-colored."

"No, it's a different color morph," Granny Gear explained. "Some are black, some are brown, and some are more yellowish. Around here, we get all three colors. Down south, there's even a pinkish variety. They call them cane-brake rattlers. Same species, though."

The snake stopped rattling, uncoiled, and crawled back into the trail, where there was a shrinking mud puddle from the rain a few nights before. It paused at the edge of the water and looked up at us, as though trying to decide whether we still posed a threat. Then it dipped its triangular head toward the surface and began to lap up water with its tongue, almost like a cat. We watched for a long moment. Then, slowly, with great dignity, the snake began to undulate its camouflage body, moving off across the ground. The rings of color on its back made hypnotizing patterns in the dappled sunlight. Eventually it crawled off into the grass at the far side of the trail.

"Wow," I said.

"Yeah, I love those critters," Granny Gear said. "There's nothing like that rattle to get your adrenaline going, though."

A few miles later, we found something that fired our adrenaline even more. I heard traffic sounds coming through the trees almost a mile before we reached it—the Palisades Interstate Parkway. The A.T. crosses other interstates, but always by using a bridge or a tunnel. Here, hikers simply have to make a mad dash. In fall, there had been hardly any traffic on the road when we had crossed. Now, though, in the middle of July, there was a steady stream of traffic: semis, tour buses, vacationers' cars. We stood at the edge of the southbound lanes, staring out across the forbidding expanse of gray concrete. The road looked enormously broad, as wide as a football field. And after the thin strip of woods, where a white blaze was just visible, there was another strip of roadway just as wide.

The sound of traffic whipping past made speech impossible. We just looked at each other, at the oncoming cars, judging distances and speeds. Isis nodded, and we ran, sprinting for our lives. My breath came in short gasps, the gray road flew past underneath—and then we were in the breakdown lane, then pelting down the path through the brush at the roadside. An eighteen-wheeler whizzed past with a sound like thunder before we reached the woods.

I leaned against a tree to catch my breath. "This is insane!"

"It was nothing like this in October," Granny Gear said.

"Not at all," Isis agreed.

We peered out of the woods. The northbound lanes looked even busier. Cautiously, we made our way to the edge of the road.

"Holy shit," I mouthed, and then we were running, flying, again. The cars that had been specks in the distance when we started across grew exponentially larger, screaming toward us. One driver leaned on his horn, nearly making me stumble with the shock of the sudden sound. When my feet touched earth again, at the far side of the Parkway, I found myself shaking with manic laughter. It reminded me of the mad, thrilling joy that had possessed me as we ran along the ridge outside Duncannon in a thunderstorm. I couldn't stop laughing until we were well inside the shade of the trees.

The rest of the day passed uneventfully, with no more snakes or interstate crossings. We stopped a few times to pick blueberries on the high ridges and wineberries in the valleys in between. Granny Gear told us about her work at the outfitter's store. We recounted some of the better stories from our north-bound hike—everything from the snow at Wayah Bald fire tower, to the Florida trip, to the Early Risers and the Leki Pole of Justice.

In the evening, Granny Gear took us back to her apartment. Her cats, fascinated with our stinky packs, nuzzled the sweat-stained fabric and curled up in the scuzzy waistbands, rolling over with delight.

Granny Gear laughed. "When I got off the Trail, they went straight for my shoes. You know, I can kind of understand where they're coming from. It's such an information-rich smell. Sure, it reeks, but it's so . . . *real*. Such an honest reek. It brings me right back to the Trail."

We took showers, ordered Chinese takeout, and told stories late into the night.

"I never told you about our first night on the Trail, did I?" Granny Gear finally said. She shook her head. "What a fiasco. Sam insisted on bringing our full packs up Katahdin. He was carrying almost eighty pounds; mine was more like seventy."

"Good Lord!" Isis said. "You can't weigh much more than 115—"

"I actually weighed about 125 at the time. That's probably my ideal weight. I think I'm still too skinny right now, but it takes a while for me to gain it back . . . So anyway, there we were on Katahdin."

I remembered the vertical rock-scrambles, the exposed places where hikers had to pull themselves up using metal bars driven into the rock. I shuddered at the thought of trying to do that while carrying more than half my body weight.

"It took us all day to reach the summit," Granny Gear continued. "By the time we got there, it was almost dark. So we just camped out on the table-land."

"You did *what?*" I asked her. The summit of Katahdin creates a weather system all of its own, like Mount Washington, unpredictable and potentially lethal.

"The rangers were furious when we came down the next morning. They read us the riot act and we had to pay a big fine." She laughed. "What a way to start the Trail. I think if I hike it again, I'll do the exact opposite. Hike northbound, go ultralight and ultra-fast. And definitely by myself."

In the morning, Granny Gear drove us into the nearest town, Fort Mont-
gomery, so we could send off some mail. I dashed off a hopeful postcard to
Tuba Man. In the brief e-mail I had read in Palmerton, he had mentioned
that he might be coming up the coast at the end of July. The dates he had
given me were quickly approaching, and I hadn't heard anything else from
him. Even after our conversation in Florida, I still felt drawn to him. I hoped
I would see him again.

We waved goodbye to Granny Gear and picked up the trail at the south
entrance to the Bear Mountain Zoo. Throngs of school children filled the
asphalt sidewalks, and several times groups of people drew us aside for the
inevitable questions: *What do you eat? Where do you sleep? How much do those
packs weigh?* We wore sandals, though, and "going incognito" helped us move
faster through the crowds.

We stopped in front of the bear exhibit, where a lazy black bear dozed in
the sun at the far side of her concrete enclosure.

"You know what they ought to do, Isis? They should have a thru-hiker
exhibit in the zoo. A shelter, where people could come by and watch us in
our natural habitat. People always want to feed zoo animals, and usually they
can't. There could be a little sign that said, 'Please feed the hikers.'"

She laughed. "I want a t-shirt that says that."

"Good idea. I doubt we'd ever get anything quite like Fat Fest, though.
That was a once-in-a-thru-hike deal."

Eventually we made our way out of the zoo and onto the Bear Mountain
Bridge, a quarter-mile span of painted I-beams crossing the Hudson. Earl
Shaffer had to pay a ten-cent toll when he crossed it in 1948, but now hikers
cross for free on a narrow pedestrian walkway. The still, gray-green surface of
the river stretched out below us. Hardly any wind stirred the sun-baked air.
Halfway across the bridge, construction workers on a catwalk above us wolf-
whistled. I grinned and waved back to them.

The heat was still strong under the shade of the forest on the far side of
the river. Sweat ran freely down my body, and in a few minutes of climbing, I
smelled as ripe as I had before my shower the day before. As I climbed, I
thought of Tuba Man: that devastating smile, the glint of laughter in his blue
eyes. The sensation of his warm shoulder leaning against me in Playfoot's Jeep
on the way to Florida. *Stop it*, I told myself. *Wishing won't bring him back. And
wishing won't make him be who you want him to be.*

At last we came out on top of the ridge. A slight breeze had risen off the
water, bringing a little relief. We stopped for a drink where a gated gravel
road crossed the trail.

"Hey, look, there's a note here. Taped to the gate," Isis said.

"Wonder who it's for."

She leaned forward to read it. Her face broke into a disbelieving smile. "No way. Guess who's waiting for us at the next road? Stitches! And—" she gave an evil grin "—Tuba Man."

"You're just reading my thoughts again. Come on, who is it really?"

She passed me the note. Sure enough, there was his familiar loopy signature, complete with a smiley face. Despite the heat of the day, I picked up my pace until I was almost running.

Isis

Even without the note, we could have guessed that there was trail magic at the road crossing. A crowd of hikers had gathered around a small silver sedan, leaning on their hiking poles and chatting in excited voices, like birds at a feeder. Stitches and Tuba Man sat in the midst of them, on the hood of the car, handing out homemade brownies. We made our way through the crowd to greet them.

"I can't believe you're here!" jackrabbit said to Tuba Man, leaning over to give him a quick hug.

"And you brought brownies! Wow, we are so spoiled," I said, hugging Stitches.

"The brownies are just an appetizer. We're taking you to town for lunch," said Tuba Man, jumping to his feet.

"It's sweet of you to offer," jackrabbit said, "but we've got a long ways to go today, and it's almost noon. Maybe we'd better picnic here with you. We've got enough food."

"Trail food." Tuba Man made a face. "I've had about enough of that for a lifetime. We're going to town!"

"Don't worry about the distance. We're going to slack you," Stitches explained. "We both have cars, so we can leave one at each trailhead and hike with you!"

After a lunch of delicious greasy eggplant subs, Tuba Man left his sedan at the road crossing where he and Stitches had met us, setting us up for a sixteen-mile slack. We all piled into Stitches's tiny Geo Metro and drove over to the RPH shelter. It was three o'clock by the time we hit the trail, hiking south.

Southbound, we had said goodbye to Compañero and Highlander at RPH. On the ridge just south of the shelter, jackrabbit had told me how much depression still haunted her. We'd fallen behind everyone who we knew, and we had faced the prospect of hiking alone for the rest of the Trail. Yellowing ferns and cold morning air had presaged the harsh and early winter we would face, though most of the trees had still held their summer green.

As we slacked up the same ridge in summer, in the company of two old friends who'd driven hundreds of miles to visit us, I thought of all we'd been through since then. Jackrabbit had struggled through her depression, only to have it strike again in winter, when the constant battle with hypothermia wore her down. In the end, though, she'd not only made it to Springer, but she'd been the one to suggest that we hike back. Our northbound hike, at this point, felt like a victory tour: wild berries, trail magic, twenty-mile days as easy as tens once were, and friends, new and old, cheering us on at every turn of the Trail.

Stitches took the lead, handing out brownies to all the nobos we met. She'd been worried that she'd have trouble going fast enough for the rest of us, since she hadn't done anything longer than a weekend hike in over a year. Her pace suited jackrabbit and me perfectly well; a steady three miles per hour was as fast as we could have comfortably walked in the afternoon's sticky heat. Only Tuba Man seemed frustrated with the speed we were going. For the first four or five miles, he brought up the rear, trading jokes with jackrabbit. A few minutes after our first snack break, though, he stopped to talk with a passing northbounder.

"I'll catch up," he said, waving the rest of us on.

As the sun set over the ridges, six miles later, we sat down for another snack break. We had begun to worry about Tuba Man—we knew he could hike faster than any of us, and he still hadn't caught up.

"Do you think maybe we should go back and look for him?" Stitches asked. "It'll be dark soon."

Just then, Tuba Man sauntered up and threw himself to the ground beside jackrabbit. "Break time?" he asked nonchalantly.

He hiked with us as far as the next valley. There, the trail crossed a road, and we could see the lights of a gas station at an intersection a tenth of a mile away.

"I have to make a call," Tuba Man said. "I think I'll go see if that store has a pay phone."

"Okay." I started to follow him.

"You don't have to wait for me," he said. "I'll see you down the trail!" He gave us a jaunty wave and sprinted toward the gas station.

For the next few miles, we walked slowly, expecting him to catch up at any minute. At one point, the A.T. swerved abruptly off an old road that it had been following. We almost missed the turn in the dark, and we worried that Tuba Man would walk right past it in his hurry to catch up with us. After a few minutes of discussion, Stitches decided to leave one of her Photon lights, switched on, dangling over the Trail at the junction.

"Do you really want to leave that here?" jackrabbit asked her.

"I'm sure he'll know it's ours and pick it up," she replied. "And I wouldn't want him to be stuck out here without a light."

An hour or so later, we were plodding along in silence when a chorus of joyful cries in high, childish voices burst out of the valley to our left. *It sounds like they just got out for recess*, I thought. *But I don't remember seeing any buildings near here on the map. Wrong time of day for recess, anyway.* The cries continued, building in pitch and intensity as they rushed toward us. There was something strange about the sound, a brittle, tremulous edge to the highest notes, that didn't seem quite human.

Coyotes. A whole family of them, setting out for the night's hunt. As soon as I realized what they were, their voices stopped. The silence of the night forest seemed far deeper than it had been ten minutes before. I strained my ears for any sound in the darkness. Pretty soon, I heard it: a slight rustle in the bushes to our left, behind us. A minute later, another rustle, this time to our right.

"Hear that?" I whispered to jackrabbit. "They're following us."

"Cool! I bet they're teaching the cubs to track."

"This must be lesson one, then," whispered Stitches. "Large noisy animals moving at a steady pace along a well-established trail."

"It's neat to think that we're being useful to coyote parents," I said.

"Yeah, but it would be kind of freaky if you were alone—being hunted, even for practice," said jackrabbit. "I hope Tuba Man's not too far behind us."

"He must have had a pretty long phone call," Stitches said. "Maybe we should wait for him for a while."

We sat on a fallen log beside the trail. The coyotes rustled around us for a few minutes, before looking for something more interesting to hunt. Another chorus of yips burst out, deep in the valley ahead of us.

After the coyotes left, we talked about sending someone back to look for Tuba Man, but decided it would be safer not to separate any further. So we waited. We sang all the songs we could think of, and recited a few long poems. After what must have been almost an hour—though it seemed like half the night—Stitches got to her feet and stretched.

"If he was behind us, he would have caught up by now," she said. "I don't think there's any point in waiting longer."

"What should we do?" I asked. "Go back and look for him?"

"We must be pretty close to the car now. I think it would be safer, this time of night, to drive to the nearest town and report him missing."

"What about the key?" jackrabbit asked. "I mean, it's Tuba's car, isn't it?"

"I have Triple A," Stitches answered. "We'll just walk down the road to the nearest house and borrow their phone. He said there's a spare key in the glove box." She shook her head. "Not that that would help much if you were locked out. But Scott, bless his heart, is not long on foresight."

"Yeah, I guess we can call Triple A," I said. I didn't remember seeing any houses near the trailhead, but I couldn't come up with any other plan. The three of us raced down the last mile and a half to the road. There sat the little blue car, with Tuba Man fast asleep in the driver's seat.

He blinked and sat up as we pounded on the doors.

"Hey, what took you so long?" he asked, rolling down the window. "I hitched over from the gas station, and I figured you'd get here an hour or two after I did."

"We were waiting for you," jackrabbit told him. "We thought you were behind us."

"You were *waiting* for me?" Tuba Man sounded incredulous. "Why'd you do that?"

We drove around for almost an hour trying to find something for dinner, but it was so late that all the restaurants were closed. Finally, Tuba Man dropped us off at RPH, promising to come back with food. When he hadn't returned by the time we had our tent set up, jackrabbit and I looked at each other, shrugged, and took the breakfast cereal out of our food bags.

I had just crawled into the tent and zipped the screen shut behind me, when headlights flashed across the clearing. The sound of rapid footsteps crossed the lawn, and Tuba Man was standing in front of our tent, a pint container in each hand.

"Are you awake?" he asked. "I brought you ice cream."

jackrabbit

"What were you *thinking* last night?" I said to Tuba Man.

"I didn't think you guys would stop and *wait* for me. I mean . . ."

"I think it's just a reflex kind of thing, you know; after hiking through winter, we wouldn't just leave somebody behind without knowing where they were."

"Huh."

"Thanks for the ice cream, though. How'd you know Cherry Garcia was my favorite?"

He shrugged and flashed that heart-stopping smile. "You told me that in Florida."

"And you remembered all this time?"

"You think I'm just a dumb blond, don't you?"

I think you're wonderful. But not in the way I hoped you would be. I laughed. "There *is* some evidence to support that theory—those fireworks, for in-stance . . ."

"Yeah, I guess that was pretty dumb. I'm not usually like that, though, really."

"Good thing," I said dryly. "Probably explains how you've reached the age of twenty-five with all your limbs intact."

"We'd better get going," Stitches said apologetically. "We've got to get this guy to Boston tonight."

"Right," Tuba Man said. "Well, hey, jackrabbit, it's been fun. Bye, Isis. You guys take care, okay?"

"Yeah, you too. Take care, Stitches. Travel safely."

After he left, the shelter seemed smaller, as though the force of his per-sonality had enlarged the room.

Isis watched the car drive away. "What a piece of work."

"He's not so bad . . ."

"You're not still mooning over him, are you?"

To my surprise, I wasn't. It had been good to see him, but I had found I was no longer attracted to him. He was so different from the mental image I had constructed over the winter, and it was that image I had fallen in love with.

My friend Aislinn arrived at the RPH shelter in midmorning.

"So good to see you," I said. "You cut your hair!" Her ash-blond hair now framed her face, short and styled; it had once been a cascade to the middle of her back. Otherwise, she looked just like she had in college: thin and petite, with a narrow face and incisive green eyes.

"Yeah, it's good to see you, too," she said. "About my hair—I found a place on the Internet called Locks of Love. If you send them ten inches of hair, they use it to make a wig for a child with leukemia. I thought, well, I don't really need it . . ."

"Aislinn, you're so *good*! It must be your Catholic upbringing."

"Oh, please!" It was an old joke from college. "I'm a *recovering* Catholic, thank you very much. Giving away my hair had nothing to do with morality or sacrifice or anything like that. I just felt like a change." She ran a hand through her newly short hair. "It was getting kind of hot, having it down all summer. And I never learned to braid it like you do, Susan."

I almost said, "Call me jackrabbit." My real name felt unreal. Having Aislinn here was even stranger. College and the Trail had seemed like two discrete worlds. It didn't seem possible that someone could step from one into the other. With her clean clothes and neat haircut, Aislinn looked completely out of place in the shelter, where grubby gear hung from every bedpost of the bunks. I tried to carry on a conversation, but it was hard to find common ground; Trail life was difficult to explain to someone who had never been a part of it. Instead, we resorted back to stories from college, reminiscing about things that had happened years ago instead of describing our current lives. Aislinn had been one of my closest friends, but I felt distant from her now. I felt us drifting apart.

For the first time in months, I thought about the southbounder Matt, who had hiked with us in Maine. *People come, people go*, he'd told me in Gorham, just before he hiked ahead of us. *Things change . . . You can't get too attached to the way things are. Attach yourself to change, because* that *is the only constant in the universe.* I could still picture his thin, freckled face and bright red hair. *Maybe it's true*, I thought. *But it's not a comfort.*

After we left the RPH Shelter, we hiked by ourselves for a few days over the rolling hills. It was the last week of July, high summer; the leaves of the oak trees hushed and shimmered in light winds. In the evenings, terrific thunderstorms battered the mountains.

It was strange to pass the places where we had stealth-camped with Compañero. It seemed like such a short time since we had crossed these hills together in late September. The last time I'd heard from him, he had been looking for a job in Maine. Perhaps we would see him again on our northbound hike. At Morgan Stewart Shelter I left a register entry commemorating one of the better in-jokes from our time with him:

7/24. Isis and jackrabbit stopping in for lunch. Tonight on Morgan Stewart Living: decorating with ramen! These versatile noodles are more than just sustenance. With a little creativity, they can become a fashion statement. Festoon your pack with delicate streamers of half-cooked ramen, and it will look simply irresistible (to mice and squirrels, anyway)! Tomorrow night: make your own emergency blanket with Pop-tart wrappers and duct tape.

On a hot, hazy afternoon, we passed Nuclear Lake. The water level had risen since fall, so the dead flats were no longer exposed. I thought I still detected a faintly unwholesome scent, a suggestion of decay and something metallic, but perhaps it was just the power of suggestion. As we came to the meadows by the lake, I heard the sound of splashing and happy voices coming through the trees.

"Isis, you don't think they're actually *swimming* there?"

Sure enough, a small group of nobos cavorted in the black water. "Come on in! The water's fine!" someone called from offshore.

"No thanks," I called back, and we kept walking. I wondered why anyone would want to swim in a place called Nuclear Lake at all. It wasn't until I checked the *Data Book* that afternoon, trying to estimate our daily mileage, that I realized the nobos in the water may not have known the name of the place. Nuclear Lake was clearly indicated on the map and given its own listing in the *Thru-Hikers' Companion*, but it wasn't even mentioned in the *Data Book*.

After a few days, we crossed the New York–Connecticut line. The thickets of tangled brush around the border were even worse than I remembered. I put on my rain jacket before I headed into the densest clumps of vines. The light drizzle descending from the clouds was hardly enough to justify it, but I had another reason. Granny Gear had mentioned that this area, on the border of New York and Connecticut, was the epicenter of Lyme disease infection. The tiny, almost invisible ticks that carry the disease cling to grasses and bushes, waiting for animals to walk past. Isis and I were careful to check our bodies for ticks whenever we stopped moving, and we checked ourselves more thoroughly at night in the tent. Even with these precautions, I didn't want my bare skin brushing against any more foliage than it had to along this section of the Trail.

We camped on the hill just outside Kent, Connecticut, and walked into town in the morning, down the slope of hemlocks and birches. The sun seemed too bright, hurting my eyes, and the half-mile walk, along a flat road, seemed much longer. *I'm becoming such a wimp*, I thought. *Maybe I've been out here too long. Maybe your body reaches a certain point, and you just can't do any more.*

The town looked much as I remembered: quiet streets with tall maples; brick and wooden buildings set back with small lawns and flower beds. This time, though, a wave of nostalgia and homesickness hit me. Kent was the first town along the Trail that really looked like New England. I thought of all the miles we had traveled and all the places we had seen before returning, and I thought of the miles that still remained ahead of us. A profound weariness settled over me.

We dropped our packs in front of the outfitters, joining the crowd of hikers already there: Polar Bear and Johnny Steel, Iculus, Dream Catcher, Flash and Stocks, and a few others.

Dream Catcher waved as we walked up. "Hey, Barefoot Sisters. Solar showers for a buck."

"Sounds good, man. How's it going?"

We exchanged the usual pleasantries. Isis went across the parking lot to the post office, and I went into the outfitter's store for a new filter cartridge and some sunscreen.

The rest of the day was consumed in the usual town chores: I sent out an e-mail to parents and friends; we took showers, bought and repackaged our resupply at the IGA, and washed clothes. The laundromat sported a collection of hostile handwritten signs: one dryer was labeled *if you break this again I won't fix it, thanks a lot moron*; another read *broke and don't ask me to pay for repairs!* I wondered how the place ever made a profit.

Outside, while we waited for the clothes to dry, Polar Bear came by with a bag full of ripe plums. He lay down on the grass beside us, and we put away the postcards we'd been writing.

"Want some fruit?"

"I'd love some! Thanks, man," I said, reaching into the paper sack.

"The only thing is," Polar Bear said, "you've got to sing me that song again."

"Not 'Dig a Hole!'" Isis groaned.

"No, no, your other one. The pretty one. You know, something about nightbirds . . ."

"Oh, sure. Definitely. It seems like we got the good end of this deal," I said, licking the plum juice from my hands.

We finished the song and Polar Bear sat back, smiling. "I love that song." Then his smile turned mischievous. "I've got the best story for you," he said.

"What is it?"

"Well, you know how Johnny Steel's always ragging on me? I found the perfect way to get back at him. A couple weeks ago, I asked him where his name came from. He said the guys at the fire station gave it to him, because he had a high resistance for heat, like steel. Something like that. So I made up this whole story about a Canadian comic book called *Johnny Steel*. About a gay superhero. He wears tights. His trademark is a pink scarf."

I laughed. It was difficult to picture Johnny Steel, with his gruff masculinity, wearing anything pink. "He *would* look good in tights."

"Oh, it gets better," Polar Bear said. "I just planted that little seed of doubt in his mind. Then, a few days ago, I met Julien." He grinned. "French-Canadian kid. He's in on the joke. I only hope I'm there when the other shoe comes down on Johnny Steel."

As usual, we ate constantly while in town: carrots from the market, pastries from the bakery on Main Street, Polar Bear's plums, a huge lunch of pizza at an Italian restaurant. I felt even more hungry than usual, a desperate kind of hunger I hadn't felt since winter. On the Trail, I had become so attuned to my metabolism that I could almost always tell how much energy I would get from a given amount of food. Recently, though, the equation had begun to break down. I wondered briefly if my body was mounting an immune response to something.

As the day wore on, my lethargy grew. I sat on the porch of the outfitter's, in the shade of a cement column, trying to motivate myself to pack up and go. Polar Bear and Johnny Steel lay on the grass nearby, eating Chinese takeout. Flash and Stocks sat on the sidewalk together, in a heated discussion of mileage and timing.

"This is ridiculous," Flash said, and his Long Island accent turned the *th* into a *d*. "I make more miles in a week at home than I do on the Trail." His clipped but rapid speech matched his spare, well-muscled frame. I remembered what he had told us at Mashipacong, that he was a half-marathon runner. Perhaps he wasn't exaggerating about the mileage.

"But Flash, man, we ain't out here to go fast an' impress the girlies. We're here to have a good time." Stocks gave an impish smile. "All the girlies walk slow, so we gotta walk slow."

"It ain't that we go slow, it's that we take all o' those days off." (I could attest to this—the two of them had passed me on the trail, numerous times, always clipping along at four miles an hour or faster. Given their pace, it was something of a wonder that we'd met them in New Jersey, 135 miles back, and they were still with us on the Trail.)

Porkchop walked up with a load of groceries. I'd met her on the Trail before, but never spent much time with her. She was in her mid-twenties, short and slender, solidly muscled, with a pageboy of dark blond curls, and she walked with a bounce in her step and seemed to wear a perpetual smile. Her little dog Frankie, a silky-haired golden mutt, trotted up to Flash, wagging her tail.

Flash petted Frankie's long ears. "What a cute doggie you are, Frankie! Yes you are!" He turned to Stocks. "See? She likes me!"

"Hi, guys," Porkchop said. "I met a local at the grocery store who's got floor space, if anybody wants to stick around town tonight."

"Sounds good!" Flash said. Stocks gave him an exasperated look, and then shrugged.

The house turned out to be just down the road from the trailhead. The owner, a man in his late fifties with a slightly owlish mournful look, showed us into the back room. Almost the whole crowd from the outfitter's had shown up; the town vortex had proved too strong for everyone but Polar Bear.

"I'm moving next week, so there's not much furniture, but you're welcome to stay here," the man said. "Watch TV, listen to the radio, take showers, use the kitchen, whatever you want."

"Thanks so much," I told him, as we helped him carry boxes out to his van. "This really means a lot to us hikers, to have a place to stay. If there's anything we can do for you, let us know."

He smiled, looking wistful, and shook his head. "Many people have been kind to me throughout my life. The least I can do is pass it on."

I ate dinner—soup and a sandwich Isis had carried from the pastry shop in town—out on the back porch. The other hikers inside had turned on the TV, and I had a headache that wouldn't quit. It was quiet back there, in the shade of old lilacs, and cool from the dampness of the ground. A skittish black-and-white cat peeked out from under the foundation, but disappeared when I turned to look.

The door creaked open behind me. "Mind if I join you?"

"Not at all."

Porkchop sat down on the steps beside me, her compact frame taking up half the space that mine did. "You're jackrabbit, right?"

"Yup. And you're Porkchop?"

"That's right." She gave a helpless laugh.

"You don't look much like a Porkchop! How'd you get the name?"

"Well, the year after I was in high school, I was part of a project called Christian Youth Outreach." She must have seen the momentary discomfort that passed over my face—I've never been a fan of proselytizing religions—because she quickly said, "My life has changed a lot since then. My priorities, my beliefs. But that year, I was with a group of other Christian kids, and we traveled all over the U.S., Europe, China, and India. We lived with families, and we traveled in a big touring bus, one of those ones with a VCR and everything. We only had a few movies, though, and the only one we all actually liked was *Groundhog Day*. Have you seen it?"

"Yeah. The one about the guy who keeps reliving the same day until he gets it right?"

"Uh-huh."

"That's a pretty repetitive movie to watch over and over."

"Oh, yeah." There was something in the way she said this, the length of the "oh" and the emphatic "yeah" that reminded me of my freshman-year roommate in college.

"Are you from Minnesota, Porkchop?"

"Wisconsin, actually." She beamed.

"But I'm distracting you from the story."

"Well, it got to the point where we knew every line in the movie, and we'd recite it to each other. There's one part where the man walks past a fat guy on the stairs of his apartment every morning, and he says—" she laughed helplessly "—he says, 'Mornin', Porkchop!' We would always say that to each other. And I was the one who laughed hardest, so eventually people on the trip just started calling me Porkchop.

"Before I started my thru-hike, I was out for a few days with my friend Matt, who was on the trip too. He'd hiked the A.T. in '99. We started talking about trail names, and he said I should be Porkchop. I told him, 'Matt, you know I'm gonna burst out laughing every time I try to introduce myself as Porkchop!' And he said, 'What better reason?'" She had such a musical, wild laugh that it was impossible not to join in. "And so I'm Porkchop."

"Excellent."

That night, when I lay on my Thermarest on the hardwood floor, sleep would not come. My head was pounding, and when I closed my eyes the room felt like a ship at sea, rocking with a faintly nauseating motion. My shoulders and neck felt stiff no matter what position I rolled into. I finally drifted off by counting not sheep but footsteps; I pictured myself climbing a mountain in New England somewhere, a slope of granite and stunted evergreens. I pictured the broken stones underfoot, and concentrated on every footfall, numbering each one, until I reached the level gray summit of sleep.

CHAPTER 8

Sick and Tired

Isis

On the morning we hiked out of Kent, we blue-blazed along the Housatonic for the first ten miles. The day heated up quickly, even along the river. I was glad to be following a level dirt road, instead of climbing up and down the ridges that the A.T. followed. Jackrabbit seemed to be having a hard day in spite of the blue-blaze; she walked with her head bent and her brow creased, as though following the smooth road was taking every ounce of her concentration. I asked how she was feeling, but she only said "tired" in a voice that implied that any further attempt at conversation would be a bigger waste of energy than she could afford at the moment.

I let it go. Whatever was wrong, she'd tell me sooner or later. We'd slow down, maybe even take a few zeros, and give her knee or shoulder or whatever it was time to rest. Her neatly written schedule, which showed us reaching Katahdin on September 15, would have to be altered again. A disappointment for her, but what were a couple days, really? Perhaps we could spend them at Upper Goose Pond Cabin in Massachusetts, the place I'd had such a hard time leaving when I passed there solo in the fall. It was only eighty miles away. I let myself slip into a daydream: the steep rocky path from the cabin, the texture of the old wooden dock beneath my feet, the cool deep water closing around my body as I dove.

Late in the morning, the dirt road became a paved road, passing through farmland and a few small towns. Blue-blazing, we caught glimpses of local culture that the Trail, in its wilderness corridor, rarely offers. Two whales' tails sculpted of wrought iron rose from a farm field beside the road. When we stopped to take pictures, a fat orange cat trotted up and wound between our ankles, purring. Farther down the road, an old man tending his flower garden waved to us, and asked if we needed any water. He vanished into his house for five minutes, then reappeared with a tray holding lemons, sugar, a pitcher of iced tea, and three tall, frosted glasses.

We bought sandwiches and ice cream for lunch at the General Store in Cornwall Bridge, then hiked up the road, back to the A.T. As soon as we hit rougher ground, jackrabbit slowed, breathing hard. I turned to ask her what was wrong, but she shot me a "don't bother me" glare before I could open my mouth. I shrugged, too contentedly full of ice cream to feel miffed, and kept walking. Five miles later, we stopped for a snack break. Jackrabbit took the granola bar I handed her, but she didn't unwrap it. She leaned against a tree with her eyes closed and sweat streaming down her forehead. I waited.

"I don't feel very well." She spoke in a small, tired voice, with no trace of the anger I'd seen in her eyes earlier.

"Are you sick to your stomach?" I asked.

"No, but I've had a pounding headache all day, and now I feel dizzy, too."

"Are you drinking enough?"

"I think so." She took out her water bottle and drained the last half liter. I consulted the *Thru-Hikers' Companion* while she ate her granola bar.

"You're in luck," I told her. "There's a hospital we can hitch to on the next road."

"A *hospital*? We can't afford a hospital!"

She had a point. Neither of us had health insurance, and the expense of an emergency room visit would put a pretty big dent in what remained of our Trail savings.

"We'll find a way to afford it," I told her. "Less restaurant meals, less overnights in towns. If you're sick, we have to do something about it."

She sighed. "It's probably just some flu that's going around. I heard another hiker back in Kent describing the same symptoms. Let's go on to the shelter."

"Are you sure?"

"It's only two miles away," she said, irritation creeping back into her voice. "Let's just go."

It took us almost an hour and a half to reach Pine Swamp Brook Lean-to.

"I see why they call it Pine *Swamp*," jackrabbit grumbled as we set down our packs in a nice sandy tent site a ways from the shelter. "Fucking mosquitoes! There're probably even more of them down at the water source. I don't know how I'll sit still long enough to filter water."

"I can get our water while you set up the tent," I offered. "They're not bothering me quite as much."

She muttered something that sounded like, "nothing bothers you, does it," and tossed her water bottles in my direction.

When I got back from the stream, ten minutes later, she was still pounding in the fly stakes, stopping after each stake to swat frenetically at her arms and legs. She heard my footsteps, and turned to face me with an expression bordering on panic.

"These fucking bugs, Isis! They're driving me crazy! I can't take it anymore."

"Go ahead and get in the tent," I told her, in the most soothing voice I could manage. "I'll sit right out here, and you can read to me while I cook."

She plunged into the tent and zipped it up behind her. I pounded in the last few stakes and took *Huckleberry Finn* out of her pack, while she huddled as far from the tent walls as she could get, clutching her knees and shivering.

"I can still hear them buzzing," she said to me as I zipped open a crack in the tent door just big enough to hand her the book.

"Pretty soon the sound of the Zip stove will drown them out," I answered.

She tried to read while I set the stove up, but she stumbled over long sentences and lost her place. After a few paragraphs she gave up and curled on the bare tent floor. I cooked, trying to keep my mind focused on the simple, comforting task at hand. Feeding the Zip stove wasn't quite enough to distract me from my worries, though. The mosquitoes were bad, but they were nothing compared with the bugs we'd dealt with on our way through Maine southbound. More recently, the no-see-ums in Pen-Mar Park had been much thicker and more pernicious than Pine Swamp Brook's insect cloud. If a few mosquitoes could make jackrabbit panic, something was wrong—something, I suspected, more serious than the flu.

She dug into our pot of polenta with as much of an appetite as ever, and for a while, I was tempted to revise my opinion. It had been a long, hot day. We'd hiked eighteen miles; she'd had a headache for most of them. Wasn't that enough to explain a moment's panic?

Later that evening, though, when I returned from hanging our food bags, I found her curled on her side with tears streaming down her face.

"What's wrong?" I asked. "Is your headache that bad? Let me get you some Tylenol."

I reached for the first aid kit, but she stopped me, grabbing my hand and pressing it to her forehead.

"Isis—do I have a fever?"

I held my hand to her head for a minute, then lifted it to mine. My forehead definitely felt cooler.

"Yeah," I told her. She drew her breath in sharply, and I added, "Not much of one; maybe a hundred."

"Isis, do you remember what we read about West Nile encephalitis? There've been cases in Connecticut, haven't there?"

I remembered that we'd been seriously worried about the West Nile virus when we first heard of it, just before we started hiking. The mosquito-borne disease had been spreading rapidly up the East Coast. Newspapers described it as an epidemic, claiming that most people who contracted the disease died within twenty-four hours. By the time we reached the Mid-Atlantic States on our northbound hike, though, most of the mosquitoes had died after the relatively dry summer. And Trail rumor, backed up by a magazine article I'd found in a hostel, reported that the mortality rate of the West Nile virus wasn't nearly as high as we'd been led to believe. Most of its victims were very old, very young, or sick with something else as well. The article speculated that most strong, healthy people who caught the disease recovered without even being diagnosed; the fever and headache, lasting about twenty-four hours, were often mistaken for symptoms of the flu.

"I'm afraid that's what I have," jackrabbit continued, without waiting for me to answer. "Headache, fever—and within twenty-four hours, you're dead."

"That's how the newspapers described it when we started southbound," I answered, surprised. "But remember that article we found later on, the one that said that not many people actually die of it?"

"The last article *I* saw said that everyone diagnosed with it had died. Isis, I'm scared. I'm afraid if I go to sleep, I won't wake up in the morning." Her voice trembled and she gripped my hand tightly.

I'd seen jackrabbit sick, injured, and grumpy about the weather a fair number of times over the past year. Her moods were pretty transparent; if she didn't complain outright, she swore, glowered, and stomped around until I could have no doubt of her unhappiness. I'd never known her to be a hypochondriac, though. On the contrary, she tended to hike even harder when she got injured, trying not to admit to herself or others just how bad it was. So if she said she was going to die, she must really believe it.

"Do you want to go back down to the road, and hitch to the hospital?" I asked her.

"We can't. No one would pick us up in the dark. Besides, I don't have the strength to walk that far."

"Okay," I said. "We'll wait till morning."

"If I'm alive in the morning," she said, her voice dull with exhaustion.

"You will be," I told her. "I'm sure you will be. Now try to get some rest."

I lay down beside her and wrapped an arm around her shoulders, trying to still her trembling. After only a few minutes, she relaxed, sighing, and her breath steadied into the slow, even rhythm of sleep.

To both of our surprise, she felt perfectly fine in the morning.

"Either you were right about West Nile virus, or else it was just the flu," she said cheerfully, as we packed up the tent. "God, it was awful, though. I was convinced I was going to die."

"I know," I said. "You told me."

"Did I really? Shit, I'm sorry. I didn't mean to say anything, but I was so scared, I guess I couldn't keep it to myself."

We hiked eight miles in the morning: more or less our usual pace. Jackrabbit still looked a bit peaked, but after her illness the day before, I was surprised at how cheerful and energetic she seemed.

Just past noon, we crossed the bridge into Falls Village and went looking for some town food for lunch. A white clapboard inn near the center of town, which seemed to have descended from the Victorian era, untouched by time, bore a sign advertising "Pizza and Pub." Adding to the incongruity, about forty large, gleaming Harleys were parked along the curb outside the building.

We leaned our packs against the porch, donned our shirts and shoes, and walked into the dining room. Gauzy white curtains drifted in and out of the open windows; Wyeth prints in gilded frames adorned the walls. Balding men in black leather, and a few heavyset women in spandex leggings and tiny, neon-colored tank tops, crowded around the polished oak tables. All the bikers glanced up as we entered. A few of them called a greeting or lifted a beer stein toward us in salutation.

"You girls want a waitress, you'll have to go back to the bar," said a man with heavy blue tattoos and a comb-over hairstyle. "There's only one of 'em here, and we're keeping 'er pretty busy."

More of the bikers filled the stools at the bar, and I put a hand to my mouth to stifle a laugh when I saw their jackets from the back. The words "Charter Oak Bike Club" encircled an image of a skull with flaming eye sockets—and a powdered George Washington wig.

The wiry, gray-haired man whose jacket I'd been studying turned around and caught me gawking.

"That's okay, you can laugh," he told me. "We won't shoot you." He looked me up and down, taking in my unkempt hair and stained clothing, and the badger claw necklace my stepfather had lent me at the beginning of our hike. "That's a pretty outlandish get-up you're wearing, yourself. You look like one of them *Survivor* types. What're you doing in Falls Village, Connecticut, if you don't mind me asking?"

"Trying to find some pizza, at the moment," jackrabbit broke in. "But hiking, for the most part. Backpacking."

"You want pizza? You need Jenny for that. Hey, Jenny! You got some customers here," he bellowed.

A pretty, slender woman with dark blond curls hurried over from the other end of the bar.

"I've got customers everywhere," she laughed. "You guys ought to warn me when you're coming through, so I can get Michelle and Deirdre in to help me out." She caught sight of me and jackrabbit. "What can I get for you?"

"Would a large veggie pizza be possible?" I asked, wondering whether Jenny was the cook as well as the sole waitress and bartender.

"Anything's possible," she said, "but it may take a while. I'll go tell Gary to fire up the oven. Can I get you a drink in the meantime?"

"Some iced tea, please," said jackrabbit. "And if you have any vegetarian appetizers that wouldn't take too long to cook."

"I'll see what I can find. Go get yourselves a table, if there are any left, and I'll be out in a minute."

We found an unoccupied two-person table under a window near the porch, and after a short search, we managed to locate two free chairs as well. Jenny came out with a tray containing a pitcher of iced tea, a loaf of garlic bread, and a large bowl of tomato and white bean salad.

"I hope this will tide you over," she said cheerily. "Gary says it'll take about twenty minutes to get the oven up to temp. If there's anything else you want while you're waiting, well, I won't make any promises, but you can always ask."

She had already vanished down the hall by the time we discovered we had no silverware. I took my little silver teaspoon from the top of my pack, and we ate the salad trading it back and forth.

"So, you ladies backpacking? On the Appalachian Trail?" It was the gray-haired man from the bar.

"Yes," jackrabbit answered, her voice guarded. He seemed friendly enough, but the *don't tell strangers where you're spending the night* rule applied even more strongly to strangers we met in a bar.

"I got a granddaughter who wants to do that," the man said. "'Course, she's only fifteen now, and by the time she graduates high school, who knows what she'll want to do. How'd you girls get started backpacking, anyway?"

We told him a few stories from our trip, and asked about his granddaughter, who turned out to be an avid kayaker and a junior champion of the local trout fishing tournament. Just after our pizza arrived, the members of the Charter Oak Bike Club began filing out of the bar.

"Hey, Charlie, whatcha doing talking to those girls?" called a tall man with a huge potbelly. "They're young enough to be your grandkids."

"I'm bragging to them about my granddaughter," he answered good-naturedly. He turned back to us. "Well, I guess we're off to the next adventure. Great meeting you."

He shook hands with each of us, then hurried out the door.

"You know," jackrabbit mused, as the sound of revving engines shook the room, "hikers have a lot in common with bikers. The freedom of the road and all that . . . We've got our own codes and symbols, our own strange way of dressing—and some people get worried, maybe with good reason, when a bunch of us descend on a town!"

The crowd in the restaurant had died down to what was probably its usual Sunday-afternoon proportions by the time we left. A few people sat at the bar: women in summer dresses and men in casual, light-colored suits. Three more men shared a table on the porch, and I overheard scraps of their conversation as I took off my sandals and strapped them onto my pack. A man with a low gravelly voice was holding forth about the difficulties of being poor in this neighborhood. He couldn't afford the kinds of things his neighbors had, and his young children were really beginning to notice the difference between their home and the houses where their friends lived.

I felt a lot of sympathy for him; western Connecticut would be a hard place to live if you were poor. We'd passed through a few middle-class neighborhoods on our blue-blaze along the river the day before, but we'd also walked by walled estates and glimpsed enormous timber frame mansions away through the trees. Today, Sunday, about half the vehicles on the roads we'd crossed were vintage sports cars in mint condition. (A cream-colored Jaguar and a flame-orange Mustang were parked in the lot beside the inn.) Falls Village itself, with its serene clapboard houses and carefully groomed lawns, emanated a sense of old East Coast elegance and prestige. *Struggling to make a living here must be frustrating, with so much wealth constantly before your eyes,* I thought to myself.

By the time we strapped on our packs, the topic of conversation had changed.

"Lovely day for a drive, isn't it?" a man with a reedy voice commented to his lunch companions.

"It certainly is," answered the deep-voiced man who had complained of being poor. "I had to get the Jaguar out of the garage so my wife could use the Mercedes, but now I'm glad I went to the trouble."

There was no trace of irony in his voice. *Well*, I thought, *I guess he's got a different definition of poverty from the one I learned.*

We only made five miles in the afternoon. Jackrabbit was flagging; the exhaustion from her bout of sickness finally catching up to her. I tried to engage her in conversation a few times, joking about the "poor" of western Connecticut, and pointing out a dragon-shaped cloud drifting over a field to our right. She answered me with a silence so stubborn and complete that it felt like anger.

Late in the day, we sat down at a stream to filter water.

"I think I've got a fever again," jackrabbit sighed.

I checked.

"You do. But you're not going to die this time, okay?"

"Ha-ha." Her voice dripped sarcasm.

"I'm sorry. I was only trying to lighten things up a bit; I didn't mean to make fun of you."

"I'm sorry too," she said. "I'm just so angry right now. At you, at the Trail, but most of all at myself. We were finally hiking at a reasonable pace, and then my body fell apart again. It's like clockwork: my hip, my foot, my knee, and now this. Whatever it is."

"This is only a temporary sickness. You'll feel better soon, and we'll make up for the miles we lost." I felt a short, sharp ache in my chest as I let go of the daydream of zeroing at Upper Goose Pond.

"It doesn't feel temporary," jackrabbit said. "It feels like my body's fighting something big. It feels like all the energy from the food I eat goes into immune response, and there's nothing left to hike with. We've done what, thirteen miles today?"

"Just about."

"I think I could hike two more miles, maximum, before I collapse with exhaustion."

We continued down the path, walking more and more slowly as evening shadows appeared between the trees.

jackrabbit

"I'm tired. I have to stop now." My own voice sounded thick and unfamiliar in my ears, as though muffled by cotton batting.

"We can't stop here." Isis was a little exasperated. "We're in Connecticut. You know stealth-camping isn't allowed here. And they have so many ridge runners . . ."

In summer, the state's sixty-mile stretch of A.T. was patrolled by four ridge runners. Only the Whites and Katahdin had a higher density of people in charge of enforcing camping rules. Just yesterday, we had met one of them, an earnest young woman who had exhorted us to always filter our water.

"I can't go on." I took my pack off and sat down by a little stream. It was close to evening; long slats of light leaned down between the dark trunks of spruces. My temples throbbed. When I tried to turn my head, pain shot through my neck and shoulders, so severe that black spots danced at the edge of my vision.

Isis sighed. "Okay. We can camp here, as long as we get out of sight of the trail. It looks like there's some level ground behind the birches there."

I opened my pack and took out the tent.

"We shouldn't set up until after dark," she said, with a puzzled frown.

Of course—it was one of the first rules for stealth-camping, especially in areas where it was illicit. How had I forgotten? Wordlessly, I closed my pack.

"We need food, though. Get your food bag out. How about you get us some water while I collect stove wood?" She left her pack by the stream and set off down the trail.

Part of me wanted to snap something mean at her retreating back. She was treating me like a child, like she had in the worst of winter when I was on the verge of hypothermia. Then I realized that I was acting just as confused and slow as I had then. The night before, I'd been convinced that I had West Nile encephalitis. I'd been fine in the morning, but now the symptoms were back: the vice-clamp headache and the soreness that spread down my back. I wondered what disease it could be.

I bent down carefully and picked up the water filter. I had a fever again; waves of alternate cold and heat shuddered through me. If I moved too fast, swarming dark threatened to overwhelm my field of vision. The light in the clearing had a weird underwater quality to it, fuzzy and spider-webbed. I blinked several times to clear my eyes, but the strangeness persisted. Evening gathered. Shadows drooped out of the heavy, tufted branches of the evergreens, and I felt suddenly, irrationally terrified by their amorphous shapes. *What's happening to me?* I wondered.

Isis came bounding down the trail as I finished filtering the last bottle of water. "Ridge runner!" she hissed.

A moment later, I heard footsteps. A young man in his twenties stepped out of the woods. He had light brown skin and a black crew cut, and he wore an olive-green uniform emblazoned with Park Service and ATC patches.

"Hi," he said. "I'm sorry I startled you back there. I'm Matt Chen, the ridge runner for this section. Mind if I join you?"

"Not at all," Isis said, reddening slightly. "I'm Isis. This is my sister, jackrabbit."

I gave a little wave, feeling not particularly sociable.

Matt slung off his well-worn pack and sat down on the bank. "Are you guys thru-hiking?"

"We're yo-yoing, actually," Isis said.

"Right on! You must be the Barefoot Sisters." (Inwardly, I groaned: the last thing I wanted right now was to field someone's questions about barefoot hiking.) But Matt just smiled at Isis's answer. "Are you planning on stealth-camping?" he asked.

"Yeah," Isis admitted. With the dark gathering in the trees, it was pretty obvious we wouldn't get much farther that night.

"I know some great stealth sites near here." He grinned, seeing the looks of surprise and relief on our faces. "I generally let thru-hikers camp wherever they want, because you guys know how to clean up after yourselves. With weekenders, it's a different story. I make them go to the established campsites. Oh, but the nearest site here is Plateau." He made a face. "I wouldn't send *anybody* to that place."

"That's right," Isis said. "We stayed there in fall. Ugh. There were night-crawlers everywhere. And that spring, just downhill from the privy—"

"—and the slope of the gravel!" Matt said. "The first and only time I stayed there, I slid down to the bottom of my tent before the night was half-over. I woke up in a little ball. And there were slugs all over my ground cloth in the morning."

My brain was running at about half-speed, but I felt like I needed to make some contribution to the conversation. "How do you like ridge running?" I asked him.

"Aside from the slugs and mosquitoes and the occasional belligerent weekender, it's a lot of fun, actually. It's really different from thru-hiking. From what I imagine thru-hiking would be, anyway. The *scale* of the experience is different. Instead of finding new scenery every day for thousands of miles, you get to know the same fifty miles of Trail really well." He gave a lopsided grin. "I actually have names for some of the rocks. All the other ridge runners think that's kind of weird."

"We have names for our gear," Isis said, setting a pot of water on the Zip stove. "The filter's called Don Juan, because in winter, before it got too cold to use it, we took turns sleeping with it so it wouldn't freeze overnight."

Matt laughed. "That's a good one." He set up his Whisperlite stove and took out a packet of long noodles. "Do you guys want to have a potluck? I've been eating rice noodles and curry for more nights than I can count."

"Yeah, that sounds good," Isis said. "I'll make couscous with pesto."

Matt and Isis traded Trail recipes as they cooked, and Matt told stories from his summer as a ridge runner. I sat back, listening to their conversation, slapping the mosquitoes that whined in my ears and brushed against my skin. I was hungry; my muscles screamed out for nourishment. But the smell of cooking food made me slightly nauseated.

Finally Matt turned to me. "Jackrabbit, are you okay?"

"Kind of. Yeah. I'm just a little out of it," I answered, again hearing my voice as though from a distance.

"You look sick," he said. "You're really pale, and you have this far-off look in your eyes."

"It's just a headache," I said.

"Are you sure? 'Cause I could take you to the hospital in the morning, if you want. I have to go in soon for a Lyme disease test. It's apparently endemic in this area; all the ridge runners have to get tested every six weeks."

"What are the symptoms of Lyme disease?" I asked him.

"I don't really know, actually. Flu-like, I guess; muscle aches and nausea and that sort of thing. It's supposed to start with a tick bite. Usually you can see a rash around the bite, like a red bull's-eye, and I haven't noticed anything like that on me." He shrugged. "I've felt fine all summer."

"Maybe that's what I have," I said. It certainly didn't feel like a normal cold, or any other disease I was familiar with. "But we've been really careful about ticks. And I haven't seen any weird rashes on me, either."

"It's worth getting it checked out, anyway," Matt said. "I could hitch to my car from the next road and pick you up."

"Yeah," Isis said. "If you're still sick in the morning, you should go."

In the morning, though, I felt fine again. Matt hiked out with us, instead of going to the hospital for his blood test; it was a perfect day to be in the mountains, with a few soft clouds traversing the arc of blue sky in a light wind. None of us wanted to leave the Trail in weather like this. When we reached the road, we just cut into the woods on the other side and kept walking, up into the rounded granite mountains. We stopped often to grab handfuls of blueberries, tiny tart pin cherries, and the plump purple seed-filled June berries. I found myself eating ravenously. My stomach rumbled, despite the big bowl of Grape-Nuts I'd eaten for breakfast.

Matt pointed out his favorite stealth sites and told us his names for the rocks and logs near the Trail: "That big pine log over there is the Nap Tree. Sometimes I'll spend an hour or two just lying there in the sun on top of it . . . Those two standing stones are The Guardians. Doesn't the forest look more mysterious behind them? It's like you could walk through and find yourself in a different world . . . See that little triangular rock sticking up in the middle of the trail? That's Ol' Anklebiter. Be careful when you walk past him; he can be spiteful. The one next to him is called Shinbarker, 'cause if Anklebiter trips you, that's right where your shin will land." He also showed us the intersections of "ridge runner blazes," old trails and gravel roads that weren't marked on the regular maps. "I have the same map that the search-and-rescue people get, so if there's an emergency on the A.T., I can get out to a road fast and get help. It's kind of cool. I feel like part of a secret club, knowing all these unmarked trails."

We stopped for lunch in the hemlock-shaded depths of Sage's Ravine, near the Connecticut-Massachusetts line, where a stream gurgled and sparkled between moss-covered rocks.

"I'm afraid this is the end of the line for me," Matt said. "The other side of the ravine is outside my territory. It's been a lot of fun hiking with you, though."

"Yeah, this has been fun," I said.

"Jackrabbit, if you start feeling bad again, I hope you'll get it checked out."

"I will. Don't worry. Thanks, Matt."

Over the next few days, the pattern repeated itself; I felt fine in the morning, full of energy and well-rested. As the day drew on, lethargy and dullness overtook me, along with the intense, throbbing headache and sore muscles.

Every morning, I convinced myself that I was recovering, but every evening I felt worse than I had the night before.

We walked over the glacier-sculpted granite peaks of Race Mountain, Mount Everett, Jug End, East Mountain. I stopped at every patch of blueberries I could find, hungrily stuffing the fruit into my mouth, and I ate as much as our resupply allowed at breakfast and lunch. By dinner, though, fatigue and nausea curbed my appetite. My muscles felt constantly weak. It seemed that the food I managed to eat was no longer giving me strength, but feeding a disease.

When we came to U.S. 7, where I had gotten back on the Trail in the fall, I had a horrible sense of foreboding. "Isis, what if I can't do it? What if this section of the Trail is too much for me? I'll never finish a thru-hike!"

She regarded me for a moment, leaning on her hiking sticks. "You've already hiked more miles than most thru-hikers do. And this section's easy. It won't give you any trouble."

We walked across the road into territory that was new to me. I pictured a cracking parchment map with engravings of dragons and flowing calligraphy spelling out *Terra Incognita*. Perhaps it was just the power of suggestion, but the dark evergreens—hemlock, spruce, pine—looked taller and more mysterious here. Pale granite rocks rose out of the forest floor in places, glimmering like ghosts between the trees.

In the evening, we hitched to the East Mountain Retreat Center. Isis had read about it in the *Companion*; a meditation center on the weekends, the place offered lodging to hikers during the week at a reasonable price. Both of us were ready for a shower and a night away from the interminable swarms of mosquitoes. The Retreat Center was a collection of yurts and a weathered wooden cabin, set in a green lawn with banks of daylilies. From the parking lot, we could look down into the valley, where the night mist was beginning to rise from the slow brown curves of the Housatonic.

A thin woman with bouncy curls stood on the porch of the cabin when we arrived, with her hands on her hips. "Welcome to East Mountain," she said. "I'm Rose, the caretaker. There's only one other hiker here tonight, so I'm putting all of you downstairs in the cabin. I live upstairs. You need anything, feel free to ask."

She led us into the building: bare wood walls, bay windows, soft cushioned furniture. It looked too clean and orderly to be a hiker hostel. Bookshelves filled the space under the windows. I glanced at the titles: *Finding Your*

Spiritual Path. The Road to Enlightenment. Hindu Mysticism. The Writings of Hildegard von Bingen.

I sank into an armchair while Isis and Rose talked. The room seemed to be swaying slightly around me, like a tree in the wind. I closed my eyes and the motion didn't stop. My shoulders and spine felt cramped up, hot and painful. Surges of fever washed over me.

"Jackrabbit, are you ill?" I recognized the deep voice, with its hint of a British accent, though I hadn't seen him since Virginia: Parypinoy. I thought I was imagining things, but I opened my eyes and he was there, his face full of concern.

"I'm okay," I finally managed. He didn't look convinced.

Isis and I took showers, and she cooked our supper on the flagstone porch. We brought the pot of macaroni inside to eat, to escape the fierce clouds of mosquitoes that had descended at dusk. I lifted the first spoonful to my mouth, trying to ignore the protests of my queasy stomach, and the room went dark.

"Isis? Parypinoy?" I said. For a moment I thought I had blacked out, but I could hear their voices. A door slammed upstairs.

"Power's out," Rose called down to us. "It happens all the time out here. Let me get you some candles."

The bright blue beam of Parypinoy's headlamp lanced through the dark. In a few minutes, Rose had lit the array of candles on the table. The room filled with their soft light; shadows danced over the wooden walls.

"Thanks," Isis said. Crickets buzzed in the long grass outside and silence settled over us.

"Parypinoy, why did you become a priest?" I asked him.

"I felt a calling when I was a young man. To serve God and the people. Are you a Christian, jackrabbit?"

"No. We were raised in a family of staunch atheists. I never felt like religion was something I needed in my life. Recently, I guess, I've started questioning that. I read a lot about different religions in college, but I could never find a path that seemed right for me, you know? I could never find dogma that felt true enough. I would describe myself as agnostic now. I *want* to believe in something. I just don't know if I *can*, having grown up without it."

Parypinoy hesitated for a moment before speaking. "I think it is necessary to have a religion, in order to find a true spiritual path," he said finally. "It is not a thing you can find by yourself. You need a community of believers who share your understanding of the world."

"I think it's an intensely personal thing," Isis protested. "I don't think you necessarily need other people around who believe the same things you do." I knew she had found her own path through Wicca, worshipping the Earth and the gods and goddesses of many religions.

"Many people choose different paths," Parypinoy said quietly, "but there is only one that leads to the salvation of the soul."

"You really believe that Christianity is the only religion that can save souls?" Isis asked him.

"I do not usually say this unless people ask me specifically. I do not want to offend anyone. But yes, I would say that Christianity, through the Catholic Church, is the only way to eternal life. There are other religions that talk about Heaven or Nirvana or some kind of afterlife. But always, in these other religions, the soul is a lonely, solitary wanderer in search of union with the divine. Enlightenment. By whatever name it is called. In Christianity the love of God reaches for everyone; we must only open our hearts to it."

In the golden candlelight, he looked so peaceful and assured that I could almost imagine the room filling up with perfect, intangible love.

Isis shook her head. "I have a hard time believing in a God who would only love those who called Him by one particular name."

"I don't know if I can imagine a God at all," I said. But when I lay down on my bunk that night, with the room spinning vertiginously around me and my headache pulsing in and out, I began to pray silently. *Dear Mother Earth, Father Sky, Great Spirit, One with Ten Thousand Names. I don't know what to call you. I don't know if I even believe in you. But I want to believe, and I am calling on you now. Help to mend what is broken in this world. Help to comfort those who grieve. Thank you for this gift, my life. Watch over us, watch over us all.*

Isis

It was only nineteen miles from the East Mountain Retreat Center to Upper Goose Pond. Pretty easy miles, as far as I recalled; I'd done fourteen of them in one day southbound, one of the longest days I'd hiked in my solo stretch. Nineteen miles. A week before, we would have thought nothing of it. If we could hike it in one day, my zero at Upper Goose Pond would be possible again. I pored over the map, trying to convince myself that we could do it. Only one long uphill, and that was less than a thousand feet. We'd hit it in the afternoon, when jackrabbit usually felt worse, which might be problematic. The last six miles were nearly level, though.

I presented my plan to jackrabbit.

"I could use a zero," she said, "but I don't know about the nineteen to get there. I *should* be able to do it."

The first four hours went well. Although we got off to a rather late start, we covered nine miles before lunch. The morning was full of small, happy coincidences that seemed to favor my plans. We found raspberries in a brushy area, and black highbush blueberries on the cliffs. A trail angel showed up at a road crossing with water, just when we'd begun to worry that we'd have to filter out of a cow pond. Wild thyme filled the meadows, its sweet, fresh scent rising up where our feet crushed it. Only a few minutes after we sat down to lunch, in the shade of an old hemlock, a familiar couple hiked up and joined us.

"Spur and Ready!" jackrabbit greeted them. "How are you guys?"

"Not too great," Ready admitted, unstrapping her pack and reaching both hands around to massage the small of her back. "My sciatica's really been bothering me. I've missed about a hundred miles of Trail."

"I'm glad you're back," said Spur, spreading peanut butter on a bagel and handing it to her. "What would I do without you, sweetheart?"

"Probably make it to Katahdin a lot faster than you will with me," Ready answered, her eyes twinkling. "Anyway, enough of my gripes. How are you guys?"

"Not that great either, I'm afraid," jackrabbit said. "I've had a headache and fever off and on for the past week."

"Hmm. Really bad in the afternoon, worse in the evening, and gone in the morning, by any chance?" Spur asked her.

"Exactly."

"Any mood swings or nightmares?"

"Nightmares, yeah. Wild ones. And I've been feeling pretty depressed lately, too. Angry over the least little things."

"Did you find a bull's-eye rash on your skin any time in the past month?" Spur asked.

She shook her head, and he continued.

"No matter. I'd guess that you have Lyme disease. I had it on my '99 hike. The rash is the easiest way to diagnose it, but that only shows up in about forty percent of cases. If I were you, I'd go to a hospital and get it checked out."

"Hopefully we can get to a hospital from Upper Goose Pond Cabin tomorrow," I said. "We're planning to zero there."

"Upper Goose Pond?" Spur asked. "That's where *we're* headed tonight. It's another ten miles. Where did you start this morning?"

"East Mountain Retreat Center."

He looked at jackrabbit. "If you can hike nineteens, I'm not sure you have Lyme disease after all. I could barely make twelves when *I* had it."

We did hike the rest of the way to the cabin, arriving just as the sun set. It was much more crowded than it had been in fall; fifteen or twenty hikers sat around the picnic table and the corners of the porch, cooking.

"Hey, Isis and jackrabbit, want some plums?" Ready called from the end of the table. "The caretaker brought them for hikers."

"Sure, I'd love one," I said, and started to make my way through the crowd.

"I'll meet you inside," jackrabbit growled. "I can't deal with all these people."

Before I could answer, she'd slipped through the screen door and hurried up the stairs to the bunkroom. I picked out a couple of plums, found the caretaker and thanked her, then followed jackrabbit upstairs. She was sitting on the furthest bunk from the stairs with her back toward me, staring out the screened window over the fire escape. I sat down next to her and offered her a plum. Her body radiated heat. She took the fruit, but shoved away the hand that I held to her forehead.

"Just leave me alone. Please. I don't want to be around people right now."

I could tell that she was struggling to keep her voice level. I wanted to ask what was wrong, but I didn't have the nerve to confront that undercurrent of fury. *Maybe she's just grumpy because she's hungry*, I told myself. *I'll go make dinner; I'm sure she'll feel better after she eats.*

By the time I carried our pot of beans and rice up the fire escape, her anger had subsided, leaving her so drained that she could barely lift the spoon to her mouth. We sat on the balcony, listening to the murmur of conversation drifting up from the porch below. We ate slowly, in silence, as we had in winter, when we needed so many calories that shoveling food into our mouths became a chore as monotonous as wading through wet snowdrifts.

Most of the other hikers had left the porch by the time we finished eating; the bunkroom was filling up behind us. I ducked inside and found our toothbrushes, pausing for a few minutes to chat with the men in the bunks next to ours. Jackrabbit gave me a smile of gratitude when I returned; she still wasn't in a mood to deal with people. I offered her a hand and she took it, pulling herself slowly to her feet.

We walked down the fire escape to brush our teeth on the empty porch, under a row of packs and food bags. Out on the pond, a single loon called and called, the first one I'd heard since—yes, since Upper Goose Pond southbound. I turned to say something to jackrabbit, but she was walking away from me, toward the steps, going to spit her toothpaste in the woods. She hit the top step and crumpled, falling down the other four and landing on her hands and knees in the dirt. In three strides I was beside her, reaching an arm around her shoulders to lift her back to her feet.

"What happened?" I asked, as I helped her up the stairs. "Did you trip?"

"I don't know what happened," she answered. "One minute, I was starting to go down the stairs, and the next minute, I was on the ground. I don't remember falling. I don't remember anything in between." She met my eyes, her brows furrowed and her lips parted, as if asking me to explain the missing seconds of her life.

"It looked to me like you tripped over something on the steps. Maybe you fainted. It's been a long day. Too long; I'm sorry." I spoke gently as I would to a hurt child, trying not to let my own fear come through my voice. "Sit here at the table while I clean up your knees. Tomorrow we'll go to the hospital."

jackrabbit

"Let's go swim in the lake," Isis said with enforced cheerfulness. "It's beautiful down there; the water's warm."

We sat at the breakfast table with a few other hikers. Thin, anemic noon sunlight came through the windows. Early in the morning, Isis had borrowed the caretaker's cell phone to try to find me a ride to the hospital. She had finally reached Mother Hen, a local trail angel who Waterfall knew, who was willing to take me into town the next day. I felt a vague resentment that Isis had been the one to make the arrangements; *I should be old enough to take care of myself*, I thought. But I was grateful, too. If I'd been hiking alone, I would probably be lying in the woods somewhere, too sick and unmotivated to move.

"No," I said dully. "I don't wanna swim." I was so tired that I couldn't imagine dragging myself back up the hillside, even if I could get down there.

She sighed. "Suit yourself. *I'm* going swimming, anyway."

I wanted to say, "don't leave me," even though I realized how melodramatic and stupid it would sound. I really didn't want her to leave, though. I knew I wouldn't be able to summon the energy to hold a conversation if any of the other hikers tried to start one. I sat in a corner by the windows, pretending to read a magazine, trying to look inconspicuous. I couldn't really concentrate. I read the same paragraph over and over and the words made no sense. The headache was starting already.

"Hey, are you one of the Barefoot Sisters?" a woman said, standing right in front of me. She was short and slightly plump, with a ponytail of glossy brown hair like a fountain on top her head. "All the other hikers said you would be here! My husband and I—have you met my husband? We're the Tourists. Debbie and Bill. We're section hiking this year . . ." Perhaps if I had met her under different circumstances, I would have found her vivacious and entertaining. But she didn't stop talking long enough for me to get a word in edgewise, and through the filter of my headache, her voice sounded querulous and braying. "We honeymooned on the Trail a few years ago. At the time, I said, 'Bill, I don't know if I can stand being with you for six months.' *Now* look at us, three years later." She gave a snort of laughter that made the windows shake.

Her husband came over, a tall, thin man dressed in khakis with a visor hat on his forehead. "So tell me. Is it true you hike barefoot?" Unlike his wife, he waited for an answer.

"Yes," I said faintly, with a pointed glance toward the magazine I was pretending to read.

He shook his head. "You know, they've made some advances in footwear in the last ten thousand years." His booming laughter was even louder than his wife's.

"We go barefoot because we like to," I said. My voice sounded sluggish and distant.

"Uh-huh. You *like* to." He shook his head. Curiosity apparently satisfied on the barefoot issue, he went on to quiz me about gear. "What kind of pack do you carry? And how much weight are we talking about? Did you ever think about switching to lighter gear? Say, a tarp instead of a tent?"

I wanted to tell the story of Toast waking up with slugs in his hair—*that's why we carry a tent!*—but I couldn't muster the energy. Instead I said, "Excuse me," and went off to look for a more secluded corner. The cabin wasn't very big, though. I settled into a different chair and picked up a tattered paperback of *The Thorn Birds.* The strings of print seemed to shift around the page before my eyes, and the cabin's wooden walls pulsed in and out in time to my headache.

After a few minutes, though, the Tourists found me again. "Isn't that a great book!" The woman crowed. "I must have read it five times! It's so romantic."

Her husband came up behind her. "What kind of stove do you carry?"

I responded to their questions with shrugs and the occasional monosyllable, and eventually they left me alone. *They probably don't think much of me, either,* I reflected.

The sky clouded over as the day wore on. The cabin became gloomy, filled with shadows. More and more hikers arrived, until every chair in the place was filled. Gear festooned the porch railings and much of the floor.

Isis came back from the lake, her long hair dripping wet. "It was so great! You should have gone."

"Hmph," I said.

"You've been down there for hours, Isis," one of the other hikers observed.

"Yeah. I only came back to put my bread in the oven." She went into the kitchen. I heard pots and pans clanking. Eventually the smell of baking bread came wafting through the room. It was a smell I usually loved, but right then it made me feel sick.

I sat back, observing the hikers. There seemed to be a haze between me and the rest of the world, a sort of gauzy curtain. A genteel Southern woman named Pack-a-sandra had finally engaged the Tourists, keeping me safe. They were deep in a discussion over the effectiveness of different kinds of rain gear. Johnny Steel settled himself on the couch, his ample frame taking up a cushion and a half.

"Where's Polar Bear?" someone asked him. The two of them had been hiking together since Virginia.

"He's up ahead," Johnny Steel said. "We had some differences of opinion. I've got a new Republican. This is Mark." The stolid, clean-shaven man in the chair next to him gave a little wave.

"Mark, buddy, I found a trail name for you," Johnny Steel said.

"I already told you, I'm not looking for a trail name. My own name suits me fine." Mark wiped off his glasses with the edge of his shirt.

"No, it's perfect," Johnny Steel insisted. "Mark Trail! Like the guy in the comic!"

"Oh, come on, Johnny Steel," Mark said.

"Johnny Steel? You are Johnny Steel?" This was a young man with rosy cheeks and short blond hair. He had a slight French accent. "Me, I am Julien. From Quebec. Tell me, Johnny Steel, have you ever read the comic?"

"*Mark Trail?*"

"No. *Johnny Steel*. It's very popular in Canada. I wondered, when I heard about you, whether you would be carrying a pink scarf . . ."

All the color drained from Johnny Steel's face. "I need a new trail name *right now*," he said with desperation. He looked wildly around the room and then seized a ballpoint pen from the end table. "Ink Pen. I will call myself Ink Pen."

Then Julien's composure cracked. He burst out laughing, nearly rolling on the floor. Bit by bit, he explained Polar Bear's plot. Everyone else in the corner began to laugh, too, tears rolling down their cheeks.

"Whatever is goin' on over there?" Pack-a-sandra spoke up in her refined Southern accent.

"Polar Bear," Johnny Steel said through stiff lips, "was trying to get me to believe my name comes from a gay superhero. He almost had me fooled, too. I could *kill* the bastard!"

Pack–a-sandra regarded him for a moment. "But Johnny Steel, you're the most heterosexual man I've ever met."

Two couples arrived, late in the day: The Honeymooners and Lightfoot and Featherweight. Honey and Moon both had curly brown hair and dark, expressive eyes; Lightfoot (the man) was tall and heavy-boned, Nordic-looking, while his wife was diminutive, with honey-blond hair a shade darker than his. More hikers whose names I didn't overhear; skinny, grubby men and women with well-defined leg muscles crowded into the room. Someone brought a dog, a scrawny black Lab that nosed around the floor looking for crumbs. Each time the door opened, more mosquitoes came in.

The strangest hiker who arrived that night was tall and gaunt, with a thin tank top plastered to his chest (it had begun to rain). He carried nothing but a fanny pack and an enormous camera case.

"Are you slacking?" one of the hikers asked him. "Where's your gear?"

"This *is* my gear," the guy said. He opened the fanny pack to show its contents: a lightweight hammock, rain gear, iodine tablets, a bag of bagels, and a bar of cream cheese. "Everything I need. I've got food, water purifier, shelter. The camera's just for fun."

"What about warm clothes?" someone else called over the hubbub of the room.

"I sleep in my rain gear to stay warm."

Every hiker learns to strike a balance between pack weight and comfort and safety. Isis and I tended toward the heavy side of the equation, though

certainly not as heavy as Big Ring and Granny Gear. I had never seen someone who erred so far on the side of pack weight reduction. I wanted to go
over and talk to him, but the room seemed to sway with every slight movement of my head, and I was afraid I would pass out again if I tried to stand up.
I wondered if he was just a fever hallucination. Other hikers seemed to be able
to see him, too, though.

"Who wants bread?" Isis said, passing around a basket of warm slices. I
took one, but I could only eat half of it. I chewed woodenly without tasting. I
went upstairs, leaning heavily on the banister, moving slowly, and lay on my
bunk. *Great Spirit, watch over the world*, I prayed. The room swam behind a
haze and went dark.

As usual, I felt marginally better in the morning. I had enough energy to
talk to people, at least. Spur and Ready came to say goodbye before they left
the cabin.

"You're going to the hospital today, right?" Spur asked me.

"Yeah."

"Good. Because the earlier you treat it, the less chance you have that it'll
become chronic."

"What?"

Spur made a grim face. "Chronic Lyme disease. Arthritis-like symptoms,
neuromuscular degeneration, depression."

"Sweetie, that's probably not what she wants to hear right now," Ready
told him.

"Yeah, but it's what you *need* to hear," he said. "That's what happens if
you don't treat it in the first couple weeks. It happened to me. I guess I'm
lucky; I didn't get any of the autoimmune stuff, but I have a real issue with
depression. Somehow the only thing that makes me happy is hiking. I
think it's the endorphins from all that exercise, or maybe just the spirit of the
Trail . . . That's why I'm out here every summer."

I remembered how he had looked when I first met him, at the Ruck in
January. On the Trail, he seemed so fully alive, so much happier than he'd
been in winter. "I already have problems with depression," I admitted. I had a
sudden flash of fear; if leaving the Trail last fall had been hard, after only a few
months of hiking, how hard would it be to leave it after more than a year?
And if I was sometimes depressed even on the Trail, how would I manage to
be happy after this hike came to an end?

"Take good care of yourself," Spur said. "That's the trick."

"And easier said than done." Ready hugged him.

"Because there's always something worth continuing for. Life can seem pretty horrible. But then—I mean, there's no good way to say it. It sounds so trite and silly. But you see a little flower or a certain kind of light on the mountains, or someone says something that's so profound, so true, you think, 'It was worth living this long just for that.'"

The dwarf irises, I thought.

"We'd better take off," Spur said. "I hope we'll see you down the trail."

"Me, too. And thanks."

"Hi, jackrabbit!"

I looked up to see Hammock Hanger, the woman who had gotten off in Shenandoah National Park with a needle in her foot.

"Hey, how are you?" I asked her.

"Good. Really good. I'm hiking again! I got back on two days ago, thirty miles back, and I haven't had any pain yet."

"That's great," I told her.

"You remember Aloha?" she asked.

"Yeah. I was there the night she got off, actually. I didn't know you guys knew each other."

"We didn't hike together very much. But then when we both had to get off . . . Well, I'd put my e-mail address in a bunch of registers. She must've copied it down. I got a note from her a few days after I got home. We've been in touch ever since. We were each other's support group, kind of."

"How is she?" I asked.

"She's okay. She's back in Hawaii. She's already climbing stairs. Her doctor thought it would be another two weeks, but she's tough. She's planning to thru-hike again next year."

"Here's to tough women who get back on the Trail," I said. "We ought to start a club."

"Jackrabbit?" Isis called from the porch. "We'd better go now so we can meet Mother Hen."

It was strange and uncomfortable to walk in the woods without my pack, without even a daypack for slacking. I realized how much I had come to depend on the added momentum, and to compensate for the weight on downhills. I felt too light without a pack, as though I might drift away from the earth. I thought of Strider's question: *What if gravity let go? It would feel like this.*

Mother Hen was a large, robust woman with a comforting smile. She drove us to the Pittsfield Hospital. While we waited in the emergency room, the sky went from blue to gray outside.

"We'll have to hike slowly for a few days while you're recovering," Isis said.

"If we can hike at all."

She ignored my pessimism. "Maybe this would be a good time for Claire to come hike with us." Our younger half sister had been planning to drive out to the Trail and meet us in the last few weeks of her summer break from college, but we hadn't finalized the plans. "I'll go give her a call while we're waiting."

I leafed through a *Good Housekeeping* from 1992. The television in the corner flickered. I could feel the headache coming on, building in intensity.

The doctor asked about my symptoms, took my pulse, set a chilly metal stethoscope on my back.

"You've been hiking the Appalachian Trail? It probably is Lyme. I've had six A.T. hikers come in with it just this summer. There's a blood test, but I'm not even going to do it. Your symptoms are pretty clear. I'll just prescribe an antibiotic for you. If that doesn't take care of it, come back in a couple weeks."

"In a couple weeks, I'll be in New Hampshire. I hope."

"They've got hospitals up there, last I heard," he said dryly. "You're not allergic to penicillin, are you?"

"Actually, I am."

"Hmm." He crumpled the prescription he'd written and tossed it into the wastebasket. "I'm going to have to put you on this other stuff . . . I don't know how expensive it is, though."

"As long as it does the trick."

"Oh, yeah. This'll take care of it."

The pills were bright blue and humongous. The first one stuck in the back of my throat and filled my mouth with an acrid, moldy taste. And they were hideously expensive—the first half of the three-week supply, all that the local pharmacy had in stock, cost well over $200.

"I won't have a cent to my name when we finish the Trail," I complained to Isis.

"I'm cutting it pretty close, too. Our mom said we could live at her place for a while, though, if we needed to, just to get our feet back under us."

Mother Hen drove us back to the trailhead and sent us off with hugs and homemade cookies. A thunderstorm broke around us as we walked back to the Upper Goose Pond Cabin. My head still ached and my neck and shoulders felt as stiff as ever. I walked through the chilly rain in a haze of fever. Perhaps the blue pills were beginning to work, though; I felt happier, less clouded. My appetite seemed to be returning; the thought of food was no longer nauseating. I nibbled one of Mother Hen's cookies. She had driven two hours out of her way to help me. *The world is so full of kind people*, I thought.

Isis

Since Connecticut, we'd been trying to get our half sister Claire to meet us on the Trail. Jackrabbit and I had both had rather prickly relationships with Claire when we were teenagers, and we hadn't seen much of her in the two years she'd been in college. We both wanted to get to know her better, now that we were all a little older and presumably wiser. Asking her to join us on the A.T. seemed like a perfect opportunity. The timing seemed right, too; when I'd reached her on the phone from Kent, a few weeks earlier, she and I had talked for hours, sharing more confidences than we had since she was a child.

We hadn't been able to come up with a plan to meet, though. Claire had a busy social schedule in the month that she was home, and jackrabbit and I had been traveling so fast that it was hard to determine where we'd be that far ahead of time. Now, though, we would have to hike some eight- and ten-mile days to let jackrabbit rest. With a logic that must have been dictated by stress, I decided that it would be a good idea to invite Claire to hike with us for the last few days of Massachusetts while we waited for jackrabbit's antibiotics to kick in.

Jackrabbit agreed. "Once the pills start working," she told me, "we'll have to hike twenties until we get to the Whites to make up for the time we've lost. Claire will be back in school by the time we reach New Hampshire, so this might be our last chance to hike with her."

When I called from the hospital in Pittsfield, Claire said that the coming weekend would be a good time for her to visit us. She would drive down on Friday and meet us in the afternoon at the Cookie Lady's blueberry farm on Washington Mountain Road. Claire looked at a road atlas while I studied the maps and *Companion*; together, we figured out the directions.

While we were in town, I also called Sarah Francis, the Upper Goose Pond Cabin caretaker who had given me and jackrabbit a place to stay last fall on the night of our reunion in Great Barrington. Sarah and I had written each other sporadically since then. I'd hoped to see her on our way through Massachusetts northbound, but my calls had never gotten through. This time she answered on the first ring.

"I'm sorry I didn't get ahold of you when we were going through Great Barrington," I said. "I'd love to see you if it's not too far to drive."

"I'm actually closer to the northern part of the Trail in Massachusetts," she answered. "I've got to work this weekend, but I should get out early on Sunday afternoon. Do you have any idea where you'll be then?"

For once, I could be pretty certain of where we'd be in three days. Our slow pace made our itinerary much more predictable than usual. An eleven, a ten, and an eight would put us in the town of Cheshire on Sunday.

"Great," Sarah said. "I'll meet you there and slack you for a day or two."

The next morning I woke before dawn and took a final swim in the still, cool pond. Saying goodbye to the cabin proved much easier this time around—we had plenty of lakes ahead of us. We were walking toward fall; by winter we'd be home. Besides, I had a new, less pleasant set of memories associated with Upper Goose Pond. Instead of the place where I'd talked with Sarah late into the evening, I thought of it as the dark crowded building in which jackrabbit and I had formed an island of pain and worry.

Our eleven-mile hike to the Cookie Lady's farm went well, if very slowly. According to the doctor, jackrabbit's antibiotics wouldn't start working for another few days. By now, though, we'd begun to learn how to cope with the disease, as we'd learned to cope with hypothermia in winter. We would start hiking just after sunrise, since the morning was jackrabbit's best time to hike. I would refrain from making cheery observations on the weather or the scenery, knowing that my comments would only aggravate jackrabbit's disease-fueled depression. I remembered Waterfall's description, at the Gathering, of how Matt had become "negative and mean" under the influence of Lyme disease. Jackrabbit was trying hard to avoid negativity, but I could see that it was an effort.

Around midday, we met an early southbounder, fast and ultralight (though not quite as ultralight as the strange man with the fanny pack and the camera case at Upper Goose Pond). He stopped and talked with us for fifteen minutes; jackrabbit's spirits rose so much that she kept talking to me for a mile after he passed us. We reached the Cookie Lady's farm just at five, and hurried up the driveway, hoping we hadn't kept our sister waiting.

No sign of Claire. The Cookie Lady's husband Roy brought us a basket of oatmeal cookies and sat with us at the picnic table, telling us about the history of the farm. The land had been farmed for over a hundred years, and some of the blueberry bushes were sixty years old. Those were his favorites, he told us, with more nuanced flavors than the recent hybrids. As I listened to him, I kept an eye on the driveway, waiting for Claire to show up. When she hadn't arrived after an hour, I explained to Roy that we were trying to meet her, and asked if I could use his phone to check if she'd changed her plans.

I made a collect call to our mom, who said that Claire hadn't left home until noon. She wouldn't reach Massachusetts until eight in the evening, at the earliest. At Roy's suggestion, I gave my mother his number so she could reach me if she heard anything more from Claire. While we waited, we picked blueberries, cooked dinner, then picked more berries. Eight o'clock came and went. Jackrabbit, tired though not as feverish as she'd been for the past few nights, rolled out her sleeping bag and went to bed early. I sat at the picnic table reading *Huckleberry Finn* in the fading evening light. Around nine, Roy came out and waved to me. I jumped to my feet, thinking I had a call. No, he explained, he hadn't heard anything from Claire, but he felt sorry for me sitting out in the yard alone. He invited me inside to wait.

Sometime around ten-thirty, Claire finally called. She was late because she'd gotten caught in rush hour traffic; she'd tried to check into a hotel only to find that they were all full for the Tanglewood Festival. Now she was lost, and angry that I hadn't given her good enough directions. Roy, who'd waited up with me, got on the phone and spent ten minutes patiently figuring out where she was, then telling her how to get to his house.

She arrived twenty minutes later. By that time, I was pretty upset with her; if she'd left home at a reasonable time or followed my directions better, I would have been in bed three hours earlier. More importantly, I wouldn't have had to impose so much on Roy's hospitality. He'd been unflaggingly cheerful, distracting me with stories from his youth in the 1930s while I waited by the phone, but I suspected that this was well past his bedtime, too.

When I heard the car pull up, though, I forgot that I'd spent the past few hours worrying. I was glad to have my sister there; glad that she'd arrived safely. I ran out to the driveway to greet her, Roy following close behind me.

"Claire! I'm so happy you got here!" I held out my arms to her as she stepped out of the car.

"Well, I'm not happy to be here." She stood up with her arms crossed. "Unfortunately, it's too late to do anything about it."

"I'm sorry your trip down was such a hassle—"

"I don't want your sympathy. Where's the bathroom?"

"Through the hall and on your right," said Roy, who'd come up behind me. Claire brushed past him without another word.

"Well, I guess you're reunited," he said to me. "I think I'll go to bed. It's late for an old man like me."

"Thanks so much for your help," I told him. "I'm sorry to have kept you up."

Claire came out ten minutes later. I offered to help her set up my solo tent, which I'd lent her for the trip.

"Tent?" she said in a tone of utter contempt. "I'd rather just sleep in the car."

"Is there anything you need?" I asked. "Are you hungry?"

"I've been hungry for the past five hours, but I'm not going to stay up and wait for you to cook me dinner." With that, she got in the car and slammed the door behind her.

I crawled into my sleeping bag beside jackrabbit, but I lay awake for probably another hour, tears streaming down my face. *I got my wish*, I thought bitterly. *I got to meet my little sister again—only to find out I don't like her.*

Claire was in much better spirits in the morning. She made no apologies for the night before, but she greeted jackrabbit with a hug. While I prepared breakfast, the two of them chatted about Claire's first backpacking expedition, a college orientation trip in Idaho. I overheard snatches of their conversation: *hideous blister on my heel! . . . Have you ever tried Cream of Wheat cereal mixed with instant pea soup? It sounds weird, but it's the best thing I ate all week . . . Oh, and I got a trail name—all the guys called me Princess.*

"So, should we call you Princess?" jackrabbit asked.

"If you want to. I mean, everyone goes by their trail names out here, don't they?"

Listening to the two of them talking together, I felt an unexpected rush of jealousy. *Go ahead, jackrabbit. Make friends with your half sister. You didn't have to deal with the Princess last night.* I was jealous of Claire, too. Jealous that jackrabbit, who'd been short-tempered with me all week under the influence of Lyme disease, had somehow managed to put on a happy face for the benefit of this haughty interloper.

The first few hours of hiking together went pretty smoothly. Jackrabbit pointed out different plants to Princess, who reciprocated by answering her questions about the region's geology. After lunch, I tried to join in the conversation. Jackrabbit was explaining to Princess the difference between hellebore, a fairly rare plant in that area, and false hellebore, which was common in the swamps. I came up with a pun that I couldn't resist sharing.

"Hey, jackrabbit—if you find hell a bore, try purgatory."

She groaned, not the usual theatrical groan with which we greeted each other's bad puns, but a God-look-what-I-put-up-with sound, the sound a teenager might make if her mother tried to tell a joke in public.

"I'm just trying for a little humor," I said. "It's been a stressful week."

"*I'm* the one who's been sick," she told me. "What do *you* have to get stressed out about?"

This was too much for me. I'd done my best to put on a good face, to be cheerful but not too cheerful, comforting but not too comforting, while jackrabbit struggled with the disease. Most of all I'd tried to hide my own feelings and not complain about how much her constant gloom and anger hurt me. "I'm stressed out *because* you've been sick," I shouted. "You're mad at me all the time; do you think that's easy? Do you think you can tell me you're going to die, and I won't care?"

My tears turned to sobs. I sat down on a rock and buried my head in my arms, trying to hide my face. I wished my sisters would just leave; I hated to break down so completely in front of both of them.

"God, don't have a cow about it," said Princess. "Susan's right, she *is* the one who's been sick."

"Go away," I told her. "Leave me alone. I don't want to see you for the rest of the day."

"Suits me," said Princess.

Jackrabbit hesitated a moment.

"Both of you," I said. "Go away."

jackrabbit

For an instant, white-hot anger flooded through me. I was tempted to scream at Isis, but I couldn't find words for what I wanted to say: *It's just like when we were kids; for anything that happens, you take the blame—and the credit—and heap it on your shoulders, and flash your long-suffering smile. You're taking my illness and making it into your own martyrdom.*

Claire looked at the two of us, our faces set in expressions of rage and grief, and she started walking. I stood there a moment longer, staring down at Isis. She looked so pitiful, crumpled in a heap beside the trail, with her head in her arms. I wanted to say something, anything, but instead I snorted with disgust. *It's all an act*, I told myself, and I turned on my heel and followed Claire down the trail.

I caught up to her at an overlook. She'd set down her pack and was munching a granola bar. In the valley below us, little lakes winked and shone, and the patchwork of fields and forest glimmered green. Claire gave me a tentative smile.

"God, I feel like such a monster," I said, almost crying. *How much of this is me*, I wondered, *and how much is the disease?*

Claire put the granola bar wrapper in her pocket and started to lift her pack.

"No, wait," I said. "Please wait."

She sat with one arm through the straps, indecision playing over her beautiful thin face.

"That's your conflict resolution strategy, isn't it?" I said. "Just get up and walk away. I wish I was that good at it."

"Conflict avoidance," she said.

I tried a smile. "We bring out the worst in each other, don't we? You know, we had one of our biggest fights when Mum came out to visit. There's just something about family, I guess."

"Something about *our* family. Or about you and Lucy, maybe. You know, it really bugs me when you guys talk about how messed-up our family was. I feel like *I* had a pretty good childhood. *I* came out of it okay."

"Better than the rest of us, I guess. You were so young during the divorce and everything."

To my surprise, tears gleamed in the corners of her eyes. "Don't think it didn't hurt me. The thing is, I managed. I put it behind me, okay? I just don't like to dwell on stuff that happened so long ago." She looked down, her fingers tracing a pattern in the surface of the rocks. "Let's talk about something else. I haven't seen you in forever. The last thing I want to do is spend our time arguing and worrying about what happened when we were kids."

"How was your summer?" I asked, a little awkwardly. We shouldered our packs and started walking.

"It was really good," she said. I couldn't see her face, but I knew her well enough to picture the smile lighting up her blue eyes. "I went on the geo department field trip to Africa. Kenya and Tanzania."

"That's what they said the last time I called home. You lucky girl. How was it?"

"We saw all kinds of cool geological things. Oh, and we saw the solar eclipse, too. It was kind of freaky. We were out on the patio of our little hotel, and the sky went all blue-black like night was falling. There were hippos that wallowed in the river behind our hotel. They make the funniest noises. Usually we'd just hear them at dusk, but they came out for the eclipse. And all the birds and insects that called at night were out too. When the light came back, it was the strangest color. All washed-out and pearly gray. The color of old dishwater, kind of, but pretty."

"What was your favorite part of the trip?"

"Oh, we got to climb Ol Doinyo Lengai."

"Ol' what?"

"Ol Doinyo Lengai. It means 'home of the gods' in Masai, I think. It's the world's only active carbonate flow volcano. The lava comes out at a cool temperature, something like a thousand degrees Fahrenheit. It looks like mud. It was erupting when we were there, blowing out these funny-looking spumes of gray stuff. It turns white when it hardens and then it floats away like soap flakes. It's really neat . . . But I nearly fell off the side of the mountain on the way up."

"What happened?"

"Well, it's kind of a long story. There was one woman on the trip, one of the adults, who I really didn't get along with. She was just kind of loud and in-your-face and—you know. Not fun to be around. A little ways up the mountain, I saw her go off to the side of the trail. I wanted to make sure she was okay, so I went over, and it turned out she was having, um, a feminine emergency. But I stayed with her, because all the guides and everybody were way out ahead. Even though she wasn't my favorite person, I didn't want her to get left behind. And then—" she rolled her eyes "—one of the *boys* on the trip came back to see if we were all right. I said, 'Sure, we're fine,' but *that woman* . . . she said 'Oh, everything's under control! We're just scattering tampons all over the mountain!' Argh!"

"Poor you," I said. "But that still doesn't explain how you almost fell off the mountain."

"Well, after that I didn't really want to be around her. I hiked out fast and got ahead with the guides. We were scouting our way across a mass wasting—landslide. That's what non-geological people call them. I like the term mass wasting, though. It has a *je ne sais quoi*. Anyway, they sent me up ahead into a little gulley. It was really steep, like forty-five degrees. I could look back down through my legs and see the plains a couple thousand feet down. I got nervous and grabbed an outcropping, but it turned out to be incompetent rock."

"Incompetent?"

"Oh, that's another good term. It means not competent to bear weight. It crumbles in your hand. So there I was. I started sliding down the gulley, and at that point I was wishing I'd stayed back there with Mrs. Scattering-Tampons-All-Over-The-Mountain and let somebody else scout the damn thing. But one of the guides caught me on the way past. We all had a good laugh about it."

We stopped at another viewpoint. I looked out over the valley, but Claire scrambled up among the slabs of white sandstone across the trail, all her attention focused on the rocks.

"Look at this! I bet this was a sea floor-shelf transition zone. There must be fossils galore in these rocks . . ."

I laughed. "And here I was admiring the view."

"No, this is really cool!"

"Claire, are you gonna go to graduate school? Because if you get this excited about rocks, you really should."

"I was thinking about it," she said. "I'd like to go some place really far away. Hawaii, maybe. Or maybe New Zealand."

"Scattering Letcher sisters all over the globe," I said dryly.

"The thought *had* occurred to me," she returned in the same tone.

The A.T. dropped down from the ridge and meandered through a valley of swamps and fir trees and little mud-brown ponds. The soft damp earth of the trail felt soothing underfoot. I began to see piles of moose droppings in the path, and once a perfect cloven hoofprint sunk in the deep mud.

"Wait, Claire," I said, and I surrounded the moose print with a square of light-colored twigs that showed up against the ground, to make sure other hikers would notice it. Claire knelt down, grinning, and spelled out *MOOSE* beside it with more sticks.

Isis finally caught up with us in midafternoon, as we followed a shady tree-lined street into the town of Dalton. We had an uneasy truce, saying little as we walked along. All the things left unsaid seemed to crackle in the air around us like a corona of electricity.

"There's a guy in town who lets hikers camp on his lawn," Isis said. "I stayed here in the fall." Her voice was tightly controlled.

"Sounds good," I said with false breeziness. But I was glad we were stopping soon. Even though the nasty blue pills were starting to work, I still felt weak and tired in the evenings. I could feel the first twinges of the headache coming on. It had been another warm day, too, even in the mountains, and here in the valley the air shimmered with heat.

"I could rest right about now," Claire said, pushing back the blue bandana on her forehead. She seemed completely unconcerned. Even after a day on the Trail, she still managed to be elegant and stylish, not a hair out of place, no sweat stains showing on her sky-blue sports bra.

The house was easy to spot: a tall white New England farmhouse with ranks of tents and tarps filling half the backyard. A slight, balding man dressed in town clothes sat on the porch, talking to the hikers assembled there. He gave a start when he saw us coming down the sidewalk. "Isis? Is that you? I heard rumors you were headed this way!"

"Hi, Tom," she said, the liveliness coming back into her voice. "It's been quite a journey. It's good to be here."

"And are these your sisters? I thought there were only two of you."

"I'm just here for a few days," Claire said, setting down her pack.

"Well, let me get you some ice cream," Tom said. Claire looked startled, and he smiled. "I do this for all the hikers. Mint chip okay?"

"Yeah, thanks," Claire said. Now she sounded a little uncomfortable and puzzled. Tom disappeared into the house. "Do people really do this kind of thing for hikers all the time?" Claire asked. "I mean, I read your postcards, but I never really thought . . . I mean, *why* would somebody do it? Open up their home to a bunch of smelly people, and then feed them, too? It's great that people do, but *why?* It's not like you're homeless or anything. It's not like it's a huge benefit to society . . ."

Isis fixed her with a glare. "*Some people* like to be kind," she said.

Claire returned a level stare. "That's quite an indictment," she answered in a prickly tone.

Tom came out of the house, smiling, with a tray bearing enormous bowls of ice cream, slices of devil's food cake, and fresh peaches. We sat down at a picnic table in front of the house.

"It's great to have you back, Isis. And your sisters. You *are* all sisters, aren't you? There's such a strong resemblance. It's wonderful to see you all together out here."

Tom's cheerful, avuncular manner defused the tension. Between bites of ice cream, Isis and I told him about our winter adventures. Even Claire listened with interest, occasionally asking a question. By the time our bowls were scraped clean, the three of us could speak to each other almost like friends.

"Thanks for the ice cream," I said to Tom. There was so much more to thank him for, but I didn't know how to put it into words.

Johnny Steel arrived as I set up the tent on Tom's lawn.

"Hey, Man of Steel," I said.

"Greetings, rabbit of jack."

"Did you see the moose footprint?"

"I did indeed. Did you see the other footprint?"

"What other footprint?"

He grinned. "Somebody put twigs around one of yours and wrote *SISTER*."

We gathered a group of hikers—Johnny Steel, Iculus, Julien, Honey and Moon, and Zirk Ziggler, who we hadn't seen since Virginia—and went looking for pizza. Our boisterous group filled the sidewalk, talking and laughing and telling raunchy jokes. Claire walked a little ways behind us, acting aloof. At the pizza place, she ordered a small salad, and she seemed mortified by the amount of food the rest of us consumed.

From the pay phone in the parking lot of the restaurant, Isis called Sarah Francis. "She's still planning to meet us in Cheshire tomorrow afternoon," Isis told us. "She said she could drive you back to your car, Claire."

"Tonight?"

"No. Tomorrow. Come on, can't you stand our company for another day?"

Claire was quiet for a moment, chewing on her lower lip and looking at the ground. "I don't think hiking is exactly my thing," she finally said.

The next day the heat was thick and stifling, and the parched wind out of the valleys offered no relief. My sisters and I walked glumly in a line, saying nothing. The day seemed interminable. The trail led up and over a lumpy ridge. Whatever beauty the landscape might have offered was concealed by my foul mood. *Why did we invite Claire out here?* I wondered. *I love her. We both love her. But somehow that love has driven a wedge between us. Isis probably thinks Claire and I are in league against her, after that first day. Nothing could be further from the truth.* For all the time I had spent talking to Claire, I didn't feel any closer to her than I had when she arrived.

I was very glad to see the town square in Cheshire, a small park shaded by enormous old maples. A few other hikers sat on the grass next to an odd monument, a concrete cylinder with an auger sunk in the top. Claire went to read the inscription.

"It commemorates the world's largest cheese," she said, beginning to smile. "The people of Cheshire made it and sent it to Thomas Jefferson when he was president. I love small New England towns."

Johnny Steel came riding up on a bicycle. "A kid at the bait shop back there just lent me this bike," he said in response to my question. "Anybody wanna go for a joyride?"

Claire jumped up and sat on the handlebars, barely balancing, shrieking with delight as Johnny Steel pedaled unsteadily down the street. They returned in a few minutes, Claire with a handful of brilliant red, white, and blue popsicles.

"Anyone want an All-American Pop?" She handed them out to the hikers, smiling. "See?" She said to Isis in an undertone. "I'm not all that bad."

Isis looked like she was blinking back tears. She was spared the need to come up with a response, though. Sarah Francis had arrived.

"Hello, Isis and jackrabbit. And you must be Claire." Sarah smiled. She was a thin, delicate woman, even thinner than I remembered from fall. Her close-cropped brown hair framed a kind, mild face with round glasses. Something in her gestures reminded me of a small lively bird, a wren or a sparrow.

As she drove, going from a two-lane highway to a narrow woods road to a gravel track, she told us about her work as a waitress and a weaver of designer fabrics.

"I love weaving. What other job can you do where you get to listen to music and talk with friends all day, and where you get to make beautiful things that will be seen all over the world? Last spring, I wove an amazing blue silk jacquard, the exact color of the sky in late summer. It was hard to work with all those slippery threads, but the fabric was so gorgeous, so light, and that *color* . . . and knowing that I was the first person on earth to see it . . . My boss never even told me who it was for, what designer, but one day in fall, I opened up the Style section of the New York Times, and there was Naomi Campbell in a blazer made out of my cloth. Of course, she'll never know who wove it, and I think it's better that way, but to know that my work is out there in the world, that's the thing . . . The hard part is, I know I won't be able to do it forever. Most professional weavers have to retire before they reach thirty-five."

"Why?" Claire asked.

"Carpal tunnel syndrome. All that repetitive stress. I've been very lucky so far, but this summer has been tough. I'm only working four days a week now.

Sometimes I have to wear a brace on my right hand. I'm looking for other work, but I know it'll be hard to find something so satisfying . . . oh, here we are."

She parked in a small pull-off on the side of the road, and we walked up the staircase of railroad ties to her house, set on the side of a steep little rise. Her deck was covered with potted plants, mostly flowers, though peas and tomatoes lined the far railing.

Sarah cooked a feast of quinoa, smoked tofu, roasted vegetables, and salad. "It's so great to have you guys visit," she said. "I just love hearing about all the adventures that hikers have. And I don't get much company, back here in the woods."

"It's wonderful to see you again," Isis said.

Sarah took Claire back to the Cookie Lady's blueberry farm to pick up her car in the morning. Claire gave a jaunty wave, her blond curls framing a picture-perfect smile, and then she was gone. I looked at Isis, feeling a hollowness in the bottom of my stomach. *Time to patch things up and move on.*

"Would you guys like to slack-pack?" Sarah asked. "See, I'm learning the hiker lingo."

"That would be great," I said.

"I could meet you in North Adams when I get off work. Five-thirty or six. I'm not sure how far it is on the Trail."

Isis looked at the map. "It's about fourteen. And we go over Greylock, the highest point in Mass." She gave me a questioning glance.

"We could do that," I said. "Excellent. Thanks."

It was hot already when we started hiking. Sweat dripped constantly down my face as we followed the trail up the shoulder of Greylock.

"Isis, I'm sorry," I finally said. "I don't know why I was such a bitch."

She sighed. "I'm sorry too. I wish the three of us could just get along. But it never happened when we were younger. Maybe it never will. At least the two of *us* understand each other."

Mostly, I wanted to say, but I held back. I was glad we were speaking again.

At the summit of Greylock, a refreshing wind blew in from the valley. Isis and I sat in the shade of Bascom Lodge, a hulking hotel/restaurant built of stone, and watched the legions of tourists swarming around the base of the immense lighthouse tower that marked the summit. There was a road up the mountain, and a steady, glittering stream of cars poured into the parking lot.

A couple of hikers we had met at Upper Goose Pond came up the walkway. I tried to dredge up their names. "Featherfoot and Lightweight?"

"Lightfoot and Featherweight," the man said with a grin. "Have you seen the water spigot?" He was carrying a pair of empty two-liter soda bottles, and he held them up to his head like moose antlers. "We're very thirsty," he said in a Monty Python accent.

Featherweight rolled her eyes. "He's been acting silly all day long. Must be the heat." She put on a funny British accent of her own. "I simply can't *bear* much more of your highjinks!"

A harried-looking man in a Hawaiian shirt marched past, followed by a pair of morose children and a scowling woman. The man turned back to Lightfoot. "Where's the summit?" He asked him. "We drove all the way out here to see the summit!"

I sat back, absolutely baffled. The tower marking the summit, by far the most prominent thing for miles around, was clearly visible from where we sat. I couldn't imagine not being able to find it.

Lightfoot regarded him with a perfectly straight face. "The summit? You must've missed it. It's back down the road a few miles." The road spiraled steadily around the mountain; from here, it would be downhill all the way.

I thought the tourist had been joking, but he gathered his family around him. "Come on, guys," he barked. "We missed it. It's back that way."

When he left, we laughed until our bellies ached.

Over the next couple days, Sarah Francis slacked us over the last few miles of Massachusetts and into Vermont. We spent one zero day at her house, when temperatures peaked at 105 in the valley. I felt stronger every day; the nasty, expensive, blue pills were finally doing their job.

We said goodbye to Sarah outside Bennington, Vermont. "Come visit us in Maine!" Isis called before Sarah drove away.

We hiked into the Green Mountains, which lived up to their name. The leaves glowed emerald, and moss dripped from the lower branches. Thick tangles of witch hobble and moose maple filled in the understory, floating their huge leaves in the gloom. Little streams murmured here and there among the rocks. Vermont's spring and summer had been wetter than usual, apparently. The sound of so much water, after months of dryness, was a beautiful thing.

That first night, we only covered three miles. It was a steep climb up from the road, almost like a notch, set with giant granite steps in its roughest pitches. We were carrying six days' worth of food, enough to get us to Woodstock, Vermont. (There was another town in between, Manchester Center, but Isis reported that the hitching was bad and the overnight options minimal there.) Between our heavy packs and the nonstop ascent, I was ready to rest when we reached the saddle of Hell Hollow Brook.

"Not the most auspicious name for a campsite," Isis said, looking around the clearing. A little creek riffled over black stones, and light came down through layer upon layer of leaves. "But it'll do."

I set up the tent out of sight of the Trail and gathered wood for the stove. It definitely wasn't the most auspicious name. I felt hopeful, though. The cloud of depression and uncertainty that had hovered around me for so long was finally beginning to dissipate. We wouldn't reach Katahdin in mid-September, with the slow pace we'd had to keep while I recovered. But for the first time in weeks, I had confidence that we would finish the Trail. *Maybe I won't be able to apply to grad school this fall,* I thought. *Something will work out, though. I'll work for a year or two, rebuild my savings. And maybe there'll be time, somewhere in there, to write down the story of our journey.*

CHAPTER 9

Jackrabbit's Thru-hike

jackrabbit

The forest revealed how far north we had come; evergreen trees, which had marked the highest elevations south of here, cloaked entire mountains in Vermont. Ranks of spruces closed in around the trail, their low branches weighted with cushions of moss. The deciduous trees, birch and beech and maple, clung to the lowlands and stream valleys. From the overlooks, we could trace watercourses on the nearby mountains by the color of the vegetation: veins of lighter, summery green cutting through the blue-black background of spruce and fir.

"Doesn't this forest look mysterious?" Isis said as we stepped across a little stream. "When I came through here southbound, a nobo told me there were rumors about hikers disappearing in these woods. Three people, over the years, he said. They just vanished. Nobody ever found a trace of them."

"It *is* kind of spooky," I said. "All these shadowy trees and the moss . . ."

"I don't think it's spooky, so much. Just mysterious. Like a fairy wood in Ireland or something. Like you could step off the path and into a different world. Or like Rip van Winkle; you fall asleep under the trees and wake up forty years later. I can imagine vanishing here."

I laughed. "You'd better not. You've got the stove, and I don't want to be eating dry, uncooked couscous all the way to Woodstock."

"You could always make a fire."

"Yeah, but you've got the matches, too."

She sighed. "Okay. No vanishing."

I heard light footsteps coming up the trail behind us, and turned to see a wiry young hiker with a light pack and shoulder-length curly brown hair. I hadn't seen him since Miss Janet's Easter party in Erwin, but he was unmistakable.

"Greensinger!" I called.

"Isis and jackrabbit! I thought I would catch you soon." He tipped his hat. "Your company is quite delightful."

"Why, thank you, sir," I said. "But what are you doing in Vermont, Greensinger? I thought you'd be in Maine by now."

"I had to get off and work for a couple weeks. I picked apples, waited tables, painted houses. Now I have enough money to finish the Trail, if I'm thrifty." He gave the wry grin that I remembered. "Hiker boxes are my friends."

He soon passed us on the uphill, skipping along the rocks. We found him at the shelter that night, though, along with another old friend: Toast.

"Hey, Mr. Toastee!" I said as we set our packs down.

"Hi there, ladies." He grinned behind his thick blond beard. "Good to see y'all."

Greensinger had dragged some dead branches to the firepit. He started breaking them up into smaller pieces. "We really ought to have a fire and tell stories tonight," he said. "After all—" he gestured at the signboard on the shelter "—this *is* Story Spring Shelter."

"Sounds good," I said.

Hikers had already claimed the space in the shelter—Honey and Moon, Lightfoot and Featherweight, and a few others I didn't recognize, plus a father out for the weekend with his two preteen sons. I found a tent site behind the shelter and set up while Isis cooked dinner.

Most of the hikers joined us at the fire that night as dusk fell. There was a slight chill in the air, and we huddled close for warmth. Toast sat on a log, with his spare t-shirt wrapped around his head like a turban. ("I don't have a hat, y'all," he explained.) The weekender and his two sons shared a rock.

"Who's got a story to start things off?" Greensinger asked.

"I've got one," Isis said. "This is a true story, and it happened right around here." She told about the three hikers who had vanished, embellishing the story with spooky details. The boys shivered and scooted closer to their father.

"I have a ghost story, too," Greensinger said. "And this is something that happened to me. On the Trail. Do you remember Tinker Cliffs, in Virginia?" The thru-hikers nodded. "It's one of the most beautiful views on the Trail," he said to the weekenders. "There's kind of a plateau with cliffs on one side, huge blocks of sandstone. A sheer drop-off to the valley. At least, that's what they say. I don't really know what it looks like, because I went through there at night." He stirred the coals with a stick and then laid it on the fire. "I was hiking by myself. It got darker and darker as I came along the ridge to Tinker Cliffs. I kept thinking I should stop and camp, but I didn't have any water. I realized I hadn't seen a white blaze in a long time. I was starting to get nervous. All of a sudden I had a strange feeling that I was being watched. Not a malevolent kind of watching, not like a predator, but a definite intelligence with its eyes on me. I seemed to see a kind of shadow, flickering in and out among the trees. I don't know whether I imagined it. It was almost completely dark by then."

"Does this story have a happy ending?" one of the kids asked, big-eyed.

Greensinger pursed his lips. "It has a *strange* ending," he finally said. "I spotted the light of a campfire, way off among the trees on my right. I heard voices over there. I thought to myself, 'Oh, good. They must be thru-hikers. At least they'll be able to tell me where the Trail is.' So I ran through the trees toward the fire. Right before I got there, I stumbled into something in the dark, and I fell. When I looked up, the fire was gone. Eventually I found my Photon—it's a kind of flashlight," he explained to the kids, and one of the other thru-hikers took one out and flashed its pale beam across the clearing. "I went looking for the fire that I'd seen. When I finally found the place, the clearing was empty." He hesitated for effect. "And the coals were stone-cold."

"Did I ever tell you about the ghost at Vandeventer?" I said. I told the legend of the woman's voice and the red-eyed bird that lands in the firepit at midnight, and I told what had happened to me. "I'm not sure if it was midnight, or even if that bird had red eyes, but I swear to God it landed right in the firepit."

"Vandeventer? In Tennessee?" Lightfoot asked. With his pale blond hair and high cheekbones, he looked like a Viking by firelight. "Oh, I'd never stay there. A friend of mine was out there last fall, just hiking for a week or so. Late October. Once I heard what happened to him there, I swore I'd never stay at that place."

"What happened?" one of the boys asked.

"Up on the ridge, a few miles before the shelter, he found a pair of dogs on the trail. One of them was some kind of hound, probably a hunting dog; the other one was bigger. Like a German shepherd, he said. They were both kind of skinny. And they were quite a few miles from any town. The guy decided he could look after them for the night, at least, and take them down to the road in the morning. So he offered them water and fed them, I don't know, some beef jerky or something. After that they followed him up the trail.

"He stayed at Vandeventer that night. And when he lay down, the dogs were right there with him. The little one, the hound, lay at his feet, and the big one put its head on his chest, and they all fell asleep. Late that night, my friend woke up and he heard the most terrible sound in the woods, right near the shelter. He said it was like a choking cough, like somebody strangling. He tried to get up and see what it was. But the little dog put a paw over his feet, and the big dog kept its head on his chest, and both of them growled whenever he tried to move. Eventually he went back to sleep. In the morning, the dogs were gone. Not even a footprint. And to this day, he has no idea what that sound was . . . Or what would've happened to him if he'd gotten up to see."

One of the boys was still listening with rapt attention, but the younger one had fallen asleep in his father's arms. "Bedtime for us," the father said. "Thanks for the stories." The older boy followed him, a bit reluctantly, back to the shelter.

"It's gettin' cold, y'all," Toast said. He ducked into the shelter and emerged with a voluminous toga of pale, silvery fabric wrapped around him. With the t-shirt turban on his head, he looked like a genie rising from a cloud of smoke.

"What *is* that, Toast?" Moon asked him. His dark eyes sparkled with barely suppressed laughter.

"It's my new sleepin' bag liner," Toast said.

I laughed. "Looks like it's big enough for two."

Toast raised an eyebrow at me and gave a slow grin. "Big enough for two if they were real close. That's why I call it the Love Sack."

The hikers around the fire whistled. When the laughter died down, the talk turned from ghost stories to adventures, a favorite topic of conversation among hikers. Isis and I told a story from our childhood.

Isis began. "When I was ten—"

"—and I was seven—"

"—our dad had a job as a yacht designer for the America's Cup. You know, that sailboat race that happens every four years? We all lived in Hawaii for a year. After that, instead of flying home, we bought a used boat and sailed across the Pacific."

"Our dad had made the crossing single-handed when he was twenty-one," I explained. "He always wanted to go back and do it again. So he took the opportunity when he had it, and brought the rest of us along."

Isis added the details. "The crossing took thirty days. About five days out, we hit the doldrums, where there's no wind, and the ocean was glassy smooth, with big sea-waves rolling through it. Albatrosses circled around us. And then we got into the trade winds and got slammed around a good bit. Nobody could keep any food down for about four days."

"Oh, it was bad," I broke in. "To this day, I still can't face canned orange juice."

"Our dad fell down the companionway in the middle of the storm, and cracked a rib—"

"—and that same night, the tiller broke, and we couldn't steer—"

"—until our mom took one of the oars and lashed it into place for that night. We took one of the seats from the dinghy and carved a replacement tiller in the morning. Our dad had to lie in his bunk for two weeks of the crossing. We were all so scared," Isis said.

"And the worst thing for me, as a kid, was that we weren't supposed to make him laugh. If he laughed, his rib hurt, so we had to be all dour and quiet down below."

"After the storm cleared, jackrabbit and I would go out on the foredeck where nobody could hear us. We'd tell all sorts of jokes to get it out of our systems."

"Our dad's rib healed up, and things got better for the last week of the crossing. And it was so beautiful, at night in the middle of the ocean. All the stars. You never forget that, once you've seen it. There are five times as many stars out there, and they all look so close you could reach out and touch them."

"We made it to Alaska at the beginning of July," Isis said.

"Near Sitka. Down on the southeast coast."

"And it was so strange and wonderful to see land again. You could smell it first. The wind changed when we were three days out, and all of a sudden it was full of this . . . green smell. Forests. Lakes. Things rotting and growing. Land smell."

"We made landfall on a little island with a gravel beach," I said. "After all that time at sea, we could hardly walk on the shore. There were these huge drift logs at the back of the beach, some of them four feet across. So of course, being kids, we went back there to play on the logs. But we couldn't walk on them. We were so used to adjusting to the rocking of the boat. I just remember how that log seemed to be moving up and down, like a boat in the waves, and I couldn't stay up on it no matter how hard I tried."

As the evening drew on, the crowd at the fire dwindled. Eventually it was down to me, Isis, Toast, Greensinger, and one other hiker who I hadn't met.

He sat a little bit apart, staring into the coals from under the brim of a beat-up leather cowboy hat. His long hair, light brown with streaks of gold, reflected the firelight.

"You must have some stories," I said to him. "And I don't think I ever got your trail name."

"I'm Disco," he said. "I guess I got some stories. Summer after I left high school, I went out West lookin' for adventure. I worked on a cattle ranch for a while. I loved the open spaces, but the pay was shit. I was there two years and barely broke even. A buddy of mine said there was good money up in Alaska, on the fishin' boats. I gave my notice at the ranch, hitchhiked up to Seattle, and got on a ferry.

"I worked on a king crab boat out of Anchorage for a few seasons. The money was great. You'd be out two weeks and make twenty thou. But the work itself—" he spat on the ground and shook his head. "It's livin' hell. Outta those two weeks you'd get maybe ten hours' sleep, total. You'd be out on the deck, gettin' tossed around, with the waves comin' in over the side. Day and night. After a while you get so you can't even tell which is which. Three days without sleep, and you start to hallucinate. Ten days, you're a wreck. Two weeks—I saw all kinds of shit out in that water. I'd see my old girlfriend wavin' to me, and I'd be about to jump overboard so I could reach her, and then she'd turn into a sea monster. Some slimy thing with too many legs. I'd see castles and cities down under the waves. More fucked up than peyote. One of the guys that was on the boat with me, he got so psycho they had to send him to the mental ward when we got back to port. All kinds of accidents happened. I was right next to a guy who cut his finger off while he was choppin' bait. He just patched the stump with duct tape and kept goin'."

The coals were beginning to die down. Disco leaned over and stirred the fire; an owl hooted softly off in the dark woods. "After a couple seasons of that," Disco continued, "I'd had enough. I started prospectin' for gold instead."

"I thought all the gold up there was mined out," I said.

Disco shook his head. "There's still gold if you know where to look. But it's not like you go out there and pan for it or anythin'. These days, all the mining's done by these big refinin' companies. They can extract it out of ore that's one or two grams per ton. Uses all kinds of chemicals and shit. My job was to go out and mark claims, make sure nobody was minin' where they weren't supposed to on company land. They'd airlift me out to these places in a helicopter, drop me off with a rifle and a month's supply of food and some campin' gear. I'd take a compass and some flaggin' tape and a can of spray paint, and mark off the edges. Some places, it was so steep I'd just punch a hole in the side of the paint can and toss it down the cliffs. And this was down in the southeast part of the state, you know, where it's basically rain forest. The worst part was this plant called devil's club."

"Oh, I remember that," Isis said. "Nasty stuff."

"Yeah," Disco grimaced at the memory. "Grows about six feet high, real thick tangles sometimes, and every single part of the plant's got thorns on it. Even the damn flowers. And these thorns, when they get in your skin, they'll break off and get infected real easy. I know a guy who fell down a mountain into a thicket of the stuff. He had to hike out four days after that, hitch down a ride with a fishin' boat that passed by. By the time he got to town, he was in such bad shape he spent two weeks in the emergency room. They took thorns outta every single part of his anatomy . . . so I was real careful of that shit. That and the bears. All kinds of grizzlies out there in the woods. I had a couple close calls with 'em, had to fire a couple warning shots and that kind of thing. Mostly, they left me alone.

"After a few years of that, the solitude started gettin' to me. I decided it was time to look for another kind of adventure. A buddy of mine had hiked the A.T. after high school. I kind of figured it might be fun."

"After everything else you've done, this probably doesn't seem like much of an adventure," I said.

"Naw." Disco smiled. "More like a vacation. But there's good people out here."

Isis

The symptoms of jackrabbit's illness—fatigue, depression, and a slow withdrawal into herself—had been so reminiscent of winter that I had fallen into that season's habits without even noticing. Tiptoeing around her, doing both our chores. Taking on as much of her weight as I could, knowing all the while that the tent poles and water filter, the packets of cheese and granola that I shifted from her pack to mine didn't make much of a difference. The thing that weighed her down the most, her depression, was something I couldn't touch.

In the few days after Claire left, jackrabbit's medication began to take effect. The transformation amazed me. Only a week before, she'd alternated between dull, bitter anger that I didn't have the strength to confront, and weakness that frightened me even more. Now, she was laughing in the rain, posing so that Disco could take a picture of us in our sports bras, shorts, and wool hats.

The rain came and went in brief gusts that shook the birch and maple leaves. Strips of wet birch bark fluttered against the trunks, white and orange and salmon-colored. We talked more than usual as we hiked, making up for the time we had lost. Jackrabbit stopped to point out a russula, a brilliant purple mushroom with a velvety cap. A few miles later, she spotted blue gentian blooming beside the trail. I told her stories from my solo hike: making blackberry pie at Dan Quinn's house, slacking a twenty with Scout the next day. Sharing a shelter with a witch, a Druid, and two military men. Getting lost in Manchester Center, with its miles of burning asphalt and outlet stores—"The *Urban* Outfitter?"

Early in the afternoon, we came to Stratton Pond. No rain was falling, although dark clouds still swirled above us. I set down my pack and waded in, trying to decide if it was warm enough for a swim. Something tickled my foot. I looked down to see a greenish-yellow newt, with two rows of orange spots along its back, nibbling at the tip of my little toe. Another brushed past my ankle. I slipped my hand under it, and it came to rest in my palm, its tiny fingers splayed and its tail fanning gently back and forth.

Hey, jackrabbit!" I called. "Check out the newts!"

She turned, halfway across the meadow to the spring trail, and came back to take a look. Soon we were both sitting on rocks at the water's edge, luring the newts to the surface with offerings of squashed mosquitoes. I let another one crawl across my palm, looking at it closely.

"The pattern of spots on their backs looks so familiar," I told jackrabbit. "Did we see this kind of newt down south?"

"I don't think so," she said. "But they do remind me of something. I've got it—those little red salamanders that come out after rain in spring and early fall. They have spots in the same pattern, only brighter. I wonder if they're related."

"They're the same species," said a voice behind us. "This is their aquatic phase." A tall, slender man with stooping shoulders stood in the meadow, only five feet away. With his round glasses and his long mane of tangled, light brown hair, he looked like a young John Lennon trying to grow dreadlocks. He was barefoot; that explained how he had managed to walk so close without us hearing him.

"I'm Jungle Jim," he said, taking a few steps forward and holding out a large, callused hand. "I'm the caretaker here this summer. Isn't it an incredible place?"

"It's lovely," I agreed. Jackrabbit and I introduced ourselves.

"The Barefoot Sisters? I'd been hoping to meet you. I figured anyone who walked barefoot on the Trail must be pretty with it. In touch with nature, I mean." Jungle Jim sat down on a rock between us, and slipped a hand into the water, letting a newt settle onto his palm. "Amazing creatures. Most folks walk by here without even noticing them. Sometimes I tell people that they're baby alligators. The tourists probably think I'm crazy, but at least it makes them stop and take a look."

Jackrabbit lifted a newt toward the surface, inspecting it carefully. "This is quite a metamorphosis. These guys are twice the size they are in their terrestrial phase, they're a completely different color, and they've got these wonderful long tadpole tails. And gills, of course. I'd hardly be more impressed if they *did* turn into alligators."

Jungle Jim smiled. "I saw one change once. I was walking up the trail when I spotted this little orange salamander running downhill just as fast as he could go. I wondered where he was going in such a hurry, so I turned around and followed him. He ran and ran, tumbling down the steep places, shoving his way through clumps of grass in the meadow, until he came to the water's edge and threw himself in. He jumped out of one element and into a completely different one, without a moment's hesitation. And then he swam away, like he'd been swimming all his life. Embracing the transformation. I'd like to be able to live that way—be so open to change that, when I was ready, I could fling myself into a new way of being without a backward glance."

A few fat drops of rain spattered onto the pond's surface, and Jungle Jim invited us back to his caretaker's tent to sit out the shower. To a long-distance hiker, the ten-by-ten foot structure of white canvas, complete with curtains and a small bookshelf, looked more like a house than a tent. A raised cot with a mattress and blankets stood against one wall, and brightly colored cushions were scattered across the floor. Jungle Jim offered us each a cushion, and set a teapot to boil on a Coleman camp stove.

"Take your pick," he said, handing us a small wooden box full of assorted tea bags. "Or would you rather have cocoa? I think I've got some in here." He produced a large tin of cocoa mix, two enamel mugs, and a box of cookies. "And how 'bout a banana? They're organic!" He pulled a large bunch off a shelf and broke one off for each of us.

"Bananas! What a treat," jackrabbit said. "How do you get them in here? Is there a road nearby that you use?"

Jungle Jim shook his head. "I have my own trail down to Manchester Center. An old woods road that doesn't show up on the maps. It's only about a ten-mile round trip. I take one day off each week and hike to town for provisions. I went just yesterday, so I still have some bananas left."

"This is all the fresh fruit you have for a week, and you're sharing it with us?" I asked. "That's so generous of you."

Jungle Jim shrugged. "I wish I had more to offer you. It's not every day that I get to have guests to tea."

"You must meet some pretty interesting people, though," jackrabbit said. "Living up here all summer."

"Oh, I do. And not all of them are thru-hikers. As a matter of fact, some of the thru-hikers—especially northbounders, once they get this close to their goal—become so focused on what they're doing that they kind of lose sight of everything. They hardly seem to be enjoying it any more. And some thru-hikers . . . well, I don't know quite how to put it. They get a sense of entitlement, I guess. I had one young woman who took the shelter fee really personally. She argued with me for two hours about whether she should have to pay six dollars—argued at me, I should say, since all I could say was, 'I work for the Green Mountain Club; I don't make their policies'—then stormed off to camp in the stealth site I'd recommended to her.

"Another time, I was hanging out at the shelter with a bunch of weekenders and section hikers. There were some really amazing people there that night; it seemed like every one of them had a story to tell. There was a man who worked for Médecins Sans Frontières; he'd just come back from a year as director of a hospital in Peru. A woman who teaches poetry at a college near here, and another woman who'd done a lot of mountaineering in the Himalayas. A couple who'd sailed halfway around the world.

"We were all cooking dinner, having a great conversation, when this young guy hiked up and asked, 'Are there any thru-hikers here?' We all shook our heads, and he went up in the loft by himself and wouldn't speak to any of us all evening. I just thought, poor guy doesn't know what he's missing. There's so much more he could get out of his hike."

"I hope I'm never that snobby," I said. I could certainly remember nights when I'd come into camp tired, and hadn't wanted to talk to anyone I didn't know. On the other hand, all of our Trail friends had been strangers only thirteen months before, and not all of them had been thru-hiking when we met. I remembered the night in Shenandoah when we'd camped with Parypinoy, the two women who had just graduated from law school, and the couple who were about to fly to Thailand for their honeymoon. *I don't think I've missed out on much of what the Trail has to offer*, I thought. *Including the wonderful people I've gotten to know.*

The rain let up after an hour or so, and we said goodbye to Jungle Jim. We'd only hiked a mile down the trail, though, when I heard running footsteps slapping on the stones behind us. I turned around to see Jungle Jim dashing toward us, with a folded square of notebook paper in one hand and a plastic-wrapped lump the size of a brick in the other. Had I forgotten something?

"I wanted to ask you a favor," Jungle Jim said, holding out the package and the paper. "My girlfriend is caretaking the shelter on Killington Peak. Her trail name is Myself, and she has a big white dog. If you see her, please give her this letter and half of this chocolate."

"Sure," I said. "What should we do with the other half?"

"Eat it, of course. The other half is for you. Thanks for taking my message to Myself!"

"Thank you for the chocolate—" I began, but he was already bounding away up the hill. He paused to wave to us at a bend in the trail, then vanished into the trees.

"Myself," mused jackrabbit, as we swung back into our long-distance gait. "I'm tempted to walk up to her and say, 'Myself! I came out on the Trail to look for you, and I've been searching for thirteen months. I'm so glad to find you at last!'" She paused for a moment. "That's probably what everyone says to her, though."

"Yeah, probably," I agreed. "Except for the part about the thirteen months."

jackrabbit

A half hour after breakfast, my stomach was growling. The bowl of Grape-Nuts I had eaten that morning hardly touched my hunger. The antibiotics were doing their job; the pounding headaches no longer plagued me. But I was still fatigued at the end of the day, and I still sensed the strange disparity between the amount of food I consumed and the amount of effort my body returned. To keep my mind off the rumblings of my stomach, I tried to notice the beauty of everything around me: the green light that filtered through the beeches, and the occasional spruce, falling in shafts through the early morning mist. The tiny orange mushrooms that peeked up through the leaves on the forest floor, and the moss carpets that covered the boulders, shining with dew.

The trail came out onto the shoulder of a paved road. Away from the cover of the forest, I squinted against the sudden brightness of the sky.

"This is the road to Manchester Center," Isis said.

"Should we hitch in?"

She frowned. "I don't think so. I mean, we're a little short on cereal, considering how hungry you've been, but it seems like a waste of time to hitch in just for another box of Grape-Nuts."

"You're right, I guess. And besides, I haven't heard any traffic at all." An SUV came chugging up the hill just then, but when the driver caught sight of us, he sped up.

"Looks like we won't get a hitch," Isis said. "Manchester Center's really not much of a hiker town, anyway. The only thing worth going in for is the breakfast restaurant."

"Please don't tell me. I don't wanna hear about food I won't get to eat."

"Okay. But if it makes you feel any better, I didn't get to go either. I just heard about it from nobos last year. It was closed by the time I got there."

We crossed the road and the trail turned sharply upward.

"Tell me again about those Vermont switchbacks," I panted to Isis's retreating back.

In about a mile we came to the Bromley Tentsite and paused to read the register. It hung in a brown box beside the trail, a tiny wire-bound notebook. Isis leaned her poles against a tree and began to read.

"The Honeymooners were here . . . Toast . . . the Tourists . . . Disco and Greensinger must still be in town."

"What have the 'Mooners got to say?" I could see almost a page of Honey's curly, ebullient handwriting. Generally, she wrote amusing entries.

"Well, I'm not so sure you want to hear it, jackrabbit."

"No, read it!"

"'What an excellent breakfast we had in M.C. this morning! We went to the New Moon Café—sobos, check it out! I had the tropical pancakes, with coconut, mango, and papaya, and a plate of veggie sausage that was out of this world! Moon had—'"

"Enough! You're right. The last thing I need is to hear about somebody else's town breakfast." As if in agreement, my stomach let out the loudest rumble of the morning.

Farther up Bromley Mountain, the trail came out on a ski slope. In high summer, it was beautiful: a swath of grass and flowers, smelling of sunshine and pollen. Bees hummed in the black-eyed Susans and Queen Anne's lace. I found myself wondering, though, what winter hikers would do here. The forest on either side of the ski slope was thick and tangled. I imagined what it would be like to beat uphill on snowshoes, burdened with a winter-weight pack, against a throng of spandex-clad skiers on their way down.

We stopped for lunch at the top of the mountain. We had only hiked five miles, but Isis was getting hungry, too. Bromley was our biggest climb of the day, about 1,800 feet from the valley floor, and the view on top was certainly spectacular. The landscape below us looked more and more like home: the glaciated granite mountains rising from a dark evergreen forest, the shimmering lakes and rivers reflecting the sky. Cloud shadows dappled the valley, moving over the land like a herd of ponderous beasts. A chilly wind whipped over the mountaintop. We took shelter behind a granite ledge in the sweet-smelling grass.

We ate our lunch—the last of our cheese rolled up in flaking tortillas, stoned wheat crackers, dried papaya, spring water still cool in our bottles. I still felt the odd sense of detachment that Lyme disease had brought, as though a thin membrane stretched between me and the rest of the world. I felt floating, distant, watching myself as I chewed the stale tortilla and unscrewed the cap of my Nalgene. My stomach still felt empty. But I knew, even as I licked the last crumbs of tortilla from my grubby fingers and picked up a stray scrap that had fallen in the grass, that I'd never known true hunger. Even in the worst short-supplied stretch, even in the depths of winter when we couldn't carry enough to sustain us, I'd always had something to scratch the surface of my hunger. Even at these times, I'd had more calories per day than much of the world's population gets.

After lunch, the day seemed to speed past. Somehow, we had walked more than three miles an hour, barefoot, for most of the early hours of afternoon. The trail was rich brown mud and fallen leaves, with little gravel to get in our way. A few stretches of bog bridges provided a change of rhythm. I amused myself by testing the different pitches of the logs as we went along, tapping my hiking sticks against each section. When Isis joined in, the trail was momentarily transformed into a giant marimba, with the *tunk, thonk, bink!* of wood on wood echoing through the forest above the softer patter of our footsteps.

The sun was low above the trees when we stopped at Lost Pond Shelter. The Honeymooners and the Tourists had already set up their tents nearby, and they greeted us as we came into the clearing. I really didn't have the energy to socialize. I climbed over the porcupine trap and dropped my pack on the dusty floorboards of the shelter, ducking under the low mouse hangers. The green spiral-bound register lay in a corner, and I commandeered it as an excuse not to have to talk. Still, fragments of the conversation outside drifted into the shadowed interior of the shelter.

"That vegetarian sausage was so great! I mean, I haven't had sausage since I stopped eating meat in '93, and this was just like I remember, only better. All those wonderful herbs in it—"

"The pancakes, though! That was the best part . . . a stack *this big* . . . but-ter . . ." I imagined Moon holding up his hands and making his kid-in-a-candy-store expression, and I almost smiled.

"Banana pancakes with chocolate sauce! I mean, it sounds gross, but, oh my God, was it ever good!" This was Debbie of the Tourists, finishing her statement with a shrill, nasal laugh.

Then came Isis's voice, somewhat sheepish. "If you guys don't mind, jackrabbit and I are kind of short-supplied. Could you, maybe, not talk about that restaurant around us?"

"Oh, I didn't know. I'm so sorry." This was Honey. I could picture the chagrin in her dark eyes.

Moon agreed. "No more breakfast talk. Sorry, Isis."

"No problem . . . you guys had no way of knowing . . ."

I turned to the last empty page of the register and scribbled a short entry, leaving a note for Greensinger in case he was behind us now. As I finished, I heard Debbie's voice outside. "I have *never* had bacon that perfect. It was so crisp and tasty. And the eggs!"

Her husband joined in. "Eggs benedict with spinach and fresh tomatoes. I mean, I've had lotsa good breakfasts in my life, but this takes the cake!"

Isis stood up; I heard the *whump!* as she shouldered her pack and the clatter of her sticks against the stones by the picnic table. "Well, jackrabbit and I had better be on our way." We had made tentative plans to go farther that night, if I was feeling up to it. When I first hit the shelter, I'd been ready to call it a night, but now I, too, was eager to put some more miles behind us.

Isis came around to the front of the shelter.

"Let's get the hell outta here," I mouthed, and she nodded fiercely.

Once we were down the trail and out of hearing range, I screamed, "Fuck their fucking breakfast!"

Isis nodded in tacit agreement; for once, she didn't say a thing about my swearing.

On the next stretch of bog bridges, we heard footsteps clunking behind us. I turned to see the slight outline of Greensinger, in his floppy leather hat with the cascade of curls beneath.

"Hail and well met, ladies," he called. "Whither are you bound?"

"Big Branch, I guess," Isis said. "We'll see how far the sunlight takes us." We could already sense the shortening of the days, and some evenings had a lingering chill; fall was coming, though the leaves were still high and green.

Greensinger passed us and bounced along the trail ahead, skipping from rock to rock with the easy grace of a hiker who carries a light pack. Not for the first time, I wished I had put more research into gear before we started. On the Trail, we had learned a great deal about modern, lightweight gear, and we'd bought a few items of it, but we couldn't afford to reoutfit ourselves completely. Most of what we carried was six or seven years old, much heavier and bulkier than the new stuff. The immensity of my pack slowed me down, especially now when the fatigue from Lyme disease still clung to me. I watched Greensinger's light frame floating above the trail, and sadness rose up in my ribcage. I thought of all the friends who had left us behind to follow their schedules; I thought of the day we'd left the Family from the North at Newfound Gap. *This trail is a trail of goodbyes*, I thought. *Who knows if we'll even see him again.*

But in a moment Greensinger paused. "I have a question for you. Just hypothetical. Do you believe it's possible to travel through space by astral projection? And if you could, would that projection of yourself have the power to influence the systems it observed? I mean, it would be a handy way around the Heisenberg Uncertainty Principle if it could work . . ."

As usual, the question was a doorway into a monologue. But this time, I welcomed it. Greensinger's mind was a storehouse of wacky but often brilliant ideas, mixed with completely untenable theories. Listening to him was like watching someone build an elaborate sand castle just ahead of the advancing tide—you knew it couldn't stand up for very long, but while the structure lasted it was beautiful to behold. And I was so glad that Greensinger hadn't decided to leave us behind that I almost could have listened to him talk about breakfast. Almost.

We found the shelter full that night, so we camped by the river on a flat patch of sand under birch trees. I pitched the tent, and Greensinger laid out his foam pad.

"I like to sleep under the stars," he said. "I just hope it doesn't rain."

"And if it does?"

He shrugged. "I pack up and go. Or I get wet."

There was a perfect swimming hole right beside us, but by the time we finished gathering stove wood and putting the tent up, it was almost dark. The chill of evening had settled, and a thin mist came off the river; there would be no swimming tonight.

Isis cooked a pot of polenta and beans, throwing in a handful of texturized vegetable protein. Though we'd gone a little short on breakfast and lunch, we had enough food for dinner. We had come almost twenty miles that day, and my hunger had grown to gargantuan proportions. The smell of dinner cooking—scents of corn and chili and garlic, blending with wood smoke—filled the clearing and made my mouth water. Greensinger was cooking an alfredo Lipton on his hobo stove. He drew a red onion and a tomato out of his pack, and Isis and I involuntarily turned to stare. Fresh vegetables were the thing we craved most on the Trail. They were ridiculously inefficient as food supply, because of all their water weight, but nothing tasted as good. We hadn't carried any in this six-day resupply.

Greensinger noticed our hungry stares. Wordlessly, he cut the two vegetables in half, and held out the halves to Isis.

"You mean it?" I said.

"Of course."

These sudden, unexpected gestures of kindness had come from so many people on the Trail, but they never ceased to amaze me. "You've renewed my faith in the human spirit," I told him, only half in jest. "How can I repay you?"

"Well, you could give me your firstborn and half your kingdom."

"My kingdom is on my back, and I don't suppose you'd want to carry it. And as for my firstborn, mmm . . . that's pretty steep, even for a tomato. I'll give you a ten percent share."

"A ten percent share in your firstborn? Deal."

"Deal." We shook hands solemnly, and then burst out laughing.

Isis

"I've been wondering about that Vermont verse you wrote for 'Dig a Hole,'" jackrabbit said as we ate a meager lunch atop White Rocks Cliff. "This state has lovely scenery and plenty of water, but 'a café at every road'? What on earth were you thinking?"

She had a point. In contrast to the Mid-Atlantic States, Vermont seemed pretty lacking in trailside delis and hot-dog stands. Even in Massachusetts, the Trail had passed within a couple hundred yards of restaurants in Dalton and Cheshire, a concession stand on top of Greylock, and a shopping center in North Adams. In our three days so far in Vermont, we'd only passed one road that led to food: the ten-mile hitch to Manchester Center.

"I think we ought to change the song," jackrabbit continued.

> If you're looking for some privacy and wilderness,
> the A.T. in Vermont might fit the bill.
> You've got miles to divest of all the things that you digest,
> but not a single town where you can refill!"

I laughed. "That could be the nobo version. Southbound, after Maine and New Hampshire, Vermont seemed full of restaurants and bakeries."

"Okay, I can see how even one or two trailside cafés would be a pleasant surprise after Maine and the Whites," jackrabbit answered. "But I haven't seen *any*. Have they all mysteriously vanished since you hiked through here?"

"They must be in the northern part of the state. Let's see . . . there was a general store with a breakfast counter in West Hartford, just eight or ten miles south of Hanover. Dan Quinn's house on Vermont 12—it's not a restaurant, but he took me to the grocery store and let me cook in his kitchen. The Inn at Long Trail, of course. And a great bakery in Killington; the ski resort there lets hikers ride the gondola down the mountain for free. This guy named Willin' went down with me, and we split an apple pie made from fresh apples that the baker had picked the day before—"

"Please don't describe it to me right now," jackrabbit broke in. "What I want to know is, where's the nearest restaurant that we can look forward to?"

"Let's see . . ." I examined the map. "Oh, yeah! Clarendon Gorge, only eight miles from here. There's a diner in an old railroad station about a quarter mile off the trail. The Whistle Stop. If we hurry, I bet we could eat dinner there, then hike on and camp at Clarendon Shelter a mile past the road."

"A diner. Do they have anything vegetarian?" jackrabbit asked.

"They make veggie burgers. And milkshakes. Really good milkshakes."

"Say no more!" Jackrabbit strapped on her pack and strode away down the trail, still chewing on her last bite of granola bar.

We made such good time that we reached the bridge at Clarendon Gorge in midafternoon, with the sun still high above us. The deep river valley wasn't the still, contemplative place I remembered from a weekday in early fall. On the near side of the river, half a dozen tents stood under the hemlocks—not thru-hikers' tents, but wide canvas pavilions in which babies napped beside their mothers, and older children lay on their bellies reading or playing with Game Boys. More people crowded around the picnic tables; the smell of someone's barbecue made my stomach growl.

From the eastern bend of the river came the shouts and splashes of people swimming, but the deep curve under the A.T. bridge seemed deserted. Hungry as I was, the opportunity to wash off the day's sweat seemed too good to pass up.

"Hey, jackrabbit," I called. "You want to stop for a swim?"

She paused, considering, then nodded. I found a path down the bank, a scramble among white marble boulders and hemlock roots. The marble bedrock at the bottom of the gorge, carved by the current into undulating, sculptural shapes, formed an otherworldly landscape. Amber-colored water pooled in the hollows, throwing flickering nets of light across the undersides of rocks. A little ways downriver, we found a pool even bigger than the one we'd seen from the bridge: swift dark water, blue-green under the shadow of the northern bank, smelling of carp. We slipped in wearing our shorts and sports bras—not quite enough privacy here to skinny-dip. Jackrabbit swam against the current, while I dove down to the underwater caves where large fish hovered in the green twilight.

Water, my element. How had I gone so long, in winter, without even enough to drink? Gliding up the deep eddies, past cave walls ribbed with patterns of shifting sunlight, I forgot all about my hunger. I felt so grateful to have made it this far, and to have Maine—with all its lakes and rivers—only one state away from me. Never mind that that state was New Hampshire, which had given us so much trouble the first time through. It would take more than a few rainy notches to discourage us now.

We swam until the wall of shadow from the north bank covered the whole pool, then strapped on our packs and clambered back up to the bridge. The sun baked our skin and clothing dry as we walked to the restaurant along the highway's shoulder. At the Whistle Stop, we ate our first hiker-sized meal in three days: veggie burgers and fries, onion rings, salads, milkshakes, pie, and ice cream. We both could have eaten more, but we stopped to make certain we wouldn't be too full to hike the last mile to the shelter.

We weren't so lucky in Killington the next day. We hurried all morning to make sure we'd have time to ride the gondola down and back; as far as I remembered, it stopped running at 4:00 in the afternoon. We reached the top of the mountain at 1:30. A uniformed attendant ushered us over to a gondola car and held the door for us as we ducked in, packs and all.

"Goin' to the Killington Mark-up?" he asked jovially. "Make sure you're back by four."

As we rode down over the mown ski trails, we caught our first glimpse of the White Mountains. From this distance, they looked like the teeth in a white shark's jawbone that I'd seen in a natural history museum when I was young. Row upon row of sharp peaks, unfolding from the northern horizon.

"So, where's the famous bakery?" jackrabbit asked as we stepped out of the gondola car. She looked around the ski resort complex: a wide expanse of blacktop, two expensive-looking restaurants, a ticket office, and a souvenir shop.

"It's in the village," I told her. "Half a mile or so downhill from here."

"Oh," she said. "You didn't tell me that we'd have to *walk* there."

"A little walking won't hurt us," I answered, nudging her shoulder.

She was too hungry to joke about it. "It's a mile out of our way." Her forehead furrowed, and I was afraid that she would insist on taking the gondola right back up the mountain and hiking on. After a minute's contemplation, she sighed. "Well, since we're here already, we might as well go to the bakery."

Killington Village turned out to be farther down the mountain than I remembered. We walked along the side of a broad, empty road, past the hotels where Willin' had stopped to ask directions. After the hotels, it seemed as if a mile went by with nothing but woods and fields. Then we passed a ski equipment store, closed for the season, on the right side, and a cluster of apartment buildings on the left, with a few closed restaurants scattered between them.

"Is it here?" jackrabbit asked hopefully.

"No, I think it's a little farther," I answered.

"It had better not be *much* farther, or we'll have to turn around and go back to the gondola before we reach it."

Twenty minutes later, we came to another group of apartments, and just beyond them, the bakery.

"It looks closed," jackrabbit said.

"That's just because there's no one on the porch," I told her. "There are tables inside, too." I set down my pack and hurried up the steps to the door. Jackrabbit was right; the bakery was closed. A sign in the window read *Open Tuesday–Sunday, 6:00 A.M. to 2:00 P.M.* By jackrabbit's watch, it was 2:15.

As a consolation prize, we bought ourselves a couple overpriced pints of ice cream in the store down the street, which must have been the place the gondola attendant referred to as the "Killington Mark-up." We could have used another cooked meal for the days ahead of us, but I balked at spending six dollars for a pair of Liptons. After we ate, I found a pay phone and called

Dan Quinn to tell him that we'd be passing VT 12 in a couple of days. I wanted to ask if I could use his kitchen again, and I was hoping that he'd let jackrabbit play his piano.

"Isis? I heard you and your sister yo-yoed. Is that true? Where are you on the Trail?"

"Killington," I told him. "Jackrabbit and I took the gondola down to pick up a little more food."

"I hope you haven't bought anything there," he said. "I can take you to a supermarket with much more reasonable prices."

"Thanks, but we're still a few days south."

"Can you be at the Inn at Long Trail tonight? Great, I'll meet you there. I can slack you the rest of the way to my place, if you'd like."

"That would be wonderful," I answered. "See you at the Inn."

By the time we caught the gondola up the mountain, a thick bank of clouds obscured the Whites, though the rest of the sky remained clear.

"That's just what they did the last time." Jackrabbit shook her head. "Remember when we saw them from Gentian Pond, southbound? There sat the Presidentials, under a perfectly clear sky. And ten minutes later, poof! Clouds over the whole range."

"You're not giving them the benefit of the doubt," I said. "For all we know, they might have taken two hours to cloud up this time."

"All *I* know is, they saw us coming and they clouded over. What does it matter how fast?" She laughed. "I'm not going to let Murphy worry me, though. I have a piano to look forward to tonight!"

We found Jungle Jim's girlfriend Myself at the shelter just after Killington Peak, sitting on the stone steps playing guitar, with a shaggy white dog the size of a bear curled at her feet. She reminded me of the Gypsies I'd seen in Southern France: a graceful dark-haired woman, dressed in several layers of rumpled skirts. She was singing "Bridge Over Troubled Water" in a soft, breathy voice, almost as if she were singing to herself, though a small audience of hikers sat on nearby rocks and stumps, listening. I waited for her to finish the song, then handed her the message and chocolate.

"How sweet of Jim to send me chocolate," she said, glancing up at me with startling blue eyes. "But a little unfair of him to ask hikers to carry something edible that far, only to give it to someone else. Will you share it with me?"

"Jim already gave us half the bar," I said, embarrassed.

"Here, have some more," Myself said. "I'm sure you're hungrier than I am." She drew a short, straight knife from her belt and chipped off big chunks of the chocolate. She offered them to the other hikers in the clearing, then handed one to each of us. "Can you sit down for a while?" she asked.

"We're meeting a friend at the Inn tonight," jackrabbit said. "But I'd love to hear you play something more before we go. I miss music."

"Do you play?" asked Myself, holding out her guitar.

Jackrabbit shook her head. "No, just piano. I'd love to learn guitar."

"You can sing, then," said Myself. "Do you know 'Sweet Baby James'?"

We sat on the warm stone for half an hour, singing together while Myself played. I added my voice to hers on the melody lines, while jackrabbit reconstructed—or invented—harmonies that wove through the songs like wind through tree branches.

"Thank you, Myself," jackrabbit said as we stood up to leave.

"You're welcome, yourself," she answered, and we all laughed.

"You know," jackrabbit said, "when I first heard your trail name, I wanted to walk up and greet you by saying, 'Myself! Just who I came to the Trail to look for! I've found you at last.'"

"That's really sweet of you. A lot of people make puns on my trail name, but no one's ever put it in such flattering terms. No one's ever brought me chocolate, either. I wonder if Jim's ever tried to send me any before." She chuckled. "I wouldn't blame the hiker who ate it all!"

"I'm glad we didn't," jackrabbit said. "It gave us a good excuse to meet you."

As the shadows of the mountains lengthened, we crossed a ski slope above the Inn at Long Trail. Where the A.T. left the open slopes and turned back into the forest, someone had posted a bright orange sign on a tree. No doubt it was intended to dissuade skiers from following the trail, but for hikers, the warning was pretty amusing. *This is an unmaintained wilderness trail. Follow it at your own risk. Be prepared to spend a night in the woods!*

We reached the Inn just before sunset. Dan came to the door and threw his arms around me. "Isis! Congratulations on your yo-yo! And this must be jackrabbit."

The introduction out of the way, he gave her a hug, too. He turned back to me. "I guess it's too late to ask you to cook dinner tonight," he said, sounding a bit glum. "I ordered some pizzas; we can pick them up on the way back. I do hope you'll have time to cook me something before you hike on, though. I've been looking forward to it ever since I heard you were doing a yo-yo.

"I've got a problem that maybe you could help me with, back at the house," he continued, as we hoisted our packs into his truck. "Woman by the name of Charlotte, wants to slack a forty from North Clarendon tomorrow. You've gotta help me talk her out of it." He looked at me beseechingly. "Isis, you slacked the twenty from here to my place last fall, so you know how hard it is. Most hikers get whipped by that stretch. I can't imagine someone trying to do it as part of a forty."

"We were thinking of slacking that twenty tomorrow. Maybe she'd be willing to hike with us, instead of doing the whole forty," I answered. "We might take a day off after the slack. I could cook you something then."

"Excellent. And if you stick around till the weekend, I can take you to Mudman's party."

"Who's Mudman?" I asked.

"He's an old friend of mine, a hiker. Lives just over the New Hampshire border. He's having a party to see off a couple of guys who've planned this crazy hike, walking all over the country for the next six years. Sheltowee and Dodger; you ever heard of them?"

"Sheltowee and Dodger's sendoff party is happening here? This weekend?" jackrabbit said. "I guess we might be taking some zeros, then!"

Dan's square, two-story farmhouse looked spacious from the outside, but on the inside, the cathedral ceilings and the maze of rooms made it seem twice the size it had appeared. Dan showed us to a bedroom I hadn't seen before, and on the way downstairs, he pointed out the door to a three-room apartment.

"My tenant's away for a few weeks. I've been painting his living room and putting new linoleum down in his kitchen."

"How big *is* this house?" I asked him. It reminded me of Irish legends of faerie hills, where opulent palaces fit into spaces no larger than a haystack.

"Big enough," Dan said with a grin.

Charlotte, a petite, fine-boned woman around thirty years old, with purple streaks in her shoulder-length black hair, met us in the kitchen.

"It's great to meet y'all," she said with a Southern drawl. "In case y'all are wonderin' about the hair, it's Kool-Aid. My brother and his girlfriend and another friend of ours all got off-trail for a concert, and we decided to dye our hair."

"What I'm wondering about is this forty-mile slack you're planning," I said.

She shrugged. "I'm gonna pick up my dog Zero at the Manchester Airport on Friday. Got too hot for him in summer, but now I'm gettin' him back. I'll have to slow down a little once he's with me, so he can get used to hikin' again. So I gotta make as many miles as I can before he gets here. I did Maryland, and I've done thirties now and then. Slackin' a forty can't be that bad."

"This one could be," I said. "It's not easy terrain."

"You could slack a twenty with these ladies tomorrow," Dan offered, "and then I'd slack you to Clarendon the day after that."

She shook her head impatiently. "My ride to Manchester's on Thursday. I've gotta get my hikin' done tomorrow."

A smile flashed across Dan's face. "If your ride is all you're worried about, don't give it another thought," he told her. "I can drive you to Manchester whenever you want to go."

"I'd hate to trouble you," Charlotte began, but he waved away her protests.

"My schedule's flexible, so it's no trouble at all. It's settled, then? You'll all slack together tomorrow?"

"Well, I guess . . ."

"Wonderful," Dan said. "A much better plan."

Dan had a carpentry job to finish in the morning, but he told us he'd be free to pick us up again that night. The three of us set off southbound from VT 12, pausing at the top of the field to pick a few blackberries. They weren't nearly as abundant as they had been the year before, but after the raspberries, blueberries, cherries, and mulberries that we'd eaten all through the Mid-Atlantic States, I wasn't about to complain.

We had just finished picking the handful or two that the patch afforded, when two muscular gray-haired men came down the trail from the woods. A black lab with a dog pack trotted beside them, tongue hanging out. I recognized one of the men: Wee Willie Prince of Whales. He wore his usual hiking costume—jeans, construction boots, and a black cotton t-shirt that read *I ain't nothin' but low-down, drunken, blue-blazin' hobo hiker trash from Hell*. He carried a pack the size of a sea-chest on his back, with a teapot, a few tarps, and a spare pair of jeans lashed to the outside of it. Without Pirate and Lone Wolf beside him to match his great height and weight, he looked like a giant out of Grimm's Fairy Tales.

"Isis and jackrabbit!" He engulfed us both in a Hobo bear hug. We introduced him to Charlotte, and he introduced his hiking partner, Mala, a wiry man about my height. Mala wore his light gray hair in two braids, and a bandana around his forehead. With his lightweight pack and nylon shorts, he looked like an ordinary thru-hiker, but his choice of companions, and his black t-shirt bearing the words *blue-blazers get off more often*, belied that impression.

"Mala," jackrabbit said, shaking his hand. "Are you a thru-hiker or a Hobo, or both?"

"I'm a Hobo at the moment." He winked at us, as though sharing a joke. "Every few years I get fed up with 'em, and I quit for a while. I think, what am I doing wasting my time with a bunch of lazy bums who don't do nothin' but hike and drink and quarrel? So I go home to my girlfriend for a month or six or seven, and then I get to missing the Trail too much. And the parties, and even the rows. So I join up again. Me and Tucker," (he reached down to pat the large black dog), "we can't seem to stay off the Trail for long . . . A thru-hiker, though? That's one thing I'm not doing any time soon. Not enough places to stop for beer up in that Hundred-Mile Wilderness. Say, how far is it to Vermont 12? Willie and me, we're doing a survey of all the local microbreweries, and we heard there's one in Woodstock that we can hitch to from there."

"Vermont 12 is right at the bottom of the meadow," I answered. "It's the next road you come to."

"Excellent! Onward in our quest for the best brew!"

"So," jackrabbit asked him, "instead of hiking the whole Trail, you hike from road to road in search of beer?"

"You got it," he answered.

"Instead of a thru-hiker, then, I should call you a brew-hiker," she joked.

"Brew-hiker! I like the sound of that! From now on, I'll be known to the world as Mala Brühiker. Spelled B-R-U with one of those funny German accents, mind you. Gotta be original. See you around, eh?"

Mala and Willie walked on down the trail, with the dog loping after them.

"Enjoy the beer," jackrabbit called.

"That's what, the third trail name you've given someone?" I asked her as we continued up the hill.

"Yeah, I've been lucky that way," she said. "Speaking of which—Charlotte, are you in the market for a trail name?"

"Actually, I've got one," Charlotte answered. "I just don't use it that much. People might take it the wrong way."

"What is it?" I asked.

"Purple Hooters."

"Wow. How'd you come by that?" jackrabbit asked her.

"Well, the Purple part is straightforward enough. That got added on when I dyed my hair. The other part comes from way back at the beginnin' of the Trail. This guy asked me what I did for a livin', and I told him I was an engineer. And he said, 'Why'd a pretty girl like you go into engineerin'?' I was so flummoxed, I just said the first thing that popped into my head. 'My life's dream was to work at Hooters,' I said, 'but they told me my boobs were too small. So I had to go for my Ph.D. instead.' There were a bunch of other hikers hangin' around, and they seemed to think it was a pretty good response. They all started callin' me Hooters after that."

We talked off and on for the rest of the morning, but by afternoon we fell silent, concentrating on the task of hiking. The trail climbed up and down steep ravines slick with mud, some only a couple hundred vertical feet, others interminable. I couldn't tell where we were on the map; I lost count of the small dirt roads that were supposed to cross the trail. It seemed like we were going at least three miles per hour, but we took three hours to cover a distance that looked like two miles on the map. *If* I was reading the landmarks right. The last mile and a half reminded me of winter—forging on after dark, bone-weary, feeling as though time had stopped and I'd never lie down again.

Dan met us on the lawn of the Inn.

"What took you so long?" he asked. "I was afraid you'd all gone on to do that forty."

"Not a chance," Charlotte said. "I'm so glad you talked me out of it."

"I thought you would be," Dan answered. "I've hiked the stretch you just did a couple of times. It usually takes me three days. Lot of little hills, and the maps are inaccurate. I have a sneaking suspicion it's more than twenty miles. Twenty-three, twenty-four, maybe. Here, throw your hiking sticks in the back of the truck. Would you like an apple? I've got some spaghetti waiting for you at home."

jackrabbit

It took a day and a half after the monster slack before I felt like walking again. Dan let us stay in his house. Isis cooked and I played the piano. The rain sheeting down from the eaves provided just enough of an excuse that I didn't feel too guilty about staying put.

On the morning of our second day at Dan's, the rain cleared and a misty, hazy sunlight came down. I sat on the back porch, talking with Mala and Wee Willie Prince of Whales. They had enjoyed the Woodstock microbrew so much that they'd decided to stick around for a few days.

"People've told me I look just like Willie Nelson," Mala said. With his long, braided gray hair and round bearded face, there was a certain resemblance.

Wee Willie made a somber face. "Did y'all hear that Willie Nelson got hit by a car?"

"No, that's terrible," I said.

"Yeah." Then a glint of amusement came into Wee Willie's dark eyes. "He was playin' 'On the Road Again.'"

"Ooh, awful!"

A white van pulled into the driveway and Sheltowee and the Artful Dodger got out. Dodger nodded to his fellow Hobos.

"Jackrabbit!" Sheltowee said. "I was hoping I'd find you and your sister here. You guys coming to the party? You're invited, too, of course," he said to the Hobos.

Isis and I finished packing and thanked Dan Quinn. We loaded ourselves into the back of Sheltowee's van with Mala and Wee Willie, ready for our next adventure.

Mudman's place was more of a camp than a house: a tiny mobile home surrounded by several pavilions made from blue tarps; a vegetable patch hacked out of the spruce woods; a spring house for water; a privy. A crowd of thru-hikers milled around under the trees, orbiting a food-laden table in front of the camper, and several dogs raced back and forth underfoot. The place reminded me of Rusty's.

"Welcome!" Mudman said. He was an amiable man in early middle age, with the slight paunch that distance hikers often develop when they stop moving for too long. "Make yourselves at home! I've got trout and salmon on the grill, and there's some bread and chips and fresh fruit on the table there. You want a beer? Plenty of beer!"

"Thanks, man." I took the ice-cold bottle from him. "This looks like a great party."

"These guys deserve it," Mudman said. "Had to have a proper send-off for an adventure like that. Man, I wish I could go with 'em."

I took a plate from the table and loaded it up with grilled trout, bread, and fresh plums. Heaven. I sat back under a tree with a pair of hikers I didn't recognize, both young women.

"Hey, I'm jackrabbit. Mind if I join you?"

"Not at all. I'm Sing-song." She had delicate features, rosy cheeks and big blue eyes, and her pale blond hair was done in dreadlocks.

"I'm Tiger Cakes," the other woman said. She had close-cropped dark brown hair and an abundance of freckles.

"That's an awesome name," I said. "How'd you get it?"

"Oh, it's a pretty good story." When Tiger Cakes grinned, she bore an amazing resemblance to my mental image of Huck Finn. "I was on a prep hike last fall with some friends of mine who'd hiked a few years earlier. And all of them were in great shape, compared to me. Our second day out, we did like eighteen miles. I was so exhausted I couldn't even think straight. We got to the campsite and one of the guys took out a package of those Little Debbie things, you know, the striped ones, with chocolate and vanilla? What are they called?"

"Zebra Cakes," Sing-song supplied.

"Right. Thanks. So anyway, I couldn't think of the right animal then, either. I just said, 'Can I have one of your Tiger Cakes?' And they decided to make it into my trail name."

"Excellent. Sing-song, how'd you get *your* name?"

"Well, when we started out, I went by Gruff. Like the billy goats. 'Cause I had a really bad cold for a few weeks, and I went around sounding all gravelly and sultry—" she lowered her voice for effect. "Hello," she rasped, then burst out laughing. "But after a while I decided I really didn't want to be known for being gruff. It's not such a positive word, you know? I like to sing, so I changed it."

"Have you guys hiked together the whole way?" I asked. Their easy camaraderie suggested that they'd known each other for a long time.

Tiger Cakes hesitated before answering. "When we started, we were *together*-together. As a couple."

"We'd been living together for a few months down in Asheville," Sing-song added. "Lesbian capital of the South."

"We kind of broke up in Virginia," Tiger Cakes continued. "But we kept hiking together. There's so much . . . I don't know how to put it. So much, like, in-your-face, testosterone-driven energy from the men on the Trail. Having another woman around helps to diffuse it."

"I can understand that," I said. "I'm straight, and it still gets to me sometimes. Hiking with my sister has been a huge help for that kind of thing."

"Oh, you must be the Barefoot Sisters!" Sing-song said. "Sheltowee was telling us all about you. How long have you been on the Trail now?"

"Almost fourteen months. It doesn't really seem that long, when I think about it. But I know it's going to be hard to leave the Trail."

"Fourteen *months*." Tiger Cakes shook her head. "I can't even imagine."

"Where are you guys on the Trail?" I asked them.

"Quite a ways back." Sing-song looked a little sheepish. "New York, actually. Bear Mountain Zoo. We're gonna hike up to Maine from here, so we can finish before the Mountain closes, and then we'll go back and fill in that section." Northbounders had already started referring to Katahdin as "the Mountain," as though to mention its name might jinx their chances of reaching it in time. Baxter State Park would close for the winter on the fifteenth of October. Any thru-hiker who failed to reach it by that date would have to postpone the climb until the next summer.

"It's gonna be kind of strange, finishing our thru-hikes in a city zoo," Sing-song said.

"Yeah," I said. "I'm gonna finish mine, at least connect the dots, when I get to Hanover."

"I thought you hiked southbound last year," Tiger Cakes said.

"I got injured and missed about two hundred miles. Hanover to Great Barrington."

"And after that you still hiked through the winter and everything?" Sing-song shook her head. "Man, you must be tough."

"Tough or stupid," I said. "The jury's still out."

Isis and I camped in the woods next to Mudman's vegetable patch, and in the morning Sheltowee and Dodger drove us back to the trailhead by Dan Quinn's barn.

"We're off to Kentucky to start our great adventure!" Sheltowee called through the window.

"Wahoo!" Dodger added.

"Best of luck," Isis and I called after them as the van pulled away. I tried to imagine what it would be like to spend six years on the road, on various trails, wandering without a fixed address. I found that I couldn't picture it.

Fifteen months would be enough. This year, when winter came, I would be happy to have a roof over my head that wasn't made of thin nylon or corrugated tin. I would be glad to have four walls, windows, and a door that I could close on the weather.

We crossed the road and started up the steep hill on the other side. A few hundred yards up the slope, a trail angel had left a cooler full of sodas. Only a few of them remained.

"Let's leave them for someone else," I said. "We've had so much magic lately."

When we found a rich patch of blackberries at the top of the next ridge, fat black clusters of fruit drooping down over the path, it felt like instant karma.

We camped that night in a clearing near Thistle Hill Shelter. A group of section hikers (recognizable by their huge, ungainly loads) and families out for the weekend had taken over the shelter. I was just as glad to be tenting; hordes of mosquitoes descended at dusk. Toast set up his tarp nearby, and we sat on the forest floor telling stories and joking until the bugs drove us in.

We rose late. I was almost reluctant to start hiking. A strange sense of foreboding filled me, as it had when we walked into Damascus northbound. Hanover was another town that had taken on mythical proportions in our southbound hike; after all the effort I had put into reaching the town as I hiked out of the Whites, more than a year ago, it didn't seem possible that I could just stroll into it. I was excited, too. When I reached the Vermont-New Hampshire line at the Connecticut River, after nearly 3,500 miles of walking, I would have seen every white blaze at least once. I would finally finish my thru-hike. I could picture that bridge with its three posts, that slow curve of river. I remembered the fiery sunset that had lit the state line when I left the Trail there last August, and somehow I couldn't imagine the place in any other light.

Isis, Toast, and I sat on logs by the firepit, eating granola out of our camping cups. The section hikers, a pair of men in their fifties or sixties, scarfed down their breakfast of Pop-tarts and prepared to leave. The older one came forward and tossed a handful of trash into the firepit: ramen and Pop-tart wrappers, a torn Ziploc, used Kleenex. He wiped his hands on his shorts and started to walk away. I noticed a patch sewn onto his bright red pack: Appalachian Mountain Club Life Member. I was speechless for a moment. How could somebody with a life membership in one of the country's oldest hiking clubs show such blatant disregard for camping etiquette?

"Excuse me," I finally managed. "Are you just going to leave that there?"

He gave me a look as though I had spoken out of turn. "What would *you* do with it?"

"Pack it out! Garbage attracts more garbage—if people see that, they'll feel like it's okay to leave all their trash in the firepit. Pretty soon this whole place will be a mess."

"Well, then," the man said, still eyeing me as though I had made a faux pas. He lit a match and flicked it into the pile of garbage. Ugly-colored flames danced over the plastic; the wet Kleenex sizzled.

"Burning plastic makes all kinds of dangerous chemicals," I said.

"Well, don't stand downwind," he retorted. He shifted his pack, cinched up the straps, and walked away.

Toast, Isis, and I watched his retreating back with expressions ranging from puzzlement to outrage.

"Well, I guess that's a reality check," I said. "It seems like, on the Trail, almost everybody's pretty considerate. To other hikers, to the environment. I guess I've come to expect so much *good* out of people. Maybe too much. But why do I feel like *I've* done something wrong for telling him off? *He* was the one who burned his damn garbage!"

Toast's comment was briefer and more to the point. "Jeez, y'all, what an asshole!"

We gathered the unburned scraps of trash and packed them out. Luckily, we didn't have far to go; it was less than five miles to West Hartford, Vermont, where we left the trash in a bin outside the post office. We stopped at the general store for a late town breakfast; the deli counter in the back served heaping plates of eggs and hash browns for $3. We sat on tall stools at the rough wooden counter.

"We can take it real easy today, y'all," Toast said while we waited for our food. "It's just another ten miles to Hanover."

"Right," I said. "And I don't really want to catch up to Mr. Garbage Burner."

"Look, the old register's still here," Isis said, taking the spiral-bound notebook from its place between the menus and the napkin dispenser. She handed it to me. "Check out the entries from last August."

I flipped back through the pages. Suddenly, I began to recognize all the handwriting: Pilgrim and Gollum, the almost-illegible sobo Porkchop. Other southbounders who I knew only from their writing, and from photographs at Harpers Ferry. Then Tenbrooks, Blue Skies, Matt, Waterfall, Blade,

Compañero. When we hiked alone in winter, we had followed all of their register entries like a lifeline, something to tie us to the rest of the world. In the West Hartford general store, I found page after page of entries addressed to me: *jackrabbit, hope you're hopping along again strong as ever . . . Word to the Barefoot Sisters: y'all rock! I hope that foot isn't slowing you down any more . . . jackrabbit, we're thinking of you . . .* I found myself blinking back tears. Here I was, more than a year later, about to finish my thru-hike at last, and the messages had finally reached me.

Isis and I put our sandals on for the final road walk into Hanover. The trail came out of the woods and followed the shoulder of a four-lane highway for a few miles. Cars hummed past, grasshoppers buzzed in the dusty grass by the roadside; the sun spread its warmth on my bare arms. The air had the slightly thick and watery quality that comes before a storm. When I saw the giant green-and-white highway sign marking the exit for Hanover, a sense of nervous expectation and barely concealed joy overcame me. I almost ran the last half mile, down to the bridge over the slow gray water of the Connecticut River. The three well-remembered concrete pylons, topped with polished granite balls, stood like sentinels above their own reflections. The bellies of storm clouds appeared in the opaque water. I looked up to see the real storms looming above the trees on the far bank. I stopped at the central post on the bridge and put my hand, once more, on the square of stone that marked the state line: VT/NH. I knelt down and leaned my forehead against the plaque, hardly believing I was there. A quiet pride glowed inside me: *I've finished the Trail.* For an instant, everything was still. Then a truck rumbled past, shaking the bridge. A mourning dove called somewhere in the forest. I stood up and kept walking: *time to find a place to stay before the storm hits.*

CHAPTER 10

Harry Potter and
the Russian Mafia

Isis

On our way into town, we took a side street over to Panarchy, the frat house where we'd stayed for half the time we'd spent in Hanover southbound. We hoped to set our packs down before going into town for food, mail, and a refill of jackrabbit's antibiotic prescription. Just as we reached the porch, a young man in a Dartmouth t-shirt hurried out the door. He caught sight of us and paused, pursing his lips.

"Sorry," he said. "We're full tonight. We can only take six hikers in the basement."

I wondered if they'd remodeled. I knew there'd been at least ten hikers there each night the year before. The basement floor, as I remembered it, was three or four times as wide as the sleeping platform of the cinderblock Tennessee shelters where a dozen of us had crowded together in winter. Maybe they only had six mattresses. Most lightweight two-person tents were narrower than a twin bed, though; six twin mattresses would be more than enough room for twelve hikers. Besides, we could lay our ground cloths and foam pads directly on the floor if we ran out of cushions.

The student noticed my confused expression. "Fire code," he explained. "Are you staying in town a few days? I can check the sign-up sheet; we might have a spot free tomorrow."

He ducked inside, then reappeared a moment later. "Sorry, we're full for the next three days. You could go inside and sit down for a minute if you want to, though. Get yourselves a glass of water from the kitchen. You could even take a shower if no one's in there. You look like you could really use a shower."

"Thanks," I said, laughing.

"It would be nice to get clean," jackrabbit said to me, "but I think we'd better head over to Alpha Theta and try to secure ourselves a bit of floor space

there. I hope *they* haven't gotten too strict about fire code. Judging by the registers lately, I'd guess there are at least thirty hikers in town tonight. We're in
the dead center of the nobo wave."

We carried our packs five blocks across town to Alpha Theta, only to find
the building locked. I knocked, and a few minutes later, a drowsy-looking
woman in a linen dress and platform heels came to the door. I could see the
blue screen of a television flickering in the curtained lounge behind her.

"What are you doing here?" she asked, her voice full of suspicion.

"We're looking for a place to stay," jackrabbit said. "I thought Alpha
Theta let hikers sleep on the lounge floor at night."

"They did that *last* year," the woman answered. "Before I was here. It
sounded like a real hassle, having strangers in your space all the time. This
year, we voted for an easier charity project."

We're lucky, I reminded myself as we walked back to town, with the thunderheads gathering above us and the dogs in people's yards barking and snap-
ping at us. *At worst, we'll have to walk a mile out of town and set up our tent in the
forest. If we really had no place to go, if we were old and ill, if we hadn't had a chance
to bathe in months instead of days, I doubt any of these clean, well-dressed students
would open their doors to us.*

I thought of a story that Pilgrim had told us when we'd met him and
Gollum for breakfast at the end of Trail Days. They'd stopped in Williams-
town, Massachusetts, to eat a town meal and wash their clothes. There weren't
any restrooms in the sandwich shop or the laundromat, so Pilgrim had walked
over to the college to see if he could use the facilities there. A security guard
had grudgingly directed him to the men's room. While he was washing his
hands, Pilgrim caught sight of his smudged, unshaven face in the mirror above
the sink. He started to wash it, too, but just then, the guard stepped through
the door.

"Don't push your luck," he told Pilgrim, taking his arm and escorting
him out of the building. "This ain't a homeless shelter."

Remembering Pilgrim's story, I counted our blessings. Packs full of high-
tech gear that allowed us to sleep outside with a minimum of discomfort, even
on cold and rainy nights. Money in our wallets and more in our savings
accounts. A direction to our lives—a path that we could follow and feel proud
of. Last but not least, parents who would drive all the way from Maine to rescue us if we got sick or injured.

I couldn't help feeling sorry for jackrabbit, though. She was still thin from
her bout of Lyme disease. After the jubilation of completing her thru-hike

had passed, her face settled into lines of glum weariness that seemed to grow deeper as each frat house turned us away. *She should be taking a shower and resting*, I thought, *not lugging her pack around the hot streets.*

As we set our packs down in front of the pharmacy, thunder rumbled in the distance.

"Murphy sent a welcoming committee," jackrabbit commented dryly, eyeing the approaching stormclouds. "How thoughtful of him."

We left our packs leaning against the side of the building, pack covers on. We'd been inside the pharmacy only a minute or two when the downpour started. After the prescription was filled, we lingered in the aisles, reading the messages on the greeting cards and checking the price of film. Rain sheeted down outside the windows.

"What should we do?" jackrabbit asked.

"Put on our rain jackets and go looking for a place to have dinner, I guess. Or we could wait under the awning until the storm lets up."

"What about a place to spend the night? There's only one other frat that I've heard of that takes hikers—*took* hikers as of last year, I should say. Tabard. The place that we avoided when we were southbound, because it had a reputation as a big-time party house."

I shrugged. "We still have a couple hours of daylight. We can go camp on the other side of the soccer field when the rain stops."

"*If* the rain stops," said jackrabbit.

"Come on, let's go find something to eat."

I stepped out on the sidewalk and glanced around. Our packs weren't there. A river of mud covered the sidewalk where we'd left them.

"Over here." A man with braided gray hair and a short beard waved at us from a wooden bench, under a nearby awning. A large, stocky black lab stood in front of him, resting its head on his knee. It was Mala and his dog, Tucker. Our packs sat on the bench behind them.

"I was afraid your gear would get wet," he said, gesturing toward the muddy sidewalk.

"It'll get wet sooner or later," jackrabbit said grimly. "Looks like we'll be sleeping in the rain tonight. But thanks for getting it out of the mud."

"You're not planning to hike out today, are you?" Mala asked. "Willie and me just got here, and Baltimore Jack's coming in tomorrow night. Party at Tabard House."

"We can't find anywhere to stay," I told him.

"You tried Tabard yet?"

I shook my head. "After the other two places turned us away, I kind of figured it would be full. Or closed to hikers."

"Tabard? Never. It's the first frat that took in hikers, way back in the seventies. It's a Trail institution. The kids there'll be delighted to meet the Barefoot Sisters." He stood up and slung jackrabbit's pack over his shoulder. "Looks like the rain's letting up now. C'mon, I'll take you over there."

The rain stopped completely as we followed Mala across town to Tabard House. By the time we turned onto the last side street, the storm had blown over and the pavement steamed in the sun. Stately brick and white clapboard buildings lined the avenue, but I could spot Tabard House from the end of the block. A ratty blue tent hung between the columns of the porch, drying. At the other end of the porch, a young woman in duct-taped sneakers played guitar. A student in a summer dress, and another wearing jeans, sat on either side of her, singing along. On the lawn beside the building, a couple of bearded hikers helped a clean-shaven kid in loafers carry bags of charcoal out to the grill.

A fluffy yellow dog trotted over to greet Tucker, and the woman playing guitar looked up.

"Porchop!" cried jackrabbit, waving at her. "And Frankie!" She reached down to scratch behind the dog's ears. "I thought you guys would be weeks ahead of us by now."

"I slowed way down," Porchop answered. She handed the guitar to the girl next to her and walked over to us. "I'm kind of dreading the Whites."

"Join the club," jackrabbit said. "Those mountains are brutal."

"I'm not really worried about them for my own sake, but I'm afraid they'd be too hard for Frankie. So I'm giving her back to her real owner, my friend Matt." She sighed. "He's coming to Hanover tomorrow to pick her up."

Frankie, who'd been investigating a flower bed with Tucker, perked up her ears when she heard Porchop say her name. She trotted back to Porchop and looked up at her with wide, dark eyes.

"Yeah, you." Porchop squatted down and took the dog's head between her hands. Frankie licked the tip of Porchop's nose, then backed away. Her tail waving like a flag, she hurried off to see what Tucker had found in the roots of the ivy.

"She'll be just as happy with Matt as she is with me," Porchop said, "but I'm going to be pretty lonely without her."

"This part of the Trail will be lonely for us, too," I said. "We had miserable weather the last time we went through, but there was always something to laugh about. We were hiking with Waterfall, our best friend southbound."

"Yeah," jackrabbit said. "Those early sobo friendships formed so quickly. It reminded me of the year I was five, when our family lived in student housing at the University of Michigan—all of a sudden, we'd moved to a neighborhood where all the kids were as weird as me. Isis and I met Waterfall in the Wilderness, and we wanted to hike the whole Trail together. Northbound, we've met a lot of great people, but we haven't hiked consistently with anyone except the Stage Crew, way down south."

"The Stage Crew?" asked Porkchop. "Luna, Six-string, Basil, and Toast? I hiked with them for a week, starting in Troutville. It was one of the best parts of my hike so far. We built a campfire and sang bluegrass songs every night, except the night of the thunderstorm."

"*The* thunderstorm?" jackrabbit asked. "As far as I remember, there was a thunderstorm every other day when we hiked through that area."

"There was only one like that. We were camped at Seeley-Woodworth Shelter; we'd stopped early because we could hear the storm coming, thunder bouncing around the clouds for at least an hour before it struck. About five in the afternoon, the sky went black and the rain just came pounding through the trees. Frankie and I dove for our tarp. We'd been under it for maybe half an hour when I heard a loud sizzle and the sound of cracking wood. It sounded like a tree was falling right nearby, but I couldn't see anything through the rain. I didn't know whether to run or stay. A second later, the tree crashed down, right between my tarp and Toast's."

"*That* storm," I said, remembering. "Jackrabbit and I saw it from our aunt's porch. We were at Seeley-Woodworth the next day."

"We must have been within a week of each other for most of the Trail," Porkchop said. "It's funny that we never really met until Kent."

Just then Mala, who'd ducked in the open door of the building as soon as we arrived, reappeared on the porch, followed by a tall young woman with dreadlocks.

"This is Leslie," he told us. "She's in charge of the place this summer. Leslie, you got room for these girls?"

Leslie eyed me and jackrabbit critically. "I might." Then her face split into a grin. "Don't look so worried. Of course we've got room for you. Come on in."

She led us down a narrow staircase into the basement. I blinked my eyes to adjust them to the light, which filtered in through a few small windows high on the wall. I didn't see any hikers, but sleeping bags and packs covered most of the fifteen or twenty mattresses that lay scattered across the floor.

"The showers are two floors up, on the left," Leslie said. "They're coed, but you can just put a sign on the door if you don't want the guys walking in. The kitchen's over in that corner." She gestured to a wide alcove at the end of the basement room. It looked relatively clean for a college dorm kitchen: no piles of dirty dishes in the sink, and no old sandwiches molding on the counters.

"If you need anything, holler. Someone'll know where to find me." Leslie gave us a quick smile, then bounded away up the stairs. Jackrabbit and I set our packs down next to a free futon in the middle of the floor. After we laid out our sleeping bags, jackrabbit went upstairs to rejoin Porkchop on the porch. I decided to explore the basement a little more. I checked out the kitchen: only three dishes lying in the bottom of the sink. Half a free shelf in the refrigerator. Plenty of pots, bowls, and serving platters stacked on the shelves. I could really cook something, if I found the time.

There was a short hall next to the refrigerator, with a door on the right-hand side standing slightly ajar. I pushed it open and looked in. Wee Willie sat on a huge, bowed couch, leaning forward to trace a line on a piece of paper spread in front of him. He glanced up and smiled at me.

"Want to see my map?" he asked. "I'm makin' a map for my book."

I sat down beside him and looked at his drawing. Two long, curved lines seemed to be coastlines; whales spouted and leapt in the narrow strip of sea between them. Dotted lines crisscrossed the continents, between the upside-down V's of mountains, the windowed squares of houses, and other, more abstruse symbols: spirals, diamonds, birds with two or three pairs of wings.

"I didn't know you were writing a book, Willie," I said. "What's it about?"

"It's about the travels of Wee Willie Prince of Whales. That's my name, but it's also the name of the character, because he's like me. He goes all over the world and has adventures. It's a different world, the one in the map, but it has some of the same trails on it. See—" he pointed to the right-hand continent "—this country here is kind of like America. There's the A.T., and there's the Sheltowee Trace that me and Pirate and Paw-paw hiked last year. We found a big nest of snakes right there—" he indicated a short, wavy line under a mountain "—so that's where Wee Willie fights with a serpent in the book."

"What's the other country?" I asked him.

"That's Vietnam. I got my name there. I was stationed in Nha Trang, and my buddies and me used to sit on the porch of a restaurant near the sea. Some days the whales went by, jumpin' and playin' way out on the edge of the horizon. More than anything I ever wanted in my life, I wanted to be out there with them. They looked as if nothin' ever made 'em sad. I told my buddies I wanted to go out there, and that's when they gave me my name. Wee Willie Prince of Whales."

Jackrabbit and I spent most of the day with Porkchop. Frankie's owner, Matt, came to pick up the dog early the next morning. We took Porkchop out to breakfast at Lou's Bakery, a favorite haunt of Waterfall's, to try to cheer her up. On the way, we stopped by the post office to pick up our mail drops. The New Hampshire maps were missing from our box; our mom had written a quick note explaining that she hadn't been able to find them in the packages we'd sent home.

"I guess we'll have to buy new ones," I said.

"They're pretty expensive," jackrabbit replied. "Can't we just use the *Data Book*?"

"I haven't used anything but the *Data Book* so far," Porkchop put in, "but a friend of mine who hiked last year told me I really ought to get the maps for New Hampshire. He said the Trail through the Whites is unblazed in places, and it can get pretty confusing if you don't have a map."

"He was right," jackrabbit said. "We followed one ridge for three miles without seeing a single blaze. And there are lots of places where the A.T. is labeled different things on the signposts: the Kinsman Ridge Trail, or the Crawford Path. In one place, it's called the Fishin' Jimmy Trail."

Porkchop giggled.

"Maybe we could buy one set of maps and hike together," I suggested. "If we've been within a week of each other for most of the Trail so far, our paces must be pretty similar."

"That sounds great," said Porkchop. "If I have you guys to hike with, I won't miss Frankie so much."

Jackrabbit smiled. "Excellent. Let's go buy a round of milkshakes to celebrate."

At the Hanover Co-op, we finished our resupply and bought a picnic lunch and spaghetti to cook for dinner. Porkchop and I got ingredients for blueberry pancakes so we could make breakfast for the whole Tabard crowd the next morning.

In the afternoon, we looked for maps. The outfitter was completely out of them, and the bookstore only had one: a small yellowish sheet showing all the trails in the southern half of the Whites. The one that twisted back and forth along the tops of all the ridges was labeled with an occasional A.T. symbol.

"I guess this'll have to do." Jackrabbit picked it up and headed over to the checkout counter. She paused halfway there, in front of a rack of paperback bestsellers. "Hey, Porkchop, have you ever read *Harry Potter?*"

Porkchop shook her head.

Jackrabbit winked at me. "I think I could carry another pound or two."

Jackrabbit started reading the first chapter of *Harry Potter and the Sorcerer's Stone* aloud while Porkchop and I cooked dinner at Tabard House. After a few pages, she put the book down to chat with Mala, Willie, and Baltimore Jack, who came in to get some beers they'd left in the fridge. As we talked, another hiker came into the kitchen: a stooped man whose long gray hair hid his face. He set a can of Vienna sausages on the counter and started rummaging through the cutlery drawer.

"Is this what you're looking for, sir?" I asked, handing him the can opener.

He looked up, and his face broke into a toothy grin. It was the creepy guy named Mike, who I'd met when I was giving out rhubarb cake, way back in Virginia.

"Rhubarb!" he said in a low, intense voice. "Tonight's my lucky night. I was in a bad mood, and I wasn't going to talk to anyone. But then a beautiful woman decided to talk to me!"

"I talk to everyone," I answered lightly. *Don't feel special*, I wanted to add.

He frowned. "Then you're not as discerning as I am. I only speak to people who I like." He gazed at me intently, running his tongue over his cracked lips. "And I like you."

"Excuse me," I said, looking away. "I have to finish cooking."

"I'll be around later," he whispered.

He grabbed his can of sausages and retreated up the stairs.

"Looks like you've got yourself an admirer," Mala joked.

"He likes you, all right," said Baltimore Jack. "Willie and I were drinking with him this afternoon, when you walked by the bar. He started talking about how you'd given him cake way back in Virginia. Guy said he'd never forgotten you."

"Your hair," added Willie. "He kept talking about the way it looked in the sunset." Willie winked at me, and all three of them laughed.

I shook my head, sighing. "Guys, this is not funny. That man frightens me. I'm not happy to be sleeping in the same room with him."

Mala's face turned serious. "I'll give you and jackrabbit the mattress that me and Tucker were using. We'll put it against the wall and Willie'll sleep next to it. I'll sleep at the foot. That guy'll have to trip over both of us to get near you."

"I'll take him to a bar tonight," Baltimore Jack offered, "and drink him under the table. He won't be able to see straight by the time he gets back here."

Jack's plan must have worked, because Creepy Mike didn't show up for the rest of the evening. Barricaded behind jackrabbit and the Hobos, I fell asleep as swiftly and easily as I usually did on the Trail. I had nightmares, though—dreams in which I ran through subterranean passages by the flickering light of torches, trying to find my way out. Drafts of cold air blew the flames out one by one, but I couldn't find an opening. When the last flames died, I stood still in the darkness. Suddenly, I felt a chilling certainty that I wasn't alone.

Something smooth and damp pressed against my face. I opened my eyes, my breath catching in my throat. By the dim predawn light, I could see a dark form looming over me: Tucker, trying to reclaim a space on the mattress he and Mala had shared the night before.

"Silly dog," I whispered, moving over to let him lie down. He nudged my cheek once more, then backed away, no longer interested. Without Tucker blocking my view of the room, I could see that there was one other person awake. Creepy Mike, his back to me, was packing his gear. In another minute he'd left, tiptoeing past the sleepers and up the stairs. Perhaps Jack and the Hobos had made it clear to him that he wasn't welcome at Tabard, or perhaps he was simply an early riser by habit. I didn't care which; I was just glad to see him go.

Once most of the other hikers were awake, Porkchop and I started cooking pancakes. Jackrabbit made a fruit salad, and Charlotte, who had come in the day before, fried some bacon for the meat-eaters. Her dog, Zero, a black-and-white husky mix with long, silky hair, sat at the edge of the kitchen floor waiting for the scraps and caresses we all found time to give him. One of his large ears stuck straight up, and the other flopped over, giving him an expression of polite inquisitiveness.

"Are you hiking out today?" Porkchop asked Charlotte, casting a wistful glance at Zero.

"Nope, I have to wait for my brother and his girlfriend." She gave a good-natured chuckle. "That's the trouble with havin' my dog back. Every-one wants to hike with *him*, not me."

"I'm sorry." Porkchop smiled ruefully. "I had the same problem when Frankie was with me."

Just as I was putting the last of the pancake batter on the griddle, Balti-more Jack woke up. He gave a yawn that sounded more like a bellow, stretched, and staggered over to the kitchen. I wondered if he really had tried to out-drink Creepy Mike; with his rumpled clothes and the dark bags under his eyes, he looked somewhat the worse for wear.

"You're just in time for breakfast," I greeted him, holding out a plate of pancakes.

"Thank you," he said, taking a few off the top of the stack. "I'll try them. But I *always* cook my own breakfast when I'm in town."

While I washed dishes, he broke a dozen eggs into a frying pan and cooked what must have been a sixteen-ounce steak in another. He scraped the eggs onto a serving platter and draped the steak across them.

"Now *this*," he said, leaning back against the counter and digging in with a fork, "*this* is what I call a breakfast."

Porkchop, jackrabbit, and I stayed in town long enough to catch the all-you-can-eat lunch buffet at the Thai restaurant—and to give Creepy Mike a good head start. When we finally left, we hiked slowly, dragging our feet in the last stretch before the Whites. Still, we were all in a cheerful mood, telling each other stories about our adventures with the Stage Crew and singing snatches of bluegrass songs as we walked. Porkchop had a lovely voice, strong and clear even when we were going uphill.

We stopped for a second lunch of apples and cheese a few miles out; it was only two and a half days' hike to Glencliff, so we had plenty of luxurious foods. Three or four hikers passed us while we ate. All of them had a hard time figuring out which way the Trail turned just before the rock we were sit-ting on. (It wasn't very clear in that place; in fact, we'd decided to stop there after getting temporarily lost on a side track that petered out twenty yards into the bushes.)

The first person to walk up the trail was Toast. He glanced to the right and left, trying to figure out which path was the A.T. Then he noticed us.

Without a word, all three of us flung out our right arms in a theatrical gesture, pointing the way.

"Purtiest Trail marker I've seen yet," said Toast, looking a little dazed. "Thank y'all."

With each consecutive hiker, our gesture became more exaggerated. After they passed, we looked at each other and collapsed in a fit of giggles. *This is going to be fun*, I thought to myself. *This is going to be a lot like hiking with Waterfall.*

jackrabbit

Porkchop hefted her gray pack after we finished lunch. "This feels so heavy," she said. "I carried my Go-lite pack from Damascus to Hanover, but with all my cold-weather gear I had to switch to this Gregory again. Oh, well." She gave a musical laugh. "This'll make me stronger. By the time we reach Katahdin, I'll be a lean, mean, hiking machine."

"You already are, Porkchop," I told her. She had the wiry, muscular build of a distance runner. "I just hope we can keep up with you."

"Oh, it shouldn't be a problem. Your legs are about twice as long as mine."

Amazingly enough, our paces matched almost exactly. Porkchop hiked between me and Isis, just like Waterfall had. Our conversation ranged from the bizarre to the profound. Porkchop told us about her journeys with the youth group, and Isis and I told stories from our hike and our earlier adventures. In the evenings, we made camp and took turns reading *Harry Potter* as we cooked dinner. Sometimes we sang songs, Porkchop's lovely voice blending with ours and the sound rising up through the dark trees.

On our second night with Porkchop, we camped at Hexacuba Shelter. Built in a hexagonal shape and large enough to sleep probably twelve hikers, it was one of the most beautiful shelters on the Trail. The open front looked out over a hillside of white birches. A few leaves already showed yellow with fall; it was late August, almost September.

"I love this part of the trail," Isis said to Porkchop. "The Dartmouth Outing Club maintains about seventy-five miles. They build the most creative shelters. Like this one. A nobo last year told me it was a Dartmouth architecture class project."

"Why a hexagon, I wonder?" Porkchop said.

Isis considered. "I think because we're right next to Mount Cube. They wanted to do a Pythagorean theme. It has a penta-privy."

Porkchop grinned. "Excellent."

"The privies around here are really works of art," Isis continued. "The D.O.C.'s best work, if you ask me. The one at Ore Hill has a drawbridge!"

"Their trail signs are pretty good, too," Porkchop said. "I liked the one we saw this morning: *Scenic Viewpoint: Beware of Tourists.*"

I did my best Crocodile Hunter impression. "Crikey! There are *tourists* everywhere down here! I've never seen so many in my *life!*"

Porkchop slipped seamlessly into an imitation of Terry, the Croc Hunter's mild-mannered wife. "Just like Steve said, the woods are full of tourists this time of year."

"Crikey! Aren't they bee-ootiful!"

"Like any other wildlife, tourists can get dangerous if they're startled, so it's really important to move slowly and speak quietly and—"

"Hand me a stick, Terry! A *bigger* stick!"

We broke down laughing.

"Ah, Porkchop," I said. "It's really fun hiking with you. I haven't laughed this hard since we were with the Stage Crew."

"Yeah, I miss the Stage Crew, too." Porkchop laughed. "Did I ever tell you about the Cove Mountain Catapult?"

"The what?"

"Well, it was the first night I ever camped with the Stage Crew. There was another hiker at the shelter named Porkchop."

"Not the southbound Porkchop of 2000? The guy whose handwriting looks like a fourth grader's on crack?"

"The same," she said. "Only now he's Old Porkchop. I defended my right to the name. There can't be two Porkchops, after all."

"How'd you decide the contest?" Isis asked.

"Well, I was cooking dinner at Cove Mountain Shelter with the Stage Crew when this guy came up. He said, 'Hi, I'm Porkchop.' I said, 'No, *I'm* Porkchop.' He said he was just hiking a section that year, but he'd already thru-hiked so he had a prior claim to it. Then Toast and Basil started shouting, 'To the catapult! To the catapult!' I didn't know what they were talking about. I was a little worried, actually, 'cause I'd just met those guys." She grinned, her dimples showing. "It turned out to be this fallen tree that had kind of a Y where you could stand with one foot on each branch. Then two people would bounce it up and down. The trick was to stay on as long as you could, and not get catapulted. Toast said the record was seven bounces. Old Porkchop stayed on for eight, and they were all saying, 'Pressure's on, Little

Porkchop!' They wanted to call me Little Porkchop, but I didn't like that name. I may be small, but I am mighty!" She made a muscleman pose.

"So how long did you stay on?" Isis asked her.

She gave a slightly guilty smile. "Fourteen bounces. By that time, Basil and Six-string were tired. They dubbed me Queen of the Catapult, and I got to keep my name." She shook her head fondly. "Stage Crew. Those guys were great."

Crossing Mount Cube in the morning, we hiked in and out of cloud layers. Horizontal bands of early sunlight illuminated the pearl-colored underside of the sky, before the sun rose higher and the clouds swallowed it. Overnight rain made the rocks shimmer: open slopes of pale gray marble with veins of red that twisted into patterns like dragons on a Chinese vase.

On the highest peak of Mount Cube, we found an old register stored in a tube of PVC pipe, tied to a stunted spruce tree. Isis sheltered the notebook with her poncho to protect it from the thin rain while we read.

"This goes back to last August," she said. "Oh, look. Here's a message from a nobo who must have heard about us."

I leaned in closer to see the faded handwriting: *If you hiked up here, you're hard-core. If you hiked up here with a pack on, you're double hard-core. If you walked up here barefoot with a pack on, you are triple hard-core and a bag of chips and I salute you.*

"That's one thing we didn't warn you about, Porkchop," I said. "We get a lot of attention. Usually it's kind of fun, but coming through the Whites last year, it got to be unpleasant sometimes. People could be really rude." I told her about the man who had taken a picture and asked Waterfall why she was in the frame. "Being our shod companion, you'll probably have to put up with a lot of crap like that."

Porkchop just laughed. "Your shod companion. I like that."

In the year since we had stayed there, the Hikers Welcome Hostel in Glencliff had changed quite a bit. The old barn was freshly painted. The backyard had an impressive set of stone benches around the fire ring, a pavilion for cooking in the rain, new carefully leveled tent sites, and several flower beds. Inside, the barn had new mattresses and bunks, and a bookshelf to hold the collection of *National Geographic*s and dog-eared paperbacks. Isis, Porkchop, and I claimed bunk space in the loft and went downstairs.

"A guitar!" Porkchop exclaimed. She gently lifted the instrument down from the wall and began to tune it.

"Isis and jackrabbit! Welcome back!" It was Big John, the hostel owner. He caught us up in a giant hug. "Great to see you! I've heard rumors you were headed this way for months. You guys are just in time for the pizza run, if you're interested."

Porkchop put the guitar down reluctantly, and we joined the crowd of hikers in Big John's van: Charlotte (a.k.a. Purple Hooters), Sing-song and Tiger Cakes, Johnny Steel, Toast, and a few other nobos I didn't know. Just before the van left the driveway, a pair of large men came running up the road from the direction of the trailhead.

"Stop the van! Stop the van! Goin' for pizza? Y'all better give this blue-blazin' Hobo hiker trash a ride!" It was Mala and Wee Willie. Big John idled in the driveway while we made room for them in the backseat.

"Good to see you guys," Mala said as he wedged into the seat between me and Isis.

"Good to see *you*, Mr. Brühiker," I replied. "Are you and Willie planning to hike the Whites?"

"Naw, not this year. Too many damn tourists up there. Think we'll go down into the Great Gulf Wilderness around Mount Washington instead, blue-blaze around a little. There's shelters back in there and everything, but you never see another person for days. Oh, but we got plans for tomorrow. We're gonna go up on Moosilauke and set a record."

"A record for what?" I asked with a little trepidation.

"Long-distance Cog mooning!" he crowed triumphantly. He raised his voice so all the hikers in the van could hear. "You guys know about the tradition of mooning the Smog Railway?"

A few hikers answered in the affirmative.

"It's the most fun I had in the Whites last August," Isis said. "We even started a secret society—the other AMC. The Association of Mooners of the Cog."

"Otherwise known," I said in a moment of inspiration, "as AssMoC."

Mala gave a wild hoot of laughter. "Ass-mock! Jackrabbit, you come up with some good ones. Maybe you can help me figure out how to celebrate my birthday in style."

"When is it?"

"Ten days."

"How old are you gonna be, anyway?"

"Fifty-three."

"You should have a kegger," I said. "How many people do you know that have had keggers for their fifty-third birthdays?"

"I like that. Oh, but you know what I oughta do?" His eyes were shining with malicious glee. "I should have a kegger in the woods. On the A.T. Yes! At Rattle River!"

"Perfect," I said. I remembered the flat, two-mile approach to the shelter from Gorham. If there was any shelter on the Trail where it would be possible to pack in a keg, that would be it. And the pool in the river just downhill from the shelter would keep it cool.

"I'll start advertising, putting up signs in the shelters and hostels and things . . . it'll be great. We'll get all the hikers in a sixty-mile radius. I'll have a birthday like nobody else's. I am, after all, Mala Brühiker!"

Back at the hostel that night, we sat around the firepit eating Ben and Jerry's out of the carton. Porkchop and Sing-song played guitar and sang in harmony. Isis and I performed all fourteen verses of "Dig a Hole," by popular request. Charlotte's dog Zero, with his one droopy ear and sweet, befuddled black-and-white face, curled up at her feet, the picture of contentment, while other dogs raced around the campsites. Crickets chirruped intermittently in the grass. For the first time since spring, I had to wear my fleece jacket; away from the fire, the night air felt bracingly cold. I was glad our mother had sent our cold-weather gear to Hanover.

I heard a van rumble into the driveway of the hostel as we packed up in the morning. The dogs all began to bark in chorus.

"You've got a visitor," Big John called to us a few minutes later.

I looked up to see a huge red dog barreling toward us. She pulled her lips back from her teeth, grinning, and thrashed her body back and forth with excitement.

"Annie?" I said. Then I spotted the bearlike man standing behind her. "Heald!" I rushed over and hugged him. Isis followed close behind.

"Thought you girls might be here," he said in his usual deadpan tone. I had forgotten how impassive he could be, and exactly how much space his enormous frame took up. "Jeez, you smell like hikers."

"Sorry," I said as we stepped back.

"It's all right. I kinda like that smell."

"So how are you, Heald?" I asked him.

"Good, now that I'm here," he said. "Out on the New Hampshire coast, ugh, it's such a freak show." He made a face. "Before today, I was working for two months straight without a day off. And how're you guys doing?"

"Good," I said. "I'm just getting over Lyme disease, but otherwise, things are great. Compared to last winter, hiking nobo has been so *easy* . . ."

"Can't wait to hit the Trail again," Heald said.

"You're not hiking through another winter, are you?"

"Yup. I'm hiking south from Greylock after Labor Day. Just like last year."

"Heald, that's hard-core!" I said.

"Naw. *You* guys are hard-core. You been out on the Trail for a whole frickin' year."

"Winter's the hardest part."

Heald sighed. "Believe me, if I had a way to make my money in winter and hike all summer . . ." Then he stopped. "Less people on the Trail in winter. Don't hafta deal with a bunch o' morons filling up all the shelters . . . Hey, I brought you something." He dug around in the back of his van and took out a long, thin cardboard box, wrapped in packing tape. It bulged in odd places. "Anything you don't wanna carry, wrap it up again and I'll send it to your folks or wherever."

"Thanks, Heald. What is it?" Isis asked.

Heald shrugged. "Just a bunch of stuff from the shop that I run. I forget what-all's in there; I was drunk when I packed it. Open it."

Isis cut the tape with her pocket knife and lifted the lid. I peered over her shoulder. The box was full of bags and packages and smaller boxes. She opened a paper bag: mood rings, beaded earrings, little silver toe rings inscribed with bare footprints. "Oh, Heald, you shouldn't have!"

I opened one of the small rectangular boxes, expecting to find a necklace, but instead I found a slender dagger with an intricately carved wooden handle. "Cool!"

"There's probably a lotta stuff like that in there," Heald said. "Whatever I couldn't sell at the shop."

We kept opening packages: balloons and party hats, candles, daggers and knives, throwing stars, even a full-sized Japanese katana.

"Heald, this is like Christmas all over again!" Isis said.

"Like an evil ninja Christmas," I said.

Heald picked up one of the remaining little boxes and handed it to my sister. "Check this one out. The Dagger of Isis." A pewter figurine of the Egyptian goddess adorned the handle. "I couldn't find nothing with a rabbit on it, 'cept for this." He handed me a silver lighter with a hare engraved on the side.

"Thanks, Heald." I flicked the switch and a little flame came out. "What does this button do?"

"Careful!" He took the lighter from me and pressed the button. A two-inch blade sprang out. "I had to get rid of these. The cops wouldn't let me sell 'em. I think they're illegal in most states." He made the blade disappear and handed it back to me.

"Uh, thanks."

He gave a rare smile. "I'm just glad some o' those blades ended up with someone who's not a total punk."

Coming from Heald, this was high praise.

Isis

Heald offered to drop us off for a southbound slack over Moosilauke, the first peak in the White Mountains. "You gotta go sobo over it," he said. "You come down the north side, you're gonna blow your knees for sure."

What with the Evil Ninja Christmas party, we got off to a very late start.

"Anyone seen Tiki?" asked Big John, as the six or seven of us who wanted to slack piled into Heald's van. "I think he wanted to go with you guys."

"Who's Tiki?" I asked.

"Tall, Asian-looking guy with a wiry little dog called Jade."

I didn't remember seeing anyone of that description around the hostel, but he sounded like he should be fairly easy to spot.

"I'll go look for him," I offered. "I was going to run back to the sink anyway and fill my extra water bottle."

The hiker sink and showers were set up in the backyard, in an open-air structure made of tarps and two-by-fours. I was halfway across the lawn when the canvas door flap opened and a tall, slender man with golden-brown skin stepped out. He shook a few drops of water from his short black hair, then met my eyes, smiling. I stopped in my tracks, noticing his high cheekbones and small, even teeth. *Uh-oh. Very handsome man. And I'm stuck with the task of telling him to hurry up.*

"Tiki?" I asked.

He nodded, his smile gleaming even more brightly.

"Um, the van's about to leave." I turned on my heel and walked back to the driveway, forgetting about the empty water bottle in my hand.

After half an hour of winding mountain highways, Heald dropped us off at Kinsman Notch, where we'd met Stitches on our southbound hike. Northbound, Kinsman lived up to our memory of it as the least notchy of notches; no sooner had we waved goodbye to Heald, than another van pulled up. Three young women and a man climbed out, tugging coolers and picnic baskets after them. They spread out a lavish picnic on the grass beside the parking lot: baskets of fresh fruit, bowls of a dozen different kinds of salad, sandwiches, and homemade brownies.

"Hikers!" one of the women called out. "Come and eat!"

"We're just slacking today," I told her. "You may as well save the trail magic for people who are really hiking."

"There's more than enough," the man said. "Come on over."

Tiki had already taken off up the mountain, with Jade bounding along beside him. The rest of us took the man up on his invitation, some just grabbing a brownie or a plum, and others sitting down for a bowl of pasta salad. Porkchop, jackrabbit, and I stayed for almost an hour, eating and chatting with the trail angels. They turned out to be a group of friends from Boston College who shared the dream of hiking the Trail someday.

"I don't know when that will be," sighed one of the women. "I'll have to look for a job to pay off my loans when I graduate. But I'm keeping myself in shape, driving out here to hike on the weekends whenever I get the chance."

"It's really generous of you to do trail magic on a beautiful day like this, when you could be climbing the mountain yourself," I said.

"Doing trail magic is even more fun," she told me, and her three friends concurred. "You get to meet all the thru-hikers and listen to their stories. It feels like you're part of the community, almost like you're out there with them. When you're just dayhiking, it's hard to get people to stop and talk."

It was nearly one o'clock when we took our leave of the trail angels. Jackrabbit and I skipped up the Trail, packless and barefoot. Although she wore sneakers, Porkchop easily matched us for agility, leaping from boulder to boulder. Every once in a while, where the trail widened in a dry stream bed, the three of us would break into a short sprint, racing each other over the rocky ground. We stopped to take pictures of the waterfalls, and to joke about the Dartmouth Outing Club's clever trail signs. *THIS TRAIL IS EXTREMELY TOUGH*, read a sign just before the biggest waterfall, a thin plume of spray cascading down fifteen or twenty feet of stone beside the A.T. *If you lack experience, please use another trail. Take special care at the cascades to avoid tragic results.* Porkchop posed beside it, her hands fanned out and her mouth gaping in mock terror at the threat of "tragic results."

Stone staircases, built from giant blocks of granite, led up the mountain beside open cliffs crossed with waterfalls. To keep ourselves amused on the steep ascent, we told all the jokes we could remember, beginning with mild ones and moving quickly to dirtier territory. I had just given the punchline to a particularly bad one when Creepy Mike appeared on the step above us.

"I like your sense of humor," he told me, smirking.

I glared up at him. "I wasn't talking to *you*," I snarled, not bothering to disguise the fury in my voice. "Get out of my way."

"Okay, sure," he mumbled, lowering his eyes and moving to the side of the stone platform.

I walked past him with my back stiff, careful not to let my shoulder touch his. Porkchop and jackrabbit followed. A quarter mile up the hill, we stopped at a stream to filter water.

"What did that guy *say* to you?" Porkchop asked. "You sure didn't cut him any slack."

"It wasn't so much what he said that time," I told her. "He's been follow-ing me around, and he's a real creep. I kept on being polite to him, partly because I felt sorry for him. And partly because I'm a snob. I felt like it was beneath my dignity to tell him off. I was hoping he'd just go away if I ignored him long enough."

"I bet he'll go away now," jackrabbit said. "If you ever directed that much anger at me, I wouldn't stop running till I hit the next state line."

She was right; that was the last I saw or heard of Creepy Mike.

From the meadows at Moosilauke's summit, we could see all the ridges of the Whites stretching away to the northeast under a cloudless sky. Jackrabbit pointed out the mountains to Porkchop.

"Those are the Kinsmans, in the front. The Trail winds along the top of them, drops into a notch, then goes over those really jagged mountains behind them. That's Franconia Ridge: Little Haystack, Lincoln, and Lafayette. And that tall one way off in the distance, with the plume of smoke rising from it— that's Mount Washington."

"Why is there smoke on top of Mount Washington?" Porkchop asked.

"Ahhh. That's the Cog Railway." Jackrabbit rubbed her hands together. "Remember what Mala said in the van last night? We thru-hikers have a way of dealing with it."

I shot half a roll of film from the summit of Moosilauke. *We'll be in the Whites for the next seven or eight days*, I thought, *but this might be the last we see of them, besides the four feet directly in front of us at any given time. Might as well take the postcard pictures while I can. This weather is far too beautiful to last.*

The sky did cloud over the next day as we hiked into the Kinsmans. To make matters worse, jackrabbit's knee, which hadn't bothered her since Tennessee, began aching as we climbed the shoulder of Mount Wolf. I tried a little Qi Gong on it, but without our mother there to encourage me, I found it hard to believe in the healing power of air and hand motions. Jackrabbit waved me away, impatient; apparently, she couldn't feel the invisible energy either. Conversation worked better; jackrabbit seemed to forget her pain as she explained Murphy to Porkchop, and told her how his Law applied to New Hampshire weather. In the last mile before Lonesome Lake, though, she limped along silently, leaning on her hiking sticks. I knew what she was thinking: the White Mountains had defeated her last time, injuring her so badly that she missed part of our southbound hike. Would they prevent her from completing her northbound hike, too?

I knew we were close to the hut when I spotted the stealth site we'd shared with Waterfall last summer. The three of us held a brief conference. None of us wanted to do work-for-stay, but Porkchop wanted to check if anyone we knew was staying at the hut.

"Besides," she said, "I've heard that the hut crews sometimes sell leftover baked goods to the hikers."

We had heard that too; we'd even seen a couple boxes on hut counters labeled *all you can eat baked goods, $1*. They'd all been empty when we came through southbound, though.

"We have to go down there to get water, anyway," jackrabbit said. "We might as well check if there's any food."

We hid our packs behind a boulder, hung our food bags, and walked the last quarter-mile to Lonesome Lake Hut. To my disappointment, I noticed that the "Revegetation Project" signs had vanished from the hut's scraggly lawn; someone must have realized how ridiculous they were. I marched up the porch steps with as much bravado as I could muster, hoping that if I looked supercilious enough, none of the hut employees would question my right to get water from their tap.

There were only a few people in the kitchen and dining area. An older man and a ten-year-old boy sat at a table, poring over a map. Two young men were chopping vegetables, and a young woman with bouncy brown curls was sweeping the floor. As soon as we stepped through the door, she set down her broom and skipped over to us, holding out her hand.

"Hi, I'm Sophie," she said. "I'm the Hut Master here. That's Drew and Ralph." The young men in the kitchen looked up, grinning. One of them waved, and the other lifted half a carrot and saluted with it. Sophie laughed merrily, then turned her attention back to us.

"Are you guys thru-hikers?" she asked.

I nodded.

"Cool! I'd love to do that some day. That's one of the reasons I applied for this job, to learn more about the Appalachian Trail. Come in and sit down. Would you like to buy some baked goods? It's supposed to be all you can eat for a dollar, but you can just put a quarter in the bowl. Whatever you want to donate." She laughed again. "It's our first week here, and we've been baking way too much."

"This is your first week here?" I asked, as she set a Plexiglas box full of cake slices down on the table beside us.

"Yeah, we're the Fall Crew. The Summer Crew just left. Say, would you guys like some tea? No charge; I'm going to make myself some anyway."

We sat and talked with Sophie for over an hour, eating slice after slice of blueberry cake, applesauce cake, and gingerbread. Once they had gotten supper in the oven, Ralph and Drew came over to sit with us too, asking about our hike and telling stories of their own camping adventures. When darkness began to fall, I stood up.

"I guess we'd better head out," I said. "It's getting late."

"Any chance I could interest you in a work-for-stay?" Sophie asked. "We haven't got any hikers tonight. There are only seventeen guests right now, so there's not too much to do. Oh, and Ralph hiked in a bottle of scotch. We're going to drink it tonight and play penny-ante poker."

"Thanks for the invitation," jackrabbit said, "but we were planning to camp out tonight."

"Okay," Sophie answered. "If you camp near here, be sure to stop by in the morning. Breakfast's at eight. We'll probably have leftovers if you come by a little later. Great to meet you all! Thanks for the stories."

All three of us thanked her warmly, and headed back to the stealth site where our packs were stashed.

"Wow, that was great!" Porkchop exclaimed. "I'm almost too full to make dinner."

"Almost?" asked jackrabbit.

"Yeah, almost. Meaning not quite. Meaning, by the time I get my tarp set up and start cooking, I'll probably be ravenous again."

I laughed, remembering how much she'd eaten in Glencliff the night before. A whole large pizza, French fries, a salad, and two pints of Ben and Jerry's. Jackrabbit and I had split a pizza, and we'd each eaten one pint of ice cream.

"Porkchop, Queen of the Hiker Appetite," I said.

"Did you do the Half-gallon Challenge?" asked jackrabbit.

"I tried. There were only two flavors of ice cream available when I went through Pine Grove Furnace. Rocky road, which I hate, and peanut butter swirl. I like peanut butter, and I like vanilla ice cream, so I thought it would be okay." She wrinkled her nose and stuck out her tongue. "Those two flavors really shouldn't be mixed. Ice cream, though . . . the thought of it's making me hungry already."

Once we'd gotten our tent set up, jackrabbit and I decided that we could stand to eat some supper, too. Much to my delight, I found a stack of neatly broken Zip stove wood under a log in the center of the stealth site—maybe even left over from the last time we'd camped there. Porkchop and I cooked while jackrabbit read aloud. Once the food was ready, we potlucked: polenta with vegetables, and rice and beans.

Porkchop gave a contented sigh as she scraped the last of the polenta from the side of the pot. "That hut crew was awesome," she said, "but I'm glad we stealthed. Having the evening to ourselves, reading and listening to the wind in the trees . . . I feel like I've got the best of both worlds."

I woke to a steady drizzle falling through the hemlocks. The foot of my sleeping bag was wet; so was the bundle of clothes I'd used as a pillow. I pulled them on, shivering, and crawled out of the tent. Porkchop had packed her tarp already. She sat cross-legged under her red Go-lite umbrella, eating a granola bar.

"What's the plan of action?" she asked cheerfully.

Jackrabbit's muffled voice came out of the tent behind me. "How 'bout we go to the hut and see if they have extra breakfast, for starters?"

"Okay. I'll meet you there." Porkchop sprang to her feet and jogged up the hill, moving with a runner's easy grace. Jackrabbit and I packed our gear and followed, a little more slowly. Jackrabbit was still limping; no doubt the weight of a wet tent and sleeping bag contributed to her discomfort. When we reached the hut porch, she shrugged off her pack with a sigh of relief. Sophie welcomed us in, ushering us over to a corner table where Porkchop was making her way through an enormous stack of pancakes. A large dish of canned peaches, a bowl of oatmeal, and two more plates of pancakes sat in front of her.

"I'm sorry I don't have time to sit down and talk," Sophie said. "I have to wash dishes. Coffee, juice, and hot chocolate are over on the counter. Help yourselves."

Once we'd taken the edge off our appetites, we debated what to do with the rest of the day. Jackrabbit and I wanted to blue-blaze down to Lafayette Place Campground in the next notch and hang around there for a while, drying our clothes. Afterward, we could hike up a trail called the Old Bridle Path, then reconnect with the A.T. at the top of Mount Lafayette. Porkchop had never blue-blazed before. She wasn't sure that she wanted to start at this point in her hike.

"You wouldn't see the views from Franconia Ridge in this weather anyway," I said.

"Come on, Porkchop, you've got to let us corrupt you," jackrabbit pleaded. "What's the good of hiking with us if you don't succumb to our evil influence?"

"Okay," Porkchop smiled. "Your 'evil influence' has been a lot of fun so far, so I guess I'll let it prevail. I'm going to be living in Massachusetts when I finish the Trail; I can always drive up and hike Franconia on a good day."

The Lafayette Place Campground seemed deserted in the rain, although tents and R.V.s filled almost all of the spaces. The few people that we saw hurried past us, garbed in rain gear from head to foot, staring in horror at our bare legs and soaking shirts. In the camp office, a taciturn woman in her thirties directed us to the laundry room. For the price of a few dryer rounds and some bottled juice from the store, she allowed us to drape our tent across a table and sit in a corner reading *Harry Potter* for three hours. By the time we packed up our gear and hiked out, our tent had dried and the rain had stopped.

The Old Bridle Path ran up a spur of Lafayette, through open birch and spruce woods. It was easy going, a trail graded for horses back when pack animals were used to carry supplies—and tourists—in the Whites. The sky seemed to lighten as we climbed; at one overlook, we could see a spot of sunlight far down in the valley. We reached cloudline just as the spruce forest thinned to alpine scrub. A brisk wind scoured the rock fields above treeline; we put on more clothes and walked quickly. The cold, blowing fog reminded me of our first time in the Whites. This time, though, the hospitality of the campground employees and hut crews made all the difference. After a mile of broken granite and stunted krummholz trees, our blue-blaze took us past Greenleaf Hut. We stopped in to warm up and check if there was anything in the leftover baked goods box. I didn't expect to have such good luck a second time, but to my surprise, the box was full of brownies. For a dollar per person, we ate our fill.

"I'm sorry," Porkchop told the Hut Master. "We almost finished off your brownies."

"Hey, that's fine by me," he answered. "If they stayed around, they'd just get stale, and we'd have to pack them down the mountain with the garbage. Would you guys like some coffee? I just made a fresh pot."

The low, blowing clouds covered the mountains all day. We descended below treeline just a few miles past Greenleaf. Out of the wind, I could stop worrying about hypothermia and enjoy the beauty of the fog-bound land-scape. The Trail climbed up and down a series of small, wooded peaks. Tufts of cloud caught in gnarled spruces, and alpine birches clung to the tops of boulders, their wet bark shining reddish black as if painted with lacquer. We set up camp half a mile shy of Garfield Shelter, in a lovely flat stealth site near the top of a mountain. The peak behind us and the thicket of spruce trees to the east sheltered us from the wind, but the ground fell away so steeply to the south and west that I felt like I was camping on a castle parapet.

jackrabbit

The cold, rainy weather continued as we hiked through the Whites. I began to wonder if I would ever see in real life the views that the post-cards advertised. This time, though, we knew the trails and springs and stealth sites well. We didn't get quite as concerned when the white blazes disappeared for three miles on Garfield Ridge. Although we missed Waterfall, we had good company; Porkchop's quirky sense of humor matched ours.

One afternoon, as thick mist swirled through the trees, we worked our way down another precipitous slope. My knee gave a few unpleasant twinges. It felt better than it had in our first few days in the Whites, but I didn't want to take any chances.

"You guys go ahead," I said. "I'll meet you down where it levels off. I've just got to take it slow for a little while."

"You sure?" Isis asked.

"Yeah, I'm sure. I don't think it's much farther, anyway."

Isis and Porkchop hiked on ahead. After a few moments, I heard voices coming from behind me through the fog: Iculus and another man.

". . . and ever since then," Iculus was saying, "I've been totally into Phish. They have this sound that, like, nobody else can copy . . . Oh, hey, jackrabbit. Have you met Tiki?"

"I think we met at that hostel in Glencliff," the other man said. "I met your sister, anyway. I'm Tiki." He was a tall, handsome Asian man with short hair that looked blue-black in the rainy light.

"Jackrabbit," I said.

"And my dog's named Jade," Tiki said. I looked around for a dog and didn't see one. Tiki sighed. "She ran off again . . . Jade! Hey, Jade, girl!"

In a few moments, the jingling of tags came through the mist, and a wiry, compact, gray dog appeared. She had tiny, vestigial-looking ears, a stubby tail, and a coat that looked too short to keep her warm in this raw weather.

"I've never seen a dog like that," I said. "Is she a mutt?"

"A *mutt*?" I thought Tiki was offended, but he started to laugh. "No, she's an American Shar-pei."

"I thought Shar-peis were all wrinkly," Iculus said.

"Chinese Shar-peis are. At least, the official breed, the ones that are recognized by the kennel club and all that. But originally, they were bred as fighting dogs. That's why they have the small ears and hardly any tail, and all that loose skin on their necks . . . Jade's got a bunch of extra skin, too, even though it doesn't show up as much on her. Don't you, girl?" Jade sat obediently, her eyes half-closed, while Tiki gently pinched a fold of skin on the back of her neck and drew it outward. She seemed to have three times as much skin as a normal dog would—it kept expanding, like the hood of a parka. When Tiki let go, though, the skin fell back into place on Jade's spare frame. It was hard to imagine where it all went.

"A friend of mine breeds Shar-peis," Tiki continued. "But a few years ago, she got really fed up with the kennel club standards. Basically, to make the dogs conform to what the breed's supposed to be, to get those big wrinkles and everything, you have to inbreed them. So she was getting beautiful dogs, but they'd have all these hereditary diseases. And they'd end up really dumb. Kind of neurotic. So this woman decided she was going to make a breed that was more like the original Shar-peis. More athletic, smarter. Not bred with their first cousins for fifteen generations. American Shar-peis. That's what Jade is."

"That's cool," Iculus said. "Dude, you never told me about that."

Tiki grinned. "Dude, you never asked."

I offered to let them pass me, since I was still walking slowly.

"No, we'll walk with you," Tiki said. "It's no problem."

Iculus vaulted down a particularly steep outcropping, then turned to watch us negotiate it. I came down cautiously, holding onto a spruce tree with one hand.

"So, Tiki," I said when we were back on level ground. "Is that your real name or a trail name?"

He laughed. "It's a trail name. Who would name their kid Tiki? My real name's Lane."

"Lane?"

"My dad used to be a race car driver."

At the foot of the slope, we found Isis and Porkchop waiting under the limbs of a large spruce tree. The drizzle thickened around us.

"Come and stealth with us," Isis said to the men. "We found a great spot back there in the woods. There must be space for twenty tents!"

"I don't want to camp in the rain again," Iculus said. "It's only, like, half a mile to that hut. Zealand Falls. I'm going to go see if they have any work-for-stay."

"Don't do it!" Isis warned him. She recounted the story of our stay at Madison last summer. "If you do work-for-stay, you sell your soul to the AMC!"

Iculus pursed his lips, considering. "They were really nice to us at that other hut, Lonesome Lake."

The drizzle turned to rain. Fat drops spattered down through the leaves and began to drip down between the branches of the spruce where we stood.

Iculus shouldered his pack. "It can't be all *that* bad."

"I'm with you, man," Tiki said to him. "C'mon, Jade." The dog rose to her feet and gave a disgruntled shake.

"The men are deserting us, Porkchop," I said.

She sighed. "Tragic."

"We still have one who won't leave us, ladies," Isis said. She held up her paperback copy of *Harry Potter and the Sorcerer's Stone*, wrapped in a Ziploc. "Good old Harry."

"Yeah," I said. The rain intensified. "And it looks like Murphy's still with us, too."

We stopped by the hut in the morning to say farewell to Tiki and Iculus—if the Zealand crew kept them working as late as the Madison crew had kept us last year, we probably wouldn't see them again for a long time. To my surprise, we found them sitting down to breakfast with the hut crew.

"Welcome!" called a young man in an AMC apron. "Are you guys thru-hikers too? Awesome! I'm Greg, the Hut Master here." He introduced the rest of the crew. "Do you guys want some breakfast? 'Cause we've got tons of food. If it doesn't get eaten, we have to pack it out. Here, let me get you some plates."

We sat down at the long wooden table. Greg served us stacks of pancakes, bowls of scrambled eggs, coffee cake, and oatmeal with brown sugar. Porkchop finished off a platter of sausages. The hut crew grew quiet as we ate. After a while I realized they were staring at us.

"Do you guys always eat that much?" someone finally asked. By now, all the bowls and serving plates had been scraped clean, even the oatmeal.

Porkchop laughed. "You must not see too many thru-hikers in here."

"Not really," Greg said. "We've been here, like, a week, and there've only been a couple of them who stayed here . . . you know, if you're still hungry, we've got some leftover calzones from last night."

"I think there's some carrot cake, too," one of the hut workers offered. "And some of that rye bread, and maybe a couple of brownies . . ."

Under the incredulous gaze of the crew, we finished off all the leftovers in the hut.

"Hey, good luck to you guys," Greg said. "Have a great time out there on the Trail. And thanks for taking care of the extra food."

"Oh, no problem. Thank *you*." Tiki patted his full stomach.

"Are we done with our work-for-stay?" Iculus asked Greg. "I mean, can we get these dishes or anything?"

"Don't worry about it. But could you sweep out the bunkroom—that is, if you don't mind?"

"Not at all," Iculus said. He and Tiki picked up brooms and headed for the next room. Isis, Porkchop and I thanked the crew for all the food and went out to the porch to wait for the guys. Streamers of cloud rose from the forest as the pale, watery sunlight strengthened.

"I had the craziest dream last night," I said, remembering. "I dreamed we went into a little town and there was no hostel, just a bed-and-breakfast kind of place. Really fancy. So I asked Isis, 'Should we get a room?' and she said, 'Well, I'm getting a room, but not with *you*. *I'm* staying with Tiki!'"

"Fat chance!" Isis laughed. "Me and Tiki? Where do you get these ideas, jackrabbit?"

I shrugged. "Beats me. And in the dream I was so upset, I turned to you—" I took Porkchop by the shoulders "—and I said, 'Porkchop, let's go shopping!'"

We had a good laugh. Porkchop knew that shopping was pretty low on my list of favorite leisure activities. The idea of Isis and Tiki getting together seemed pretty ludicrous, too.

"Really, you're the lucky one as far as Trail romances go," Isis said to me.

"Whatever! I haven't had a single one. Black Forest doesn't count."

"No, but there are a lot more *possibilities* for you. All the guys out here are your age, just out of college. Or even younger. Iculus must be, like, twenty. Old ladies like me and Porkchop—" twenty-six and twenty-seven "—just don't have that many options."

"Tiki's twenty-eight," Porkchop said with a naughty smile.

At this point, almost simultaneously, the three of us realized that we hadn't heard a broom in quite a while. We fell silent, wondering exactly how much of the discussion had been overheard. When the guys came out of the hut, though, they acted as though nothing had happened.

"Was that sweet or what?" Iculus said. "All that food, and all we had to do was wash a few dishes, sweep the floor. The hut people were really fun to hang out with, too. Isis, I don't know where you got your ideas about work-for-stay."

"Madison," she said sourly.

"I think it's partly 'cause it's a new crew," I said. "How long did Greg say they'd been there? Like a week? Not long enough to get tired of stinky thru-hikers. They were still impressed with our superhuman eating powers."

The clouds lifted as we walked from Zealand down into Crawford Notch. Tiki, Iculus, and Porkchop started a vigorous discussion on the relative merits of *Die Hard* and *Die Hard II*. Never having seen either movie, Isis and I hung back, looking at the scenery. For the first time, I caught sight of the cliffs around us. Sheer gray walls of glacier-scraped rock towered a thousand feet above the clusters of birches at their base. Streams and sheets of water left on the cliffs began to glow like gold foil in the sun. Suddenly, I could see why people loved the White Mountains.

By the time we reached the road in Crawford Notch, the sky was fully blue and warm sunlight streamed through the trees. Isis checked the *Companion* as we stood in the parking lot. "There's a snack bar just a mile down the road," she said. "It's some kind of state historical site. I bet they have ice cream. Let's go!"

The place did have ice cream, thirty flavors. Without any consultation, though, all five of us ordered White Russian. Porkchop was the last to emerge from the snack bar. When we all saw her cone, the same rich off-white color as the rest of ours, we broke down laughing.

"What?" she said. Then she noticed. "It's a conspiracy! You were reading my mind!"

"Yes," Tiki said. "We're the mafia. The Russian Mafia."

"I am Boris," Iculus said. He crossed two strands of his long hair under his nose like a mustache.

"Then I am Natasha," I said. "Bor-ees, my darlink!" I licked the side of my ice cream cone just in time to stop a drip.

"What's another good Russian name?" Isis mused. "There was an exchange student at Colby named . . . Natalya! I'll be Natalya!"

Iculus let go of his fake mustache and rubbed his temples. "Darlinks, your names are so very seem-ilar. You are confusink me!"

"I want to be that girl, what's-her-name," Porkchop said. "That tiny little girl who won the Olympic figure-skating championships . . . Oksana! I always thought that was a great name."

"You even look like her, a little," I said. "Tiki, what's your Russian Mafia name?"

He crunched down the last of his ice cream cone and grinned. "I am Vladimir," he said with a bad Russian accent. "Vlad the Impaler." He made a lewd gesture with his hiking poles. Isis blushed.

We ate on the porch of the snack bar, leaning back against our packs. Across the road from the park, a pond mirrored the sheer face of Webster Cliffs, broken into ripples where winds skittered across the surface. When we had finished our ice cream, we looked around the little park: a handful of brown-painted buildings on a square of shabby grass, surrounding an old cellar hole. The stark face of the cliffs loomed up behind us, and scattered blocks of stones from old landslides showed among the trees. Porkchop read the informational signs and reported back to us.

"This is the Willey House Historical Site," she said. "Apparently there was a family homestead here in the 1800s. A landslide came down into the valley one night. The house—that old cellar hole is all that's left now—the house was untouched, but when the neighbors came to check on the Willeys, they were all gone. Vanished. They must have run out of the house and been crushed."

"What an awful story!" Isis said.

"Yeah." Porkchop shuddered. "Reminds me of that night when Toast and I were in our tarps, and that tree came down right next to us. I guess it's a good thing neither of us moved. But can you imagine, lying in your bed at night, and suddenly you hear this awful grinding and rumbling sound of stone coming down from the cliffs . . ."

"Horrible," Isis agreed. "But it's just like New Hampshire to make it into a tourist attraction. This state is so perverse. Did you know they have discount liquor stores on the interstate? And those license plates that say 'live free or die'? I heard they're made in prisons!"

"Come on, New Hampshire's not so bad," Iculus said. "I mean, every state has their own little weird things . . ."

"We had a pretty bad time here as sobos," I said. "Did we ever tell you about the word 'notch'?" I gave a quick explanation of how it had become an expletive. "We got notched over so many times—by the weather, injuries, outdated *Companion* prices, unsympathetic hut workers . . . by the time I got through New Hampshire sobo, I thought I'd never come back here. Once through the Whites was enough for me."

"And here we go again," Isis said with an expressive shrug.

We stealth-camped that night on the shoulder of Webster Cliffs, over-looking Crawford Notch. New Hampshire seemed to be doing its best to dispel our negative impressions. A cloudless sunset cast a fine orange glow over the expanses of open rock, casting the spider-webbing of dark cracks into brilliant relief. As night settled, a host of stars leaped into view, close and innumerable, scattered across the indigo dome above us. The silhouettes of jagged mountains stretched out all around us like slumbering animals, furred with evergreens or scaly with broken cliffs, blending with the edge of the sky at full dark.

Isis

The Russian Mafia hiked together for most of the morning. From an over-look on the Webster Cliff Trail, where we stopped for a snack break, we had a spectacular view of the Presidentials. The southern ridge of them curved away to our left: Pierce, Franklin, Washington. Muscular green ridges, scarred with landslides and topped with a wide tawny swath of alpine meadow and bare stone. Farther away, the weathered granite peaks of Adams and Madison showed through the gaps in the ridge. A single cloud, the only one in the whole sky, perched squarely atop Mount Washington. The highest tower of the observatory peeked over the top of it, all reflective glass and wires. Against the pristine backdrop of the mountains, this one sign of technology looked incongruous and vaguely threatening.

By midday, it was clear that we wouldn't have time to make it over both Washington and Madison in a single day—not if we wanted time to find a campsite below treeline on the other side. Iculus wanted to do work-for-stay at Lakes of the Clouds Hut. Tiki offered to hike ahead to reserve bunk space for the rest of us in the basement room there known as "the Dungeon." Porkchop, jackrabbit, and I followed at a more leisurely pace, stopping to take pictures and examine the thickets of krummholz spruce, the foot-high birches and willows, and the carpet of saxifrage growing between the rocks.

We reached the hut a few hours before sunset. The air was still warm, and the sky completely cloudless. To the north, the bald dome of Mount Washington caught the late afternoon light. Only a mile and a half away from us, and thirteen hundred vertical feet. We could be there in less than an hour. But where would that put us when the sun set? Even on a warm, clear night, it would be hard to follow the Trail through the rock fields around Mount Adams. I remembered one stretch where someone had (accidentally, I hoped) marked the A.T. with blue blazes for a couple hundred yards: confusing even by daylight.

And then there was the weather. I'd seen how fast it could change. I shivered, gazing up at the serene golden dome. The rest of the Presidentials could wait until morning. As for the summit of Mount Washington, it was one place on earth where I hoped never to set foot again. Jackrabbit and I had been planning to blue-blaze around it ever since we decided to yo-yo. A magazine article about Native American sacred sites that Bob had shown us at Kincora had confirmed my feelings about the place. According to the article, the Native American name of Mount Washington meant "forbidden holy place." Native people believed that it was the domain of spirits, where humans should never trespass.

We found Iculus in the hut kitchen wearing an AMC apron; he'd gotten his work-for-stay. Tiki sat at a table nearby, playing cards with two other hikers. I didn't recognize one of them, a thin man in his forties with a bushy beard and round glasses. The other was tall and sturdy with short curly brown hair: Johnny Steel.

"Hey, Barefoot Sisters! And Porkchop!" Johnny Steel exclaimed. "Tiki warned me that we'd be sharing the Dungeon with you. Scary."

The older man stood up and held out his hand. "Hi, I'm Awol," he said. "I'm staying in the Dungeon, too."

"Awol and I have been hiking together," Johnny Steel announced. "I ran out of Republicans when Mark left me behind, so I decided to try a retired navy officer for a hiking partner. He's not that easy to make fun of, but at least he puts up with my attempts."

"We're about to start a new round of hearts," said Tiki, winking at me. "Shall I deal you in?"

"Actually, I'm kind of hungry," I told him. "Do you know if there's anything in the baked goods box?"

"We ate most of the cheesecake brownies," Johnny Steel said, "but I think there might be some bread."

"Bread?!"

Jackrabbit, Porkchop and I made a beeline for the box. There were four or five large brownies in it, and—almost too good to be true—an entire loaf of whole wheat bread. We put our $3 in the bowl on the counter, divided the loaf into three chunks, and went outside to eat them. What with the bread and brownies, and some soup that the hut crew sold us, we didn't have to cook anything that night. We sat on a stone wall at the edge of the hut's courtyard, snacking and taking turns reading *Harry Potter*, until the sun went down in the valley below us. Before the bands of yellow and orange had faded from the western horizon, the moon rose behind us in a pale lavender sky. We watched the first stars flicker into view, before descending to the Dungeon.

The ten-foot-square windowless room, located under the hut's kitchen, lived up to its name. It was furnished with ancient plywood bunks, not even large enough to sit up in, stacked three deep on the south and east walls. Our packs took up most of the remaining space. We left the door open as long as possible; a smell that seemed too foul to ascribe to hiker gear hung in the damp, chilly air.

"So, who wants to join AssMoC, the Association of Mooners of the Cog?" jackrabbit asked the guys as we rolled out our sleeping bags. "It's the *other* AMC."

"Polar Bear told me about that," Johnny Steel said, "but I thought it was one of those crazy Trail rumors. Either that or he was trying to set me up, like he did with that comic book story."

"It's a thru-hiker tradition," jackrabbit told him. "We did it last year."

"You mean you *mooned* someone? You and Isis?" asked Tiki. "And you're going to do it again?" He paused for a moment, and I wondered if we'd scandalized him. He was already lying in his bunk, with Jade curled up beside him; I couldn't see his face in the darkness. "Count me in," he said, with unmistakable glee.

"Johnny Steel?" asked jackrabbit.

"If this is a setup, I'll use all my superpowers to bring the perpetrators to justice!" came Johnny Steel's voice.

"It can't be a setup if we're all doing it together," Porkchop answered.

"Thanks, Johnny Steel," jackrabbit said. "I knew we could count on you. What about you, Awol?"

"Mooning isn't really my style," answered Awol, "but I'll hold your cameras and take pictures if you want."

"Some documentation would be nice," jackrabbit said. "You can be an honorary member of AssMoC."

"Thanks, I guess," Awol told her, sounding somewhat taken aback.

"First you talk me into mooning the Cog, and now you're going to let Awol take a picture of the event?" Johnny Steel said to jackrabbit. "I knew it would be dangerous to spend a night in the Dungeon with you!"

In the morning, we opened the door of the Dungeon to find clouds blowing over the ridge in a stiff east wind.

"I knew Murphy had something up his sleeve," jackrabbit said. "Mount Washington looked far too friendly yesterday. Sure you don't want to join us in a blue-blaze?" she asked Porkchop.

"I want to follow the A.T. for this section," Porkchop said. "Joining Ass-MoC is enough corruption for me, for today."

The hut didn't have too many guests, so the crew let us eat breakfast at a spare table next to the windows. The baked goods box had miraculously refilled overnight, with dozens of huge oatmeal cookies left over from dessert. Four or five of them made a hiker-sized meal. Iculus, who'd been let off early because there wasn't much work to do, came over and joined us. With all of the rest of us encouraging him, jackrabbit quickly persuaded him to join the mooning party. Over breakfast, we planned our raid on the train. Jackrabbit and I would skirt around the side of the mountain, on the trail we'd almost taken after we mooned the Cog with Waterfall. We'd hike a little ways up the A.T., meeting the others where the Trail came closest to the tracks.

Jackrabbit and I hiked with Porkchop for the first mile. Clouds rolled across the mountain, fluffy and white at the top but dark gray on the undersides. Between them, patches of blue sky opened above us. Long vistas of ridge and valley cleared then vanished again. The two ponds that gave Lakes of the Clouds Hut its name reflected the colors of the tumultuous sky, silver and steel and fleeting scraps of blue. The peak of Mount Washington, ahead of us, remained engulfed in fog of a decidedly threatening shade of gray.

Just before our side trail split off, we came to a scratched enamel sign reading:

STOP

The area ahead has the worst weather in America. Many have died there from exposure, even in the summer. Turn back now if the weather is bad.

I took a picture of Porkchop huddling in front of it, umbrella deployed, with the clouds on Mount Washington roiling in the background.

The sky was clearer on the western side of the mountain, out of the wind. As jackrabbit and I followed the blue-blaze across slopes of granite scree, we caught glimpses of the whole range to the south and west of us. Clouds capped each peak and streamed down between them, so that if I squinted, they seemed like much higher mountains, covered with glaciers and the plumes of avalanches. Behind them, the sky shone a hazy blue. We walked in and out of sunlight, the granite slabs cold beneath our feet.

As we crossed under the Cog tracks, the clouds closed around us again. We hurried up the A.T., to the place where we'd planned to meet, and bundled into all our warm clothes to wait. We'd only been there five or ten minutes when the others arrived, hurrying down the mountain.

"It wasn't raining on top," Porkchop reported, "but that wind was *cold*. I didn't want to stick around too long."

A shrill whistle sounded in the valley. Pretty soon, we could hear the steady chug of the approaching train. Awol collected cameras as the other six of us lined up beside the tracks.

With so many of us mooning, it was even more fun than the first time. The Cog passengers laughed and cheered, leaning out the window with video cameras. This conductor didn't look nearly as angry as the one we'd mooned with Waterfall. He was a good aim, though; one chunk of coal hit Tiki squarely on the ass, leaving a black streak that he proudly showed off to anyone willing to look.

So much for making an environmental statement about the amount of coal the Cog is wasting, I thought. *We're probably part of the draw.* I didn't really care, though. We were having fun, and the passengers certainly seemed to be entertained.

The feeling of exhilaration stayed with me for the rest of the day as we scrambled over boulder fields in rising wind and patchy sunlight. We stopped at Madison Hut for lunch. It was a completely different experience from our first visit there, when we'd huddled in a corner of the crowded room, hoping that we might be allowed to sleep on the floor. Now the wide dining hall was almost empty; most of the guests were out hiking for the afternoon. The hut crew sold us soup and bread for a dollar per person, and sat down to eat lunch with us. When we finished off the first pot of soup, one of the crew members went into the kitchen to make another one.

Johnny Steel got into a deep conversation with the Hut Master, who was seated next to him. When the rest of us got up to leave, he announced that he was going to do a work-for-stay.

"Come on, Johnny Steel," jackrabbit chided him. "It's one in the afternoon. We have miles to make!"

"Nope, I'm staying," Johnny Steel said. "This might be my only chance."

"To do what, eat a seventh bowl of soup?"

"You'll see. I'll tell you when I catch up to you. And then, maybe, you won't laugh at me."

The rumor reached us before Johnny Steel himself caught up. A few days later, a hiker told me that Johnny Steel had packed up all of Madison's food for the week, a job usually shared by two or three people. He'd carried four or five pack loads, each probably close to a hundred pounds, up the steep trail from the valley floor. The Hut Master had tried to talk him into an easier work-for-stay, but he had insisted.

jackrabbit

We raced down the shoulder of Mount Madison, running over the slope of broken stones as fast as we could. Thunderheads loomed up over the bald dome of Mount Washington, and we didn't want to get caught above treeline when they hit. A fierce wind rushed up the slope, a force so strong we could use it for balance. We spread our arms against it and leaped from rock to rock. My sore knee seemed to have healed; not even the jarring landings bothered me now.

"This is so fun," Porkchop laughed, yelling over the roar of the wind. "This is—oh, shoot!" She tripped on the edge of a stone block and sprawled forward.

"Porkchop, are you okay?" Isis ran back to help her.

"Oh, yeah, I'll be fine." Porkchop picked herself up, a bit gingerly. Blood dripped from a scrape on her right knee, and her palms were both red from abrasion, but she was smiling. "What a rush! I felt like I was flying. Guess I flew a little low." She laughed and stood up, and in a moment she was running again, faster than before.

The storm didn't hit the valley until after dark. By then, we were safely ensconced in our tarps and tents in a stealth site down in Pinkham Notch.

Rain came down in buckets, sloshing down through the trees, transforming our campsite into a tributary of the nearby creek. After a night like that, the Russian Mafia was ready for a trip to town. We dragged the piles of brush back into our stealth site and walked to the AMC camp by the road at the bottom of the notch.

The sounds of cars and voices came through the woods long before we reached the place. The collection of brown-painted lodges, the restaurant and gift shop, the wide expanse of asphalt, looked just like I remembered. Groups of tourists, mostly dressed in spotless L.L. Bean attire, strolled on the concrete walkways. As our bedraggled crew reached the parking lot, washed-out sunlight began to paint the woods around us. Off in the direction of Mount Washington, though, baleful dark clouds still filled the sky.

Tiki found a pay phone and called all the hostels in Gorham. "Hikers Paradise has free shuttles to here," he reported. "It's twelve bucks a night. They take dogs, too." He reached down and patted Jade.

"Sounds good," Iculus said. He brushed back a strand of his dark, curly hair, which was beginning to look oiled. "I could really use a shower."

Porkchop laughed. "Look at us! I think we all could." It was true. Our bare legs were covered with grime from the wet trail, and even with the cool late summer weather, our clothes bore sweat stains. Porkchop's scraped knee had left an ugly streak of dried blood down her shin. We drew a few stares from the crowd of tourists in the parking lot.

"You know what I want?" Tiki said. "White Russians! First thing when I get to town, I'm going to the liquor store."

"Sounds good to me," I said.

"Pardon me . . ." an impeccably dressed woman came up the walkway. "I saw you come out of the woods a few moments ago, and I just *had* to ask. Are the two of you really hiking barefoot? With those enormous packs? Why on *earth* would you do a thing like that?"

Isis began the explanation. "It feels really good, sometimes, when you're walking in soft mud, or grass, or smooth rocks. And you get better traction than you have in boots. And your feet stay healthy; they don't stink—"

"But . . ." the woman arched her eyebrows. "You get *dirty!*"

"Can't argue with that," I said.

A few minutes later, a young man came up, staring at our mud-covered feet. "Nice *boots*," he said.

"Thanks," I told him. "They were a birthday present."

Hikers Paradise offered a few bunkrooms, a bathroom, and a lovely kitchen, up a rickety wooden staircase from a motel at the west end of town. The décor was straight out of the seventies—mustard yellow, orange, and pea green—but the place looked comfortable, and the price was right. The five of us got a bunkroom to ourselves.

After a quick shower at the hostel, our first stop in town was the supermarket: Grape-Nuts and powdered milk; crackers, peanut butter, and dried fruit; the usual assortment of prepackaged rice and noodle dishes. A loaf of bread and a few apples as treats. Isis, Porkchop, and I picked up ingredients for quesadillas, since it would be cheaper to cook at the hostel than to eat out. We all handed Tiki some crumpled bills, and he added bottles of Kahlua, vodka, and cream to his cart full of hiker fare and dog snacks.

On the way to check out, wrestling with my cart's sticky wheel, I nearly ran into another thru-hiker. (I could tell he was a hiker from his thick beard and disheveled clothing, and the corded muscles of his legs. Most people in the supermarket, I imagined, could have guessed as much from smell alone, but I was so used to my own aroma that I hardly noticed other hikers' funk.)

"Sorry about that," I said, steering the cart aside just in time.

"Oh, no prob . . . hey, jackrabbit! Haven't seen you in forever!"

I thought a moment, studying his curly dark brown hair and round face. He looked thinner than I remembered, but I hadn't seen him since Erwin. "Digger? How are you, man?"

"I'm good, pretty good. I got myself a new trail name, actually," he said. "These days I go by Buttah."

"There's gotta be a story behind that."

"Yup." He looked a little embarrassed. "It was on the way out of Damascus. I went to the Side Track for lunch, and I had soup and a roll. They must've brought me twenty of those little butter packets, you know? And I was like, 'I can't let these go to waste.' So I put as much butter on that roll as it would hold, and I put the rest in my pocket."

"Hope it wasn't a warm day," I said.

"No, the weather was decent. One of those cooler spring days, you know? It would have been fine, actually, except that about halfway up that hill, coming out of town, I took a fall. Ten butter packets all over my shorts, and it was another week before I could do laundry. And the thing was, I was hiking with five other guys at the time. None of them would let me live it down. So that's my name now." He gave a self-deprecating smile.

"Where are you staying in town, Buttah?"

"I'm over at the Barn."

"Aw, we're at Hikers Paradise." The two hostels were at opposite ends of town, more than a mile apart. "Well, I hope we'll meet up on the Trail. Say, Buttah, are you going to Mala's party?"

"That kegger in the woods? You mean it's real?"

"It's totally real. Real as hiker funk. I was there when he planned it."

Buttah shook his head. "This Trail. Just when I think it can't get any stranger. Yeah, I guess I can stick around a few days for a keg party. Maybe I'll go camp at Rattle River."

"Cool. Spread the word—this party's not just a Trail rumor. Hey, it's good to see you, man."

"Yeah. Likewise."

Back at the hostel, Iculus started mixing White Russians while the rest of us chopped vegetables and grated cheese for supper.

"That ought to be enough vodka," he said, filling half the pitcher with it.

"Borees, you vill get all uf us trunk!" I said in my breathy Natasha voice.

"Isn't that the idea?" Tiki said. He took a half-sized can of something out of his shopping bag and started opening it with his pocket knife. An unpleasant aroma drifted into the room.

"Tiki, what *is* that?" Isis asked him.

"Potted Meat Product. Tasty, eh?" He held it up. "I feed a can of this stuff to Jade in every town." The dog appeared from under the table and gave him a pleading look, wagging her stubby tail. "It's actually called Potted Meat *Food* Product. Just to make it clear, I guess. They changed the label a few months ago. Oh, the ingredients are great, too. Look: partially defatted fatty pork tissue, mechanically separated chicken—"

"Partially defatted fatty pork tissue?"

"It used to be even better. Before they changed the label, it was 'partially defatted fatty pork fat.'" He scooped out a lump of the gelatinous meat substance with his Lexan spoon and tossed it in Jade's general direction. She made a spring-coiled leap and caught it in midair. "Good girl. You like that, don't you?"

"Partially defatted fatty pork fat," I mused. "That's got such a nice ring to it."

"Keeps her coat nice and shiny. Helps her keep the weight on, too. I'll have to feed her more of it when it gets cold."

"Ladies, I haff trinks for you," Iculus announced. He passed us tall glasses of White Russians.

After our supper of quesadillas, the drinking started in earnest. Pitcher after pitcher of White Russians disappeared. Our Russian accents degenerated, and our stories became more ribald than ever. I awarded Tiki an Ass-MoC Medal of Valor for his unfortunate encounter with a lump of Cog Railway coal; I traced the AMC logo off a brochure from the hotel downstairs and transposed a few elements of it, adding some extra letters, a train car, a set of tracks, and the stick figure of a mooning hiker.

"AssMoC lives! Pour me another one, Vladimir!" Isis cried, slamming her cup down on the table in front of Tiki.

He lifted the pitcher. It was empty. Tiki surveyed the bottles on the windowsill and sighed. "No more vodka. Haff to make liquor run. Come, Comrade Jade. Top secret mission for us."

Tiki returned sooner than we had expected. I heard his footsteps coming up the stairway outside.

"C'mon back and join the party, sailor!" Isis called. She'd been flirting with Tiki all evening.

Tiki's voice sounded strained. "I can't come in. Jade got sprayed by a skunk. She's out here in the parking lot, stinking to high heaven . . ."

"Tiki, you're hilarious," Isis said.

"No, really, I'm not joking," he said. "Damn dog! She chases everything that moves." Then the stench came up through the doorway, thick and rank, eye-watering.

"Oh, shit, you're serious," Porkchop said. Then she started laughing. We all laughed, drunk and silly, and eventually even Tiki joined in.

"Tomato juice," Isis said when she caught her breath. "It's s'posed to neutralize skunk spray."

Tiki swore. "The grocery store's like half a mile away. Think it's closed by now, anyway."

"Liquor store's not that far," I said. "Bloody Mary mix."

Jade spent the night on the porch, huddled up in a pile of newspapers. The Bloody Mary mix seemed to have reduced the smell a little, but she was certainly pungent by morning light. She was in a foul mood, too, growling at Tiki when he went out to feed her breakfast.

"Whoo-ee! You are one stinky puppy, Jade," he observed. "One skanky, skunked-out dawg." He saw me standing in the doorway. "Jackrabbit, you might know the answer to this. You studied biology, right?"

"Yeah . . ."

"That stuff that a skunk sprays . . . doesn't it come out of the ass?"

I stifled a laugh. "Well . . . it comes out of the musk glands, which are on either side of the, you know, anus. But yeah, I guess you could say it comes out of the ass."

"Skunk ass," he said, almost to himself. "My dog got skunk-assed. Skassed. You know what, Jade? After 1,800 miles, you got yourself a trail name. Skass Dawg. How do you like that, Skassy?"

Jade shifted in her pile of newspapers and let out a throaty growl.

Tiki turned to me. "I don't think she likes it at all."

In the motel restaurant, the waitress came to take our orders. "You guys must be hikers," she said. "Any of you interested in the Breakfast Challenge?"

"What is it, exactly?" Tiki asked her.

She smiled and smoothed down her apron. "Well, if you can finish it by yourself in under an hour, it's free. Otherwise, you owe us ten dollars." She took a deep breath. "It's six eggs any style, six pieces of toast (white or wheat), four pancakes, four pieces of French toast, six sausages, six strips of bacon, three bananas, and an orange. Plus all the coffee you can drink."

We paused for a few moments, imagining that amount of food. I remembered how Blade had vanquished the Stomper the last time we'd been in Gorham. I wasn't eager to see any of my companions do an encore to that performance.

"Has anybody ever finished it?" Tiki asked.

"There was a fellow last year that did. Big strapping young gentleman, came through in August. But he didn't look too good afterwards."

To my great relief, no one took the Challenge. The regular breakfasts were ample enough, anyway: three-egg omelets with hash browns and toast; thick stacks of pancakes; enormous slices of French toast. Plus all the coffee we could drink.

Tiki had to give Jade a few more tomato juice baths before the Hikers Paradise shuttle driver would allow her in the van. Even then, and even with all the windows down, it was a stinky ride. The view was amazing, though. Where the highway crested a ridge, we saw the White Mountains rising all around us under a perfectly clear sky, their saw-toothed, ragged peaks and glacier-scraped flanks looking so close we could touch them.

I was a little nervous about Wildcat Mountain. It was where I had slipped, and with one step prevented myself from hiking the whole A.T. as a south-bounder. Sleepy the Arab had told me that his first northbound hike had ended there. The mountain loomed above the parking lot in Pinkham Notch, a mass of almost-vertical stone with the sun behind it. But the white blazes led up it, and I followed them as I had for more than 3,500 miles.

At first, we hiked in a line: Tiki and Jade (who scrambled up the rocks like a pro—I envied her low center of gravity), Iculus, Porkchop, Isis, and I. Tiki stopped after a few minutes, though.

"You guys go on ahead. I drank too much coffee this morning—got to take a leak."

After a short while, Iculus did the same.

"Boys," Porkchop laughed.

"Well, think about it," Isis said, reaching up to pull herself onto a higher rock ledge. "Out in the woods, they can pee just about anywhere they want to. They don't really *need* any bladder control out here. We women have to be a little more, shall we say, discrete. So we never lose the skill of holding it." Isis and I hadn't mastered Simply Seeking's technique of peeing standing up—the prospect of training accidents, with laundry facilities so far apart, was too daunting.

"Yeah, that was a weird thing I noticed at Trail Days," I said. "There was a line three blocks long for the *men's* room."

I was amazed by how short the climb seemed. We pulled ourselves up hand over hand with tree roots and tiny ledges, clambered up rock steps, scampered across open slopes. In a little less than an hour, we stood atop the first peak of Wildcat Mountain. I wasn't even breathing hard. I felt a surge of strength and certainty fill my frame as I looked out over the valley to the monumental sweep of the Presidential Range. *I can do this. Look what I've already done.*

Porkchop, Isis, and I sat down on a rock, waiting for the men.

"Did I ever teach you *Hava na Shira*?" Porkchop asked. "It's a round." She sang and we repeated it, phrase by phrase. We could almost sing it in three-part harmony by the time Tiki and Iculus came up the trail.

"You three are like sirens," Iculus said. "Always singing a merry tune."

Isis laughed. "You know what the sirens did, don't you, Iculus? They lured sailors to their deaths with their beautiful voices."

"Oh, yeah. Well, I didn't mean you're deadly or anything like that. I just meant you're always singing."

"Excuse me," came a voice from the trail. I looked up to see a man in spotless khakis with a golden retriever on a leash. (Jade growled and the dog slunk back.) "Is this the trail that goes down to the notch?"

"Yup," Porkchop told him. The rest of us were silent, wondering where this apparition straight out of an L.L. Bean catalog had come from.

"Is it a really rough trail? Because I was thinking of taking Bailey down there. But he's afraid of heights."

"Uh, yeah, it's pretty rough," Porkchop told him. "Pretty steep. I don't know about going down it with a dog."

"Thanks," the man said. "I guess I'll go back then."

I was puzzled—I didn't remember the path up the other side being any easier. From what I recalled of the topo map, I didn't think there were *any* easy approaches to Wildcat Mountain. I was even more puzzled when we rounded a bend in the trail and found a family with three small children.

"Quincy! Delaney! Morgan! Let these people go by!" the mother said. She stepped well away from the path, as if Jade's odor were contagious.

The mystery was solved when we came over the crest of the next ridge and saw a gondola, like the one we'd ridden on Killington, ferrying people up and down the mountain. The huge platform where they disembarked was right next to the A.T. For a few hundred yards around it, the trail was full of tourists. The lenses of countless cameras pointed back toward the massif of Mount Washington behind us.

"Crikey!" Porkchop whispered. "The Dartmouth Outing Club never warned us about *this* place!"

"I didn't even know this thing was here," Isis said. It was hard to imagine not spotting that platform—but all I remembered from my last trip up Wildcat Mountain was a tunnel of swirling clouds. "I guess they must not run the gondola on foggy days."

All afternoon, we kept looking back at the Presidential Range. The tourists on Wildcat certainly had a reason to point their cameras in that direction. The huge, curving sweep of stone seemed to fill half the horizon. Forests on the mountain's lower flanks gave way to scarred and blasted rock, sheer cliffs and jumbles of gray stone stacked up and up, lifting to the bright sky. From a distance, the auto road was a tiny zigzag scratch, barely visible, and the summit buildings looked flea-sized, insignificant compared to the wilderness around them.

Our last view of the Presidentials came just before sunset, from the summit of Carter Dome. Late light rimmed the mountains, a thousand harsh and stunning shades of gold and purple. The scene had the same fierce beauty as the Grayson Highlands in winter: splendor and menace in equal measure; the beauty of wilderness. I took one last look as the light began to fade from the sky, and then I turned and walked down the trail, back into the woods.

We stealthed at Zeta Pass, filtering water out of a scummy puddle between the roots of a spruce tree. Shadows thickened under the limbs of the evergreens, and the first few stars glimmered among the feathery branches by the time I had the tent set up. I read a chapter of *Harry Potter* aloud as Isis cooked our pot of rice and beans. My memory strayed back to the night we had spent here with Waterfall, more than a year ago. So much had happened in that time. On the Trail, I had been forced to recognize the limits of my strength. I had also expanded those limits beyond what I had imagined possible. I remembered the pride I had felt when we finished the Maryland Challenge; my elation at the border of New Hampshire when I had finally finished a thru-hike; the sense of strength that had filled me just that morning after racing up the side of Wildcat Mountain. In the darkened campsite, I felt powerful and content.

It was a chilly night at Zeta Pass. For the first time since winter, I pulled my mummy bag up around my head. Skass Dawg, exiled from Tiki's tent, moaned and whined until he let her into the vestibule. All of us were slow to get moving in the morning; somehow the cold put a new edge on our usual hiker hobble.

"Can't take the cold like I used to," I commented as I packed up the tent, jumping from foot to foot in an effort to stay warm. "Maybe I should start eating that partially defatted fatty pork fat, too."

"Wha?" Porkchop mumbled from her tarp nearby. I heard her sleeping bag unzip as she sat up and stretched. "Jackrabbit, were you talking to me?"

I laughed. "No, I was talking about Jade's favorite town food. Remember? Partially defatted fatty pork fat."

"Wow. I *really* wasn't awake." Her musical laughter drifted out into the clearing. I heard the rustle of nylon as she opened her food bag. "Oh! Little Debbie snacks for breakfast!" She yawned. "Time to refat the partially defatted fatty Porkchop."

By now, dawn light slanted between the trees. Chickadees and finches hopped about in the branches, twittering; the chirring call of a red squirrel drifted back from somewhere in the forest. Isis, Porkchop, Tiki, and I sat on logs around the campsite, eating breakfast, but there was no sign of life from Iculus's tent.

"Jackrabbit, what'd you do to Iculus last night?" Tiki said. "You tired the poor kid out."

"Me? Whatever!"

"Boris and Natasha, sitting in a tree . . ." he sang.

I decided to get in on the act. "I luff him," I said in my Natasha voice, low and husky. "My Borees . . . Borees, my darlink," I called out. "Vake up! Borees, ze train is leavink!"

Iculus unzipped his tent door, bleary-eyed. "Are you spreading nasty rumors about me again, Tiki?"

"Borees! Tell him, it is only ze truth! It is luff, Borees, true luff!"

Iculus shook his head. "Oh man. I ought to go back to sleep."

We heard loud, boisterous voices coming through the woods well before Rattle River Shelter. It was four in the afternoon and the party had already started. Mala came to meet us, red-faced and laughing, a Nalgene of dark beer in his hand.

"Hey, it's the Barefoot Sisters! And Porkchop! And—" he peered at Iculus and Tiki "—a couple of other hikers!"

"Happy birthday, Mala," I said.

"We got beer down at the creek. None of that watery mass-produced shit—I got a whole keg of Sam Adams!"

We left our packs in the shelter and took our water bottles down to the creek. Sure enough, a huge silver keg rested in a pool of the Rattle River. Toast stood knee-deep in the water, operating the tap.

"Hey, y'all," he said.

"Mr. Toastee!"

He grinned. "I love it when the ladies call me Mr. Toastee. Hand me your water bottle, jackrabbit." He filled it with beer.

"Whoah! That's plenty, Toast. Thanks. So how in hell did you get a keg out here in the woods, anyway?"

He grinned. "Wasn' easy, y'all. There was a bunch of us; me and Wee Willie, Dream Catcher, guy named Spider. A couple others; I forget their names. Mala didn't carry it, 'cause it's *his* birthday, after all. We rigged up a stretcher, kind of, with the keg on the middle. Still took us a good two hours to get here." He rolled his shoulders. "I swear, y'all, that's the last time I'm carryin' that much weight *anywhere*. Isis, gimme that bottle and I'll fill it for ya."

"Just halfway, Toastee," she said. "I had a few too many White Russians in Gorham."

A crowd was beginning to assemble in the clearing in front of the shelter: Buttah, Dream Catcher, Greensinger, Sing-song and Tiger Cakes, Ranger Kain from Shenandoah, and a handful of other thru-hikers I didn't know. I met Spider, a rail-thin young man with shaved blond hair and deep-set eyes. He demonstrated how he got his trail name—hanging upside down from the rafters of the shelter.

"I was a rock climber in my former life," he said dryly, clinging to the beams. Then he flipped down neatly and landed on his feet. "Now I hike."

"*What* is going on here?" I looked out into the clearing to see an irate man with a bulging, heavy pack. His clothes and shoes looked brand new. The woman beside him, slim and stylishly coifed, stood back and waited for an explanation.

"It's a party!" One of the hikers yelled. "Yee-haw!"

Spider looked over at me. "I think there's going to be trouble," he said in an undertone, "unless we make those two feel welcome." He stepped out of the shelter and spoke to them in a cheery voice. "Hi! I'm Spider. Welcome to Mala's fifty-third birthday kegger extravaganza. The beer's down at the stream; help yourselves."

The man wasn't buying it. "My wife and I are out here for three days to enjoy the wilderness," he spluttered, "and *what* do we find at the shelter? A bunch of filthy drunks!"

"That's taking it a little far, don't you think?" Greensinger said to him. "We're certainly all filthy, but not all of us are quite drunk. Yet."

The man turned purple.

Spider tried to salvage the situation. "There are some really nice campsites just half a mile upstream. It's not much farther; you could camp there. That way the noise from the party wouldn't bother you."

The man threw down his pack. "We are camping *right here*," he said through clenched teeth. "My *wife* is *tired*. And you can rest assured, Spider, the authorities will hear about your little shenanigans!"

The woman convinced him to move to one of the tent sites behind the shelter, at least, so they would be out of the main staging area for the party.

Spider sat on the edge of the shelter's sleeping platform after the week-enders left, rubbing his temples. "That didn't go well at all," he said. "Now they think *I'm* responsible!"

"Come on, Spider," I said. "What 'authorities' are they possibly going to bring down on you? The freakin' Imp Campsite caretaker?"

He laughed a little. "Yeah, I doubt this'll end up on my permanent record . . . I can kind of see where they're coming from, though."

"I guess I can, too. If I was just out here for a weekend, this definitely isn't what I'd like to find at my campsite. But when you're out here for so long . . . I guess thru-hikers start to miss the vices of civilization after a while." I thought back to winter, the night when we had camped with Yogi, Yurtman, and the Family from the North just south of Max Patch. Yogi had turned up the volume on his pocket radio, filling the clearing with staticky pop hits. If I had just been out for a few days, it would have been the last thing I wanted to hear. As it was, with the ice in the trees and the chilly wind, that inane music had been the perfect distraction after a long day. Here at Rattle River, the loud, raucous voices of hikers in the clearing and the Nalgene of dark beer in my hand had the same kind of appeal; we'd given up the pretense of a wilderness experience in exchange for a human experience.

The rain returned and followed us over the Mahoosuc range, north of Gorham. September had come. Fall colors had begun to paint a few scattered trees; birch leaves sported golden tips, and wetland maples here and there glowed with cool flames. Droplets of water silvered the limbs of spruce and fir trees. At the summits of the granite peaks, tiny stunted krummholz trees clung to the stones, and heath bogs on the high ridges showed the smoldering red of cranberry leaves and sphagnum moss.

I had forgotten how steep and rough the trail became in the last few miles of New Hampshire. We clambered over an obstacle course of enormous stone blocks and steep pitches of rock, sometimes helped along by ladders or iron handles. Tiki had to lift Skass Dawg by the scruff of her neck and the extra skin on her rump to get her over the toughest places. (The skunk smell still clung to her fur, but now it was only perceptible from a few feet away.)

On the afternoon of the second day after Mala's party, a strong wind whipped across the bare summits of the mountains, tossing the clouds away to the west. Sunlight reflected back from every surface in a million tiny sparkles; the shadows of the last clouds raced across the valleys in ever-shifting patches of dark green. In the bogs, thin sedges and the white puffs of cotton grass danced in the wind, bent almost double. Looking to the north, I could see the landscape of Maine at last; patched with clear-cuts, stained with the smoke of paper mills, sliced apart by roads, the Great North Woods was a diminished wilderness. But I sensed wildness in it still, in the touch of ice in the wind, the cry of ravens, the vast spread of mountains blued with distance: *this is the land I return to, time after time. This is home.* In the clearing at the state line, Isis and I leaned down to kiss the ground.

CHAPTER 11

September

jackrabbit

We stayed at Full Goose Shelter, five miles inside the Maine–New Hampshire line. The last rays of the sun, horizontal and saffron-colored, came through the spruce branches as I filtered water at the spring. By the time I stood up to carry my clattering load of water bottles back to the shelter, it was almost dark. I saw the first stars between the branches. The days were shortening perceptibly; every evening the chill grew stronger.

Someone had started a fire in the pit in front of the shelter, and by its light I recognized many friends: Iculus and Tiki, Greensinger, Toast, Disco, and Spider. Porkchop and Isis sat off to one side, singing quietly.

Another hiker came into the clearing. "Any space in the shelter?" he asked.

"Buttah, is that you?" I said.

"Yup."

"Didn't recognize you in the dark."

"I think there's still some space," Spider said. "Buttah, do you know all these people?"

"I think so. Almost. Wait a sec. Who's that on the far side of the fire?"

Spider gave a broad grin. "Buttah, meet Toast. Toast, Buttah."

Porkchop laughed. "*I* was always looking for someone named Apple-sauce!"

Isis cooked a pot of polenta over the fire, and we perched on a rock together to eat. Just as we dipped our spoons into the steaming pot, a horren-dous snore shook the air around us.

"Who *is* that?" I asked.

"Section hiker," Toast said in a tone of regret. "He's right next to me in the shelter."

Isis stared up at the night sky for a few moments. "Looks like it'll stay clear," she said. "I think I'll just move my stuff to that tent platform behind the shelter and sleep out."

"Sounds good," I said.

The snoring intensified, a ragged, irregular sound. Tiki looked up from his pot of ramen. "Mind if I join you guys?"

Isis smiled. "Not at all."

Late that night, I woke up to the sound of the rising wind. It took me a moment to realize where I was—instead of the familiar blue tent walls above me, I saw the enormous, shaggy outlines of spruce trees and a swatch of dark sky spatter-painted with stars. Without my contact lenses, everything blurred a little bit. The moon floated over us, bright as a streetlamp; cool night wind brushed my face. In all the time we had spent on the Trail, this was the first night I had slept in the open without either tent or shelter. Lying there in the dappled moonlight, with nothing but dark air between me and the night forest, I couldn't help thinking that I'd missed out a little.

I rolled over to go back to sleep, and I caught sight of Isis and Tiki on the platform beside me, fast asleep. Their faces leaned together, almost touching; my sister's long hair fanned out around them both like silver water. They were holding hands.

The snoring section hiker was up early. Whistling cheerfully (a sound almost as interminable as his nocturnal symphony), he ate breakfast, packed, and left before seven. The thru-hikers took a little longer to get moving.

"I never heard a snore like that one, y'all," Toast commented, rubbing his eyes. "Every once in a while he'd stop, and I'd think, 'Great, I can get some rest!' Then he'd start right back up again."

"Yeah, that was pretty remarkable," Greensinger agreed. "I kept thinking he'd implode. One long inhale and *poof!*—no more section hiker!"

Disco laughed. "Still, it woulda been nice to get some sleep before the Notch."

"Mahoosuc Notch isn't really that bad," I said. "People say it's the hardest mile on the Trail. I guess it would be if you were on crutches. Or if you were Bill Erwin." Bill, a legally blind man who had thru-hiked in the early nineties, was a legend in the Trail community. "But for the average thru-hiker, especially the average nobo, it shouldn't be that tough. It's a big rock jumble, basically. Like a giant, mile-long jungle gym. You just have to take your pack off every once in a while. Oh, and watch out for the Icy Breath of Doom."

Buttah sat on a rock outside the shelter with a cigarette dangling from his lips. He was shirtless, wrapped in his green sleeping bag from the waist down. "Icy Breath of Doom?"

Spider caught sight of him and laughed. "You look like a mermaid, Buttah." Buttah just sat there staring from heavy-lidded eyes, puffing on his cigarette, with three days' worth of stubble on his face, until Spider revised his opinion. "Like the smoking, male version of a mermaid," he appended.

"What is this Icy Breath of Doom, jackrabbit?" Buttah asked again.

I told him about the ice that collects in the caves at the bottom of the Notch and stays around all summer. "I don't know if there'll still be anything there, though," I said. "That was the end of July; this is September."

I watched Isis and Tiki as we packed up, to see whether I had just imagined last night's tableau. They treated each other with the same offhand camaraderie that all of us shared, though. It didn't seem like anything had happened between them.

Mahoosuc Notch looked much as I remembered: giant blocks of lichen-speckled stone, some the size of houses and others like small cars, heaped haphazardly in the floor of a steep-sided valley. Even the weather was similar, a gray sky that cast a flat illumination over the rocks and moss. Water trickled and dripped somewhere far down below us. The air was warmer, though, without the ghostly, subterranean wafts of cold that had greeted us as sobos; the Icy Breath of Doom had, indeed, subsided. Also, as southbounders we had gone through the Notch alone, and this time we had a group of companions. Toast and Spider leaped from rock to rock and hung from tree branches, cracking jokes and laughing. Greensinger raced ahead, hiding in caves and jumping out to startle people. Tiki stayed back with Jade, helping her across the gaps between the stones. Isis, Porkchop, and I stopped in the largest caves, testing their acoustic properties by singing. The traverse of Mahoosuc Notch was one of our slowest miles on the Trail, but also one of the most entertaining.

Isis

Our second time through southern Maine, we stayed with Honey and Bear, a retired couple who had befriended the Family from the North and helped them out at the beginning of their hike. Honey and Bear ran a mysterious hostel called The Cabin, supposedly located in Andover. I'd heard about it from many other hikers, but I couldn't remember seeing it anywhere on the two or three streets that made up the town. The Family had put us in touch with Honey and Bear last winter, and they'd told us to call when we got near the Maine-New Hampshire border. I'd reached Bear from Gorham,

and he'd warmly invited us, and all the friends we were hiking with, to stay at
The Cabin as long as possible.

"I'll send a shuttle to pick you up at Grafton Notch, so you can slack
Baldpate Mountain as well as Wyman and Moody," Bear had said. "And
you've got to take at least one zero. We can go over to the lake if it's good
weather, take a picnic."

I couldn't help running up a calculation in my head. Thirty-mile shuttle.
Two days of slacking, and a zero. All of the town meals we'd eat in that stretch
of time.

"I'd love to spend some time with you guys," I told Bear. "But we're running kind of short on money at this end of our hike, and so are most of the
people we're hiking with. Do you have any work-for-stay available?"

"Your friends could help out in the garden," Bear said, "or chop some
firewood. There's always something to do. As for you and jackrabbit, don't
even think about money. Paul and Mary told me how much you guys helped
them in the winter. It's the least we can do to repay you."

I opened my mouth to protest. I wanted to tell him what a debt of gratitude we owed to all of the trail angels, hostel owners, and fellow hikers who'd
helped us in our hike—the Family not the least among them. I could never
repay all the people who'd given me food, water, or encouragement just when
I needed it most. The best I could do was to accept the help that was given
me, and look for an opportunity to pass it on to the next person in need.

"Thanks, Bear," I told him. "I'm looking forward to meeting you and
Honey."

A huge red pickup was waiting at the trailhead when we climbed down
Grafton Notch. Mala hopped out of the driver's seat, grinning.

"This here's the Cabin shuttle. Swanky, ain't it? I'm taking a few weeks off
from hiking to hang out with Bear and drive it for him. Hop on board, everyone, and hurry up. Don't wanna keep supper waiting."

"Honey and Bear are making supper?" I asked.

"You bet they are. A feast, to welcome the Barefoot Sisters."

Toast, Spider, Tiki, and I climbed into the back of the truck with Jade,
whose stench had died down to a relatively bearable stale-coffee smell. Buttah,
jackrabbit, and Porkchop crammed into the front with Mala. Just as the truck
pulled out of the parking lot, Greensinger strolled down the trail. Jackrabbit
leaned over and said something to Mala. He stopped, and Greensinger hopped
in the back with me and Tiki.

Ten miles or so outside of Andover, Mala turned in at a driveway lined with pines, leading to a broad swath of lawn. The handsome three-story building at the end of the drive was indeed a log cabin, though its decorative woodwork and the beds of marigolds in the dooryard made it looked more like a chalet. Two young women in sundresses sat in plastic chairs on the lawn, sipping glasses of lemonade. One of them, a tall redhead, wore a silver cardboard crown. Beside the women, two bearded men lounged in the grass. One was shirtless, the other wore a plaid shirt, shorts, and a visor. All four of them came over to greet us while we unloaded our packs from the van.

"Hey! Isis and jackrabbit!" The shirtless man was Jack, from Elmer's. He introduced us to his girlfriend, Ramblin' Rose, a pretty, thin woman with pale blond hair and glasses. They had come up for a month to hike Maine.

"We've only hiked a few days so far," Ramblin' Rose admitted. "We've been at The Cabin for almost a week. It's so hard to leave this place."

The other hikers were Abacus and Mummy-toe, a couple who we'd met briefly in Virginia, but never hiked with.

"Great town clothes," I told Abacus, the woman in the crown.

"Thanks." She curtsied, lifting the hem of her blue-and-white checkered dress with her pinkies extended. "I call this outfit The Royal Tablecloth." She giggled. "The Cabin's got a whole closet full of loaner clothing. Stuff for hikers to borrow while their clothes are in the laundry. Some of it's just shorts and t-shirts, but some of it's, like, kilts and kimonos and somebody's old prom dress."

The door of The Cabin swung open with a thump. A tall, fit man with ruddy cheeks and a trimmed gray beard stood in the doorway, smiling from ear to ear. A woman with a round, cheerful face and curly white hair followed close behind him.

"Welcome, welcome," said the man. "I'm Earle, and this is my wife Margie, though most folks call us Bear and Honey. Now, which of you are the Barefoot Sisters? Ah, I thought so. So good to have you here at last." He shook hands with me and jackrabbit, and Honey gave us each a hug.

"You all probably want to get cleaned up before dinner," Bear continued, addressing the whole crowd of hikers. "There's a shower by the bunkroom downstairs, and another on the third floor. Help yourselves to the loaner clothing in the hostel closet. I'll give you a quick tour, and then I've got to run upstairs to start the water boiling. Give me a heads-up when the last person's in the shower, so I can throw the lobsters in the pot."

"Lobsters?" whispered someone behind me.

"Yes. A lobster cookout to welcome our friends to The Cabin." Bear beamed at me and jackrabbit.

It was all I could do not to gape in astonishment. Already, Bear and Honey had invited us to stay with them for three days, and bring along as many of our friends as we wanted. Now they were putting on a lobster feed for all of us.

"Wow. Thanks," I finally said.

"Thank you for coming." Honey spoke in a soft voice, with a trace of a Maine accent, the r on the end of "for" almost vanishing into an h-sound. "We've been looking forward to this for months."

Inside The Cabin, Bear showed us around the hostel on the lowest floor. Just to the right of the door, three couches were grouped around a wide-screen TV, forming a living room area. Beyond that was the kitchen/wash-room, with a refrigerator, stove, and dishwasher at one end, and a washing machine and dryer at the other. Across from the door we'd come through, Bear pointed out the hostel bathroom and the famous loaner closet. Down the hall was a room full of bunks the size of twin beds, all neatly made up with sheets and blankets.

"And the hiker box is over there on the counter," Bear continued. "Help yourself to anything you need." I glanced inside it, seeing the usual bags of mysterious grains and white powder, but also boxes of instant dinners and granola that looked fresh off the supermarket shelf. And in one corner, a ragged paperback copy of *Harry Potter and the Chamber of Secrets*—just in time; we'd finished the first volume in the series last night. I took the book with me as we left the common room.

On the way back toward the living room, Bear indicated a closed door on the side of the hall. "That's the private room for couples." He smiled benevolently at me and Tiki, who were at the head of the line. "Jack and Ramblin' Rose are using it right now, but you two can have it as soon as they hike out."

I glanced at Tiki, startled. We were certainly headed in the direction of "seeking fellowship in the wilderness." We'd lain beside each other at Full Goose Shelter, in our separate sleeping bags, whispering jokes and stories after the others fell asleep. We flirted pretty shamelessly when we were hiking close to each other, but I didn't know what gestures could have convinced Bear that we were a couple already. I remembered jackrabbit's dream the night we camped near Zealand Falls Hut. Did everybody know these things before I did?

Tiki returned my glance, his straight, dark eyebrows raised and his lips curved in a playful smile: *Well, how 'bout it?* I shrugged, smiling back: *Why not? We don't have a lot of time left; we may as well make the best of it.*

I turned to Porkchop and jackrabbit. "I guess you'll have to go shopping now," I told them.

Each of us claimed a bunk, and we took turns with the showers. I was lucky and drew the upstairs shower, giving me a chance to see the rest of The Cabin. The living room, decorated in a blue-and-white nautical theme, had a cathedral ceiling; next to it, an open staircase led to the third floor. Sunlight slanted through the skylights and the stained-glass window high on the living room wall, making the varnished wood and brasswork glow. The bathroom itself, with its lacy curtains and decorative tiles, seemed far too luxurious for a hiker washing off five days' worth of sweat and grime. As I watched the streams of mud run off my feet, I felt like a fairy-tale character elevated from peasant to princess overnight: awkward, and a little in awe of my own luck.

I dressed in a blouse and skirt from the loaner closet and went downstairs just in time to help Honey carry the bread and salad to the table. There must have been twenty people gathered in the dining room: our friends, more hikers I didn't know, and several of Honey and Bear's neighbors. Tiki helped Mala serve the lobsters, while Bear walked around the table, passing out ears of corn and making sure everyone was comfortable. Honey brought in a summer squash casserole, in case any of us were serious vegetarians. I sat next to her, and we traded stories about the Family from the North.

"Do you have any idea where they are now?" Honey asked me.

I told her what I'd heard from Lash at Trail Days; they were staying in a friend's cabin in Georgia, doing some carpentry work in lieu of rent.

"They left Georgia in early summer," Honey said. "I got a postcard from Mary. She said they'd hitched across country to visit her mother in Kansas. After that, they planned to go back to the island where Paul and Mary met— somewhere in the Caribbean, I think. There's a valley there, with waterfalls and caves and a long sand beach, where people from all over the world camp and live off the land. Mary told me about it, when they stopped here in the first month of their hike."

"She told me about it, too," I said. "In the middle of winter. It sounded like paradise to both of us, then. I hope they make it there." I could hardly imagine the challenges of crossing oceans and national borders with five children, no money, and no I.D.s. I'd seen how the Family worked together, though. If there was a way, they'd find it. I smiled to myself, picturing the seven of them camped on a tropical beach, fishing and gathering wild fruit and sharing their campfires with other wanderers.

(Whether they parted the sea with their hiking sticks, or hitched a ride on a boat or a cargo plane, they did make it. In late October we got a postcard from Mary, emblazoned with a spectacular tropical sunset. *We are so happy*; she wrote, *at last we have come home. We take walks on the beach and in the mountains. The children go barefoot all the time. I make jewelry to sell, and Paul catches fish. Write us care of our friend.* But she neglected to leave an address, and none of our mutual Trail friends had heard from them.)

The next morning, after a breakfast of blueberry pancakes, home fries, and omelets, Mala drove the eight of us who wanted to slack Baldpate back to the trailhead. Buttah, who hadn't had a chance to do his laundry yet, had asked Bear if he could hike in some of the loaner clothing. Bear had told him certainly—the loaner clothes were there for hikers; we could do anything we wanted with them. Hearing this, most of our slacking party had borrowed clothes from the closet. Buttah's outfit was one of the most prosaic: baggy green shorts, a sleeveless orange t-shirt, and wraparound shades. Porkchop wore a blouse with a loud black-and-white floral pattern, lavender Hawaiian-print shorts, and a seven-foot-long purple scarf. Jackrabbit had on a turquoise shirt and a splotchy pastel mini skirt ("très eighties high school dance," Buttah commented). She'd started the day in a pale purple wig, but thought that it would be too hot to wear while hiking. At our trailhead photo-op, Mala wore the wig. With his skinny gray braids hanging down from the mop of lavender curls, he looked like Long John Silver trying to hide in a nursing home. I'd found a wool skirt, a cream-colored blouse with ruffles at the neck and sleeves, and a sweater vest: turn-of-the-century schoolmarm chic. Greensinger's outfit took the cake, though—a long black satin bathrobe over a kilt.

It was a lovely September day, clear and warm once the sun rose high enough to burn off the dew. My schoolmarm outfit rapidly lost its modesty: first the sweater vest came off, then I unbuttoned the blouse. Pretty soon I was hiking along quite comfortably in skirt and bra—a lacy white undergarment from the loaner closet, rather than the sports bra I usually wore, but it covered at least as much skin as a bikini would have. Jackrabbit, too, stripped down to bra and skirt, and most of the men took their shirts off. Shocking, I'm sure, if there'd been any tourists to see us, but we seemed to have the mountain to ourselves.

We spread out a picnic on the granite ledges near the peak. After lunch, none of us were in a hurry to leave. We took pictures of each other in the afternoon version of our loaner outfits: Greensinger with his kilt and farmer's tan, and Buttah, the only one of us to have put on a layer during our lunch break, looking like a mafioso with his black windbreaker rolled up to the elbows and his shades. Then we all took a siesta, lying on the warm, smooth rocks.

We'd been there perhaps an hour, when a hiker I hadn't seen since Tennessee came strolling up the mountain from the north. It was Patch, named for Max Patch, the kind, quiet young man I'd talked to all evening when jackrabbit and I first met him at Kincora. His coffee-colored skin had darkened a shade over the summer, and he looked a bit older than I had thought him when we first met; the bright sunlight revealed creases around his eyes when he smiled.

"This looks like a good place for a break." He lowered his pack to the ground, and it landed with a muffled thud. It didn't seem any lighter than it had been at Kincora; in fact, the half-sized guitar case strapped to the outside was new since then.

"Patch!" I hurried over to hug him. "Great to see you again! How's your hike going?"

"Wonderful. So good, I don't know how I'll go back to the world." He smiled ruefully. "Nowhere I've ever lived has been like the Trail. Every hour I see something new and beautiful. But more than that—I've gotten used to being trusted by strangers. Before I hiked, I was a pro tennis coach. People treated me with respect if they knew my name, but otherwise . . . On the Trail, complete strangers invite me to dinner, just because I'm carrying a pack."

"Hey, Patch!" Porkchop came skipping over, followed by jackrabbit. "I haven't seen you since Virginia. I'm so glad you've caught up!"

"I haven't caught up, really," Patch explained. "I'm doing a flip-flop. I've been hiking slowly, eight- or ten-mile days, to try to make the Trail last as long as possible. But I wanted to see Katahdin before the park closed, so I caught a ride up from Pennsylvania a few weeks ago."

"So you're going south?" Porkchop asked. "This is all we're going to see of you?"

"Hike back to Katahdin with us," jackrabbit suggested. "If you cover the same ground twice, you'll be on the Trail even longer than you planned."

Patch chuckled. "When I finish my first thru-hike, you can try talking me into a yo-yo. Right now, I want to get through the Whites before the first snowfall."

"There must be a way we can spend more time together," I said. "We're staying at a hostel called The Cabin in Andover. It's a wonderful place. There are plenty of bunks free. Maybe we could get the shuttle driver to pick you up at Grafton Notch this evening."

"I'm sure we could talk Mala into swinging over there," jackrabbit said. "Will you stay with us, Patch?"

"I'd love to," he said, "as long as it's not any trouble to your friend to pick me up."

We came across Mala late in the afternoon, sitting by a waterfall about a mile above East B Hill Road, where he'd planned to pick us up.

"Sorry we're late," I told him. "We met an old friend on Baldpate, and we spent a long time talking."

"No problem. It gives me a good excuse to hike up here myself and take a look at the scenery." He gestured to the waterfall, liquid amber in the afternoon light, splashing down a rock face streaked orange and gold with iron ore.

"We were hoping—I mean, could we ask you a big favor, Mala?" jackrabbit asked.

"Anything I can do, I'd be glad to," he answered.

"Well, the friend we met on the mountain—guy by the name of Patch—he'll be in Grafton Notch tonight. We were hoping you could stop by there and pick him up so he could come back to The Cabin with us."

Mala's face clouded over. "Now that is a problem, I'm afraid. Grafton Notch is a forty-minute drive from here, almost as long as it is from The Cabin. And Honey's expecting us back for supper at seven."

I exchanged a worried glance with Porkchop. We had promised Patch that we'd meet him. On the other hand, it had been pretty thoughtless of me to pledge Mala's services to the effort without asking him first.

Mala caught my eye and grinned. "Nothing we can't handle, though. Tell ya what. I'll drive you all back to The Cabin for dinner, like Honey told me to. Then I'll go out to Grafton Notch and pick up your friend."

"*We* could drive out there," jackrabbit offered, "if Bear would trust us to borrow his truck."

"Bear would *give* you his truck, if you needed it," Mala said. "Him and Honey think the world of you. I'd never hear the end of it, though, if I let you skip dinner to run the hiker shuttle. No, you stay at The Cabin, and I'll drive out to the Notch. Don't give it another thought."

I couldn't help thinking about it, though. I'd made a pretty big presumption, one that would cost Mala an hour and a half of his evening, as well as the chance to sit down to dinner on time. Was I getting spoiled by all the trail magic I'd been given?

Honey had made us an enormous pot of spaghetti. Jackrabbit, Porkchop, and I helped her carry the plates down the hall from the kitchen to the dining room. Some old friends of Honey and Bear's, a couple in their fifties who'd hiked northbound five or six years before, had shown up for a visit. The dining room was even more crowded than it had been the evening before. I wondered whether Honey and Bear fed that many people every night in summer. It couldn't be easy, or inexpensive, to provide for us all. The hostel had a nominal fee of $20 a night—a pretty good deal, considering that it included breakfast and dinner, showers, laundry, and a bed with clean sheets. Looking around the table, though, I realized that at least three-quarters of the people there were guests, or working for the cost of their stays. Like so many other hostels along the Trail, The Cabin seemed to be about ten percent business and ninety percent a labor of love.

Mala arrived just as we were finishing dessert, bringing with him not only Patch, but also Sing-song and Tiger Cakes. Jackrabbit sprang up to greet them and introduce them to our hosts, while I hurried to the kitchen to get Mala a plate of spaghetti.

"Have you eaten yet?" Honey was asking Patch, when I came back into the dining room.

"Yes, thank you, I cooked dinner with these ladies in Grafton Notch, just before Mala picked us up."

"Well, let me get you a slice of pie, dear," Honey said.

"Hey, good to see you," I said, sitting down next to Tiger Cakes.

"It's great to see *you*," she answered. "And it's great to be here. When me and Sing-song met Patch in Grafton, he told me you were staying at an awesome hostel, somewhere around Andover, and you were going to send someone over to pick him up. It sounded like one of those crazy Trail rumors—you know how it is, when you're out in the middle of the woods and night's falling, everything quiet and still, and somebody hikes by and tells you there's a trail magic cookout just a quarter mile farther on? You just can't believe it's there, until you're close enough to smell things frying and see the lantern lights. Even then, you can't quite believe it's for you. So there we were, cooking sweet 'n' sour Lipton rice on our hobo stoves like any other night. When it got real late, even Patch figured something had come up and you couldn't make it. We were about to set up our tents, when Mala pulled into the parking lot, and just like that—" she snapped her fingers "—we're here. Every time I think I get used to this Trail, something new and amazing happens. Wow, pie! Thanks so much, ma'am," she said, as Honey set a generous slice in front of her.

Buttah and Spider hiked out the next day, but the rest of us took a zero. Porkchop, jackrabbit, and I wanted to spend some time with Patch, and we also hoped to figure out what our group could do in terms of work-for-stay. So far, we'd stacked a few things in the dishwasher and made our own beds: less work than might be expected of high school students living at home. Porkchop had offered to wash the pots and pans for two nights in a row, but Bear had told her not to worry about it.

"Just enjoy yourself," he'd said. "Margie and I want you to feel at home."

Tiki was getting restless too. "These are good people," he'd told me, "but I'm afraid we're taking advantage of their kindness. I want to find some way to help them out."

So did I. I decided that cooking was the best skill I had to offer. On the morning of our zero, I told Honey how much I missed being in the kitchen, and asked her if she might allow me to make supper that night.

"There'll be about twenty-five people," she'd told me, sounding doubtful. "It's a big job to cook for that many."

"I'll make the dessert," Tiki offered. "I've got a great recipe for rum cake. That way Isis won't have to do all the work."

I gave him a speculative glance. "Are you really going to help, or are you just going to distract me?"

"A little of both, I hope," he said with a wink.

"I've cooked for twenty-five before," I told Honey. "I'd really love to do it."

"Okay, dear. Let me get you some money for groceries."

With a great deal of effort, I discouraged her from paying for the groceries. Jackrabbit, Porkchop, Tiki and I had already decided to pool the money we were saving by not eating in restaurants or paying for accommodations in Andover, and put on a feast. Tiki borrowed Bear's truck and we drove over to town to pick up groceries: salmon and asparagus, mushrooms, white wine, cream. Onions, oranges, and carrots for the soup. Milk and eggs, butter, sugar, and flour for the bread and cake. With Tiki's help, I filled the grocery cart, looking forward to the afternoon's work.

Porkchop was sitting out on the lawn when we got back, trying to teach jackrabbit to play Patch's guitar. Sing-song and Tiger Cakes had found another guitar; they were over at the picnic table, singing "Shady Grove."

"Bear only let me weed one of the flower beds before he told me to go relax and play some music," Porkchop told me. "Patch and Greensinger are building a new raised bed for the vegetable garden, but I bet he'll tell them they've done enough any minute now."

Sure enough, Greensinger came around the corner of the house as she spoke, wiping the sawdust off his hands. Patch followed him a few minutes later.

"That wasn't much of a work-for-stay," he said. "But Bear wouldn't give me anything else to do."

"I could use some helpers," I told him.

Pretty soon, the kitchen was full of hikers chopping vegetables, flipping crêpes, and kneading the bread dough. Porkchop, Sing-song, and jackrabbit formed a singing dish brigade, washing the pots and putting them away as soon as I finished with them. By midafternoon, we had everything ready for assembly, so we went out on the lawn to play some more music. Mala, who'd taken a run to the trailheads to see if any hikers needed a ride, returned with Johnny Steel, Lightfoot, and Featherweight. Iculus and Dream Catcher were also in town, he reported, staying at the Andover Guest House. Hopefully, we'd meet them on the trail.

Almost everyone dressed up for dinner. Jackrabbit donned the lavender wig again, along with a fuchsia sarong. Porkchop wore a little white satin dress with the tag still dangling from the armpit, a child-sized red acrylic cap, and her long purple scarf. She'd tried to give the scarf to Johnny Steel, but he refused. ("Wrong color," he'd told her in his deadpan voice. "Mine's s'posed to be pink.") Jack wore a red, blue, and green striped bathrobe, and sipped dark beer out of a tiny sherry glass. Abacus had come up with a Princess Leia outfit: a flowing white dress, felt boot liners with zippers up the fronts, and black earmuffs. Beside her, Mummy-toe looked resplendent in a three-piece suit, cowboy hat, and string tie.

Tiki and I carried the food in, course after course. Chilled carrot-orange soup and loaves of golden challah, mushroom-asparagus crêpes, salmon poached in white wine, salad with lemon and garlic dressing. It was a luxury to prepare a meal like this, to have time and money and so many helping hands. Serving the food, I felt at home, comfortable in a way that I hadn't felt in a long time. Conversation flowed past me like a brook, steady and joyful. The setting sun's warm light poured through the window at the end of the room, lighting the faces of all the friends, new and old, gathered around the table. There was Porkchop, who had made our return to the Whites the best part of our northbound trip so far. Greensinger, who had shared fresh vegetables with us when we were short-supplied. Patch, whose boundless sense of wonder made me see the world through new eyes. Tiki, who would soon be my lover. There were our hosts, Honey and Bear. And jackrabbit, my oldest friend of all. I hoped that with this meal, I could give something of myself to all of them.

The only cloud on the evening was an argument between Greensinger and Mala, several hours after dinner. I was upstairs in the living room, looking at a scrapbook that Honey was making to send to the Family, if they ever settled down long enough to receive mail. Mala must have had a few beers; his rumbling voice seemed to shake the floorboards. I recognized the other, quieter voice as Greensinger's. I didn't know who had started the quarrel, but I wanted to try to calm Mala down. Beneath all his intellectual posturing— *probably that was what offended Mala*, I thought—Greensinger was eighteen years old and prone to depression. Getting yelled at like that could really hurt him. I started to rise to my feet. Bear sprang up immediately, saying that he'd settle the matter, and hurried away downstairs. After Bear's intercession, I heard no more raised voices, but Greensinger left The Cabin before dawn. Patch, the only person up at that hour besides Bear and Honey, borrowed the truck to drive him back to the trail.

Tiger Cakes, Porkchop, Tiki, jackrabbit, and I slacked over Wyman and Moody Mountains, getting a late start. Patch, who'd agreed to take one more day off before continuing south, walked with us. He had never slacked; he'd carried his eighty- to ninety-pound pack for every step of the Trail. ("I'm used to it," he'd told me with a shrug. "It feels good, to have everything I need with me, to be able to stop and set up my tent anywhere.") Now he was taking great delight in hiking with a daypack.

"I see why people slackpack," he told me. "The woods look different, this way. I have more time to notice the trees, when I'm not putting so much energy into each step. I hiked through here just a few days ago, but I feel like I'm walking this stretch for the first time."

Patch's calm good spirits comforted me. I was worried about Green-singer—he must have been really upset to have left so early, without saying goodbye to any of us. The note he left in the Hall Mountain Lean-to register did little to dispel my fears, though it made no mention of his quarrel with Mala. *There are dark forces stirring in the world*, he wrote. *To all my friends behind: I am hiking fast to Katahdin, alone. I can find no peace, even on the Trail. I am haunted by foreboding. I wish you luck, and strength, to face the dark days that are at hand.*

The language was straight out of *Lord of the Rings*, but I had known Greensinger long enough to recognize that he framed some of his strongest emotions in those terms. Remembering my own struggle with depression during my teenage years, I wished that I could catch up to him, to reassure him. *The dark days come, but sooner or later, they pass away.* I looked over at jackrabbit, who was sitting on the porcupine trap, teaching Porkchop a song in close harmony. She had been deeply depressed when she got off the Trail, and again in winter, and again, recently, because of Lyme disease. I had never been able to comfort her; in fact, at the worst of times, my presence seemed to make her even more angry and withdrawn. Now she laughed as she missed a note, and laughed again, with delight, when she and Porkchop both got the first line perfect. My heart ached for her, her fragile happiness.

The afternoon was hot for September, the air humid and still. The six of us climbed up Moody, the last long ascent of the day, in a silent line. I was deep in my own thoughts and worries; when I saw a hiker with a daypack walking toward me, I simply stood aside to let him pass.

"Isis! Honey and Bear told me I could find you guys here."

I looked up. It was Compañero. I knew him immediately by his tall, lanky frame and the thoughtful smile on his narrow face. Jackrabbit called out his name and hurried up the trail to give him a hug. We introduced him to Pork-chop, Tiki, Patch, and Tiger Cakes.

"What brings you to Andover?" jackrabbit asked Compañero.

"Hoping to find you guys." He smiled. "Actually, I live near here now. I'm working at a hospital about thirty miles away. I had a day off, so I thought I'd come out to the Trail and look for you. I called The Cabin—I figured you might stay there—and Bear told me where you were hiking today."

"Wow, it's great to see you," I said. "How long has it been? Since RPH Shelter last fall?"

Compañero nodded. "Almost a year."

"Can you stick around for a while and hike with us tomorrow?" jack-rabbit asked. "We've got so much to catch up on."

"I have to be at work tomorrow morning," Compañero said. "But there's something I wanted to ask you about. Some of my coworkers have been telling me about an organic farmers' fair that's going on at the end of the month. I have a long weekend then . . ."

"The Common Ground Fair!" jackrabbit said. "We used to go every year when we were kids. It's great; you should definitely go if you have the time free."

"What I wanted to ask is, would you like to go with me?"

"Of course—but—we're hiking with other people—"

"Maybe you could talk some of them into coming along."

Compañero drove us to The Cabin and stayed for dinner. On his way home, he took Patch back to Grafton Notch; Patch wanted to camp out there so he could get an early start. Jack and Ramblin' Rose had also left that day, along with Abacus and Mummy-toe. For the first time, Tiki and I had a room to ourselves. After weeks of flirtation with no privacy, it should have been a relief. Instead, we were shy with each other, sitting in the hostel's common room until late, drinking the beers that Mala kept passing around. When we finally closed the door behind us, amid the whistles and laughter of other half-drunk hikers, we were too tired to do more than undress and exchange a few fumbling kisses.

Perhaps an hour later, I woke up, needing to pee. I slipped on the bathrobe I'd taken from the loaner closet, and stepped out into the hall. The party was still in full swing. Johnny Steel, Mala, and a few hikers I didn't know sat around on the couches, watching a football game on TV. The table in between them was covered with empty bottles. A whiff of rank smoke hung in the air—not cigarette or marijuana. Perhaps someone had dropped something on the stove. I glanced into the kitchen; all the burners were off. *Whatever it was, someone must have taken care of it*, I thought.

I nearly bumped into Mala as I stepped out of the bathroom.

"Sorry," I said, stepping aside to let him pass.

He stood there looking at me, his head tilted a little to one side. *Uh-oh, he's totally drunk and probably looking for someone to flirt with*, I thought. *I'm too tired to deal with this right now.* The smell of smoke seemed to be getting stronger. I wasn't really in a mood to deal with that, either, but it seemed like I was going to have to; everyone else was still engrossed in the game. After a minute, Mala nodded to himself.

"I know wha' you are," he slurred, beaming up at me. "I can tell. Anyone look at me, and they'd think I was jus' a drunk ol' redneck. But I studied Buddhism a long time ago. That's where my name comes from; it's a string of beads, used for Buddhist prayers. But you know that . . . All I'm tryin' to say is, I studied enough to know I ain't gonna be enlightened in this life." He threw his head back and guffawed, then looked at me, instantly serious again. "I recognize them that are, though. I wanna thank you for comin' back. To help us. We're gonna need all the help we can get."

I stared back at him, at a loss for words.

"Don' worry," he said, beaming again. "You don' have to say anythin'. I *know*."

Just then, jackrabbit dashed past us, her eyes wild and her tangled hair streaming behind her. She was holding her nose with one hand; in the other, she held out a smoking red lump of knit fabric at arm's length. She thrust the cloth under the faucet, and turned it on full blast.

"Phew," she said, removing her hand from her nose. Then, raising her voice, "Somebody open a couple windows please?"

"Okay," said Mala, lumbering off across the room.

"What *is* that thing you were carrying?" I asked, peering at the mass of soggy fabric in the sink.

"I don't know," jackrabbit answered groggily. "I don't have my contacts in. I woke up and the room was all smoky. At first I thought the house was burning, but then I noticed *that thing* on the lamp."

Porchop appeared in the bathroom doorway, looking as sleepy as jackrabbit.

"What's going on?" she asked.

Jackrabbit gestured toward the cloth in the sink, and started to explain.

"Uh-oh." Porchop looked sheepish. "That's my hat. That little knit cap from the loaner closet that I've been wearing. Man, I must have been really drunk when I went to bed."

"How on earth did your hat get on the lamp?" Jackrabbit sounded more puzzled than grumpy.

"Well, I was really tired, so I tried to go to bed around eleven-thirty. I left the light on, 'cause most of the other hikers were still partying. But it was so bright, I couldn't get to sleep. So I turned off the overhead and turned on my bedside lamp. That was a little better. Then I had the bright idea of putting my hat over the lampshade, to reduce it to a nice red glow. After that, I went to sleep. I woke up to the bright light again, and a lot of nasty smoke." She gave jackrabbit an apologetic smile. "I guess my hat wasn't very fireproof. Thanks for putting it in the sink."

"Sure, anytime," said jackrabbit, looking a little bemused. "I think I'm going to go back to bed right now, though."

I lay next to Tiki, unable to sleep. *It would be nice if I really were enlightened,* I thought. *Then perhaps I could decipher the strange mood that's come over us all.*

I must have dozed off, because I was awakened by Mala's shout. His voice came from outside; he was probably standing in the driveway. "There will be a reckoning!" he screamed at the night sky. "There will be a fuckin' reckoning!"

We were all awake early, though none of the hikers appeared to have gotten much rest. Bear and Honey greeted us as cheerfully as ever; they seemed to have been oblivious to the previous night's carousing. In fact, Bear enthusiastically invited us to stay another day or two at The Cabin, offering to slack us over the Bemis Range.

"You can't leave so soon," Bear said. "We were hoping you'd be able to take another zero with us. You've got more than a month before Katahdin closes."

I felt restless, eager to be covering ground again. But Honey and Bear had been so kind to us that I had a hard time refusing their offer. I looked at jackrabbit.

"I don't know if we can take a zero," she told Bear, "but I'd love to slack another day, if you're sure it wouldn't be any trouble."

"No trouble at all," Bear said, clapping her on the shoulder. "We're glad to have you."

We started hiking just a little after eight. It promised to be another hot day; I was already sweating in my shorts and sports bra as we hiked up the first long hill. Tiki suggested that we blue-blaze down the Bemis Stream Trail and reconnect with the A.T. via an old railroad bed, instead of following all the PUDs along the ridgeline. Jackrabbit and I decided to go with him; Porkchop, Johnny Steel, Sing-song, and Tiger Cakes, who were all slacking with us, agreed to meet us where the Trail intersected with the railroad bed.

The Bemis Stream Trail was clearly marked and well maintained where it branched off from the A.T. Once we descended to the valley, though, the trail became indistinguishable from the moose and bear paths that crisscrossed the forest floor. We waded across a murky stream, looking for blazes, and found instead the end of a logging road.

"This road *looks* like it's going north," jackrabbit said.

I frowned. "It's going north here, but it might curve around and go off to the east."

"I'm sure it'll connect to other roads," Tiki said. "Come on, this'll be much faster than trying to follow the stream out."

We set off, following the road through a parched landscape: cut-over forest, scrub, and meadows already yellowing with fall. The hot sky curved above us, not a cloud or even a vapor trail in sight. Here and there, a cricket buzzed in the sweetfern or a yellow-shafted flicker flew in low arcs over the road. The clear-cut land and the white, dusty web of roads seemed empty, devoid of human life, as if the civilization that made them had vanished overnight. After a few miles, the road branched, then branched again. We stayed to the left, skirting along the edge of the Bemis Range, until we found the old railroad bed and followed it back to the Trail.

Under the shade of the trees, we ate a snack and waited for the others. They arrived half an hour behind us: the PUDs on the ridge must have made pretty slow going on such a hot day.

"I think you guys got the better deal," Tiger Cakes told me and Tiki and jackrabbit, wiping the sweat off her forehead and sitting down on a boulder beside the road.

"We've been attacked! We've been attacked!" I looked up. It was a hiker named Stoker, who we'd met a couple times before: a man about my age with balding black hair and a trimmed beard. He was flying down the trail toward us, waving his arms and shouting at the top of his lungs. In one hand, he held a purple portable radio like the one Yogi used to dance to. "We've been attacked," he repeated, stumbling to a halt in front of us and gasping for breath.

I jumped to my feet, muscles tensing. I noticed that everyone around me had done the same. *A bear must have gotten into somebody's pack*, I thought. *Good thing there are enough of us here to chase it away.*

"Where?" I asked Stoker, "What happened?"

jackrabbit

"What's happening?" Isis asked again. "Who's been attacked? Stoker, what's going on?"

He paused to catch his breath. "The United States is under attack," he said, his face pale. "Somebody bombed the World Trade Center. No, they flew a plane into it. Two planes. And one in the Pentagon. Another plane crashed somewhere in Pennsylvania." He paused, listening to his radio. "They have no idea who did it, or why. Bush is calling it an act of war. They don't know how many people are dead. Maybe tens of thousands . . .'"

That morning, I hadn't known or cared what day of the month it was. Now, it was a date that would be burned into my memory, into the memory of everyone who lived through it: it was September 11, 2001.

I sat down heavily on the bank of the gravel road, under the dappled shade of yellowing maples, feeling waves of panic and disbelief wash over me. I saw Isis, beside me, clutch at a handful of earth as though its solidity could somehow sustain her. The sky overhead was still the same shade of pale blue; the same golden light came down between the leaves. The day felt changed, though, the scene around me suddenly fragile and illusory, as though it was painted on glass and could shatter and shift without warning.

We walked the last half mile to the paved road, numb with disbelief. Bear was standing by his truck in the parking lot. "I guess you guys know what happened," he said, seeing our stricken faces.

We rode back to the hostel in silence: Isis and I, Sing-song and Tiger Cakes, Tiki, Porkchop, Johnny Steel. (Stoker had decided to stay on the Trail.) All the way back along the winding mountain roads, past glowing hillsides of fall maples and flat blue lakes that shimmered in the sun, I tried to reconcile the disaster with the world I knew. For the last fifteen months, I had lived in the Trail world, where friendships and trust came easily. Disagreements were generally solved by walking away. I had become more of an optimist, more trusting in the basic goodness of humanity, than I had ever been in my life. With the horrific events of the morning, I felt this newfound hope sliding away. The radio in Bear's truck droned on and on, numbering the dead and speculating on causes. It didn't seem real to me yet; it seemed like a nightmare from which we all might somehow awaken.

Back at The Cabin, we sat in the lounge downstairs, watching television. The names and faces of firefighters flashed across the screen. Johnny Steel sat back on the couch, anguish in his dark blue eyes, his fists clenched. "I knew some of those guys," he said. "I went to fire academy with them. I wish I could be there. I wish I could be there and *do* something. I am so *powerless* here." He glanced around the little room like a trapped animal.

I remembered Tony, the New York firefighter we had met at Harriman State Park. Just a kid, barely out of his teens. *Where was he? Where were Spike and Caveman?*

"Six thousand," the television commentator was saying, "or perhaps even more. It will take days, maybe months, before we can be certain. Let's show the footage again."

The camera cut away to a long shot of the two towers. The plane came like a wedge of shadow from the right-hand edge of the screen, in slow motion. For an instant the plane's nose touched its own reflection, smoothly meeting its image on the building's glass facade. Then the plane went into the building, crumpling into a fireball of eerie, horrible beauty. I half-expected it to reemerge from the far side of the skyscraper, a cartoon plane, magically reassembled from its fragments, but nothing came out. The sky at the far edge of the tower remained pale and still, empty, unchanged. Then my mind caught up with me. I realized I had just witnessed the deaths of thousands of people. I didn't stay to watch the second plane hit the other tower, or the buildings burn and collapse. I had seen enough.

I clapped a hand over my mouth to keep from screaming. The walls of the room seemed to be closing in; the air was too thick to breathe. I ran into the bunkroom, where the only light came from the high windows at the back. Somehow, the cool darkness was a comfort. I huddled in the far corner of the room, hugging my shoulders and rocking back and forth, sobbing. I felt as if all my illusions about the goodness of humanity had shattered with the buildings. I had begun to trust in the power of goodwill and kindness. But the power of destruction, the power of hate, was so much vaster and more direct. How could trail magic and camaraderie counteract the kind of implacable rage that made people fly planes into buildings? I closed my eyes and the terrible image played out, again and again, seared into the back of my eyelids.

"Jackrabbit?" I looked up to see Isis standing over me. "Jackrabbit, are you okay?" I realized it was fully dark now; the only light in the room was the rectangle of pale yellow coming through the doorway from the next room. I wondered how long I had been there. "Jackrabbit, are you okay? Talk to me."

I shook my head, numb with pain and terror. I was afraid that if I opened my mouth, the darkness inside me would come pouring out. Isis sat down next to me but I shrank back. When I opened my eyes again, she was gone. I stayed there, racked with sobs, feeling trapped inside myself. I tried to pray, but it felt as futile as pounding on the locked door of an empty house.

Isis came back sometime later—minutes, hours, I wasn't sure. She pressed a phone to my ear.

"Susan? Sweetie?" It was my mother's voice. I hadn't thought there were any more tears in me, but now they were released. "Listen to me," she said, and her voice was fierce with conviction, concentrated, like my sister's voice in the depths of winter. "Listen to me. You can't let them win, whoever did this. If you lose yourself in depression, you're letting them win."

"How can there be so much hate in the world?" I finally managed. "Why is it like this now?"

"Oh sweetie. It's always been like this. Every generation has to deal with horror and hate. Remember the Holocaust. Pearl Harbor, the firebombing of Dresden, Hiroshima. Cambodia."

"How do people just go on, after . . ."

"People do, honey. It's what we have to do. We pick up the pieces and we go on. Because—" her voice became thin and quiet, edged with tears. "Because it's the only thing we *can* do. We have to realize that there's still light in the world, there's still beauty." Her voice grew strong again. "You have to keep *living*, sweetheart. Keep hoping. Keep loving your life, because it's the only life you have. Don't let hate win. Okay, sweetie? Okay?"

"Okay," I whispered. The room seemed to relax into more manageable dimensions. "I love you, Mum."

"I love you more than all the stars." It was an old game, one we hadn't played since I was very young.

"More than all the fall leaves on all the maples," I said.

"More than all the little flowers in spring."

"More than all the footsteps I've taken on the Trail."

"Love *is* stronger," she said. "I believe that with every fiber of my being. I think you have to believe it to stay sane."

"I want to believe," I said.

"Believe. Are you going to keep hiking?"

"I don't know. There doesn't seem to be any point, anymore."

"Stay on the Trail," she said. "Don't give up your dream because of this. Don't let them win."

I felt stronger as I hung up the phone. The walls still seemed to waver around me, as though not quite real, but I could breathe freely again. I wanted to anchor myself to the world again, somehow. *Music*, I thought. *Music*. I went upstairs to the living room, where an electronic keyboard sat on an end table.

The evening before, as we waited for dinner, I had played a little concert for Lightfoot and Featherweight. They had wandered in as I was finishing a fugue from the *Well-tempered Clavier*.

Featherweight had flashed her sweet smile. "Hi, jackrabbit. We have a request."

"I don't know many things off the top of my head. I'll give it a try, though."

"This is our favorite song," Lightfoot said.

"When we started dating, we were both in college. We went out for coffee or something. Then he asked me back to his room, 'cause he wanted to play a song for me. He said it was his absolute favorite song. He put the CD on, and I said, 'No way! That's my favorite piece of music, too!'"

"Friends of ours played it at our wedding."

"What is it?" I asked them.

"Pachelbel's *Canon.*"

"Oh, I can play that!"

They had sat back on the couch, intertwined, lost in reverie, while my hands remembered the music. The living room had filled with the sound, a melody three centuries old and somehow still as new as the day it was written. Thinking about the mystery and wonder of music, of love, I had been so happy.

The evening of September 11, I plugged in the keyboard and played the first few notes of the "Prelude" from Bach's *English Suite No. 2.* As soon as I started, though, it felt wrong. I couldn't go on. I didn't want to bring that glorious and unsullied music into a world that seemed so changed. So diminished.

Porchop came to the door, carrying a guitar. There were tear-stains down her cheeks. "Do you want to come sing with us, jackrabbit? We're out in the kitchen."

"I don't know if I *can* sing."

"At least come eat some dinner. We saved you a veggie burger and some salad."

I had felt sick all afternoon, but to my surprise, I could eat. Afterward, Isis and Porchop and I sang our old songs, with Porchop's skillful guitar accompaniment.

"Do you know any Indigo Girls?" she asked us. "I was thinking about 'Secure Yourself to Heaven.'"

Our fragile, tear-choked voices filled the kitchen. I wished that I could believe in something like Heaven. I thought of Parypinoy's description of God's love reaching out through the universe. I tried to imagine it, but every time I closed my eyes, the horrible image flashed back: the plane went into the building and it didn't come out. How could a God of love, how could any God, sanction this?

I looked around the kitchen. The lamp was turned down low. Golden light glimmered on the polished wood cabinets and the tile floor. The sound of our singing hung in the air, and I imagined how the sound waves traveled forever outward, thinning until they vanished. *This is the only life I have*, I thought. *Let it be beautiful. Let me come to understand the beauty in it, and let that be enough.*

I sent an e-mail to Spike and Caveman—Isis had been trying to call them for hours, but all the lines to New York were busy. I also sent one to the fire-fighter, Tony. I hoped he was alive, but I didn't pray. I couldn't pray any more.

Dawn came. Shafts of light descended to the bunkroom from the windows. I could hear birds calling in the trees outside. For an instant, on waking, I forgot about the events of the day before. It was another beautiful fall day on the Trail. As I rolled over, preparing my hiker-hobbled muscles to jump down from the upper bunk, the memory came rushing back to me. Blackness swam around the edges of my vision. I held tightly to the headboard of the bunk, afraid of falling, and I focused on my breathing until the horror subsided a little. Looking around the room, I was astounded that the surface of everything maintained its continuity: the same light on the sleeping faces of my companions; the same cool air with faint smells of concrete and carpeting, wood and wool and hikers; the sound of birdsong and wind stirring the leaves outside the windows.

I put on my fleece jacket over the hiking clothes I'd slept in, and walked upstairs to the computer. There was a message from Caveman. He and Spike were alive and well, but they'd had to seal their windows with tape to keep out the acrid plume of smoke. *In all of my thoughts*, he wrote, *hikers kept coming to mind: people who would emerge from the woods to see the news footage of the recent past, a stark contrast to the world of the Trail . . . It's so hard to believe that you were just visiting us and that something like this can happen at any time, anywhere.*

There was no message from Tony. *He's probably still working*, I thought. *Too busy to check his e-mail.* At least, that was what I tried to tell myself, but uglier thoughts kept forcing their way into my mind.

Downstairs, someone had turned on the television. I couldn't look at the screen, dreading what I might see there. The bland, impossibly cheerful voice of the commentator droned on: "All flights have been grounded; American airspace is closed. We don't know whether more attacks are planned. Officials are concerned about the possibility of chemical and biological agents . . . Preliminary investigations indicate that a group of Islamic fundamentalists may be responsible. Stay tuned for the latest breaking news."

I couldn't listen any more. I went into the bunkroom to pack. More than anything, I wanted to be back on the Trail, following the white blazes. I desperately needed the simplicity and purity of Trail life, where each footstep brought me closer to a goal. *It could happen at any time, anywhere*, I thought. *But I can't sit here and wait for it. I need the illusion, at least, that I'm accomplishing something. That I'm making my life into something meaningful.*

It was a subdued group that left the hostel that morning: Isis and Porkchop and I; Tiki, Toast, Johnny Steel. The weather had cooled overnight. A brisk wind came between the spruce trees. The landscape seemed to be half water: the wind-scuffed expanses of Moxie Pond and Sabbath Day Pond (which would have been called lakes in any other state), and countless smaller tarns nestled into the peat bogs beside the trail. The sky seemed preternaturally blue and flawless. It took me a moment to realize why: no jet contrails, from horizon to horizon.

We camped at Little Swift River Pond. There was no river, swift or otherwise, but a wide mud-bottomed pond stretched out beside the campsite, rimmed with spindly spruce trees. A pair of battered aluminum canoes lay in the undergrowth, with paddles stowed beneath them. Isis and Porkchop wrestled one to the edge of the water, and I helped Johnny Steel launch the other. I jumped into my sister's boat, though, when we had them both floating.

"C'mon, jackrabbit," Johnny Steel said with a wink. "You don't wanna take a ride in my canoe?"

"You're a very attractive man, Johnny Steel," I said. "And very interesting. But Isis and Porkchop have an even *more* interesting guy in their boat—Harry Potter!"

Isis held up the book, laughing, and we paddled to the far shore to read out loud as the sun went down. The surface of the water became smooth in the evening calm, reflecting every needle of the trees along the shore. My sister's voice rose and fell. I lost myself in the story, so immersed in the adventures of fictional eleven-year-olds that I didn't hear Johnny Steel paddle up beside us.

"You girls see the swamp donkey?"

I almost jumped at the sound of his voice. "The what?"

"Swamp donkey. Moose," he explained. "C'mon. I'll show you where she is."

"Swamp donkey," Porkchop said, grinning. "I like that."

Isis put the book down and we paddled along beside his canoe. Around a small curve of the shore, we saw the moose. She was a female, without antlers, but still an undeniably impressive animal. Her massive brown frame, sunk halfway in the water, was larger than a horse's body. She looked up as we came into view, her scooplike ears swiveling around, water dripping from her bulbous nose and the load of pondweeds caught in her jaws.

"Awesome," Porkchop whispered. "I've never seen one in the wild before."

The momentum of our boats kept sliding us forward, until we could see the separate hairs of her shaggy brown coat.

"Don't get too close," Johnny Steel cautioned. "Moose can have a temper."

It was hard to imagine that this placid-looking animal could be dangerous, but I had heard enough cautionary tales from outdoorsmen in Maine and Alaska. I dug my paddle into the still brown pondwater to bring us to a halt. We snapped pictures as the sun went down. At first the moose flapped her ears with annoyance each time someone's shutter clicked, but eventually she ignored us and went back to her dinner. She ducked her head underwater and emerged with clumps of dripping vegetation in her mouth. We could hear the crunching and grinding of her teeth. I sat back and watched the moose eating: so powerful, so unconcerned.

Back at the campsite, we found Disco sitting beside a fire. Isis sat next to him, cooking dinner, but he didn't seem to be in a mood to talk. Toast and Porkchop and I told jokes and stories, laughing, taking refuge in the traditions of Trail life. The sounds of our voices, the wind in the trees, the slow progress of evening across the sky seemed so much more real than the nightmare taking place in the outside world.

Sing-song and Tiger Cakes came up the trail at dusk. They set up their tarps at the far edge of the clearing and came over to the fire.

"Hey, guys," I said. "Do you know everybody here?"

"Most of 'em," Tiger Cakes said, flicking off her headlamp and sitting down on a log by the fire. "I don't think I know this guy."

"I'm Johnny Steel." He extended a hand.

"Johnny Steel!" Sing-song said. "We heard you were a gay superhero!"

"News travels fast," he said, with a small ironic lift of his eyebrows. His reaction had changed quite a bit, I noticed, since that night at Upper Goose Pond when he had frantically sought a new trail name.

"So is it true?" Tiger Cakes said. "'Cause gay people could really use some representation in the superhero community. I mean, there's all kinds of speculation about Batman and Robin, but they're not exactly out of the closet."

Johnny Steel sat back, his expression hovering between resignation and amusement. "Johnny Steel isn't gay himself," he finally said. "But he's a super-hero who helps gay people out. Like, if there was a gay person caught in a burning building somewhere, I'd fly up and rescue them."

The image of burning buildings, with no hope of escape, came back to all of us, horrible and immediate.

"Johnny Steel, where does your name really come from?" I asked him in the silence that followed.

"The brothers at the fire academy in Missouri gave it to me—we all called each other brothers. Professional firefighters do; it's like a secret club or some-thing. A brotherhood. Anyway, the steel part of my name came from my heat tolerance, I always thought. I was kind of notorious that way. The fire acad-emy had this hot room, where you'd go in with all your gear for simulations. They'd crank it up so it was like being in a burning house. And I could spend longer in there than anybody else. I'd come out of there with my eyebrows singed off under my helmet, and I wouldn't even have noticed." He laughed a little. "Probably not the smartest thing, to fry my brain like that . . . But I was good at it, you know? First thing in my life I could remember being really good at. Steel's got the highest melting point of any regular building material, so they started calling me Mr. Steel."

He reached into the fire, bare-handed, and picked up a burning log. Without urgency, he set it down in another part of the fire.

"How do you *do* that?" Porkchop asked him.

"It's really not that hard. You look for the dark places. Those are the parts that aren't as hot. You just pick it up by the dark spots and don't touch the orange." He moved another log, careful but unhurried. No one else was will-ing to try it, though.

I took his hand and studied it by the light of my headlamp: his blunt fin-gers were slightly sooty, but uninjured and cool to the touch. "I can see where the steel part of your name comes from," I said. "What about the Johnny part?"

"I always figured it came from John 15:13. It's a Bible verse I carried with me all the time, taped in my helmet. A lot of firefighters do. I'm not religious or anything; I just kept it with me 'cause it seemed so fitting."

He went over to his pack and returned with a wrinkled index card. By the light of his headlamp, I could see that the edges were brown and curled from exposure to heat. Johnny Steel's cramped, angular handwriting spelled out, *John 15:13. Greater love hath no man than this, that a man lay down his life for his friends.*

"I wish I could be in New York," he said suddenly, savagely. "I could *do* something there. There's a tradition in the fire house that if a brother's lost in the line of duty, nobody leaves the site until his remains are found for a proper burial. Two hundred and some years of firefighting in this country, the tradition's never been broken. And now it's shot to hell."

The stars came out as they would any other night, points of brightness against a velvet sky. I looked around the fire at the faces of my friends. Fear and uncertainty were mirrored in everyone's eyes.

"Whatever happens," Disco said, "whatever comes out of this, it's not going to be good. Violence like that, it's a disease. When it gets out in the world, it doesn't stop. Thousands more people are gonna die."

"What can we do against that kind of hate?" I said.

Disco shrugged. "Keep doin' what you're doin'. The world's full of good people. Be one of 'em and help keep it that way. As for me, I can't take this so-called civilization any more. Think I'll go back to minin' in Alaska for a while. Soon as I get a little money together, I'm gonna find me an island somewhere. A place where I don't have to deal with people."

"What about the Trail?" Isis asked him. "Don't you want to finish the Trail?"

He shook his head. "Not any more. There's things I'll miss, sure. But I was never in it to finish the Trail, anyway. I was out here 'cause I got tired of bein' alone all the time. Right now, I figure I've seen enough of what people can do to each other to last me a good long time. Think I'll hitch out tomorrow from the next road, try to get down to Boston. Hitch across the country if I can; get on a ferry in Seattle and go back where I belong."

"I feel like I belong here," Isis said quietly. "Even if the world all goes to hell in a handbasket tomorrow. Right here, right where we are, is where *I* want to be."

A loon called, off somewhere in the distance. We could hear the splashing footsteps of the moose foraging at the edge of the pond. Inside our little circle of firelight, I felt, for the moment, safe.

Isis

We passed the road into Rangeley in midmorning. No one felt ready for another town stop. It was a damp day, not raining yet, but chilly in a way that permeated our clothing, making even our sweat feel cold. Two miles past the road, a thin white plume of smoke rose from the firepit at Piazza Rock Shelter. We walked over to investigate, and found the shelter empty.

"Some idiot left his fire going," muttered Johnny Steel, but instead of putting it out, he stirred the coals and added some sticks from the pile beside the firepit. The rest of us fanned out through the woods, gathering armloads of branches. Johnny Steel built the fire up until it roared, and we stood around it, eating our morning snacks. Strange, to have a fire by daylight. I watched the pale flames flicker along the edges of the wood, trying to keep my mind off the image from the television screen. *Warmth. A blessing, today.*

"My hero," jackrabbit said to Johnny Steel, holding her hands out over the flames.

"I'm not a hero," he answered quietly. "I'm just good with fire."

We crossed Saddleback in blowing fog, walking fast over the bare rock above treeline. Even under the forest cover, small gusts of wind reached down and lifted the hair on the back of my neck. The damp ground made my toes go numb; I was tempted to put my sandals on for warmth. We were still a few miles from Poplar Ridge Lean-to when the sky began to darken—we must have spent longer than I realized at Johnny Steel's fire.

I heard a snatch of whistled music through the trees, and a moment later a hiker came around a bend in the trail, walking toward us. A tall man with a mop of light-colored curls—could it be Tuba Man? I remembered how he'd appeared out of the dusk on the day before we reached Springer. No; this guy was older, thinner than Tuba Man, but I knew I'd seen him before.

"Isis?" he said. "Isis and jackrabbit!"

"Breaking Wind! What are you doing in Maine?" I asked. "Are you yo-yoing?"

"No, I'm flip-flopping. Completing my hike. I was off all summer."

"Were you working?" jackrabbit asked him.

"I was raising a fawn."

"How'd you end up doing that?"

"Well, I have a friend who runs a wildlife rehabilitation center. I was off the Trail, visiting him, when somebody gave him a newborn fawn. He asked me if I'd like to take care of it."

"Wow! Will you tell us about it?"

"Sure, but I'm getting cold standing here," he said. "I'll walk to the shelter with you and stay there tonight. It's only a mile or so back."

We walked in single file through the dusk, while Breaking Wind told us about his summer pretending to be the fawn's mother: feeding her from a bottle, racing through the woods beside her, showing her where to find fresh grass and twigs.

"I couldn't see anyone or speak out loud for three months," he told us. "I had to teach her to be afraid of other people."

Tiki ran out of dog food for Jade a day's hike before Stratton. We were staying on Sugarloaf, in the hexagonal ski lodge known as the Octagon. Across the valley, the ridge of the Bigelows seemed to fill the horizon, rosy in the evening light.

"I'm going to have to blue-blaze down to the ski resort," Tiki said. "Hitch into Stratton and stay in a hotel." He turned to me. "Do you want to come?"

I looked out at the mountains, mauve and orange and gold, and didn't answer him right away. I wished I could stay in that glass tower with its view of the mountains for months, singing rounds with jackrabbit and Porkchop. I wasn't ready to face the world and find out what new disasters might have happened in our absence. But I would have to, tomorrow at the latest. A night alone with Tiki might make the transition easier. And he wanted me to go with him. I turned away from the window, smiling at him.

We dressed for an expedition; hats and jackets and tattered rain pants. Although the sky was clear, the northern side of the mountain lay in shadow. The wind slammed against us, almost knocking us off our feet. At the top, the ski trail was covered in fist-sized chunks of rock that slipped loose as we stepped on them, clattering away down the steep slope. Across from us, the Bigelows darkened to a rich purple color and seemed to rise higher and higher over our heads. Soon we reached the beginner slopes, long narrow meadows thick with raspberry canes, not yet mown for the winter season. Jade skipped far out ahead of us, chasing butterflies. She, at least, seemed delighted to be headed to town.

The only thing open in the ski resort was a restaurant, a black-tie place by the looks of it. There didn't seem to be any cars on the road.

"Let's go to dinner," Tiki said. "Maybe one of the waiters can give us a lift to Stratton afterward, if any of them live there."

I wasn't dressed to eat in a place like that, and I hadn't even showered. Besides, it would be expensive. But I shrugged and smiled at Tiki. "That sounds like a good idea."

We stripped off our excess clothing, choosing the least dirty layers to put back on. I pulled out the little bottle of rose-scented hand lotion that I kept in my pack and rubbed some on my face and hands, hoping its mild perfume would mask my body odor enough that I wouldn't offend the other diners. Tiki tied Jade's leash to a railing next to our packs, and draped his fleece over her.

"Town tonight," he promised. "Potted meat product." She wagged her stubby tail, then tucked her paws under herself like a cat and closed her eyes.

The hostess who seated us took no notice of our ragged clothes—perhaps hikers blue-blazed down to this restaurant often. Our waiter, too, took our orders with perfect equanimity.

"Drinks?" he asked, after we'd read off a list of appetizers and entrées. Tiki ordered a bottle of wine.

"Is there anything else I can get you?" the waiter asked.

"Well, this may be a bit of a stretch—"

"Try me," he said, smiling.

"We just hiked down the mountain," I told him, "and we're hoping to get into Stratton tonight. So if you know of anyone in the kitchen or on the wait staff who's going that way, could you please tell them we're looking for a ride?"

"I'm headed to town myself," he answered. "I'd be glad to take you when I get off tonight."

"Thanks so much," I said.

A few minutes later, the hostess came over to our table. "I'm sorry to disturb you," she said, "but we're about to hold a vigil for the victims of the terrorist attacks. If you'd like to join us, please meet me in the courtyard, out the back door and on your left."

She went on to the next table. I wasn't sure what she meant by "vigil." I didn't know if I could stomach a lot of prayer, a lot of rhetoric. Even with my close friends, I hadn't been able to talk about it much. I needed time to mourn before trying to put it into words. *This vigil is important to someone here,* I told myself, *and I will honor that.* I stood up, and Tiki, across the table, did the same. We waited in the narrow concrete courtyard with a growing crowd of waiters, diners, and kitchen staff. Overhead, stars had begun to come out. A bitter wind blew down between the buildings. The hostess appeared and handed out candles with paper cups around them. One of the waiters walked around the circle, lighting them.

"Now we're just going to have a moment of silence," the hostess said.

A quiet sigh went up from the group as we bowed our heads over the candles. Standing shoulder to shoulder with the strangers from the table beside us, with the wind whipping at our candle flames, I felt a strange lightening in my chest. *This is, for all of us, a chance to mourn.*

jackrabbit

After Isis and Tiki left the Octagon, Johnny Steel and I sat close to the giant cast iron stove, breaking up the pile of dead wood we had hauled in earlier in the afternoon. Porkchop stood at the back of the room, perusing a map on the wall and comparing it with the shapes of the mountains outside.

"You guys, I think I see it!" Porkchop called. We came over and looked where she was pointing. A thin sliver of a mountain hovered on the horizon in the rich, failing light, distant but unmistakable: Katahdin.

"I think you're right," I said, feeling a kind of nervous energy rise inside me.

"Are you sure?" Johnny Steel said. "It's, like, two hundred miles from here."

"Two hundred by the A.T.," I said. "But the Trail loops around a lot in the Wilderness. As the crow flies, it's more like sixty or seventy."

We all stared at the distant wedge of stone, low sunlight flaring along its edge. Porkchop's face was full of wonder, entranced. My own face, I'm sure, reflected something more like regret; I didn't want our endpoint to be so real, so close. When the Trail ended, I would have to face the outside world in all its meaningless brutality. I didn't know if I had the strength.

Johnny Steel stared out at Katahdin for a few moments, too, but his face was entirely impassive. "Got to keep the fire going," he said, rubbing his hands together. "It's gonna get cold tonight."

There was a message board on the wall next to the map, with a single nearly spent dry-erase marker hanging on a string. In winter, no doubt, the board was used for reporting ski conditions and trail closures. In summer, it had become an unofficial A.T. register. There was hardly any space, but we wrote out our names and the date along the bottom edge: *Man of Steel, Rabbit of Jack, Chop of Pork, 9/14/01.* In one of the upper corners, someone—Iculus?—had scribbled *partially defatted fatty pork fat.* I smiled.

Porkchop and I had a potluck; she made bowtie pasta with homemade sauce that she had dehydrated. She added strips of dried tomato sauce, dark as fruit leather, to a pot of boiling water before she poured in the noodles. She claimed to be sick of it, but the rich marinara tasted infinitely better, to my mind, than the pot of pesto mashed potatoes that I cooked up. We offered to share with Johnny Steel.

"You're a vegetarian, aren't you, jackrabbit? All of my food's got meat in it."

"I'd almost rather eat meat than these infernal potatoes."

"These are actually pretty good, jackrabbit," Porkchop said, licking her spoon. "Where'd you get the idea to mix pesto and potatoes?"

"It was Toast's recipe, actually," I said. "The original was creamy pesto grits, but it's hard to find grits this far north."

All the little rituals of Trail life were comforting: boiling water, feeding the fire; inflating my air mattress and laying out my sleeping bag on the floor. The biggest comfort was our singing. After dinner, when the stars came out all around us and the wind howled louder in the eaves, Porkchop and I sang a few rounds. The harmonies sounded sparse without Isis, though. I hoped she had made it down the ski trail before sunset. I realized it was the first night in more than a year that we had spent apart.

Frost from our breath covered all the windows of the lodge in the morning. I woke early and watched the light change from gray to pink to gold, refracted as though coming through stained glass. Frost covered the floorboards, too, and it was hard to get myself motivated to roll out of my sleeping bag. The cold made my stiff muscles complain.

Johnny Steel got up a few minutes after me. He put on all his warm clothes and stepped out onto the concrete balcony in front of the ski lodge. "Jackrabbit, check this out!" he called. A chilling gust of wind came through the half-open door.

I followed him out into the clear brilliance of the morning. The cold wind was electric, alive, shocking me awake. The whole top of the mountain sparkled with frost, millions of diamonds. An inch-deep puddle at the edge of the balcony had frozen solid.

"It's beautiful," I said over the sound of the wind. But it was also a good reminder that winter was returning fast. I looked again toward the far-off silver crest of Katahdin. Standing there in the cold, I didn't feel so sorry that the Trail was coming to an end. I didn't know if I would be strong enough for whatever was waiting out in the world beyond the A.T. But I knew that I wouldn't be strong enough, even if I had the money, for another winter on the Trail.

We packed our gear and ate a quick breakfast, standing up, stamping our feet to stay warm. I took one last look around the Octagon. The plate glass windows cleared as the sun melted the frost. I could already see clouds gathering above the White Mountains, southwest of us, but the northern sky remained clear. Lakes in the valleys shimmered white-gold; the dark green flanks of the mountains faded to blue with distance, quiet under the bright sky. *That's where we're going*, I thought. *Until the last white blaze.*

Below treeline and out of the wind, the air felt twenty degrees warmer. The trail led up and down steep, wooded mountains, with descents and rock-scrambles almost as treacherous as the notches of New Hampshire. Between the trees, we glimpsed an occasional view of the valley. A few maples in the swamps blazed with fall color.

For some reason, the day seemed to drag on and on. None of us had much enthusiasm for hiking; we could barely summon the energy to converse. Finally Porkchop stopped and sat down on a log by the side of the trail.

"I've got to stop and eat something," she said. "I feel totally drained."

"Me, too." I dropped my pack and sat next to her.

"I'm gonna go on," Johnny Steel said. We heard his tramping footsteps going down the path for a few moments, and then the sound faded.

"This is silly," Porkchop said. "I usually enjoy being out here so much, but today it's just not fun. There's this little voice in the back of my head that says, 'Porkchop—'" she laughed a little at the sound of her name—"'why are you out here when you could be in town, resting and eating yummy food?'"

"I've been having the same kinds of thoughts," I admitted. "I think it's something to do with Isis and Tiki going into town when we didn't."

"Maybe," she said. "But we get to feel virtuous for white-blazing, anyway."

"Small consolation. White-blazing, greasy town food." I made a gesture of weighing the two in my hands. "I think I'd choose the town food, at this point. But we're only, like, three miles from Stratton, and the quickest way there is the path we're on. Do you want part of this Clif bar, Porkchop?"

"Is that one of the carrot cake ones?"

"Yeah."

"No, thanks. Kind of you to offer, but I just don't like them as much as I used to. You know, when I first tasted one, I thought, 'Wow! Just like carrot cake. This is great!' But after six months . . .'"

"They get a little old," I said, crunching down the last few bites and taking a swig from my water bottle.

We stood up and kept walking. After a few minutes, I heard something large crashing through the underbrush beside the trail, and an odd, resonant, nasal sound, like someone grunting and blowing his nose at the same time. *What in the world is Johnny Steel doing?* I wondered.

Porkchop, just ahead of me, stopped and made a small noise of alarm. "Oh . . ." she backed up a few steps, nearly bumping into me, and in that time my brain realized what was standing in the trail, less than fifteen feet away: not Johnny Steel, but an enormous bull moose. His rack of antlers stretched from one side of the trail to the other. I could smell his thick, mammalian stench, with undertones of moss and rotting vegetation, from where I stood. The moose stopped making his odd sound when his beady brown eyes fixed on Porkchop and me. He shook his head, pawing the ground, and swiveled his ears. For an instant I was afraid he would charge straight toward us. Those antlers looked big enough to scoop us both up and fling us into the trees. The moose turned aside, though, and crashed off into the underbrush, kicking up his heels as he disappeared.

"Wow!" Porkchop said. "At first I thought it was Johnny Steel making that funny noise."

"Me, too! I had no idea a moose could do that. I can't even imitate that sound. It was like a Wagnerian tenor with a head cold." We looked at each other for a moment, and then we broke down laughing.

"Oh, that was wonderful!" Porkchop said. "I guess now we know why we were still hiking. Town has its perks, but out here on the Trail you never know what you'll find next. Moose opera."

Isis

Tiki's sister's boyfriend Nigel met us in Stratton. He'd been a chef in New York, but his restaurant, just a block from the World Trade Center, had closed after the terrorist attacks. Instead of looking for a new job, he'd asked Tiki if he could come out and hike the rest of Maine with him.

"Nigel's an athlete," Tiki told me. "He works out at the gym, like, every day. I don't know how well he'll deal with the lack of showers, but he'll keep up with us."

Medium height and slender, with a short, dark beard and an Afro, Nigel looked like a hiker already. He fit in well with the hiker crowd, too, playing hacky-sack in the parking lot with Dream Catcher, Tiki, and Tiger Cakes, and trading lines of rhyme with Beer Poet, a friend of Johnny Steel's. Quite a group of us gathered at the White Wolf Inn, a rickety wooden building that looked like it had been borrowed from the set of a Western, except for its coat of brilliant turquoise paint. The Honeymooners sat together on the porch, wearing town clothes that rivaled the outfits from The Cabin's loaner closet: satin shirts in brilliant paisley prints, a sarong for her and a pair of green wind pants for him. Charlotte was there, too, along with the whole contingent of people with Kool-Aid-dyed hair. She introduced us to her brother Tommy, whose longish hair was dyed a wild shade of green, his girlfriend Berry, whose thick ponytail was streaked with blue, and their friend Sticker Dan, who had dyed both his hair and beard dandelion yellow.

Julien came in a few minutes after jackrabbit and Porkchop, wheeling his pack along in a grocery cart that he'd found across town. "I have found a new way to hike," he told us. "No more of *carrying* my pack—now I push it."

Tiki and I had already gotten the groceries; all we had left to do was put our clothes in the laundry and repackage our food, a three-day supply to take us to Caratunk, where we'd meet Compañero to go to the Common Ground Fair. None of us seemed in a hurry to do the chores. Porkchop, Sing-song, jackrabbit, and I sat on the edge of the porch, trying to see if we could remember anything in four-part harmony. Beer Poet and Julien joined the game of hacky-sack. Johnny Steel sat down on the porch. Jackrabbit went over to talk to him; pretty soon, they were engaged in a friendly tussle, pitting her Tae Kwon Do moves against his firefighter's self-defense training and the dirty tricks he'd picked up in bar fights.

"Hey, no fair!" I heard my sister holler.

"Nobody fights fair on the street," came Johnny Steel's voice. "You think somebody's gonna . . . oof!" I looked over to see him sprawled on the ground.

We all went to dinner together, putting our tables together in a row that stretched halfway across the restaurant.

"What to eat, what to eat?" mused Johnny Steel, poring over the wild game section of the menu. It was his turn to order; the waitress tapped her pen on the paper.

"I will have . . ." he closed his eyes and brought his finger down on the paper, then opened them to see where it had landed. "Braised quail!" he announced triumphantly.

What the waitress eventually brought him was the smallest quail I'd ever seen. While everyone else had heaping platters of burgers and fries or deep casserole dishes of lasagna, great big strapping Johnny Steel got a bird the size of a robin, lying on its back in a pile of lettuce leaves.

"It's the pink scarf special," Julien joked.

Johnny Steel, desperately signaling the waitress, ignored him.

"I'd like a couple burgers with my quail," he called out. "And an order of fries, and whatever else you've got, please."

In the end, Johnny Steel got to finish Nigel's lasagna as well as his own meal. Though he fit in with the hiker crowd in most other respects, Nigel had yet to develop the Appetite. I wondered how he'd do with the actual hiking.

Jackrabbit, Porkchop, Tiki, Nigel, and I left town late the next afternoon, after dawdling over our chores and going back to the restaurant for lunch. (Jackrabbit tried to persuade Johnny Steel to hike out with us, but he claimed that he needed at least another day's worth of town food to make up for his meager dinner the night before. "I'll catch up," he'd promised. "Once I regain my strength, I'll fly!") We hiked the five miles of steady uphill to Horns Pond Lean-to. Nigel dropped behind pretty quickly, and Tiki slowed down to stay with him. They arrived half an hour after the rest of us. Nigel looked tired but cheerful.

He fared slightly worse the next day, a ten over peaks of the Bigelows. We ate lunch with Julien on Avery Peak, enjoying the view of Flagstaff Lake in the valley below us and the mountains stretching to the horizon on either side. Nigel stayed on the peak to rest a while after we finished eating. Tiki waited with him, and we didn't see them again until they came into Little Bigelow Lean-to an hour after dark, more than two hours after the rest of us had arrived. Nigel hardly spoke while he set up his stove, and he went to bed as soon as he had eaten.

In the morning, we reviewed our options. We had to reach the Kennebec River by two o'clock the next afternoon to catch Steve's ferry in time to meet Compañero in Caratunk. Twenty-one miles, in a day and a half. Jackrabbit, Porkchop, and I wanted to hike the seventeen to Pierce Pond and spend some time there in the morning. I remembered how lovely the shelter was, with its grove of red pines and the rock ledge overlooking the lake. Nigel was pretty sure he couldn't hike that far in one day; he and Tiki planned to camp a few miles before the shelter.

The five of us hiked together all morning, along with Julien and Sing-song. We stopped for a late lunch and a swim at East Carry Pond, only seven miles from Pierce Pond.

"This is it for me," Nigel said, lying back on the narrow sand beach. "I'll catch up tomorrow."

"This *is* a lovely place," Sing-song said. "I'll probably camp near here, too."

Julien had wandered off down the beach, looking for skipping stones. Porkchop, jackrabbit, and I hiked on alone, just the three of us for the first time since the Whites. We gathered firewood, set up our tent and Porkchop's tarp by the water, and sat on the shore to eat our potluck supper. Tommy and Berry, the only occupants of the shelter, joined us for the meal. While we ate, we watched the sun set over the pond, patches of gold dancing on the water, reflected off the undersides of the clouds. There were no loons this time, but we sang our own songs late into the night.

A rustling and stomping of feet woke me, some hours after we had gone to bed. *Did Tiki and Nigel decide to night-hike after all?* I wondered sleepily. It would be good to spend the morning with them.

The rising sun bathed the far shore in rich yellow light for a few minutes before disappearing into a cloud bank. A few red maple crowns and yellow birches stood out against the green hillside, their leaves already changed. After the clouds dulled the light on the opposite shore, jackrabbit and I walked up the hill to the shelter. I was surprised to see that Tommy and Berry were still the only hikers in the lean-to.

"Was that you guys up late last night?" I asked. "I thought I heard some-body else hike in."

"That was Johnny Steel and the Beer Poet," Berry told me. "They just stopped in to check the register."

"At eleven o'clock at night? Where were they going?" asked jackrabbit.

"They were planning to camp on the bank of the Kennebec," Tommy said.

"What for?" I asked. "Steve's ferry doesn't start running until ten in the morning."

"They started at Horns Pond yesterday," Berry said. "I think they hiked all that way just to see if they could do it. Johnny Steel said that ever since he missed his chance to do the Maryland Challenge, he's been meaning to hike a long day somewhere."

"Horns Pond to the Kennebec?" Jackrabbit whistled. "That's a thirty . . . no, more like thirty-one! They could have picked an easier place to do it."

We took full advantage of our morning off, building a fire and making pot after pot of tea. Porkchop and I went for a quick swim; this time, I couldn't lure jackrabbit in. The water was stunningly cold, making my whole skin tin-gle—an "alive check," Porkchop called it. We huddled by the fire afterward, taking turns reading to each other from *Harry Potter.* Then we pooled all the cookable food we had left, making ourselves a big pot of Lipton alfredo and pasta primavera with half a stick of cheese chopped into it. Jackrabbit skimmed through the register while the pot steamed above the coals.

"All it says is, 'Johnny Steel and the Beer Poet were here at ten-thirty, completing our epic hike from Horns Pond to the Kennebec!'" she reported indignantly. "The Beer Poet didn't even write a poem."

"I guess you'll have to come up with one for him," I said.

"I was just thinking I might," she said, scribbling in the register. Ten minutes later, she recited her handiwork for us.

> Listen, my children, and I'll reveal
> the midnight hike of Johnny Steel—
> the Man of Steel and the Poet of Beer
> hiked all the way from Horns Pond to here,
> and then, to complete their epic trek,
> they marched on down to the Kennebec!
> Thirty-one miles from dawn to dark,
> and the first ten, at least, were no walk in the park.
> Why did they do it? Were they drunk?
> What lured them to Caratunk?
> The answer is known to them alone,
> but I'd say it was testosterone!

jackrabbit

The Kennebec River ran deep and swift on the day we arrived as north-bounders. Light-filled water the color of bronze and amber rippled over its bed of stones. Steve Longley, the ferryman, waved from the far bank and pushed his canoe into the water. He crossed the river standing up, his tall, slim body expertly balanced in the back of the canoe. I remembered him from our southbound trip, a laconic philosopher with an air of quiet confidence.

Steve remembered us, too. "The Barefoot Sisters." He nodded to our companions, Porkchop, Tiki, and Nigel. "People said you'd be headed this way today. I brought you something." He held out a grease-stained paper bag with a tantalizing smell. "Egg rolls from the Chinese place down the road in Bingham."

"Thanks, Steve," I said. "That's really generous of you." I remembered spotting Caratunk on a road map of Maine. It was almost twenty miles from the nearest town of any size. Steve must have had a long drive to bring us the food.

He shrugged. "You guys have come quite a ways."

We divided up the egg rolls and handed chunks to our hiking companions. Isis offered a piece to Steve, but he declined, a glint of amusement in his eyes.

Nigel and Porkchop rode in the first boatload, then Tiki and Skass Dawg. (Jade's skunky miasma had faded, but the name had stayed with her.) Skassy looked decidedly unhappy as she climbed into the canoe; Tiki had to keep a tight hold on her leash. Then it was our turn. Steve brought the canoe back and glided to a stop in the marshy ground at the edge of the river.

"Put your packs in the middle and get the lifejackets on," he said. "You know the drill."

"Did you bring a couple of guys over early this morning?" I asked him. I hoped Johnny Steel and Beer Poet hadn't tried to ford the river after their thirty-miler. "One of them was tall, kind of stocky, curly short brown hair; the other's really skinny with longish blond hair and a beard."

To my relief, he nodded. "First thing in the morning. They told me about their long hike yesterday."

"I'm glad to hear they got over the river okay."

"Oh yeah. Water level's been pretty high the past few weeks; nobody's tried to ford in quite a while . . . Isis, paddle on the downstream side, if you would."

We moved out into the current. Steve steadied the canoe against the rush of water. "I'm glad you guys made it back safe," he said. "You must've had a few adventures since the last time I saw you."

"Quite a few," Isis said. "We were out all winter, dealing with frostbite and hypothermia, and when we got to Georgia in March, we decided to just turn around and come back. It's been great. I never imagined it would be like this."

"Not much farther now," Steve said. "One hundred and fifty-one miles to go when you set foot on that far bank."

"It's amazing," I said. "The closer we get to the end of the Trail, the more . . . *final* everything seems. I think, 'how many more mountains will I climb? How many more times will I set up my tent in the woods?' It's like everything's bathed in a different kind of light. Even this crossing. It becomes like a kind of legend, almost, like you're Charon ferrying us across the Styx—"

"Please don't say that." His voice was grim and tightly controlled. "Please don't compare me to Charon, ferrying the dead. In the first few days, the bridges were closed and they had to bring people off in ferries. Remains of people. My cousin was on the first plane that hit."

For an instant, I felt the same sensation that had overtaken me on the logging road when we first heard of the attacks. The world around me seemed illusory, a thin backdrop that might shatter and spin into nothingness. The image of the plane and the building, etched into my memory, seemed to hover in the air over the wide, golden river.

"I'm so sorry," I said. "I had no idea."

"You had no way to know." His voice was softer now. We proceeded in silence; the only sound was the slap and gurgle of water against the hull. Slowly the ghastly images faded from my mind.

"I remember what you said last summer, when you brought us across," I offered. "That it's never the same river twice."

"That's true," he said. I looked back to where he stood in the stern. There was a distant, haunted look in his eyes. "I'll tell you something else that's true. We all find our own way to ride the river. And this is something I can't claim is true, but I believe it: it's harder on the ones who stay afloat than the ones who go down."

The nose of the canoe slid gently up the bank and Isis stepped out.

"Thank you, Steve," I said. "I'm so sorry to hear about your cousin."

"We ride the river, jackrabbit. We take what the river brings us; we find our own way to cross."

We stayed at the Caratunk House, the elegant bed-and-breakfast where we had spent a night as southbounders. Then, we had stayed in a private room with handmade lace curtains across the windows and doilies on the end tables. This time, we stayed in the bunkhouse to save money—decidedly less luxurious, but still comfortable and well-appointed.

Julien lay on the couch, watching a *South Park* episode on the widescreen TV, when we came in. "The Barefoot Sisters!" he said. "And the famous Porkchop, and Tiki with his Skass Hound. And Nigel—how do you like the Trail, Nigel?"

Nigel grinned. "Man, the Trail's kind of kicking my ass right now, but I love it out here."

"Hey, Julien," Isis said. "Want to come to the Common Ground Fair with us? We're getting off tomorrow with a friend."

"Come on, Julien," I said. "It's the best of American culture."

"Better than *South Park*?" He smiled. "Me, I thought this was the best your country had to offer." On the screen, someone had, once again, killed Kenny.

"Worlds better than *South Park*," I said.

Julien considered. "I do not think I can."

"Oh, you have to!" Isis said. "It'll be so much fun."

Julien's face turned serious. "No, I really cannot go. My visa expires in two weeks. I need to finish the Trail. If I show up at the border, looking like I do now, with an expired visa . . . your government, I think, they would put me in jail."

"They're not being *that* strict, are they?" I said. "I mean, Julien, your socks might be classifiable as a biological weapon, but they're not going to lock you up for being a few days late on your visa."

Nigel made a grim face. "You haven't been watching the news much, have you? They're tossing all kinds of people in jail on less of a pretext than that. It's crazy, man. So much bad shit in the world out there. You guys are damn lucky to be out of it all, right now."

"It is horrible, horrible, what happened," Julien said.

"More horrible things coming down the pipeline," Nigel answered.

I thought of what Disco had said at Little Swift River Pond, before he left the Trail: *whatever comes out of this, it's not going to be good. Violence like that, it's a disease. When it gets out in the world, it doesn't stop.*

I shuddered. "Please, can we talk about something else?" My voice came out higher than I meant it to, sounding like a child's, scared and pleading. "I'm sorry." I managed to get my voice back under control. "I just have a hard time with it right now."

"I think we all do," Tiki said quietly.

"Hey, there's a guitar here!" Porkchop exclaimed. She sat down on one of the bunks and began to tune the strings. "Jackrabbit, what was that harmony you were working on for 'I'll Fly Away'?"

Compañero came to the hostel in the late morning to pick us up for the Fair. He got out of the car, smiling broadly, still as lean and wiry as he had been on the Trail.

"Isis and jackrabbit! So good to see you. And I think I met the rest of you on Moody Mountain, but remind me of your names . . ."

Porkchop, Tiki, and Nigel introduced themselves.

"I talked to your mom," he said to Isis and me. "We're planning to meet up at a campground near the Fair. Your stepdad's coming, too. They sound like fun people." He turned to our companions. "I think there'll be space for all of us, if you can fit four across in the backseat. This car's bigger than it looks." He patted the station wagon's open door.

We loaded our gear and climbed into the car. With everyone's packs in the trunk and Jade lying across our laps in the backseat, there was ample space.

"So how are things going, Compañero?" I asked him.

"Fairly well, considering. I found a good job as a pharmacist in a hospital out in western Maine. The pay's a bit lower than what I made in Georgia, but the environment is so much better. I can be out in the mountains, hiking, any time I want. I'm closer to my family in Connecticut, too. In times like this, I'm grateful to be near them."

Woods and fields unwound beside the highway, and the broad Kennebec flowed beside us, steel-gray under an overcast sky.

"Do you hear anything from Highlander?" I asked Compañero. I remembered our Mount Everett expedition as if it had been yesterday.

"Not much," he said. "He finished the Trail in June. Last I heard, he was back in San Francisco looking for a job. Highlander." Compañero chuckled. "That man could sing like nobody else. And all those Ogden Nash poems he knew . . ."

"When I first met him, I thought there was no way he'd thru-hike," Isis said. "But he had more grit than most people."

"I guess you never can predict that kind of thing," I said. "You never know how someone will adapt to Trail life."

"Yeah, man," Tiki said. "I never thought I'd see Nigel out here."

"Guess your sister hasn't told you much about me," Nigel said with a small smile.

"Oh, Natalie's told me plenty. I always thought you were a city boy, though."

"Not really. I mean, I grew up in the city. New York. But I feel like I have to get out of it every once in a while, you know? I mean, even before all this shit went down. There's something so . . . soul-suffocating in a city. I have to get back to the woods. I was out of town, actually, when the attacks happened. I drove back in to make sure Natalie was okay. And it was crazy—there were all these blockades, and police checks, and things . . . it got to the point where I was like, 'man, I'd better go into the next 7-11 bathroom I find and shave off my 'fro.' Couldn't do anything about the color of my skin, though . . . I got to the apartment and picked up Natalie, and we left. We just took off. She's back with her folks in North Carolina, and me . . . I needed to clear my head. Breathe some air that didn't have that cloud of . . . God, I don't want to think about it. I just want to leave it behind."

I clenched my fists tightly and took a deep breath. I hadn't come nearly as close to the site of the disaster as Nigel had, but the aftershocks of it had ripped through my world, too.

"Sorry," Nigel said after a moment. "Here I am trying to forget it, and it keeps coming back. I should talk about something else. If I was gonna thru-hike, what's a good month to start?"

We kept to the safe, neutral territory of Trail stories and hiking lore, a self-contained world we could all step into and forget the chaos outside.

A light rain began as we reached the campground, a collection of RVs and shabby plots of grass at the edge of a lake. We met our mom at the tent site that Compañero had reserved. Rain beaded up in her graying dark blond hair. I hadn't seen her since she'd hiked the Roans with us in spring. She looked older now, almost fragile, but her blue eyes still held the same youthful light. We jumped out of the car and hugged her.

"Oh, sweeties. It is so, so wonderful to see you." She held us tightly, as though to convince herself we were real and truly present. Then she let go and introduced herself to the rest of our group. "I feel like I know you already," she said. "The girls have told me so much about you."

"Uh-oh," Tiki said with his impish little-boy smile.

Our stepdad, David, stood back at first, shy with so many people. His pale blue eyes sparkled under the brim of a baseball cap. A few wisps of long white hair had escaped from his ponytail.

I ran over to hug him. "I missed you, Davidoo."

He grinned at the old nickname. "I missed you, too . . . jackrabbit. Are you coming home after the Trail?"

"For a while, anyway."

"Good. You can tell me about all your adventures while we stack the cordwood for winter."

"You mean you guys still haven't gotten the wood stacked? You said they delivered it in August!"

He shrugged. "We wanted to save some work for you guys, so you could feel useful around the house."

"Considerate of you," I laughed. "David, come meet our friends from the Trail. This is Porkchop, and Tiki, and Nigel."

"David?" Porkchop said. "Wow, you look just like Paul Newman!"

He grinned, his shyness fading a little. "My momma always said I should be in pictures . . ."

"Well, you *are*, David," I said. "He's just behind the camera instead of on screen," I explained to the rest of the hikers. "David has an independent film company. Documentaries, mostly."

"A really small company," David said. "My friend Gunnar's the writer and producer. I do the camera work and editing."

"They run it out of a barn in our backyard," Isis added.

Our mom leaned on David's shoulder. "He keeps saying he'll retire, but then another project comes along."

The rain picked up, blurring the view across the lake. David enlisted Compañero's help in setting up a tarp above the picnic table while the rest of us set up our tents. Our mom went to her car and retrieved a cooler, a cast iron kettle, and an enormous basket of vegetables.

"These are all from our garden—peppers, carrots, tomatoes, pole beans. All organic. My girls always say they miss vegetables when they're out in the woods. Try some of these for your first course! I'll start the chili cooking."

Normally the sound of rain on the tent would keep me awake, anxious about the next day's hike and the amount of weight the wet tent would add to my pack. Tonight, though, I was so happy, so grateful for the company of friends and family, that I didn't mind the sound at all. I went to sleep smiling.

I hadn't been to the Common Ground Fair since high school, but it was exactly like I remembered. The Fair had been an annual event since the early seventies, celebrating rural life, traditional crafts, and organic farming. Aside from the crowds of people in brightly-colored modern clothing, nearly every-thing on the fairgrounds seemed to have come through a time warp from the nineteenth century. Instead of Ferris wheels and roller coasters, the Fair offered hay rides, gardening demonstrations, music, political speeches, live-stock shows, and tents full of hand-crafted pottery, jewelry, and clothing.

A steady stream of people filed through the main gate. Our mom and David went to see a Native American basketry demonstration; Tiki and Nigel headed in the opposite direction to watch a horse race. Porkchop stayed with me and Isis. We walked past the farmers' market, where the stalls displayed potatoes, carrots, garlic, squash and pumpkins, herbs, apples, watermelons, and anything else Maine's brief growing season would support. (One farm had even managed to grow artichokes and sweet potatoes, normally native to much warmer climates.) The colors of the produce seemed twice as bright, jewel-like, under the low, rainy sky.

"I'm hungry," I said.

Porkchop laughed. "We're hikers. Are we ever *not* hungry?"

We bought a medium-sized watermelon and ate it as we walked, carving pieces out with Isis's pocketknife. We maneuvered through the crowds to the food vendors' area, where the aroma of roasting meat and frying vegetables filled the air. It was still early, so the lines were short. In an hour's time, we'd eaten falafel sandwiches, egg rolls, Thai curry, deep-fried shiitake mushrooms, and an enormous order of French fries.

Porkchop rubbed her flat belly. "Dessert."

We found a stall selling pastries, and the three of us split an entire blueberry pie. As we ate it, licking the juice from our fingers, we watched the sheepdog demonstration. A pair of shaggy black-and-white border collies moved the sheep around with a minimum of effort, making them weave around cones and go through a chute. The dogs barely moved; instead, they crouched as though hunting and stared at the sheep with a feral intensity.

"They make it look easy, don't they?" the dog handler said through a megaphone. "Let's bring some of you humans out and see how well you do. I need some volunteers to herd these sheep through the chute. Now, the only rule is, you can't grab the sheep's wool, because that hurts them. You can hold them like this—" he demonstrated, bending down and crooking his arm around a sheep's neck "—but not too tightly. Who wants to be a human sheepdog?"

He chose six kids from the legion of volunteers. They ran onto the field and instant pandemonium ensued—sheep scurried in all directions, except where they were supposed to go. Kids dashed here and there across the field. Eventually the group of sheep reassembled itself at the far end of the paddock. Two older children had managed to hold onto one of the sheep, a boy with an arm around its neck and a girl pushing on its rump. They almost reached the chute, but the sheep broke away and trotted to the far end of the field to join its companions. The little flock grazed peacefully, ignoring the now-exhausted children.

"You see? It's not as easy as it looks!" the man said.

But then one of the kids figured it out. A small boy dropped down to his hands, staring fiercely at the sheep, just as the border collies had. The rest of the kids copied him, directing the sheep with the force of their gazes. The flock began to move in a rough bunch. The children herded the sheep in the direction of the chute, and two or three of the animals actually went through it. A roar of applause came from the crowd around the field.

The dog handler shook his head. "Smart kids. Well done." Then he called the dogs back with a complicated series of whistles, and in less than thirty seconds they had brought all the sheep through the chute and right to where he stood.

I shook my head. "What an interesting species we belong to. Who knows what we'd be capable of, if we didn't put so much energy into wiping ourselves out."

The rain picked up, and we went into the exhibition hall. By the doorway, the winner of the giant pumpkin contest displayed its blue ribbon: a pale, fat, lopsided squash big enough to fill a bathtub, weighing in at 278 pounds.

"Let's take it for our next resupply!" Porkchop said. "I bet we could get all the way to Katahdin eating that thing!"

We walked around the tables, looking at countless varieties of fruits and vegetables laid out on paper plates. They ranged from the familiar—picture-perfect jalapeños and carrots and apples—to the bizarre: knobby purple heirloom potatoes from Ecuador, red-and-yellow striped tomatoes, skinny gourds six feet long, and watermelons with delicate yellow-flecked patterns like stars on their dark green skin. Along the walls, racks of preserves and pickles stood beside handmade quilts and lace samplers.

At the far end of the exhibition hall, a crowd had gathered around a man at a podium. We edged closer to hear his words over the sound of rain on the roof.

"We don't need another war," he was saying. "War has a way of perpetuating itself. What we need is an international police effort to bring the perpetrators to justice. And we also need an international dialogue about the causes and consequences of violence like this. With an act so reprehensible, so unthinkable, you have to ask, what's behind this absolute hatred? The first step toward preventing terrorism has to be *understanding* . . ."

I cheered along with the rest of the crowd, feeling a kind of hope returning to me. *So there are people in the rest of the world who believe in the power of dialogue and community. Maybe it's not just the Trail.* These were the first hopeful words I had heard about the situation, and it was the first time that the thought of the attack hadn't given me a rising sense of panic.

"The next few months will be a critical time," the speaker continued. "We can only hope that our leaders will act with courage, compassion, and the careful consideration of the effects their actions will have in the future."

After the speech, Porkchop, Isis, and I felt hungry again. We returned to the pie stall and bought another one, strawberry rhubarb. I felt as though an enormous burden had been lifted from me—*to be able to speak about terrorism, not with the knee-jerk reactions of anguish and rage, but to say instead, where do we go from here?*

Back on the Trail, we hiked the short stretch between Caratunk and Monson in two days. On the open granite ledges of Moxie Bald, I remembered meeting Tenbrooks and watching the "fireworks" of thunderstorms move in across the valley. This time, the low-hanging clouds posed no danger; it was too late in the season for lightning. I looked out over the land: miles of rounded, glacier-scoured mountains with the soft blue-green of spruce forests. Southward, the unmistakable symmetry of the Bigelow Range rose in the middle distance: Avery, West Peak, the twin summits of the Horns. Down in the valley, the still surface of Moxie Pond reflected its fringe of trees and the island in its center, exactly as it had when we were southbound. Then the clouds lifted a little. Shafts of sunlight came down, ethereal, casting momentary light on patches of the landscape. The wet limbs of spruce trees below us glowed for an instant, outlined in gold, until the clouds closed in again.

We camped by the outlet of Bald Mountain Pond, where loons traded their haunting songs back and forth all night. Nigel went to bed early, tired from a long day of hiking. Isis and Tiki went back to Tiki's tent. (Jade, exiled for a different reason than skassiness now, loped around the edges of the campsite, sulking.) I sat up by the fire with Porkchop.

"I can't believe how fast this has all gone," she said, adding another branch to the fire.

"I can't either. Tomorrow, we'll have ten days left." At the Fair, Isis and I had made plans to meet our family at Katahdin on October 3. The date was fixed; our once-endless journey had suddenly become finite.

"Ten days." She hugged her knees to her chest. "I guess we'll have to make the most of it while it lasts, right?"

We sang a few songs as the fire burned lower. Then the rain came and we headed for our tents.

Mist covered the surface of the pond in the morning. The sun rose red-gold behind the curtain of haze; lily pads on the surface shone like small, bright coins. By the time we had packed and eaten breakfast, the sky was clear over the lake. The leaves above us were now half green and half painted with autumn colors. All day, we walked through a brilliant patchwork of translucent hues.

We reached Monson in the early afternoon. In town, we had decided to stay at the Pie Lady's. When we stayed in Monson as southbounders, Mr. Shaw's injunctions to avoid the town's other hostel had been constant and quite vehement. I was kind of wondering what the Pie Lady was like—I didn't imagine that anyone could be quite so unbalanced as Mr. Shaw had suggested and still manage to run a business. Besides, Shaw's Boarding House didn't take dogs. Isis wanted to stay with Tiki, and he had Jade.

The Pie Lady's house was an old three-story Victorian on the edge of town that had seen better days. The white paint on the clapboards was beginning to peel, and grass sprouted up from cracks in the cement walkway to her front steps. There was a welcoming sign hung out front, though, with a hand-painted picture of a steaming pie.

Iculus, Dream Catcher, Stoker, and Charlotte came out of the house as we approached. Charlotte's dog, Zero, tethered to the front steps, wagged his tail when he saw us. He and Jade had a friendly skirmish on the lawn.

"Hey, guys!" I said. "Where's the Pie Lady?"

"She made a grocery run," Iculus said. "She should be back soon."

"I'm curious . . . what's she like?"

Stoker made an inscrutable face. "She's okay. A little . . . high-strung, maybe."

"Woman's a psycho," Dream Catcher said.

"Just don't piss her off," Stoker suggested.

"Dream Catcher, what'd you do?" I asked him.

"I didn't *do* anything. I just said something."

"He'd heard a rumor that she and Keith Shaw had been high school sweethearts," Charlotte said. "He asked her about it. She kinda flipped out."

"Makes good pies, though," Stoker said philosophically, holding up an empty tin.

A car pulled into the driveway and a skinny, short-haired woman, probably in her mid-sixties, stepped out. Dream Catcher backed away slightly.

"You all want rooms tonight?" she said in a low, gravelly smoker's voice. "We got space."

"That would be great," Isis said.

"That dog's gonna hafta stay in the kennel out back," she said to Tiki. "No animals in the house."

The Pie Lady led us inside and up the rickety stairwell. The house had a musty, lived-in smell, but the rooms were clean and relatively cheap. I shared a room with Porkchop and Nigel, across the hall from Isis and Tiki.

"Shower's downstairs across from the kitchen," the Pie Lady said. "I've got Internet upstairs, for anybody that uses it . . . Apple pie's in the oven. Ten bucks a pie, two bucks a slice. But damned if I can remember the last hiker who just bought a slice . . . Breakfast's at seven-thirty and don't be late."

She left and hobbled down the stairs. She was certainly brusque, I reflected as I unpacked and collected my dirty laundry, but she didn't seem so bad.

We spent the rest of the day repairing gear, cleaning our water bottles, washing clothes, and assembling our resupply for the last leg of our journey. We planned to take eight days through the Wilderness this time; slow, for northbounders, but a lot more comfortable than the twelve days we'd taken at the beginning. Our packs would be about forty pounds when we left town, much better than our southbound fifty-five. The town chores were so automatic now, just like the chores of setting up camp. It was hard to believe this was the last time we would do them on the Trail.

We polished off the Pie Lady's apple crumble in the middle of the afternoon, and then went in search of supper. The restaurant in the laundromat, where we had eaten such wonderful pizza last summer, was closed for the season now. We went to the convenience store at the gas station instead, up a hill at the edge of town, where the pizza was overpriced and undercooked. I turned my back on the television that yammered in the corner of the dining area. It was impossible to ignore the poster of a Middle Eastern man's face, superimposed onto a rifle target, that hung on the wall. I recognized him from the headlines and photos in the newspapers stacked by the checkout counter: Osama bin Laden. I shivered, looking away. *Violence propagating like a disease in the world.*

It rained all night and into the next day. At breakfast, Dream Catcher came down from his room a few minutes late.

The Pie Lady came in from the kitchen, her hands on her hips. "I was about to clear your place away. I've got half a mind not to serve you anyway! You've got no respect for other people's time."

"What? I was just, like, thirty seconds late . . ." Dream Catcher's voice revealed a tinge of annoyance. Stoker shot him a warning look, but he didn't catch it.

The Pie Lady gathered herself up. "I've been up since four in the morning, baking, to get breakfast on the table for you, and what do you do? You disrespect me and you badmouth me! I tell you, I've got half a mind to throw your breakfast out on the street and let you eat out there!"

"Those muffins look lovely!" Stoker said quickly. "Are they blueberry? My favorite!"

Dream Catcher took this opportunity to slide into his chair.

The Pie Lady pursed her lips. "Yup, they're blueberry," she said shortly, and bustled back into the kitchen. She returned a moment later with a platter of pancakes and a pan of runny eggs, which she slopped out onto our plates with a minimum of ceremony.

I took a muffin from the basket. The edges were golden brown and perfectly done, but when I tried to cut it in half the knife slipped: the center of the muffin was frozen. The Pie Lady's hostel had its charms, I decided, but if I ever hiked through Monson again I'd probably go back to Shaw's.

After breakfast, I packed up quickly and used the Pie Lady's computer. I tried to type an e-mail to my friends, describing the last few weeks of our hike. So much of it was still too raw to put into words. I finally cobbled something together and hit "send." I was about to log out, but I noticed one more piece of mail in my inbox. Someone named Antonios, with an unfamiliar Greek surname. Nothing in the subject line. *Probably another piece of spam*, I thought, but I opened it anyway:

Wed, 19 Sep 2001 08:44:37

Your concern is touching and appreciated. I am untouched by the mercy of fate however I have seen sights that I hope you and your sister never ever have to face. You two are a great encouragement and help myself and my friends realize our want to go to the trail. I have spent the last week digging bodies and parts of bodies from the steel and dust ghost of a building I knew would outlive me. It's a memory that will never leave me. I know a few things, and one of them is that I want to follow in the footsteps of Isis and Jackrabbit through the trail, under the stars, through the mountains and clean my soul. I want to go backpacking. I think of you and your sister often. Stay safe and cherish every second of the life you have been graced with. Even when the bugs bite and it's ramen noodles for dinner, again. I hope to see both of you on the trail and our biggest concern can be where Orion lays in the sky. I am not usually this heavy but these are not usual times. Thank you again for your concern and feel free to write again. I may be in Maine soon.

> *Bag a mountain for me,*
> *—TONY*

Tears streamed down my face as I shut down the computer, but they were tears of relief. Outside the window, the rain pounded down as hard as ever. Fog rose from the wet ground, making the streets of Monson look gauzy and unreal, like a half-developed Polaroid. It was terrible to think of Tony, so young, sifting through the ruins for the bodies of the dead. But he was alive. He was alive.

"Are you ready?" the Pie Lady shouted from downstairs. "I'm not going to wait all day! The shuttle to the trailhead's leaving!" I grabbed my pack and ran down the staircase.

CHAPTER 12

The Greatest Mountain

jackrabbit

The rain continued all day after we hiked out of Monson, and thick mist hung between the trees, dulling the sound of falling water. Occasionally wind stirred the branches with a low sigh, bringing down a fresh curtain of rainwater. It was cold, too, probably forty-five degrees. Tiki and Nigel fell behind after a short time, and Isis, Porkchop, and I were alone in the woods. None of us felt like talking; we were all lost in our own thoughts. The weather seemed to mirror my mood: subdued, but with an edge of worry. I tried not to imagine what was happening in the outside world.

In midafternoon, we stopped at Wilson Valley Lean-to for a snack. It took a moment for my eyes to adjust to the gloom of the shelter's interior. Three hikers, wrapped in their sleeping bags, leaned against the back wall.

"Hey, guys." Jack and his girlfriend Ramblin' Rose waved.

"What's up?" I said.

Jack stretched and yawned. "Nothing much. Nasty day to be out hiking, isn't it?"

"Not the greatest," Porkchop agreed. "But any day on the Trail has some redeeming virtues." She slung her pack off and sat down on the porcupine trap. "Who else is back there?" She peered into the shelter.

The other hiker stirred and looked up. "Spider," he croaked. It was him, all right; I recognized his pale blond hair and narrow face. He looked awful, though. His cheeks were sunken to the point of gauntness, and the spark I remembered was gone from his eyes.

"Spider the Keg Outlaw?" I said.

He gave a feeble laugh. "The same."

"Long time no see. I have to say, though, you don't look so good. Are you okay?"

He coughed. "I'm not feeling so great. Nasty cold. I've been here for two days, just hunkering down and resting. If I feel good enough tomorrow, I'll keep hiking north. Otherwise, I'll just go back to Monson."

"You have enough food?" Isis asked him.

"Yeah, I'll be fine."

"You've got some time before the Mountain closes," I said. The approach to Katahdin would be open for another twenty days, if the trails weren't blocked by snow.

"I know I've got time. But I'm running out of money. And motivation." He coughed again. "I guess I just don't want it to be over. Even if I was feeling fine, I might turn around here and hike out. That way I'll have some . . . I don't know, some feeling of control over the whole thing. Like it's my decision to end my hike, not some outside factor like the white blazes ending. And like I can come back next year, and this will still be waiting for me."

"I can see where you're coming from," I said. "Southbound, I almost quit the Trail ten miles from Springer. I probably would have, if there'd been a road to hitch out from. But it's worth it to finish. It really is."

"I'll see," he said.

"I hope you feel better, Spider," I told him.

"You guys staying here tonight?" Ramblin' Rose asked us. "There's plenty of space. The roof only leaks a little bit; we patched the worst holes with duct tape."

I glanced at my watch. It was 3:30, earlier than I had thought; the dark, low-hung clouds made it look like evening already.

"I don't know," I said. "I'd like to put a few more miles behind us if we can. It's less than five to the lean-to at Long Pond Stream."

"I guess so," Isis said, and Porkchop nodded. "We'll see you guys down the trail. Good luck, Spider."

The rain intensified as we left the shelter. I had a few second thoughts as we started down the mud-slick path. My rain gear clung damply to my skin. After two thousand miles, my Frogg Toggs had given up their water-repelling ability just as my Gore-Tex had on our southbound trip. But I was glad to be moving again. I had fond memories of Long Pond Stream Lean-to, a shelter of hewn logs set on a hillside among hemlocks, with a clear, leaping stream nearby for water. We had met Tenbrooks and his little dog Molly there last summer.

A few miles down the trail, Porkchop stopped abruptly. "Shoot! Jack-rabbit, are my sandals still on the outside of my pack? I took them off when I got my snacks out at that shelter, and I can't remember if I put them back."

"I don't see them," I said.

"Oh, man. I must have left them. I'm just gonna leave my pack here and run back." She slung her pack off and set it against a tree, pulling up the rain cover over the straps.

"Are you sure?" Isis said. "I could go back with you."

"No, that's okay. I feel like going fast, anyway."

"I'll wait here for you, then," Isis said.

"If you want to." Porkchop took off down the trail with the easy, loping stride of a cross country runner.

I jogged in place, trying to stay warm.

"You go ahead, jackrabbit," Isis told me. "You can get us some space in the shelter and start filtering water." She unpacked the filter and handed it to me, along with her extra water bottles.

"Okay," I said reluctantly, stowing Don Juan and the bottles in my pack. "I'm not sure if I like us being split up on a day like this. Hypothermia weather. Stay warm, okay?"

Isis was putting on her hat and gloves. "I'll be fine. Go on."

I walked alone through the dripping woods. It was almost dusk when I reached the shelter. Under the limbs of the hemlocks, shadows were thickening. The rain continued, strong as ever. I saw the beams of several headlamps in the shelter interior and the blue flame of a Whisperlite stove.

"Hello!" I called. "Any room in the shelter?"

"Oh, I don't think so," said an unfamiliar woman's voice. She sounded so cheerful that I thought she was kidding, but when I looked closer I saw that she was right. There were at least eight people packed shoulder to shoulder along the floorboards.

"Jackrabbit! How're you?" It was Featherweight, curled up in her sleeping bag, warm and dry. Lightfoot sat beside her, reading the register.

"Fine," I managed. I wasn't really in a mood for small talk. "I've gotta find water before it gets totally dark." I remembered the little stream, off to the left of the shelter. A week ago, after the dry summer we'd had, I wouldn't have trusted it. After all this rain, though . . .

"The stream's dry," said another voice I recognized—Moon. He, too, sounded happy and content. "The nearest place is that creek at the bottom of the hill. Less than half a mile, I think."

Stands to reason that they're so upbeat, I thought sourly. *They all have a place out of the rain tonight.*

"So, how's your hike going, jackrabbit?" Honey asked. "I haven't seen you in a while."

"It's been okay," I said. I gathered up all the water bottles and the filter, glad for an excuse not to talk any more. I knew it would take an effort for me to stay civil.

Down at the river, I perched on a rock ledge above a narrow chute where water roiled and foamed between smooth walls of rock. Rain lashed down all around me. The whole landscape—river, rocks, hillside, trees—became a montage of dark grays. The filter needed a new cartridge; it was an effort to get any water out of it at all. I pumped the handle savagely. *It just figures that the shelter's full of people. My own damn fault for wanting to make a few more miles. But damn, I hate being wet. Lying down wet and waking up wet and knowing I'll have to carry a wet tent in the morning . . .*

After I had filled six bottles, my arm cramped up. I sat back, resting. The roar of the water in the gorge filled the air. My anger had subsided a little. *Where do I get the idea that I'm entitled to shelter space, anyway?* I thought. *I'm as bad as Lash and Black Forest in Maryland, telling the Boy Scouts to move out. I should be grateful that I'm on the Trail at all. Consider the alternative. Consider the alternative.* But my mind balked at the image that came back to me with this phrase: the fireman Tony, sorting through the rubble. *The steel and dust ghost of a building I knew would outlive me,* he had written. I hugged my knees to my chest and stared down into the churning water. It seemed impossible that such a world could coexist with this one. I tried to be grateful, but all I could manage was tired and worried. And sad.

I found a pair of marginally flat tent sites behind the shelter. One had a ten-degree slant to it and four large spruce roots running crosswise, and the other boasted a sagging center with a puddle three inches deep. I set up our tent on the wet site, figuring that it would keep out groundwater better than Porkchop's tarp. As I laid out my foam pad and sleeping bag, though, I could see dark patches of water already soaking through the tent floor. *So much for that.*

I returned to the shelter with a few handfuls of Zip stove wood just as Isis and Porkchop arrived, late and dripping wet. People in the shelter called out various greetings. From the monosyllables that my hiking companions returned, it was evident that they weren't up for much of a conversation with the warm, dry people, either. The three of us hung up our packs and sat on the porcupine trap to cook. It was cold; I realized I could see my breath by the light of my headlamp. We tried to stay out of the rain, but now and then the wind drove the line of drips from the eaves straight back in our faces. The Zip stove smoked and sputtered, even though I'd peeled the wet bark off the twigs.

"Did you get your sandals, Porkchop?" I asked her.

She shook her head, looking more glum than I'd ever seen her. "I got about halfway back to the shelter, and I just thought, 'This is dumb. Here I am, running through the woods, miles from town, with no med kit, no warm clothes, no water even. What if something happens?' So I turned around and came back. It wasn't worth it for a pair of sandals."

"Did you run into Tiki and Nigel?"

"No. I think they must've stayed at that last shelter." She gave a tired laugh. "They were smart."

A gust of wet wind overturned Porkchop's pot of ramen and doused her alcohol stove. She put her head in her hands. "This is *not* my day."

"We've got some extra couscous," Isis said. She took another Ziploc out of her food bag. "You can eat with us tonight."

"You sure?"

"We always have extra food. It's a habit left over from winter, I guess."

The couscous was a little watery from the rain that had fallen in, but it tasted wonderful in the raw cold of the evening. After supper, the rain continued unabated. It rattled the tin roof and cascaded from the eaves in a constant sheet.

Isis sighed. "Let's wait and see if it lets up a little." She took the candle lantern from her pack and lit it. The shelter filled up with soft orange light. (Our mom had brought the lantern back to us at the Fair, remembering our descriptions of how it had brightened our winter evenings. "I thought you might want it again," she'd said. "It's starting to get dark early out there.") I could see the faces of the other hikers now: Honey and Moon, Lightfoot and Featherweight, and a pair of unfamiliar couples.

"What a lovely lantern," one of the women said. I recognized her voice—she was the one who had told me the shelter was full. She had long red hair that gleamed in the low light. "I'm Karen, by the way, and this is my husband, Tim." The bearded man beside her waved.

"And we're Weebles and Tahogie," the other woman said. Her face was in shadow from where I sat, so I couldn't see her clearly, but she had a bright, youthful voice. "We got our names when we were trying on packs. Mine's from that old song, you know, 'weebles wobble but they don't fall down.'" She laughed.

"When I was getting my gear for this hike," Tahogie said, "I must have tried on twenty packs looking for one that would actually fit." He had a deep, slightly gruff voice. "I finally found that one—" he gestured toward a large pack hung on the wall, which looked gray-green in the candlelight. "It fit perfectly, but darned if I could pronounce the name of the thing. It's called a—what is it, honey? I *still* can't remember."

"Tioga," Weebles supplied.

"Right. But I kept calling it 'Tahogie,' so that became my name."

"Cool," Porkchop said, with more enthusiasm than I could have mustered.

Conversation faltered. I stared out into the curtain of rain, now glittering orange with the light of the candle lantern. If anything, it was falling harder than before. I started to hum to myself, softly.

"Is that 'The Water Is Wide'?" Karen asked.

In answer, I sang the first verse. Karen joined in with a subtle harmony. At the chorus, Tim and Tahogie's bass voices joined in.

"Do you know 'The Sally Gardens'?" Weebles asked when we finished.

We sang for hours as the rain pounded down outside. Karen and Weebles taught us some new rounds, and we invented harmonies for spirituals and folk songs. Our voices blended into a rich tapestry of sound, filling the shelter as the lantern filled it with light.

Finally Isis yawned. "I don't want to know how late it is. I'm fading."

"Let's sing one more song, then," Karen said. "Let's do 'The Water Is Wide' again." This time, everyone in the shelter sang, and the sound of rain on the roof was lost behind our voices.

> The water is wide; I cannot cross over,
> and neither have I wings to fly.
> Build me a boat that will carry two,
> and both shall row, my love and I.

The puddle in the middle of the tent had grown and spread, soaking into the underside of my sleeping bag, but I was happy anyway. Our songs had transformed the night from a miserable, wet, lonely evening, to one of the best nights I could remember on the Trail.

I arranged my fleece jacket as a pillow, trying to keep it out of the wet area, and took out my contact lenses. "Good night, Isis."

"Good night."

In the dark tent, listening to the sound of the rain, I lay awake for a while. Images and phrases flashed through my mind: *the water is wide. (The golden Kennebec, water shot through with light)—put your packs in the middle and get the life-*

jackets on. We all ride the river. (The creek at the foot of the hill, pale in the dusk, and the sound of so much water.) Fasten up your earthly burdens. River Jordan is deep and cold. I cannot cross over. Build me a boat that will carry two, and both shall row . . .

For the first time since September 11, I found myself capable of prayer. I couldn't imagine an all-powerful god anymore. Instead, I imagined an all-loving god, one who could only watch the destruction of his kingdom and mourn. The image was full of sadness, but it brought me a kind of peace. *Great Spirit*, I prayed. *Thank you for this beautiful day. Whatever power is in you, may it be enough to keep hate from destroying us all.*

The morning dawned clear and almost warm. The hillside came alive with fall colors. Through the screen of the tent door, I could see a brilliant collage of gold and red. I had woken up in a puddle four inches deep, with my entire left side soaking wet, but somehow I was still in a good mood. I pulled my sleeping bag out of the tent after me to wring out some of the water.

Just upslope, Porkchop emerged from her tarp, yawning and stretching. Her hair was a wild mass of curls. "What a night! I had the Mississippi flowing through my tarp!"

"Well, we've got Lake Superior in *our* tent," I boasted cheerfully.

Porkchop peered into the entrance as Isis sloshed her way out. "Wow! That *is* a lot of water. Good thing it's such a beautiful morning."

The rest of the hikers had left the shelter by the time we got there to retrieve our packs. I started to stuff the sopping-wet tent into the bottom of my pack, but Isis shook her head.

"We ought to wait for Tiki and Nigel."

"Right. That'll give us some time to dry out, anyway."

I hung the tent over one of the rafters, and we used the bear line to string up Porkchop's tarp and all our sleeping bags in the clearing. Isis fetched a pot of water from the stream near the shelter—it was running, finally—and made a pot of tea to go with our breakfast. I sat on the porcupine trap, reading *Harry Potter* aloud.

It was almost noon when Tiki and Nigel arrived.

"Hey, ladies," Tiki said. He gave Isis a quick kiss. "Porkchop, did you leave these at the last shelter?" He held up a pair of Tevas.

"My sandals! Tiki, you're awesome."

We hiked up the shoulder of Barren Mountain together. Last spring, I had heard hikers wax rhapsodic about the view from Barren Ledges. When we had arrived as southbounders, though, we'd seen nothing but fog. This time, the view was everything I had hoped for. From the curving slope of polished granite, we could see rounded mountains on three sides, their slopes painted with fall colors. In the valley, Lake Onawa's smooth surface mirrored the pale blue of the sky, the water darkening in patches where breezes raced across it.

Nigel stood at the edge of the drop-off, staring into the distance. He looked more peaceful than he had in a long time. "That's awesome. All the blisters and everything, it's worth it for that." He smiled at Tiki. "Thanks for letting me tag along, man."

"I'm glad you came."

Dusk caught up to us early, as we traversed the ambiguously numbered peaks of the Barren-Chairback range.

"This has *got* to be Third Mountain," Nigel said. "I've been counting."

"We had the same problem as sobos," I told him. "There are peaks in here that don't have numbers. This one we're on right now, if memory serves, is the one we called Mount Three-and-a-half Kicking-ass."

"You got the kicking-ass part right." Nigel sighed as he reached for a tree root to haul himself up a particularly steep stretch. "Where's the next shelter, anyway?"

"Chairback Gap," Tiki said. "It's another couple miles."

"It'll be dark!"

"We could night-hike it."

"These mountains are too beautiful to night-hike through," Isis said. "Let's sleep out. I remember some ledges on top of Third Mountain that would be perfect. Monument Cliffs."

I looked up at the sky, calculating. There were streamers of high cirrus, indicating another storm in two or three days, but no immediate foul-weather signs. Then another possible problem came to mind. "What about water?"

Isis pursed her lips, thinking. "After all that rain, there'll be puddles. We've drunk out of puddles before."

There was, indeed, a puddle behind Monument Cliffs. The water was brownish stained and had a mossy taste, even after passing through the filter, but after so long on the Trail, we weren't picky. Even Nigel drank it without comment.

We sat on the ledges as a purple sunset flared in the west, reflected in the lakes down below. Looking out over the landscape, I felt an indescribable sense of longing. I wished I could hold that moment forever, frozen in time, whole and incorruptible. But the light faded gradually; a little wind rustled the tops of the nearby spruce trees and the stars came out.

We woke to a chilly morning, with gray wisps of fog blowing through the trees maybe twenty feet above us. The pearly light gave way to dawn; a window of brilliant orange opened in the eastern sky, just above the dark spruces, and horizontal light leaked into the valley, turning the treetops incandescent red and gold. Early mist silvered the surfaces of the lakes; the far mountains, still wreathed in fog, loomed indistinct and soft.

Porkchop had already packed by the time I got out of my sleeping bag. "I think I'm going to take off," she said. "It's lovely here, but it's kind of chilly. And—" she made a face. "I found a slug on my sleeping bag."

"Ick! I didn't think they could get across granite ledges."

"It's been wet for a few days." She shrugged. "But in the slug's defense, it was one of the least sluggy slugs I've ever encountered."

Isis

We caught up to Porkchop after only an hour of hiking; she'd stopped to eat breakfast at an overlook. It was early, but we decided to stop for a snack too. Tiki unfolded his map. He'd heard there was a blue-blaze somewhere around the next road, and he and Nigel were interested in taking it.

"Yep, there it is," Tiki exclaimed. "You hike down the valley there, then you take that logging road . . . you turn left at the bridge there, and connect back up to the Trail on the other side of the Whitecap Range. Looks like it cuts out a lot of rough terrain."

Jackrabbit leaned over and took a look. "It cuts out a lovely section of trail, too, if I remember correctly. There's the Hermitage—" she pointed to a valley a little ways ahead of us "—one of the only stands of old-growth forest in the state. And just beyond it is this beautiful slate gorge, Gulf Hagas, that our friend Waterfall told us about. It's not exactly on the Trail, but I want to make a loop through it. After Gulf Hagas there's Whitecap. On a good day, you get an awesome view of Katahdin from there."

Nigel sighed. "Sounds great, but my blisters are killing me. If there's an easier way out of here, I'm going to have to take it."

"I'm with you, man," said Tiki, throwing an arm around his shoulders. "I mean, I feel fine, but I'm hiking with *you*. You're practically my brother."

I felt only a flicker of sadness as I watched the two of them walk away down the side trail together. Since Monson, I had felt myself drawing away from him, emotionally as well as physically. I knew my time with him was running out, but, more importantly, our hike was running out. *Ours*, meaning mine and jackrabbit's. After all the miles and seasons, quarrels and celebrations, we had only a week left as hiking partners. Porkchop's company added to our friendship, but a romantic relationship took too much of my energy away. I was grateful to have Nigel with us—the time he and Tiki spent together, renewing their friendship, gave me a better excuse to quietly step away.

From the south bank of the Pleasant River, the Hermitage looked like an ordinary patch of woods: stately pines and hemlocks leaning over a narrow forest stream. Only when we were knee-deep in the river, picking our way slowly over the slippery rocks of the ford, did the perspective of the scene fall into place. Hemlocks three feet thick curved over the water, and straight white pines three times the height of a house clustered behind them. In their shade, I felt as if I had walked into a painting of the Hudson River School.

On the north shore, the trail curved along the bank of the river. Porkchop, who'd taken her sneakers off to ford the river, kept them off as we walked the soft, swampy trail through the Hermitage. All three of us left bare footprints in the mud. We stopped for lunch in a wide, sunny clearing opened by the fall of a single pine. Through the trees, we could see the river's far shore, with its fifty-year-old forest. The shift in perspective made the Pleasant seem as wide as the Kennebec. It looked like a river from another era, shadowed by virgin forest on both its banks.

We spent most of the afternoon following a side trail up the river, along the edge of Gulf Hagas. Southbound, jackrabbit and I had passed the trail to Gulf Hagas late in the evening of our first thirteen-mile day, hurrying to find a place to camp. Northbound, we had plenty of time for the side trip; we had only five miles to hike to Carl A. Newhall Lean-to, where we were planning to spend the night. (Tiki and Nigel were planning to meet us the next evening at East Branch Lean-to.)

The trail took us along the edge of cliffs, past miles and miles of waterfalls where white spray plunged down over slabs of polished black slate. Dark pools swirled in their rounded basins, fifty feet below us, the spirals of foam on their surfaces echoing the patterns of moss and lichen on the cliffs. Spruce and pine forests seemed to spill over the edges of the gorge; trees leaned out into space and clung to narrow shelves of stone along the cliff faces. Here and there the leaves of a young birch shone like gold against the muted greens and the luminous scarlet of the maples. Of all the side trails we had taken on our northbound hike, this was the most beautiful by far.

A group of section hikers moved over to make room for us, sliding their packs and sleeping bags closer together, when we reached Carl A. Newhall Lean-to. We unpacked quietly, trying not to disturb a man who was already asleep in one corner of the shelter. We chatted with the section hikers while we cooked. They had graduated from college that spring, and one of them was going to Morocco with the Peace Corps in a month.

"I'll come back and hike the whole Trail," she told us, sounding a little wistful. "One of these years."

The section hikers had gone to sleep, and Porkchop, jackrabbit, and I were rolling out our own sleeping bags by the time the mice came out. At first, they scampered back and forth along the rafters, keeping out of the beams of our headlamps. Soon, though, a particularly bold one had worked its way down the string of our mouse-hanger. I watched it wrap its tail tightly around the string, swing itself over the edge of the tuna can, and grab hold of the stick beneath it. In a minute, it was clinging to the neck of my food bag, trying to bite through the fabric. I grabbed the register notebook and thumped it against the food bags, knocking the mouse off. By the time I returned to my foam pad, another one was climbing down the string.

I looked at the other two mouse hangers. They must have been better-designed, with slipperier strings or some other innovation, because the mice seemed to be focusing their assault on ours. With the shelter this crowded, though, all of the mouse hangers were loaded down. I couldn't move our food bags to safer hangers without displacing someone else's. I batted the second mouse off our bags and tried to figure out if anything in our gear could deter them during the night. *No number ten cans to put in place of the tuna can. No Hav-a-Hart traps, and from the looks of it, I'd need a raccoon-sized trap to contain all the mice in this shelter, anyway. No cat. Maybe, if I have enough duct tape, I could wrap it inside out around the string . . .*

I opened the outer pocket of my pack, keeping on eye on the mouse hanger. In the top of the pouch was the $3 plastic poncho I'd bought in Gorham after my last rain jacket wore out. I wrapped it around our food bags right below the tuna can and tied it off as tightly as I could. The mice didn't give up easily: I fell asleep to an intermittent, satisfying *swwwish plunk!* sound as mouse after mouse slid down the poncho and landed on the ground.

The next day, my twenty-seventh birthday, we hiked over the Whitecap Range in wind and fog. Southbound, these mountains had offered us our last view of Katahdin. I had hoped to catch a glimpse of the Mountain here, but in this weather we couldn't see much more than the tall spruces on either side of the path. We bundled up in all our layers, from hats to sandals; above tree-line, the air felt uncomfortably close to the temperature where the fog would turn to ice rime.

Tiki and Nigel caught up with us at Logan Brook Lean-to, where we stopped for a late lunch.

"Hi, guys," jackrabbit said. "I thought you'd be way ahead of us, with that shortcut you took on the logging roads."

Tiki made a face. "We got lost. Those roads are a lot farther out than they look like on the map. We've been running all morning, trying to catch up with you."

"But we saw moose, man. Don't forget we saw a lot of moose." Nigel looked pretty cheerful for someone who'd been running uphill on blisters all morning. I'd been worried about him keeping up with us for the rest of the Wilderness, but I began to revise my opinion. Perhaps, after a little over a week on the Trail, Nigel was already in long-distance hiker shape.

"Jade didn't like the moose much," Tiki said. "Did you, Skassy?" Hearing her nickname, Jade bounced back and forth, pawed the ground in front of Tiki, then went into a tizzy chasing her own short tail.

"Man, that dog has too much energy for anyone," Nigel said, shaking his head slowly. "I could go to sleep right now, after that hike we did this morning."

"It's only four more miles to the shelter," Tiki encouraged him. "All downhill."

It was an easy hike down the mountain, through white birch forest with an understory of witch hobble, its saucer-sized leaves turning a rainbow of startling colors from deep reddish purple to peach. The clouds thinned as we walked; by the time we reached East Branch Lean-to, the sky above us was completely clear. We found a crowd of old friends gathered around the firepit: Sing-song and Tiger Cakes, Jack and Ramblin' Rose, Iculus, Dream Catcher, Stoker and Charlotte. Stoker had collected a three-foot-high pile of branches; he was busy balancing sticks around a clump of birch bark in the firepit. I sat down on a stump next to Sing-song and Tiger Cakes and unpacked the Zip stove.

"Happy birthday, Isis!" Tiger Cakes greeted me. "It is today, isn't it? Tiki told me about it back in Monson, when he was looking for a card."

"Thank you!" I laughed. Tiki, Porkchop, and jackrabbit had all bemoaned the fact that they couldn't find me a proper birthday card in Monson. Every time we'd gone to the general store, they'd sorted through the card rack, joking about the possibilities: a cartoon of a wrinkled old woman in front of a mirror, which said, "Don't worry, you're not as old as you look," or a photo of a scantily clad young woman with a word balloon over her head saying "Hey big guy, I'm all yours for your birthday."

"It's your birthday? Wow, I didn't know," said Dream Catcher. "What can I do for you?" He sounded apologetic, as though he'd been invited to a party and had forgotten to bring a gift.

"I don't know. Tell me a story, or read me a poem, or something."

"Can I read you a poem, too?" asked Jack. "I've got one I wrote at Overmountain Shelter. It's about ghosts in an old tobacco barn."

"I've got a new song I've been working on," offered Sing-song.

"I'll come up with something," Dream Catcher promised. "Just give me an hour or so." He picked up the register notebook and sat with it in a corner of the shelter, sucking on the end of a pencil as he concentrated.

"Don't look," Porkchop told me.

We'd just finished dinner; we were still sitting around the fire. I turned off my headlamp and put my hands over my eyes. The murmur of conversations was punctuated by the scratch and hiss of a match lighting.

"Okay, you can look again!" came Porkchop's voice.

She'd stuck a birthday candle in a stack of hermit cookies that she'd secretly carried from Monson. Jackrabbit handed out sparklers, and everyone started singing "Happy Birthday."

"I've got my poem," Dream Catcher announced, as I handed out slices of hermit. "You're going to have to be patient with me, though, 'cause I never wrote a poem before." He picked up the register and read slowly, stumbling a little over his own words: a simple, heartfelt paean to the beauty of the autumn woods.

After Dream Catcher, everyone took turns singing, reading poems they carried with them, or telling stories of their favorite moments on the Trail. Tiger Cakes recited a fierce love poem, rhythmic and full of dazzling turns of phrase.

"That was awesome," Porkchop told her. "Who wrote it?"

"I did," Tiger Cakes answered. It was the first time I'd ever heard her sound shy.

"Wow. You should send your work to a literary magazine," jackrabbit said.

"I've already published a few poems," Tiger Cakes admitted.

Tiki gave me a card he'd bought at the Common Ground Fair, with a pen-and-ink drawing of an exuberant barefoot woman holding a birthday cake. Somehow, he'd managed to pass it around the campfire without my noticing; everyone there had signed it. In it, jackrabbit had written an Antonio Machado poem that I'd often heard her recite, and her own translation:

> Traveler, your footsteps make
> the only path: the path you take.
> Traveler, there is no path—
> the path unwinds beneath your feet,
> and turning for a backward view
> you find the pathway closed to you—
> we travel, yet cannot retreat.
> Traveler, there is no path;
> the sea is crossed with ships' bright wakes.

jackrabbit

Frost covered the ground in the morning, coating the dry spruce needles and pine duff with bright shards. It glittered on the shadowed side of the tent fly and the back of the shelter. I pulled on my hat, wool shirt, and wind pants against the cool of the morning. Down at the slow-flowing stream, when I went to filter our water for the day, wisps of frost-smoke rose from the amber-colored surface. I dipped my hand into the water, and found it warmer than the air.

Back at the lean-to, Sing-song and Tiger Cakes were making a breakfast fit for royalty. A Nalgene full of hot chocolate was cooling on the picnic table. Pots of scrambled eggs and grits simmered on their alcohol stoves, and Tiger Cakes had coaxed the coals in the firepit back to life to fry a pan of what looked like sausage.

"I thought you guys were vegetarians," I said.

Tiger Cakes grinned, brushing back a strand of her short brown hair with a sooty hand. "We are. This is veggie sausage. You know, the powdered kind you mix up?"

"Wow! Where'd you get all this great food?"

"Out of the hiker box at Shaw's. Best one I've seen yet!"

Another reason to stay there next time I go through Monson, I thought.

"Eggs are ready," Sing-song called. "Girl, you got soot on your face!"

Tiger Cakes examined her reflection in a pot lid and wiped her forehead with a sleeve. A small smudge of black remained above her left eyebrow.

"It's still there." Sing-song indicated the spot on her own face.

Tiger Cakes shrugged. "It'll make me look tough. Keep the riffraff away."

They sat down to breakfast. Isis and I joined them at the table. We made a pot of cocoa, too, to go with our Grape-Nuts. Sing-song and Tiger Cakes offered us a few bites of the veggie sausage, which seemed far too delicious to have come from a hiker box.

By the time we finished eating, most of the other hikers had packed up and left. The morning mist off the river was disappearing as the sun warmed the air. I heard footsteps coming up the path. It was Baltimore Jack. I hadn't seen him since Hanover, but he was easy to recognize: broad-shouldered and stocky, slightly grizzled-looking, with three days' worth of salt-and-pepper stubble. A cigarette dangled from his lips. He wore a much-abused pair of khaki shorts and a black t-shirt with a two-by-six white blaze on the front.

"Morning, Jack," I said.

He appeared not to notice. Instead of answering, he walked over to the shelter and sat down on the porcupine trap, leafing through the register. "Oh, Isis and jackrabbit were here last night," he murmured to himself.

"And we're *still* here, Jack," I said, a bit louder. "Good morning."

"Well, hello, dear. I thought you were weekenders, staying at the shelter so late in the morning. I don't generally speak to weekenders any more. And pardon me for saying so, but you look terribly outré in that Earl Shaffer shirt."

I looked down at my wool shirt, which was beginning to unravel at the elbows and armpits. Earl Shaffer, the first thru-hiker, had carried famously low-tech gear on his 1948 and 1998 hikes—including, I realized, a wool shirt much like this one. Even though I knew Jack hadn't intended it as a compliment, I was secretly pleased by the comparison.

"Come on, Jack," I said. "You of all people should know not to judge by appearances. How many times have you hiked the Trail now?"

"This is my sixth thru-hike. I've walked most of the Trail seven times, but the first time through—" his tone switched to severe disapproval "I *blue-blazed*."

"So you don't think a thru-hike counts unless you follow all the white blazes?" I asked him.

"It doesn't," he said flatly. "The Trail is the Trail. If you don't follow it, you're not a thru-hiker."

I felt tempted to argue, but I knew it would do no good. I'd talked to other people—purists, in Trail lingo—who insisted on following every white blaze, but I'd never met one quite so fanatical as Baltimore Jack. I decided to change the subject.

"Are you hiking again next year?"

He coughed, a hacking, rattling smoker's cough. "No. Never again. I've had enough." But there was something in his eyes that suggested otherwise. I remembered what Mala had told me about Baltimore Jack: *Oh, every year the guy says he won't hike again. Then April rolls around, and he's back at Springer Mountain with the rest of the pack.*

"What about you?" Baltimore Jack asked. "Are you going to hike again, jackrabbit?"

Plenty of people had asked me this in the past few months. My answers had fluctuated according to my mood: *of course, maybe, no way in hell.* The real answer was something I generally kept to myself: *yes, I hope, but not for a good long time.* Right now, though, I had the best response yet.

"If I do," I said, "I'll have to change my name to *Baltimore* jackrabbit."

A slow smile spread across his face. "That's a good one."

The air warmed up as the sun climbed the powder-blue sky. I tied my Earl Shaffer shirt to the outside of my pack as we started up the shoulder of Little Boardman Mountain. We came to a stand of brown ash trees, their yellow leaves and slim branches forming a kind of gateway above the trail. Two ravens swooped between the branches in graceful, silent flight. To the Native tribes of Maine, I knew, ravens represented messengers from the spirit world. As these two flew past, I had a sudden flash of knowledge; I pictured the path to Katahdin stretching out, clear and bright through the glowing fall woodlands before me. I knew then, for the first time in the entire hike, that I would finish the Trail.

On the far side of Little Boardman, we passed the first place where we had stealth-camped as southbounders. The fallen leaves of maples and birches had painted the clearing with daubs of orange, red, and gold. I had remembered the stealth site as a tiny, inhospitable place, but now it appeared welcoming and spacious, much larger than some of the clearings where we had pitched our tent in the past fifteen months. I could easily recall how I had lain awake, on our first night alone in the woods, startled at every sound, straining my ears for an early warning of bears or unfriendly humans. Now, as I stood in the little clearing, listening to the wind in the treetops and the cawing of ravens far off, it seemed the most natural thing in the world to set up a tent in the wilderness, to sleep on the side of a mountain in a temporary shelter made of cloth. *I belong here,* I thought. *This space of woods, and a thousand others like it, is more home to me than any drab apartment out in the "real world" could ever be. And that world, with its currents of horror and hate, scares me so much more than this space of leafy ground in the middle of nowhere.*

Isis

We reached Antlers Tentsite late in the day. The light fell in glowing bars between the red pine trunks, but the air felt decidedly Octobery—no way I was going to brave the leeches for a swim this time. By the time jackrabbit had set up the tent and I'd hung our bear line, the sun had set. A chill, steady wind blew off the lake. We cooked our dinner on the leeward shore of the point and went to bed early.

I woke just as the sky lightened. The wind had died during the night; mist rose like steam from the glassy surface of the lake. The sun came up in a yellow circle of haze, backlighting the rocks and trees. A family of merganser ducks swam by close to shore, ignoring me as I snapped pictures. As the sun rose higher, the haze above the surface gradually cleared, and the trees all around the lake cast perfect reflections on the still water.

Jackrabbit and Porkchop joined me on the shore for breakfast. We tried to wake Tiki and Nigel—we'd planned to hike a twenty to Rainbow Stream Lean-to, and wanted to get an early start—but the only response we got was a growl from Jade, followed by a louder growl from Tiki. Not wanting to press the point, the three of us packed up and hiked out by ourselves.

The air temperature had risen only a few degrees when we passed a white sand beach on the far side of Lower Jo-Mary Lake. Porkchop stopped and glanced up and down the Trail, her eyes sparkling.

"I don't think anyone's coming," she said. "The others were pretty sound asleep when we left the campsite. How 'bout an alive check?"

"It's *cold*," I complained. My toes, numb since I took my sandals off to hike, had just begun to feel the tingle of returning circulation.

"That's good; the leeches will all be frozen." Jackrabbit, not usually a big fan of cold water, was already unfastening her pack. The three of us stripped down, giggling, and sprinted for the water. There was a five or six foot drop-off just a little ways out from the shore; all three of us dove together. The water was breathtakingly cold, instant-headache cold, but at the same time, it felt wonderfully cleansing. Besides, as jackrabbit had said when she convinced me to do the Maryland Challenge, it could be pretty fun to do something stupid with a bunch of friends. We rose to the surface sputtering, our giggles changing to shrieks that must have wakened Tiki and Nigel across the water. Back on the shore, the air felt warm and soft as a towel fresh from the dryer.

We stopped for a morning snack break on the shore of Pemadumcook Lake. Suddenly, there was Katahdin, rising over the level land like a cathedral over wheat fields. Tiki caught up with us there. He stood looking across the lake for a few minutes, then whistled softly.

"Jack told me you could see the Mountain from here," he said. "I thought it would be some little lump on the horizon that someone would point to and say, 'There's Katahdin.' That thing looks like a chunk of the Himalayas, minus the snow. I've come all this way, and now I'm not sure I'm ready to hike that."

Tiki fell behind us again in the afternoon, waiting for Nigel. Jackrabbit, Porkchop, and I reached Rainbow Stream Lean-to as the sun sank below the trees. The day's hike had gone smoothly; as usual, it felt good to stretch our legs into a twenty-mile pace after a lot of short days. At the shelter, Stoker was already tending a roaring fire. Charlotte sat beside him, her hand on his knee. Iculus and Dream Catcher were there, too, rolling out their sleeping bags in the shelter.

It was a subdued fire that night, compared to the campfire on my birthday. The stories people told had a melancholy edge to them that reminded me of the night we'd camped at Pierce Pond southbound, when the first group of friends we'd hiked with was beginning to split apart. Stoker and Charlotte, who'd only been a couple since Monson, and who would soon be returning to homes several thousand miles apart, didn't say much. They sat close together, feeding the fire, and absentmindedly patting Zero, who was curled up at their feet. I spared a thought for Tiki, who must have set up his tent with Nigel somewhere back there in the dark. *Would it have been harder to let go of him, if I'd been hiking alone?* I felt a twinge of guilt as I wondered: *Is it harder for him to let go than it is for me? We never talked about it.* I turned my attention back to the campfire. Only two more days on the Trail. Only one more night. I didn't want to waste a minute of it indulging in regrets. Stoker had just thrown an armload of sticks on the fire, and slipped off to his tent with Charlotte. The rest of us talked for a few more hours, telling stories about mountains we'd climbed and trips we'd taken long ago: places we'd been and would likely never return to.

jackrabbit

Porkchop, Isis, and I left the shelter early, as the rest of the hikers packed up. In the morning, we passed Rainbow Deadwaters, the mosquito swamp that had lived up to the "deadwater" part of its name when we hiked past it southbound. Now, it had become a rainbow; the reflections of thousands of maples hung in the mirrored surfaces of the pools, with the vivid indigo sky seeping between the branches. All day, as we walked, the colors of the forest around us intensified, growing in brilliance and variety. The canopy seemed to have burst into flame: orange and yellow and red in a million unnamed hues. Leaves drifted down through the air and blanketed the trail. Beside the path, the large leaves of witch hobble showed a panoply of colors: pale green, peach and maroon, flaming scarlet, and purple, splotched across each leaf in irregular patches. I felt drunk with beauty, saturated, as though I could not absorb anything more.

In the early afternoon, we came to Hurd Brook Lean-to. It was an unassuming structure, probably fifty years old, and its rough logs bore the marks of time.

"The last shelter on the A.T.," Porkchop said quietly.

Isis stopped short. "That's right. I'd forgotten. You know, it's funny. I keep thinking the Trail will go on and on. It's hard for me to imagine living in a place where water comes from a faucet, where you can eat things you don't have to carry for forty miles."

"Yeah," I said. "Think about *houses*. Won't that be weird? To have a room you can stand up in, and move around. A room that stays in the same place every night. And all the *things* you can have in that room."

I sat down on the porcupine trap and left a few quick messages in the register for friends who might still be behind us: Sleepy the Arab, Spider, the errant members of the Stage Crew. Then I closed the register and simply sat there, trying to capture all the sensations in my mind. *The last shelter.* The scents of old pine and cedar wood, dried earth, the rank perfume of my sweat and my grungy pack. The feeling of the age-worn logs underneath me, smooth and cool; the sun streaming through the branches and dappling my face; the chilly shadows in the interior of the shelter. The sound of wind in the spruce boughs; water, far off; a tiny rustle from the roof that might have been a rodent. Mouse hangers, their ropes sweat-stained green and brown, dangling from the rafters. Out from the mouth of the shelter, I could just glimpse a blaze down the trail, beckoning from the gray, cracked bark of a spruce. I felt a mixture of regret and excitement that was hard to pin down: we were almost finished. We had almost accomplished what few people ever have a chance to attempt. But after this, how could we go back to the world beyond the Trail?

We walked on through cedar swamps and low hummocks of spruce, toward the end of the Wilderness. The last hundred miles of the Trail had formed a lazy S-shape, winding among large lakes. I was grateful for those curves in the path: they had made it all last a little longer. But now we were less than twenty miles from Katahdin. I remembered the view of the Mountain from Pemadumcook Lake, how it had loomed huge and incontrovertible over the water. *The name comes from the Penobscot language*, I remembered. *Ket-adene, greatest mountain.* I had seen higher mountains on this hike, but none so deserving of the name. Katahdin rises out of low-lying swamps and lake country, the highest mountain for nearly a hundred miles in any direction. It creates its own weather, drawing down clouds out of a blue sky to wreath its summit in gray. Penobscot legends say that the spirits convene there when clouds cover the peak. *This chapter of my life is almost over*, I thought. *I'm glad that it will end in such a place.*

A little wind stirred the forest canopy, bringing down a swirl of red maple leaves. *And what will the next part of my life be like?* I wondered. *It's October already; too late to apply to grad schools this fall. I'm not even sure if I want to go to grad school. And in what, anyway? Music or biology? I haven't studied music for more than a year now; I've touched a piano maybe once a month. But I'm pretty far behind in biology, too. The field changes so fast that half of what I learned will be obsolete by now.* I sighed. I had hoped that the Trail would give me a chance to figure out what I wanted to do with my life, or at least with the next few years. Instead, I'd become so caught up in the life of the Trail, living in the moment, that I'd hardly given a thought to my future. *Another two hundred miles, maybe*, I told myself. *Then I'd manage to figure it all out.*

A strange sound came filtering through the woods. My mind took a handful of seconds to identify the hum and rush, the clattering and bumping: traffic. Logging trucks bound for Millinocket, thumping over Abol Bridge with their loads of thin spruce trees. From the road crossing, I knew, it was only fifteen miles to the peak of Katahdin. Fifteen point one. *If I'm going to have an epiphany, it better happen soon*, I thought. But there was only the sound of the trucks on the road, getting closer and closer until I could see the asphalt between the trees.

Isis

A sign posted at the road crossing before Abol Bridge warned us: *no camping at Daicey Pond without reservations.* In smaller print, it stated that reservations could only be obtained by appearing in person at the Baxter State Park headquarters in Millinocket, between the hours of 8 A.M. and 4 P.M. weekdays. It was 3:15. After a brief conference, Porkchop and I decided to try to hitch to town in search of camping reservations at Daicey or Katahdin Stream, some extra food for our last couple days, and the third *Harry Potter* book. (We had just finished reading the second one.) Jackrabbit, who wasn't feeling ready to leave the woods, elected to stay and guard our backpacks.

We tried hitching from the parking lot of the Abol Bridge Campground store. After fifteen minutes, we were about to give up, when an enormous pickup squealed to a halt in front of us. A pair of middle-aged men in camo descended from it.

"You ladies want a ride to town?" asked the one who'd been driving.

"We were hoping to get to the park headquarters . . ." Porchop began.

"Hop right on in," the man told us. "Al and me have to pick up some drinks at the store; we'll just be a minute."

Porchop and I looked at each other and shrugged. We were running pretty short on time; we might not make it to the park office before it closed. But I didn't know of any other way that we could camp in Baxter legally. It was worth a try. We both climbed into the backseat of the cab. Five minutes later, the men came out of the store, each carrying a six-pack of beer.

"You want a drink?" asked the one named Al, popping open a can. His friend at the wheel opened another beer and took a few swigs before revving up the engine.

"What a weekend!" he exclaimed, zooming down the road with one hand around his beer can and the other balanced on top the wheel. He turned around in his seat to grin at me and Porchop. "You sure you girls don't want a beer?"

Twenty hair-raising minutes later, he dropped us off in front of the park headquarters. We raced across the parking lot, a few minutes to four, only to find the door already locked; the rangers must have gone home early.

"Well, I guess we'll just have to wing it," Porchop said. "See if we can hitch out from Katahdin Stream tomorrow or something. In the meantime, I'm pretty hungry. Do you know of any good restaurants in this town?"

After the cute little Trail towns of New England—and especially after a week in the Wilderness—Millinocket looked like a truck stop from the wrong side of the highway. We had to negotiate several parking lots and a four-lane road before we found a pizza place in a nearby mall. We ordered half a dozen calzones: some to eat, some to take back to jackrabbit, and some for the next day's hike. While we waited, I went looking for a pay phone to call my mother and make the final arrangements for her to pick us up in two days.

After dinner, Porchop and I looked up bookstores in the phone book and walked back and forth across town trying to find them. None were open so late. Finally, we went into the local supermarket to buy some fresh fruit for the following day. There, on a shelf by the checkout line, we finally found *Harry Potter and the Prisoner of Azkaban*. I tried not to think how few chapters we'd have time to read together.

By the time we finished shopping, it was getting dark. Unwilling to risk a hitch at that hour, we called a taxi from a gas station pay phone.

"Where'd you say you wanted to go, deah?" asked a woman with a heavy Maine accent. "Abol Bridge? That's way out in the woods, deah. Well, all right. I'll send someone right ovah."

We sat down on the curb and read to each other by the glare of a street-light. Half an hour later, the pay phone rang. A scraggly-looking man in a leather vest, who'd been leaning against a car smoking a cigarette, picked it up. *Uh-oh, drug deal*, I thought. *I don't want to be in the middle of this.* I started to put the book away. The man in the leather vest set the phone down, and looked toward us.

"I think it's for you," he rasped.

It was the taxi dispatcher. "The guy I was gonna send for ya, he got a flat. I'll have someone out they-ah in a minute, though. I just didn't want ya to think I'd forgotten ya."

In a few minutes, a battered brown station wagon pulled up in front of us.

"You the girls going to Abol?" asked the driver. "Well, hop on in; I can get you there. You must be hikers on the Appalachian Trail."

"Do you get a lot of calls from hikers?" I asked him, as I slid into the passenger's seat.

"Hikers, hunters, you name it. And this town has the only topless bar in northern Maine, so we get a lot of business from that. Taking the customers out there, but also, the girls call us to drive 'em around . . . One time, we had a new guy in the fleet. Didn't know his way around town real good. So we sent him out there and gave him directions to walk right in, backstage. Of course we'd warned the girls he was coming, and they were ready for 'im. Didn't have a lick of clothing on. Poor guy was still blushing four hours later when he drove into the lot to change shifts."

The car careened down narrower and narrower roads, the headlights flashing across marsh scrub and dead trees as we bounced over potholes.

"I know a shortcut here," said the driver. He took a sharp left turn onto an even bumpier gravel road. "Gotta go slow, though. There's a lotta moose. The tourists, sometimes they pay me to just drive around out here, looking for moose. One time I had this couple from California in the car. We'd been all over the back roads, and hadn't seen nothing, when I come around a cor-ner and there's a big cow moose, standing in the middle of the road. Well, the Californians were all happy; they leaned out the window and snapped a lot of pictures. Then they wanted to go back to town, but that moose wasn't getting out of the road. I honked, and she just stamped her hoof at me. So I says to myself, 'I'll just roll forward, real slow, and pretty soon she'll *have* to get out of the way.' I rolled forward until the bumper was almost touching the backs of her knees. But she didn't budge. She just bent her legs a little bit, and damned if she didn't pee all over the hood of my car. Well, me and the tourists had a good laugh about that one, but I wasn't laughing the next week, nor the week after. That stuff got down in the radiator, and the whole car smelled like moose pee for a month."

The headlights shone on a large body of water, a lake perhaps, close by the road. I didn't remember any lakes between Abol Bridge and Millinocket.

"Is this still the shortcut?" I asked the driver.

"Nope," he answered. "We're almost there."

"Abol Bridge? The campground with the gas station in front of it?"

"Oh, Abol *Bridge*. Thought you said Abol Campground. Abol Bridge is another five miles around the mountain, but we can't get there from here. I'll have to drive back out the way I came."

By the time we got to the campground, jackrabbit had set up our tent and eaten supper long ago, but she was hungry enough to make short work of the cold spinach calzone that Porkchop and I had brought her.

Nigel and Tiki still hadn't caught up the next morning, so the three of us hiked on to Daicey Pond by ourselves, stopping to skinny-dip in a quick-flowing stream. The sun felt so warm that we lay on the granite ledges beside the stream to dry out, then dove in again. We walked slowly through the forest of spruce and moose maple, passing small ponds and muskegs with amber-colored water.

We ate lunch at a picnic table by Daicey Pond, under the shadow of Katahdin. From Pemadumcook Lake, it had dominated the horizon; now, its summit loomed above us like the crest of a giant wave about to break. I could see the scars of landslides on its sheer gray flanks.

The ranger at Daicey, a different one from the soft-spoken man whose words had encouraged us the year before, reassured us about the availability of campsites at Katahdin Stream.

"Not many people besides thru-hikers staying there this time of year, except on weekends. Just talk to the ranger when you get there. At worst, you'll have to walk a quarter-mile down the road to the new lean-tos."

He was right; there was almost no one but thru-hikers at the campground when we arrived. There were plenty of tent sites to choose from, and even a few lean-tos we could have used if it had been raining. We reserved a space next to our campsite for Tiki and Nigel, who came in after dark.

Nigel looked exhausted. "Man, I wouldn't have made it if Tiki hadn't been talking to me the whole time," he said. "I'm sleeping in tomorrow."

"I think I might sleep in too," Tiki said.

"I'll see you later, then." I walked over and gave him a kiss on the cheek. "Jackrabbit, Porkchop, and I are planning to start up at dawn." I didn't add that our mother was coming to pick us up on the other side of the mountain; if he started late I might not see him at all. With all the emotion of the Trail's end, I didn't have the courage for goodbyes.

After supper, we joined a bunch of the other hikers for a campfire. Porkchop mixed up an instant Jell-O cheesecake that she'd bought in Millinocket and passed it around. The songs and the stories didn't flow the way they usually did, though. People sat in silence, or made jokes that were in poor taste, even for hikers. Perhaps everyone was nervous, preparing for the long hike tomorrow, but to me it seemed like most of us were skipping ahead, already off the Trail in our minds. The common goal that had bound us, only two nights before, had become the point at which we would all split apart.

jackrabbit

Isis, Porkchop, and I rose before dawn on the morning of October 3, 2001. The rest of the hikers in the campsite were still asleep. Frost glittered in the beams of our headlamps as we packed up, and the sound of gravel crunching underfoot seemed unnaturally loud in the predawn stillness. We took our heavier items of gear—tent, tarp, sleeping bags, stoves—and stashed them on the front porch of the ranger station. Even after thousands of miles, none of us wanted to hike Katahdin with a full pack.

"This is it," Porkchop whispered.

We walked to the meadow at the center of the campground so we could watch the Mountain as we ate breakfast. Katahdin was visible first as a great triangle of black space, blocking out the stars, above the dim outlines of the trees. Gradually, rose-colored light leaked out from the eastern horizon, the stars vanished one by one, and the Mountain differentiated itself from the sky. From this angle, it looked almost volcanic: a sharp pyramid of scarred gray stone, edged in reddish light. Tiny leopard-spots of cloud gathered in the air above the summit.

"We heard the weather report in town the other night," Isis told me. "It's supposed to be good in the morning and clouding up later on."

"Good thing we're getting an early start," I said.

The trees around the meadow went from gray to luminescent reds and oranges as the first rays of the sun touched down. We signed in at the trailhead register, a clipboard with spaces for date, time, name, and address.

"There's a column here that says 'day use/overnight,'" Porkchop said. "I almost marked overnight, but then I thought, 'Wait a second. We're dayhikers now.'"

"It's strange, isn't it?" Isis said. "We're just dayhikers. Just like everybody else."

Above the register, a signpost gave the distance to a few landmarks. At the bottom of the list: *Baxter Peak, Mount Katahdin: 5.2.*

Shadows lingered in the understory of the forest, under the vibrant leaves of the witch hobble, but it was light enough to hike barefoot without our headlamps. My feet shaped themselves instinctively to the cold stones. I scarcely noticed the effort of climbing.

The maples and birches of the stream valley gave way to spruce and fir; the evergreens shrank to stunted krummholz, clinging to the spaces between boulders. We climbed steadily, hauling ourselves up hand over hand among the enormous blocks of gray granite. At treeline, where the last misshapen spruces ended, we paused to put on our jackets. A fierce wind whipped around the curve of the mountain, and here on the western side, the shadow of the summit still cast a chill around us. Looking toward the lesser mountains behind us, we could see rugged cliffs and ranks of trees outlined starkly in the horizontal yellow light. The immense shadow of Katahdin filled the valley, blue against the gold birches, receding toward the foot of the slope as we watched. I knew the shadow moved because the sun was rising, but it was difficult not to attribute some motivation to Katahdin itself: the Mountain drawing its mysteries back into its stone heart.

The trail turned sharply upward, following the steep, rock-jumbled scarp of the Hunt Spur. The sky above the peak was almost clear; the clouds we had seen in the early morning had vanished. I looked up at the bulk of the mountain looming over us. We couldn't see the summit yet, but I knew it was there, less than three miles away. Ahead of us stretched the final climb of the entire journey.

Not much time for my epiphany, I thought. Slowly, I gave up the hope that my future would be revealed in marvelous clarity, a pathway as bright and distinct before me as the white blazes shining from the stones of Katahdin. Instead, I felt a gathering of joy and pride, and underneath it, a great sense of peace: the infinite, solid, and imperturbable peace of the Mountain.

We scrambled up the last few stones of the Hunt Spur and onto the table-land, a flat expanse strewn with lichen-covered stones of pink and gray granite. We could see the summit now, a low rise less than a mile away. In the clear light, every rock etched its shadow on the ground. Low grasses danced in the wind, and the cushion-shaped mounds of potentilla and saxifrage hunkered beside the trail. I pictured the exponential progression: thousands of miles, hundreds, tens, single digits. Then it became tenths, hundredths, as we dashed forward across the broken stone of the ridge. Isis and I clasped hands and ran together for the last few hundred yards, until we stood before the wooden A-frame sign:

KATAHDIN   5268 ft.
Northern Terminus of the Appalachian Trail

Thoreau Spring	*1.0*
Katahdin Stream Campground	*5.2*
Maine-New Hampshire State Line	*281.4*
Springer Mountain, Georgia	*2160.2*

"We're here," I said. "We really did it." I reached out to touch the brown-painted wood, almost fearing that it was a dream, that my hand would pass right through it and I would wake to find myself back in our tent, somewhere in New Jersey. But the wood was solid, cool beneath my palm, as solid as the rocks under my bare feet. Isis and I embraced in front of the sign, tears running freely down our cheeks.

"We made it," Porkchop said, and we expanded our hug to make room for her.

"I just can't believe it's over," Isis said.

We took photos at the sign, laughing and crying. I wished there was some profound observation I could make, or some quote appropriate to the occasion, but I found myself at a loss for words. Porkchop was the only one who came up with something.

"'Fox in socks, our GAME is done, sir; thank you for a lot of fun, sir!'" She laughed helplessly, the way she had laughed when she first introduced herself as Porkchop. "It's from Dr. Seuss. It was the only thing I could think of."

I looked around the barren, wind-blasted summit. We seemed to be on top of the world, standing more than four thousand feet above the surrounding plain. On the south side of the Mountain, the valley floor glowed with maples and birches in their full fall glory, transmuted by distance into an abstract patchwork of colors. Countless lakes, scattered across the land below us, shone like disks of white-hot metal. The north side of Katahdin had been carved by glaciers into a gigantic cirque, with the jewel-like Chimney Pond set in its center. The pond shivered from dark reflections of the mountain to bright ripples of sky as the wind played across its surface. All around the inside of the cirque, the bones of the mountain were laid bare, great gray pillars of granite and heaps of broken stone.

"Should we hike the Knife Edge?" I asked. The Knife Edge Trail runs along the rim of the cirque, on a ridge less than a foot wide at its narrowest point, with a three-thousand-foot drop on either side. We had planned to hike it if the weather allowed. To hike the Knife Edge in bad weather, though, is to invite disaster.

"I think we could," Porkchop said. "The sky's almost clear . . ." but she stopped, frowning. "No, it's not." In the few minutes that we had stood there, the clouds had returned. Wisps of vapor collected in the air above us and twined together, disappearing as the wind carried them away from the peak. Fantastic shapes appeared, swirled, and vanished: arcs, veils, dark wings.

"Look," Isis whispered, pointing. Above the approach to the Knife Edge, a slowly revolving spiral of clouds hovered in the air. It remained there, steady and perfectly formed, for almost thirty seconds before the wind snatched it away.

"I think it's the spirits of the Mountain," she said. "Welcoming us home."

Physics and meteorology might have a different explanation for it, I thought, *but that's the one I'd like to believe, too.*

We shouldered our packs, under the ceiling of dancing clouds, and walked across the Knife Edge and into the rest of our lives.